T0237687

Mathematical Pictures at a Data Science Exhibition

In the past few decades, heuristic methods adopted by big tech companies have complemented existing scientific disciplines to form the new field of Data Science. This text provides deep and comprehensive coverage of the mathematical theory supporting the field. Composed of 27 lecture-length chapters with exercises, it embarks the readers on an engaging itinerary through key subjects in data science, including machine learning, optimal recovery, compressive sensing (also known as compressed sensing), optimization, and neural networks. While standard material is covered, the book also includes distinctive presentations of topics such as reproducing kernel Hilbert spaces, spectral clustering, optimal recovery, compressive sensing, group testing, and applications of semidefinite programming. Students and data scientists with less mathematical background will appreciate the appendices that supply more details on some of the abstract concepts.

SIMON FOUCART is Professor of Mathematics at Texas A&M University, where he was named Presidential Impact Fellow in 2019. He has previously written, together with Holger Rauhut, the influential book *A Mathematical Introduction to Compressive Sensing* (2013).

Mathematical Pictures
at a
Data Science Exhibition

SIMON FOUCART
Texas A&M University

CAMBRIDGE
UNIVERSITY PRESS

University Printing House, Cambridge CB2 8BS, United Kingdom

One Liberty Plaza, 20th Floor, New York, NY 10006, USA

477 Williamstown Road, Port Melbourne, VIC 3207, Australia

314–321, 3rd Floor, Plot 3, Splendor Forum, Jasola District Centre,
New Delhi – 110025, India

103 Penang Road, #05–06/07, Visioncrest Commercial, Singapore 238467

Cambridge University Press is part of the University of Cambridge.

It furthers the University's mission by disseminating knowledge in the pursuit of
education, learning, and research at the highest international levels of excellence.

www.cambridge.org
Information on this title: www.cambridge.org/9781316518885
DOI: 10.1017/9781009003933

© Simon Foucart 2022

This publication is in copyright. Subject to statutory exception
and to the provisions of relevant collective licensing agreements,
no reproduction of any part may take place without the written
permission of Cambridge University Press.

First published 2022

A catalogue record for this publication is available from the British Library.

ISBN 978-1-316-51888-5 Hardback
ISBN 978-1-009-00185-4 Paperback

Cambridge University Press has no responsibility for the persistence or accuracy of
URLs for external or third-party internet websites referred to in this publication
and does not guarantee that any content on such websites is, or will remain,
accurate or appropriate.

Pour Jeanne, à nouveau,

and now also for Émile and Léopold

Contents

vii

Preface

Traditional scientific disciplines have lately been complemented by heuristics adopted in big tech companies to form the new field of Data Science. Now making its way into university curricula, this loosely defined field immediately brings computer science and statistics to mind. But mathematics, too, plays a central role by laying foundations and developing new theories. This book focuses on the subfield of Mathematical Data Science. Since its content is also loosely defined, a selection of topics was made to provide summaries only of Machine Learning, Optimal Recovery, Compressive Sensing (also known as Compressed Sensing), Optimization, and Neural Networks.

Audience: This book is intended for mathematicians who wish to know bits and pieces about Data Science. Ideally, it will convince them that there is some elegant theory behind this trendy field. Although the book may also be valuable for genuine data scientists in search of mathematical sophistication, it should primarily serve as a resource for a graduate course on Data Science given in a department of mathematics. In brief, the most important word of the title is the first one.

Theme: The common thread throughout this book is the processing of data given in the form

$$y_i = f(x^{(i)}), \qquad i \in [1:m],$$

toward the ultimate goal of learning/approximating/recovering[1] the unknown function f. In PART ONE (Machine Learning), one mostly thinks of the $x^{(i)}$ as independent realizations of a random variable and one targets results valid in expectation or with high probability. In PART TWO (Optimal Recovery), one thinks instead of the $x^{(i)}$ as fixed entities and one targets results valid

---

[1] The favored terminology seems to depend on one's inclination and training.

xiii

with certainty in a worst-case setting, given some side information about f. In PART THREE (Compressive Sensing), this side information conveys e.g. that f is a linear function depending on few variables. In this framework, it is actually possible to recover f exactly. A shared concern in these first three parts is complexity (sample or information complexity), i.e., the minimal number m of data that makes the learning/approximation/recovery task possible. The task almost invariably requires solving a minimization program, so PART FOUR (Optimization) reviews the necessary material. Finally, PART FIVE (Neural Networks) studies tools for the approximation of f that have recently proved very effective in Deep Learning.

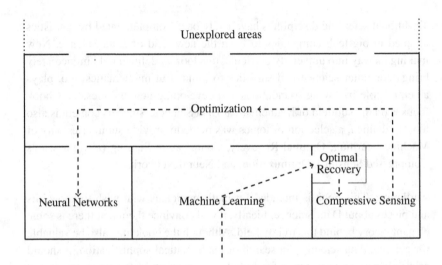

Figure 0.1 Map of the exhibition.

Content: The field of Data Science is too vast to be covered in a single book. As a matter of fact, each of the five parts picked out here is by itself worth a whole book, if not more. The executive summaries for each of the five parts suggest further readings that go into further detail. The selection of topics was merely dictated by my personal taste and interests. The route through the selected topics is metaphorically similar to an exhibition's itinerary; see Figure 0.1. Indeed, we enter through a hall (of Machine Learning) where the brightest lights lead us; continuing our path, we stumble upon a vestibule (of Optimal Recovery) filled with charming but neglected works, before arriving at a chamber (of Compressive Sensing) that we are particularly fond of; pausing for a while, we realize that the previous rooms were all connected to the large court (of Optimization) that we visit next; finally, as time runs out, we decide to come back later to see some unexplored areas, but we cannot avoid a stop at the most fashionable parlor (of Neural Networks).

Unexplored Areas: Many important topics are left out of this biased overview of mathematical Data Science. They include data assimilation (Law et al., 2015), data streams (Muthukrishnan, 2005), uncertainty quantification (Smith, 2013), reinforcement learning (Sutton and Barto, 2018), and topological data analysis (Dey and Wang, 2022), among others.

Novelty: Some of the topics covered here can already be found in book form in other places. This is particularly true for PART ONE, whose novelty lies mostly in the presentation. Other topics are unlikely to appear elsewhere. For instance, PART TWO is rather uncommon—the content of Chapter 10 there is found only in research articles. PART THREE is original as its presentation relies fully on a modified version of the standard restricted isometry property. This property plays the central role in the exposition of One-Bit Compressive Sensing offered in Chapter 17, which follows the survey article (Foucart, 2017). Most of PART FOUR is rather standard, except Chapter 22 where semidefinite programming techniques are applied to Optimal Recovery. The ingredients of PART FIVE are currently scattered around the literature. Finally, a sizable appendix is included in order to make the text almost self-contained, so that outside references are not required in the main text (with the exception of a few footnotes). It can serve as a toolkit for mathematical scientists who lack a formal training in high-dimensional geometry, probability theory, functional analysis, matrix analysis, or approximation theory. The results recalled in the appendix are of course not new, but some proofs may be innovative (e.g. the von Neumann trace inequality, the Birkhoff theorem). Some other results may not be very familiar (e.g. the Korovkin theorem, the Kolmogorov theorem).

Computational illustrations: Arguably, the field of Data Science would be inconsequential without computations. Although this book focuses on theory, most of its chapters are accompanied by unpretentious implementations, both in MATLAB and in Python. They can be found at

github.com/foucart/Mathematical_Pictures_at_a_Data_Science_Exhibition

Acknowledgment: This book originated from the lecture notes I wrote for a graduate course entitled Topics in Mathematical Data Science and delivered at Texas A&M University in Fall 2019 and in Fall 2020. Its completion was eased by a course development grant from the Texas A&M Institute of Data Science. The first bricks were actually laid while I was visiting the Institute for Foundations of Data Science at the University of Wisconsin–Madison during a sabbatical semester in Spring 2019. I am indebted to both these institutes for their support. I am also grateful to be associated with various grants from the NSF (DMS-1622134, DMS-1664803, CCF-1934904, DMS-2053172) and from the ONR (N00014-20-1-2787). Finally, I wish to thank a few colleagues for their feedback during the book's development, namely Radu Balan, Albert Cohen, Rémi Gribonval, Mark Iwen, Philipp Petersen, Sebastien Roch, Jan Vybíral, and Stephan Wojtowytsch.

Notation

Commonly Used Notation

$[i:j]$	the set $\{i, i+1, \ldots, j\}$ of integers from i to j
$\mathbb{N}$	the set $\{0, 1, 2, \ldots\}$ of natural numbers, including 0
$\mathbb{N}^*$	the set $\{1, 2, 3, \ldots\}$ of natural numbers, excluding 0
$\mathbb{Z}$	the set of integers
$\mathbb{Q}$	the set of rational numbers
$\mathbb{R}$	the set of real numbers
$\mathbb{C}$	the set of complex numbers
i	the imaginary unit $\sqrt{-1}$
$\mathcal{A}, \mathcal{S}, \mathcal{X}$	generic sets
$\mathcal{S}^c$	the complement of $\mathcal{S}$ (relative to $\mathcal{X} \supseteq \mathcal{S}$, i.e., $\mathcal{X} \setminus \mathcal{S}$)
$\mathcal{S} \Delta \mathcal{S}'$	the symmetric difference $(\mathcal{S} \cup \mathcal{S}') \setminus (\mathcal{S} \cap \mathcal{S}')$ of $\mathcal{S}$ and $\mathcal{S}'$
$\mathbb{1}_{\text{event}}$	the number equal to 1 if event is true and to 0 otherwise
$\mathbb{1}_{\mathcal{S}}$	the indicator function of a set $\mathcal{S}$ (so that $\mathbb{1}_{\mathcal{S}}(x) = \mathbb{1}_{\{x \in \mathcal{S}\}}$); it can also represent a vector in $\{0, 1\}^n$ when $\mathcal{S} \subseteq [1:n]$
$\|\mathcal{S}\|$	the cardinality of a finite set $\mathcal{S}$
F, X	generic vector spaces
span$(\mathcal{S})$	the linear subspace spanned by a set $\mathcal{S} \subseteq F$
conv$(\mathcal{S})$	the convex hull of a set $\mathcal{S} \subseteq F$
Ex$(\mathcal{S})$	the set of extreme points of a set $\mathcal{S} \subseteq F$
cl$(\mathcal{X})$	the closure of a set $\mathcal{S} \subseteq F$
vol$(\mathcal{S})$	the volume of a set $\mathcal{S} \subseteq F$
H	a Hilbert space
$\langle x, x' \rangle$	the inner product between two vectors $x, x' \in H$
$\mathcal{S}^{\perp}$	the linear space orthogonal to the set $\mathcal{S} \subseteq H$
$P_{\mathcal{V}}$	the orthogonal projector onto the linear subspace $\mathcal{V}$
T^*	the adjoint of a linear operator T defined on H

$\|x\|_F$	the norm of a vector $x \in F$
$\text{dist}_F(x, \mathcal{S})$	the distance from $x \in F$ to a subset $\mathcal{S}$ of F
$B(c, r)$	the ball centered at $c \in F$ with radius $r \geq 0$
B_F	the unit ball $B(0, 1)$ of a normed space F
F^*	the dual space of a normed space F
ℓ_p^n	the space $\mathbb{R}^n$ or $\mathbb{C}^n$ normed with $\|x\|_p = \left[\sum_{i=1}^n |x_i|^p \right]^{1/p}$
B_p^n	the unit ball of the space ℓ_p^n
$(e_1, \ldots, e_n)$	the canonical basis for $\mathbb{R}^n$ or $\mathbb{C}^n$
$[x_1; \ldots; x_n]$	a column vector with entries $x_1, x_2, \ldots, x_n$
$F(\mathcal{X}, \mathcal{Y})$	the space of functions from a set $\mathcal{X}$ to a set $\mathcal{Y}$
$C(\mathcal{X})$	the space of continuous functions from $\mathcal{X}$ to $\mathbb{R}$
$C^k(\mathcal{X})$	the space of k-times continuously differentiable functions
$L_p(\mathcal{X})$	the space of functions with integrable pth power
$W_p^k(\mathcal{X})$	the Sobolev space of functions with kth derivative in $L_p(\mathcal{X})$
$\mathcal{K}_{\text{Lip}}$	the set of functions f with Lipschitz constant $|f|_{\text{Lip}} \leq 1$
δ_x	the evaluation functional at a point $x \in \mathcal{X}$
μ, ν	generic Borel measures
$\mathcal{M}(\mathcal{X})$	the set of Borel measures on $\mathcal{X}$
$\mathcal{M}_+(\mathcal{X})$	the set of nonnegative Borel measures on $\mathcal{X}$
$\mathcal{P}_n$	the space of algebraic polynomials of degree $\leq n$
$\mathcal{T}_n$	the space of trigonometric polynomials of degree $\leq n$
A, B, X	generic matrices
$A_{i,j}$	the entry of a matrix A on the ith row and jth column
A^*	the adjoint of a matrix A, defined by $A_{i,j}^* = \overline{A_{j,i}}$
$A^\top$	the transpose of a matrix A, defined by $A_{i,j}^\top = A_{j,i}$
$A^{-\top}$	the matrix $(A^{-1})^\top = (A^\top)^{-1}$
$\text{diag}[x_1; \ldots; x_n]$	a diagonal matrix with diagonal entries $x_1, x_2, \ldots, x_n$
$\lambda_j(A)$	the jth eigenvalue of A (in nonincreasing order)
$\sigma_j(A)$	the jth singular value of A (in nonincreasing order)
$A \succeq 0$	means that the matrix A is positive semidefinite
$\langle A, B \rangle_F$	the Frobenius inner product between $A, B \in \mathbb{R}^{m \times n}$
$\|A\|_F$	the Frobenius norm of $A \in \mathbb{R}^{m \times n}$
$\|A\|_{2 \to 2}$	the operator norm of $A \in \mathbb{R}^{m \times n}$, i.e., $\sigma_1(A)$
$\|A\|_*$	the nuclear norm $A \in \mathbb{R}^{m \times n}$, i.e., $\sum_{i=1}^m \sigma_i(A)$
$\ker(A)$	the null space of (a matrix or linear map) A
$\text{ran}(A)$	the range of (a matrix or linear map) A
$u * v$	the (discrete or continuous) convolution product of u and v
$\log_2(x)$	the logarithm in base 2 of $x \in (0, +\infty)$
$\ln(x)$	the natural logarithm (in base e) of $x \in (0, +\infty)$
$\exp(x)$	the exponential of $x \in \mathbb{R}$

$\lfloor x \rfloor$	the floor of $x \in \mathbb{R}$, i.e., the integer satisfying $x - 1 < \lfloor x \rfloor \le x$
$\lceil x \rceil$	the ceiling of $x \in \mathbb{R}$, i.e., the integer satisfying $x \le \lceil x \rceil < x + 1$
$\mathbb{P}[\mathcal{E}]$	the probability of an event $\mathcal{E}$
$\mathbb{E}[Z]$	the expectation of a random variable Z
$\mathbb{V}[Z]$	the variance of a random variable Z
$\mathcal{N}(0, \sigma^2)$	the normal distribution with mean zero and variance σ^2
g	a standard gaussian random variable, i.e., $g \sim \mathcal{N}(0, 1)$

Machine-Learning-Specific Notation

$\mathcal{X}$	the set where the instances $x^{(i)}$ (aka datapoints) live
$\mathcal{Y}$	the set where the targets y_i (aka observations) live, often $\mathcal{Y} = \mathbb{R}$, $\mathcal{Y} = \{0, 1\}$, or $\mathcal{Y} = \{-1, +1\}$
$\mathcal{H}$	a hypothesis class, i.e., a subset of $F(\mathcal{X}, \mathcal{Y})$
Loss	a function from $\mathcal{Y} \times \mathcal{Y}$ into $[0, +\infty)$ such that $L(y, y) = 0$
$\mathrm{Risk}_f(h)$	the risk of a predictor $h \in \mathcal{H}$ given $f \in F(\mathcal{X}, \mathcal{Y})$
S	an element of $(\mathcal{X} \times \mathcal{Y})^m$ representing a sample
$\widehat{\mathrm{Risk}}_S(h)$	the empirical risk of $h \in \mathcal{H}$ relative to S
$\varepsilon_{\mathrm{app}}$	the approximation error
$\varepsilon_{\mathrm{est}}$	the estimation error
$m_{\mathcal{H}}(\varepsilon, \delta)$	the sample complexity
$\mathrm{vc}(\mathcal{H})$	the Vapnik–Chervonenkis dimension of $\mathcal{H} \subseteq F(\mathcal{X}, \{0, 1\})$
K	a kernel, i.e., a symmetric function defined on $\mathcal{X} \times \mathcal{X}$

Optimal-Recovery-Specific Notation

$\mathcal{K}$	the model set
Q	a quantity of interest, typically a linear map
λ_i	the ith observation functional, often equal to $\delta_{x^{(i)}}$
Λ	the observation map
Δ	a recovery map
$\mathrm{Err}_{\mathcal{K}, Q}(\Lambda, \Delta)$	the worst-case error of Δ (for Q over $\mathcal{K}$ given Λ)
$\mathrm{Err}^*_{\mathcal{K}, Q}(\Lambda)$	the intrinsic error (for Q over $\mathcal{K}$ given Λ)
$\mathrm{Err}^0_{\mathcal{K}, Q}(\Lambda)$	the null error (for Q over $\mathcal{K}$ given Λ)
$\mathrm{Err}^*_{\mathcal{K}, Q}(m)$	the mth minimal intrinsic error (for Q over $\mathcal{K}$)
$m_{\mathcal{K}, Q}(\varepsilon, d)$	the information complexity
$\mathrm{Var}_{HK}(f)$	the variation of f (in the sense of Hardy and Krause)
$\mathrm{Disc}^*(\mathfrak{X})$	the star discrepancy of a finite set $\mathfrak{X}$

Compressive-Sensing-Specific Notation

Σ_s^N	the set of s-sparse vectors in $\mathbb{R}^N$ or $\mathbb{C}^N$
$\text{supp}(x)$	the support of a vector x in $\mathbb{R}^N$ or $\mathbb{C}^N$
S	an index set, i.e., a subset of $[1:N]$
x_S	the vector x whose entries outside of S are zeroed out
H_s	the hard thresholding operator with parameter s
A	an $m \times N$ observation matrix
A_S	the submatrix of A with columns indexed by S^c removed
$\mathcal{A}$	an observation map (defined on a space of matrices)
μ	the coherence of a matrix
δ	ℓ_1-restricted isometry constant of a matrix or linear map
α	lower ℓ_1-restricted isometry constant of a matrix or linear map
β	upper ℓ_1-restricted isometry constant of a matrix or linear map
Δ	a recovery map
$d^m(\mathcal{K}, F)$	the mth Gelfand width of a set $\mathcal{K}$ in a space F
$\chi(v)$	the binary vector with ith entry given by $\mathbb{1}_{\{v_i > 0\}}$

Optimization-Specific Notation

$(x^t)_{t \geq 0}$	a sequence of vectors produced by some iterative algorithm
∇f	the gradient of a multivariate function f
L	the Lagrangian of a minimization program
λ, v	the dual optimization variables, aka Lagrange mutipliers
C^*	the dual cone of a set C
$\text{Toep}_\infty(u)$	the infinite symmetric Toeplitz matrix built from $(u_n)_{n \geq 0}$
$\text{Toep}_{N+1}(u)$	the finite symmetric Toeplitz matrix built from $(u_n)_{n=0}^N$

Neural-Networks-Specific notation

ϕ	a generic activation function
ReLU	the rectified linear unit defined by $\text{ReLU}(x) = \max\{x, 0\}$
n_ℓ	the width of the ℓth layer
$x^{[\ell]}$	the state vector at the ℓth layer
$W^{[\ell]}$	the weight matrix (in $\mathbb{R}^{n_\ell \times n_{\ell-1}}$) producing the ℓth layer
$b^{[\ell]}$	the bias vector (in $\mathbb{R}^{n_\ell}$) producing the ℓth layer
$\mathcal{N}_\phi$	the linear space of functions generated by shallow networks
$\mathcal{N}_\phi^n$	the set of functions generated by width-n shallow networks
$\mathcal{N}_\phi^{n,L}$	the set of functions generated by width-n, depth-L networks

PART ONE

MACHINE LEARNING

Executive Summary

What exactly constitutes Data Science is not universally agreed upon, but it is certainly inseparable from Machine Learning. Some would even consider Data Science as a subfield of Machine Learning—its intersection with application domains. This book adopts a different viewpoint: Data Science is seen as incorporating the field of Machine Learning.

A necessarily incomplete outline of this vast field is presented in the first of the book's five parts. It starts by considering the scenario of supervised learning, in which a to-be-learned function f is available only through point values $y_i = f(x^{(i)})$ at datapoints $x^{(1)}, \ldots, x^{(m)}$. In Statistical Learning Theory, these datapoints are assumed to be realizations of some hidden random variable. Chapter 1 introduces the main notions attached to this theory, in particular the PAC-learning framework. Chapter 2 scrutinizes the concept of VC-dimension, in anticipation of its connection to the problem of binary classification, where the labels y_i take only two values. Chapter 3, of a technical nature, makes this connection precise by establishing the fundamental theorem of PAC-learning. Chapter 4 continues to probe the problem of binary classification but drops the statistical setting. It proposes some tools—in particular, support vector machines—to separate datapoints and it also acquaints the readers with kernel methods. Chapter 5 takes a careful look at the associated reproducing kernel Hilbert spaces. Chapter 6 concludes the tour of supervised learning by way of a few peeks at the regression problem, featuring real-valued labels y_i. Chapter 7 turns to the scenario of unsupervised learning, in which the labels are absent: the task examined there consists in exploiting similarity information about the datapoints to cluster them in a meaningful way. Finally, Chapter 8 presents common techniques to deal with the hindering high-dimensionality of datapoints.

Readers in search of a more detailed exposition to Machine Learning are referred to the books by Shalev-Shwartz and Ben-David (2014) and Mohri et al. (2018). For more targeted reading, they can also consult the books by Hastie et al. (2009), Scholkopf and Smola (2001), and Vershynin (2018).

1

Rudiments of Statistical Learning Theory

In the scenario considered in the next few chapters, data reach a learner in the form

$$y_i = f(x^{(i)}), \qquad i \in [1:m].$$

Both the *instances* $x^{(i)} \in X$ and the *targets* $y_i \in \mathcal{Y}$ are known to the learner. It is often the case that $X \subseteq \mathbb{R}^d$ is made of vectors containing d *features*, overlooking here how these features are created, and that $\mathcal{Y}$ is a discrete set whose elements represent certain classes, in which case the y_i are called *labels*. The postulate of statistical learning theory is that $x^{(1)}, \ldots, x^{(m)}$ come as independent realizations of a single random variable—whose distribution is not available to the learner. The implicit assumption that the targets y_i depend deterministically on the instances $x^{(i)}$ via $y_i = f(x^{(i)})$ for some function $f : X \to \mathcal{Y}$ could be relaxed. It is indeed usual, although not examined in this book, to consider the couples $(x^{(i)}, y_i) \in X \times \mathcal{Y}$ as independent realizations of a random variable (x, y) with a distribution on $X \times \mathcal{Y}$ for which $\mathbb{E}[y|x] = f(x)$.

1.1 True and Empirical Risks

The learner's objective is to exploit the data given through the *training sample* $S = ((x^{(1)}, y_1), \ldots, (x^{(m)}, y_m))$ and to produce a function $h_S : X \to \mathcal{Y}$, called a *predictor*, as a substitute for the unknown function $f : X \to \mathcal{Y}$. The map $\Delta : S \in (X \times \mathcal{Y})^m \mapsto h_S \in F(X, \mathcal{Y})$ does not need to be computationally feasible at this point, so Δ is referred to as a *learning map* rather than a learning algorithm. The performance of a given predictor $h \in F(X, \mathcal{Y})$ is assessed by how small its *risk* is. The latter, also called the *generalization error*, is defined relative to a loss function by

$$\mathrm{Risk}_f(h) := \mathbb{E}[\mathrm{Loss}(h(x), f(x))], \tag{1.1}$$

where the expectation is taken over a random variable x whose distribution is the one that generated the $x^{(i)}$. The *loss function*, defined on $\mathcal{Y} \times \mathcal{Y}$ and taking values in $[0, \infty)$, should be small when its two inputs are close and large when they are far. For *binary classification*, i.e., the situation where $\mathcal{Y} = \{0, 1\}$ or $\mathcal{Y} = \{-1, +1\}$, a popular choice is the *0/1-loss*, given by

$$\text{Loss}_{0/1}(y, y') = \mathbb{1}_{\{y \neq y'\}} = \begin{cases} 1 & \text{if } y \neq y', \\ 0 & \text{if } y = y'. \end{cases}$$

For *regression*, i.e., the situation where $\mathcal{Y} = \mathbb{R}$, a popular choice is the *square loss*, given by

$$\text{Loss}_{\text{sq}}(y, y') = (y - y')^2.$$

Notice that the learner does not have access to the true risk defined in (1.1), since the distribution generating $x^{(1)}, \ldots, x^{(m)}$ is not available. But the training sample $S = ((x^{(1)}, y_1), \ldots, (x^{(m)}, y_m))$ supplies an ersatz known as the *empirical risk*, which is defined by

$$\widehat{\text{Risk}}_S(h) := \frac{1}{m} \sum_{i=1}^{m} \text{Loss}(h(x^{(i)}), y_i).$$

Without constraint on $h \in F(X, \mathcal{Y})$, minimizing the empirical risk is easy: one can create a predictor h_S yielding $\widehat{\text{Risk}}_S(h_S) = 0$ by forcing $h_S(x^{(i)}) = y_i$ for each $i \in [1 : m]$ and choosing $h_S(x)$ arbitrarily for $x \notin \{x^{(1)}, \ldots, x^{(m)}\}$, e.g. as a constant there. However, such a predictor will not generalize well, in the sense that the true risk (aka generalization error) will not be small.

This phenomenon is attenuated by calling upon a prior belief that realistic predictors are close to functions from a certain *hypothesis class* $\mathcal{H} \subseteq F(X, \mathcal{Y})$. Thus, with the constraint that h belongs to $\mathcal{H}$, the *empirical risk minimization* strategy offers the natural learning map defined by

$$\Delta_{\mathcal{H}}^{\text{erm}} : S \in (X \times \mathcal{Y})^m \mapsto \operatorname*{argmin}_{h \in \mathcal{H}} \widehat{\text{Risk}}_S(h) \in \mathcal{H}.$$

The risk of this empirical risk minimizer decomposes as

$$\text{Risk}_f(\Delta_{\mathcal{H}}^{\text{erm}}(S)) = \varepsilon_{\text{app}} + \varepsilon_{\text{est}},$$

i.e., as the sum of the *approximation error* $\varepsilon_{\text{app}} \geq 0$ and the *estimation error* $\varepsilon_{\text{est}} \geq 0$, respectively given by

$$\varepsilon_{\text{app}} := \inf_{h \in \mathcal{H}} \text{Risk}_f(h),$$

$$\varepsilon_{\text{est}} := \text{Risk}_f(\Delta_{\mathcal{H}}^{\text{erm}}(S)) - \inf_{h \in \mathcal{H}} \text{Risk}_f(h).$$

The approximation error ε_{app} is independent of the sample S and reflects how well f can be approximated by elements from the given hypothesis class. The estimation error ε_{est} is the object of the considerations that follow.

1.2 PAC-Learnability

In the *probably approximately correct* (PAC for short) framework, one attempts to make ε_{est} smaller than a prescribed accuracy $\varepsilon \in (0, 1)$ with a prescribed confidence $\delta \in (0, 1)$. It is sometimes required to do so via an efficient learning algorithm, i.e., an algorithm whose runtime is polynomial in ε^{-1}, δ^{-1}, and the sizes of the problem. This is not enforced in the formal definition below, in which the probability is taken over $x^{(1)}, \ldots, x^{(m)}$, understood as independent random variables.

Definition 1.1 A hypothesis class $\mathcal{H} \subseteq F(\mathcal{X}, \mathcal{Y})$ is called *PAC-learnable* with respect to a loss function Loss: $\mathcal{Y} \times \mathcal{Y} \to [0, \infty)$ if there exists a learning map $\Delta: S \in (\mathcal{X} \times \mathcal{Y})^m \mapsto h_S \in \mathcal{H}$ such that, for all $f: \mathcal{X} \to \mathcal{Y}$ and all $\varepsilon, \delta \in (0, 1)$,

$$\mathbb{P}\left[\text{Risk}_f(h_S) - \inf_{h \in \mathcal{H}} \text{Risk}_f(h) \leq \varepsilon \right] \geq 1 - \delta,$$

independently of the probability distribution on $\mathcal{X}$, provided that

$$m \geq m_{\mathcal{H}}(\varepsilon, \delta)$$

for some $m_{\mathcal{H}}: (0, 1)^2 \to \mathbb{N}^*$ growing at most polynomially in ε^{-1} and δ^{-1}.

The smallest possible function $m_{\mathcal{H}}$ appearing in this definition is referred to as the *sample complexity*. For binary classification with the 0/1-loss, it would have been equivalent to state the definition with Δ specifically taken to be the empirical risk minimization map. This will be revealed by the fundamental theorem of PAC-learning in Chapter 3. As a prelude to this theorem, the next result shows that a class of boolean functions that is finite is automatically PAC-learnable for the 0/1-loss. This is an example of a distribution-free result, since no assumption on the underlying probability distribution is made.

Proposition 1.2 *Given a finite set* $\mathcal{H} \subseteq F(\mathcal{X}, \{0, 1\})$ *and a loss function with values in* $[0, 1]$, *the empirical risk minimization strategy provides a learning map* $S \in (\mathcal{X} \times \mathcal{Y})^m \mapsto h_S \in \mathcal{H}$ *such that, for all boolean functions* $f: \mathcal{X} \to \{0, 1\}$ *and all* $\varepsilon, \delta \in (0, 1)$,

$$\mathbb{P}\left[\text{Risk}_f(h_S) - \inf_{h \in \mathcal{H}} \text{Risk}_f(h) \leq \varepsilon \right] \geq 1 - \delta \qquad (1.2)$$

provided that

$$m \geq \frac{2\ln(2|\mathcal{H}|/\delta)}{\varepsilon^2}. \tag{1.3}$$

Proof The inequality (1.2) shall be established in the equivalent form

$$\mathbb{P} := \mathbb{P}[\operatorname{Risk}_f(h_S) - \operatorname{Risk}_f(h_*) > \varepsilon] \leq \delta, \tag{1.4}$$

where $h_* \in \mathcal{H}$ is chosen so that $\operatorname{Risk}_f(h_*)$ is equal to $\inf_{h \in \mathcal{H}} \operatorname{Risk}_f(h)$ (or is arbitrarily close to it in case the infimum is not achieved). From the definition of empirical risk minimization, one observes that $\widehat{\operatorname{Risk}}_S(h_S) \leq \widehat{\operatorname{Risk}}_S(h_*)$ and, in turn, that

$$
\begin{aligned}
\operatorname{Risk}_f(h_S) - \operatorname{Risk}_f(h_*) &= (\operatorname{Risk}_f(h_S) - \widehat{\operatorname{Risk}}_S(h_S)) + (\widehat{\operatorname{Risk}}_S(h_S) - \operatorname{Risk}_f(h_*)) \\
&\leq (\operatorname{Risk}_f(h_S) - \widehat{\operatorname{Risk}}_S(h_S)) + (\widehat{\operatorname{Risk}}_S(h_*) - \operatorname{Risk}_f(h_*)) \\
&\leq 2 \sup_{h \in \mathcal{H}} |\widehat{\operatorname{Risk}}_S(h) - \operatorname{Risk}_f(h)|.
\end{aligned}
$$

As a consequence, one has

$$
\begin{aligned}
\mathbb{P} &\leq \mathbb{P}\left[\sup_{h \in \mathcal{H}} |\widehat{\operatorname{Risk}}_S(h) - \operatorname{Risk}_f(h)| > \frac{\varepsilon}{2}\right] \\
&= \mathbb{P}\left[|\widehat{\operatorname{Risk}}_S(h) - \operatorname{Risk}_f(h)| > \frac{\varepsilon}{2} \text{ for some } h \in \mathcal{H}\right]. \tag{1.5}
\end{aligned}
$$

For a fixed $h \in \mathcal{H}$, the *Hoeffding inequality* (see Theorem B.6) yields

$$
\begin{aligned}
&\mathbb{P}\left[|\widehat{\operatorname{Risk}}_S(h) - \operatorname{Risk}_f(h)| > \frac{\varepsilon}{2}\right] \\
&= \mathbb{P}\left[\left|\frac{1}{m}\sum_{i=1}^{m} \operatorname{Loss}(h(x^{(i)}), f(x^{(i)})) - \mathbb{E}[\operatorname{Loss}(f(x), h(x))]\right| > \frac{\varepsilon}{2}\right] \\
&\leq 2\exp\left(-\frac{\varepsilon^2 m}{2}\right),
\end{aligned}
$$

having used the fact that the random variables $\operatorname{Loss}(h(x^{(i)}), f(x^{(i)}))$ take values in $[0, 1]$. A union bound in (1.5) now implies that

$$\mathbb{P} \leq 2|\mathcal{H}|\exp\left(-\frac{\varepsilon^2 m}{2}\right).$$

This is bounded above by δ exactly when $m \geq 2\ln(2|\mathcal{H}|/\delta)/\varepsilon^2$, i.e., when Condition (1.3) is fulfilled. $\qquad\square$

1.3 Validation

With m and δ being fixed, it is apparent from (1.3) that enlarging the class $\mathcal{H}$ has the effect of increasing (a bound on) the estimation error ε_{est}. At the same time, enlarging the class $\mathcal{H}$ has the effect of decreasing the approximation error ε_{app}. Thus, in order to keep the total error $\varepsilon_{app} + \varepsilon_{est}$ low, a compromise is to be found for the size of $\mathcal{H}$. This observation exemplifies the *bias-complexity tradeoff*. In more general situations, it remains intuitive that a small hypothesis class is not flexible enough to perform well on the sample (this phenomenon is called *underfitting*), while a large hypothesis class can match the sample perfectly but perform poorly on other datapoints (this phenomenon is called *overfitting*); see Figure 1.1 for an illustration.

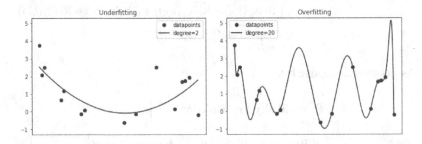

Figure 1.1 Data fitting with univariate polynomials results in underfitting when the degree is low (left) and in overfitting when the degree is high (right).

Even after having decided on a hypothesis class $\mathcal{H}$ and a learning map Δ, the learner will still find it difficult to evaluate the true risk of the predictor $h = \Delta(\mathcal{S})$, as the definition (1.1) involves two unknown entities: the function f and the distribution over which the expectation is taken. The natural ersatz $\widehat{\text{Risk}}_S$ is not a reliable substitute for $\text{Risk}_f(h)$ because the learning map Δ is designed to make this empirical risk small, yet its performance on unseen datapoints remains uncertain. A heuristic workaround consists in partitioning the sample $\mathcal{S}$ into a *training set* $\mathcal{T}$ and a *validation set* $\mathcal{V}$. The training set $\mathcal{T}$ is used to produce the predictor $h = \Delta(\mathcal{T})$, whose performance is then assessed by the empirical risk $\widehat{\text{Risk}}_{\mathcal{V}}(h)$ relative to the validation set $\mathcal{V}$. *Cross-validation* actually consists in partitioning $\mathcal{S}$ into K groups $\mathcal{U}_1, \ldots, \mathcal{U}_K$ of roughly equal size and to repeat, for each $k \in [1:K]$, the above procedure with $\mathcal{S} \setminus \mathcal{U}_k$ and $\mathcal{U}_k$ as training and validation sets, respectively.

Exercises

1.1 Given $h \in F(X, Y)$, verify that the expectation of the empirical risk over the independent random variables $x^{(1)}, \ldots, x^{(m)}$ agrees with the true risk, i.e., that $\mathbb{E}[\widehat{\text{Risk}}_S(h)] = \mathbb{E}[\text{Loss}(h(x), f(x))]$. Verify also that its variance satisfies $\mathbb{V}[\widehat{\text{Risk}}_S(h)] = \mathbb{V}[\text{Loss}(h(x), f(x))]/m$.

1.2 Let $\mathcal{H}$ be the hypothesis class of *affine functions* on $\mathbb{R}^d$, i.e., of functions of the form

$$x \in \mathbb{R}^d \mapsto a_0 + a_1 x_1 + \cdots + a_d x_d \in \mathbb{R}.$$

For the square loss, observe that the empirical risk minimization strategy reduces to the least-squares problem of minimizing $\|y - Xa\|_2^2$ over all $a \in \mathbb{R}^{d+1}$ for some matrix $X \in \mathbb{R}^{m \times (d+1)}$ to identify.

1.3 Let a sample S be partitioned into a training set $\mathcal{T}$ and a validation set $\mathcal{V}$. Considering the hypothesis class of affine functions and the square loss, let $h_{\mathcal{T}}$ denote the empirical risk minimizer relative to $\mathcal{T}$. Prove that the expected empirical risk of $h_{\mathcal{T}}$ is no larger on $\mathcal{T}$ than on $\mathcal{V}$, i.e., that

$$\mathbb{E}\big[\widehat{\text{Risk}}_{\mathcal{T}}(h_{\mathcal{T}})\big] \leq \mathbb{E}\big[\widehat{\text{Risk}}_{\mathcal{V}}(h_{\mathcal{T}})\big],$$

with expectation taken over all the independent random variables $x^{(i)}$.

1.4 When (x, y) is a random variable over $X \times Y$, the *risk* of a predictor $h \colon X \to Y$ is defined relative to a loss function via

$$\text{Risk}(h) := \mathbb{E}[\text{Loss}(h(x), y)],$$

with expectation now taken jointly over x and y.

For regression with the square loss, defining $f(x) := \mathbb{E}[y|x]$ to be the conditional probability of y given x, establish the identity

$$\text{Risk}(h) = \text{Risk}(f) + \mathbb{E}\big[(h(x) - f(x))^2\big],$$

showing that f is an optimal predictor.

For classification with the 0/1-loss, prove that an optimal predictor is given by the *Bayes predictor* defined for $x \in X$ by

$$f(x) = \begin{cases} 1 & \text{if } \mathbb{P}[y = 1|x] \geq \mathbb{P}[y = 0|x], \\ 0 & \text{otherwise.} \end{cases}$$

2

Vapnik–Chervonenkis Dimension

While the concept of dimension usually applies to sets, the concept of *Vapnik–Chervonenkis dimension*, or VC-dimension for short, applies to families of sets (as subsets of some bigger set X). Since one can identify a subset of X with its indicator function via the correspondence between $S \subseteq X$ and $\mathbb{1}_S \in F(X, \{0, 1\})$, the concept of VC-dimension applies in a similar way to families of boolean functions. This is the viewpoint taken in Machine Learning, where a family of boolean functions is thought of as a hypothesis class. The fundamental theorem of PAC-learning, to be covered in the next chapter, will reveal the importance of the concept of VC-dimension: a hypothesis class is PAC-learnable if and only if it has a finite VC-dimension.

2.1 Definitions

Here is the formal definition of *VC-dimension* that adopts the viewpoint of boolean functions.

Definition 2.1 Let $\mathcal{H}$ be a family of boolean functions defined on a set X. A subset $\mathcal{Y}$ of X is said to be *shattered* by $\mathcal{H}$ if any $g: \mathcal{Y} \to \{0, 1\}$ takes the form $g = h_{|\mathcal{Y}}$ for some $h \in \mathcal{H}$. The VC-dimension of $\mathcal{H}$ is the largest size of a subset shattered by $\mathcal{H}$. In short,

$$\mathrm{vc}(\mathcal{H}) = \sup \{m \in \mathbb{N}^* : \tau_{\mathcal{H}}(m) = 2^m\},$$

where the *shatter function* (aka *growth function*) is defined by

$$\tau_{\mathcal{H}}(m) = \max_{|\mathcal{Y}|=m} \left|\{h_{|\mathcal{Y}}, h \in \mathcal{H}\}\right|.$$

By adopting the viewpoint of sets rather than boolean functions, one can repeat the definition of VC-dimension as the equivalent statement below, which

10

shows more distinctly that $\emptyset$ is always shattered by $\mathcal{H}$ and that X is shattered by $\mathcal{H}$ if and only if $\mathcal{H}$ consists of all subsets of X.

Definition 2.2 Let $\mathcal{H}$ be a family of subsets of a set X. A subset $\mathcal{Y}$ of X is said to be *shattered* by $\mathcal{H}$ if any subset $\mathcal{Z} \subseteq \mathcal{Y}$ takes the form $\mathcal{Z} = \mathcal{Y} \cap S$ for some $S \in \mathcal{H}$. The VC-dimension of $\mathcal{H}$ is the largest size of a subset shattered by $\mathcal{H}$. In short,

$$\mathrm{vc}(\mathcal{H}) = \sup\{m \in \mathbb{N}^* : \tau_{\mathcal{H}}(m) = 2^m\},$$

where the *shatter function* (aka *growth function*) is defined by

$$\tau_{\mathcal{H}}(m) = \max_{|\mathcal{Y}|=m} |\{\mathcal{Y} \cap S, S \in \mathcal{H}\}|.$$

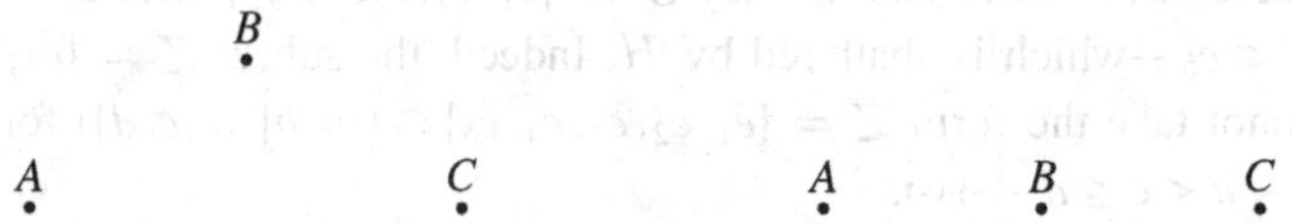

Figure 2.1 The set on the left is shattered by the family of disks, while the set on the right is not, since $\{A, C\}$ cannot equal the intersection of $\{A, B, C\}$ with a disk.

2.2 Examples

To understand the concept of VC-dimension, it is best to work through a few examples. Notice that, in view of the previous definition(s), to establish that a family $\mathcal{H}$ has a VC-dimension equal to d, one needs to prove that

(i) there is a set $\mathcal{Y}$ of size d which is shattered by $\mathcal{H}$ (not necessarily that all sets of size d are shattered by $\mathcal{H}$)—this says that $\mathrm{vc}(\mathcal{H}) \geq d$;
(ii) there is no set $\mathcal{Y}$ of size $d + 1$ which is shattered by $\mathcal{H}$—this says that $\mathrm{vc}(\mathcal{H}) \leq d$.

Example 2.3 For intervals, the VC-dimension equals 2.

Proof Let $\mathcal{H}$ be the family of subsets of $\mathbb{R}$ made of finite intervals $[a, b]$ with $-\infty < a \leq b < +\infty$. The two points below show that $\mathrm{vc}(\mathcal{H}) = 2$.

(i) There is a set of size 2—in fact, any set $\mathcal{Y} = \{c, e\}$ with $c < e$—which is shattered by $\mathcal{H}$. Indeed, picking $d \in (c, e)$,

$$\emptyset = \{c, e\} \cap [d, d], \qquad \{c\} = \{c, e\} \cap [c, d], \qquad (2.1)$$

$$\{c, e\} = \{c, e\} \cap [c, e], \qquad \{e\} = \{c, e\} \cap [d, e]. \qquad (2.2)$$

(ii) There is no set of size 3—say $\mathcal{Y} = \{c, d, e\}$ with $c < d < e$—which is shattered by $\mathcal{H}$. Indeed, the subset $\mathcal{Z} = \{c, e\}$ of $\mathcal{Y}$ cannot take the form $\mathcal{Z} = \{c, d, e\} \cap [a, b]$ for some $-\infty < a \leq b < +\infty$.   □

Example 2.4   For pairs of intervals, the VC-dimension equals 4.

Proof   Let $\mathcal{H}$ be the family of subsets of $\mathbb{R}$ made of unions $[a, b] \cup [c, d]$ of two intervals with $-\infty < a \leq b < c \leq d < +\infty$. The two points below show that $\mathrm{vc}(\mathcal{H}) = 4$.

   (i) There is a set of size 4—in fact, any set $\mathcal{Y}$ of size 4—which is shattered by $\mathcal{H}$. Indeed, careful consideration as in (2.1) and (2.2) above reveal that any of the 16 subsets of $\mathcal{Y}$ can be obtained as the intersection of $\mathcal{Y}$ with a pair of intervals.

   (ii) There is no set of size 5—say $\mathcal{Y} = \{e_1, e_2, e_3, e_4, e_5\}$ with $e_1 < e_2 < e_3 < e_4 < e_5$—which is shattered by $\mathcal{H}$. Indeed, the subset $\mathcal{Z} = \{e_1, e_3, e_5\}$ of $\mathcal{Y}$ cannot take the form $\mathcal{Z} = \{e_1, e_2, e_3, e_4, e_5\} \cap ([a, b] \cup [c, d])$ for some $-\infty < a \leq b < c \leq d < +\infty$.   □

Example 2.5   For half-spaces in $\mathbb{R}^n$, the VC-dimension equals $n + 1$.

Proof   Let $\mathcal{H}$ be the family of subsets of $\mathbb{R}^n$ made of half-spaces determined by an equation $\langle w, x \rangle - b \geq 0$ for some $w \in \mathbb{R}^n$ and $b \in \mathbb{R}$. Equivalently, the family $\mathcal{H}$ consists of half-spaces $S_{\widetilde{w}} = \{x \in \mathbb{R}^n : \langle \widetilde{w}, \widetilde{x} \rangle \geq 0\}$ for some $\widetilde{w} \in \mathbb{R}^{n+1}$, where $\widetilde{x} = [x; 1] \in \mathbb{R}^{n+1}$ represents the vector $x \in \mathbb{R}^n$ padded with a one in the last position. The two points below show that $\mathrm{vc}(\mathcal{H}) = n + 1$.

   (i) There is a set of size $n + 1$ which is shattered by $\mathcal{H}$—for instance, the set $\mathcal{Y} = \{0, e_1, \ldots, e_n\}$. Indeed, in the case $\mathcal{Z} = \{e_i, i \in I\}$ for some $I \subseteq [1 : n]$, one has $\mathcal{Z} = \mathcal{Y} \cap S_{\widetilde{w}}$ with $\widetilde{w} = [\mathbb{1}_I; -1]$, and in the case $\mathcal{Z} = \{0\} \cup \{e_i, i \in I\}$ for some $I \subseteq [1 : n]$, one has $\mathcal{Z} = \mathcal{Y} \cap S_{\widetilde{w}}$ with $\widetilde{w} = [-\mathbb{1}_{I^c}; 0]$.

   (ii) There is no set of size $n+2$—say $\mathcal{Y} = \{x_1, \ldots, x_{n+2}\}$—which is shattered by $\mathcal{H}$. Indeed, since $\widetilde{x}_1, \ldots, \widetilde{x}_{n+2}$ are $n + 2$ vectors in $\mathbb{R}^{n+1}$, they cannot be linearly independent, so there must exist $(c_1, \ldots, c_{n+2}) \neq (0, \ldots, 0)$ such that $c_1 \widetilde{x}_1 + \cdots + c_{n+2}\widetilde{x}_{n+2} = 0$. Considering the index sets I^+ and I^- defined by $I^{\pm} = \{i \in [1 : n + 2] : \pm c_i > 0\}$, which are both nonempty, one writes

$$\sum_{i \in I^+} c_i \widetilde{x}_i = \sum_{i \in I^-} (-c_i) \widetilde{x}_i. \tag{2.3}$$

If $\mathcal{Y}$ was shattered by $\mathcal{H}$, then there would exist some $\widetilde{w} \in \mathbb{R}^{n+1}$ such that $\{x_i, i \in I^-\} = \{x_1, \ldots, x_{n+2}\} \cap S_{\widetilde{w}}$, so $\langle \widetilde{w}, \widetilde{x}_i \rangle \geq 0$ for $i \in I^-$ and $\langle \widetilde{w}, \widetilde{x}_i \rangle < 0$ for $i \in I^+$. Taking the inner product of (2.3) with $\widetilde{w}$, the left-hand side would be negative and the right-hand side would be nonnegative, which is of course a contradiction.   □

It is possible to derive the VC-dimension exactly for further examples, e.g. in the plane

- for circles, the VC-dimension equals 3;
- for axis-aligned rectangles, the VC-dimension equals 4;
- for convex k-gons, the VC-dimension equals $2k + 1$.

2.3 Sauer Lemma

It is now time to have a closer look at the *shatter function* $\tau_{\mathcal{H}}$. According to Definitions 2.1 and 2.2, if this function grows polynomially, i.e., if it is bounded above by a polynomial, then the VC-dimension of the family $\mathcal{H}$ has to be finite. The next result, known as the *Sauer lemma* (aka the Sauer–Shelah lemma or the Sauer–Shelah–Perles lemma), conversely demonstrates that a finite VC-dimension implies a polynomial growth for the shatter function. Thus, there are only two possible behaviors for the asymptotic growth of the shatter function: either exponential or polynomial.

Lemma 2.6 *If* $\mathrm{vc}(\mathcal{H}) = d$ *and* $m \geq d$, *then*

$$\tau_{\mathcal{H}}(m) \leq \sum_{k=0}^{d} \binom{m}{k} \leq \left(\frac{em}{d}\right)^d.$$

Proof The second inequality involves elementary observations: the estimate

$$\binom{m}{k} = \frac{m(m-1)\cdots(m-k+1)}{k!} \leq \frac{m^k}{k!} = \left(\frac{m}{d}\right)^k \frac{d^k}{k!}$$

is used together with the fact that $d \leq m$ in

$$\sum_{k=0}^{d} \binom{m}{k} \leq \sum_{k=0}^{d} \left(\frac{m}{d}\right)^k \frac{d^k}{k!} \leq \left(\frac{m}{d}\right)^d \sum_{k=0}^{\infty} \frac{d^k}{k!} = \left(\frac{m}{d}\right)^d e^d.$$

For the first inequality, one isolates an observation known as the *Pajor lemma*, namely:

if X is a finite set, then any family $\mathcal{H}$ of boolean functions on X has size

$$|\mathcal{H}| \leq |\{\mathcal{Y} \subseteq X : \mathcal{Y} \text{ is shattered by } \mathcal{H}\}|. \tag{2.4}$$

Assuming (2.4) is established, applying it not to the original family $\mathcal{H}$ of the lemma but to $\mathcal{H}_{|\mathcal{Y}} := \{h_{|\mathcal{Y}} : h \in \mathcal{H}\}$, where $\mathcal{Y}$ has size $|\mathcal{Y}| = m$, one obtains

$$|\{h_{|\mathcal{Y}} : h \in \mathcal{H}\}| \leq |\{\mathcal{Y}' \subseteq \mathcal{Y} : \mathcal{Y}' \text{ is shattered by } \mathcal{H}\}|.$$

Recalling that no $\mathcal{Y}'$ of size $\geq d + 1$ can be shattered by $\mathcal{H}$, one sees that

$$|\{h_{|\mathcal{Y}} : h \in \mathcal{H}\}| \leq |\{\mathcal{Y}' \subseteq \mathcal{Y} : |\mathcal{Y}'| \leq d\}| = \sum_{k=0}^{d} \binom{m}{k}.$$

Taking the maximum over $\mathcal{Y}$ gives the desired result.

Thus, it remains to prove (2.4), which is done by induction on $n = |X|$. The base case $n = 1$ holds because, when $|X| = 1$, there are only two boolean functions on X, so that $|\mathcal{H}| \leq 2$, and because $\emptyset$ is always shattered by $\mathcal{H}$ while X is shattered by $\mathcal{H}$ if and only if $|\mathcal{H}| = 2$. Assume now that the induction hypothesis holds up to $n - 1$, $n \geq 2$. Let X be a set of size n and let $\mathcal{H}$ be a family of boolean functions on X. For an arbitrary $x \in X$, write $X = \{x\} \cup X'$ with $|X'| = n - 1$, and consider two families $\mathcal{H}_0$ and $\mathcal{H}_1$ of boolean functions on X' defined by

$$\mathcal{H}_{0/1} = \{h_{|X'}, \ h \in \mathcal{H}, \ h(x) = 0/1\}.$$

Consider also two families $\mathcal{F}_0$ and $\mathcal{F}_1$ of subsets of X' defined by

$$\mathcal{F}_{0/1} = \{\mathcal{Y}' \subseteq X' : \mathcal{Y}' \text{ is shattered by } \mathcal{H}_{0/1}\}.$$

By the induction hypothesis, one has $|\mathcal{H}_{0/1}| \leq |\mathcal{F}_{0/1}|$, and hence

$$|\mathcal{H}| = |\mathcal{H}_0| + |\mathcal{H}_1| \leq |\mathcal{F}_0| + |\mathcal{F}_1| = |\mathcal{F}_0 \cup \mathcal{F}_1| + |\mathcal{F}_0 \cap \mathcal{F}_1|.$$

It is claimed that $|\mathcal{F}_0 \cup \mathcal{F}_1| \leq |\mathcal{F}'|$ and that $|\mathcal{F}_0 \cap \mathcal{F}_1| \leq |\mathcal{F}''|$, where

$$\mathcal{F}' := \{\mathcal{Y} \subseteq X : \mathcal{Y} \text{ is shattered by } \mathcal{H} \text{ and } x \notin \mathcal{Y}\},$$
$$\mathcal{F}'' := \{\mathcal{Y} \subseteq X : \mathcal{Y} \text{ is shattered by } \mathcal{H} \text{ and } x \in \mathcal{Y}\}.$$

To justify the first claim, consider $\mathcal{Y}' \in \mathcal{F}_0 \cup \mathcal{F}_1$. One has $\mathcal{Y}' \subseteq X$, $x \notin \mathcal{Y}'$, and $\mathcal{Y}'$ is shattered by either $\mathcal{H}_0$ or $\mathcal{H}_1$, which implies that it is shattered by $\mathcal{H}$, thus $\mathcal{Y}' \in \mathcal{F}'$. This means that $\mathcal{F}_0 \cup \mathcal{F}_1 \subseteq \mathcal{F}'$, and in particular $|\mathcal{F}_0 \cup \mathcal{F}_1| \leq |\mathcal{F}'|$. To justify the second claim, consider $\mathcal{Y}' \in \mathcal{F}_0 \cap \mathcal{F}_1$. One has $\mathcal{Y}' \subseteq X$, $x \notin \mathcal{Y}'$, and $\mathcal{Y}'$ is shattered by $\mathcal{H}_0$ and by $\mathcal{H}_1$, which implies that $\mathcal{Y} = \{x\} \cup \mathcal{Y}'$ is shattered by $\mathcal{H}$, thus $\mathcal{Y} \in \mathcal{F}''$. Since distinct $\mathcal{Y}' \in \mathcal{F}_0 \cap \mathcal{F}_1$ give rise to distinct $\mathcal{Y} = \{x\} \cup \mathcal{Y}' \in \mathcal{F}''$, it follows that $|\mathcal{F}_0 \cap \mathcal{F}_1| \leq |\mathcal{F}''|$. With both claims now justified, one derives that

$$|\mathcal{H}| \leq |\mathcal{F}'| + |\mathcal{F}''| = |\{\mathcal{Y} \subseteq X : \mathcal{Y} \text{ is shattered by } \mathcal{H}\}|,$$

which is the induction hypothesis for n. This concludes the proof. $\square$

Exercises

2.1　Show that $vc(\mathcal{H}) \le \log_2(|\mathcal{H}|)$ for a finite family $\mathcal{H}$.

2.2　Given two families $\mathcal{H}$ and $\mathcal{H}'$ of subsets of a set X, prove that

$$\max\{vc(\mathcal{H}), vc(\mathcal{H}')\} \le vc(\mathcal{H} \cup \mathcal{H}') \le vc(\mathcal{H}) + vc(\mathcal{H}') + 1.$$

2.3　Prove the correctness of the VC-dimensions stated for the families of circles, of axis-aligned rectangles, and of convex k-gons.

2.4　Example 2.5 could have been justified by invoking the *Radon theorem*: any set of $n + 2$ points in $\mathbb{R}^n$ can be partitioned into two subsets whose convex hulls intersect. Establish this theorem.

3

Learnability for Binary Classification

This chapter is devoted to the awaited *fundamental theorem of PAC-learning* and to its proof. Here is the statement.

Theorem 3.1 *For a hypothesis class $\mathcal{H} \subseteq F(X, \{0, 1\})$ of boolean functions, the following properties are equivalent when using the 0/1-loss:*

(i) *$\mathcal{H}$ has finite VC-dimension;*
(ii) *$\mathcal{H}$ has the uniform convergence property;*
(iii) *empirical risk minimization is a successful PAC-learning map;*
(iv) *$\mathcal{H}$ is PAC-learnable.*

The implication (iii)$\Rightarrow$(iv) is straightforward. Once the uniform convergence property is formally defined below, the implication (ii)$\Rightarrow$(iii) will be easy. The implications (i)$\Rightarrow$(ii) and (iv)$\Rightarrow$(i) are the difficult ones.

3.1 Uniform Convergence Property

This section is devoted to the proof of the implication (ii)$\Rightarrow$(iii). One starts by defining the *uniform convergence property*, recalling that the randomness stems from the datapoints $x^{(1)}, \ldots, x^{(m)}$ in the sample S, which are viewed as independent identically distributed random variables.

Definition 3.2 A hypothesis class $\mathcal{H} \subseteq F(X, \mathcal{Y})$ has the *uniform convergence property* with respect to a loss function $\text{Loss}: \mathcal{Y} \times \mathcal{Y} \to [0, \infty)$ if, for all $f: X \to \mathcal{Y}$ and all $\varepsilon, \delta \in (0, 1)$,

$$\mathbb{P}\left[\sup_{h \in \mathcal{H}} \left| \text{Risk}_f(h) - \widehat{\text{Risk}}_S(h) \right| \le \varepsilon \right] \ge 1 - \delta$$

independently of the probability distribution on X, provided that

$$m \geq \widetilde{m}_{\mathcal{H}}(\varepsilon, \delta)$$

for some $\widetilde{m}_{\mathcal{H}} : (0,1)^2 \to \mathbb{N}^*$ growing at most polynomially in ε^{-1} and δ^{-1}.

Assume now that (ii) holds. Given $f : X \to \{0,1\}$ and $\varepsilon, \delta \in (0,1)$, consider the favorable situation where

$$\left| \mathrm{Risk}_f(h) - \widehat{\mathrm{Risk}}_S(h) \right| \leq \frac{\varepsilon}{2} \qquad \text{for all } h \in \mathcal{H}, \tag{3.1}$$

which occurs with probability at least $1 - \delta$ when $m \geq \widetilde{m}_{\mathcal{H}}(\varepsilon/2, \delta)$. Denote by $h_S \in \mathcal{H}$ the output of the empirical risk minimization algorithm, so that $\widehat{\mathrm{Risk}}_S(h_S) \leq \widehat{\mathrm{Risk}}_S(h)$ whenever $h \in \mathcal{H}$. Using (3.1) for $h_S \in \mathcal{H}$ and for any $h \in \mathcal{H}$, one has

$$\mathrm{Risk}_f(h_S) \leq \widehat{\mathrm{Risk}}_S(h_S) + \frac{\varepsilon}{2} \leq \widehat{\mathrm{Risk}}_S(h) + \frac{\varepsilon}{2} \leq \mathrm{Risk}_f(h) + \frac{\varepsilon}{2} + \frac{\varepsilon}{2}.$$

Taking the infimum over $h \in \mathcal{H}$, one obtains

$$\mathrm{Risk}_f(h_S) \leq \inf_{h \in \mathcal{H}} \mathrm{Risk}_f(h) + \varepsilon.$$

Since the latter occurs with probability at least $1 - \delta$ when $m \geq \widetilde{m}_{\mathcal{H}}(\varepsilon/2, \delta)$, empirical risk minimization appears as a successful PAC-learning map with sample complexity $m_{\mathcal{H}}(\varepsilon, \delta) \leq \widetilde{m}_{\mathcal{H}}(\varepsilon/2, \delta)$, and hence (iii) holds.

3.2 Finite VC-Dimension Implies PAC-Learnability

This section is devoted to the proof of the implication (i)$\Rightarrow$(ii). Therefore, one assumes from now on that (i) holds, i.e., that $d := \mathrm{vc}(\mathcal{H}) < +\infty$. The goal is to prove that, given $f : X \to \{0,1\}$ and $\varepsilon, \delta \in (0,1)$,

$$\mathbb{P} := \mathbb{P}\left[\sup_{h \in \mathcal{H}} \left| \mathrm{Risk}_f(h) - \widehat{\mathrm{Risk}}_S(h) \right| > \varepsilon \right] \leq \delta \tag{3.2}$$

when it is assumed that

$$m \geq \frac{4e^2}{\varepsilon^2}\left(d \ln\left(\frac{e}{\varepsilon}\right) + \ln\left(\frac{1}{\delta}\right) \right). \tag{3.3}$$

This goal is achieved by relating the tail probability $\mathbb{P}$ to the expectation of the associated random variable, i.e., to

$$\mathbb{E} := \mathbb{E}\left[\sup_{h \in \mathcal{H}} \left| \mathrm{Risk}_f(h) - \widehat{\mathrm{Risk}}_S(h) \right| \right].$$

One could invoke the *Markov inequality* (Lemma B.1) to write $\mathbb{P} \leq \mathbb{E}/\varepsilon$ and bound $\mathbb{E}$ from above, but this would entail a stronger condition than (3.3). Relying on the almost optimal[1] condition (3.3) calls for extra sophistication. Nonetheless, one must still bound the expectation $\mathbb{E}$, which is done below in four steps. The first step introduces an independent copy $\bar{\mathbf{x}} = (\bar{x}^{(1)}, \ldots, \bar{x}^{(m)})$ of the sequence $\mathbf{x} = (x^{(1)}, \ldots, x^{(m)})$. Writing $\bar{\mathfrak{X}} = \{\bar{x}^{(1)}, \ldots, \bar{x}^{(m)}\}$ to parallel the random set $\mathfrak{X} = \{x^{(1)}, \ldots, x^{(m)}\}$ and $\bar{S} = ((\bar{x}^{(1)}, f(\bar{x}^{(1)})), \ldots, (\bar{x}^{(m)}, f(\bar{x}^{(m)})))$ to parallel the random sample $S = ((x^{(1)}, f(x^{(1)})), \ldots, (x^{(m)}, f(x^{(m)})))$, one has

$$
\begin{aligned}
\mathbb{E} &= \mathbb{E}_{\mathbf{x}} \left[\sup_{h \in \mathcal{H}} \left| \mathbb{E}_{\bar{\mathbf{x}}} \left[\widehat{\mathrm{Risk}}_{\bar{S}}(h) - \widehat{\mathrm{Risk}}_S(h) \right] \right| \right] \\
&\leq \mathbb{E}_{\mathbf{x}} \left[\sup_{h \in \mathcal{H}} \mathbb{E}_{\bar{\mathbf{x}}} \left| \widehat{\mathrm{Risk}}_{\bar{S}}(h) - \widehat{\mathrm{Risk}}_S(h) \right| \right] \\
&\leq \mathbb{E}_{\mathbf{x}} \mathbb{E}_{\bar{\mathbf{x}}} \left[\sup_{h \in \mathcal{H}} \left| \widehat{\mathrm{Risk}}_{\bar{S}}(h) - \widehat{\mathrm{Risk}}_S(h) \right| \right] \\
&= \mathbb{E}_{\mathbf{x}, \bar{\mathbf{x}}} \left[\sup_{h \in \mathcal{H}} \left| \frac{1}{m} \sum_{i=1}^m \xi_{\mathbf{x}, \bar{\mathbf{x}}, i}(h) \right| \right],
\end{aligned}
$$

where the random variables $\xi_{\mathbf{x}, \bar{\mathbf{x}}, 1}(h), \ldots, \xi_{\mathbf{x}, \bar{\mathbf{x}}, m}(h) \in \{-1, 0, 1\}$ are defined by

$$
\xi_{\mathbf{x}, \bar{\mathbf{x}}, i}(h) = \mathrm{Loss}_{0/1}(h(x^{(i)}), f(x^{(i)})) - \mathrm{Loss}_{0/1}(h(\bar{x}^{(i)}), f(\bar{x}^{(i)})).
$$

The second step introduces independent *Rademacher variables* $\epsilon_1, \ldots, \epsilon_m$, i.e., random variables taking values -1 or $+1$ with equal probability, and exploits the fact that $\xi_{\bar{\mathbf{x}}, \mathbf{x}, i}(h) = -\xi_{\mathbf{x}, \bar{\mathbf{x}}, i}(h)$ to arrive at

$$
\mathbb{E} \leq \mathbb{E}_{\epsilon} \mathbb{E}_{\mathbf{x}, \bar{\mathbf{x}}} \left[\sup_{h \in \mathcal{H}} \left| \frac{1}{m} \sum_{i=1}^m \epsilon_i \xi_{\mathbf{x}, \bar{\mathbf{x}}, i}(h) \right| \right] = \mathbb{E}_{\mathbf{x}, \bar{\mathbf{x}}} \mathbb{E}_{\epsilon} \left[\sup_{h \in \mathcal{H}_{|\mathfrak{X} \cup \bar{\mathfrak{X}}}} \left| \Xi_{\mathbf{x}, \bar{\mathbf{x}}, \epsilon}(h) \right| \right], \quad (3.4)
$$

where the random variable $\Xi_{\mathbf{x}, \bar{\mathbf{x}}, \epsilon}(h) \in [-1, 1]$ is defined by

$$
\Xi_{\mathbf{x}, \bar{\mathbf{x}}, \epsilon}(h) = \frac{1}{m} \sum_{i=1}^m \xi_{\mathbf{x}, \bar{\mathbf{x}}, i}(h) \, \epsilon_i.
$$

The third step involves fixing both $\mathbf{x}$ and $\bar{\mathbf{x}}$ to bound the expectation (over ϵ) of the above supremum. This relies on evaluating, for each $h \in \mathcal{H}_{|\mathfrak{X} \cup \bar{\mathfrak{X}}}$, the

---

[1] More involved techniques allow one to derive an upper bound of order $\varepsilon^{-2}(d + \ln(1/\delta))$ for the sample complexity, which is matched by a lower bound of the same order; see e.g. Chapter 28 of Shalev-Shwartz and Ben-David (2014).

moment generating function of $\Xi_{\mathbf{x},\bar{\mathbf{x}},\epsilon}(h)$ *at* $t \in \mathbb{R}$ *via*

$$\mathbb{E}[\exp(t\Xi_{\mathbf{x},\bar{\mathbf{x}},\epsilon}(h))] = \mathbb{E}\left[\prod_{i=1}^{m}\exp\left(\frac{t\xi_{\mathbf{x},\bar{\mathbf{x}},i}(h)}{m}\epsilon_i\right)\right] = \prod_{i=1}^{m}\mathbb{E}\left[\exp\left(\frac{t\xi_{\mathbf{x},\bar{\mathbf{x}},i}(h)}{m}\epsilon_i\right)\right]$$

$$= \prod_{i=1}^{m}\left(\frac{1}{2}\exp\left(\frac{t\xi_{\mathbf{x},\bar{\mathbf{x}},i}(h)}{m}\right) + \frac{1}{2}\exp\left(-\frac{t\xi_{\mathbf{x},\bar{\mathbf{x}},i}(h)}{m}\right)\right)$$

$$\leq \prod_{i=1}^{m}\exp\left(\frac{t^2\xi_{\mathbf{x},\bar{\mathbf{x}},i}(h)^2}{2m^2}\right) \leq \prod_{i=1}^{m}\exp\left(\frac{t^2}{2m^2}\right) = \exp\left(\frac{t^2}{2m}\right).$$

In view of Proposition B.5, one arrives at

$$\mathbb{E}_\epsilon\left[\sup_{h \in \mathcal{H}_{|\bar{\mathbf{x}} \cup \bar{\mathbf{x}}}}\left|\Xi_{\mathbf{x},\bar{\mathbf{x}},\epsilon}(h)\right|\right] \leq \sqrt{\frac{2\ln(2|\mathcal{H}_{|\bar{\mathbf{x}} \cup \bar{\mathbf{x}}}|)}{m}}. \tag{3.5}$$

Since $|\mathcal{H}_{|\bar{\mathbf{x}} \cup \bar{\mathbf{x}}}| \leq \tau_\mathcal{H}(2m)$ by the definition of the *shatter function*, an application of the *Sauer lemma* (Lemma 2.6) gives $|\mathcal{H}_{|\bar{\mathbf{x}} \cup \bar{\mathbf{x}}}| \leq (2em/d)^d$. Taking (3.3) into account, one obtains $2|\mathcal{H}_{|\bar{\mathbf{x}} \cup \bar{\mathbf{x}}}| \leq (m/d)^{2d}$ and in turn

$$\frac{2\ln(2|\mathcal{H}_{|\bar{\mathbf{x}} \cup \bar{\mathbf{x}}}|)}{m} \leq \frac{2\ln\left((m/d)^{2d}\right)}{m} = \frac{4\ln(m/d)}{m/d}. \tag{3.6}$$

The fourth and final step consists in collecting the above estimates to bound, through some slight technicality, the expectation $\mathbb{E}$ by a fraction of ε. The estimates (3.4), (3.5), and (3.6) indeed combine to give

$$\mathbb{E} \leq \eta(m/d), \qquad \text{where} \quad \eta(t) := 2\sqrt{\ln(t)/t}.$$

Remarking that η is decreasing on $[e, \infty)$, with $\eta(e) = 2/\sqrt{e}$, one can consider $t_\varepsilon \geq e$ such that $\eta(t_\varepsilon) = 2\varepsilon/e$. From

$$t_\varepsilon = \left(\frac{e}{\varepsilon}\right)^2\ln(t_\varepsilon) \leq \left(\frac{e}{\varepsilon}\right)^2\sqrt{t_\varepsilon},$$

it follows that $t_\varepsilon \leq (e/\varepsilon)^4$, and in turn that

$$t_\varepsilon \leq \frac{4e^2}{\varepsilon^2}\ln\left(\frac{e}{\varepsilon}\right).$$

Condition (3.3) then implies $m/d \geq t_\varepsilon$, and hence $\eta(m/d) \leq \eta(t_\varepsilon)$. Therefore, one has

$$\mathbb{E} \leq \frac{2}{e}\varepsilon \leq \frac{3}{4}\varepsilon.$$

Now that a bound on $\mathbb{E}$ has been obtained, one turns to the estimation of the tail probability (3.2), noticing first that

$$\mathbb{P} = \mathbb{P}\left[\sup_{h \in \mathcal{H}}\left|\text{Risk}_f(h) - \widehat{\text{Risk}}_S(h)\right| - \mathbb{E} > \varepsilon - \mathbb{E}\right]$$

$$\leq \mathbb{P}\left[\sup_{h \in \mathcal{H}}\left|\text{Risk}_f(h) - \widehat{\text{Risk}}_S(h)\right| - \mathbb{E} > \frac{\varepsilon}{4}\right].$$

Next, one observes that if $\mathbf{x}$ and $\bar{\mathbf{x}}$ differ at only one index $i \in [1:m]$, then

$$\sup_{h \in \mathcal{H}}\left|\text{Risk}_f(h) - \widehat{\text{Risk}}_S(h)\right| - \sup_{h \in \mathcal{H}}\left|\text{Risk}_f(h) - \widehat{\text{Risk}}_{\bar{S}}(h)\right|$$

$$\leq \sup_{h \in \mathcal{H}}\left|\widehat{\text{Risk}}_S(h) - \widehat{\text{Risk}}_{\bar{S}}(h)\right|$$

$$= \sup_{h \in \mathcal{H}}\frac{1}{m}\left|\text{Loss}_{0/1}(h(x^{(i)}), f(x^{(i)})) - \text{Loss}_{0/1}(h(\bar{x}^{(i)}), f(\bar{x}^{(i)}))\right|$$

$$\leq \frac{1}{m}.$$

Finally, an application of the *McDiarmid inequality* (Theorem B.9) implies that

$$\mathbb{P} \leq \exp\left(-\frac{m\varepsilon^2}{8}\right).$$

The latter is bounded by δ since $m \geq (8/\varepsilon^2)\ln(1/\delta)$, which is a consequence of (3.3). Thus, the desired inequality (3.2) holds and the proof is complete.

3.3 No-Free-Lunch Theorem

This section is devoted to the proof of the implication (iv)$\Rightarrow$(i). It is a direct consequence of Lemma 3.3 below, sometimes referred to as the *no-free-lunch theorem*. Indeed, if (iv) holds, i.e., if $\mathcal{H}$ is PAC-learnable, then the probability in (3.7) can be made smaller than $1/4$ when $m \geq \widetilde{m}(1/4, 1/5)$, say. To avoid a contradiction with the statement of the lemma, it is then necessary for $\mathcal{H}$ to have finite VC-dimension, i.e., for (i) to hold.

Lemma 3.3 *Let $\mathcal{H} \subseteq F(\mathcal{X}, \{0, 1\})$ be a hypothesis class of boolean functions having infinite VC-dimension. For any integer $m \geq 1$ and any learning map $S \in (\mathcal{X} \times \mathcal{Y})^m \mapsto h_S \in \mathcal{H}$, there is a probability distribution and a function $f \in F(\mathcal{X}, \{0, 1\})$ such that, relative to the 0/1-loss, one has*

$$\mathbb{P}\left[\text{Risk}_f(h_S) - \inf_{h \in \mathcal{H}}\text{Risk}_f(h) > \frac{1}{4}\right] \geq \frac{1}{4}. \tag{3.7}$$

Proof Since $vc(\mathcal{H}) = +\infty$, there is a subset $\mathcal{Y}$ of $\mathcal{X}$ with size $|\mathcal{Y}| = 8m$, say, which is shattered by $\mathcal{H}$, i.e., $\mathcal{H}_{|\mathcal{Y}} = F(\mathcal{Y}, \{0, 1\})$. Therefore, for any function $f \in F(\mathcal{X}, \{0, 1\})$, there exists $h \in \mathcal{H}$ such that $h(x) = f(x)$ whenever $x \in \mathcal{Y}$, and hence whenever the distribution of random x's is supported on $\mathcal{Y}$. One actually chooses the uniform distribution over this set $\mathcal{Y}$. This ensures in particular that

$$\inf_{h \in \mathcal{H}} \mathrm{Risk}_f(h) = \inf_{h \in \mathcal{H}} \mathbb{E}_x[\mathrm{Loss}_{0/1}(h(x), f(x))] = 0.$$

In this way, the objective is reduced to proving that

$$\mathbb{P}\left[\mathrm{Risk}_f(h_S) > \frac{1}{4}\right] \geq \frac{1}{4}$$

for some $f \in F(\mathcal{X}, \{0, 1\})$. In view of Lemma B.2, it suffices to show that

$$\mathbb{E}[\mathrm{Risk}_f(h_S)] \geq \frac{7}{16}$$

for some $f \in F(\mathcal{Y}, \{0, 1\})$. Note that one now thinks of f as a function defined on $\mathcal{Y}$ rather than on $\mathcal{X}$, since its values on $\mathcal{X} \setminus \mathcal{Y}$ are inconsequential. The existence of such a function f will follow as soon as one establishes that

$$\overline{\mathbb{E}} := \frac{1}{2^{|\mathcal{Y}|}} \sum_{f \in F(\mathcal{Y}, \{0,1\})} \mathbb{E}[\mathrm{Risk}_f(h_S)] \geq \frac{7}{16}. \tag{3.8}$$

The latter can be seen by writing very explicitly, with $S_{\mathbf{x}, f}$ denoting the sample built from $\mathbf{x} \in \mathcal{Y}^m$ and $f \in F(\mathcal{Y}, \{0, 1\})$, that

$$\begin{aligned}
\overline{\mathbb{E}} &= \frac{1}{2^{|\mathcal{Y}|}} \sum_{f \in F(\mathcal{Y}, \{0,1\})} \frac{1}{|\mathcal{Y}|^m} \sum_{\mathbf{x} \in \mathcal{Y}^m} \mathrm{Risk}_f(h_{S_{\mathbf{x},f}}) \\
&= \frac{1}{2^{|\mathcal{Y}|}} \sum_{f \in F(\mathcal{Y}, \{0,1\})} \frac{1}{|\mathcal{Y}|^m} \sum_{\mathbf{x} \in \mathcal{Y}^m} \frac{1}{|\mathcal{Y}|} \sum_{x \in \mathcal{Y}} \mathrm{Loss}_{0/1}(h_{S_{\mathbf{x},f}}(x), f(x)) \\
&\geq \frac{1}{|\mathcal{Y}|^m} \sum_{\mathbf{x} \in \mathcal{Y}^m} \frac{1}{|\mathcal{Y}|} \sum_{x \in \mathcal{Y} \setminus \mathbf{x}} \frac{1}{2^{|\mathcal{Y}|}} \sum_{f \in F(\mathcal{Y}, \{0,1\})} \mathrm{Loss}_{0/1}(h_{S_{\mathbf{x},f}}(x), f(x)).
\end{aligned}$$

Noticing that, when fixing $\mathbf{x} \in \mathcal{Y}^m$ and $x \in \mathcal{Y} \setminus \mathbf{x}$, there are as many functions $f \in F(\mathcal{Y}, \{0, 1\})$ for which $\mathrm{Loss}_{0/1}(h_{S_{\mathbf{x},f}}(x), f(x)) = 1$ (i.e., $f(x) \neq h_{S_{\mathbf{x},f}}(x)$) as there are functions $f \in F(\mathcal{Y}, \{0, 1\})$ for which $\mathrm{Loss}_{0/1}(h_{S_{\mathbf{x},f}}(x), f(x)) = 0$ (i.e., $f(x) = h_{S_{\mathbf{x},f}}(x)$), one derives that

$$\overline{\mathbb{E}} \geq \frac{1}{|\mathcal{Y}|^m} \sum_{\mathbf{x} \in \mathcal{Y}^m} \frac{1}{|\mathcal{Y}|} \sum_{x \in \mathcal{Y} \setminus \mathbf{x}} \frac{1}{2} \geq \frac{1}{|\mathcal{Y}|^m} \sum_{\mathbf{x} \in \mathcal{Y}^m} \frac{7m}{8m} \frac{1}{2} = \frac{7}{16}.$$

This is the lower bound required in (3.8). $\qquad \square$

Exercises

3.1 Observe that the finite union of PAC-learnable hypothesis classes of boolean functions is also PAC-learnable. What can be inferred about its sample complexity?

3.2 The *Rademacher complexity* of a set $\mathcal{A} \subseteq \mathbb{R}^m$ is defined by

$$\text{Rad}(\mathcal{A}) = \mathbb{E}\left[\frac{1}{m} \sup_{a \in \mathcal{A}} \sum_{i=1}^{m} \epsilon_i a_i\right],$$

where $\epsilon_1, \ldots, \epsilon_m$ are independent Rademacher variables. When $\mathcal{A}$ is a finite set, establish the following estimate, known as the *Massart lemma*:

$$\text{Rad}(\mathcal{A}) \leq \frac{\sqrt{2 \ln(|\mathcal{A}|)}}{m} \sup_{a \in \mathcal{A}} \|a\|_2.$$

3.3 Given a hypothesis class $\mathcal{H}$ of boolean functions, with $h_S \in \mathcal{H}$ denoting the output of the empirical risk minimization algorithm with respect to the 0/1-loss, observe that

$$\mathbb{E}\left[\text{Risk}_f(h_S) - \inf_{h \in \mathcal{H}} \text{Risk}_f(h)\right] \leq 4\,\mathbb{E}\left[\text{Rad}(\mathcal{A}_S)\right],$$

where both expectations are over the independent identically distributed $x^{(i)}$ in the sample S and where the random set $\mathcal{A}_S \subseteq \mathbb{R}^m$ is given by $\mathcal{A}_S = \{[\text{Loss}_{0/1}(h(x^{(1)}), f(x^{(1)})); \ldots ; \text{Loss}_{0/1}(h(x^{(m)}), f(x^{(m)}))], h \in \mathcal{H}\}.$

3.4 Extend the fundamental theorem of PAC-learning to n-ary classification. For $\mathcal{H} \subseteq F(\mathcal{X}, \{0, 1, \ldots, n-1\})$, the VC-dimension is to be replaced by the *Natarajan dimension*, i.e., the largest size of a subset $\mathcal{Y}$ of $\mathcal{X}$ shattered by $\mathcal{H}$, meaning here that there are $f, g \in F(\mathcal{Y}, \{0, 1, \ldots, n-1\})$ such that, for any subset $\mathcal{Z} \subseteq \mathcal{Y}$, one can find some $h \in \mathcal{H}$ for which $h(x) = f(x) \neq g(x)$ for all $x \in \mathcal{Z}$ and $h(x) = g(x) \neq f(x)$ for all $x \in \mathcal{Y} \setminus \mathcal{Z}$. As for the Sauer lemma, it can be substituted by the *Natarajan lemma*: *for a finite set X of size m, if $\mathcal{H} \subseteq F(X, \{0, 1, \ldots, n-1\})$ has a Natarajan dimension $d \leq m$, then $|\mathcal{H}| \leq \sum_{k=0}^{d} \binom{m}{k}\binom{n}{2}^k \leq (2n^2 m/d)^d$.*

4

Support Vector Machines

This chapter focuses once more on *binary classification*, but it abandons the probabilistic viewpoint in favor of a deterministic viewpoint. In this context, unequivocal guarantees will be obtained under some reasonable separability assumptions on the training examples. Precisely, in the scenario considered in this chapter, instances $x^{(1)}, \ldots, x^{(m)}$ belonging to some set $\mathcal{X} \subseteq \mathbb{R}^d$ come with labels $y_1, \ldots, y_m$ belonging to a binary set, chosen here to be $\{-1, +1\}$ instead of $\{0, 1\}$. It is assumed that the labels were created by setting $y_i = 1$ when the instance $x^{(i)}$ belonged to some (unknown) region of $\mathbb{R}^d$. The objective then consists in learning such a region whose ideally simple boundary separates the positively labeled instances and the negatively labeled instances. Thus, when a new instance (say, a picture) arrives, its label (say, a bike or a car) can be automatically determined.

4.1 Linear Separability

A natural assumption posits that the training examples $(x^{(1)}, y_1), \ldots, (x^{(m)}, y_m)$ are *linearly separable*, meaning that there is an affine hyperplane separating the $x^{(i)}$ for which $y_i = +1$ from the $x^{(i)}$ for which $y_i = -1$. Of course, this assumption is not always met, a counterexample being supplied with $d = 2$ by $y_i = \text{sgn}(x_1^{(i)} x_2^{(i)})$. But when it is met, the goal is simply to find an affine hyperplane H in $\mathbb{R}^d$, parametrized by $w \in \mathbb{R}^d$ and $b \in \mathbb{R}$ through its equation $\langle w, x \rangle - b = 0$, that separates the data. Since such an H divides $\mathbb{R}^d \setminus H$ into two regions, namely $\{x \in \mathbb{R}^d : \langle w, x \rangle - b > 0\}$ and $\{x \in \mathbb{R}^d : \langle w, x \rangle - b < 0\}$, the data $((x^{(1)}, y_1), \ldots, (x^{(m)}, y_m))$ is correctly separated by such a hyperplane if $\langle w, x^{(i)} \rangle - b > 0$ when $y_i = +1$ and $\langle w, x^{(i)} \rangle - b < 0$ when $y_i = -1$, i.e., if $y_i(\langle w, x^{(i)} \rangle - b) > 0$ for all $i \in [1:m]$. By renormalizing w and b, one can therefore write the *linear separability* assumption as:

> *There exist $w^* \in \mathbb{R}^d$ and $b^* \in \mathbb{R}$ such that* $\min_{i \in [1:m]} y_i(\langle w^*, x^{(i)} \rangle - b^*) \geq 1.$　(4.1)

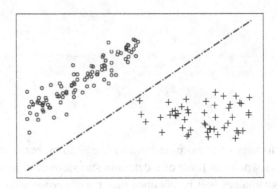

Figure 4.1 A hyperplane separating the data $(x^{(1)}, y_1), \ldots, (x^{(m)}, y_m)$ represented by circles when $y_i = -1$ and by crosses when $y_i = +1$.

Under this linear separability assumption, a separating hyperplane—which is clearly not unique—can be found by solving a linear feasibility problem (see Chapter 20 for more details on the subject). This task can be performed by relying on an all-purpose optimization solver after introducing a dummy objective function, e.g. the constant 1, thus solving

$$\underset{w \in \mathbb{R}^d, b \in \mathbb{R}}{\text{minimize }} 1 \quad \text{subject to} \quad y_i(\langle w, x^{(i)} \rangle - b) \geq 1 \quad \text{for all } i \in [1:m].　(4.2)$$

Optimization solvers are in fact not necessary to find a separating hyperplane, as one can instead apply the *perceptron algorithm* shown below. Its description and analysis use the notation (previously introduced in Chapter 2)

$$\widetilde{w} := [w; -b] \in \mathbb{R}^{d+1}, \qquad \widetilde{x}^{(i)} = [x^{(i)}; 1] \in \mathbb{R}^{d+1},$$

so that $\langle w, x^{(i)} \rangle - b = \langle \widetilde{w}, \widetilde{x}^{(i)} \rangle$ for all $i \in [1:m]$.

- start with some initial $\widetilde{w}^{(0)} \in \mathbb{R}^{d+1}$, often chosen as $\widetilde{w}^{(0)} = 0$;
- for each $t \geq 0$, if there is an $i \in [1:m]$ such that $y_i \langle \widetilde{w}^{(t)}, \widetilde{x}^{(i)} \rangle \leq 0$, then set

$$\widetilde{w}^{(t+1)} = \widetilde{w}^{(t)} + \frac{y_i}{\|\widetilde{x}^{(i)}\|_2^2} \widetilde{x}^{(i)};$$

- stop when $y_i \langle \widetilde{w}^{(t)}, \widetilde{x}^{(i)} \rangle > 0$ for all $i \in [1:m]$.

Theorem 4.1 *If the data* $(x^{(1)}, y_1), \ldots, (x^{(m)}, y_m)$ *are linearly separable, then the perceptron algorithm initialized with* $\widetilde{w}^{(0)} = 0$ *returns an affine hyperplane that correctly separates the data in a number of iterations bounded by*

$$T \leq \lceil R^2 \|\widetilde{w}^*\|_2^2 \rceil,$$

where $R := \max_{i \in [1:m]} \|\widetilde{x}^{(i)}\|_2$ *and* $\widetilde{w}^* := [w^*; -b^*]$ *with* w^* *and* b^* *as in (4.1).*

Proof Let T be the iteration index where no more misclassification occurs. For $t < T$, since there is an $i \in [1:m]$ such that $y_i \langle \widetilde{w}^{(t)}, \widetilde{x}^{(i)} \rangle \leq 0$, one has

$$\|\widetilde{w}^{(t+1)} - \widetilde{w}^*\|_2^2 = \left\| \widetilde{w}^{(t)} - \widetilde{w}^* + \frac{y_i}{\|\widetilde{x}^{(i)}\|_2^2} \widetilde{x}^{(i)} \right\|_2^2$$

$$= \|\widetilde{w}^{(t)} - \widetilde{w}^*\|_2^2 + \frac{1}{\|\widetilde{x}^{(i)}\|_2^2} + 2 \frac{y_i}{\|\widetilde{x}^{(i)}\|_2^2} \langle \widetilde{w}^{(t)} - \widetilde{w}^*, \widetilde{x}^{(i)} \rangle$$

$$\leq \|\widetilde{w}^{(t)} - \widetilde{w}^*\|_2^2 + \frac{1}{\|\widetilde{x}^{(i)}\|_2^2} - 2 \frac{y_i}{\|\widetilde{x}^{(i)}\|_2^2} \langle \widetilde{w}^*, \widetilde{x}^{(i)} \rangle.$$

Keeping in mind that (4.1) forces $y_i \langle \widetilde{w}^*, \widetilde{x}^{(i)} \rangle \geq 1$, one deduces that

$$\|\widetilde{w}^{(t+1)} - \widetilde{w}^*\|_2^2 \leq \|\widetilde{w}^{(t)} - \widetilde{w}^*\|_2^2 - \frac{1}{\|\widetilde{x}^{(i)}\|_2^2} \leq \|\widetilde{w}^{(t)} - \widetilde{w}^*\|_2^2 - \frac{1}{R^2}.$$

By immediate induction, it follows that

$$\|\widetilde{w}^{(T)} - \widetilde{w}^*\|_2^2 \leq \|\widetilde{w}^{(0)} - \widetilde{w}^*\|_2^2 - \frac{T}{R^2}.$$

If $T > \lceil R^2 \|\widetilde{w}^*\|_2^2 \rceil$, then one would obtain $\|\widetilde{w}^{(T)} - \widetilde{w}^*\|_2^2 < 0$, which is, of course, impossible. One therefore concludes that $T \leq \lceil R^2 \|\widetilde{w}^*\|_2^2 \rceil$. □

Advantageously, the perceptron algorithm can also be executed for data that arrive in a streaming fashion; see Exercise 4.3.

4.2 Hard and Soft SVM

The linear feasibility problem (4.2) and the perceptron algorithm both tend to produce separating hyperplanes that can be close to some training examples (as in Figure 4.1), hence they are not robust to data perturbation. For the sake of robustness, one would like to select a separating hyperplane that stays as far away from the examples as possible. To do so, one introduces the notion of *margin* for an affine hyperplane $H_{w,b}$ of equation $\langle w, x \rangle - b = 0$ relative to the datapoints $x^{(1)}, \ldots, x^{(m)}$, as defined by

$$\text{margin}(H_{w,b}, \{x^{(1)}, \ldots, x^{(m)}\}) = \min_{i \in [1:m]} \text{dist}_{\ell_2}(x^{(i)}, H_{w,b})$$

$$= \min_{i \in [1:m]} \frac{|\langle w, x^{(i)} \rangle - b|}{\|w\|_2},$$

where the last equality stands because $\text{dist}_{\ell_2}(x, H_{w,b}) = |\langle w, x \rangle - b|/\|w\|_2$ for any $x \in \mathbb{R}^d$. Since the margin is unchanged when $[w; -b]$ is multiplied by a nonzero scalar, one may assume that $\min_{i \in [1:m]} |\langle w, x^{(i)} \rangle - b| = 1$, so under the separation constraint that $y_i(\langle w, x^{(i)} \rangle - b) > 0$, maximizing the margin is equivalent to maximizing $1/\|w\|_2$ subject to $\min_{i \in [1:m]} y_i(\langle w, x^{(i)} \rangle - b) = 1$, or to $\min_{i \in [1:m]} y_i(\langle w, x^{(i)} \rangle - b) \geq 1$. Thus, finding the separating hyperplane with the largest possible margin is done by solving the following quadratic optimization program, called *hard SVM*:

$$\underset{w \in \mathbb{R}^d, b \in \mathbb{R}}{\text{minimize}} \ \|w\|_2 \quad \text{s.to} \quad y_i(\langle w, x^{(i)} \rangle - b) \geq 1 \quad \text{for all } i \in [1:m]. \quad (4.3)$$

With (w^*, b^*) denoting a solution to this minimization problem, the points $x^{(j)}$ for which $\text{dist}_{\ell_2}(x^{(j)}, H_{w^*,b^*}) = \text{margin}(H_{w^*,b^*}, \{x^{(1)}, \ldots, x^{(m)}\})$ are called *support vectors*. The terminology of support vector machines is rooted in the following observation.

Proposition 4.2 *A vector $w^* \in \mathbb{R}^d$ solving* (4.3) *is unique and belongs to the linear span of the support vectors.*

Proof Let (w^*, b^*) denote a solution to the program (4.3) and let v denote its minimal value. Considering another solution (w', b') to (4.3), one readily sees that $((w^* + w')/2, (b^* + b')/2)$ is also a feasible point for (4.3), and hence that $v \leq \|(w^* + w')/2\|_2 \leq \|w^*\|_2/2 + \|w'\|_2/2 = v/2 + v/2 = v$. Thus, equality occurs all the way through, and particularly in the triangle inequality. This implies that $w' = w^*$, justifying the uniqueness of w^*.

Next, let $J := \{j \in [1:m] : |\langle w^*, x^{(j)} \rangle - b^*| = \min_{i \in [1:m]} |\langle w^*, x^{(i)} \rangle - b^*|\}$ be the index set associated with support vectors and let $\mathcal{V} := \text{span}\{x^{(j)}, j \in J\}$ be the linear span of the support vectors. For $u \in \mathcal{V}^\perp$ and $t \in \mathbb{R}$ with $|t|$ small enough, one easily observes that $(w^* + tu, b^*)$ is a feasible point for (4.3), and hence that

$$\|w^*\|_2^2 \leq \|w^* + tu\|_2^2 = \|w^*\|_2^2 + 2t\langle w^*, u \rangle + t^2\|u\|_2^2.$$

For the latter to hold whenever $|t|$ is small enough, one must have $\langle w^*, u \rangle = 0$. Since this is valid for any $u \in \mathcal{V}^\perp$, one concludes that $w^* \in (\mathcal{V}^\perp)^\perp = \mathcal{V}$, as announced.   □

It is now time to examine the situation where the data are not exactly linearly separable. In this case, there is no feasible point for the hard SVM (4.3). To remedy this issue, the constraints are relaxed to $y_i(\langle w, x^{(i)} \rangle - b) \geq 1 - \xi_i$ for some $\xi_i \geq 0$, but large ξ_i are penalized by adding them to the objective function. Therefore, with a parameter $\lambda > 0$ that can be selected by the learner, one considers the minimization problem called *soft SVM*:

$$\underset{w \in \mathbb{R}^d, b \in \mathbb{R}, \xi \in \mathbb{R}^m}{\text{minimize}} \ \|w\|_2^2 + \frac{1}{\lambda} \sum_{i=1}^{m} \xi_i \quad \text{s.to} \ \ y_i(\langle w, x^{(i)} \rangle - b) \geq 1 - \xi_i$$

$$\text{and} \ \ \xi_i \geq 0 \quad \text{for all } i \in [1:m]. \quad (4.4)$$

Note that each constraint on ξ_i in fact reads $\xi_i \geq \max\{0, 1 - y_i(\langle w, x^{(i)} \rangle - b)\}$, so that $\sum_{i=1}^{m} \xi_i$ is as small as possible when each ξ_i takes on this lower bound. Thus, the soft SVM can also be formulated as

$$\underset{w \in \mathbb{R}^d, b \in \mathbb{R}}{\text{minimize}} \ \|w\|_2^2 + \frac{1}{\lambda} \sum_{i=1}^{m} \max\{0, 1 - y_i(\langle w, x^{(i)} \rangle - b)\}.$$

Given that the term $\max\{0, 1 - y_i(\langle w, x^{(i)} \rangle - b)\}$, called the *hinge loss*, is a convex function of (w, b), this formulation has the form of an unconstrained convex optimization program.

4.3 Kernel Trick

Even in situations where the data are emphatically not linearly separable, it is still conceivable that they can be linearly separated after transforming them via a *feature map* $\phi \colon \mathcal{X} \to \mathbb{R}^D$ where $D > d$. In other words, it is conceivable that there is an hyperplane in $\mathbb{R}^D$ for which the positively labeled $\phi(x^{(i)})$ lie on one side and the negatively labeled $\phi(x^{(i)})$ lie on the other side. Applying either hard SVM or soft SVM in $\mathbb{R}^D$, one arrives at a minimization of the type

$$\underset{w \in \mathbb{R}^D, b \in \mathbb{R}}{\text{minimize}} \ F(\|w\|_2^2) + G((\langle w, \phi(x^{(i)}) \rangle - b)_{i=1}^{m}), \quad (4.5)$$

for an increasing function $F \colon \mathbb{R}_+ \to \mathbb{R}$ and a function $G \colon \mathbb{R}^m \to \mathbb{R} \cup \{+\infty\}$ that can encapsulate possible constraints by taking an infinite value when some constraints $y_i(\langle w, \phi(x^{(i)}) \rangle - b) \geq 1$ are not met. The following observation, known as the *representer theorem*, has an important consequence to be pointed out below.

Theorem 4.3 *There is a solution* $(w^*, b^*) \in \mathbb{R}^D \times \mathbb{R}$ *to the program* (4.5) *for which* $w^* \in \text{span}\{\phi(x^{(1)}), \dots, \phi(x^{(m)})\}$.

Proof Let (w, b) denote a solution to (4.5) and let w^* denote the orthogonal projection of w onto the space $\mathrm{span}\{\phi(x^{(1)}), \ldots, \phi(x^{(m)})\}$. One immediately sees that (w^*, b) is also a solution to (4.5), because $\langle w^*, \phi(x^{(i)})\rangle - b = \langle w, \phi(x^{(i)})\rangle - b$ for all $i \in [1:m]$ and because $\|w^*\|_2 \le \|w\|_2$, so that $F(\|w^*\|_2^2) \le F(\|w\|_2^2)$. □

The aforementioned important consequence of the representer theorem is the fact that a solution to (4.5) can be sought in the form $w = \sum_{j=1}^m a_j \phi(x^{(j)})$, leading to the alternative optimization problem

$$\underset{a \in \mathbb{R}^m, b \in \mathbb{R}}{\text{minimize}} \ F\left(\sum_{i,j=1}^n a_i a_j \langle \phi(x^{(i)}), \phi(x^{(j)})\rangle\right) + G\left(\left(\sum_{j=1}^m a_j \langle \phi(x^{(j)}), \phi(x^{(i)})\rangle - b\right)_{i=1}^m\right).$$

This is significant for two reasons: first, the number of optimization variables has gone from D to m, which can be quite beneficial when ϕ maps into a very high dimensional space; second, an explicit expression for the feature map ϕ is not needed, so long as the *kernel* $K(x, x') = \langle \phi(x), \phi(x')\rangle$ can be evaluated at the datapoints. Two commonly used kernels are now highlighted and illustrated by Figures 4.2 and 4.3 in the toy situation $d = 2$.

Example 4.4 The degree-n (inhomogeneous) *polynomial kernel*, given by

$$K(x, x') = (1 + \langle x, x'\rangle)^n, \qquad x, x' \in \mathbb{R}^d,$$

is associated with a feature map $\phi\colon \mathbb{R}^d \to \mathbb{R}^{[0:d]^n}$. Its coordinates are given by

$$(\phi(x))_{(j_1, \ldots, j_n)} = \prod_{i=1}^n x_{j_i}, \qquad x \in \mathbb{R}^d.$$

Proof Using the convention $x_0 = x_0' = 1$, the kernel can be written as

$$K(x, x') = \left(\sum_{j=0}^d x_j x_j'\right)^n = \sum_{(j_1, \ldots, j_n) \in [0:d]^n} \prod_{i=1}^n x_{j_i} x_{j_i}' = \langle \phi(x), \phi(x')\rangle.$$

Note that the dimension $D = (d+1)^n$ is typically much larger than m. □

Example 4.5 The *gaussian kernel*, given for some $\sigma > 0$ by

$$K(x, x') = \exp\left(-\frac{\|x - x'\|_2^2}{2\sigma^2}\right), \qquad x, x' \in \mathbb{R}^d,$$

is associated with a feature map $\phi\colon \mathbb{R}^d \to \mathbb{R}^{[1:d]^*}$, where $[1:d]^*$ denotes the set of finite sequences on $[1:d]$. Its coordinates are given by

$$(\phi(x))_{(j_1, \ldots, j_n)} = \frac{\exp(-\|x\|_2^2/(2\sigma^2))}{\sqrt{n!}\sigma^n} \prod_{i=1}^n x_{j_i}, \qquad x \in \mathbb{R}^d.$$

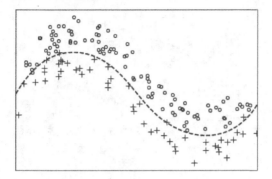

Figure 4.2 Data separated by a soft SVM using the degree-3 polynomial kernel.

Proof The kernel can be written as

$$K(x, x') = \exp\left(-\frac{\|x\|_2^2 + \|x'\|_2^2}{2\sigma^2}\right) \exp\left(\frac{\langle x, x'\rangle}{\sigma^2}\right)$$

$$= \sum_{n=0}^{\infty} \frac{\exp(-(\|x\|_2^2 + \|x'\|_2^2)/(2\sigma^2))}{n!\sigma^{2n}} \langle x, x'\rangle^n$$

$$= \sum_{n=0}^{\infty} \frac{\exp(-(\|x\|_2^2 + \|x'\|_2^2)/(2\sigma^2))}{n!\sigma^{2n}} \left(\sum_{j=1}^{d} x_j x'_j\right)^n$$

$$= \sum_{n=0}^{\infty} \frac{\exp(-(\|x\|_2^2 + \|x'\|_2^2)/(2\sigma^2))}{n!\sigma^{2n}} \sum_{(j_1,\dots,j_n)\in[1:d]^n} \prod_{i=1}^{n} x_{j_i} x'_{j_i}$$

$$= \sum_{n=0}^{\infty} \sum_{(j_1,\dots,j_n)\in[1:d]^n} \frac{\exp(-\|x\|_2^2/(2\sigma^2))}{\sqrt{n!}\sigma^n} \prod_{i=1}^{n} x_{j_i} \times \frac{\exp(-\|x'\|_2^2/(2\sigma^2))}{\sqrt{n!}\sigma^n} \prod_{i=1}^{n} x'_{j_i}$$

$$= \langle \phi(x), \phi(x')\rangle.$$

Note that the feature space has a dimension which is infinite in this case. □

Exercises

4.1 Given data $(x^{(1)}, y_1), \dots, (x^{(m)}, y_m) \in \mathbb{R}^d \times \{-1, +1\}$ and a hyperplane of equation $\langle w^*, x\rangle - b^* = 0$ separating these data according to (4.1), verify that the perturbed hyperplanes of equation $\langle w, x\rangle - b = 0$ also separates these data provided that $\|w - w^*\|_2 \max_{i\in[1:m]} \|x^{(i)}\|_2 + |b - b^*| < 1$.

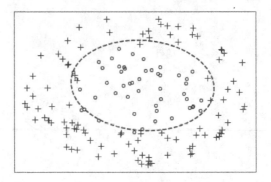

Figure 4.3 Data separated by a soft SVM using the gaussian kernel.

4.2   For a hyperplane $H_{w,b}$ of equation $\langle w, x \rangle - b = 0$, verify the identity $\text{dist}_{\ell_2}(x, H_{w,b}) = |\langle w, x \rangle - b|/\|w\|_2$ for any $x \in \mathbb{R}^d$.

4.3   When linearly separable data arrive in a streaming fashion—i.e., first $x^{(1)}$ arrives before y_1, then $x^{(2)}$ arrives before y_2, then $x^{(3)}$ arrives before y_3, etc.—the interest does not lie in separating the data at the end, but in predicting the correct label of a newly arriving $x^{(i)}$ on the fly. A variant of the *perceptron algorithm* allows one to perform this task with few errors. The variant reads:

> - start with some initial $\widetilde{w}^{(0)} \in \mathbb{R}^{d+1}$;
> - for each $t \geq 1$, receive $x^{(t)}$ and compute $\widehat{y}_t = \text{sgn}\langle \widetilde{w}^{(t)}, \widetilde{x}^{(t)} \rangle$;
> - receive y_t and
>   - if $\widehat{y}_t = y_t$, then the prediction was correct, so do nothing;
>   - if $\widehat{y}_t \neq y_t$, then the prediction was incorrect, so set
>
> $$\widetilde{w}^{(t)} = \widetilde{w}^{(t-1)} + \frac{y_t}{\|\widetilde{x}^{(t)}\|_2^2}\widetilde{x}^{(t)}.$$

Using the notation of Theorem 4.1, check that the number of incorrect predictions is bounded by $\lceil R^2 \|\widetilde{w}^*\|_2^2 \rceil$.

4.4   Skip forward to Section 21.3 and derive that the dual of the *hard SVM* takes the form

$$\underset{a \in \mathbb{R}^m}{\text{maximize}} \sum_{i=1}^{m} a_i - \frac{1}{2}\sum_{i,j=1}^{m} a_i a_j y_i y_j \langle x^{(i)}, x^{(j)} \rangle \quad \text{s.to} \quad \sum_{i=1}^{m} a_i y_i = 0$$

$$\text{and} \quad a \geq 0.$$

5

Reproducing Kernel Hilbert Spaces

The polynomial and gaussian kernels encountered in Chapter 4 go hand in hand with vector spaces of functions which are particularly well suited for Data Science tasks, i.e., function spaces where point evaluations make perfect sense and where an inner product structure prevails—these are reproducing kernel Hilbert spaces. This chapter aims at elucidating the connection between a symmetric function of two (multivariate) inputs, loosely called a *kernel*, and such a function space. First, it will be shown that a reproducing kernel Hilbert space gives rise to a positive semidefinite kernel. Next, it will be conversely shown that a positive semidefinite kernel gives rise to a reproducing kernel Hilbert space. Finally, under an added condition on the positive semidefinite kernel, a construction of the reproducing kernel Hilbert space associated with the kernel will be outlined.

5.1 Abstract Definition

The vague suggestion given above for what constitutes a reproducing kernel Hilbert space is formalized in the following definition.

Definition 5.1 A Hilbert space H of functions defined on a set X is called a *reproducing kernel Hilbert space* over X if, for each $x \in X$, the point evaluation at x is a continuous linear functional, i.e., if there exists some $C_x \geq 0$ such that

$$|f(x)| \leq C_x \|f\|_H \qquad \text{for all } f \in H. \tag{5.1}$$

This is a nontrivial definition, since (5.1) is not satisfied in every Hilbert space of functions. It is not satisfied in $L_2[-1, 1]$ because point evaluations are not even well defined there. It is not satisfied in $C[-1, 1]$ equipped with the Hilbert structure of $L_2[-1, 1]$ either, because the evaluation δ_0 at 0, say, is not

31

a continuous linear functional. Indeed, if $f_n\colon x \in [-1,1] \mapsto \max\{0, 1 - n|x|\}$ denote the tent function vanishing outside $[-1/n, 1/n]$, one has

$$f_n \xrightarrow{L_2} 0 \qquad \text{but} \qquad \delta_0(f_n) = 1 \not\rightarrow \delta_0(0).$$

As already alluded to, a reproducing kernel Hilbert space induces a function of two inputs with some specific properties.

Theorem 5.2 *If H is a reproducing kernel Hilbert space over a set X, then there is a unique kernel $K\colon X \times X \to \mathbb{R}$ enabling the reproducing property*

$$f(x) = \langle K(\cdot, x), f\rangle_H \qquad \text{for all } x \in X \text{ and all } f \in H. \tag{5.2}$$

Moreover, the kernel K is a positive semidefinite function,[1] *in the sense that, for any $m \geq 1$ and any $x^{(1)}, \ldots, x^{(m)} \in X$, the $m \times m$ matrix with entries $K(x^{(i)}, x^{(j)})$, $i, j \in [1 : m]$, is positive semidefinite.*

Proof Given $x \in X$, the existence of a unique element $K(\cdot, x) \in H$ yielding the reproducing property (5.2) is just an application of the *Riesz representation theorem* for Hilbert spaces (Theorem C.2). Note that taking $f = K(\cdot, x')$ in the reproducing property (5.2) gives

$$K(x, x') = \langle K(\cdot, x), K(\cdot, x')\rangle_H \qquad \text{for all } x, x' \in X.$$

The symmetry of K then follows from the symmetry of the inner product. Finally, given $x^{(1)}, \ldots, x^{(m)} \in X$, one observes that, for any $v \in \mathbb{R}^m$,

$$\sum_{i,j=1}^{m} v_i v_j K(x^{(i)}, x^{(j)}) = \sum_{i,j=1}^{m} v_i v_j \langle K(\cdot, x^{(i)}), K(\cdot, x^{(j)})\rangle_H$$

$$= \left\langle \sum_{i=1}^{m} v_i K(\cdot, x^{(i)}), \sum_{j=1}^{m} v_j K(\cdot, x^{(j)}) \right\rangle_H$$

$$= \left\| \sum_{i=1}^{m} v_i K(\cdot, x^{(i)}) \right\|_H^2 \geq 0.$$

This establishes the positive semidefiniteness of the kernel K. □

In a reproducing kernel Hilbert space with a kernel K which is furthermore a *positive definite function*, in the sense that, for any $m \geq 1$ and any distinct $x^{(1)}, \ldots, x^{(m)} \in X$, the $m \times m$ matrix with entries $K(x^{(i)}, x^{(j)})$, $i, j \in [1 : m]$, is positive definite instead of merely positive semidefinite, interpolation is always

---

[1] Beware of the terminology: positive semidefinite functions are often called positive definite functions in the literature.

possible. Precisely, given $x^{(1)}, \ldots, x^{(m)} \in \mathcal{X}$ and $y_1, \ldots, y_m \in \mathbb{R}$, one can always find a function f in the datapoint-dependent form

$$f = \sum_{j=1}^{m} c_j K(\cdot, x^{(j)})$$

satisfying the interpolatory conditions

$$f(x^{(i)}) = y_i \qquad \text{for all } i \in [1:m]. \tag{5.3}$$

One can see that the statement is equivalent to the invertibility of the linear map $c \in \mathbb{R}^m \mapsto [\sum_{j=1}^{m} c_j K(x^{(1)}, x^{(j)}); \ldots; \sum_{j=1}^{m} c_j K(x^{(m)}, x^{(j)})] \in \mathbb{R}^m$, which holds because its matrix, i.e., the matrix with entries $K(x^{(i)}, x^{(j)})$, is positive definite. This interpolatory success contrasts with interpolatory failure using a fixed, datapoint-independent vector space (e.g. of multivariate polynomials). Indeed, the *Mairhuber–Curtis theorem*[2] indicates that if $d \geq 2$ and if $\mathcal{X} \subseteq \mathbb{R}^d$ contains an interior point, then there is no vector space $\mathcal{V}$ with $m := \dim(\mathcal{V}) \geq 2$ such that the interpolatory conditions (5.3) can be met by some $f \in \mathcal{V}$ for any choice of $x^{(1)}, \ldots, x^{(m)} \in \mathcal{X}$ and $y_1, \ldots, y_m \in \mathbb{R}$.

5.2 Moore–Aronszajn Theorem

As a converse to Theorem 5.2, it is natural to wonder about the more practical question: starting with a positive semidefinite kernel K, is there a reproducing kernel Hilbert space with K as its reproducing kernel? The following result, known as the *Moore–Aronszajn theorem*, reveals that the answer is affirmative.

Theorem 5.3 *If $K \colon \mathcal{X} \times \mathcal{X} \to \mathbb{R}$ is a positive semidefinite kernel, then there exists a unique reproducing kernel Hilbert space H whose reproducing kernel coincides with K.*

The proof is more involved than the proof of Theorem 5.2 and is broken down in a series of lemmas.

Lemma 5.4 *Given functions $f = \sum_{i=1}^{m} a_i K(\cdot, x^{(i)})$ and $g = \sum_{j=1}^{n} b_j K(\cdot, \bar{x}^{(j)})$, the expression*

$$\langle f, g \rangle_{H_0} := \sum_{i=1}^{m} \sum_{j=1}^{n} a_i b_j K(x^{(i)}, \bar{x}^{(j)}) \tag{5.4}$$

defines an inner product on the vector space $H_0 := \text{span}\{K(\cdot, x), x \in \mathcal{X}\}$.

---

[2] See Chapter 1 of Cheney and Light (2009) and the references therein.

Proof One first has to verify that the expression (5.4) is well defined, i.e., that it does not depend on the particular representations $f = \sum_{i=1}^{m} a_i K(\cdot, x^{(i)})$ and $g = \sum_{j=1}^{n} b_j K(\cdot, \bar{x}^{(j)})$ of $f \in H_0$ and $g \in H_0$ as finite linear combinations of some $K(\cdot, x)$, $x \in X$. To see the independence with respect to the representation of g, say, one simply observes that

$$\langle f, g \rangle_{H_0} = \sum_{i=1}^{m} a_i \left(\sum_{j=1}^{n} b_j K(\cdot, \bar{x}^{(j)}) \right)(x^{(i)}) = \sum_{i=1}^{m} a_i g(x^{(i)}).$$

Next, to prove that (5.4) defines a legitimate inner product, one has to prove that $\langle f, f \rangle_{H_0} = 0$ implies $f = 0$, the other defining properties of an inner product being readily verified. Thus, consider $f = \sum_{i=1}^{m} a_i K(\cdot, x^{(i)})$ such that $\langle f, f \rangle_{H_0} = 0$, i.e., $\sum_{i,j=1}^{m} a_i a_j K(x^{(i)}, x^{(j)}) = 0$. For any $x^{(0)} \in X$ and $a_0 \in \mathbb{R}$, notice that the positive semidefiniteness of K yields

$$0 \le \sum_{i,j=0}^{m} a_i a_j K(x^{(i)}, x^{(j)}) = a_0^2 K(x^{(0)}, x^{(0)}) + 2a_0 \sum_{j=1}^{m} a_j K(x^{(0)}, x^{(j)})$$

$$= a_0^2 K(x^{(0)}, x^{(0)}) + 2a_0 f(x^{(0)}).$$

Given that the latter is nonnegative for any $a_0 \in \mathbb{R}$, one derives that $f(x^{(0)}) = 0$, and since this is true for any $x^{(0)} \in X$, the conclusion $f = 0$ follows. □

For any $x \in X$, the definition (5.4) applied to $g = K(\cdot, x)$ leads to the identity $\langle f, K(\cdot, x) \rangle_{H_0} = f(x)$ valid for any $f \in H_0$. In turn, this reproducing property implies that

$$|f(x)| \le \|K(\cdot, x)\|_{H_0} \|f\|_{H_0} = K(x, x)^{1/2} \|f\|_{H_0}, \tag{5.5}$$

so that the point evaluation at x is a continuous linear functional on the space H_0. However, this space is not yet the reproducing kernel Hilbert space hunted for because it might not be *complete*. In order to guarantee completeness, it shall be enlarged to the space H made of pointwise limits of Cauchy sequences in H_0, namely to

$$H := \{ f \in F(X, \mathbb{R}) : \text{there is a Cauchy sequence } (f_n)_{n \ge 0} \text{ in } H_0$$
$$\text{such that } f_n(x) \xrightarrow[n \to \infty]{} f(x) \text{ for all } x \in X \}. \tag{5.6}$$

Before extending the inner product (5.4) from H_0 to H, it is useful to isolate the following observation.

Lemma 5.5 *If $(h_n)_{n \ge 0}$ is a Cauchy sequence in H_0 that converges pointwise to the zero function, then*

$$\|h_n\|_{H_0} \xrightarrow[n \to \infty]{} 0.$$

Proof Let $\varepsilon > 0$ be given. By the boundedness of Cauchy sequences, there is a constant $C > 0$ such that $\|h_n\|_{H_0} \leq C$ for all $n \geq 0$. Since $(h_n)_{n\geq 0}$ is a Cauchy sequence, some $n' \geq 0$ exists such that $\|h_n - h_{n'}\|_{H_0} \leq \varepsilon^2/(2C)$ whenever $n \geq n'$. Writing $h_{n'}$ as $h_{n'} = \sum_{i=1}^m a_i K(\cdot, x^{(i)})$, one then considers $n'' \geq 0$ such that $|h_n(x^{(i)})| \leq \varepsilon^2/(2\|a\|_1)$ for all $i \in [1:m]$ whenever $n \geq n''$. It follows that, for $n \geq \max\{n', n''\}$,

$$\|h_n\|_{H_0}^2 = \langle h_n - h_{n'}, h_n \rangle_{H_0} + \langle h_{n'}, h_n \rangle_{H_0}$$

$$\leq \|h_n - h_{n'}\|_{H_0}\|h_n\|_{H_0} + \sum_{i=1}^m a_i h_n(x^{(i)})$$

$$\leq \frac{\varepsilon^2}{2C}C + \sum_{i=1}^m |a_i|\frac{\varepsilon^2}{2\|a\|_1} = \frac{\varepsilon^2}{2} + \frac{\varepsilon^2}{2} = \varepsilon^2.$$

In other words, one has $\|h_n\|_{H_0} \leq \varepsilon$ whenever $n \geq \max\{n', n''\}$, which is the desired result. □

The above lemma facilitates the argument for the extension of the inner product (5.4) to the space H.

Lemma 5.6 *Given f and g which are pointwise limits of Cauchy sequences $(f_n)_{n\geq 0}$ and $(g_n)_{n\geq 0}$ in H_0, the expression*

$$\langle f, g \rangle_H := \lim_{n\to\infty} \langle f_n, g_n \rangle_{H_0} \qquad (5.7)$$

defines an inner product on the vector space H.

Proof As in the proof of Lemma 5.4, one first has to verify that the expression (5.7) is well defined, meaning here that the limit of $\langle f_n, g_n \rangle_{H_0}$ exists and is independent of the choice of Cauchy sequences $(f_n)_{n\geq 0}$ and $(g_n)_{n\geq 0}$. To justify the existence, it is enough to check that $(u_n)_{n\geq 0} := (\langle f_n, g_n \rangle_{H_0})_{n\geq 0}$ is a real-valued Cauchy sequence, which is seen from

$$\sup_{k\geq 0} |u_n - u_{n+k}| = \sup_{k\geq 0} |\langle f_n, g_n - g_{n+k} \rangle_{H_0} + \langle f_n - f_{n+k}, g_{n+k} \rangle_{H_0}|$$

$$\leq \|f_n\|_{H_0} \sup_{k\geq 0} \|g_n - g_{n+k}\|_{H_0} + \sup_{k\geq 0} \|f_n - f_{n+k}\|_{H_0} \sup_{k\geq 0} \|g_{n+k}\|_{H_0}$$

$$\xrightarrow[n\to\infty]{} 0.$$

To justify the independence, suppose e.g. that f is the pointwise limit of two Cauchy sequences $(f_n)_{n\geq 0}$ and $(f_n')_{n\geq 0}$ in H_0. One needs to show that $\langle f_n, g_n \rangle_{H_0}$ and $\langle f_n', g_n \rangle_{H_0}$ have the same limit, which is seen from

$$|\langle f_n, g_n \rangle_{H_0} - \langle f_n', g_n \rangle_{H_0}| = |\langle f_n - f_n', g_n \rangle_{H_0}| \leq \|f_n - f_n'\|_{H_0}\|g_n\|_{H_0}$$

$$\xrightarrow[n\to\infty]{} 0,$$

where Lemma 5.5 was used for the Cauchy sequence $(h_n)_{n\geq 0} = (f_n - f'_n)_{n\geq 0}$.

Next, to prove that (5.7) defines a legitimate inner product, one has to prove that $\langle f, f \rangle_H = 0$ implies $f = 0$. Thus, for $f \in H$ with $\langle f, f \rangle_H = 0$, consider a Cauchy sequence $(f_n)_{n\geq 0}$ in H_0 converging pointwise to f. By (5.7), notice that $\lim_{n\to\infty} \|f_n\|^2_{H_0} = 0$. For any $x \in X$, the inequality (5.5) then yields

$$|f(x)| = \lim_{n\to\infty} |f_n(x)| \leq K(x,x)^{1/2} \lim_{n\to\infty} \|f_n\|_{H_0} = 0.$$

This means that $f(x) = 0$ for any $x \in X$, i.e., that $f = 0$, as required. $\square$

The definition (5.7) of the inner product on H contains some implicit and important information: given $f \in H$, if $(f_n)_{n\geq 0}$ is a Cauchy sequence in H_0 that converges pointwise to f, then the convergence is also valid relative to the norm on H. Indeed,

$$\|f - f_n\|_H = \lim_{k\to\infty} \|f_{n+k} - f_n\|_{H_0} \leq \sup_{k\geq 0} \|f_{n+k} - f_n\|_{H_0} \xrightarrow[n\to\infty]{} 0. \tag{5.8}$$

This implies in particular that H_0 is dense in H. The final lemma of the series establishes the completeness of H.

Lemma 5.7 *The vector space H defined in (5.6) and equipped with the inner product (5.7) is complete.*

Proof Let $(f_n)_{n\geq 0}$ be a Cauchy sequence in H. The goal is to show that $(f_n)_{n\geq 0}$ converges to some $f \in H$, i.e., to some pointwise limit of a Cauchy sequence in H_0. By denseness of H_0 in H, for any $n \geq 0$, one can find $g_n \in H_0$ such that $\|f_n - g_n\|_H \leq 1/(n+1)$, say. Then, for $k \geq 0$,

$$\|g_n - g_{n+k}\|_{H_0} = \|g_n - g_{n+k}\|_H \leq \|g_n - f_n\|_H + \|f_n - f_{n+k}\|_H + \|f_{n+k} - g_{n+k}\|_H$$

$$\leq \frac{2}{n+1} + \|f_n - f_{n+k}\|_H,$$

which implies that $(g_n)_{n\geq 0}$ is a Cauchy sequence in H_0. Note then that $(g_n)_{n\geq 0}$ has a pointwise limit: indeed, for any $x \in X$, the real-valued sequence $(g_n(x))_{n\geq 0}$ is a Cauchy sequence by virtue of (5.5). Denoting this pointwise limit by $f \in H$, the final claim is that $(f_n)_{n\geq 0}$ converges to f relative to the norm on H. This simply follows from $\|f - f_n\|_H \leq \|f - g_n\|_H + \|g_n - f_n\|_H$, coupled with the facts that $\|f - g_n\|_H \to 0$, obtained exactly as in (5.8), and that $\|g_n - f_n\|_H \leq 1/(n+1)$. $\square$

The necessary series of lemmas having been established, one can finally turn to the proof of the Moore–Aronszajn theorem, stating that a positive semidefinite kernel gives rise to a reproducing kernel Hilbert space.

Proof of Theorem 5.3 By virtue of Lemmas 5.6 and 5.7, it is acquired that the function space H is a complete inner product space, i.e., a Hilbert space. Next, for $x \in X$, with $f \in H$ being the pointwise limit of some Cauchy sequence $(f_n)_{n \geq 0}$ in H_0, one has

$$|f(x)| = \lim_{n \to \infty} |f_n(x)| \leq K(x, x)^{1/2} \lim_{n \to \infty} \|f_n\|_{H_0} = K(x, x)^{1/2} \|f\|_H,$$

where the inequality (5.5) and the definition (5.7) were used. Thus, each point evaluation at x is a continuous linear functional on H. This justifies the fact that H is a reproducing kernel Hilbert space. To verify that its reproducing kernel coincides with K, one must show that $f(x) = \langle K(\cdot, x), f \rangle_H$ whenever $x \in X$ and $f \in H$. With $(f_n)_{n \geq 0}$ denoting a Cauchy sequence in H_0 converging pointwise to f, and hence also in norm, this follows from the reproduction property on H_0 via

$$\langle K(\cdot, x), f \rangle_H = \lim_{n \to \infty} \langle K(\cdot, x), f_n \rangle_{H_0} = \lim_{n \to \infty} f_n(x) = f(x).$$

Finally, it remains to prove that H is unique. To this end, consider a reproducing kernel Hilbert space H' whose reproducing kernel coincides with K. One must have $K(\cdot, x) \in H'$ for all $x \in X$, so that $H_0 \subseteq H'$, and in turn $H \subseteq H'$. The equality $H = H'$ is shown by establishing that the orthogonal complement of H in H' reduces to $\{0\}$. To see this, one can simply observe that a function f in this orthogonal complement must satisfy $f(x) = \langle K(\cdot, x), f \rangle_{H'} = 0$ for any $x \in X$, i.e., $f = 0$. $\square$

5.3 Mercer Theorem

The polynomial and gaussian kernels encountered in Chapter 4 had the form $K(x, x') = \langle \phi(x), \phi(x') \rangle$ for some feature map ϕ taking values in a Hilbert space. The observation that

$$\sum_{i,j=1}^{m} a_i a_j \langle \phi(x^{(i)}), \phi(x^{(j)}) \rangle = \left\| \sum_{i=1}^{m} a_i \phi(x^{(i)}) \right\|^2 \geq 0$$

shows that such a kernel K is positive semidefinite. Thus, the Moore–Aronszajn theorem ensures that there is a unique reproducing kernel Hilbert space H_K possessing K as its reproducing kernel. However, the arguments did not offer an effective construction of the space H_K. One will see very soon that such a construction can be derived as a consequence of the *Mercer theorem* proved below with many omitted details.[3]

---

[3] The omitted details can be found in König (1986), in particular in Theorem 3.a.1 there.

Theorem 5.8 *Let μ be a finite nonnegative Borel measure on a set X and let $K\colon X \times X \to \mathbb{R}$ be a continuous and positive semidefinite kernel satisfying $K \in L_\infty(X \times X, \mu \times \mu)$. Then there exist an orthonormal basis $(\phi_n)_{n \geq 1}$ for $L_2(X, \mu)$ and an absolutely summable sequence $(\lambda_n)_{n \geq 1}$ of nonnegative numbers such that K has the (absolutely and uniformly) convergent expansion*

$$K(x, x') = \sum_{n=1}^{\infty} \lambda_n \phi_n(x) \phi_n(x'), \qquad x, x' \in X. \tag{5.9}$$

Proof (Sketch) The above conditions guarantee that $K \in L_2(X \times X, \mu \times \mu)$, which allows one to define an operator T on $L_2(X, \mu)$ by setting

$$T(f)(x) = \int_X K(x, x') f(x') d\mu(x') \tag{5.10}$$

for all $f \in L_2(X, \mu)$ and all $x \in X$. This operator, called a *Hilbert–Schmidt integral operator*, is self-adjoint and compact. Furthermore, the fact that the kernel K is continuous and positive semidefinite implies that the operator T is positive semidefinite, in the sense that $\langle T(f), f \rangle_{L_2(X, \mu)} \geq 0$ for all $f \in L_2(X, \mu)$. By the *spectral theorem*, there exist a square-summable sequence $(\lambda_n)_{n \geq 1}$ and an orthonormal basis $(\phi_n)_{n \geq 1}$ for $L_2(X, \mu)$, with each ϕ_n being an eigenvector of T associated with the eigenvalue $\lambda_n \geq 0$. The eigendecomposition of T reads, for $f \in L_2(X, \mu)$ and $x \in X$,

$$T(f)(x) = \sum_{n=1}^{\infty} \lambda_n \left(\int_X \phi_n(x') f(x') d\mu(x') \right) \phi_n(x), \tag{5.11}$$

with equality so far understood in the sense of $L_2(X, \mu)$. Now, the boundedness condition imposed on K implies (after some work) that the sequence $(\lambda_n)_{n \geq 1}$ is absolutely summable and that $\sup \{\|\phi_n\|_{L_\infty(X, \mu)}, n \geq 1\}$ is finite. Therefore, comparing (5.10) and (5.11) justifies the absolutely and uniformly convergent expansion (5.9).   □

Keeping the above notation, one further assumes that the kernel K is positive definite, implying that none of the eigenvalues $\lambda_n \geq 0$ equal zero. One then defines the space

$$H_K = \left\{ f \in L_2(X, \mu) : \sum_{n=1}^{\infty} \frac{\langle \phi_n, f \rangle_{L_2(X, \mu)}^2}{\lambda_n} < +\infty \right\}.$$

This is a Hilbert space equipped with the inner product

$$\langle f, g \rangle_{H_K} = \sum_{n=1}^{\infty} \frac{\langle \phi_n, f \rangle_{L_2(X, \mu)} \langle \phi_n, g \rangle_{L_2(X, \mu)}}{\lambda_n}, \qquad f, g \in H_K.$$

Each point evaluation at $x \in \mathcal{X}$ is seen to be a continuous linear functional by writing, for any $f \in H_K$,

$$f(x) = \sum_{n=1}^{\infty} \langle \phi_n, f \rangle_{L_2(\mathcal{X},\mu)} \phi_n(x) \leq \left[\sum_{n=1}^{\infty} \frac{\langle \phi_n, f \rangle_{L_2(\mathcal{X},\mu)}^2}{\lambda_n} \right]^{1/2} \left[\sum_{n=1}^{\infty} \lambda_n \phi_n(x)^2 \right]^{1/2}$$

$$= \|f\|_{H_K} K(x,x)^{1/2},$$

where the expansion (5.9) was used with $x' = x$ in the last step. Fixing $x \in \mathcal{X}$, the expansion (5.9) also implies that $\langle \phi_n, K(\cdot, x) \rangle_{L_2(\mathcal{X},\mu)} = \lambda_n \phi_n(x)$ for all $n \geq 1$, from where it follows that $K(\cdot, x) \in H_K$ with $\|K(\cdot, x)\|_{H_K}^2 = K(x,x)$. In turn, one obtains, for any $x \in \mathcal{X}$ and any $f \in H_K$,

$$f(x) = \sum_{n=1}^{\infty} \langle \phi_n, f \rangle_{L_2(\mathcal{X},\mu)} \phi_n(x) = \sum_{n=1}^{\infty} \langle \phi_n, f \rangle_{L_2(\mathcal{X},\mu)} \frac{\langle \phi_n, K(\cdot, x) \rangle_{L_2(\mathcal{X},\mu)}}{\lambda_n}$$

$$= \langle f, K(\cdot, x) \rangle_{H_K}.$$

All in all, it has now been shown that H_K is the reproducing kernel Hilbert space—an explicitly constructed one—whose kernel coincides with K.

Exercises

5.1   Verify that the following kernels are positive semidefinite:
- $K(x, x') = \cos(x - x')$, $x, x' \in \mathbb{R}$,
- $K(x, x') = 1/(x + x')$, $x, x' \in (0, \infty)$,
- $K(x, x') = \exp(\langle x, x' \rangle / \sigma^2)$, $x, x' \in \mathbb{R}^d$,
- $K(x, x') = \exp(-\|x - x'\|_2 / \sigma)$, $x, x' \in \mathbb{R}^d$.

5.2   Given two positive semidefinite kernels K_1 and K_2, show that the sum $K_1 + K_2$, the product $K_1 \times K_2$, and the tensor product $K_1 \otimes K_2$ are also positive semidefinite kernels. For the latter two properties, it is useful to first prove the *Schur product theorem*, stating that the entrywise product of two positive semidefinite matrices is also positive semidefinite.

5.3   Given a positive semidefinite kernel $K \colon \mathcal{X} \times \mathcal{X} \to \mathbb{R}$, prove that the *normalized kernel* defined by

$$K^{\text{nzed}}(x, x') = \begin{cases} \dfrac{K(x, x')}{K(x, x)^{1/2} K(x', x')^{1/2}} & \text{if } K(x, x) > 0 \text{ and } K(x', x') > 0, \\ 0 & \text{otherwise,} \end{cases}$$

is a positive semidefinite kernel taking values in $[-1, 1]$. Verify that the normalized kernel for $K(x, x') = \exp(\langle x, x' \rangle / \sigma^2)$ is the *gaussian kernel*.

5.4   Verify that $(x, x') \in [0, 1]^2 \mapsto 1 + \min\{x, x'\} \in \mathbb{R}$ is the reproducing kernel for the Sobolev space $W_2^1[0, 1]$ equipped with the inner product $\langle f, g \rangle = f(0)g(0) + \int_0^1 f'g'$.

5.5   Given a supspace $\widetilde{H}$ of a reproducing kernel Hilbert space H over a set X, observe that $\widetilde{H}$ is itself a reproducing kernel Hilbert space. Describe its reproducing kernel $\widetilde{K}$ in terms of the reproducing kernel K of H. For the special case $\widetilde{H} = \{f \in H : f(u) = 0\}$ where $u \in X$ satisfies $K(u, u) > 0$, verify that the kernel $\widetilde{K}$ is given by

$$\widetilde{K}(x, x') = K(x, x') - \frac{K(x, u)K(u, x')}{K(u, u)}, \qquad x, x' \in X.$$

6

Regression and Regularization

Previous chapters concentrated on binary classification, where the set of labels contained exactly two elements, typically $\mathcal{Y} = \{0, 1\}$ or $\mathcal{Y} = \{-1, +1\}$. This chapter now takes a look at the *regression* problem, where $\mathcal{Y} = \mathbb{R}$, meaning that the labels $y_1 = f(x^{(1)}), \ldots, y_m = f(x^{(m)})$ are real-valued. The empirical risk minimization strategy from Chapter 1 will be examined first. Next, the plain strategy will be enhanced by the introduction of a regularization term. Finally, a regression approach of dealing with classification problems will be presented.

6.1 Empirical Risk Minimization

As a reminder, given a sample $\mathcal{S} = ((x^{(1)}, y_1), \ldots, (x^{(m)}, y_m))$ where $y_i = f(x^{(i)})$ for every $i \in [1 : m]$, the empirical risk minimization strategy consists in outputting a predictor $h_{\mathcal{S}} = \Delta_{\mathcal{H}}^{\mathrm{erm}}(\mathcal{S}) \in \mathcal{H}$ by minimizing over $h \in \mathcal{H}$ the empirical risk

$$\widehat{\mathrm{Risk}}_{\mathcal{S}}(h) = \frac{1}{m} \sum_{i=1}^{m} \mathrm{Loss}(h(x^{(i)}), y_i).$$

The hypothesis class selected here is the vector space of all *affine functions* on $\mathbb{R}^d$. In other words, still using the notation $\widetilde{x} := [x; 1] \in \mathbb{R}^{d+1}$ associated with $x \in \mathbb{R}^d$, the hypothesis class is the set

$$\mathcal{H}_{\mathrm{aff}} = \{h_w : x \in \mathbb{R}^d \mapsto \langle w, \widetilde{x} \rangle, \ w \in \mathbb{R}^{d+1}\}.$$

When the square loss $\mathrm{Loss}_{\mathrm{sq}}(y, y') = (y - y')^2$ is used, as is often the case, the empirical risk of the predictor h_w becomes the *mean-square error*

$$\frac{1}{m} \sum_{i=1}^{m} (\langle w, \widetilde{x}^{(i)} \rangle - y_i)^2 = \frac{1}{m} \|\widetilde{X}^\top w - y\|_2^2,$$

41

where the columns of the *augmented data matrix* $\widetilde{X}$ are the augmented data-points $\widetilde{x}^{(1)}, \ldots, \widetilde{x}^{(m)}$, so that

$$\widetilde{X} = \left[\begin{array}{ccc} \widetilde{x}^{(1)} & \cdots & \widetilde{x}^{(m)} \end{array}\right] = \left[\begin{array}{ccc} x^{(1)} & \cdots & x^{(m)} \\ \hline 1 & \cdots & 1 \end{array}\right] \in \mathbb{R}^{(d+1)\times m}.$$

Thus, empirical risk minimization reduces here to the *least-squares problem*

$$\underset{w\in\mathbb{R}^{d+1}}{\text{minimize}} \ \|\widetilde{X}^\top w - y\|_2^2, \tag{6.1}$$

with solution(s) $\widehat{w}$ being characterized by the *normal equations*

$$\widetilde{X}\widetilde{X}^\top \widehat{w} = \widetilde{X}y. \tag{6.2}$$

This characterization is easily derived geometrically (see Figure 6.1) from the orthogonality of $\widetilde{X}^\top \widehat{w} - y$ to the space $\text{ran}(\widetilde{X}^\top) = \{\widetilde{X}^\top v, v \in \mathbb{R}^{d+1}\}$. Indeed, the identity $\widetilde{X}\widetilde{X}^\top \widehat{w} - \widetilde{X}y = 0$ follows from the fact that, for any $v \in \mathbb{R}^{d+1}$,

$$0 = \langle \widetilde{X}^\top \widehat{w} - y, \widetilde{X}^\top v\rangle = \langle \widetilde{X}(\widetilde{X}^\top \widehat{w} - y), v\rangle.$$

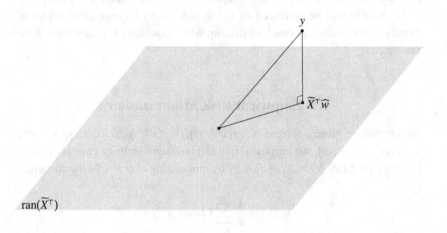

Figure 6.1 $\widetilde{X}^\top \widehat{w}$ is the orthogonal projection of y onto the space $\text{ran}(\widetilde{X}^\top)$.

In the *overparametrized regime* $d + 1 > m$ (more parameters than data), the matrix $\widetilde{X}\widetilde{X}^\top \in \mathbb{R}^{(d+1)\times(d+1)}$ is never invertible. Therefore, if the normal equations (6.2) possess a solution, then it is not unique. And most of the time, the normal equations do possess a solution, because $\widetilde{X}^\top \widetilde{X} \in \mathbb{R}^{m\times m}$ is typically invertible, so $\widehat{w} = \widetilde{X}(\widetilde{X}^\top \widetilde{X})^{-1}y$ readily solves (6.2). Notice incidentally that this solution yields an empirical risk equal to zero. In the *underparametrized regime* $d + 1 \leq m$ (less parameters than data), the situation is quite different since it is the matrix $\widetilde{X}\widetilde{X}^\top \in \mathbb{R}^{(d+1)\times(d+1)}$ which is typically invertible, so that the normal equations (6.2) have the unique solution $\widehat{w} = (\widetilde{X}\widetilde{X}^\top)^{-1}\widetilde{X}y$.

For other loss functions, e.g. $\text{Loss}_p(y, y') = |y - y'|^p$ with $p \in [1, \infty)$, the empirical risk minimization strategy turns into the minimization of $\|\widetilde{X}^\top w - y\|_p$ over all $w \in \mathbb{R}^{d+1}$. This is a convex optimization program which can be solved efficiently, but its solution $\widehat{w}$ (unique for $p \in (1, \infty)$) does not have an explicit form unless $p = 2$. It is still possible, though, to give an orthogonality-like characterization of $\widetilde{X}^\top \widehat{w}$; see Exercise 6.1.

6.2 Regularization

Solutions to the empirical risk minimization (6.1) are sometimes considered too "complex", so one attempts to promote "simpler" solutions by adding a *regularizer* to the empirical risk. For instance, to promote solutions with a small ℓ_2-norm, it is natural to consider the *Tikhonov regularization*

$$\underset{w\in\mathbb{R}^{d+1}}{\text{minimize}} \|\widetilde{X}^\top w - y\|_2^2 + \lambda^2\|w\|_2^2 \tag{6.3}$$

for some *tuning parameter* $\lambda > 0$. The minimization program (6.3), also called *ridge regression*, is solved by interpreting (6.3) as the standard least-squares problem

$$\underset{w\in\mathbb{R}^{d+1}}{\text{minimize}} \left\| \begin{bmatrix} \widetilde{X}^\top \\ \lambda\,\text{Id} \end{bmatrix} w - \begin{bmatrix} y \\ 0 \end{bmatrix} \right\|_2^2. \tag{6.4}$$

By considering the normal equations for (6.4), one sees that (6.3) has a unique solution given by

$$\widehat{w} = (\widetilde{X}\widetilde{X}^\top + \lambda^2 I_{d+1})^{-1}\widetilde{X}y,$$

where the matrix $\widetilde{X}\widetilde{X}^\top + \lambda^2 I_{d+1}$ is invertible because it is positive definite.

Instead of $\lambda^2\|w\|_2^2$, another popular choice of regularizer is $\lambda\|w\|_1$, leading to the *LASSO* (short for Least Absolute Shrinkage and Selection Operator) program

$$\underset{w\in\mathbb{R}^{d+1}}{\text{minimize}} \|\widetilde{X}^\top w - y\|_2^2 + \lambda\|w\|_1. \tag{6.5}$$

In the overparametrized regime, the LASSO promotes solutions with a few nonzero entries, i.e., sparse solutions. The following observation hints in this direction.

Theorem 6.1 *The optimization program* (6.5) *admits a solution with at most m nonzero entries.*

Proof   Among all possible solutions to (6.5), let $w^{(0)}$ be one with the smallest number of nonzero entries. Denoting by $J = \{j \in [1:d+1] : w_j^{(0)} \neq 0\}$ its support, one shall prove that the columns of $\widetilde{X}^\top$ indexed by J are linearly independent. Since the columns in question are vectors $\mathbb{R}^m$, this will force $|J| \leq m$, which is the desired result. Thus, assume by contradiction that the columns of $\widetilde{X}^\top$ indexed by J are linearly dependent, meaning that there is a nonzero vector $u \in \mathbb{R}^{d+1}$ supported on J and such that $\widetilde{X}^\top u = 0$. For each $t \in \mathbb{R}$, one introduces the vector $w^{(t)} = w^{(0)} + tu$. In view of $\widetilde{X}^\top w^{(t)} = \widetilde{X}^\top w^{(0)}$ and of $\|\widetilde{X}^\top w^{(0)} - y\|_2^2 + \lambda\|w^{(0)}\|_1 \leq \|\widetilde{X}^\top w^{(t)} - y\|_2^2 + \lambda\|w^{(t)}\|_1$, one must have $\|w^{(0)}\|_1 \leq \|w^{(t)}\|_1$. It follows that, whenever t is small enough in absolute value (precisely, whenever $|t| \leq \min\{|w_j^{(0)}|/|u_j|, \; j \in J : u_j \neq 0\} =: |w_\ell^{(0)}|/|u_\ell|)$,

$$\sum_{j \in J} |w_j^{(0)}| \leq \sum_{j \in J} |w_j^{(t)}| = \sum_{j \in J} \mathrm{sgn}(w_j^{(0)} + tu_j)(w_j^{(0)} + tu_j)$$

$$= \sum_{j \in J} \mathrm{sgn}(w_j^{(0)})(w_j^{(0)} + tu_j) = \sum_{j \in J} |w_j^{(0)}| + t \sum_{j \in J} \mathrm{sgn}(w_j^{(0)})u_j.$$

This can occur only when $\sum_{j \in J} \mathrm{sgn}(w_j^{(0)})u_j = 0$. In this case, all the $w^{(t)}$ with $|t| \leq |w_\ell^{(0)}|/|u_\ell|$ are also minimizers of (6.5). For $t = -w_\ell^{(0)}/u_\ell$, one has $w_\ell^{(t)} = 0$, so that the minimizer $w^{(t)}$ has fewer than $|J|$ nonzero entries. This is impossible according to the definition of $w^{(0)}$, providing the required contradiction.   □

Another favorable choice of regularizer is $\lambda^2\|w\|_1^2$, i.e., the square of the LASSO regularizer, leading to the program

$$\underset{w \in \mathbb{R}^{d+1}}{\text{minimize}} \; \|\widetilde{X}^\top w - y\|_2^2 + \lambda^2\|w\|_1^2. \tag{6.6}$$

Decomposing the optimization variable as $w = w^+ - w^-$ with $w^+ \geq 0$ and $w^- \geq 0$, this program can advantageously be reformulated as the *nonnegative least-squares problem*

$$\underset{w^+, w^- \in \mathbb{R}^{d+1}}{\text{minimize}} \; \left\| \begin{bmatrix} \widetilde{X}^\top & | & -\widetilde{X}^\top \\ \lambda \mathbf{1}^\top & | & \lambda \mathbf{1}^\top \end{bmatrix} \begin{bmatrix} w^+ \\ w^- \end{bmatrix} - \begin{bmatrix} y \\ 0 \end{bmatrix} \right\|_2^2 \quad \text{subject to } w^+ \geq 0, w^- \geq 0. \tag{6.7}$$

6.3 Classification via Regression

Faced with a classification task, a common approach for assigning a class to a datapoint $x \in \mathbb{R}^d$ consists first in producing, for each class, a likelihood that the datapoint belongs to that class and then in outputting the class with the maximal likelihood. In this way, the task turns into the regression problem of predicting a nondiscrete quantity, namely a vector $p \in \mathbb{R}^n$ of likelihoods

$p_1, \ldots, p_n \geq 0$ with $p_1 + \cdots + p_n = 1$. In the case of binary classification, which involves two classes labeled by -1 and $+1$, say, one thus has to produce some $p(x) \in [0, 1]$ to represent the likelihood that x belongs to the positively labeled class. In *logistic regression*, it is assumed that the logarithm of the odd $\omega(x) = p(x)/(1 - p(x))$ is an affine function of $x \in \mathbb{R}^d$. After some algebraic manipulation, this assumption translates into the adoption of the hypothesis class $\mathcal{H} = \{h_w, w \in \mathbb{R}^{d+1}\}$, where

$$h_w(x) = \frac{\exp(\langle w, \widetilde{x} \rangle)}{1 + \exp(\langle w, \widetilde{x} \rangle)} = \frac{1}{1 + \exp(-\langle w, \widetilde{x} \rangle)}.$$

The loss function evaluated at $y = h_w(x) \in [0, 1]$ and $y' \in \{-1, +1\}$ is designed to take the value 0 when $y = 1$ and $y' = +1$ and when $y = 0$ and $y' = -1$, and the value $+\infty$ when $y = 1$ and $y' = -1$ and when $y = 0$ and $y' = +1$. This requirement is fulfilled by the *logistic loss* defined asymmetrically on $[0, 1] \times \{-1, +1\}$ by

$$\text{Loss}_{\text{logi}}(y, y') = \log_2(1 + \exp(-y' \ln(\omega))), \qquad \omega = \frac{y}{1 - y}.$$

Given the sample $((x^{(1)}, y_1), \ldots, (x^{(m)}, y_m))$ with labels $y_1, \ldots, y_m \in \{-1, +1\}$, the empirical risk minimization strategy now leads to the optimization program

$$\underset{w \in \mathbb{R}^{d+1}}{\text{minimize}} \frac{1}{m} \sum_{i=1}^{m} \log_2(1 + \exp(-y_i \langle w, \widetilde{x}^{(i)} \rangle)). \tag{6.8}$$

This program is solvable in practice because the objective is a convex function of $w \in \mathbb{R}^{d+1}$. To see this, notice that the functions $t \mapsto \ln(1 + \exp(-y't))$, $y' = \pm 1$, are both convex on $\mathbb{R}$, since the derivatives $t \mapsto -y'/(1 + \exp(y't))$ are both increasing functions of $t \in \mathbb{R}$.

Exercises

6.1   For $p \in (1, \infty)$, prove that $\widehat{w} \in \mathbb{R}^{d+1}$ is a solution to

$$\underset{w \in \mathbb{R}^{d+1}}{\text{minimize}} \|\widetilde{X}^\top w - y\|_p^p$$

if and only if

$$\widetilde{X}(\text{sgn}(\widetilde{X}^\top \widehat{w} - y)|\widetilde{X}^\top \widehat{w} - y|^{p-1}) = 0,$$

with the understanding that the sign, absolute value, and $(p - 1)$st power functions act entrywise on a vector.

6.2   Given a matrix $A \in \mathbb{R}^{n \times (d+1)}$ with $\ker(A) \cap \ker(\widetilde{X}^\top) = \{0\}$, find an explicit expression for the solution to the regularized program

$$\underset{w \in \mathbb{R}^{d+1}}{\text{minimize}} \|\widetilde{X}^\top w - y\|_2^2 + \lambda^2 \|Aw\|_2^2.$$

6.3   Verify carefully the equivalence between the minimization programs (6.6) and (6.7). Observe that there is a solution with at most m nonzero entries.

6.4   Prove that the *Tikhonov regularization* with parameter $\lambda \geq 0$, namely the unconstrained optimization program

$$\underset{w \in \mathbb{R}^{d+1}}{\text{minimize}} \ \|\widetilde{X}^\top w - y\|_2^2 + \lambda^2 \|w\|_2^2, \tag{6.9}$$

and the constrained optimization programs with parameters $\eta, \tau \geq 0$ given by

$$\underset{w \in \mathbb{R}^{d+1}}{\text{minimize}} \ \|w\|_2^2 \qquad \text{subject to } \|\widetilde{X}^\top w - y\|_2^2 \leq \eta^2, \tag{6.10}$$

$$\underset{w \in \mathbb{R}^{d+1}}{\text{minimize}} \ \|\widetilde{X}^\top w - y\|_2^2 \qquad \text{subject to } \|w\|_2^2 \leq \tau^2, \tag{6.11}$$

have essentially the same sets of solutions. More precisely, prove that a solution $\widehat{w}$ to (6.9) with $\lambda > 0$ solves (6.10) with $\eta = \|\widetilde{X}^\top \widehat{w} - y\|_2 \geq 0$, a solution $\widehat{w}$ to (6.10) with $\eta \geq 0$ solves (6.11) with $\tau = \|\widehat{w}\|_2 \geq 0$, and a solution $\widehat{w}$ to (6.11) with $\tau > 0$ solves (6.9) with some $\lambda \geq 0$.

7

Clustering

The learning tasks discussed so far, namely classification and regression, were examples of *supervised learning*, where some labels $y_1, \ldots, y_m$ came with the instances $x^{(1)}, \ldots, x^{(m)}$. This chapter examines an example of *unsupervised learning*, where labels are not available. Instead, the learner is given points $x^{(1)}, \ldots, x^{(m)}$ together with values $s(x^{(i)}, x^{(j)}) \in [0, 1]$ or $d(x^{(i)}, x^{(j)}) \in [0, \infty]$ measuring similarity or dissimilarity between $x^{(i)}$ and $x^{(j)}$. Total similarity is characterized by $s(x, x') = 1$ or $d(x, x') = 0$ and total dissimilarity by $s(x, x') = 0$ or $d(x, x') = \infty$. For instance, if dist is a distance function, one could take $s(x, x') = \exp(-\text{dist}(x, x')^2)$ and $d(x, x') = \text{dist}(x, x')$. With a parameter k that may or may not be an input of a clustering procedure, the goal is to produce k *clusters* $C_1, \ldots, C_k$ that partition $\mathfrak{X} = \{x^{(1)}, \ldots, x^{(m)}\}$ in a meaningful way, so that points in the same cluster are more similar than points in different clusters. Three successful strategies—single-linkage, center-based, and spectral—will be presented, despite the intuitive feeling that this clustering problem is not well-posed. This feeling can be backed up by some impossibility results, such as the one below, prevailing when too much is asked of the clustering procedure.

Theorem 7.1 *No clustering procedure F taking as inputs a set $\mathfrak{X}$ of points and a dissimilarity function d can be simultaneously:*

(i) rich: *for any $\mathfrak{X}$ and any partition $\mathfrak{C}$ of $\mathfrak{X}$, there is some d such that $F(\mathfrak{X}, d) = \mathfrak{C}$;*

(ii) consistent: *for any $\mathfrak{X}$ and any d, d', if $d'(x, z) \leq d(x, z)$ whenever x and z are in the same cluster of $F(\mathfrak{X}, d)$ and $d'(x, z) \geq d(x, z)$ whenever x and z are in different clusters of $F(\mathfrak{X}, d)$, then $F(\mathfrak{X}, d') = F(\mathfrak{X}, d);$*

(iii) scale-invariant: *for any $\mathfrak{X}$ and any d, if $\alpha > 0$, then $F(\mathfrak{X}, \alpha d) = F(\mathfrak{X}, d)$.*

Proof Suppose by contradiction that there is a procedure F satisfying (i), (ii), and (iii) simultaneously. Let us consider a finite set $\mathfrak{X}$ of size $|\mathfrak{X}| \geq 3$. By (i), let d, d' be such that $\{\{x\}, x \in \mathfrak{X}\} = F(\mathfrak{X}, d) \neq F(\mathfrak{X}, d')$. Next, select $\alpha > 0$ such that $\alpha \, d'(x, z) \geq d(x, z)$ for all $x, z \in \mathfrak{X}$. Given that distinct x and z are always in different clusters of $F(\mathfrak{X}, d)$, (ii) then implies that $F(\mathfrak{X}, \alpha d') = F(\mathfrak{X}, d)$. By (iii), one deduces that $F(\mathfrak{X}, d') = F(\mathfrak{X}, d)$, which is a contradiction. □

7.1 Single-Linkage Clustering

In spite of general negative results, clustering can be performed faithfully for some specific configurations of points via e.g. the *single-linkage algorithm*, described as follows:

- start with the partition $\mathfrak{C}^{(0)} = \{C_1^{(0)} = \{x^{(1)}\}, \ldots, C_m^{(0)} = \{x^{(m)}\}\}$;
- for each $t \geq 0$, identify clusters $C_i^{(t)}$ and $C_j^{(t)}$ that minimize

$$\text{dist}(C, C') := \min_{x \in C, x' \in C'} \text{dist}(x, x')$$

  over $C \neq C' \in \mathfrak{C}^{(t)}$ and merge them into one cluster in $\mathfrak{C}^{(t+1)}$, leaving the other clusters unchanged;
- stop after $m - k$ steps and output the partition $\mathfrak{C}^{(m-k)}$ containing k clusters.

The favorable situations where single linkage succeeds include the ones where intra-cluster distances are always smaller than inter-cluster distances, as illustrated in Figure 7.1 below and shown in Theorem 7.2.

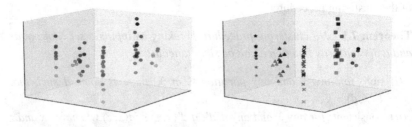

Figure 7.1 Datapoints that are organized in well-separated clusters (left) can be grouped into the original clusters using the single-linkage algorithm (right).

Theorem 7.2 *If $\mathfrak{X}$ is partitioned into k clusters $C_1^*, \ldots, C_k^*$ such that*

$$\max_{h \in [1:k]} \max_{x \neq x' \in C_h^*} \operatorname{dist}(x, x') < \min_{\ell \neq \ell' \in [1:k]} \operatorname{dist}(C_\ell^*, C_{\ell'}^*), \tag{7.1}$$

then the single linkage algorithm outputs the partition $\mathfrak{C}^* = \{C_1^*, \ldots, C_k^*\}$.

Proof The plan is to establish by induction on $t \in [0 : m - k]$ that each $C_i^{(t)}$, $i \in [1 : m - t]$, is included in $C_{\ell^{(t)}(i)}^*$ for some $\ell^{(t)}(i) \in [1 : k]$. The result for $t = m - k$ then yields the required conclusion. The base case $t = 0$ being clear, one assumes that the induction hypothesis holds up to some $t < m - k$. To prove that it holds for $t + 1$, it is enough to show that clusters $C_i^{(t)}$ and $C_j^{(t)}$ minimizing $\operatorname{dist}(C, C')$ over $C \neq C' \in \mathfrak{C}^{(t)}$ are included in the same cluster C_ℓ^*. Suppose that this is not the case, i.e., that $\ell^{(t)}(i) \neq \ell^{(t)}(j)$. Then, in view of $C_i^{(t)} \subseteq C_{\ell^{(t)}(i)}^*$, of $C_j^{(t)} \subseteq C_{\ell^{(t)}(j)}^*$, and of the assumption (7.1), one has

$$\operatorname{dist}(C_i^{(t)}, C_j^{(t)}) \geq \operatorname{dist}(C_{\ell^{(t)}(i)}^*, C_{\ell^{(t)}(j)}^*) > \operatorname{dist}(x, x')$$

for any $x \neq x'$ belonging to the same cluster C_h^*. Now, since $m - t > k$, the map $\ell^{(t)}$ defined on $[1 : m - t]$ and taking values in $[1 : k]$ cannot be injective, and hence there exist $i' \neq j' \in [1 : m - t]$ such that $\ell^{(t)}(i') = \ell^{(t)}(j') =: h$. Picking $x \in C_{i'}^{(t)} \subseteq C_h^*$ and $x' \in C_{j'}^{(t)} \subseteq C_h^*$, it follows that

$$\operatorname{dist}(C_i^{(t)}, C_j^{(t)}) > \operatorname{dist}(x, x') \geq \operatorname{dist}(C_{i'}^{(t)}, C_{j'}^{(t)}),$$

which contradicts the choice of i and j. Thus, one has $\ell^{(t)}(i) = \ell^{(t)}(j) =: \ell$, so the cluster $C_i^{(t)} \cup C_j^{(t)}$ newly created in $\mathfrak{C}^{(t+1)}$ is included in C_ℓ^*. This shows that the induction hypothesis holds for $t + 1$ and concludes the inductive proof. □

7.2 Center-Based Clustering

The second procedure to be briefly covered, called *center-based clustering*, relies on the notion of centers $c_1, \ldots, c_k$ of clusters $C_1, \ldots, C_k$, as characterized by

$$C_i = \{x \in \mathfrak{X} : \operatorname{dist}(x, c_i) < \operatorname{dist}(x, c_j) \text{ for all } j \neq i\}. \tag{7.2}$$

The centers are heuristically chosen to minimize the objective function

$$\operatorname{Obj}(\mathfrak{X}, c_1, \ldots, c_k) = \sum_{i=1}^{k} \sum_{x \in C_i} \operatorname{dist}(x, c_i)^2. \tag{7.3}$$

This strategy is called *k-means clustering*. There are some variants: without the squares, it becomes *k-median clustering*; with centers constrained to lie in $\mathfrak{X}$, it becomes *k-medoids clustering*; etc. In the case of Euclidean distance, and for a fixed cluster C_i, note that the point c minimizing $\sum_{x \in C_i} \text{dist}(x, c)^2$ is the barycenter c_i of C_i, which is given by

$$c_i = \frac{1}{|C_i|} \sum_{x \in C_i} x. \tag{7.4}$$

Indeed, in view of $\|c_i - c\|_2^2 \geq 0$ and of $\sum_{x \in C_i} (x - c_i) = 0$, one has

$$\sum_{x \in C_i} \|x - c\|_2^2 = \sum_{x \in C_i} \|x - c_i + c_i - c\|_2^2$$

$$= \sum_{x \in C_i} \left(\|x - c_i\|_2^2 + \|c_i - c\|_2^2 + 2\langle x - c_i, c_i - c \rangle \right)$$

$$\geq \sum_{x \in C_i} \|x - c_i\|_2^2 + 2\left\langle \sum_{x \in C_i} (x - c_i), c_i - c \right\rangle$$

$$= \sum_{x \in C_i} \|x - c_i\|_2^2.$$

Alternating between relation (7.2), creating clusters from centers, and relation (7.4), creating barycenters from clusters, leads to the *Lloyd algorithm*:

- start with arbitrary centers $c_1^{(0)}, \ldots, c_k^{(0)}$;
- for each $t \geq 0$, form clusters $C_1^{(t)}, \ldots, C_k^{(t)}$ via

$$C_i^{(t)} = \{x \in \mathfrak{X} : \|x - c_i^{(t)}\|_2 < \|x - c_j^{(t)}\|_2 \text{ for all } j \neq i\}$$

  and compute their centers $c_1^{(t+1)}, \ldots, c_k^{(t+1)}$ via

$$c_i^{(t+1)} = \frac{1}{|C_i^{(t)}|} \sum_{x \in C_i^{(t)}} x;$$

- stop at a predefined halting criterion.

While the algorithm is not necessarily guaranteed to produce the "correct" partition, one can establish, at the very least, that the objective function (7.3) decreases along the iterations.

Proposition 7.3 *For each $t \geq 0$, the iterates of the Lloyd algorithm satisfy*

$$\text{Obj}(\mathfrak{X}, c_1^{(t+1)}, \ldots, c_k^{(t+1)}) \leq \text{Obj}(\mathfrak{X}, c_1^{(t)}, \ldots, c_k^{(t)}).$$

Proof For each $x \in \mathfrak{X}$, let $c_{i(x)}^{(t+1)}$ denote the center $c_i^{(t+1)}$ closest to x. According to the definitions of the objective function and of the clusters $C_1^{(t+1)}, \ldots, C_k^{(t+1)}$, one has

$$
\begin{aligned}
\mathrm{Obj}(\mathfrak{X}, c_1^{(t+1)}, \ldots, c_k^{(t+1)}) &= \sum_{i=1}^{k} \sum_{x \in C_i^{(t+1)}} \|x - c_i^{(t+1)}\|_2^2 \\
&= \sum_{x \in \mathfrak{X}} \|x - c_{i(x)}^{(t+1)}\|_2^2 \\
&= \sum_{i=1}^{k} \sum_{x \in C_i^{(t)}} \|x - c_{i(x)}^{(t+1)}\|_2^2 \\
&\leq \sum_{i=1}^{k} \sum_{x \in C_i^{(t)}} \|x - c_i^{(t+1)}\|_2^2 \\
&\leq \sum_{i=1}^{k} \sum_{x \in C_i^{(t)}} \|x - c_i^{(t)}\|_2^2 \\
&= \mathrm{Obj}(\mathfrak{X}, c_1^{(t)}, \ldots, c_k^{(t)}),
\end{aligned}
$$

where the last two inequalities followed from the very definitions of $c_{i(x)}^{(t+1)}$ and of $c_i^{(t+1)}$, respectively. $\square$

7.3 Spectral Clustering

In the final procedure to be examined, namely *spectral clustering*, the points $x^{(1)}, \ldots, x^{(m)}$ are thought of as vertices of a weighted undirected graph whose edges have weights $W_{i,j} = s(x^{(i)}, x^{(j)})$. The heuristic behind spectral clustering is a link between the clusters and the spectrum of the symmetric weighted adjacency matrix $W \in \mathbb{R}^{m \times m}$, or rather with the *graph Laplacian*

$$
L := D - W \in \mathbb{R}^{m \times m},
$$

where $D \in \mathbb{R}^{m \times m}$ is a diagonal matrix with diagonal entries $D_{i,i} = \sum_{j=1}^{m} W_{i,j}$. The following observation illustrates this heuristic.

Proposition 7.4 *The graph Laplacian possesses the eigenvalue* 0*, which is a multiple eigenvalue if and only if the graph is disconnected.*

Proof Let C be a connected component of the graph, so that $W_{i,j} = 0$ if $i \in C$

and $j \notin C$. One calculates, for any $i \in [1:m]$,

$$(L\mathbb{1}_C)_i = \sum_{j \in C} L_{i,j} = \sum_{j \in C} D_{i,j} - \sum_{j \in C} W_{i,j}$$

$$= \begin{cases} D_{i,i} - \sum_{j=1}^m W_{i,j} & = 0 \quad \text{if } i \in C, \\ 0 - 0 & = 0 \quad \text{if } i \notin C. \end{cases}$$

This shows that 0 is an eigenvalue for L with eigenvector $\mathbb{1}_C$. In particular, if the graph has several connected components, then 0 is a multiple eigenvalue.

For the converse, one makes use of the crucial (and easy to verify, starting from the right-hand side) observation that

$$\langle Lv, v \rangle = \frac{1}{2} \sum_{i,j=1}^m W_{i,j}(v_i - v_j)^2 \qquad \text{for all } v \in \mathbb{R}^m.$$

In this way, if v is an eigenvector associated with the eigenvalue 0, then $Lv = 0$ forces $W_{i,j}(v_i - v_j)^2 = 0$ for all $i, j \in [1:m]$. Thus, when i and j are connected ($W_{i,j} > 0$), the entries v_i and v_j have the same value. Therefore, for a connected graph, all the entries of v must have the same value, i.e., v is a multiple of $\mathbb{1}$. This means that 0 is a simple eigenvalue. $\square$

In order to state convincing results about spectral clustering, the setting is further restricted. Precisely, one assumes that the undirected graph associated with $x^{(1)}, \ldots, x^{(m)}$ is unweighted (i.e., $W_{i,j}$ is either 0 or 1) and that there are only two clusters, also referred to as communities here, each having size $m/2$ (assuming m is even). These communities are groups of vertices tending to be more connected if they belong to the same community. More formally, the *stochastic block model* with parameters $q > p$ is adopted: for any $i, j \in [1:m]$,

$$\mathbb{P}[W_{i,j} = 1] = \mathbb{P}[x^{(i)} \text{ and } x^{(j)} \text{ are connected}]$$

$$= \begin{cases} q & \text{if } x^{(i)} \text{ and } x^{(j)} \text{ are in the same community,} \\ p & \text{if } x^{(i)} \text{ and } x^{(j)} \text{ are in different communities.} \end{cases}$$

The clustering is done according to the signs of the eigenvector associated with the largest eigenvalue of an auxiliary matrix built from W:

- compute the leading eigenvector $v \in \mathbb{R}^m$ for the matrix $W - \omega \mathbb{1}\mathbb{1}^\top$, where $\omega := \sum_{i,j=1}^m W_{i,j}/m^2$;
- return the two communities given as $\{i \in [1:m] : v_i > 0\}$ and $\{i \in [1:m] : v_i \leq 0\}$.

Theorem 7.5 *Under the stochastic block model with parameters $q > p$, it occurs with failure probability at most $\exp(-m/4)$ that the two communities are identified by the above procedure with fewer than $C/(q-p)^2$ errors.*

Proof The random quantity ω has expectation $\mathbb{E}[\omega] = (q+p)/2$. As for the random matrix W, its expectation takes the form, up to a proper ordering of the vertices,

$$\overline{W} := \mathbb{E}[W] = \begin{bmatrix} q & \cdots & q & | & p & \cdots & p \\ & \vdots & & | & & \vdots & \\ q & \cdots & q & | & p & \cdots & p \\ p & \cdots & p & | & q & \cdots & q \\ & \vdots & & | & & \vdots & \\ p & \cdots & p & | & q & \cdots & q \end{bmatrix}.$$

Thus, the expectation of the random matrix $Z := W - \omega \mathbb{1}\mathbb{1}^\top$ takes the form, up to the same proper ordering of the vertices,

$$\overline{Z} := \mathbb{E}[Z] = \frac{q-p}{2} \begin{bmatrix} +1 & \cdots & +1 & | & -1 & \cdots & -1 \\ & \vdots & & | & & \vdots & \\ +1 & \cdots & +1 & | & -1 & \cdots & -1 \\ -1 & \cdots & -1 & | & +1 & \cdots & +1 \\ & \vdots & & | & & \vdots & \\ -1 & \cdots & -1 & | & +1 & \cdots & +1 \end{bmatrix}$$

$$= \frac{(q-p)m}{2} uu^\top, \tag{7.5}$$

where the ℓ_2-normalized vector $u \in \mathbb{R}^m$ has entries $u_i = +1/\sqrt{m}$ when i is in the first community and $u_i = -1/\sqrt{m}$ when i is in the second community. While (7.5) provides the eigendecomposition of $\overline{Z}$, the eigendecomposition of Z is written (with a leading eigenvector $v = v_1$ chosen such that $\langle u, v \rangle \geq 0$) as

$$Z = \lambda_1 v_1 v_1^\top + \lambda_2 v_2 v_2^\top + \cdots + \lambda_m v_m v_m^\top.$$

According to Proposition B.10, the operator norm of the symmetric random matrix $Z - \overline{Z}$, whose entries lie in $[-3/2, 3/2]$, is controlled with overwhelming probability by a constant multiplied by $\sqrt{m}$. Precisely, the choices $\delta = 1/3$ and $t = 3$ yield

$$\mathbb{P}\left[(2/3)\|Z - \overline{Z}\|_{2\to 2} > 12\sqrt{m}\right] \leq \exp(-m/4).$$

Placing oneself in the likely situation where $\|Z - \overline{Z}\|_{2\to 2} \leq 18\sqrt{m}$, one obtains

$$\|(Z - \overline{Z})u\|_2^2 \leq \|Z - \overline{Z}\|_{2\to 2}^2 \|u\|_2^2 \leq 18^2 m. \tag{7.6}$$

The consequence (D.4) of the *Weyl inequality* also ensures that the eigenvalues of Z satisfy, for any $i \geq 2$,

$$|\lambda_i(Z)| = |\lambda_i(Z) - \lambda_i(\bar{Z})| \leq \|Z - \bar{Z}\|_{2 \to 2} \leq 18\sqrt{m}.$$

Under the assumption that $m \geq (108/(q - p))^2$, it follows that, for any $i \geq 2$,

$$|\langle (Z - \bar{Z})u, v_i \rangle| = \left| \lambda_i(Z)\langle u, v_i \rangle - \frac{(q - p)m}{2}\langle u, v_i \rangle \right|$$

$$\geq \frac{(q - p)m}{2}\left(1 - \frac{36}{(q - p)\sqrt{m}} \right)|\langle u, v_i \rangle|$$

$$\geq \frac{(q - p)m}{3}|\langle u, v_i \rangle|.$$

From here, one deduces that

$$\|(Z - \bar{Z})u\|_2^2 = \sum_{i=1}^{m}\langle (Z - \bar{Z})u, v_i \rangle^2 \geq \sum_{i=2}^{m}\frac{(q - p)^2 m^2}{9}\langle u, v_i \rangle^2$$

$$= \frac{(q - p)^2 m^2}{9}((1 - \langle u, v \rangle^2) \geq \frac{(q - p)^2 m^2}{9}(1 - \langle u, v \rangle)$$

$$= \frac{(q - p)^2 m^2}{18}\|u - v\|_2^2. \tag{7.7}$$

Combining (7.6) and (7.7) gives

$$\|u - v\|_2^2 \leq \frac{18^3}{(q - p)^2 m}.$$

Now, since an index belonging to the set $I := \{i \in [1:m] : \text{sgn}(u_i) \neq \text{sgn}(v_i)\}$ leads to $|u_i - v_i| \geq |u_i| = 1/\sqrt{m}$, one has

$$\|u - v\|_2^2 \geq \sum_{i \in I}|u_i - v_i|^2 \geq \frac{|I|}{m}.$$

Therefore, one arrives at $|I| \leq 18^3/(q - p)^2$. Given that I is the set of indices where errors occur, the announced result is proved with a constant $C = 18^3$ when $m \geq (108/(q - p))^2$. When $m \leq (108/(q - p))^2 = 2(18^3)/(q - p)^2$, the result is more direct because the number of errors is always at most $m/2$. $\quad\square$

Exercises

7.1 Which of the richness, consistency, and scale-invariance properties fail(s) for the single-linkage algorithm as presented in Section 7.1?

7.2 As a mixture of the single-linkage algorithm and the Lloyd algorithm, the *Ward algorithm* iteratively produces some partitions $\mathfrak{C}^{(1)}, \ldots, \mathfrak{C}^{(m-k)}$ of $\mathfrak{X} = \{x^{(1)}, \ldots, x^{(m)}\}$. It begins with $\mathfrak{C}^{(0)} = \{\{x^{(1)}\}, \ldots, \{x^{(m)}\}\}$ and, for $t \in [0 : m - k - 1]$, it merges into $\mathfrak{C}^{(t+1)}$ the clusters $C \neq C' \in \mathfrak{C}^{(t)}$ that minimize the increase in the k-means objective function (7.3), i.e.,

$$\sum_{x \in C \cup C'} \text{dist}(x, c'')^2 - \sum_{x \in C} \text{dist}(x, c)^2 - \sum_{x \in C'} \text{dist}(x, c')^2,$$

where c, c', and c'' represent the barycenters of C, C', and $C \cup C'$, respectively. Observe that the above increase in the objective function can also be expressed as $(|C||C'|/|C \cup C'|) \|c - c'\|^2$.

7.3 As a natural clustering strategy, one could aim at outputting a partition $\mathfrak{C}^* = \{C_1^*, \ldots, C_k^*\}$ of $\mathfrak{X}$ that minimizes the objective function

$$\text{Obj}(\mathfrak{X}, \mathfrak{C}) = \max_{i \in [1:k]} \max_{x, x' \in C_i} \text{dist}(x, x')$$

over all partitions $\mathfrak{C} = \{C_1, \ldots, C_k\}$ of $\mathfrak{X}$. Although this constitutes an NP-hard problem, a simple algorithm solves it approximately. Namely, consider centers $c_1, \ldots, c_k \in \mathfrak{X}$ defined recursively with $c_1 \in \mathfrak{X}$ arbitrary and with $c_{i+1} \in \mathfrak{X}$ chosen as a maximizer of $\min\{\text{dist}(x, c_h), h \in [1 : i]\}$. Prove that the partition $\mathfrak{C} = \{C_1, \ldots, C_k\}$ with clusters C_i deduced from the centers c_i as in (7.2) satisfies $\text{Obj}(\mathfrak{X}, \mathfrak{C}) \leq 2\text{Obj}(\mathfrak{X}, \mathfrak{C}^*)$.

7.4 Show that the number of connected components of a weighted undirected graph equals the multiplicity of the eigenvalue 0 for its graph Laplacian.

7.5 State and prove a spectral clustering result extending Theorem 7.5 to two communities of unequal sizes.

8

Dimension Reduction

Learning scenarios commonly take place in a situation (never rendered by a picture!) where the ambient dimension of the datapoints $x^{(1)}, \ldots, x^{(m)} \in \mathbb{R}^d$ far exceeds their number, i.e., $d \gg m$. This situation occurs both in the context of supervised learning, especially if the $x^{(i)}$ are replaced by some $\phi(x^{(i)})$ for a feature map $\phi: \mathbb{R}^d \rightarrow \mathbb{R}^D$ with $D > d$ (see Chapter 4), and in the context of unsupervised learning, where the pairwise distances $\|x^{(i)} - x^{(j)}\|_2$ often play a prominent role (see Chapter 7). Thus, one instantly faces some computational obstacles—for a start, determining one of these pairwise distances exactly has a high cost proportional to d. This chapter examines three possible ways to reduce the dimension d while preserving some relevant information, namely principal component analysis, the Johnson–Lindenstrauss lemma, and locally linear embedding.

8.1 Principal Component Analysis

Given datapoints $x^{(1)}, \ldots, x^{(m)} \in \mathbb{R}^d$, it is intuitive that the dimension d could be reduced at least to m, since any m points live in a linear space of dimension m. In fact, it is realistic to believe that these datapoints live close to a linear space of even smaller dimension $k \ll m$. The best k-dimensional space, in the sense of cumulative squared euclidean distances, is obtained from the singular value decomposition of the *data matrix*

$$X = \left[x^{(1)} | \cdots | x^{(m)} \right] \in \mathbb{R}^{d \times m}. \tag{8.1}$$

The result is stated formally below.

Theorem 8.1 *A k-dimensional linear subspace $\mathcal{W}$ of $\mathbb{R}^d$ that minimizes*

$$\sum_{i=1}^{m} \text{dist}_{\ell_2}(x^{(i)}, \mathcal{W})^2 \qquad (8.2)$$

is given by $\text{span}\{u_1, \ldots, u_k\}$*, where* $u_1, \ldots, u_m \in \mathbb{R}^d$ *are the left singular vectors appearing in the singular value decomposition* $X = \sum_{j=1}^{m} \sigma_j u_j v_j^\top$.

Proof Let $\mathcal{W}$ be a k-dimensional subspace of $\mathbb{R}^d$ with orthonormal basis $(w_1, \ldots, w_k)$, say. Let $P_{\mathcal{W}}$ denote the (matrix of) the orthogonal projector from $\mathbb{R}^d$ onto $\mathcal{W}$, so that $P_{\mathcal{W}} x = \sum_{j=1}^{k} \langle w_j, x \rangle w_j = (\sum_{j=1}^{k} w_j w_j^\top) x$ for any $x \in \mathbb{R}^d$. In view of $\text{dist}_{\ell_2}(x, \mathcal{W}) = \|x - P_{\mathcal{W}} x\|_2$, the objective function (8.2) takes the form

$$\sum_{i=1}^{m} \|x^{(i)} - P_{\mathcal{W}} x^{(i)}\|_2^2 = \sum_{i=1}^{m} \|\text{column}_i(X - P_{\mathcal{W}} X)\|_2^2 = \|X - P_{\mathcal{W}} X\|_F^2.$$

Since $P_{\mathcal{W}} X = (\sum_{j=1}^{k} w_j w_j^\top) X$ has rank at most k and since, by the *Eckart–Young theorem* (Theorem D.11) or simply by Remark D.12, the best rank-k approximation is obtained by truncating the singular value decomposition, one has

$$\|X - P_{\mathcal{W}} X\|_F^2 \geq \left\| X - \sum_{j=1}^{k} \sigma_j u_j v_j^\top \right\|_F^2.$$

Summing over $j \in [1:k]$ the identity $\sigma_j u_j v_j^\top = u_j u_j^\top \sum_{\ell=1}^{m} \sigma_\ell u_\ell v_\ell^\top = u_j u_j^\top X$, one arrives at $\sum_{j=1}^{k} \sigma_j u_j v_j^\top = P_{\mathcal{U}} X$, where $\mathcal{U} := \text{span}\{u_1, \ldots, u_k\}$. Therefore, one concludes that $\|X - P_{\mathcal{W}} X\|_F^2 \geq \|X - P_{\mathcal{U}} X\|_F^2$, i.e., that $\mathcal{U}$ is a k-dimensional subspace minimizing the objective function under consideration. □

Substituting each datapoint $x^{(i)}$, living in the high-dimensional space $\mathbb{R}^d$, by its orthogonal projection $\widehat{x}^{(i)} = P_{\mathcal{U}}(x^{(i)})$, living in the low-dimensional space $\mathcal{U} = \text{span}\{u_1, \ldots, u_k\}$, constitutes a reasonable dimension reduction process. The method is commonly called *principal component analysis*, abbreviated as *PCA*, due to a statistical interpretation to be elucidated right now. For this interpretation, consider a random vector $x \in \mathbb{R}^d$ whose distribution generated the datapoints $x^{(1)}, \ldots, x^{(m)}$. Its *covariance matrix* is the symmetric matrix

$$\text{cov}(x) = \mathbb{E}\left[(x - \mathbb{E}[x])(x - \mathbb{E}[x])^\top\right] \in \mathbb{R}^{d \times d}.$$

Making the assumption that the distribution has mean zero, this covariance matrix reduces to $\text{cov}(x) = \mathbb{E}[x x^\top]$. One would like to find the first principal component u_1, understood as the direction presenting the maximal variance. Note that the variance of the random vector $x \in \mathbb{R}^d$ projected on a direction $u \in \mathbb{R}^d$, i.e.,

$$\mathbb{V}[\langle x, u \rangle] = \mathbb{E}[\langle x, u \rangle^2] = \mathbb{E}[u^\top x x^\top u] = u^\top \text{cov}(x) u,$$

reduces to the *Rayleigh quotient* of $\mathrm{cov}(x)$ at u, whose maximizer is known e.g. as a consequence of the *Courant–Fischer theorem* (see (D.1) with $i = 1$). Thus, one deduces that the first principal component u_1 is the leading eigenvector of $\mathrm{cov}(x)$. Next, one would like to find the second principal component u_2, understood as the direction orthogonal to u_1 presenting the maximal variance. By virtue of

$$\max_{\substack{u \perp u_1 \\ \|u\|_2=1}} u^\top \mathrm{cov}(x)u \leq \max_{\|u\|_2=1} u^\top (\mathrm{cov}(x) - \lambda_1(\mathrm{cov}(x))u_1 u_1^\top)u = \lambda_2(\mathrm{cov}(x)),$$

one easily derives that the second principal component u_2 is the second leading eigenvector of $\mathrm{cov}(x)$. In general, the jth principal component u_j is the jth leading eigenvector of $\mathrm{cov}(x)$. Now, since one does not have access to $\mathrm{cov}(x)$, the latter is replaced by the *empirical covariance matrix*

$$\widehat{C} = \frac{1}{m} \sum_{i=1}^m x^{(i)} x^{(i)\top} = \frac{1}{m} XX^\top \in \mathbb{R}^{d \times d},$$

where X still denotes the data matrix (8.1). The true principal components are then replaced by the eigenvectors of $XX^\top$, i.e., the left singular vectors of X that appeared in Theorem 8.1.

Remark 8.2 The above consideration could wrongly suggest obtaining the principal components by performing an eigendecomposition on the big matrix $XX^\top \in \mathbb{R}^{d \times d}$. This is definitely not advised. Indeed, in view of the large size of d, it is a much better idea, in terms of computational cost, to perform an eigendecomposition on the small matrix $X^\top X \in \mathbb{R}^{m \times m}$. The eigenvectors of the latter are the right singular vectors v_j of X, while the eigenvectors of the former are the left singular vectors u_j of X—the principal components—which can simply be deduced from the v_j via $Xv_j = \sigma_j u_j$. Moreover, when the datapoints are of the form $\phi(x^{(i)})$ for some feature map ϕ associated with a kernel K, the entries of the small matrix $X^\top X$ are

$$(X^\top X)_{i,j} = \langle \phi(x^{(i)}), \phi(x^{(j)}) \rangle = K(x^{(i)}, x^{(j)}), \qquad i, j \in [1:m].$$

As with other kernel methods, it is then possible to perform PCA without an explicit knowledge of the feature map by relying only the kernel. This strategy is called *kernel PCA*.

8.2 Johnson–Lindenstrauss Lemma

Generating substitutes $\widehat{x}^{(1)}, \ldots, \widehat{x}^{(m)}$ for the datapoints $x^{(1)}, \ldots, x^{(m)}$ from a low-dimensional linear space $\mathcal{W}$ can be carried out with much less effort put into the creation of $\mathcal{W}$ than PCA: a random space $\mathcal{W}$ is very likely to do the trick of approximately preserving pairwise distances. The dimension of $\mathcal{W}$, which is independent of d, scales only logarithmically in the number m of datapoints and quadratically in the inverse of the desired distortion δ. This is the so-called *Johnson–Lindenstrauss lemma*, stated as Corollary 8.4 below. It is deduced from the following concentration inequality.

Lemma 8.3   *Let $x \in \mathbb{R}^d$ and $\delta \in (0, 1)$. If $A \in \mathbb{R}^{k \times d}$ is a random matrix whose entries are independent mean-zero gaussian variables with variance $1/k$, then*

$$\mathbb{P}\left[\left|\|Ax\|_2^2 - \|x\|_2^2\right| > \delta\|x\|_2^2\right] \le 2\exp\left(-\left(\frac{\delta^2}{4} - \frac{\delta^3}{6}\right)k\right). \tag{8.3}$$

Proof   For any $i \in [1:k]$, recalling that a linear combination of independent gaussian random variables is still gaussian, one can write

$$(Ax)_i = \sum_{j=1}^d A_{i,j}x_j = \frac{\|x\|_2}{\sqrt{k}}g_i,$$

where g_i denotes a standard gaussian random variable (i.e., it has mean zero and variance one). Then, since $\|Ax\|_2^2 = \sum_{i=1}^k (Ax)_i^2$, one has

$$\mathbb{P}\left[\|Ax\|_2^2 > (1+\delta)\|x\|_2^2\right] = \mathbb{P}\left[\sum_{i=1}^k g_i^2 \ge k(1+\delta)\right]$$

$$= \mathbb{P}\left[\exp\left(u\sum_{i=1}^k g_i^2\right) > \exp\left(uk(1+\delta)\right)\right],$$

where $u > 0$ will be chosen later. Using the *Markov inequality* (Lemma B.1), the independence of the random variables $g_1, \dots, g_k$, and the expression (B.5) for the moment generating function $t \mapsto \mathbb{E}[\exp(tg^2)]$ of a squared standard gaussian random variable, one obtains

$$\mathbb{P}\left[\|Ax\|_2^2 > (1+\delta)\|x\|_2^2\right] \le \frac{\mathbb{E}[\exp(u\sum_{i=1}^k g_i^2)]}{\exp(uk(1+\delta))} = \frac{\mathbb{E}[\prod_{i=1}^k \exp(ug_i^2)]}{\prod_{i=1}^k \exp(u(1+\delta))}$$

$$= \prod_{i=1}^k \frac{\mathbb{E}[\exp(ug_i^2)]}{\exp(u(1+\delta))} = \left(\frac{1/\sqrt{1-2u}}{\exp(u(1+\delta))}\right)^k.$$

Making the (optimal) choice $u = \delta/(2(1+\delta))$, for which $1 - 2u = 1/(1+\delta)$ and

$\exp(u(1 + \delta)) = \exp(\delta/2)$, it follows that

$$\mathbb{P}\left[\|Ax\|_2^2 > (1 + \delta)\|x\|_2^2\right] \leq \left(\frac{1 + \delta}{\exp(\delta)}\right)^{k/2} \leq \exp\left(-\frac{\delta^2}{2} + \frac{\delta^3}{3}\right)^{k/2}$$

$$= \exp\left(-\left(\frac{\delta^2}{4} - \frac{\delta^3}{6}\right)k\right),$$

where the inequality $\ln(1 + \delta) \leq \delta - \delta^2/2 + \delta^3/3$ was used. A similar estimate for $\mathbb{P}[\|Ax\|_2^2 < (1 - \delta)\|x\|_2^2]$ is derived in exactly the same fashion, leading to (8.3) in view of the fact that $\left|\|Ax\|_2^2 - \|x\|_2^2\right| > \delta\|x\|_2^2$ occurs either when $\|Ax\|_2^2 > (1 + \delta)\|x\|_2^2$ or when $\|Ax\|_2^2 < (1 - \delta)\|x\|_2^2$. □

With the concentration inequality (8.3) in place, dimension reduction in the sense of Johnson–Lindenstrauss is now achieved by taking each substitute $\tilde{x}^{(i)} = A(x^{(i)})$ to live in the k-dimensional range of a random matrix $A \in \mathbb{R}^{k \times d}$.

Corollary 8.4 *Let* $x^{(1)}, \ldots, x^{(m)} \in \mathbb{R}^d$ *and* $\delta \in (0, 1/2)$, *say. If*

$$k \geq 18 \frac{\ln(m)}{\delta^2} \tag{8.4}$$

and if $A \in \mathbb{R}^{k \times d}$ *is a random matrix whose entries are independent mean-zero gaussian variables with variance* $1/k$, *then*

$$(1 - \delta)\|x^{(i)} - x^{(j)}\|_2^2 \leq \|A(x^{(i)}) - A(x^{(j)})\|_2^2 \leq (1 + \delta)\|x^{(i)} - x^{(j)}\|_2^2$$

holds for all $i \neq j \in [1 : m]$ *simultaneously with probability at least* $1 - 1/m$.

Proof Fixing $i \neq j \in [1 : m]$ and setting $x^{(i,j)} := x^{(i)} - x^{(j)} \in \mathbb{R}^d$, Lemma 8.3 ensures that

$$\mathbb{P}\left[\left|\|A(x^{(i,j)})\|_2^2 - \|x^{(i,j)}\|_2^2\right| > \delta\|x^{(i,j)}\|_2^2\right] \leq 2\exp\left(-\frac{\delta^2 k}{6}\right),$$

where the fact that $\delta^3/6 \leq \delta^2/12$ when $\delta \leq 1/2$ was used. Now, unfixing the pair (i, j), one deduces by way of a union bound that

$$\mathbb{P}\left[\left|\|A(x^{(i,j)})\|_2^2 - \|x^{(i,j)}\|_2^2\right| > \delta\|x^{(i,j)}\|_2^2 \text{ for some } i \neq j \in [1 : m]\right]$$

$$\leq \binom{m}{2} 2\exp\left(-\frac{\delta^2 k}{6}\right) \leq m^2 \exp\left(-3\ln(m)\right) = \frac{1}{m}.$$

The latter means that with probability at least $1 - 1/m$, one has

$$\left|\|A(x^{(i)} - x^{(j)})\|_2^2 - \|x^{(i)} - x^{(j)}\|_2^2\right| \leq \delta\|x^{(i)} - x^{(j)}\|_2^2$$

for all $i \neq j \in [1 : m]$ simultaneously. This is the desired conclusion. □

8.3 Locally Linear Embedding

Principal component analysis and Johnson–Lindenstrauss embedding are both instances of linear dimension reduction techniques, in the sense that the substitutes $\widehat{x}^{(1)}, \ldots, \widehat{x}^{(m)}$ are obtained from the datapoints $x^{(1)}, \ldots, x^{(m)}$ by applying a linear transformation with values in a low-dimensional linear space. They are not appropriate when $x^{(1)}, \ldots, x^{(m)}$ congregate instead along a nonlinear manifold—the "Swiss roll" being a typical example; see Figure 8.1. In such a case, one can use one of many nonlinear dimension reduction techniques, which often offer strong heuristics in spite of limited theoretical guarantees (owing to the fact that the manifold itself has to be discovered). Although local multidimensional scaling (local MDS), isometric feature mapping (isomap), and Laplacian eigenmaps all deserve to be mentioned, the focus here is on *locally linear embedding* (LLE) for the simplicity of its exposition. As its name suggests, this method tries to preserve local linear relationships between neighboring datapoints.

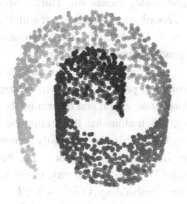

Figure 8.1 A set of three-dimensional datapoints lying close to a two-dimensional nonlinear manifold.

Requiring two integer parameters k and n with $k \leq n \leq d$, the method outputting substitutes $\widehat{x}^{(1)}, \ldots, \widehat{x}^{(m)} \in \mathbb{R}^k$ for the inputs $x^{(1)}, \ldots, x^{(m)} \in \mathbb{R}^d$ proceeds as follows:

- for each $i \in [1:m]$, create an index set J_i of n (approximate) nearest neighbors of $x^{(i)}$;
- for each $i \in [1:m]$, define $w^{(i)} \in \mathbb{R}^{J_i}$ as a solution to

$$\operatorname*{minimize}_{w \in \mathbb{R}^{J_i}} \left\| x^{(i)} - \sum_{j \in J_i} w_j x^{(j)} \right\|_2 \quad \text{s.to} \quad \sum_{j \in J_i} w_j = 1;$$

- define $\bar{x}^{(1)}, \ldots, \bar{x}^{(m)} \in \mathbb{R}^k$ as solutions to

$$\operatorname*{minimize}_{z^{(1)},\ldots,z^{(m)} \in \mathbb{R}^k} \sum_{i=1}^{m} \left\| z^{(i)} - \sum_{j \in J_i} w_j^{(i)} z^{(j)} \right\|_2^2 \quad \text{s.to} \quad \sum_{i=1}^{m} z^{(i)} = 0,$$

$$\text{and} \quad \sum_{i=1}^{m} z^{(i)} z^{(i)\top} = I_k.$$

Before giving more details about each of these three steps, here is an intuitive explanation. First, one identifies a local patch around each datapoint. Second, one approximates this patch as a low-dimensional affine space by means of weights that minimize an objective function invariant under rotation, rescaling, and (thanks to the constraint) translation. Third, one creates a global low-dimensional system of coordinates agreeing best with the all the weights while enforcing the system to be (thanks to the first constraint) centered at the origin and (thanks to the second constraint) orthogonal.

Concerning the first step, creating the index set J_i is not an issue: there are highly efficient algorithms to perform such a *nearest neighbors* search. With a straightforward approach, one would first determine the distances $\|x^{(i)} - x^{(j)}\|_2$ for all $i \neq j \in [1:m]$, which alone has the prohibitive computational cost of $\Theta(m^2 d)$ when d is very large. This cost can easily be lowered to $\Theta(m^2 \ln(m))$ if one settles for n approximate nearest neighbors, i.e., neighbors $x^{(\ell)}$ satisfying $\|x^{(i)} - x^{(\ell)}\|_2 \leq 2 \max\{\|x^{(i)} - x^{(j)}\|_2, j \in J_i\}$, say. For this, it suffices to consider a Johnson–Lindenstrauss embedding $A \colon \mathbb{R}^d \to \mathbb{R}^k$, $k \asymp \ln(m)$, and to perform the n nearest neighbors search on $A(x^{(1)}), \ldots, A(x^{(m)}) \in \mathbb{R}^k$. Thus, if ℓ belongs to the index set $\widehat{J_i}$ of n nearest neighbors to $A(x^{(i)})$, one has

$$\|x^{(i)} - x^{(\ell)}\|_2^2 \leq \frac{1}{1-\delta} \|A(x^{(i)}) - A(x^{(\ell)})\|_2^2$$

$$\leq \frac{1}{1-\delta} \max\{\|A(x^{(i)}) - A(x^{(j)})\|_2^2, j \in \widehat{J_i}\}$$

$$\leq \frac{1}{1-\delta} \max\{\|A(x^{(i)}) - A(x^{(j)})\|_2^2, j \in J_i\}$$

$$\leq \frac{1+\delta}{1-\delta} \max\{\|x^{(i)} - x^{(j)}\|_2^2, j \in J_i\},$$

yielding $\|x^{(i)} - x^{(\ell)}\|_2 \leq 2 \max\{\|x^{(i)} - x^{(j)}\|_2, j \in J_i\}$ with the choice $\delta = 3/5$.

Concerning the second step, solving an optimization program is actually not necessary. Indeed, assuming invertibility of the matrix $G^{(i)} \in \mathbb{R}^{n \times n}$ with entries $G^{(i)}_{j,\ell} = \langle x^{(i)} - x^{(j)}, x^{(i)} - x^{(\ell)} \rangle$, $j, \ell \in J_i$, the solution is given by

$$w^{(i)} = \gamma (G^{(i)})^{-1} \mathbb{1}, \qquad \text{where } \gamma = \frac{1}{\sum\limits_{j,\ell \in J_i} (G^{(i)})^{-1}_{j,\ell}} \quad \text{and} \quad \mathbb{1} = \begin{bmatrix} 1 \\ \vdots \\ 1 \end{bmatrix} \in \mathbb{R}^n.$$

To see this, one introduces a matrix $M \in \mathbb{R}^{d \times n}$ with columns $x^{(i)} - x^{(j)} \in \mathbb{R}^d$, $j \in J_i$, to write the objective function as $\left\| \sum_{j \in J_i} w_j (x^{(i)} - x^{(j)}) \right\|_2 = \|Mw\|_2$. The minimal property of $w^{(i)}$ is equivalent to $\|M(w^{(i)} - v)\|_2 \geq \|M(w^{(i)})\|_2$ for all $v \in \mathcal{V} = \mathbb{1}^\perp$, so that 0 is the best approximant to $Mw^{(i)}$ from $M(\mathcal{V})$. This implies that $Mw^{(i)} \perp M(\mathcal{V})$, i.e., that $M^\top M w^{(i)} \perp \mathcal{V}$. Since $G^{(i)} = M^\top M$, the latter reads $G^{(i)} w^{(i)} = \gamma \mathbb{1}$ for some $\gamma \in \mathbb{R}$. It simply remains to multiply on the left by $(G^{(i)})^{-1}$ and to determine γ from the condition $\sum_{j \in J_i} w^{(i)}_j = 1$.

Finally, the third step also does not require solving an optimization problem. Indeed, if $W \in \mathbb{R}^{m \times m}$ denotes the sparse matrix whose ith column is equal to $w^{(i)}$ on J_i and 0 outside J_i, and if $u_1, \dots, u_m \in \mathbb{R}^m$ are the eigenvectors of $(I_m - W)(I_m - W)^\top$ associated with eigenvalues sorted, as usual, in nonincreasing fashion, then

$$\left[\widetilde{x}^{(1)} \big| \cdots \big| \widetilde{x}^{(m)} \right] = \begin{bmatrix} u_{m-k}^\top \\ \vdots \\ u_{m-1}^\top \end{bmatrix}.$$

To see this, one observes that, with $Z := [z^{(1)}, \dots, z^{(m)}] \in \mathbb{R}^{k \times m}$, the objective function reads

$$\|Z(I_m - W)\|_F^2 = \mathrm{tr}\left((I_m - W)^\top Z^\top Z (I_m - W) \right) = \mathrm{tr}\left((I_m - W)(I_m - W)^\top Z^\top Z \right).$$

The constraint $\sum_{i=1}^m z^{(i)} = 0$ says that the k rows of Z are orthogonal to $\mathbb{1} \in \mathbb{R}^m$. Incidentally, the trailing eigenvector u_m equals $\mathbb{1}/\sqrt{m}$, since $\sum_{j \in J_i} w^{(i)}_j = 1$ for all $i \in [1:m]$ reads $W^\top \mathbb{1} = \mathbb{1}$, and hence $(I_m - W)^\top \mathbb{1} = 0$. As for the constraint $\sum_{i=1}^m z^{(i)} z^{(i)\top} = I_k$, interpreted as $ZZ^\top = I_k$, it means that the k rows of Z form an orthonormal system. By completing the system made of $\mathbb{1}/\sqrt{m}$ and the rows of Z to form an orthonormal basis of $\mathbb{R}^m$, one creates an orthogonal matrix $Q \in \mathbb{R}^{m \times m}$ of the form $Q = [\mathbb{1}^\top/\sqrt{m}; Z; \widetilde{Z}]$. Since $Q^\top Q = I_m$ reads $\mathbb{1}\mathbb{1}^\top/m + Z^\top Z + \widetilde{Z}^\top \widetilde{Z} = I_m$, the objective function becomes

$$\mathrm{tr}\left((I_m - W)(I_m - W)^\top (I_m - \mathbb{1}\mathbb{1}^\top/m) \right) - \mathrm{tr}\left((I_m - W)(I_m - W)^\top \widetilde{Z}^\top \widetilde{Z} \right).$$

Thus, minimizing the objective function becomes equivalent to maximizing

$\text{tr}((I_m - W)(I_m - W)^\top \widetilde{Z}^\top \widetilde{Z})$ subject to $\widetilde{Z}\widetilde{Z}^\top = I_{m-k-1}$. This constraint imposes $\sigma_\ell(\widetilde{Z}^\top \widetilde{Z}) = 1$ for $\ell \in [1:m-k-1]$ and $\sigma_\ell(\widetilde{Z}^\top \widetilde{Z}) = 0$ for $\ell \in [m-k:m]$, in which case the *von Neumann trace inequality* (Theorem D.8) implies that

$$\text{tr}\left((I_m - W)(I_m - W)^\top \widetilde{Z}^\top \widetilde{Z}\right) \le \sum_{\ell=1}^{m-k-1} \sigma_\ell((I_m - W)(I_m - W)^\top),$$

with equality occurring when the rows of $\widetilde{Z}$ coincides with $u_1, \ldots, u_{m-k-1}$. Keeping in mind that $u_m = 1/\sqrt{m}$, this optimal situation occurs when the rows of Z are equal to $u_{m-k}, \ldots, u_{m-1}$, as announced.

Exercises

8.1 Determine a k-dimensional affine subspace $\mathcal{W}$ of $\mathbb{R}^d$ that best fits the datapoints $x^{(1)}, \ldots, x^{(m)} \in \mathbb{R}^d$ in the sense of the cumulative squared euclidean distances (8.2).

8.2 Let $x^{(1)}, \ldots, x^{(m)} \in \mathbb{R}^d$ be independent identically distributed random vectors with mean μ and covariance matrix $C \in \mathbb{R}^{d \times d}$. When μ is known, an unbiased estimator for C is given by $m^{-1} \sum_{i=1}^m (x^{(i)} - \mu)(x^{(i)} - \mu)^\top$. When μ is not known but estimated by $\widehat{\mu} = m^{-1} \sum_{i=1}^m x^{(i)}$, prove that an unbiased estimator for C is given instead by

$$\widehat{C} = \frac{1}{m-1} \sum_{i=1}^m (x^{(i)} - \widehat{\mu})(x^{(i)} - \widehat{\mu})^\top,$$

i.e., prove that $\mathbb{E}[\widehat{C}] = C$.

8.3 Extend the Johnson–Lindenstrauss lemma to the case where the entries of the random matrix $A \in \mathbb{R}^{k \times m}$ are independent mean-zero subgaussian variables with variance $1/k$.

8.4 Observe that LLE can be interpreted as a kernel PCA, i.e., that it amounts to finding the k largest eigenvalues of the (not explicitly given) positive semidefinite matrix

$$(I_m - \mathbb{1}\mathbb{1}^\top/m)(\lambda_{\max} I_m - M)(I_m - \mathbb{1}\mathbb{1}^\top/m),$$

where $M = (I_m - W)(I_m - W)^\top$ is the matrix encountered in LLE's final step and where $\lambda_{\max}$ is its largest eigenvalue.

PART TWO

OPTIMAL RECOVERY

Executive Summary

While Machine Learning automatically jumps to mind when discussing Data Science, the older and lesser-known topic of Optimal Recovery rarely does. It should nonetheless be an inevitable part of Data Science. Indeed, the scenario is again that of a to-be-recovered function f which is observed through point values $y_i = f(x^{(i)})$. However, the datapoints are considered fixed entities and not realizations of a random variable, so the performance of recovery methods is assessed not via generalization errors, but via worst-case errors instead. Note a subtle switch in terminology: "learning" has been replaced by "recovering".

Chapter 9 gives a synopsis of the theory behind Optimal Recovery, with a focus on situations where recovery procedures that are certifiably optimal over a model set can be chosen as linear maps. Chapter 10 particularizes the analysis to a newly considered model set based on approximation capabilities, emphasizing the computational realizability of optimal recovery procedures. Chapter 11 presents two examples showing that observation procedures can sometimes be chosen in an optimal way, too, revealing in passing that adaptive observations are generally not superior. In Chapter 12, the phenomenon known as curse of dimensionality is precisely defined via the notion of information complexity. It highlights two scenarios for the integration problem: one where the curse strikes, and one where it is avoided. Chapter 13 further examines the integration problem by way of quasi-Monte Carlo methods, which features deterministic rather than random evaluation points.

An overview of classic Optimal Recovery can be found in Micchelli and Rivlin (1977). The more recent results linked to approximability models are mostly taken from Binev et al. (2017) and DeVore et al. (2019). Concerning the examples of optimal observation procedures, the integration of Lipschitz functions was resolved in (Sukharev, 1979), while the description of the Hilbert setting can be found in Novak and Woźniakowski (2008). This is also where the results on information-based complexity were taken from—note that the missing piece for the integration of trigonometric polynomials was uncovered only recently in Vybíral (2020). For more on quasi-Monte Carlo methods, readers are referred to the survey by Dick et al. (2013).

9

Foundational Results of Optimal Recovery

In the scenario considered in the next few chapters, although data still come as

$$y_i = f(x^{(i)}), \qquad i \in [1:m],$$

it is not assumed that $x^{(1)}, \ldots, x^{(m)}$ are independent realizations of a random variable. Instead, the $x^{(i)}$ are now prescribed points whose location might be unfavorable: this cannot be controlled. But one still hunts for good—in fact, optimal—ways to recover f (or merely a quantity depending on f) from the data. This quest is meaningless without further assumption on f: think of the many different ways to fit a univariate function through a finite set of points; see Figure 9.1. There must be an added model assumption, which is an educated belief about properties of realistic functions f.

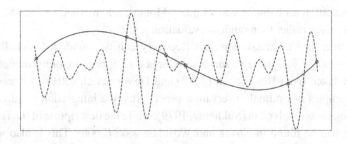

Figure 9.1 There are infinitely many ways to fit a univariate function through a finite set of points (circles), some of them (solid curve) probably more natural than others (dashed curve).

9.1 Models, Errors, and Optimality

In the problem statement below, the objective is formalized in a more abstract setting. Instead of viewing f genuinely as a function, one considers it more generally as an element of a normed linear space F. The point evaluations of f at the $x^{(i)}$ are then replaced by the applications of linear functionals $\lambda_i \in F^*$ to f, yielding

$$y_i = \lambda_i(f), \qquad i \in [1:m].$$

The data $y_1, \ldots, y_m \in \mathbb{R}$, called *observations* (aka *a posteriori information*), are summarized as $y = \Lambda(f)$, where $\Lambda \colon f \in F \mapsto [\lambda_1(f); \ldots; \lambda_m(f)] \in \mathbb{R}^m$ is referred to as the *observation map*. As for the educated belief about f, called *co-observation* (aka *a priori information*), it is encapsulated by the assumption that f belongs to a known subset $\mathcal{K}$ of F, referred to as a *model set*. Given the available information, the goal can be to fully approximate f or merely to estimate a quantity $Q(f)$ depending on f. Although the setting allows for arbitrary quantities of interest $Q \colon F \to Z$, one often thinks of the cases where Q is the identity and where Q is a linear functional as particularly relevant instances. The approximation of $Q(f)$ is obtained by applying a *recovery map* $\Delta \colon \mathbb{R}^m \to Z$ to $y = \Lambda(f) \in \mathbb{R}^m$. When $Q = \mathrm{Id}$, the map $\Delta \colon \mathbb{R}^m \to F$ could be *data-consistent*, meaning that $\Lambda(\Delta(y)) = y$ for all $y \in \mathbb{R}^m$, or *model-consistent*, meaning that $\Delta(y) \in \mathcal{K}$ for all $y \in \mathbb{R}^m$, or both, or neither. It is not required to be computationally feasible at this point (which is why the common terminology of "algorithm" is avoided). One now needs to assess the performance of the recovery map Δ given the observation map Λ. For a single $f \in \mathcal{K}$, the error incurred by approximating $Q(f)$ with $\Delta(y)$, $y = \Lambda(f)$, is $\|Q(f) - \Delta(\Lambda(f))\|$. To account for varying $f \in \mathcal{K}$, one adopts a worst-case viewpoint and defines the *worst-case error* (aka *distortion*) of Δ over $\mathcal{K}$ as

$$\mathrm{Err}_{\mathcal{K},Q}(\Lambda, \Delta) = \sup_{f \in \mathcal{K}} \|Q(f) - \Delta(\Lambda(f))\|.$$

The term *optimal recovery map* designates a recovery map $\Delta^{\mathrm{opt}} \colon \mathbb{R}^m \to Z$ for which $\mathrm{Err}_{\mathcal{K},Q}(\Lambda, \Delta^{\mathrm{opt}})$ equals

$$\mathrm{Err}^*_{\mathcal{K},Q}(\Lambda) = \inf_{\Delta \colon \mathbb{R}^m \to Z} \mathrm{Err}_{\mathcal{K},Q}(\Lambda, \Delta), \tag{9.1}$$

which is called the *intrinsic error* (for the evaluation of Q over the model set $\mathcal{K}$ given the observation map Λ).

There is a related notion of optimality, namely the notion of local optimality. Precisely, a recovery map $\Delta^{\mathrm{opt}} \colon \mathbb{R}^m \to Z$ is called *locally optimal* if $\Delta^{\mathrm{opt}}(y)$

minimizes the *local worst-case error* at any $y \in \Lambda(\mathcal{K})$, i.e., if

$$\Delta^{\text{opt}}(y) \in \underset{z \in Z}{\text{argmin}} \quad \underset{f \in \mathcal{K}, \Lambda(f)=y}{\sup} \|Q(f) - z\| \qquad \text{for all } y \in \Lambda(\mathcal{K}).$$

Such a $\Delta^{\text{opt}}(y) \in Z$ is called a *Chebyshev center* of the set $Q(\mathcal{K} \cap \Lambda^{-1}(\{y\}))$, since it is seen, almost tautologically, to be (one of) the center(s) of a smallest ball in Z containing $Q(\mathcal{K} \cap \Lambda^{-1}(\{y\}))$. Such a ball is called a *Chebyshev ball*.

Although there is little hope to determine the exact intrinsic error exactly in general, it can be related in many situations to the more amenable quantity

$$\text{Err}^0_{\mathcal{K},Q}(\Lambda) = \underset{f \in \ker(\Lambda) \cap \mathcal{K}}{\sup} \|Q(f)\|. \tag{9.2}$$

This appears as the local worst-case error at zero of the zero recovery map and hence is termed the *null error* (for the evaluation of Q over $\mathcal{K}$ given Λ).

Proposition 9.1 *Let $Q: F \to Z$ be a linear quantity of interest. If the model set $\mathcal{K} \subseteq F$ is symmetric—i.e., if $-\mathcal{K} = \mathcal{K}$—then*

$$\text{Err}^0_{\mathcal{K},Q}(\Lambda) \leq \text{Err}^*_{\mathcal{K},Q}(\Lambda). \tag{9.3}$$

Furthermore, if $\mathcal{K}$ is also convex—i.e., if $(1/2)\mathcal{K} + (1/2)\mathcal{K} \subseteq \mathcal{K}$—then

$$\text{Err}^*_{\mathcal{K},Q}(\Lambda) \leq 2\,\text{Err}^0_{\mathcal{K},Q}(\Lambda). \tag{9.4}$$

Proof Assume first that $\mathcal{K}$ is symmetric. For a recovery map $\Delta: \mathbb{R}^m \to Z$ and an element $f \in \ker(\Lambda) \cap \mathcal{K}$, one observes that $\text{Err}_{\mathcal{K},Q}(\Lambda, \Delta) \geq \|Q(f) - \Delta(0)\|$ and $\text{Err}_{\mathcal{K},Q}(\Lambda, \Delta) \geq \|Q(-f) - \Delta(0)\|$, so that

$$\|Q(f)\| = \frac{1}{2}\|(Q(f) - \Delta(0)) - (Q(-f) - \Delta(0))\|$$

$$\leq \frac{1}{2}(\|Q(f) - \Delta(0)\| + \|Q(-f) - \Delta(0)\|)$$

$$\leq \text{Err}_{\mathcal{K},Q}(\Lambda, \Delta).$$

Taking the supremum over $f \in \ker(\Lambda) \cap \mathcal{K}$ yields $\text{Err}^0_{\mathcal{K},Q}(\Lambda) \leq \text{Err}_{\mathcal{K},Q}(\Lambda, \Delta)$, then taking the infimum over $\Delta: \mathbb{R}^m \to Z$ yields the desired inequality (9.3).

Assume now that $\mathcal{K}$ is also convex. Considering a recovery map $\Delta: \mathbb{R}^m \to Z$ which assigns to any $y \in \Lambda(\mathcal{K})$ an element $Q(g_y) \in Z$ for some (arbitrary) $g_y \in \mathcal{K}$ such that $\Lambda(g_y) = y$, one has

$$\text{Err}^*_{\mathcal{K},Q}(\Lambda) \leq \underset{f \in \mathcal{K}}{\sup} \|Q(f) - \Delta(\Lambda(f))\| = \underset{f \in \mathcal{K}}{\sup} \|Q(f) - Q(g_{\Lambda(f)})\|$$

$$= 2 \underset{f \in \mathcal{K}}{\sup} \left\| Q\left(\frac{1}{2}f - \frac{1}{2}g_{\Lambda(f)}\right) \right\|.$$

With $h := (1/2)f - (1/2)g_{\Lambda(f)}$, noticing that $\Lambda(h) = (1/2)\Lambda(f) - (1/2)\Lambda(f) = 0$ and that $h \in (1/2)\mathcal{K} + (1/2)\mathcal{K} \subseteq \mathcal{K}$, one obtains

$$\mathrm{Err}^*_{\mathcal{K},Q}(\Lambda) \le 2 \sup_{h \in \ker(\Lambda) \cap \mathcal{K}} \|Q(h)\| = 2\,\mathrm{Err}^0_{\mathcal{K},Q}(\Lambda),$$

which is the desired inequality (9.4). □

Remark 9.2 Whenever the intrinsic and null errors $\mathrm{Err}^*_{\mathcal{K},Q}(\Lambda)$ and $\mathrm{Err}^0_{\mathcal{K},Q}(\Lambda)$ are involved, it is implicitly assumed that $(\lambda_{1|\mathcal{K}}, \ldots, \lambda_{m|\mathcal{K}})$ constitutes a linearly independent system. If not, then $\lambda_{m|\mathcal{K}}$, say, would be a linear combination of $\lambda_{1|\mathcal{K}}, \ldots, \lambda_{m-1|\mathcal{K}}$ and the mth observation made on $f \in \mathcal{K}$ would be redundant, so that the observation map $f \in F \mapsto [\lambda_1(f); \ldots; \lambda_{m-1}(f)] \in \mathbb{R}^{m-1}$ would be considered instead.

9.2 Linearity of Optimal Recovery Maps

As is about to be revealed, Proposition 9.1 can be improved by showing that the intrinsic error (9.1) and the null error (9.2) coincide in at least two important situations, namely when F is a Hilbert space and when Q is a linear functional. In both situations, an added bonus emerges from the fact that one can find a linear optimal recovery map. The latter situation is considered first.

Theorem 9.3 *Let $Q: F \to \mathbb{R}$ be a linear functional. If the model set $\mathcal{K} \subseteq F$ is symmetric and convex, then the intrinsic error for the evaluation of Q over $\mathcal{K}$ given Λ satisfies*

$$\mathrm{Err}^*_{\mathcal{K},Q}(\Lambda) = \mathrm{Err}^0_{\mathcal{K},Q}(\Lambda).$$

Moreover, there exists an optimal recovery map which is linear.

Proof Consider the symmetric convex set defined by

$$C = \{[Q(f); \lambda_1(f); \ldots; \lambda_m(f)], f \in \mathcal{K}\} \subseteq \mathbb{R}^{m+1}.$$

Setting $e^0 := \mathrm{Err}^0_{\mathcal{K},Q}(\Lambda)$, one notices that $[e^0; 0; \ldots; 0]$ is a boundary point of C. The supporting hyperplane theorem (Theorem C.8) implies the existence of $(c_0, c_1, \ldots, c_m) \ne (0, 0, \ldots, 0)$ such that $c_0 Q(f) + c_1 \lambda_1(f) + \cdots + c_m \lambda_m(f) \le c_0 e^0$ for all $f \in \mathcal{K}$. In view of Remark 9.2, one can assume that $c_0 \ne 0$. Then, the invariance under $f \leftrightarrow -f$ yields $|Q(f) - \sum_{i=1}^m c'_i \lambda_i(f)| \le e^0$ for all $f \in \mathcal{K}$, where $c'_i := -c_i/c_0$ for $i \in [1:m]$. For the linear recovery map $\Delta: \mathbb{R}^m \to \mathbb{R}$ defined by $\Delta(y) = \sum_{i=1}^m c'_i y_i$, one consequently obtains $\mathrm{Err}_{\mathcal{K},Q}(\Lambda, \Delta) \le e^0 \le \mathrm{Err}^*_{\mathcal{K},Q}(\Lambda)$, where the last inequality was (9.3). This justifies the two statements of the theorem. □

One continues by considering the situation where F is a Hilbert space, which corresponds to the case $T = \mathrm{Id}_H$ in the result below. The result essentially says that linear optimal recovery maps exist over ellipsoidal model sets.

Theorem 9.4 *Let $Q: F \to Z$ be a linear quantity of interest. In addition, let $T: F \to H$ be a linear map with values in a Hilbert space H and such that $\ker(T) \cap \ker(\Lambda) = \{0\}$. If the model set $\mathcal{K} = T^{-1}(B_H)$ is the preimage by T of the unit ball of H, then the intrinsic error for the evaluation of Q over $\mathcal{K}$ given Λ satisfies*

$$\mathrm{Err}^*_{\mathcal{K},Q}(\Lambda) = \mathrm{Err}^0_{\mathcal{K},Q}(\Lambda). \tag{9.5}$$

Moreover, there exists an optimal recovery map which is linear.

As a matter of fact, the result is a consequence of the following easy but important observation.

Lemma 9.5 *Let $Q: F \to Z$ be a linear quantity of interest and let $\mathcal{K} \subseteq F$ be a symmetric and convex model set. If $\Delta: \mathbb{R}^m \to F$ is a data-consistent map which satisfies $f - \Delta(\Lambda(f)) \in \mathcal{K}$ whenever $f \in \mathcal{K}$, then $\mathrm{Err}^*_{\mathcal{K},Q}(\Lambda) = \mathrm{Err}^0_{\mathcal{K},Q}(\Lambda)$ and $Q \circ \Delta: \mathbb{R}^m \to Z$ is an optimal recovery map.*

Proof For $f \in \mathcal{K}$, the two assumptions on the recovery map Δ translate into $f - \Delta(\Lambda(f)) \in \ker(\Lambda) \cap \mathcal{K}$, so that

$$\|Q(f) - (Q \circ \Delta)(\Lambda(f))\| = \|Q(f - \Delta(\Lambda(f)))\| \leq \mathrm{Err}^0_{\mathcal{K},Q}(\Lambda).$$

Taking the supremum over $f \in \mathcal{K}$ gives $\mathrm{Err}_{\mathcal{K},Q}(\Lambda, Q \circ \Delta) \leq \mathrm{Err}^0_{\mathcal{K},Q}(\Lambda)$. Then, in view of $\mathrm{Err}^0_{\mathcal{K},Q}(\Lambda) \leq \mathrm{Err}^*_{\mathcal{K},Q}(\Lambda)$, one concludes that $Q \circ \Delta$ is an optimal recovery map and that $\mathrm{Err}^*_{\mathcal{K},Q}(\Lambda) = \mathrm{Err}^0_{\mathcal{K},Q}(\Lambda)$. $\square$

Proof of Theorem 9.4 Consider the map $\Delta: \mathbb{R}^m \to F$ defined for $y \in \mathbb{R}^m$ by

$$\Delta(y) = \underset{f \in F}{\mathrm{argmin}} \, \|T(f)\| \qquad \text{subject to } \Lambda(f) = y. \tag{9.6}$$

To see that $\Delta(y)$ is uniquely defined, given two minimizers $f_1, f_2 \in F$, the strict convexity of the objective function implies that $T(f_1) = T(f_2)$, and then $f_1 = f_2$ follows from $f_1 - f_2 \in \ker(T) \cap \ker(\Lambda) = \{0\}$. Now, observe that the constraint in (9.6) implies that $\Lambda(\Delta(y)) = y$ for any $y \in \mathbb{R}^m$, i.e., that Δ is data-consistent. Next, observe that $T(\Delta(y))$ is orthogonal to the space $T(\ker(\Lambda))$ for any $y \in \mathbb{R}^m$, which is due to the fact that, for all $h \in \ker(\Lambda)$, $t \in \mathbb{R}$, and with f_y temporarily denoting $\Delta(y)$, one has

$$\|T(f_y)\|^2 \leq \|T(f_y + th)\|^2 = \|T(f_y)\|^2 + 2t\langle T(f_y), T(h)\rangle + O(t^2).$$

The orthogonality condition ensures the linearity of Δ. Indeed, for $c_1, c_2 \in \mathbb{R}$

and $y_1, y_2 \in \mathbb{R}^m$, one must verify that $h := c_1\Delta(y_1) + c_2\Delta(y_2) - \Delta(c_1y_1 + c_2y_2)$ is the zero vector. Since h belongs to $\ker(\Lambda)$, one knows that $T(h)$ is orthogonal to $T(\Delta(y_1))$, $T(\Delta(y_2))$, and $T(\Delta(c_1y_1 + c_2y_2))$, and hence to $T(h)$ itself. This implies that $\|T(h)\| = 0$, i.e., $h \in \ker(T)$, which in conjunction with $h \in \ker(\Lambda)$ yields $h = 0$, as expected. Finally, for $f \in F$, in view of $f - \Delta(\Lambda(f)) \in \ker(\Lambda)$, one deduces that

$$\|Tf\|^2 = \|T(f - \Delta(\Lambda(f))) + T(\Delta(\Lambda(f)))\|^2$$
$$= \|T(f - \Delta(\Lambda(f)))\|^2 + \|T(\Delta(\Lambda(f)))\|^2$$
$$\geq \|T(f - \Delta(\Lambda(f)))\|^2.$$

In particular, one obtains $\|T(f - \Delta(\Lambda(f)))\| \leq 1$ whenever $\|T(f)\| \leq 1$, i.e., $f - \Delta(\Lambda(f)) \in \mathcal{K}$ whenever $f \in \mathcal{K}$. Lemma 9.5 now ensures the equality (9.5) between intrinsic and null errors, as well as the optimality of the linear recovery map $Q \circ \Delta: \mathbb{R}^m \to Z$. □

9.3 An Extremal Property of Splines

It might be unclear how to solve (9.6) computationally when F is infinite-dimensional, but there are situations where the solution can be made explicit. The most striking example involves *spline functions*, thus explaining why the term *spline algorithm* is sometimes used for (9.6). In this case, the observation functionals are point evaluations and T represents the second derivative acting on functions in a Sobolev space. The problem corresponds to minimizing the strain energy of a curve constrained to pass through a prescribed set of points. The solution, a cubic spline, was mechanically produced by draftsmen using a thin pliable rod constrained by metal ducks. The term spline was the name of the device and ultimately became the generic name for univariate piecewise polynomial functions satisfying some smoothness conditions at their break-points. As established below, the result generalizes to derivatives of arbitrary order k, thus providing a computable optimal recovery maps associated with the model set

$$\mathcal{K} = \{f \in W_2^k[a, b] : \|f^{(k)}\|_{L_2[a,b]} \leq 1\}.$$

Theorem 9.6 Let $W_2^k[a, b]$ denote the Sobolev space *consisting of functions* $f \in L_2[a, b]$ *whose derivatives* $f', \ldots, f^{(k)}$ *are also square-integrable. For* $m \geq k$, *given points* $x^{(1)} < \cdots < x^{(m)} \in (a, b)$ *and given values* $y_1, \ldots, y_m \in \mathbb{R}$, *the program*

$$\underset{f \in W_2^k[a,b]}{\text{minimize}} \|f^{(k)}\|_{L_2[a,b]} \qquad \text{subject to } f(x^{(i)}) = y_i, \ i \in [1:m],$$

has a unique solution, called natural spline, *which is defined as the piecewise polynomial function with breakpoints at* $x^{(1)}, \ldots, x^{(m)}$, *of degree* $< 2k$ *on each* $(x^{(i)}, x^{(i+1)})$, *of degree* $< k$ *on* $(a, x^{(1)})$ *and* $(x^{(m)}, b)$, *of global smoothness* C^{2k-2}, *and which fulfills the interpolatory conditions* $f(x^{(1)}) = y_1, \ldots, f(x^{(m)}) = y_m$.

Proof Let $f_y \in W_2^k[a, b]$ denote the piecewise polynomial function obeying the listed conditions, assuming for the moment its existence and uniqueness. Given $f \in W_2^k[a, b]$ fulfilling $f(x^{(1)}) = y_1, \ldots, f(x^{(m)}) = y_m$, the goal is to prove that $\|f^{(k)}\|_{L_2[a,b]} \geq \|f_y^{(k)}\|_{L_2[a,b]}$. Setting $x^{(0)} = a$ and $x^{(m+1)} = b$, and considering some $h \in \ker(\Lambda)$, successive integrations by parts give, for any $i \in [0:m]$,

$$\int_{x^{(i)}}^{x^{(i+1)}} f_y^{(k)} h^{(k)} = \sum_{j=1}^{k} (-1)^{j-1} \left[f_y^{(k+j-1)} h^{(k-j)} \right]_{x^{(i)}}^{x^{(i+1)}} + (-1)^k \int_{x^{(i)}}^{x^{(i+1)}} f_y^{(2k)} h.$$

The latter integral equals zero since the polynomial piece of f_y on $(x^{(i)}, x^{(i+1)})$ has degree $< 2k$. Thus, summing over $i \in [0:m]$ yields

$$\int_a^b f_y^{(k)} h^{(k)} = \sum_{j=1}^{k} (-1)^{j-1} \sum_{i=0}^{m} \left[f_y^{(k+j-1)} h^{(k-j)} \right]_{x^{(i)}}^{x^{(i+1)}}$$

$$= \sum_{j=1}^{k} (-1)^{j-1} \Big\{ f_y^{(k+j-1)}(b_-) h^{(k-j)}(b_-) - f_y^{(k+j-1)}(a_+) h^{(k-j)}(a_+)$$

$$+ \sum_{i=1}^{m} \big(f_y^{(k+j-1)}(x_-^{(i)}) h^{(k-j)}(x_-^{(i)}) - f_y^{(k+j-1)}(x_+^{(i)}) h^{(k-j)}(x_+^{(i)}) \big) \Big\}.$$

In view of $f_y^{(k+j-1)}(b_-) h^{(k-j)}(b_-) = f_y^{(k+j-1)}(a_+) h^{(k-j)}(a_+) = 0$ for $j \in [1:k]$ because the polynomial pieces of f_y have degree $< k$ on $(a, x^{(1)})$ and on $(x^{(m)}, b)$, in view of the continuity of $f_y^{(k+j-1)} h^{(k-j)}$ at $x^{(1)}, \ldots, x^{(m)}$ for $j \in [1:k-1]$ because of the C^{2k-2} smoothness of f_y, and in view of $f_y^{(2k-1)}(x_-^{(i)}) h(x_-^{(i)}) = 0$ and $f_y^{(2k-1)}(x_+^{(i)}) h(x_+^{(i)}) = 0$ because $h \in \ker(\Lambda)$, one derives that

$$\langle f_y^{(k)}, h^{(k)} \rangle_{L_2[a,b]} = \int_a^b f_y^{(k)} h^{(k)} = 0. \tag{9.7}$$

The special choice $h = f - f_y \in \ker(\Lambda)$ shows that $f_y^{(k)}$ is orthogonal to $f^{(k)} - f_y^{(k)}$, from where the required inequality $\|f^{(k)}\|_{L_2[a,b]} \geq \|f_y^{(k)}\|_{L_2[a,b]}$ is deduced via

$$\|f^{(k)}\|_{L_2[a,b]}^2 = \|(f^{(k)} - f_y^{(k)}) + f_y^{(k)}\|_{L_2[a,b]}^2 = \|f^{(k)} - f_y^{(k)}\|_{L_2[a,b]}^2 + \|f_y^{(k)}\|_{L_2[a,b]}^2$$

$$\geq \|f_y^{(k)}\|_{L_2[a,b]}^2.$$

It remains to show that f_y as defined above exists and is unique. To do so, one must verify that the linear map $\Lambda_{|S} : s \in S \mapsto [s(x^{(1)}); \ldots ; s(x^{(m)})] \in \mathbb{R}^m$ is an isomorphism, where S denotes the space of C^{2k-2} piecewise polynomial functions with breakpoints at $x^{(1)}, \ldots, x^{(m)}$, of degree $< 2k$ on each $(x^{(i)}, x^{(i+1)})$, and of degree $< k$ on $(a, x^{(1)})$ and $(x^{(m)}, b)$. It is not hard to see that S has dimension m. A loose argument consists in counting the free parameters for each interval $(x^{(i)}, x^{(i+1)})$, for the interval $(a, x^{(1)})$, and for the interval $(x^{(m)}, b)$, and subtracting the number of smoothness conditions imposed at each $x^{(i)}$, to find that there are $2k \times (m-1) + k + k - (2k-1) \times m = m$ degrees of freedom. Thus, one only needs to prove that $\Lambda_{|S}$ is injective. Let then $s \in \ker(\Lambda)$, so that $s = f_0$ using the above notation. The identity (9.7) written with $h = s$ then reads $\|s^{(k)}\|^2_{L_2[a,b]} = 0$, i.e., $s^{(k)} = 0$. The function s now appears as a polynomial of degree $< k$ having $m \geq k$ roots, so $s = 0$ (incidentally, this is the argument justifying that $\ker(T) \cap \ker(\Lambda) = \{0\}$). Thus, the injectivity of $\Lambda_{|S}$ is established, which concludes the proof. $\qquad\square$

Theorem 9.6 extends beyond the univariate setting. The explicit solutions of the optimization program are then provided by the so-called *thin plate splines*.[1]

Exercises

9.1 Prove that the set of (locally) optimal recovery maps for the evaluation of a quantity of interest $Q: F \to Z$ over a model set $\mathcal{K} \subseteq F$ given an observation map $\Lambda: F \to \mathbb{R}^m$ is a convex set.

9.2 Let C be a closed convex subset of a Hilbert space H. Prove that C must contain the Chebyshev center(s) f^* of C, characterized by

$$\sup_{f \in C} \|f - f^*\| \leq \sup_{f \in C} \|f - g\| \qquad \text{for all } g \in H.$$

9.3 Suppose that a set $C \subseteq F$ is symmetric about some $f^* \in F$, i.e., that $2f^* - f \in C$ whenever $f \in C$. Show that f^* is a Chebyshev center of C.

9.4 Improve Theorem 9.4 by showing that the recovery map (9.6) is in fact locally optimal.

9.5 Suppose that elements $f \in \mathcal{K}$ are observed via $y = \Lambda(f) + e$ with error vectors e belonging to some uncertainty set $\mathcal{E}$. Observe that this situation formally reduces to the standard situation by writing the worst-case error of a recovery map $\Delta: \mathbb{R}^m \to Z$ over $\mathcal{K}$ and $\mathcal{E}$ as

$$\sup_{\substack{f \in \mathcal{K} \\ e \in \mathcal{E}}} \|Q(f) - \Delta(\Lambda(f) + e)\| = \text{Err}_{\widetilde{\mathcal{K}}, \widetilde{Q}}(\widetilde{\Lambda}, \Delta)$$

for some $\widetilde{\mathcal{K}}$, $\widetilde{Q}$, and $\widetilde{\Lambda}$ to be determined.

---

[1] The reader is referred to Wendland (2004) for more details on the subject.

10
Approximability Models

The model set $\mathcal{K} = \{f \in W_2^k[a,b] : \|f^{(k)}\|_{L_2} \leq 1\}$, encountered at the end of the previous chapter, imposes smoothness. Smoothness can alternatively be characterized in terms of approximability. This is made precise by the *Jackson theorem* (aka the *direct theorem*) and the *Bernstein theorem* (aka the *inverse theorem*). They are stated here (and proved in Appendix E) for 2π-periodic functions to be approximated by elements of the space

$$\mathcal{T}_n = \text{span}\{1, \cos, \sin, \ldots, \cos(n\cdot), \sin(n\cdot)\}$$

of *trigonometric polynomials* of degree at most n.

Theorem 10.1 *Let a function f be defined on $\mathbb{T}$ and let $k \geq 0$ be an integer.*

- Jackson: *If $f \in C^k(\mathbb{T})$, then $\text{dist}_{C(\mathbb{T})}(f, \mathcal{T}_n) \leq c_f \, n^{-k}$ for all $n \geq 1$.*
- Bernstein: *For any $\alpha \in (0,1)$, if $\text{dist}_{C(\mathbb{T})}(f, \mathcal{T}_n) \leq c_f \, n^{-(k+\alpha)}$ for all $n \geq 1$, then the kth derivative $f^{(k)}$ exists and is α-Hölder continuous.*

After the introduction of a model set suggested by this rough equivalence smoothness-approximability, the focus will be put on the two situations where the existence of linear optimal recovery maps has already been established: the ones involving Hilbert spaces and involving linear functionals as quantities of interest. In both situations, it will be shown that the exact intrinsic error can be computed and that the linear optimal recovery maps become practical algorithms.

10.1 The Model Set

In light of the connection between smoothness and approximability revealed by Theorem 10.1, one can view $\cap_{n \geq 1}\{f \in C(\mathbb{T}) : \text{dist}_{C(\mathbb{T})}(f, \mathcal{T}_n) \leq cn^{-k}\}$ as another model set forcing C^k-continuity. The model at the heart of this chapter actually consists of a single set from this intersection, but with $\mathcal{T}_n$ replaced by an arbitrary linear subspace $\mathcal{V}$ of a normed space F and with cn^{-k} replaced by an arbitrary parameter $\varepsilon > 0$. The main message to be delivered is the computability of optimal recovery maps associated with the *approximability set*

$$\mathcal{K} := \{f \in F : \text{dist}(f, \mathcal{V}) \le \varepsilon\}. \tag{10.1}$$

In hindsight, this model makes completely explicit an assumption that may occur implicitly, e.g. through the choice of hypothesis classes that are expected to yield small approximation errors. Many numerical procedures also involve such implicit assumptions. For instance, when producing a quadrature formula $\sum_{i=1}^{m} a_i f(x^{(i)})$ to estimate the integral of a function $f \in F$ (say, $F = C(\mathbb{T})$), one presumes that f is well approximated by elements from $\mathcal{V}$ (say, $\mathcal{V} = \mathcal{T}_n$), i.e., that $\text{dist}(f, \mathcal{V})$ is small, then one selects the coefficients $a_1, \ldots, a_m$ so that the quadrature formula is exact on $\mathcal{V}$, and one finally derives an estimation bound featuring $\text{dist}(f, \mathcal{V})$.

The choice of a suitable approximation space $\mathcal{V}$ obviously depends on the elements f of interest, but also on the observation map $\Lambda \colon F \to \mathbb{R}^m$ at hand. Indeed, suppose e.g. that there exists $v \in \mathcal{V}$ with $\Lambda(v) = 0$. Then, fixing some $f_0 \in \mathcal{K}$, all the $f_t \colon f_0 + tv$, $t \in \mathbb{R}$, belong to the model set $\mathcal{K}$ and share the same observation vector $\Lambda(f_0)$, leading to unbounded recovery errors. For this reason, the space $\mathcal{V}$ is chosen to satisfy the condition

$$\ker(\Lambda) \cap \mathcal{V} = \{0\}. \tag{10.2}$$

This condition legitimates the introduction of the quantity

$$\mu_{\mathcal{V}, Q}(\Lambda) := \sup_{u \in \ker(\Lambda) \setminus \{0\}} \frac{\|Q(u)\|}{\text{dist}(u, \mathcal{V})}, \tag{10.3}$$

dubbed the *compatibility indicator* between the model and the observation process. Its relevance transpires through the easily verifiable identity

$$\text{Err}^0_{\mathcal{K}, Q}(\Lambda) = \mu_{\mathcal{V}, Q}(\Lambda)\, \varepsilon, \tag{10.4}$$

which decouples the null error as the product of the compatibility indicator and the approximability parameter. Given that the model set (10.1) is symmetric and convex, Proposition 9.1 guarantees that, whenever the quantity of interest $Q \colon F \to Z$ is linear, the intrinsic error satisfies

$$\mu_{\mathcal{V}, Q}(\Lambda)\, \varepsilon \le \text{Err}^*_{\mathcal{K}, Q}(\Lambda) \le 2\, \mu_{\mathcal{V}, Q}(\Lambda)\, \varepsilon.$$

With this in mind, one can produce a (not necessarily computable) near-optimal recovery map as $Q \circ \Delta \colon \mathbb{R}^m \to Z$, where $\Delta \colon \mathbb{R}^m \to F$ is defined, for any $y \in \mathbb{R}^m$, by

$$\Delta(y) \in \operatorname*{argmin}_{f \in F} \operatorname{dist}(f, \mathcal{V}) \quad \text{subject to } \Lambda(f) = y. \qquad (10.5)$$

Indeed, the required estimate $\operatorname{Err}_{\mathcal{K},Q}(\Lambda, Q \circ \Delta) \leq 2 \operatorname{Err}^*_{\mathcal{K},Q}(\Lambda)$ is deduced from the following chain of inequalities, valid for any $f \in \mathcal{K}$:

$$\begin{aligned}
\|Q(f) - (Q \circ \Delta)(\Lambda(f))\| &= \|Q(f - \Delta(\Lambda(f)))\| \\
&\leq \mu_{\mathcal{V},Q}(\Lambda) \operatorname{dist}(f - \Delta(\Lambda(f)), \mathcal{V}) \\
&\leq \mu_{\mathcal{V},Q}(\Lambda) \left[\operatorname{dist}(f, \mathcal{V}) + \operatorname{dist}(\Delta(\Lambda(f)), \mathcal{V}) \right] \\
&\leq \mu_{\mathcal{V},Q}(\Lambda) \left[\operatorname{dist}(f, \mathcal{V}) + \operatorname{dist}(f, \mathcal{V}) \right] \\
&\leq 2 \mu_{\mathcal{V},Q}(\Lambda) \varepsilon.
\end{aligned}$$

10.2 Optimality in a Hilbert Setting

When F is a Hilbert space, the near-optimal recovery map stemming from (10.5) turns out to be genuinely optimal. In view of Lemma 9.5, this could be seen by verifying that $f - \Delta(\Lambda(f)) \in \mathcal{K}$ whenever $f \in \mathcal{K}$. The following result shows a little more, namely that the recovery map is locally optimal. Below, the notation $P_{\mathcal{V}}$ stands for the orthogonal projector onto the space $\mathcal{V}$.

Theorem 10.2 *Let $F = H$ be a Hilbert space and let $Q \colon H \to Z$ be a linear quantity of interest. The recovery map $Q \circ \Delta \colon \mathbb{R}^m \to Z$, where $\Delta \colon \mathbb{R}^m \to H$ is defined for any $y \in \mathbb{R}^m$ by*

$$\Delta(y) \in \operatorname*{argmin}_{f \in H} \|f - P_{\mathcal{V}}(f)\| \quad \text{subject to } \Lambda(f) = y, \qquad (10.6)$$

is locally optimal over the model set (10.1), i.e., for any $y \in \Lambda(\mathcal{K})$ and for any $z \in Z$,

$$\sup_{f \in \mathcal{K} \cap \Lambda^{-1}(\{y\})} \|Q(f) - z\| \geq \sup_{f \in \mathcal{K} \cap \Lambda^{-1}(\{y\})} \|Q(f) - (Q \circ \Delta)(y)\|.$$

Proof Fixing $y \in \mathbb{R}^m$ and writing f^* for $\Delta(y)$, while abbreviating $\mu_{\mathcal{V},Q}(\Lambda)$ simply as μ, the goal is to prove on the one hand that

$$\sup_{f \in \mathcal{K} \cap \Lambda^{-1}(\{y\})} \|Q(f) - Q(f^*)\| \leq \mu \left[\varepsilon^2 - \|f^* - P_{\mathcal{V}}(f^*)\|^2 \right]^{1/2} \qquad (10.7)$$

and on the other hand that, for any $z \in Z$,

$$\sup_{f \in \mathcal{K} \cap \Lambda^{-1}(\{y\})} \|Q(f) - z\| \geq \mu \left[\varepsilon^2 - \|f^* - P_{\mathcal{V}}(f^*)\|^2 \right]^{1/2}. \qquad (10.8)$$

Besides being orthogonal to $\mathcal{V}$, the element $f^\star - P_\mathcal{V}(f^\star)$ is also orthogonal to $\ker(\Lambda)$. Indeed, for any $u \in \ker(\Lambda)$ and any $t \in \mathbb{R}$, the expression

$$\|f^\star + tu - P_\mathcal{V}(f^\star + tu)\|^2$$
$$= \|f^\star - P_\mathcal{V}(f^\star)\|^2 + 2t\langle f^\star - P_\mathcal{V}(f^\star), u - P_\mathcal{V}(u)\rangle + O(t^2)$$

is minimized when $t = 0$, which forces $\langle f^\star - P_\mathcal{V}(f^\star), u - P_\mathcal{V}(u)\rangle = 0$, i.e., $\langle f^\star - P_\mathcal{V}(f^\star), u\rangle = 0$. Now, considering $f \in \mathcal{K} \cap \Lambda^{-1}(\{y\})$ written for some $u \in \ker(\Lambda)$ as $f = f^\star + u$, the fact that $f \in \mathcal{K}$ reads

$$\varepsilon^2 \geq \|f - P_\mathcal{V}(f)\|^2 = \|f^\star - P_\mathcal{V}(f^\star) + u - P_\mathcal{V}(u)\|^2$$
$$= \|f^\star - P_\mathcal{V}(f^\star)\|^2 + \|u - P_\mathcal{V}(u)\|^2.$$

Rearranging the latter gives

$$\text{dist}(u, \mathcal{V}) = \|u - P_\mathcal{V}(u)\| \leq \left[\varepsilon^2 - \|f^\star - P_\mathcal{V}(f^\star)\|^2\right]^{1/2}.$$

It remains to take the definition (10.3) of μ into account in order to bound $\|Q(f) - Q(f^\star)\| = \|Q(u)\|$ and to arrive at (10.7).

Now, in order to establish (10.8), one first selects $u \in \ker(\Lambda)$ such that

$$\|Q(u)\| = \mu \, \text{dist}(u, \mathcal{V}), \tag{10.9}$$

$$\|u - P_\mathcal{V}(u)\| = \left[\varepsilon^2 - \|f^\star - P_\mathcal{V}(f^\star)\|^2\right]^{1/2}. \tag{10.10}$$

Next, considering $f^\pm := f^\star \pm u$, it is clear that $f^\pm \in \Lambda^{-1}(\{y\})$, while $f^\pm \in \mathcal{K}$ follows from

$$\|f^\pm - P_\mathcal{V}(f^\pm)\|^2 = \|(f^\star - P_\mathcal{V}(f^\star)) \pm (u - P_\mathcal{V}(u))\|^2$$
$$= \|f^\star - P_\mathcal{V}(f^\star)\|^2 + \|u - P_\mathcal{V}(u)\|^2 \doteq \varepsilon^2.$$

Therefore, for any $z \in Z$, one has

$$\sup_{f \in \mathcal{K} \cap \Lambda^{-1}(\{y\})} \|Q(f) - z\| \geq \max\{\|Q(f^+) - z\|, \|Q(f^-) - z\|\}$$

$$\geq \frac{1}{2}(\|Q(f^+) - z\| + \|Q(f^-) - z\|)$$

$$\geq \frac{1}{2}\|Q(f^+ - f^-)\| = \|Q(u)\|.$$

Finally, taking (10.9) and (10.10) into account finishes to justify (10.8). □

The above proof did not establish the linearity of the recovery map (10.6). Its linearity will be apparent from the more explicit expression (10.11) presented in the next proposition. There, each $u_i \in H$, $i \in [1:m]$, denotes the *Riesz representer* of λ_i, which is characterized by $\lambda_i(f) = \langle u_i, f\rangle$ for all $f \in H$.

By the linear independence of $(\lambda_1, \ldots, \lambda_m)$, the system $(u_1, \ldots, u_m)$ forms a basis for $\mathcal{U} := \text{span}\{u_1, \ldots, u_m\} = \ker(\Lambda)^\perp$. Let also $(v_1, \ldots, v_n)$ denote a basis for $\mathcal{V}$. One introduces the *Gramian* $G_u \in \mathbb{R}^{m \times m}$ of $(u_1, \ldots, u_m)$, the *Gramian* $G_v \in \mathbb{R}^{n \times n}$ of $(v_1, \ldots, v_n)$, and the *cross-Gramian* $C \in \mathbb{R}^{m \times n}$ of $(u_1, \ldots, u_m)$ and $(v_1, \ldots, v_n)$. Their entries are given, for $i, i' \in [1:m]$ and $j, j' \in [1:n]$, by

$$(G_u)_{i,i'} = \langle u_i, u_{i'} \rangle = \lambda_i(u_{i'}),$$
$$(G_v)_{j,j'} = \langle v_j, v_{j'} \rangle,$$
$$C_{i,j} = \langle u_i, v_j \rangle = \lambda_i(v_j).$$

The matrices G_u and G_v are positive definite and in particular invertible. The matrix C has full rank thanks to the condition (10.2) that $\ker(\Lambda) \cap \mathcal{V} = \{0\}$.

Proposition 10.3 *The locally optimal recovery map* (10.6) *can be explicitly expressed, for any $y \in \mathbb{R}^m$, via*

$$\Delta(y) = \sum_{i=1}^{m} a_i u_i + \sum_{j=1}^{n} b_j v_j, \tag{10.11}$$

where the coefficient vectors $a \in \mathbb{R}^m$ and $b \in \mathbb{R}^n$ are given by

$$b = (C^\top G_u^{-1} C)^{-1} C^\top G_u^{-1} y \quad \text{and} \quad a = G_u^{-1} y - G_u^{-1} C b. \tag{10.12}$$

Proof From the previous proof, with $f^\star$ still representing $\Delta(y)$, one recalls that $f^\star - P_{\mathcal{V}}(f^\star)$ is orthogonal to $\ker(\Lambda)$. Since $\ker(\Lambda)^\perp = \mathcal{U}$, this implies that

$$f^\star - P_{\mathcal{V}}(f^\star) = \sum_{i=1}^{m} a_i u_i \qquad \text{for some } a \in \mathbb{R}^m.$$

Taking inner products with $v_1, \ldots, v_n$ leads to $0 = C^\top a$. Then, expanding $P_{\mathcal{V}}(f^\star)$ on $(v_1, \ldots, v_n)$, one obtains

$$f^\star = \sum_{i=1}^{m} a_i u_i + \sum_{j=1}^{n} b_j v_j \qquad \text{for some } b \in \mathbb{R}^n. \tag{10.13}$$

Taking inner products with $u_1, \ldots, u_m$ leads to $y = G_u a + Cb$ and in turn to $C^\top G_u^{-1} y = C^\top G_u^{-1} C b$ after having multiplied by $C^\top G_u^{-1}$. The latter yields the expression for b in (10.12), while the former yields the expression for a. $\square$

Although only the Gramian G_u appeared above, the Gramian G_v comes into play below in a result that indicates how the compatibility indicator (10.3) can be computed for the full approximation problem. These Gramians reduce to the identity matrices I_m and I_n in case the bases $(u_1, \ldots, u_m)$ and $(v_1, \ldots, v_n)$ can be chosen as orthonormal bases, possibly after an orthonormalization procedure (if such a procedure can be carried out exactly).

Theorem 10.4 *If $F = H$ is a Hilbert space and $Q = \mathrm{Id}$ is the identity of H, then the compatibility indicator between the model (10.1) and the observation process is explicitly given by*

$$\mu_{\mathcal{V},\mathrm{Id}}(\Lambda) = \frac{1}{\left[\lambda_{\min}(G_v^{-1/2} C^\top G_u^{-1} C G_v^{-1/2})\right]^{1/2}}. \tag{10.14}$$

Proof The starting point is the observation, deduced from Exercise 10.3, that

$$\frac{1}{\mu_{\mathcal{V},\mathrm{Id}}(\Lambda)} = \inf_{v \in \mathcal{V}} \frac{\|P_{\mathcal{U}}(v)\|}{\|v\|}.$$

Next, one writes the singular value decomposition of $G_u^{-1/2} C G_v^{-1/2} \in \mathbb{R}^{m \times n}$ as

$$G_u^{-1/2} C G_v^{-1/2} = P \Sigma Q^\top,$$

where $\Sigma = \mathrm{diag}[\sigma_1, \dots, \sigma_n] \in \mathbb{R}^{m \times n}$ and where $P \in \mathbb{R}^{m \times m}$ and $Q \in \mathbb{R}^{n \times n}$ are orthogonal matrices. The systems $(\widetilde{u}_1, \dots, \widetilde{u}_m)$ and $(\widetilde{v}_1, \dots, \widetilde{v}_n)$, defined for $i \in [1:m]$ and $j \in [1:n]$ by

$$\widetilde{u}_i = \sum_{i'=1}^{m} (G_u^{-1/2} P)_{i',i}\, u_{i'} \quad \text{and} \quad \widetilde{v}_j = \sum_{j'=1}^{n} (G_v^{-1/2} Q)_{j',j}\, v_{j'},$$

are claimed to be orthonormal bases for $\mathcal{U}$ and $\mathcal{V}$, respectively. Indeed, one observes e.g. that, for $i, k \in [1:m]$,

$$\begin{aligned}
\langle \widetilde{u}_i, \widetilde{u}_k \rangle &= \sum_{i',k'=1}^{m} (G_u^{-1/2} P)_{i',i} (G_u^{-1/2} P)_{k',k} (G_u)_{i',k'} \\
&= ((G_u^{-1/2} P)^\top G_u (G_u^{-1/2} P))_{i,k} = (P^\top P)_{i,k} = \delta_{i,k}.
\end{aligned}$$

One also observes that, for $i \in [1:m]$ and $j \in [1:n]$,

$$\begin{aligned}
\langle \widetilde{u}_i, \widetilde{v}_j \rangle &= \sum_{i'=1}^{m} \sum_{j'=1}^{n} (G_u^{-1/2} P)_{i',i} (G_v^{-1/2} Q)_{j',j} C_{i',j'} \\
&= ((G_u^{-1/2} P)^\top C (G_v^{-1/2} Q))_{i,j} = \Sigma_{i,j} = \sigma_i \delta_{i,j}.
\end{aligned}$$

Thus, for $v \in \mathcal{V}$ written as $v = \sum_{j=1}^{n} b_j \widetilde{v}_j$, one has

$$\|P_{\mathcal{U}}(v)\|^2 = \sum_{i=1}^{m} \langle \widetilde{u}_i, v \rangle^2 = \sum_{i=1}^{m} \left(\sum_{j=1}^{n} b_j \langle \widetilde{u}_i, \widetilde{v}_j \rangle \right)^2 = \sum_{i=1}^{n} b_i^2 \sigma_i^2$$

$$\geq \min\{\sigma_1, \dots, \sigma_n\}^2 \|v\|^2.$$

Noticing that equality can be achieved, it follows that $1/\mu_{\mathcal{V},\mathrm{Id}}(\Lambda)$ equals the smallest singular value of $G_u^{-1/2} C G_v^{-1/2}$, i.e., the square root of the smallest eigenvalue of $(G_u^{-1/2} C G_v^{-1/2})^\top (G_u^{-1/2} C G_v^{-1/2}) = G_v^{-1/2} C^\top G_u^{-1} C G_v^{-1/2}$. This is the result announced in (10.14). $\qquad\square$

10.3 Optimality for Linear Functionals

Not imposing the normed space F to be a Hilbert space anymore, one turns to the situation where the quantity of interest is a linear functional. It is already known that there is an optimal recovery map which is a linear functional, and the following result provides a way to construct such an optimal recovery map. It is worth noting that the construction is independent of the approximability parameter $\varepsilon > 0$.

Theorem 10.5 *If the quantity of interest* $Q\colon F \to \mathbb{R}$ *is a linear functional, then a linear optimal recovery map over the model set* (10.1) *takes the form*

$$\Delta^{\star}\colon y \in \mathbb{R}^m \mapsto \sum_{i=1}^m a_i^{\star} y_i \in \mathbb{R}, \tag{10.15}$$

where the vector $a^{\star} = [a_1^{\star}; \ldots; a_m^{\star}] \in \mathbb{R}^m$ *is a solution to*

$$\underset{a \in \mathbb{R}^m}{\text{minimize}} \left\| Q - \sum_{i=1}^m a_i \lambda_i \right\|^* \quad \text{s.to} \quad \sum_{i=1}^m a_i \lambda_i(v) = Q(v) \quad \text{for all } v \in \mathcal{V}. \tag{10.16}$$

Proof According to both Theorem 9.3 and (10.4), the intrinsic error becomes $\mathrm{Err}_{\mathcal{K},Q}^*(\Lambda) = \mu\,\varepsilon$, where the notation μ stands for $\mu_{\mathcal{V},Q}(\Lambda)$. Thus, it is sufficient to show that the worst-case error of $\Delta^{\star}$ satisfies $\mathrm{Err}_{\mathcal{K},Q}(\Lambda, \Delta^{\star}) \leq \mu\,\varepsilon$. With κ denoting the minimal value of the optimization program (10.16), the plan is to prove the inequalities

$$\mathrm{Err}_{\mathcal{K},Q}(\Lambda, \Delta^{\star}) \leq \kappa\,\epsilon \qquad \text{and} \qquad \kappa \leq \mu. \tag{10.17}$$

The first inequality in (10.17) is easy to justify: for $f \in \mathcal{K}$, select $v \in \mathcal{V}$ such that $\|f - v\|$ equals $\mathrm{dist}(f, \mathcal{V})$, so that $\|f - v\| \leq \varepsilon$, then use the constraint from (10.16) to write

$$\left| Q(f) - \sum_{i=1}^m a_i^{\star} \lambda_i(f) \right| = \left| Q(f - v) - \sum_{i=1}^m a_i^{\star} \lambda_i(f - v) \right|$$

$$\leq \left\| Q - \sum_{i=1}^m a_i^{\star} \lambda_i \right\|^* \|f - v\| \leq \kappa\,\varepsilon,$$

and finally take the supremum over $f \in \mathcal{K}$ to arrive at the desired inequality.

Justifying the second inequality in (10.17) requires more work. Introducing a linear functional λ defined on the subspace $\ker(\Lambda) \oplus \mathcal{V}$ of F by

$$\lambda(u) = Q(u) \quad \text{for all } u \in \ker(\Lambda), \qquad \lambda(v) = 0 \quad \text{for all } v \in \mathcal{V},$$

one relies on the *Hahn–Banach extension theorem* (Theorem C.10) to consider a norm-preserving extension $\overline{\lambda} \in F^*$ of $\lambda \in (\ker(\Lambda) \oplus \mathcal{V})^*$. Because $Q - \overline{\lambda}$

vanishes on $\ker(\Lambda)$, one has $Q - \widetilde{\lambda} = \sum_{i=1}^m \widetilde{a}_i \lambda_i$ for some $\widetilde{a} \in \mathbb{R}^m$. Then, because $\widetilde{\lambda}$ vanishes on $\mathcal{V}$, one has $\sum_{i=1}^m \widetilde{a}_i \lambda_i(v) = Q(v)$ for all $v \in \mathcal{V}$. It follows that

$$\kappa \leq \left\| Q - \sum_{i=1}^m \widetilde{a}_i \lambda_i \right\|^* = \left\| \widetilde{\lambda} \right\|^* = \left\| \lambda \right\|_{\ker(\Lambda) \oplus \mathcal{V}}^* = \sup_{\substack{u \in \ker(\Lambda) \\ v \in \mathcal{V}}} \frac{|\lambda(u - v)|}{\|u - v\|}$$

$$= \sup_{\substack{u \in \ker(\Lambda) \\ v \in \mathcal{V}}} \frac{|Q(u)|}{\|u - v\|} = \sup_{u \in \ker(\Lambda)} \frac{|Q(u)|}{\text{dist}(u, \mathcal{V})} = \mu,$$

which is precisely the desired inequality. $\qquad\square$

It is worth pointing out that the construction of the optimal recovery map needs to be performed only once, after which calculating $\Delta^\star(y)$ via (10.15) for each fresh observation vector $y \in \mathbb{R}^m$ is immediate. Therefore, resources can be allocated to solve (10.16) once and for all in an offline stage, even if it is rather costly. Solving (10.16) may actually be out of reach in general, but it is certainly feasible for some important examples, e.g. when F is a reproducing kernel Hilbert space. The example showcased below concerns the case where F is the space $C(X)$ of continuous functions defined on a compact set X. If the observations functionals $\lambda_1, \ldots, \lambda_m$ are point evaluations at distinct points $x^{(1)}, \ldots, x^{(m)} \in X$ and if the quantity of interest Q is also a point evaluation at some $x^{(0)} \notin \{x^{(1)}, \ldots, x^{(m)}\}$, then the problem (10.16) reduces to the efficiently solvable ℓ_1-minimization

$$\underset{a \in \mathbb{R}^m}{\text{minimize}} \sum_{i=1}^m |a_i| \quad \text{s.to} \quad \sum_{i=1}^m a_i v_j(x^{(i)}) = v_j(x^{(0)}) \quad \text{for all } j \in [1:n], \quad (10.18)$$

where $(v_1, \ldots, v_n)$ denotes a basis for $\mathcal{V}$. This is a consequence of the fact that $\|Q - \sum_{i=1}^m a_i \lambda_i\|^* = 1 + \sum_{i=1}^m |a_i|$: the $\leq$-part is simply the triangle inequality, while the $\geq$-part relies on the *Tietze extension theorem* (Theorem C.4) in order to guarantee the existence of a function $f \in C(X)$ with $\|f\|_{C(X)} = 1$, $f(x^{(0)}) = 1$, and $f(x^{(i)}) = -\text{sgn}(a_i)$, $i \in [1:m]$, so that

$$\left\| Q - \sum_{i=1}^m a_i \lambda_i \right\|^* \geq f(x^{(0)}) - \sum_{i=1}^m a_i f(x^{(i)}) = 1 + \sum_{i=1}^m |a_i|.$$

The same reduction remains valid if the quantity of interest was replaced by the integral $Q(f) = \int_X f$. Notice that, by a property of ℓ_1-minimizers established in Remark 20.3 or in Theorem 6.1 by formally taking $\lambda = \infty$, (one of) the solution(s) to (10.18) is n-sparse, meaning that only $n \leq m$ observations are used by the optimal recovery map (10.15).

Again considering an observation map $\Lambda_x: C(X) \to \mathbb{R}^m$ associated with point evaluations at $x^{(1)}, \ldots, x^{(m)}$, applying the procedure (10.15) and (10.16) to $Q(f) = f(x^{(0)}) \in X$ for each $x^{(0)} \in X$ allows one to establish (at the expense of some technicalities to ensure that the functions $x^{(0)} \mapsto a_i^\star$ are continuous[1]) the existence of a linear optimal recovery map $\Delta^\star \colon \mathbb{R}^m \to C(X)$ for the full approximation problem, i.e., for $Q = \mathrm{Id}$. It can also be proved that the intrinsic error again decouples as the product of the compatibility indicator and the approximability parameter, i.e., that $\mathrm{Err}^*_{\mathcal{K},\mathrm{Id}}(\Lambda_\mathbf{x}) = \mu_{\mathcal{V},\mathrm{Id}}(\Lambda_\mathbf{x})\,\varepsilon$. Incidentally, the *compatibility indicator* takes a somewhat explicit form here.

Theorem 10.6 *Let $F = C(X)$ be the space of continuous functions on a compact set X. The compatibility indicator between the model (10.1) and the observation map associated with point evaluations at $x^{(1)},\ldots,x^{(m)} \in X$ is given by*

$$\mu_{\mathcal{V},\mathrm{Id}}(\Lambda_\mathbf{x}) = 1 + \sup_{v \in \mathcal{V}} \frac{\|v\|_{C(X)}}{\max_{i \in [1\,:\,m]} |v(x^{(i)})|}. \tag{10.19}$$

Proof Let η denote the supremum appearing in (10.19). For $f \in \ker(\Lambda_\mathbf{x})$ and $v \in \mathcal{V}$ such that $\mathrm{dist}(f,\mathcal{V}) = \|f - v\|_{C(X)}$, one observes that

$$\frac{\|f\|_{C(X)}}{\mathrm{dist}(f,\mathcal{V})} = \frac{\|f\|_{C(X)}}{\|f - v\|_{C(X)}} \le 1 + \frac{\|v\|_{C(X)}}{\|f - v\|_{C(X)}} \le 1 + \frac{\|v\|_{C(X)}}{\max_{i \in [1\,:\,m]} |(f - v)(x^{(i)})|}$$

$$= 1 + \frac{\|v\|_{C(X)}}{\max_{i \in [1\,:\,m]} |v(x^{(i)})|} \le 1 + \eta.$$

Taking the supremum over $f \in \ker(\Lambda_\mathbf{x})$ shows the $\le$-part of (10.19).

To verify the $\ge$-part, select $v \in \mathcal{V}$ such that $\max\{|v(x^{(1)})|,\ldots,|v(x^{(m)})|\} = 1$ and $\|v\|_{C(X)} = \eta$. Picking $x_\star \in X$ such that $|v(x_\star)| = \|v\|_{C(X)}$ (one can assume that $x_\star \notin \{x^{(1)},\ldots,x^{(m)}\}$, otherwise one slightly perturbs it and replaces η with $\eta - \delta$ for some arbitrary small $\delta > 0$), the *Tietze extension theorem* guarantees the existence of $h \in C(X)$ such that $\|h\|_{C(X)} = 1$, $h(x_\star) = \mathrm{sgn}(v(x_\star))$, and $h(x^{(i)}) = -v(x^{(i)})$ for all $i \in [1\,:\,m]$. Then, since $f := h + v \in \ker(\Lambda_\mathbf{x})$, writing

$$\mu_{\mathcal{V},\mathrm{Id}}(\Lambda_\mathbf{x}) \ge \frac{\|f\|_{C(X)}}{\mathrm{dist}(f,\mathcal{V})} \ge \frac{\|h + v\|_{C(X)}}{\|h\|_{C(X)}} \ge |h(x_\star) + v(x_\star)|$$

$$= 1 + |v(x_\star)| = 1 + \eta$$

shows the $\ge$-part of (10.19). □

For the $(2n + 1)$-dimensional space $\mathcal{V} = \mathcal{T}_n$ of trigonometric polynomials of degree at most n and for evaluations at equispaced points $\theta_1,\ldots,\theta_m$ on $\mathbb{T}$, the

---

[1] See DeVore et al. (2019) for the necessary details.

supremum appearing in (10.19) is well understood. For instance, one has

$$\mu_{T_n,\mathrm{Id}}(\Lambda_\theta) \asymp \ln(m) \qquad \text{when } 2n + 1 = m,$$
$$\mu_{T_n,\mathrm{Id}}(\Lambda_\theta) \asymp 1 \qquad \text{when } n \le c\,m,$$

which is in accordance with the general fact that $\mu_{\mathcal{V},Q}(\Lambda)$ increases when the space $\mathcal{V}$ is enlarged. Since $\mathcal{V}$ can be chosen by the user, this increase is to be balanced with a decrease of the approximation parameter ε in order to make the intrinsic error $\mathrm{Err}^*_{\mathcal{K},Q}(\Lambda)$ small.

Exercises

10.1 Observe that the condition (10.2) forbids overparametrization, i.e., that it forces $\dim(\mathcal{V}) \le m$. Verify also the identity (10.4) expressing the null error as a product of the compatibility indicator and the approximability parameter.

10.2 Given a linear subspace $\mathcal{V}$ of a Hilbert space H, extend Theorem 10.2 to the model set

$$\mathcal{K} = \{f \in F : \mathrm{dist}(Tf, \mathcal{V}) \le \varepsilon\}$$

relative to a linear map T taking values in H.

10.3 Given two subspaces $\mathcal{Y}$ and $\mathcal{Z}$ of a Hilbert space, prove that

$$\sup_{y \in \mathcal{Y}} \frac{\|y\|^2}{\|P_{\mathcal{Z}^\perp}(y)\|^2} = \left[\inf_{z \in \mathcal{Z}} \frac{\|P_{\mathcal{Y}^\perp}(z)\|^2}{\|z\|^2} \right]^{-1}.$$

10.4 Determine the optimal recovery map from Theorem 10.5 when F is a reproducing kernel Hilbert space, the observations are point evaluations, and the quantity of interest is an integral.

10.5 In case the observation functionals are evaluations at m equispaced points $\theta_1, \ldots, \theta_m \in \mathbb{T}$, show that $\mu_{T_n,\mathrm{Id}}(\Lambda_\theta) \le C$ when $n \le c\,m$ with constants $c, C > 0$ to be determined. The *Bernstein inequality* will be useful here: proved in Exercise E.4, it states that $\|p'\|_{C(\mathbb{T})} \le n\|p\|_{C(\mathbb{T})}$ for all $p \in \mathcal{T}_n$.

11

Ideal Selection of Observation Schemes

In the previous two chapters, the functionals $\lambda_1, \ldots, \lambda_m \in F^*$ associated with the observation map Λ were considered fixed entities. The objective consisted in determining the intrinsic error $\mathrm{Err}^*_{\mathcal{K},Q}(\Lambda)$ and uncovering optimal recovery maps that are efficiently computable. In this chapter, it is now assumed that the user is free to select suitable observation functionals $\lambda_1, \ldots, \lambda_m \in F^*$. Can one then determine a way to do so optimally? Put differently, one aims at achieving the infimum in

$$\mathrm{Err}^*_{\mathcal{K},Q}(m) := \inf \{ \mathrm{Err}^*_{\mathcal{K},Q}(\Lambda), \Lambda \text{ is a linear map from } F \text{ to } \mathbb{R}^m \}.$$

Two cases where the answer is affirmative are highlighted below, namely the Hilbert setting and the integration of Lipschitz functions, the latter prompting an aside on adaptive observations.

11.1 Hilbert Setting

In a Hilbert space H, when one is interested in the full approximation problem over an ellipsoidal model set, an optimal observation scheme can be made explicit. Such a situation is covered by the case $F = Z$ and $Q = \mathrm{Id}$ of the statement below.

Theorem 11.1 *Let $Q: F \to Z$ be a linear quantity of interest taking values in a Hilbert space Z. If the model set $\mathcal{K}$ is the preimage by an isomorphism $T: F \to H$ of the unit ball of a Hilbert space H, i.e., $\mathcal{K} = T^{-1}(B_H) \subseteq F$, then the mth minimal intrinsic error for the evaluation of Q over $\mathcal{K}$ is the $(m + 1)$st largest singular value of QT^{-1}. In other words,*

$$\mathrm{Err}^*_{\mathcal{K},Q}(m) = \sigma_{m+1}(QT^{-1}). \tag{11.1}$$

Moreover, with $(v_1, \ldots, v_m)$ *denoting the leading m right singular vectors of* QT^{-1}, *the linear functionals* $\lambda_1 = \langle v_1, T(\cdot) \rangle, \ldots, \lambda_m = \langle v_m, T(\cdot) \rangle$ *give rise to an optimal observation map* Λ.

Proof Given $\Lambda: F \to \mathbb{R}^m$, invoking Theorem 9.4 and the definition (9.2) of the null error, one has

$$\mathrm{Err}^*_{\mathcal{K},Q}(\Lambda)^2 = \mathrm{Err}^0_{\mathcal{K},Q}(\Lambda)^2 = \sup_{\substack{f \in \ker(\Lambda) \\ \|T(f)\| \leq 1}} \|Q(f)\|^2 = \sup_{\substack{v \in \ker(\Lambda T^{-1}) \\ \|v\| \leq 1}} \|(QT^{-1})(v)\|^2$$

$$= \sup_{\substack{v \in \ker(\Lambda T^{-1}) \\ \|v\| \leq 1}} \langle Q_T^* Q_T v, v \rangle,$$

where Q_T stands for QT^{-1}. According to an infinite-dimensional analog of the *Courant–Fischer theorem*, whose finite-dimensional version is given in (D.1), the above quantity minimized over all linear maps $\Lambda: F \to \mathbb{R}^m$ is the $(m + 1)$st largest eigenvalue of the positive semidefinite operator $Q_T^* Q_T: H \to H$. Since this is the square of the $(m + 1)$st largest singular values of $Q_T: H \to Z$, the result (11.1) is acquired if one is willing to take the required minimax characterization of eigenvalues for granted.

If not, an unfolded argument is rather straightforward. Let $(v_1, v_2, \ldots, v_n, \ldots)$ denote an orthonormal basis for H which consists of eigenvectors of $Q_T^* Q_T$ corresponding to eigenvalues $\mu_1 \geq \mu_2 \geq \cdots \geq \mu_n \geq \cdots \geq 0$. Because the $(m + 1)$-dimensional space span$\{v_1, \ldots, v_{m+1}\}$ has a nontrivial intersection with the m-codimensional space $\ker(\Lambda T^{-1})$, one can consider a normalized element $v \in \ker(\Lambda T^{-1}) \cap \mathrm{span}\{v_1, \ldots, v_{m+1}\}$. Writing it as $v = c_1 v_1 + \cdots + c_{m+1} v_{m+1}$ and observing that $\|v\|^2 = 1$ enforces $c_1^2 + \cdots + c_{m+1}^2 = 1$, one derives that

$$\langle Q_T^* Q_T v, v \rangle = \left\langle \sum_{i=1}^{m+1} c_i Q_T^* Q_T(v_i), \sum_{i=1}^{m+1} c_i v_i \right\rangle = \left\langle \sum_{i=1}^{m+1} c_i \mu_i v_i, \sum_{i=1}^{m+1} c_i v_i \right\rangle = \sum_{i=1}^{m+1} c_i^2 \mu_i$$

$$\geq \mu_{m+1} \sum_{i=1}^{m+1} c_i^2 = \mu_{m+1}.$$

Based on the relation between eigenvalues of $Q_T^* Q_T$ and singular values of Q_T, this establishes the inequality $\mathrm{Err}^*_{\mathcal{K},Q}(\Lambda)^2 \geq \sigma_{m+1}(Q_T)^2$ for all observation maps $\Lambda: F \to \mathbb{R}^m$. To see how this inequality can be turned into an equality with an appropriate choice of Λ, observe in particular that one needs the ability to select $v_{m+1} \in \ker(\Lambda T^{-1})$. This can be done by taking $\lambda_i = \langle v_i, T(\cdot) \rangle$ for $i \in [1:m]$, since then $\lambda_i(T^{-1} v_{m+1}) = \langle v_i, T(T^{-1} v_{m+1}) \rangle = \langle v_i, v_{m+1} \rangle = 0$. In this case, for any $v \in \ker(\Lambda T^{-1}) = \mathrm{span}\{v_{m+1}, \ldots, v_n, \ldots\}$ with $\|v\| \leq 1$, one easily verifies that $\langle Q_T^* Q_T v, v \rangle \leq \mu_{m+1}$. The conclusion follows. $\square$

11.2 Integration of Lipschitz Functions

The intrinsic error can also be minimized explicitly for a specific real-valued linear quantity of interest, namely the integral. In this context, it should first be pointed out that some restrictions are necessary concerning the type of realistic observations. Indeed, without such restrictions, one could select the integral as one of the observation functionals, leading to an intrinsic error trivially equal to zero. Therefore, only point evaluations of the form $\lambda_i(f) = f(x^{(i)})$ are permitted in the integration problem considered below. The result is actually more powerful than expected, as it even minimizes over adaptive observations. An observation scheme is called *adaptive* when the choice of an observation functional depends on the results of previous observations, namely when

$$\lambda_i = \lambda_{i;(\lambda_1,y_1),\dots,(\lambda_{i-1},y_{i-1})}, \qquad i \geq 2. \tag{11.2}$$

A more formal discussion on adaptivity vs. nonadaptivity is deferred after the statement and proof of the main result about integration of *Lipschitz functions*.

Theorem 11.2 *Let* $F = C([0,1]^d)$ *be the space of continuous functions defined on* $[0,1]^d$ *and let* $\mathcal{K}_{\mathrm{Lip}} \subseteq F$ *be the model set consisting of functions with* Lipschitz *seminorm at most one, i.e.,*

$$\mathcal{K}_{\mathrm{Lip}} := \left\{ f \in F : |f|_{\mathrm{Lip}} := \sup_{x \neq x' \in [0,1]^d} \frac{|f(x) - f(x')|}{\|x - x'\|_\infty} \leq 1 \right\}.$$

If the quantity of interest is the linear functional Int *giving the integral, i.e.,* $\mathrm{Int}(f) = \int_{[0,1]^d} f$, *then, whenever* $m = n^d$ *for some integer n, one has*

$$\inf \left\{ \mathrm{Err}^*_{\mathcal{K}_{\mathrm{Lip}},\mathrm{Int}}(\Lambda_x), \; x^{(1)}, \dots, x^{(m)} \in [0,1]^d \right\} = \frac{d}{2d+2} \left(\frac{1}{m} \right)^{1/d}, \tag{11.3}$$

while the lower estimate $\mathrm{Err}^*_{\mathcal{K}_{\mathrm{Lip}},\mathrm{Int}}(\Lambda_x) \geq (d/(2d+2))m^{-1/d}$ *remains valid without condition on m and even for adaptive choices of* $x^{(1)}, \dots, x^{(m)}$.

Proof Assume first that $m = n^d$ and that $\Lambda_x \colon F \to \mathbb{R}^{n \times \cdots \times n}$ is the evaluation map on the *d*-fold tensor product of a regular one-dimensional *n*-point grid (see Figure 11.1 for an illustration), i.e.,

$$\Lambda_x(f) = \left[f\left(\frac{i_1 - 1/2}{n}, \dots, \frac{i_d - 1/2}{n} \right); \; i_1, \dots, i_d \in [1:n] \right].$$

Consider also the recovery map $\Delta \colon \mathbb{R}^{n \times \cdots \times n} \to \mathbb{R}$ outputting the average of an

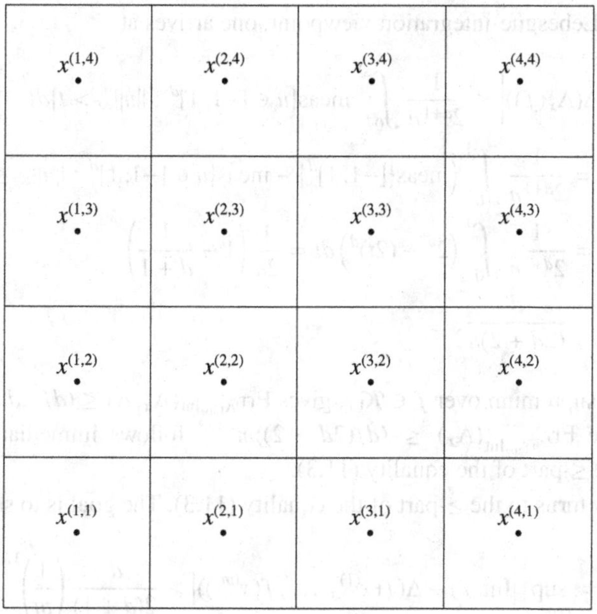

Figure 11.1 The n^d evaluation points $x^{(i)} = [(i_1 - 1/2)/n, \ldots, (i_d - 1/2)/n]$ used for the proof of the $\leq$-part of (11.3) when $d = 2$ and $n = 4$.

input vector $y \in \mathbb{R}^{n \times \cdots \times n}$. For any function $f \in F$ with $|f|_{\mathrm{Lip}} \leq 1$, one has

$$\left| \mathrm{Int}(f) - \Delta(\Lambda_x(f)) \right| = \left| \sum_{i_1,\ldots,i_d=1}^{n} \int_{\prod_{j=1}^{d}\left[\frac{i_j-1}{n}, \frac{i_j}{n}\right]} \left(f(x) - f\left(\frac{i_1 - 1/2}{n}, \ldots, \frac{i_d - 1/2}{n}\right) \right) dx \right|$$

$$\leq \sum_{i_1,\ldots,i_d=1}^{n} \int_{\prod_{j=1}^{d}\left[\frac{i_j-1}{n}, \frac{i_j}{n}\right]} \left| f(x) - f\left(\frac{i_1 - 1/2}{n}, \ldots, \frac{i_d - 1/2}{n}\right) \right| dx$$

$$\leq \sum_{i_1,\ldots,i_d=1}^{n} \int_{\prod_{j=1}^{d}\left[\frac{i_j-1}{n}, \frac{i_j}{n}\right]} \left\| x - \left(\frac{i_1 - 1/2}{n}, \ldots, \frac{i_d - 1/2}{n}\right) \right\|_{\infty} dx$$

$$= \sum_{i_1,\ldots,i_d=1}^{n} \int_{[-1,1]^d} \frac{\|u\|_{\infty}}{(2n)^{d+1}} du$$

$$= \frac{1}{2^{d+1}n} \int_{[-1,1]^d} \|u\|_{\infty} du,$$

where changes of variables were performed in the second-to-last step. Next, adopting a Lebesgue-integration viewpoint, one arrives at

$$\left|\text{Int}(f) - \Delta(\Lambda_x(f))\right| \leq \frac{1}{2^{d+1}n} \int_0^\infty \text{meas}\{u \in [-1,1]^d : \|u\|_\infty > t\}dt$$

$$= \frac{1}{2^{d+1}n} \int_0^1 \left(\text{meas}\{[-1,1]^d\} - \text{meas}\{u \in [-1,1]^d : \|u\|_\infty \leq t\}\right)dt$$

$$= \frac{1}{2^{d+1}n} \int_0^1 \left(2^d - (2t)^d\right)dt = \frac{1}{2n}\left(1 - \frac{1}{d+1}\right)$$

$$= \frac{d}{(2d+2)n}.$$

Taking the supremum over $f \in \mathcal{K}_{\text{Lip}}$ gives $\text{Err}_{\mathcal{K}_{\text{Lip}}, \text{Int}}(\Lambda_x, \Delta) \leq (d/(2d+2))n^{-1}$, from where $\text{Err}^*_{\mathcal{K}_{\text{Lip}}, \text{Int}}(\Lambda_x) \leq (d/(2d+2))m^{-1/d}$ follows immediately. This justifies the $\leq$-part of the equality (11.3).

One now turns to the $\geq$-part of the equality (11.3). The goal is to show that

$$e := \sup_{f \in \mathcal{K}_{\text{Lip}}} \left|\text{Int}(f) - \Delta(f(x^{(1)}), \dots, f(x^{(m)}))\right| \geq \frac{d}{2(d+1)}\left(\frac{1}{m}\right)^{1/d}$$

for any recovery map $\Delta: \mathbb{R}^m \to \mathbb{R}$ and evaluation points $x^{(1)}, \dots, x^{(m)} \in [0,1]^d$, which can possibly be chosen adaptively. So let $x^{(1)} \in [0,1]^d$ be arbitrary and let $x^{(2)}, \dots, x^{(m)} \in [0,1]^d$ be subsequently generated by the adaptive process resulting from the observation of the zero function. These are also the points generated when observing $\pm f$, where the function f is defined by

$$f(x) = \text{dist}_{\ell_\infty}(x, \{x^{(1)}, \dots, x^{(m)}\}), \qquad x \in [0,1]^d.$$

Since both f and $-f$ belong to $\mathcal{K}_{\text{Lip}}$, one has

$$e \geq \frac{1}{2}\left|\text{Int}(f) - \Delta(0, \dots, 0)\right| + \frac{1}{2}\left|\text{Int}(-f) - \Delta(0, \dots, 0)\right|$$

$$\geq \frac{1}{2}\left|(\text{Int}(f) - \Delta(0, \dots, 0)) - (\text{Int}(-f) - \Delta(0, \dots, 0))\right|$$

$$= \left|\text{Int}(f)\right|.$$

It is therefore enough to prove that

$$\widetilde{e} := \int_{[0,1]^d} \text{dist}_{\ell_\infty}(x, \{x^{(1)}, \dots, x^{(m)}\})dx \geq \frac{d}{2(d+1)}\left(\frac{1}{m}\right)^{1/d}. \tag{11.4}$$

To see this, one again adopts a Lebesgue-integration viewpoint and performs the following calculations involving a parameter $u > 0$ determined at the end:

$$\widetilde{e} = \int_0^\infty \text{meas}\{x \in [0,1]^d : \text{dist}_\infty(x, \{x^{(1)}, \ldots, x^{(m)}\}) > t\}dt$$

$$\geq \int_0^u \left(\text{meas}\{[0,1]^d\} - \text{meas}\left\{ \cup_{i=1}^m \{x \in [0,1]^d : \|x - x^{(i)}\|_\infty \leq t\}\right\}\right)dt$$

$$\geq \int_0^u \left(1 - m(2t)^d\right)dt = u - m2^d \frac{u^{d+1}}{d+1}.$$

The latter is maximized when $u = 1/(2m^{1/d})$, which leads to the lower bound announced in (11.4). □

11.3 Adaptivity Does Not Help Much

The phenomenon highlighted by Theorem 11.2 is rather surprising because adaptive schemes intuitively seem more powerful than nonadaptive schemes. This phenomenon is not restricted to the integration of Lipschitz functions. Indeed, the following result, shown using arguments similar to the ones found at the end of the previous proof, establishes that the adaptive and nonadaptive settings often yield comparable worst-case errors.

Theorem 11.3 *Let $Q: F \to Z$ be a linear quantity of interest. If the model set $\mathcal{K}$ is symmetric and convex, then the mth minimial adaptive and nonadaptive intrinsic errors, as defined by*

$$\text{Err}_{\mathcal{K},Q}^{*,\text{(non)ada}}(m) := \inf\{\text{Err}_{\mathcal{K},Q}^*(\Lambda), \Lambda: F \to \mathbb{R}^m \text{ (non)adaptive linear map}\},$$

are essentially the same, in the sense that

$$\text{Err}_{\mathcal{K},Q}^{*,\text{ada}}(m) \leq \text{Err}_{\mathcal{K},Q}^{*,\text{nonada}}(m) \leq 2\,\text{Err}_{\mathcal{K},Q}^{*,\text{ada}}(m).$$

Proof The leftmost inequality simply translates the fact that any nonadaptive observation scheme can also be interpreted as an adaptive scheme. To prove the rightmost inequality, consider an adaptive observation map Λ associated with $\lambda_1, \ldots, \lambda_m \in F^*$ generated according to (11.2). One then defines nonadaptive linear functionals $\widetilde{\lambda}_1, \ldots, \widetilde{\lambda}_m \in F^*$ by $\widetilde{\lambda}_1 = \lambda_1$ and

$$\widetilde{\lambda}_i = \lambda_{i;(\widetilde{\lambda}_1,0),\ldots,(\widetilde{\lambda}_{i-1},0)}, \qquad i \in [2:m].$$

For $f \in \mathcal{K} \cap \ker(\widetilde{\Lambda})$, the adaptive observations made on $\pm f \in \mathcal{K}$ are all zero, and hence, for any recovery map $\Delta: \mathbb{R}^m \to Z$,

$$\text{Err}_{\mathcal{K},Q}(\Lambda, \Delta) \geq \frac{1}{2}\|Q(f) - \Delta(0,\ldots,0)\| + \frac{1}{2}\|Q(-f) - \Delta(0,\ldots,0)\| \geq \|Q(f)\|.$$

By taking the supremun over $f \in \mathcal{K} \cap \ker(\widetilde{\Lambda})$, the definition of the null error yields

$$\mathrm{Err}^*_{\mathcal{K},Q}(\Lambda, \Delta) \geq \mathrm{Err}^0_{\mathcal{K},Q}(\widetilde{\Lambda}) \geq \frac{1}{2}\mathrm{Err}^*_{\mathcal{K},Q}(\widetilde{\Lambda}),$$

where the last inequality was established in Proposition 9.1. Next, taking the infimum over Δ leads to $\mathrm{Err}^*_{\mathcal{K},Q}(\Lambda) \geq (1/2)\,\mathrm{Err}^*_{\mathcal{K},Q}(\widetilde{\Lambda}) \geq (1/2)\mathrm{Err}^{*,\mathrm{nonada}}_{\mathcal{K},Q}(m)$. Finally, by taking the infimum over the adaptive map Λ, one concludes that $\mathrm{Err}^{*,\mathrm{ada}}_{\mathcal{K},Q}(m) \geq (1/2)\mathrm{Err}^{*,\mathrm{nonada}}_{\mathcal{K},Q}(m)$, as required.   □

It is worth pointing out, as would be revealed by a careful examination of the above proof, that the minimal adaptive and nonadaptive intrinsic errors $\mathrm{Err}^{*,\mathrm{ada}}_{\mathcal{K},Q}(m)$ and $\mathrm{Err}^{*,\mathrm{nonada}}_{\mathcal{K},Q}(m)$ are actually equal to one another as soon as the intrinsic and null errors $\mathrm{Err}^*_{\mathcal{K},Q}(\Lambda)$ and $\mathrm{Err}^0_{\mathcal{K},Q}(\Lambda)$ coincide for any observation map $\Lambda \colon F \to \mathbb{R}^m$. As a reminder from Chapter 9, this is known to occur in at least two important situations, namely when Q is a linear functional and when $\mathcal{K}$ is an ellipsoidal subset of a Hilbert space.

Exercises

11.1 Prove that an optimal observation map $\Lambda \colon F \to \mathbb{R}^m$ is not unique. Start by noticing that $\Gamma \circ \Lambda \colon F \to \mathbb{R}^m$ is also an optimal observation map whenever the linear map $\Gamma \colon \mathbb{R}^m \to \mathbb{R}^m$ is invertible. Continue by showing that in general $\mathrm{ran}(\Lambda^*) = \mathrm{span}\{\lambda_1, \ldots, \lambda_m\}$ is not unique either.

11.2 Let $(\phi_n)_{n\geq 1}$ be an orthonormal basis for a Hilbert space H. Given a non-increasing sequence $(\gamma_n)_{n\geq 1}$ of positive numbers, one considers a model set $\mathcal{K}$ defined by

$$\mathcal{K} := \left\{ f \in H : \sum_{n=1}^{\infty} \frac{1}{\gamma_n^2}\langle \phi_n, f \rangle^2 \leq 1 \right\}.$$

For the full approximation problem, prove that the mth minimal intrinsic error over $\mathcal{K}$ is just $\mathrm{Err}^*_{\mathcal{K},\mathrm{Id}}(m) = \gamma_{m+1}$ and find an optimal observation map.

11.3 Given weights $\gamma_1 \geq \gamma_2 \geq \cdots \geq \gamma_d = 1$, extend Theorem 11.2 to the model set

$$\mathcal{K} := \left\{ f \in C([0,1]^d) : \sup_{x \neq x' \in [0,1]^d} \frac{|f(x) - f(x')|}{\max_{j \in [1:d]} \gamma_j |x_j - x'_j|} \leq 1 \right\}$$

by establishing that $\mathrm{Err}^*_{\mathcal{K},\mathrm{Int}}(\Lambda_x) \geq (\gamma_1 \gamma_2 \cdots \gamma_d)^{1/d}(d/(2d+2))m^{-1/d}$ for any $x^{(1)}, \ldots, x^{(m)} \in [0,1]^d$, with equality possible when $\gamma_1, \gamma_2, \ldots, \gamma_d$ are integers and when $m = \gamma_1 \gamma_2 \cdots \gamma_d n^d$ for some integer $n \geq 1$.

11.4 When $\mathcal{K}$ is a symmetric and convex model set in a Hilbert space H, observe that the mth minimal intrinsic error for the full approximation problem over $\mathcal{K}$ coincides with the mth *Gelfand width* of $\mathcal{K}$ relative to H, as defined by

$$d^m(\mathcal{K}, H) := \inf_{\text{codim}(\mathcal{U}) \leq m} \sup_{f \in \mathcal{K} \cap \mathcal{U}} \|f\|_H.$$

In addition, when F is the space H but endowed with a different norm and when $\mathcal{K}$ is the unit ball of the dual space F^*, prove that the mth minimal intrinsic error also coincides with the mth *Kolmogorov width* of the unit ball of H relative to F, as defined by

$$d_m(B_H, F) := \inf_{\dim(\mathcal{V}) \leq m} \sup_{f \in B_H} \inf_{v \in \mathcal{V}} \|f - v\|_F.$$

For the latter, it is useful to remark that $v \in \mathcal{V}$ is a best approximant to f from $\mathcal{V}$ for the norm on F if and only if $\|f - v\|_F = \lambda(f)$ for some linear functional $\lambda \in F^*$ satisfying $\|\lambda\|_F^* \leq 1$ and $\lambda_{|\mathcal{V}} = 0$.

12

Curse of Dimensionality

The previous chapter provided an example of a model set $\mathcal{K} \subseteq F$ together with a quantity of interest Q—the set of d-variate Lipschitz functions with $|f|_{\text{Lip}} \leq 1$ together with the integral—for which the decay of the minimal intrinsic error for the evaluation of Q over $\mathcal{K}$ could be precisely evaluated as the number m of observations increases. From a different perspective, reminiscent of the sample complexity encountered in Chapter 1, this precise determination also indicates how large m should be to enable the approximation of $Q(f)$ with a prescribed accuracy $\varepsilon > 0$ for all $f \in \mathcal{K}$. Thus, one defines the *information complexity* of the problem defined by $\mathcal{K}$ and Q as

$$m_{\mathcal{K},Q}(\varepsilon, d) := \min \{m \in \mathbb{N}^* : \text{Err}^*_{\mathcal{K},Q}(m) \leq \varepsilon\}. \tag{12.1}$$

The field of *information-based complexity* examines specifically the behavior of $m_{\mathcal{K},Q}(\varepsilon, d)$ with the number d of variables of the underlying functions. After formally defining some notions associated with the curse of dimensionality, two examples are carefully analyzed: one where the curse strikes (integration of trigonometric polynomials) and one where it can be avoided (integration in weighted Sobolev spaces).

12.1 Notions of Tractability

The typical behaviors of the information complexity (12.1) are characterized through their level of tractability, as elucidated below.

Definition 12.1 A problem determined by a model set $\mathcal{K}$ and a quantity of interest Q (and possibly the type of permitted observations) is said to be:
- *intractable* if $m_{\mathcal{K},Q}(\varepsilon, d)$ depends exponentially on ε^{-1} or d;
- *tractable* if $m_{\mathcal{K},Q}(\varepsilon, d) \leq C\varepsilon^{-\alpha} d^{\beta}$ for some positive constants C, α, β;
- *strongly tractable* if $m_{\mathcal{K},Q}(\varepsilon, d) \leq C\varepsilon^{-\alpha}$ for some positive constants C, α.

The *curse of dimensionality* occurs when the problem is intractable, more precisely when the exponential dependence of $m_{K,Q}(\varepsilon, d)$ is on d, not on ε^{-1}. The integration of Lipschitz functions, for instance, suffers from the curse of dimensionality if *standard observations* (i.e., point evaluations) are used. Indeed, it was established in Theorem 11.2 that

$$\inf \left\{ \mathrm{Err}^*_{K_{\mathrm{Lip}},\mathrm{Int}}(\Lambda_x),\ x^{(1)}, \ldots, x^{(m)} \in [0, 1]^d \right\} = \frac{d}{2(d+1)} \left(\frac{1}{m} \right)^{1/d}.$$

This is seen to be less than or equal to $\varepsilon > 0$ as soon as $2^d (1 + 1/d)^d m \geq \varepsilon^{-d}$, so that

$$m^{\mathrm{standard}}_{K_{\mathrm{Lip}},\mathrm{Int}}(\varepsilon, d) = \left\lceil \frac{1}{2^d (1 + 1/d)^d} \varepsilon^{-d} \right\rceil \underset{d \to \infty}{\sim} \frac{1}{2^d e} \varepsilon^{-d}.$$

The fact that the information complexity grows exponentially in d means that the curse of dimensionality prevails. It also prevails for the L_∞-approximation of Lipschitz functions using standard observations, since the ability to perform L_∞-approximation with accuracy $\varepsilon > 0$ automatically implies the ability to perform integration with accuracy $\varepsilon > 0$.

Two further instances of integration problems will be examined next in connection with the curse of dimensionality. They both involve some standard calculations in reproducing kernel Hilbert spaces, which are isolated below.

Lemma 12.2 *Let H be a reproducing kernel Hilbert space over a set X and let K be its kernel. For the integration problem that uses an observation map $\Lambda_x \colon H \to \mathbb{R}^m$ associated with evaluation points $x^{(1)}, \ldots, x^{(m)} \in X$, a recovery map $\Delta \colon y \in \mathbb{R}^m \mapsto \sum_{i=1}^m c_i y_i \in \mathbb{R}$ has worst-case error over the unit ball of H given by*

$$\mathrm{Err}_{B_H,\mathrm{Int}}(\Lambda_x, \Delta)^2 = \left\| h_{\mathrm{Int}} \right\|^2 - 2 \sum_{i=1}^m c_i h_{\mathrm{Int}}(x^{(i)}) + \sum_{i,j=1}^m c_i c_j K(x^{(i)}, x^{(j)}),$$

where $h_{\mathrm{Int}} \in H$ denotes the Riesz representer *of the integration functional.*

Proof The integration error of a single function $f \in B_H$ is the absolute value of

$$\int_X f - \sum_{i=1}^m c_i f(x^{(i)}) = \langle h_{\mathrm{Int}}, f \rangle - \sum_{i=1}^m c_i \langle K(\cdot, x^{(i)}), f \rangle = \left\langle h_{\mathrm{Int}} - \sum_{i=1}^m c_i K(\cdot, x^{(i)}), f \right\rangle.$$

Thus, the worst-case error $e := \mathrm{Err}_{B_H,\mathrm{Int}}(\Lambda_x, \Delta)$ of Δ over B_H becomes

$$e = \sup_{\|f\| \leq 1} \left| \left\langle h_{\mathrm{Int}} - \sum_{i=1}^m c_i K(\cdot, x^{(i)}), f \right\rangle \right| = \left\| h_{\mathrm{Int}} - \sum_{i=1}^m c_i K(\cdot, x^{(i)}) \right\|.$$

Taking the squares and expanding the right-hand side leads to

$$e^2 = \|h_{\text{Int}}\|^2 - 2 \sum_{i=1}^{m} c_i \langle K(\cdot, x^{(i)}), h_{\text{Int}} \rangle + \sum_{i,j=1}^{m} c_i c_j \langle K(\cdot, x^{(i)}), K(\cdot, x^{(j)}) \rangle$$

$$= \|h_{\text{Int}}\|^2 - 2 \sum_{i=1}^{m} c_i h_{\text{Int}}(x^{(i)}) + \sum_{i,j=1}^{m} c_i c_j K(x^{(i)}, x^{(j)}),$$

which is the announced result.   □

12.2 Integration of Trigonometric Polynomials

In comparison with the integration of Lipschitz functions discussed earlier, the manifestation of the curse of dimensionality discussed here is more surprising, because the space $H \subseteq F([0,1]^d, \mathbb{R})$ of d-variate functions under consideration has a finite dimension. It is taken to be the space

$$H = \text{span}\{f_1 \otimes f_2 \otimes \cdots \otimes f_d, \ f_1, \ldots, f_d \in \{1, \cos(2\pi \cdot), \sin(2\pi \cdot)\}\} \quad (12.2)$$

spanned by d-fold tensor products of degree-1 trigonometric polynomials. It is endowed with a Hilbert structure by defining an inner product through

$$\langle f_1 \otimes \cdots \otimes f_d, g_1 \otimes \cdots \otimes g_d \rangle_H = \langle f_1, g_1 \rangle \cdots \langle f_d, g_d \rangle,$$

where $\langle \cdot, \cdot \rangle$ is the inner product on $\text{span}\{1, \cos(2\pi \cdot), \sin(2\pi \cdot)\}$ making the system $(1, \cos(2\pi \cdot), \sin(2\pi \cdot))$ orthonormal. In fact, one can check (the verification is left to the reader as Exercise 12.3) that H is a reproducing kernel Hilbert space with kernel given, for $x, x' \in [0,1]^d$, by

$$K(x, x') = \prod_{k=1}^{d} \left[1 + \cos(2\pi(x_k - x_k')) \right] = 2^d \prod_{k=1}^{d} \cos^2(\pi(x_k - x_k')). \quad (12.3)$$

The curse of dimensionality is materialized by the exponential dependence on d of the information complexity, as established below.

Theorem 12.3 *The integration problem over the unit ball of the space* (12.2) *is intractable using standard observations, since the information complexity satisfies*

$$m_{B_H, \text{Int}}^{\text{standard}}(\varepsilon, d) \geq (1 - \varepsilon^2) 2^d.$$

Proof By linearity of an optimal recovery map (Theorem 9.3), the conclusion will be acquired as soon as one proves that

$$\inf_{x^{(1)}, \ldots, x^{(m)} \in [0,1]^d} \ \inf_{\Delta = \langle c, \cdot \rangle} \text{Err}_{B_H, \text{Int}}(\Lambda_x, \Delta)^2 \begin{cases} = 0 & \text{if } m \geq 2^d, \\ \geq 1 - m2^{-d} & \text{if } m \leq 2^d. \end{cases} \quad (12.4)$$

Indeed, when $m < (1 - \varepsilon^2)2^d$, according to the second case in (12.4), the squared worst-case error cannot be smaller than $1 - m2^{-d} > 1 - (1 - \varepsilon^2) = \varepsilon^2$. To justify (12.4), one starts by invoking Lemma 12.2 while observing that the Riesz representer of the integration functional is $h_{\text{Int}} = 1$ to arrive at

$$e_{x,c}^2 := \text{Err}_{B_H,\text{Int}}(\Lambda_x, \Delta)^2 = 1 - 2 \sum_{i=1}^m c_i + \sum_{i,j=1}^m c_i c_j K(x^{(i)}, x^{(j)})$$

for any observation map Λ_x associated with points $x^{(1)}, \ldots, x^{(m)} \in [0,1]^d$ and recovery map $\Delta = \langle c, \cdot \rangle$ featuring coefficients $c_1, \ldots, c_m$. One claims that it is enough to establish the lower bound

$$\sum_{i,j=1}^m c_i c_j K(x^{(i)}, x^{(j)}) \geq \frac{2^d}{m} \left(\sum_{i=1}^m c_i \right)^2. \tag{12.5}$$

Indeed, setting $\gamma := \sum_{i=1}^m c_i$, it will follow that

$$e_{x,c}^2 \geq 1 - 2\gamma + \frac{2^d}{m} \gamma^2 = 1 - \frac{m}{2^d} + \frac{2^d}{m} \left(\gamma - \frac{m}{2^d} \right)^2 \geq 1 - \frac{m}{2^d}.$$

This is meaningful only when $m \leq 2^d$. When $m \geq 2^d$, one can actually obtain $e_{x,c}^2 = 0$ by taking $\{x^{(1)}, \ldots, x^{(2^d)}\} = \{0, 1/2\}^d$, $c_1 = \cdots = c_{2^d} = 2^{-d}$, and $c_{2^d+1} = \cdots = c_m = 0$. Altogether, this will prove the required estimate (12.4).

At this point, it remains to justify the inequality (12.5). To this end, one introduces a kernel $\widetilde{K}$ satisfying $\widetilde{K}^2 = K$, namely

$$\widetilde{K}(x, x') = 2^{d/2} \prod_{k=1}^d \cos(\pi(x_k - x_k')), \qquad x, x' \in [0,1]^d.$$

This kernel $\widetilde{K}$ is positive semidefinite because each $\cos(\pi(x_k - x_k'))$ defines a positive semidefinite kernel on $[0,1]$ (see Exercise 5.1) and because the tensor product of positive semidefinite kernels is a positive semidefinite kernel (see Exercise 5.2). As such, the matrix $A \in \mathbb{R}^{m \times m}$ with entries $A_{i,j} = \widetilde{K}(x^{(i)}, x^{(j)})$ is positive semidefinite, and hence it can be written as $A = BB^\top$ for some $B \in \mathbb{R}^{m \times m}$. From here, one writes

$$\sum_{i,j=1}^m c_i c_j K(x^{(i)}, x^{(j)}) = \sum_{i,j=1}^m c_i c_j (A_{i,j})^2 = \sum_{i,j=1}^m c_i c_j \left(\sum_{\ell=1}^m B_{i,\ell} B_{j,\ell} \right)^2$$

$$= \sum_{i,j=1}^m c_i c_j \sum_{\ell,\ell'=1}^m B_{i,\ell} B_{j,\ell} B_{i,\ell'} B_{j,\ell'} = \sum_{\ell,\ell'=1}^m \sum_{i,j=1}^m c_i B_{i,\ell} B_{i,\ell'} c_j B_{j,\ell} B_{j,\ell'}$$

$$= \sum_{\ell,\ell'=1}^m \left(\sum_{i=1}^m c_i B_{i,\ell} B_{i,\ell'} \right)^2 \geq \sum_{\ell=1}^m \left(\sum_{i=1}^m c_i B_{i,\ell}^2 \right)^2,$$

where one simply discarded the terms indexed by $\ell \neq \ell'$ in the last inequality. Then, using the usual comparison between the ℓ_1-norm and the ℓ_2-norm on $\mathbb{R}^m$, namely $\|v\|_1^2 \leq m\|v\|_2^2$ for $v \in \mathbb{R}^m$, it follows that

$$\sum_{i,j=1}^{m} c_i c_j K(x^{(i)}, x^{(j)}) \geq \frac{1}{m}\left(\sum_{\ell=1}^{m}\sum_{i=1}^{m} c_i B_{i,\ell}^2\right)^2 = \frac{1}{m}\left(\sum_{i=1}^{m} c_i \sum_{\ell=1}^{m} B_{i,\ell}^2\right)^2$$

$$= \frac{1}{m}\left(\sum_{i=1}^{m} c_i A_{i,i}\right)^2 = \frac{1}{m}\left(\sum_{i=1}^{m} c_i \widetilde{K}(x^{(i)}, x^{(i)})\right)^2 = \frac{2^d}{m}\left(\sum_{i=1}^{m} c_i\right)^2.$$

The required lower bound (12.5) has been obtained. $\qquad\square$

Remark 12.4   As Exercise 12.2 demonstrates, the rate at which the minimal intrinsic error decays with the number m of observations is tied to tractability, but it does not tell the whole story. The previous proof provides a rather striking illustration: despite a decay rate (12.4) as good as one can hope for, the problem is intractable because this ideal rate kicks in only when m exceeds a threshold which is exponential in d.

12.3 Integration in Weighted Sobolev Spaces

To finish on an optimistic note, one now highlights a situation where the curse of dimensionality can be bypassed. This feat is made possible by attributing more influence to some variables than to others, which is done by introducing weights $\gamma_1 \geq \gamma_2 \geq \cdots \geq \gamma_d > 0$. Precisely, one considers the *Sobolev space* $H = W_2^{(1,\ldots,1)}[0, 1]^d$ of functions whose derivatives of maximal order one are all square-integrable on $[0, 1]^d$, i.e.,

$$H = \left\{ f \in F([0, 1]^d, \mathbb{R}) : \frac{\partial^{|U|} f}{(\partial x)_U} \in L_2[0, 1]^d \text{ for all } U \subseteq [1 : d] \right\}. \tag{12.6}$$

Here, for a subset U of $[1 : d]$, the notation $(\partial x)_U$ represented $\prod_{k \in U} \partial x_k$. Also using the notation $\gamma_U \in \mathbb{R}$ to represent the product $\prod_{k \in U} \gamma_k$ (with $\gamma_\emptyset := 1$) and $x_U \in [0, 1]^d$ to represent the vector with entries $(x_U)_k = x_k$ when $k \in U$ and $(x_U)_k = 1$ when $k \notin U$, the space H is endowed with a Hilbert norm defined by

$$\|f\|^2 = \sum_{U \subseteq [1:d]} \frac{1}{\gamma_U} \int_{[0,1]^d} \left(\frac{\partial^{|U|} f}{(\partial x)_U}(x_U)\right)^2 dx, \qquad f \in H.$$

One can check (the verification is again left to the reader as Exercise 12.3) that H is a reproducing kernel Hilbert space whose kernel is given by

$$K(x, x') = \prod_{k=1}^{d} \left[1 + \gamma_k \min\{1 - x_k, 1 - x'_k\} \right], \qquad x, x' \in [0, 1]^d. \qquad (12.7)$$

The following result shows that tractability is achieved when the weights γ_k decrease fast enough.[1]

Theorem 12.5 *The integration problem over the unit ball of the space* (12.6) *is tractable using standard information when* $\gamma_1 + \cdots + \gamma_d \leq C \ln(d)$ *for some absolute constant* $C > 0$.

Proof With the recovery map $\Delta \colon \mathbb{R}^m \to \mathbb{R}$ fixed throughout the proof and given by $\Delta(y) = m^{-1} \sum_{i=1}^{m} y_i$, the conclusion will be acquired as soon one proves that

$$e^2 := \inf_{x^{(1)}, \ldots, x^{(m)} \in [0,1]^d} \mathrm{Err}_{B_H, \mathrm{Int}}(\Lambda_x, \Delta)^2 \leq \frac{1}{m} \prod_{k=1}^{d} \left(1 + \frac{\gamma_k}{2} \right). \qquad (12.8)$$

Indeed, since the right-hand side is bounded by $\exp\left((\gamma_1 + \cdots + \gamma_d)/2\right)/m$, one even derives that:

- if $\gamma_1 + \cdots + \gamma_d \leq C \ln(d)$, then one has $e^2 \leq d^{C/2}/m$, which implies that $m_{B_H, \mathrm{Int}}^{\mathrm{standard}}(\varepsilon, d) \leq d^{C/2} \varepsilon^{-2}$: tractability prevails;
- if $\gamma_1 + \cdots + \gamma_d \leq C$, then one has $e^2 \leq \exp(C/2)/m$, which implies that $m_{B_H, \mathrm{Int}}^{\mathrm{standard}}(\varepsilon, d) \leq \exp(C/2)\varepsilon^{-2}$: strong tractability prevails.

To justify (12.8), one starts by invoking Lemma 12.2 for $c_1 = \cdots = c_m = 1/m$ to arrive at

$$e_x^2 := \mathrm{Err}_{B_H, \mathrm{Int}}(\Lambda_x, \Delta)^2 = \left\| h_{\mathrm{Int}} \right\|^2 - \frac{2}{m} \sum_{i=1}^{m} h_{\mathrm{Int}}(x^{(i)}) + \frac{1}{m^2} \sum_{i,j=1}^{m} K(x^{(i)}, x^{(j)}) \quad (12.9)$$

for any observation map Λ_x associated with points $x^{(1)}, \ldots, x^{(m)} \in [0, 1]^d$. One need not determine the Riesz representer h_{Int} of the integration functional explicitly, as one can simply rely on

$$\left\| h_{\mathrm{Int}} \right\|^2 = \int_{[0,1]^d} h_{\mathrm{Int}} = \int_{[0,1]^d \times [0,1]^d} K(x, x') dx dx'.$$

To justify these identities, one recalls that $\langle h_{\mathrm{Int}}, f \rangle = \int_{[0,1]^d} f$ for any $f \in H$, so choosing $f = h_{\mathrm{Int}}$ yields the leftmost identity while choosing $f = K(\cdot, x)$

---

[1] It is shown that boundedness of $(\gamma_1 + \cdots + \gamma_d)/\ln(d)$ implies quasi-Monte Carlo tractability. The original paper by Sloan and Woźniakowski (1998) also established that unboundedness of this quantity implies quasi-Monte Carlo intractability.

before integrating over $x \in [0,1]^d$ yields the rightmost identity. Therefore, returning to (12.9) and taking expectations over random points $x^{(1)}, \ldots, x^{(m)}$ independently and uniformly distributed in $[0,1]^d$—in other words, integrating over $x^{(1)}, \ldots, x^{(m)} \in [0,1]^d$—one obtains

$$\mathbb{E}(e_x^2) = \left\|h_{\text{Int}}\right\|^2 - \frac{2}{m} \sum_{i=1}^{m} \int_{[0,1]^d} h_{\text{Int}}(x^{(i)}) dx^{(i)}$$

$$+ \frac{1}{m^2} \left(\sum_{i=1}^{m} \int_{[0,1]^d} K(x^{(i)}, x^{(i)}) dx^{(i)} + \sum_{\substack{i,j=1 \\ i \neq j}}^{m} \int_{[0,1]^d \times [0,1]^d} K(x^{(i)}, x^{(j)}) dx^{(i)} dx^{(j)} \right)$$

$$= \left\|h_{\text{Int}}\right\|^2 - 2\left\|h_{\text{Int}}\right\|^2 + \frac{1}{m} \int_{[0,1]^d} K(x,x) dx + \left(\frac{m^2 - m}{m^2}\right) \left\|h_{\text{Int}}\right\|^2$$

$$\leq \frac{1}{m} \int_{[0,1]^d} K(x,x) dx.$$

This guarantees the existence of points $x^{(1)}, \ldots, x^{(m)}$ (without providing them) for which

$$e_x^2 \leq \frac{1}{m} \int_{[0,1]^d} K(x,x) dx = \frac{1}{m} \prod_{k=1}^{d} \int_0^1 \left[1 + \gamma_k(1 - x_k)\right] dx_k = \frac{1}{m} \prod_{k=1}^{d} \left(1 + \frac{\gamma_k}{2}\right).$$

Since $e^2 = \inf \{e_x^2 : x^{(1)}, \ldots, x^{(m)} \in [0,1]^d\}$, the bound (12.8) is now justified and the proof is complete. $\qquad\square$

Exercises

12.1 For a problem determined by a model set $\mathcal{K}$ and a quantity of interest Q, observe that the minimal intrinsic error, as a function of $m \in \mathbb{N}^*$, and the information complexity, as a function of $\varepsilon > 0$, are essentially inverse functions to one another. In particular, if $\text{Err}^*_{\mathcal{K},Q}(m)$ is strictly decreasing with m, notice that $m_{\mathcal{K},Q}(\text{Err}^*_{\mathcal{K},Q}(m), d) = m$ for any $m \in \mathbb{N}^*$.

12.2 Consider a problem with minimal intrinsic error decaying according to

$$c_d m^{-r} \leq \text{Err}^*_{\mathcal{K},Q}(m) \leq C_d m^{-r}, \qquad m \geq 1,$$

for a fixed exponent $r > 0$ and some constants c_d, C_d depending on d. Prove that the problem suffers from the curse of dimensionality when $c_d \geq \gamma^d$ for some $\gamma > 1$ and is tractable when $C_d \leq d^\kappa$ for some $\kappa \geq 0$.

12.3 Verify that the spaces (12.2) and (12.6) are reproducing kernel Hilbert spaces with kernels given by (12.3) and (12.7), respectively. It may be useful to skip forward to Lemma 13.5 and its proof.

12.4 Given a reproducing kernel Hilbert space over a compact set $\mathcal{X}$ with a continuous kernel K, show that the Riesz representer of the integration functional is given by

$$h_{\text{Int}}(x) = \int_{\mathcal{X}} K(x, x')dx', \qquad x \in \mathcal{X}.$$

Find its explicit expression for the weighted Sobolev space (12.6).

13
Quasi-Monte Carlo Integration

The previous chapter highlighted that the curse of dimensionality is avoidable for the integration in weighted Sobolev spaces using a *Monte Carlo* rule, i.e., a quadrature rule of the type

$$\int_{[0,1]^d} f \approx \frac{1}{m} \sum_{i=1}^{m} f(x^{(i)}), \tag{13.1}$$

where $x^{(1)}, \ldots, x^{(m)}$ are random points chosen independently from the uniform distribution on $[0, 1]^d$. For a fixed function f, Monte Carlo rules are known (see Exercise 13.1 for a proper statement) to yield an integration error of the type

$$\left| \int_{[0,1]^d} f - \frac{1}{m} \sum_{i=1}^{m} f(x^{(i)}) \right| \leq \frac{C_f}{\sqrt{m}}, \tag{13.2}$$

valid in expectation and in turn with high probability. Importantly, the rate $m^{-1/2}$ is independent on the number d of variables. Here, one aims for results in the same vein but with a deterministic rather than a probabilistic perspective. This is what is meant by a *quasi-Monte Carlo* rule: a quadrature rule with equal weights as in (13.1) but with points $x^{(1)}, \ldots, x^{(m)}$ chosen deterministically. Advantageously, the error bound (13.2) will not be tied to a fixed function anymore and, as will be shown, the rate $m^{-1/2}$ can even be improved. Such refinements are made possible thanks to the Koksma–Hlawka inequality, which decouples the integration error as a product of a term—the discrepancy— involving the locations of the points only and a term—the variation—involving the regularity of the function only. One shall first introduce these two terms, then establish the Koksma–Hlawka inequality, and conclude by uncovering point sets having small discrepancy.

102

13.1 Variation and Discrepancy

For a univariate function $f \in F([0, 1], \mathbb{R})$, the notion of *variation* causes no ambiguity: rather intuitively, it is defined as

$$\text{Var}(f) = \sup_{n \geq 1} \sup_{0 \leq x_0 < \cdots < x_n \leq 1} \sum_{j=1}^{n} |f(x_j) - f(x_{j-1})|.$$

When f is continuously differentiable, the variation becomes the integral of $|f'|$, as the reader is invited to verify in Exercise 13.2. For multivariate functions $f \in F([0, 1]^d, \mathbb{R})$, there are several ways to extend the notion of variation. In the sense of *Vitali*, instead of stating the definition in its full generality, one simply mentions that it becomes

$$\text{Var}_V(f) = \int_{[0,1]^d} \left| \frac{\partial^d f}{\partial x_1 \cdots \partial x_d}(x) \right| dx,$$

whenever the integrand makes sense and is integrable. It is another meaning of variation, introduced below, which is favored in this chapter.

Definition 13.1 The *variation* of a function $f \in F([0, 1]^d, \mathbb{R})$, in the sense of *Hardy and Krause*, is

$$\text{Var}_{HK}(f) = \sum_{U \subseteq [1:d]} \text{Var}_V \left(f_{|\mathcal{F}_U^d} \right),$$

where $\mathcal{F}_U^d$ is a face of $[0, 1]^d$ given by $\mathcal{F}_U^d = \{x \in [0, 1]^d : x_k = 1 \text{ for } k \notin U\}$. When $f \in F([0, 1]^d, \mathbb{R})$ is smooth enough, this variation of f simply becomes

$$\text{Var}_{HK}(f) = \sum_{U \subseteq [1:d]} \int_{\mathcal{F}_U^d} \left| \frac{\partial^{|U|} f}{(\partial x)_U}(x) \right| dx.$$

The notion of *discrepancy* (more precisely, of geometric discrepancy[1]) of a set of points $x^{(1)}, \ldots, x^{(m)} \in [0, 1]^d$ for a subset $S \in [0, 1]^d$ quantifies how well the integral of the indicator function $\mathbb{1}_S$ is approximated by a quasi-Monte Carlo rule at the points $x^{(1)}, \ldots, x^{(m)}$, so that

$$\text{disc}(\{x^{(1)}, \ldots, x^{(m)}\}, S) = \text{vol}(S) - \frac{1}{m} |\{i \in [1:m] : x^{(i)} \in S\}|.$$

The discrepancy of the set $\{x^{(1)}, \ldots, x^{(m)}\}$ for a family $\mathfrak{S}$ of subsets of $[0, 1]^d$ is then

$$\text{Disc}(\{x^{(1)}, \ldots, x^{(m)}\}, \mathfrak{S}) := \sup_{S \in \mathfrak{S}} \left| \text{disc}(\{x^{(1)}, \ldots, x^{(m)}\}, S) \right|.$$

---

[1] As opposed to combinatorial discrepancy, also covered in the books by Chazelle (2001) and Matousek (2009).

Cases of particular interest include the family of boxes $[a, b) = \prod_{k=1}^{d}[a_k, b_k)$ for $a, b \in \mathbb{R}^d$. In fact, one only considers here the special instance $a = 0$, for which the discrepancy takes a special name.

Definition 13.2 The *star discrepancy* of a set of points $x^{(1)}, \ldots, x^{(m)} \in [0, 1]^d$ is

$$\mathrm{Disc}^*(\{x^{(1)}, \ldots, x^{(m)}\}) := \sup_{x \in [0,1]^d} \left| \mathrm{disc}(\{x^{(1)}, \ldots, x^{(m)}\}, [0, x)) \right|.$$

In other words, the star discrepancy appears as the supremum norm of the *star discrepancy function* of the set $\{x^{(1)}, \ldots, x^{(m)}\}$, defined for $x \in [0, 1]^d$ by

$$\mathrm{disc}^*(\{x^{(1)}, \ldots, x^{(m)}\}, x) = x_1 \cdots x_d - \frac{1}{m}\left|\{i \in [1:m] : x^{(i)} \in [0, x)\}\right|. \quad (13.3)$$

Although the star discrepancy function is neither monotone nor continuous, it can be reliably estimated at a given point if it is known at two nearby points, as revealed in a lemma that will prove useful later.

Lemma 13.3 *If* $[0, x^-) \subseteq [0, x) \subseteq [0, x^+)$, *then*

$$\left|\mathrm{disc}^*(\{x^{(1)}, \ldots, x^{(m)}\}, x)\right| \le \max_{\pm} \left|\mathrm{disc}^*(\{x^{(1)}, \ldots, x^{(m)}\}, x^{\pm})\right| + \sum_{k=1}^{d}(x_k^+ - x_k^-).$$

Proof By monotonicity of both terms making the star discrepancy function, one has on the one hand

$$\mathrm{disc}^*(\{x^{(1)}, \ldots, x^{(m)}\}, x) \le x_1^+ \cdots x_d^+ - \frac{1}{m}\left|\{i \in [1:m] : x^{(i)} \in [0, x^-)\}\right|$$

$$= \mathrm{disc}^*(\{x^{(1)}, \ldots, x^{(m)}\}, x^-) + (x_1^+ \cdots x_d^+ - x_1^- \cdots x_d^-),$$

and on the other hand

$$\mathrm{disc}^*(\{x^{(1)}, \ldots, x^{(m)}\}, x) \ge x_1^- \cdots x_d^- - \frac{1}{m}\left|\{i \in [1:m] : x^{(i)} \in [0, x^+)\}\right|$$

$$= \mathrm{disc}^*(\{x^{(1)}, \ldots, x^{(m)}\}, x^+) - (x_1^+ \cdots x_d^+ - x_1^- \cdots x_d^-).$$

Setting $\gamma = \max_{\pm} |\mathrm{disc}^*(\{x^{(1)}, \ldots, x^{(m)}\}, x^{\pm})|$ and $\delta = (x_1^+ \cdots x_d^+ - x_1^- \cdots x_d^-)$, these inequalities imply that $-\gamma - \delta \le \mathrm{disc}^*(\{x^{(1)}, \ldots, x^{(m)}\}, x) \le \gamma + \delta$, i.e., $|\mathrm{disc}^*(\{x^{(1)}, \ldots, x^{(m)}\}, x)| \le \gamma + \delta$. It remains to suitably bound the quantity δ. To do so, one writes γ as the telescoping sum

$$\gamma = \sum_{k=1}^{d}(x_1^+ \cdots x_k^+ x_{k+1}^- \cdots x_d^- - x_1^+ \cdots x_{k-1}^+ x_k^- \cdots x_d^-)$$

$$= \sum_{k=1}^{d} x_1^+ \cdots x_{k-1}^+ (x_k^+ - x_k^-) x_{k+1}^- \cdots x_d^- \le \sum_{k=1}^{d}(x_k^+ - x_k^-),$$

which is the required bound. $\qquad \square$

13.2 Koksma–Hlawka Inequality

As alluded to earlier, one of the main ingredients for the analysis of quasi-Monte Carlo methods is an inequality that separates the contributions of the quadrature points and of the function to be integrated. This inequality, known as the *Koksma–Hlawka inequality*, is now formally stated.

Theorem 13.4 *Given $f \in C([0,1]^d)$ and $x^{(1)}, \ldots, x^{(m)} \in [0,1]^d$, one has*

$$\left| \int_{[0,1]^d} f - \frac{1}{m} \sum_{i=1}^{m} f(x^{(i)}) \right| \leq \mathrm{Disc}^*(\{x^{(1)}, \ldots, x^{(m)}\}) \, \mathrm{Var}_{HK}(f).$$

Thus, considering the model set $\mathcal{K} = \{f \in C([0,1]^d) : \mathrm{Var}_{HK}(f) \leq 1\}$, one derives that the worst-case integration error over $\mathcal{K}$ satisfies

$$\mathrm{Err}_{\mathcal{K},\mathrm{Int}}(\Lambda_x, \Delta) \leq \mathrm{Disc}^*(\{x^{(1)}, \ldots, x^{(m)}\}),$$

where the observation map Λ_x is associated with the points $x^{(1)}, \ldots, x^{(m)}$ and the recovery map Δ is given by $\Delta(y) = m^{-1} \sum_{i=1}^{m} y_i$ for any $y \in \mathbb{R}^m$. Selecting the low-discrepancy points put forward in the next section, one can subsequently bound the mth minimal intrinsic error using standard observations as

$$\mathrm{Err}_{\mathcal{K},\mathrm{Int}}^{*,\mathrm{standard}}(m) \leq C \frac{\ln(m)^{d-1}}{m}.$$

At first sight, this may appear as an excellent rate. Indeed, overlooking the logarithmic factor, one could be tempted to think that this specific model set $\mathcal{K}$ overcomes the curse of dimensionality. This is misleading: the huge number $m \approx (d \ln(d))^{d-1}$ of observations is not even enough to produce an error bound that decays to zero as d increases.

Returning to the Koksma–Hlawka inequality and its justification, one stresses that it is deduced as a direct consequence of the following result, known as the *Zaremba identity*.

Lemma 13.5 *Given a function $f \in C([0,1]^d)$ whose derivatives of maximal order one are all integrable and given points $x^{(1)}, \ldots, x^{(m)} \in [0,1]^d$, one has*

$$\int_{[0,1]^d} f - \frac{1}{m} \sum_{i=1}^{m} f(x^{(i)}) = \sum_{U \subseteq [1:d]} (-1)^{|U|} \int_{\mathcal{F}_U^d} \mathrm{disc}^*(\{x^{(1)}, \ldots, x^{(m)}\}, x) \frac{\partial^{|U|} f}{(\partial x)_U}(x) dx.$$

Proof One shall prove a stronger identity, understood in a distributional sense, namely

$$\int_{[0,1]^d} g_1'(x_1) \cdots g_d'(x_d) f(x) dx$$

$$= \sum_{U \subseteq [1:d]} (-1)^{|U|} \int_{\mathcal{F}_U^d} g_1(x_1) \cdots g_d(x_d) \frac{\partial^{|U|} f}{(\partial x)_U}(x) dx, \qquad (13.4)$$

valid when the univariate functions $g_1, \ldots, g_d$ satisfy $g_k(0) = 0$ and $g_k(1) = 1$. Specifying this identity to functions defined by $g_k(x) = x$ and $g_k(x) = \mathbb{1}_{\{x > x_k^{(i)}\}}$ yields

$$\int_{[0,1]^d} f(x) dx = \sum_{U \subseteq [1:d]} (-1)^{|U|} \int_{\mathcal{F}_U^d} x_1 \cdots x_d \frac{\partial^{|U|} f}{(\partial x)_U}(x) dx,$$

$$f(x^{(i)}) = \int_{[0,1]^d} \delta_{x^{(i)}}(x) f(x) dx = \sum_{U \subseteq [1:d]} (-1)^{|U|} \int_{\mathcal{F}_U^d} \mathbb{1}_{\{x^{(i)} \in [0,x)\}} \frac{\partial^{|U|} f}{(\partial x)_U}(x) dx,$$

having used $\delta_{x^{(i)}}(x) = \delta_{x_1^{(i)}}(x_1) \cdots \delta_{x_d^{(i)}}(x_d)$ and $\mathbb{1}_{\{x^{(i)} \in [0,x)\}} = \mathbb{1}_{\{x_1 > x_1^{(i)}\}} \cdots \mathbb{1}_{\{x_d > x_d^{(i)}\}}$. These identities combine to give

$$\int_{[0,1]^d} f(x) dx - \frac{1}{m} \sum_{i=1}^m f(x^{(i)})$$

$$= \sum_{U \subseteq [1:d]} (-1)^{|U|} \int_{\mathcal{F}_U^d} \left(x_1 \cdots x_d - \frac{1}{m} \sum_{i=1}^m \mathbb{1}_{\{x^{(i)} \in [0,x)\}} \right) \frac{\partial^{|U|} f}{(\partial x)_U}(x) dx.$$

In view of the definition (13.3) of the star discrepancy function, the latter is nothing else than the Zaremba identity. Thus, it remains to justify (13.4). One proceeds by induction on $d \geq 1$. The base case $d = 1$ reads

$$\int_0^1 g'(x) f(x) dx = g(1) f(1) - \int_0^1 g(x) f'(x) dx,$$

which holds by virtue of $g(0) = 0$. One assumes at present that the induction hypothesis holds up to $d - 1$, $d \geq 2$. To prove that it holds for d, one writes, with $\bar{x} := x_{[1:d-1]}$,

$$\int_{[0,1]^d} g_1'(x_1) \cdots g_d'(x_d) f(x) dx$$

$$= \int_{[0,1]^{d-1}} g_1'(x_1) \cdots g_{d-1}'(x_{d-1}) \left[\int_0^1 g_d'(x_d) f(\bar{x}, x_d) dx_d \right] d\bar{x}$$

$$= \int_{[0,1]^{d-1}} g_1'(x_1) \cdots g_{d-1}'(x_{d-1}) \left[f(\bar{x}, 1) - \int_0^1 g_d(x_d) \frac{\partial f}{\partial x_d}(\bar{x}, x_d) dx_d \right] d\bar{x}$$

$$=: I - J.$$

The two implicitly defined terms I and J are transformed using the induction hypothesis. Firstly, the term labeled I is

$$
\begin{aligned}
I &= \int_{[0,1]^{d-1}} g_1'(x_1) \cdots g_{d-1}'(x_{d-1}) f(\bar{x}, 1) d\bar{x} \\
&= \sum_{\bar{U} \subseteq [1:d-1]} (-1)^{|\bar{U}|} \int_{\mathcal{F}_{\bar{U}}^{d-1}} g_1(x_1) \cdots g_{d-1}(x_{d-1}) \frac{\partial^{|\bar{U}|} f}{(\partial x)_{\bar{U}}} (\bar{x}, 1) d\bar{x} \\
&= \sum_{\substack{U \subseteq [1:d] \\ d \notin U}} (-1)^{|U|} \int_{\mathcal{F}_U^d} g_1(x_1) \cdots g_{d-1}(x_{d-1}) g_d(x_d) \frac{\partial^{|U|} f}{(\partial x)_U} (x) dx.
\end{aligned}
$$

Secondly, the term labeled J is

$$
\begin{aligned}
J &= \int_0^1 \left(\int_{[0,1]^{d-1}} g_1'(x_1) \cdots g_{d-1}'(x_{d-1}) \frac{\partial f}{\partial x_d} (\bar{x}, x_d) d\bar{x} \right) g_d(x_d) dx_d \\
&= \int_0^1 \left(\sum_{\bar{U} \subseteq [1:d-1]} (-1)^{|\bar{U}|} \int_{\mathcal{F}_{\bar{U}}^{d-1}} g_1(x_1) \cdots g_{d-1}(x_{d-1}) \frac{\partial^{|\bar{U}|+1} f}{(\partial x)_{\bar{U}} \partial x_d} (\bar{x}, x_d) d\bar{x} \right) g_d(x_d) dx_d \\
&= \sum_{\bar{U} \subseteq [1:d-1]} (-1)^{|\bar{U}|} \int_{\mathcal{F}_{\bar{U}}^{d-1} \times [0,1]} g_1(x_1) \cdots g_{d-1}(x_{d-1}) g_d(x_d) \frac{\partial^{|\bar{U}|+1} f}{(\partial x)_{\bar{U} \cup \{d\}}} (\bar{x}, x_d) d\bar{x} dx_d \\
&= - \sum_{\substack{U \subseteq [1:d] \\ d \in U}} (-1)^{|U|} \int_{\mathcal{F}_U^d} g_1(x_1) \cdots g_{d-1}(x_{d-1}) g_d(x_d) \frac{\partial^{|U|} f}{(\partial x)_U} (x) dx.
\end{aligned}
$$

Since a subset U of $[1:d]$ satisfies either $d \notin U$ or $d \in U$, subtracting the expressions obtained for I and J shows that the induction hypothesis holds for d. This completes the proof. $\qquad\square$

13.3 Low-Discrepancy Sets

The final goal of this chapter is to uncover sets of m deterministic points whose star discrepancy is small, precisely of order $\ln(m)^{d-1}/m$. This order is better than the order $1/\sqrt{m}$ obtained if $x^{(1)}, \ldots, x^{(m)}$ were chosen as random points drawn independently from the uniform distribution on $[0,1]^d$. Indeed, when

$x \in [0, 1]^d$ is fixed, one can calculate

$$\mathbb{E}[\, \text{disc}^*(\{x^{(1)}, \dots, x^{(m)}\}, x)^2] = \mathbb{E}\Bigg[(x_1 \cdots x_d)^2 - \frac{2}{m} x_1 \cdots x_d \sum_{i=1}^{m} \mathbb{1}_{\{x^{(i)} \in [0,x)\}}$$

$$+ \frac{1}{m^2}\Bigg(\sum_{i=1}^{m} \mathbb{1}_{\{x^{(i)} \in [0,x)\}} + \sum_{\substack{i,j=1 \\ i \neq j}}^{m} \mathbb{1}_{\{x^{(i)} \in [0,x)\}} \mathbb{1}_{\{x^{(j)} \in [0,x)\}} \Bigg) \Bigg]$$

$$= (x_1 \cdots x_d)^2 - \frac{2}{m}(x_1 \cdots x_d) m(x_1 \cdots x_d)$$

$$+ \frac{1}{m^2}(m(x_1 \cdots x_d) + (m^2 - m)(x_1 \cdots x_d)^2)$$

$$= \frac{1}{m}(x_1 \cdots x_d)(1 - x_1 \cdots x_d).$$

Therefore, taking e.g. $x_1 = \cdots = x_d = 2^{-1/d}$ shows that the squared star discrepancy is on average bounded below by $1/(4m)$. As for constructions of better-than-random point sets, one only focuses on the Halton–Hammersley set below, merely mentioning lattice rules and digital nets and sequences in passing.[2] The construction involves the *radical inverse function* ϕ_b in base $b \geq 2$ defined from the b-ary expansion of an integer $h \geq 0$ via:

$$\text{if} \qquad h = \sum_{j=1}^{\infty} a_j b^{j-1} = a_1 + a_2 b + a_3 b^2 + \cdots,$$

$$\text{then} \qquad \phi_b(h) = \sum_{j=1}^{\infty} \frac{a_j}{b^j} = \frac{a_1}{b} + \frac{a_2}{b^2} + \frac{a_3}{b^3} + \cdots \in [0, 1).$$

The sequence $\phi_b(0), \phi_b(1), \dots, \phi_b(h), \dots$ is called the *van der Corput* sequence in base b. The *Halton sequence* is the multidimensional analog: given bases $b_1, \dots, b_d \geq 2$, its elements are

$$x^{(i)} = [\phi_{b_1}(i - 1); \dots; \phi_{b_d}(i - 1)] \in [0, 1)^d, \qquad i \geq 1.$$

In the following result, showing that the first m points of the Halton sequence have low star discrepancy, the bases are often chosen as the smallest d prime numbers.

Theorem 13.6 *If the integers $b_1, \dots, b_d \geq 2$ are pairwise coprime, then the set of first $m \geq 4$ points of the Halton sequence in bases $b_1, \dots, b_d$ satisfies*

$$\text{Disc}^*(\{x^{(1)}, \dots, x^{(m)}\}) \leq C \frac{\log_2(m)^d}{m},$$

where the constant C depends on $b_1, \dots, b_d$, e.g. as $C = 2^d b_1 \cdots b_d + 1$.

---

[2] A comprehensive treatment can be found in the book by Dick and Pillichshammer (2010).

Proof The objective is to show that

$$|\text{disc}(\{x^{(1)}, \ldots, x^{(m)}\}, x)| = \left| x_1 \cdots x_d - \frac{1}{m} |\{i \in [1:m] : x^{(i)} \in [0, x)\}| \right|$$

$$\leq C' \frac{\log_2(m)^d}{m} \tag{13.5}$$

independently of $x \in [0, 1]^d$. For any $k \in [1:d]$, let n_k represent the number of b_k-ary digits needed to express all the integers $(i - 1)$, $i \in [1:m]$, so that n_k is characterized by $b_k^{n_k-1} \leq m - 1 \leq b_k^{n_k} - 1$, i.e., $b_k^{n_k-1} < m \leq b_k^{n_k}$, which means that

$$n_k = \lceil \log_{b_k}(m) \rceil = \left\lceil \frac{\log_2(m)}{\log_2(b_k)} \right\rceil.$$

One claims that it is sufficient to establish (13.5) in the particular cases where $x = [\ell_1/b_1^{n_1}; \ldots; \ell_k/b_k^{n_k}]$ for some integers $\ell_k \in [1 : b_k^{n_k}]$. Indeed, for an arbitrary $x \in [0, 1]^d$, one can select integers $\ell_k \in [1 : b_k^{n_k}]$ such that each x_k belongs to the interval $[(\ell_k - 1)/b_k^{n_k}, \ell_k/b_k^{n_k}]$. Lemma 13.3 then ensures that

$$|\text{disc}(\{x^{(1)}, \ldots, x^{(m)}\}, x)| \leq C' \frac{\log_2(m)^d}{m} + \sum_{k=1}^{d} \frac{1}{b_k^{n_k}} \leq C' \frac{\log_2(m)^d}{m} + \frac{d}{m}.$$

This right-hand side is bounded by $C(\log_2(m)^d)/m$ with $C := C' + 1$, by virtue of $d \leq \log_2(m)^d$ when $m \geq 4$. Therefore, it remains to establish (13.5) when $x_k = \ell_k/b_k^{n_k}$ with $\ell_k \in [1 : b_k^{n_k}]$. Setting $I := \{i \in [1:m] : x^{(i)} \in [0, x)\}$, this reduces to proving that

$$\left| \frac{\ell_1}{b_1^{n_1}} \cdots \frac{\ell_d}{b_d^{n_d}} - \frac{|I|}{m} \right| \leq C' \frac{\log_2(m)^d}{m}. \tag{13.6}$$

Note that $i \in I$ if and only if $\phi_{b_k}(i-1) < \ell_k/b_k^{n_k}$ for all $k \in [1:d]$. Consequently, given $k \in [1:d]$, one can assume that $\ell_k \leq b_k^{n_k} - 1$, for otherwise $\ell_k = b_k^{n_k}$ effectively means to decrease the dimension from d to $d - 1$. Thus, the b_k-ary expansion of ℓ_k reads

$$\ell_k = \beta_{k,1} b_k^{n_k-1} + \beta_{k,2} b_k^{n_k-2} + \cdots + \beta_{k,n_k-1} b_k + \beta_{k,n_k}$$

for some $\beta_{k,1}, \ldots, \beta_{k,n_k} \in [1 : b_k - 1]$. Likewise, the b_k-ary expansion of $i - 1$, $i \in [1:m]$, reads

$$i - 1 = a_{k,n_k}^{(i-1)} b_k^{n_k-1} + a_{k,n_k-1}^{(i-1)} b_k^{n_k-2} + \cdots + a_{k,2}^{(i-1)} b_k + a_{k,1}^{(i-1)}$$

for some $a_{k,n_k}^{(i-1)}, \ldots, a_{k,1}^{(i-1)} \in [1 : b_k - 1]$. Now, the condition $i \in I$, written as $b_k^{n_k} \phi_{b_k}(i - 1) < \ell_k$, becomes

$$a_{k,1}^{(i-1)} b_k^{n_k-1} + \cdots + a_{k,n_k-1}^{(i-1)} b_k + a_{k,n_k}^{(i-1)} < \beta_{k,1} b_k^{n_k-1} + \cdots + \beta_{k,n_k-1} b_k + \beta_{k,n_k}$$

for all $k \in [1:d]$. Fixing this index k, the above condition is fulfilled if and only if one of the following mutually exclusive conditions is fulfilled:

$$a_{k,1}^{(i-1)} = \alpha_{k,1} \qquad \text{for some } \alpha_{k,1} \in [0:\beta_{k,1} - 1];$$

$$a_{k,1}^{(i-1)} = \beta_{k,1}, a_{k,2}^{(i-1)} = \alpha_{k,2} \qquad \text{for some } \alpha_{k,2} \in [0:\beta_{k,2} - 1];$$

$$\vdots$$

$$a_{k,1}^{(i-1)} = \beta_{k,1}, \ldots, a_{k,n_k-1}^{(i-1)} = \beta_{k,n_k-1}, a_{k,n_k}^{(i-1)} = \alpha_{k,n_k} \quad \text{for some } \alpha_{k,n_k} \in [0:\beta_{k,n_k} - 1].$$

The jth condition prescribes the first j digits of $i - 1$ in base b_k, so it reads $i - 1 \equiv h_{\alpha_{k,j}} \pmod{b_k^j}$ for some integer $h_{\alpha_{k,j}}$. It follows that

$$\mathcal{I} = \bigcup_{\substack{j_1 \in [1:n_1] \\ \alpha_{1,j_1} \in [0:\beta_{1,j_1}-1]}} \cdots \bigcup_{\substack{j_d \in [1:n_d] \\ \alpha_{d,j_d} \in [0:\beta_{d,j_d}-1]}} \{i \in [1:m] : i - 1 \equiv h_{\alpha_{k,j_k}} (\bmod\, b_k^{j_k}), \ k \in [1:d]\},$$

with disjoint sets appearing in this union. By the Chinese remainder theorem, the system of congruences defining each of these sets has a unique solution modulo $\pi := b_1^{j_1} \cdots b_d^{j_d}$, say $s \in [0:\pi - 1]$. Hence, the set in question has the form $\{s, s+\pi, \ldots, s+(q-1)\pi\}$ with $s+(q-1)\pi \leq m-1 < s+q\pi$, so its cardinality q obeys $m/\pi - (1 + s)/\pi < q \leq m/\pi - (1 + s)/\pi + 1$, i.e., $q = m/(b_1^{j_1} \cdots b_d^{j_d}) + \theta$ with a perturbation $\theta \in [-1, 1]$. Adding these perturbations into a cumulative perturbation Θ, one obtains

$$|\mathcal{I}| = \sum_{j_1 \in [1:n_1]} \cdots \sum_{j_d \in [1:n_d]} \beta_{1,j_1} \cdots \beta_{d,j_d} \frac{m}{b_1^{j_1} \cdots b_d^{j_d}} + \Theta$$

$$= m\left(\sum_{j_1 \in [1:n_1]} \frac{\beta_{1,j_1}}{b_1^{j_1}}\right) \cdots \left(\sum_{j_d \in [1:n_d]} \frac{\beta_{d,j_d}}{b_d^{j_d}}\right) + \Theta = m\frac{\ell_1}{b_1^{n_1}} \cdots \frac{\ell_d}{b_d^{n_d}} + \Theta.$$

This is a reformulation of the desired estimate (13.6), by virtue of

$$|\Theta| \leq n_1 b_1 \cdots n_d b_d \leq 2\log_2(m)b_1 \cdots 2\log_2(m)b_d = C' \log_2(m)^d,$$

with constant $C' = 2^d b_1 \cdots b_d$ yielding $C = 2^d b_1 \cdots b_d + 1$. $\qquad\square$

Although an order $\ln(m)^{d-1}/m$ has been promised, only the order $\ln(m)^d/m$ has been delivered so far. The promised order can be achieved with the related *Hammersley set*, whose points $x^{(1)}, \ldots, x^{(m)} \in [0, 1)^d$ consists of

$$x^{(i)} = [\phi_{b_1}(i - 1); \ldots; \phi_{b_{d-1}}(i - 1); (i - 1)/m], \qquad i \in [1:m].$$

The justification relies on the simple trick outline in Exercise 13.4, working for other sequences as well. Despite the advantage of the Hammersley set in terms of discrepancy, the Halton sequence may still be preferred for another reason: if the integral of f has already been estimated using m points and if one wants to refine the estimation using $m' > m$ points, them only $m' - m$ new point evaluations of f are needed with the Halton sequence, whereas m' new point evaluations are required with the Hammersley set.

Exercises

13.1 Given a function $f \in C([0, 1]^d)$, let $x^{(1)}, \ldots, x^{(m)}$ be random points drawn independently from the uniform distribution on $[0, 1]^d$. Prove that

$$\mathbb{E}\left[\left(\int_{[0,1]^d} f - \frac{1}{m} \sum_{i=1}^m f(x^{(i)})\right)^2\right] = \frac{\sigma^2(f)}{m},$$

where $\sigma^2(f) := \int_{[0,1]^d} f^2 - \left(\int_{[0,1]^d} f\right)^2$ denotes the variance of f. Proceed by establishing that, for any $t > 0$,

$$\mathbb{P}\left[\left|\int_{[0,1]^d} f - \frac{1}{m} \sum_{i=1}^m f(x^{(i)})\right| > \frac{t\sigma(f)}{\sqrt{m}}\right] \le \frac{1}{t^2}.$$

13.2 For a univariate function f which is continuously differentiable on $[0, 1]$, verify carefully that

$$\mathrm{Var}(f) = \int_0^1 |f'(x)| dx.$$

13.3 Introducing exponents $p, p' \in [1, \infty]$ such that $1/p + 1/p' = 1$ and weights $\gamma_U > 0$ associated with each $U \subseteq [1 : d]$, establish the following generalization of the *Koksma–Hlawka inequality*: given $f \in C([0, 1]^d)$ and $x^{(1)}, \ldots, x^{(m)} \in [0, 1]^d$, one has

$$\left|\int_{[0,1]^d} f - \frac{1}{m} \sum_{i=1}^m f(x^{(i)})\right| \le \mathrm{Disc}^*_{p,\gamma}(\{x^{(1)}, \ldots, x^{(m)}\}) \, \mathrm{Var}_{HK,p',\gamma}(f),$$

where the discrepancy and variation have been replaced by

$$\mathrm{Disc}^*_{p,\gamma}(\{x^{(1)}, \ldots, x^{(m)}\}) = \left[\sum_{U \subseteq [1:d]} \gamma_U^{p-1} \int_{\mathcal{F}_U^d} |\mathrm{disc}^*(\{x^{(1)}, \ldots, x^{(m)}\}, x)|^p dx\right]^{1/p},$$

$$\mathrm{Var}_{HK,p',\gamma}(f) = \left[\sum_{U \subseteq [1:d]} \frac{1}{\gamma_U} \int_{\mathcal{F}_U^d} \left|\frac{\partial^{|U|} f}{(\partial x)_U}(x)\right|^{p'} dx\right]^{1/p'}.$$

13.4 Given $x^{(1)}, \ldots, x^{(m)} \in [0, 1)^d$, consider the points $\widetilde{x}^{(1)}, \ldots, \widetilde{x}^{(m)} \in [0, 1)^{d+1}$ defined by $\widetilde{x}^{(i)} = [x^{(i)}; (i - 1)/m]$. Prove that

$$\mathrm{Disc}^*(\{\widetilde{x}^{(1)}, \ldots, \widetilde{x}^{(m)}\}) \le \frac{1}{m}\left(\max_{\ell \in [1:m]} \ell \, \mathrm{Disc}^*(\{x^{(1)}, \ldots, x^{(\ell)}\}) + 1\right).$$

PART THREE

COMPRESSIVE SENSING

Executive Summary

Data Science often takes place in the realm of Big Data. Still, operating in the realm of Small Data is not infrequent. There, observations are scarce, so that learning/recovering a function f from the limited a posteriori information may seem hopeless. But a lifeline comes from the a priori information. Suppose e.g. that f is known to be a linear function depending on a few variables, i.e., that $f(x) = \langle v, x \rangle$ where v is a vector with only a few nonzero entries. Thus, the observations $f(x^{(i)})$ made on f become linear measurements $\langle v, x^{(i)} \rangle$ made on the sparse vector v. Exploiting a small number of linear measurements to recover sparse vectors precisely constitutes the standard Compressive Sensing problem.

In Chapter 14, it is shown that the above scenario actually allows one to recover sparse vectors exactly and ℓ_1-minimization is proposed as a suitable recovery procedure. Chapter 15 turns to the complexity of the problem, i.e., to the minimal number of observations necessary for a stable recovery procedure to exist. Chapter 16 extends the theory from the vector world to the matrix world, where sparse is replaced by low-rank and ℓ_1-minimization by nuclear norm minimization. Chapter 17 studies an extremely quantized version of the standard problem in which the observations are available only through their signs. Finally, Chapter 18 is a self-contained vignette of a boolean analog of Compressive Sensing known as (nonadaptive) Group Testing.

A comprehensive treatment of Compressive Sensing can be found in the book by Foucart and Rauhut (2013), see also Eldar and Kutyniok (2012). The perspective taken here is slightly different because it is based on a restricted isometry property from ℓ_2 to ℓ_1 rather than from ℓ_2 to ℓ_2. This makes it possible to swiftly cover the scenario of One-Bit Compressive Sensing using arguments proposed in the survey (Foucart, 2017). It also facilitates the analysis of low-rank recovery from rank-one measurements. As for Group Testing, most (but not all) of the included material can be found in the book by Du and Hwang (2000). The summary presented here follows Foucart (2019).

14

Sparse Recovery from Linear Observations

In the standard Compressive Sensing problem, one acquires high-dimensional vectors $x \in \mathbb{R}^N$ via nonadaptive linear observations

$$y_i = \langle a^{(i)}, x \rangle, \qquad i \in [1:m].$$

With $A \in \mathbb{R}^{m \times N}$ denoting the matrix whose rows are (the transposes of) the vectors $a^{(1)}, \ldots, a^{(m)} \in \mathbb{R}^N$, this a posteriori information is summarized as

$$y = Ax \in \mathbb{R}^m.$$

Since $m < N$—in practice, $m \ll N$—there are infinitely many vectors $z \in \mathbb{R}^N$ satisfying the observation constraint $Az = y$. But some a priori information about the solution $x \in \mathbb{R}^N$ is also available: realistic vectors $x \in \mathbb{R}^N$ are (close to being) *sparse*, meaning that, for some small integer s, one has

$$\|x\|_0 := |\operatorname{supp}(x)| \le s, \qquad \operatorname{supp}(x) := \{j \in [1:N] : x_j \ne 0\}.$$

The goal is to recover those s-sparse vectors $x \in \mathbb{R}^N$ from the observations $y = Ax$, i.e., to find efficient recovery maps $\Delta : \mathbb{R}^m \to \mathbb{R}^N$ such that

$$\Delta(Ax) = x \qquad \text{whenever } x \in \Sigma_s^N := \{z \in \mathbb{R}^N : \|z\|_0 \le s\}. \tag{14.1}$$

In practice, stronger guarantees incorporating observations errors and sparsity defect are also targeted. Nonetheless, even the idealized quest (14.1) cannot be achieved for every observation matrix $A \in \mathbb{R}^{m \times N}$. Fortuitously, a central assumption in Compressive Sensing is the freedom to select observations with favorable properties. As revealed below, these favorable properties depend only on the null space of A and are realizable with a number m of observations large enough compared to the sparsity s. First, the property linked to a natural but impractical recovery method will be isolated. Then, the property linked to a popular recovery method based on convex optimization will be highlighted.

116

Finally, it will be shown that the latter is a consequence of a (nonstandard) restricted isometry property.

14.1 ℓ_0-Minimization

As already apparent in (14.1), instead of looking at the recovery of a particular s-sparse vector $x \in \mathbb{R}^N$ from the observation vector $y = Ax \in \mathbb{R}^m$, $m \ll N$, the emphasis is placed on the possibility of recovering every s-sparse vector x from $y = Ax$. A moment of reflection shows that this aspiration is similar to asking that every s-sparse x acquired as $y = Ax$ is the unique s-sparse solution to $Az = y$, or that it is the unique solution to the ℓ_0-*minimization program*

$$\underset{z \in \mathbb{R}^N}{\text{minimize}} \; \|z\|_0 \qquad \text{subject to } Az = y. \tag{P_0}$$

This program constitutes an impractical recovery method, though: one cannot hope for much better than a naive combinatorial search consisting in testing all the $N + \cdots + \binom{N}{s}$ possible supports of size at most s, as it is known that (P_0) is a NP-hard problem. Nonetheless, the theoretical understanding of the success of the program (P_0) for s-sparse recovery is informative.

Proposition 14.1 *For $A \in \mathbb{R}^{m \times N}$, the following properties are equivalent:*

(i) *every $x \in \Sigma_s^N$ is the unique minimizer of $\|z\|_0$ subject to $Az = Ax$;*
(ii) *the null space $\ker(A)$ does not contain any nonzero $2s$-sparse vector.*

Proof (i)$\Rightarrow$(ii). Suppose that there is a nonzero $u \in \Sigma_{2s}^N$ such that $Au = 0$. Writing $u = v - w$ for distinct $v, w \in \Sigma_s^N$ and noticing that $Av = Aw =: y$, it is evidently impossible for v and w to both be the unique minimizer of $\|z\|_0$ subject to $Az = y$.

(ii)$\Rightarrow$(i). Suppose that $x \in \Sigma_s^N$ is observed via $y = Ax$ and let $x^\sharp \in \mathbb{R}^N$ be a minimizer of $\|z\|_0$ subject to $Az = y$. In view of $Ax^\sharp = Ax$ and $x^\sharp \in \Sigma_s^N$, one sees that $u := x - x^\sharp \in \ker(A) \cap \Sigma_{2s}^N$. This implies that $u = 0$, i.e., that $x = x^\sharp$. □

The minimal value of m making (ii)—hence theoretical s-sparse recovery—possible equals $2s$. Indeed, put differently, (ii) says that any $2s$ columns of A are linearly independent as vectors in $\mathbb{R}^m$, which forces $m \geq 2s$. Conversely, practical recovery procedures based on only $m = 2s$ consecutive discrete Fourier observations can be devised; see Exercise 15.1. Such a procedure is bound to suffer from inherent instability, though, as revealed in Chapter 15. But increasing slightly the number m of well-chosen observations creates enough room for efficient and stable recovery methods.

14.2 ℓ_1-Minimization

One such efficient and stable recovery method comes about when convexifying the program (P_0), thus considering the following ℓ_1-*minimization program*, also known as the *basis pursuit*:

$$\underset{z \in \mathbb{R}^N}{\text{minimize}} \ \|z\|_1 \qquad \text{subject to } Az = y. \tag{P_1}$$

An intuitive explanation for the success of (P_1) is the fact that it automatically possesses m-sparse solutions: this can be seen with arguments encountered in the proof of Theorem 6.1 or exposed in Remark 20.3. With a terminology to be made more precise in Chapters 19 and 20, the program (P_1), which appears as a convex optimization program, can further be recast as a linear program by doubling the size of the optimization variable. There are two options to do so: one consists in introducing a vector $c \in \mathbb{R}^N$ of *slack variables* such that $c \geq |z|$ and the other consists in introducing two nonnegative vectors z^+, z^- of *slack variables* such that $z^+ - z^- = z$ and $z^+ + z^- = |z|$. This leads to the linear programs

$$\underset{z,c \in \mathbb{R}^N}{\text{minimize}} \ \sum_{j=1}^{N} c_j \qquad \text{s.to} \quad Az = y, \ -c \leq z \leq c,$$

$$\underset{z^+,z^- \in \mathbb{R}^N}{\text{minimize}} \ \sum_{j=1}^{N} (z_j^+ + z_j^-) \qquad \text{s.to} \quad A(z^+ - z^-) = y, \ z^+ \geq 0, \ z^- \geq 0.$$

In any case, the success of (P_1) is again characterized by a property of $\ker(A)$, known as the *null space property* of order s.

Theorem 14.2 *For $A \in \mathbb{R}^{m \times N}$, the following properties are equivalent:*

(i) every $x \in \Sigma_s^N$ is the unique minimizer of $\|z\|_1$ subject to $Az = Ax$;

(ii) for all $v \in \ker(A) \setminus \{0\}$ and $S \subseteq [1:N]$ with $|S| \leq s$, one has $\|v_S\|_1 < \|v_{S^c}\|_1$.

Proof (i)$\Rightarrow$(ii). Let $v \in \ker(A) \setminus \{0\}$ and $S \subseteq [1:N]$ with $|S| \leq s$. The fact that $Av = 0$ leads to $A(-v_{S^c}) = A(v_S)$. Since $v_S \in \Sigma_s^N$, it must be the unique ℓ_1-minimizer, implying that $\|v_S\|_1 < \| - v_{S^c}\|_1 = \|v_{S^c}\|_1$.

(ii)$\Rightarrow$(i). Let $x \in \Sigma_s^N$ and $z \in \mathbb{R}^N$ be distinct from x and satisfy $Az = Ax$. With $S := \text{supp}(x)$ and $v := x - z \in \ker(A) \setminus \{0\}$, one has

$$\|x\|_1 \leq \|x - z_S\|_1 + \|z_S\|_1 = \|v_S\|_1 + \|z_S\|_1$$
$$< \|v_{S^c}\|_1 + \|z_S\|_1 = \|z_{S^c}\|_1 + \|z_S\|_1 = \|z\|_1,$$

which proves that x is indeed the unique ℓ_1-minimizer. $\qquad\qquad\square$

As a side note, the null space property (ii) can equivalently be stated as:

(ii') for all $v \in \ker(A) \setminus \{0\}$ and for an index set S of s largest absolute entries of v, one has $\|v_S\|_1 < \|v\|_1/2$;

(ii") for all $v \in \ker(A) \setminus \{0\}$ and for an index set S of s largest absolute entries of v, one has $\|v\|_1 < 2\|v_{S^c}\|_1$.

Given a column-normalized matrix $A = [A_1 | \cdots | A_N] \in \mathbb{R}^{m \times N}$, the null space property holds if the *coherence* $\mu(A)$ of A is small enough. Precisely, with the coherence being defined when $\|A_1\|_2 = \cdots = \|A_N\|_2 = 1$ as

$$\mu(A) := \max_{j \neq k} |\langle A_j, A_k \rangle|,$$

the null space property holds if $\mu(A) < 1/(2s - 1)$. However, this condition can be met only[1] if $m \gtrsim s^2$, far from a coveted linear scaling of m in s. Overcoming this *quadratic barrier* is possible through the introduction of a stronger tool than the coherence and known as the restricted isometry property.

14.3 ℓ_1-Restricted Isometry Property

The usual theory of Compressive Sensing is built on a version of the restricted isometry property featuring the ℓ_2-norm as an inner norm. Instead, a version featuring the ℓ_1-norm as an inner norm shall be exploited here. This version will also play a crucial role in the theory of One-Bit Compressive Sensing presented in Chapter 17.

Definition 14.3 A matrix $A \in \mathbb{R}^{m \times N}$ is said to satisfy the ℓ_1-*restricted isometry property* of order s with constant $\delta \in (0, 1)$ if

$$(1 - \delta)\|z\|_2 \leq \|Az\|_1 \leq (1 + \delta)\|z\|_2 \qquad \text{for all } z \in \Sigma_s^N.$$

Under this ℓ_1-restricted isometry property, the null space property also holds, and so exact recovery of sparse vectors by ℓ_1-minimization becomes possible. A little more is established below.

Theorem 14.4 *If $A \in \mathbb{R}^{m \times N}$ satisfies the ℓ_1-restricted isometry property of order $9s$ with constant $\delta < 1/5$, then it also satisfies a strengthened version of the null space property of order s, namely: for all $v \in \mathbb{R}^N$ and $S \subseteq [1 : N]$ with $|S| = s$,*

$$\|v_S\|_2 \leq \frac{\rho}{2\sqrt{s}}\|v\|_1 + \tau\|Av\|_1 \tag{14.2}$$

with some constants $\rho \in (0, 1)$ and $\tau \in (0, +\infty)$ depending only on δ.

[1] Details can be found in Chapter 5 of Foucart and Rauhut (2013).

Proof Let $v \in \mathbb{R}^N$ and S be an index set of s largest absolute entries of v. With $t := 9s$, let $T_0 \supseteq S$ be an index set of t largest absolute entries of v. After T_0, one proceeds with the *sort-and-split technique* to define sets $T_1, T_2, \ldots$ of size t in such a way that

$\qquad$ T_1 contains indices of next t largest absolute entries of v,

$\qquad$ T_2 contains indices of next t largest absolute entries of v,

$\qquad$ etc.

By comparing averages, it is easily seen that, for all $k \geq 1$,

$$\|v_{T_k}\|_2 \leq \frac{1}{\sqrt{t}}\|v_{T_{k-1}}\|_1.$$

Then, invoking the ℓ_1-restricted isometry property of order t several times, one can write

$$\|v_{T_0}\|_2 \leq \frac{1}{1-\delta}\|Av_{T_0}\|_1 = \frac{1}{1-\delta}\left\|A\left(v - \sum_{k \geq 1} v_{T_k}\right)\right\|_1$$

$$\leq \frac{1}{1-\delta}\left(\sum_{k \geq 1}\|Av_{T_k}\|_1 + \|Av\|_1\right)$$

$$\leq \frac{1+\delta}{1-\delta}\sum_{k \geq 1}\|v_{T_k}\|_2 + \frac{1}{1-\delta}\|Av\|_1$$

$$\leq \frac{1+\delta}{1-\delta}\frac{1}{\sqrt{t}}\sum_{k \geq 1}\|v_{T_{k-1}}\|_1 + \frac{1}{1-\delta}\|Av\|_1$$

$$\leq \frac{1+\delta}{1-\delta}\frac{1}{\sqrt{t}}\|v\|_1 + \frac{1}{1-\delta}\|Av\|_1. \tag{14.3}$$

Keeping $t = 9s$ and $\delta < 1/5$ in mind, while also taking $\|v_S\|_2 \leq \|v_{T_0}\|_2$ into account, one derives the required result with $\rho = 2(1 + \delta)/(3(1 - \delta)) < 1$ and $\tau = 1/(1 - \delta) \leq 5/4$. $\qquad\square$

Remark 14.5 A look back at the above proof reveals that the conclusion holds under the condition

$$\alpha\|z\|_2 \leq \|Az\|_1 \leq \beta\|z\|_2 \qquad \text{for all } z \in \Sigma_t^N$$

as soon as the constants $\beta \geq \alpha > 0$ and the integer parameter t satisfy $\beta/\alpha < \gamma$ and $t \geq 4\gamma^2 s$ for some $\gamma > 1$.

Matrices $A \in \mathbb{R}^{m \times N}$ satisfying the ℓ_1-restricted isometry property of order t with constant $\delta \in (0, 1)$ exist as soon as $m \geq C(\delta)t \ln(eN/t)$. Theorem B.11 in Appendix B indeed establishes that, with overwhelming probability, a random matrix with independent $\mathcal{N}(0, (\pi/2)/m^2)$ entries fits the bill. It is also worth pointing out that property (14.2), known as the ℓ_2-*robust null space property*, guarantees[2] that, for any $x, z \in \mathbb{R}^N$ and any $p \in [1, 2]$,

$$\|x - z\|_p \leq \frac{C}{s^{1-1/p}}\left(\|z\|_1 - \|x\|_1 + 2\operatorname{dist}_{\ell_1}(x, \Sigma_s^N)\right)$$
$$+ D s^{1/p-1/2}\|A(x - z)\|_1. \tag{14.4}$$

With these ingredients in place, the following flagship result is easily justified.

Theorem 14.6 *Let $m \geq cs\ln(eN/s)$ and let $A \in \mathbb{R}^{m \times N}$ be a random matrix populated by independent mean-zero gaussian entries with standard deviation $\sqrt{\pi/2}/m$. With probability at least $1 - 2\exp(-c'm)$, the following statement holds simultaneously for all $x \in \mathbb{R}^N$ and $e \in \mathbb{R}^m$:*
if $y = Ax + e$ with $\|e\|_1 \leq \eta$, then $x \in \mathbb{R}^N$ is approximately recovered by a solution $x^\sharp \in \mathbb{R}^N$ to

$$\underset{z\in\mathbb{R}^N}{\text{minimize}} \|z\|_1 \qquad \text{subject to } \|y - Az\|_1 \leq \eta$$

with error bounded as

$$\|x - x^\sharp\|_1 \leq C \operatorname{dist}_{\ell_1}(x, \Sigma_s^N) + D\sqrt{s}\,\eta, \tag{14.5}$$
$$\|x - x^\sharp\|_2 \leq \frac{C}{\sqrt{s}} \operatorname{dist}_{\ell_1}(x, \Sigma_s^N) + D\eta. \tag{14.6}$$

The constants $c, c', C, D > 0$ are absolute.

Remark 14.7 The estimates (14.5) and (14.6) are more often encountered with η representing an ℓ_2-bound on the observation error $y - Ax$ rather than an ℓ_1-bound (and with $x^\sharp$ denoting an ℓ_1-minimizer subject to the ℓ_2-constraint $\|y - Az\|_2 \leq \eta$ rather than the ℓ_1-constraint $\|y - Az\|_1 \leq \eta$). The inconsistency is only apparent and is due to the normalization of the matrix A, and hence of the observation error. Indeed, one typically uses gaussian matrices $\widetilde{A}$ whose entries have standard deviation $1/\sqrt{m}$, so that $A = (c/\sqrt{m})\widetilde{A}$, $c = \sqrt{\pi/2}$, and an ℓ_2-bound $\widetilde{\eta}$ on the error $\widetilde{y} - \widetilde{A}x$ leads to an ℓ_1-bound $\eta \leq c\widetilde{\eta}$ on the error $y - Ax = (c/\sqrt{m})(\widetilde{y} - \widetilde{A}x)$ by virtue of $\|u\|_1 \leq \sqrt{m}\|u\|_2$ for any $u \in \mathbb{R}^m$. Therefore, with the typical normalization, the estimates (14.5) and (14.6) for an ℓ_1-minimizer under proper ℓ_1-constraint become valid with η representing an ℓ_2-bound on the observation error in the right-hand sides. As a matter of fact, with the typical normalization, one can even replace $x^\sharp$ by a minimizer of $\|z\|_1$ subject to the equality constraint $Az = y$ (which is useful when the magnitude of the observation error cannot be estimated) and still guarantee a

---

[2] Details can be found in Theorem 4.25 of Foucart and Rauhut (2013).

recovery error bounded in ℓ_2, say, as

$$\|x - x^\#\|_2 \leq \frac{C}{\sqrt{s}} \; \mathrm{dist}_{\ell_1}(x, \Sigma_s^N) + D \|e\|_2. \tag{14.7}$$

The argument relies on another property of gaussian matrices, known as the quotient property.[3]

Exercises

14.1 Let $A \in \mathbb{R}^{m \times N}$ with $m < N$. Prove that, when $p > 1$, there is a 1-sparse vector $x \in \mathbb{R}^N$ which is not a minimizer of $\|z\|_p$ subject to $Az = Ax$.

14.2 For a column-normalized matrix $A \in \mathbb{R}^{m \times N}$, verify that the coherence condition $\mu(A) < 1/(2s - 1)$ implies the null space property of order s.

14.3 Given a index set $S \subseteq [1 : N]$, a norm $\|\cdot\|$ on $\mathbb{R}^m$, and constants $\rho \in (0, 1)$ and $\tau \in (0, +\infty)$, show that a matrix $A \in \mathbb{R}^{m \times N}$ satisfies

$$\|v_S\|_1 \leq \rho \|v_{S^c}\|_1 + \tau \|Av\| \quad \text{for all } v \in \mathbb{R}^N,$$

which is called the ℓ_1-*robust null space property* relative to the set S with constants ρ and τ and with respect to the norm $\|\cdot\|$, if and only if

$$\|x - z\|_1 \leq \frac{1 + \rho}{1 - \rho}(\|z\|_1 - \|x\|_1 + 2\|x_{S^c}\|_1) + \frac{2\tau}{1 - \rho}\|A(z - x)\| \quad \text{for all } x, z \in \mathbb{R}^N.$$

14.4 Establish an analog of Theorem 14.4 under a version of the *restricted isometry property* featuring the ℓ_2-norm as an inner norm. Precisely, prove that the null space property of order s holds as soon as

$$(1 - \delta)\|z\|_2^2 \leq \|Az\|_2^2 \leq (1 + \delta)\|z\|_2^2 \quad \text{for all } z \in \Sigma_{\kappa s}^N$$

for some integer $\kappa \geq 1$ and constant $\delta \in (0, 1)$ to be determined.

---

[3] Details can be found in Theorem 11.9 of Foucart and Rauhut (2013).

15

The Complexity of Sparse Recovery

As just revealed in Chapter 14, it is theoretically possible to exactly recover any s-sparse vector $x \in \mathbb{R}^N$ from $m = 2s$ nonadaptive linear observations, while s-sparse recovery with stronger desiderata is achievable via ℓ_1-minimization when m is slightly larger, namely proportional to $s \ln(eN/s)$. Can the stronger desiderata be fulfilled when m is only proportional to s, maybe via another recovery map? The purpose of this chapter is to give a negative answer to this question, thus showing that the results brought forward in Compressive Sensing are optimal. This is to be justified as soon as the desiderata of stability and robustness are spelled out. Asides on the notions of Gelfand width and ℓ_2-stability will follow.

15.1 Limitations Imposed by Stability and Robustness

Informally, *stability* refers to the reliability of the recovery despite deviation from sparsity, thus corresponding to the term $\mathrm{dist}_{\ell_1}(x, \Sigma_s^N)$ in (14.5), (14.6), and (14.7)—one would talk about ℓ_1-stability to emphasize that the ℓ_1-norm is used to measure the distance to sparse vectors. *Robustness* refers to the reliability of the recovery despite observation errors, thus corresponding to the term $\|e\|_2$ in (14.7), say. Robustness is a somewhat stronger property than stability, as uncovered by the result below, whose hypothesis is fulfilled by typically normalized gaussian matrices; see Exercise B.3.

Proposition 15.1 *Let $A \in \mathbb{R}^{m \times N}$ be an observation matrix for which there is a constant $\gamma > 0$ such that $\|Ax\|_2 \le \gamma \|x\|_2$ whenever $x \in \Sigma_s^N$ and let $\Delta: \mathbb{R}^m \to \mathbb{R}^N$ be a recovery map. If the pair (A, Δ) provides robustness at sparsity level $2s$, then it provides stability and robustness at sparsity level s.*

Proof Suppose that, for any $2s$-sparse $x \in \mathbb{R}^N$ and any $e \in \mathbb{R}^m$, one has

$$\|x - \Delta(Ax + e)\|_2 \leq D\|e\|_2. \tag{15.1}$$

Now consider a not necessarily sparse vector $x \in \mathbb{R}^N$ and let $T \in [1:N]$ be an index set of $2s$ largest absolute entries of x. Writing $Ax + e = Ax_T + e'$ where $e' := Ax_{T^c} + e$, one can apply (15.1) to the $2s$-sparse vector x_T and obtain

$$\|x_T - \Delta(Ax + e)\|_2 = \|x_T - \Delta(Ax_T + e')\|_2 \leq D\|e'\|_2 \leq D\|Ax_{T^c}\|_2 + D\|e\|_2.$$

It follows that

$$\|x - \Delta(Ax + e)\|_2 \leq \|x_{T^c}\|_2 + \|x_T - \Delta(Ax + e)\|_2$$
$$\leq \|x_{T^c}\|_2 + D\|Ax_{T^c}\|_2 + D\|e\|_2. \tag{15.2}$$

It remains to bound $\|x_{T^c}\|_2$ and $\|Ax_{T^c}\|_2$ in terms of $\text{dist}_{\ell_1}(x, \Sigma_s^N)$. Both bounds can be derived via the *sort-and-split technique*. Let $S_0, S_1, S_2, \ldots$ be index sets of size s selected so that S_0 corresponds to s largest absolute entries of x, S_1 to next s largest absolute entries of x, etc. Since $T = S_0 \cup S_1$, one has

$$\|x_{T^c}\|_2 = \left\| \sum_{k \geq 2} x_{S_k} \right\|_2 \leq \sum_{k \geq 2} \|x_{S_k}\|_2 \leq \sum_{k \geq 2} \frac{\|x_{S_{k-1}}\|_1}{\sqrt{s}}$$
$$\leq \frac{\|x_{S_0^c}\|_1}{\sqrt{s}} = \frac{1}{\sqrt{s}} \text{dist}_{\ell_1}(x, \Sigma_s^N); \tag{15.3}$$

$$\|Ax_{T^c}\|_2 = \left\| \sum_{k \geq 2} Ax_{S_k} \right\|_2 \leq \sum_{k \geq 2} \|Ax_{S_k}\|_2 \leq \sum_{k \geq 2} \gamma\|x_{S_k}\|_2 \leq \gamma \sum_{k \geq 2} \frac{\|x_{S_{k-1}}\|_1}{\sqrt{s}}$$
$$\leq \gamma \frac{\|x_{S_0^c}\|_1}{\sqrt{s}} = \gamma \frac{1}{\sqrt{s}} \text{dist}_{\ell_1}(x, \Sigma_s^N). \tag{15.4}$$

Substituting (15.3) and (15.4) into (15.2) leads to the desired stable and robust estimate of type (14.7). $\qquad\square$

The above proposition explains why the main result of this chapter is stated below by focusing on stability only.

Theorem 15.2 *If there exists a pair (A, Δ) of observation matrix $A \in \mathbb{R}^{m \times N}$ and recovery map $\Delta: \mathbb{R}^m \to \mathbb{R}^N$ which provides stability at sparsity level s for some $p \in [1, 2]$, i.e., if*

$$\|x - \Delta(Ax)\|_p \leq \frac{C}{s^{1-1/p}} \text{dist}_{\ell_1}(x, \Sigma_s^N) \quad \text{for all } x \in \mathbb{R}^N, \tag{15.5}$$

then the number of linear observations satisfies

$$m \geq c\, s \ln\left(\frac{eN}{s}\right) \tag{15.6}$$

for some positive constant c depending only on C.

The key to the argument is a combinatorial lemma whose usefulness can be certified by the fact that it has been independently uncovered and exploited by various authors for a few decades.

Lemma 15.3 *One can find*

$$K \geq \left(\frac{N}{4s}\right)^{s/2} \tag{15.7}$$

subsets $S_1, \ldots, S_K$ *of* $[1:N]$, *each of size* s, *with small pairwise intersections, in the sense that*

$$|S_k \cap S_\ell| < \frac{s}{2} \qquad \text{whenever } k \neq \ell \in [1:K]. \tag{15.8}$$

Proof Let S denote the family of subsets of $[1:N]$ with size s. Starting from $\mathcal{A}_0 = \emptyset$, one defines $S_1, \ldots, S_K \in S$ and $\mathcal{A}_1, \ldots, \mathcal{A}_K \subseteq S$ via

- $S_k \in S \setminus (\mathcal{A}_0 \cup \ldots \cup \mathcal{A}_{k-1})$,
- $\mathcal{A}_k = \{S \in S : |S \cap S_k| \geq s/2\}$,

the process stopping when $S \setminus (\mathcal{A}_0 \cup \cdots \cup \mathcal{A}_K) = \emptyset$, i.e., $S = \mathcal{A}_1 \cup \cdots \cup \mathcal{A}_K$. By construction, one has $|S_k \cap S_1| < s/2, \ldots, |S_k \cap S_{k-1}| < s/2$ for all $k \in [1:K]$, so that (15.8) is fulfilled. Moreover, in view of $S = \mathcal{A}_1 \cup \cdots \cup \mathcal{A}_K$, one has

$$|S| \leq K \max_{k \in [1:K]} |\mathcal{A}_k|, \qquad \text{i.e.,} \qquad K \geq \frac{1}{\max_{k \in [1:k]} |\mathcal{A}_k| / \binom{N}{s}}. \tag{15.9}$$

Now, for any $k \in [1:K]$, one observes that

$$\frac{|\mathcal{A}_k|}{\binom{N}{s}} = \frac{\sum_{t=\lceil s/2 \rceil}^{s} \binom{s}{t}\binom{N-s}{s-t}}{\binom{N}{s}} = \sum_{t=\lceil s/2 \rceil}^{s} \binom{s}{t} \frac{\binom{N-s}{s-t}}{\binom{N}{s}}.$$

Taking into account that, for $t \leq s$,

$$\frac{\binom{N-s}{s-t}}{\binom{N}{s}} = \frac{(N-s)(N-s-1)\cdots(N-2s+t+1)}{N(N-1)\cdots(N-s+1)} s(s-1)\cdots(s-t+1)$$

$$\leq \frac{s\cdots(s-t+1)}{N\cdots(N-t+1)} \leq \left(\frac{s}{N}\right)^t,$$

one arrives at

$$\frac{|\mathcal{A}_k|}{\binom{N}{s}} \leq \sum_{t=\lceil s/2 \rceil}^{s} \binom{s}{t}\left(\frac{s}{N}\right)^t \leq \left(\frac{s}{N}\right)^{\lceil s/2 \rceil} \sum_{t=0}^{s} \binom{s}{t} \leq \left(\frac{s}{N}\right)^{s/2} 2^s = \left(\frac{4s}{N}\right)^{s/2}.$$

Substituting the latter into (15.9) yields the desired estimate (15.7). □

Proof of Theorem 15.2 Let $S_1, \ldots, S_K$ be the index sets from Lemma 15.3. For each $k \in [1 : K]$, one introduces an ℓ_1-normalized s-sparse vector $x^{(k)} \in \mathbb{R}^N$ whose entries are

$$x_j^{(k)} = \begin{cases} 1/s & \text{if } j \in S_k, \\ 0 & \text{if } j \notin S_k. \end{cases} \tag{15.10}$$

With $\rho < 1/(2(C+1))$, one considers the subsets $E_1, \ldots, E_K$ of $\mathbb{R}^m$ defined by

$$E_k = A\left(x^{(k)} + \rho\left(B_1^N \cap \frac{1}{s^{1-1/p}} B_p^N\right)\right).$$

One claims that these sets are all disjoint. Indeed, if there was an element in $E_k \cap E_\ell$, $k \neq \ell$, say, $y = A(x^{(k)} + \rho z) = A(x^{(\ell)} + \rho z')$ with $z, z' \in B_1^N \cap B_p^N / s^{1-1/p}$, then

$$
\begin{aligned}
\|x^{(k)} - x^{(\ell)}\|_p &\leq \|x^{(k)} + \rho z - \Delta(y)\|_p + \|x^{(\ell)} + \rho z' - \Delta(y)\|_p + \|\rho z - \rho z'\|_p \\
&\leq \frac{C}{s^{1-1/p}}\left(\operatorname{dist}_{\ell_1}(x^{(k)} + \rho z, \Sigma_s^N) + \operatorname{dist}_{\ell_1}(x^{(\ell)} + \rho z', \Sigma_s^N)\right) + \rho\|z - z'\|_p \\
&\leq \frac{C}{s^{1-1/p}}(\|\rho z\|_1 + \|\rho z'\|_1) + \rho(\|z\|_p + \|z'\|_p) \leq \frac{2C\rho}{s^{1-1/p}} + \frac{2\rho}{s^{1-1/p}} \\
&< \frac{1}{s^{1-1/p}},
\end{aligned}
$$

which would contradict the fact that $\|x^{(k)} - x^{(\ell)}\|_p = (1/s)|S_k \Delta S_\ell|^{1/p} > 1/s^{1-1/p}$. One also claims that all the E_k are contained in $(1+\rho)A(B_1^N \cap B_p^N / s^{1-1/p})$, which is justified by the fact that all the vectors $x^{(k)}$ belong to $B_1^N \cap B_p^N / s^{1-1/p}$. From these two claims, one derives that

$$\sum_{k=1}^K \operatorname{vol}(E_k) = \operatorname{vol}\left(\bigcup_{k=1}^K E_k\right) \leq \operatorname{vol}\left((1+\rho)A(B_1^N \cap B_p^N / s^{1-1/p})\right).$$

With $\mathcal{V} := \operatorname{vol}(A(B_1^N \cap B_p^N / s^{1-1/p}))$ and $r := \operatorname{rank}(A)$, this inequality reads $K\rho^r \mathcal{V} \leq (1+\rho)^r \mathcal{V}$. In view of $K \geq (N/4s)^{s/2}$ and of $r \leq m$, this implies that

$$\left(\frac{N}{4s}\right)^{s/2} \leq \left(1 + \frac{1}{\rho}\right)^m, \qquad \text{so that} \qquad \frac{s}{2}\ln\left(\frac{N}{4s}\right) \leq m\ln\left(1 + \frac{1}{\rho}\right).$$

One has thus arrived at $m \geq c' s \ln(N/4s)$ with c' depending only on C via ρ. To derive the conclusion in its exact form, some technical work is still needed. Specifically, keeping in mind that $m \geq 2s$ must be fulfilled, one has

$$m \geq c' s \ln\left(\frac{eN}{s}\right) - c' s \ln(4e) \geq c' s \ln\left(\frac{eN}{s}\right) - \frac{c' \ln(4e)}{2} m.$$

Rearranging the latter gives

$$\left(1 + c' \frac{\ln(4e)}{2}\right) m \geq c' s \ln\left(\frac{eN}{s}\right),$$

and in turn $m \geq cs \ln(eN/s)$ with c depending only on C via c'. $\qquad \square$

Interestingly, Lemma 15.3 allows one to prove that $m \geq c \, s \ln(eN/s)$ is also necessary if one targets sparse recovery without even requiring stability but insisting on the recovery map to be ℓ_1-minimization.

Proposition 15.4 *If there exists an observation matrix $A \in \mathbb{R}^{m \times N}$ such that every $2s$-sparse vector $x \in \mathbb{R}^N$ is a minimizer of $\|z\|_1$ subject to $Az = Ax$, then the number of linear observations satisfies*

$$m \geq c \, s \ln\left(\frac{eN}{s}\right)$$

for some absolute constant $c > 0$.

Proof Let $x^{(1)}, \ldots, x^{(K)}$ be still defined as in (15.10). Working in the *quotient space* $\ell_1^N / \ker(A)$ equipped with the norm $\|[z]\| := \inf\{\|z'\|_1 : Az' = Az\}$, the ℓ_1-minimality of $2s$-sparse vectors guarantees that, for any $k \neq \ell \in [1:K]$,

$$\|[x^{(k)}] - [x^{(\ell)}]\| = \|[x^{(k)} - x^{(\ell)}]\| = \|x^{(k)} - x^{(\ell)}\|_1 > 1.$$

One also has $\|[x^{(k)}]\| = 1$ for any $k \in [1:K]$. Thus, the points $[x^{(1)}], \ldots, [x^{(K)}]$ form a 1-separating subset of the unit ball of the r-dimensional quotient space $\ell_1^N / \ker(A)$, $r \leq m$. According to Theorem A.5, this implies that $K \leq 3^r \leq 3^m$. The conclusion follows by taking the logarithm and proceeding along lines similar to the end of the previous proof. $\qquad\square$

15.2 Gelfand Width of the ℓ_1-Ball

The stability of sparse recovery has unsuspected connections with the fields of Optimal Recovery and of Banach space geometry. These connections are indeed surprising because the results in these fields do not involve sparsity at all. Here is a result from Optimal Recovery.

Theorem 15.5 *The mth minimal intrinsic error for full approximation in ℓ_2^N over the unit ℓ_1^N-ball satisfies, for $m \leq N$,*

$$\mathrm{Err}^*_{B_1^N, \mathrm{Id}_{\ell_2^N}}(m) \asymp \min\left\{1, \sqrt{\frac{\ln(eN/m)}{m}}\right\}.$$

Proof For the upper estimate, the result is clear if $m < C \ln(eN/m)$, $C \geq 18e$ being a constant chosen later. Indeed, considering the observation map $\Lambda = 0$ and the recovery map $\Delta = 0$ yields $\mathrm{Err}_{B_1^N, \mathrm{Id}_{\ell_2^N}}(\Lambda, \Delta) = \sup_{x \in B_1^N} \|x\|_2 = 1$. Now, assuming that $m \geq C \ln(eN/m)$, one defines $s := \lceil m/(C \ln(eN/m)) \rceil \geq 1$. One has $m \geq (C/2)s \ln(eN/m)$, so that $m \geq (C/2)s$, and hence $9s/m \leq 18/C \leq 1/e$. In turn, it follows that

$$
\begin{aligned}
m &\geq \frac{C}{2} s \ln\left(\frac{eN}{9s}\right) + \frac{Cm}{18} \frac{9s}{m} \ln\left(\frac{9s}{m}\right) \\
&\geq \frac{C}{2} s \ln\left(\frac{eN}{9s}\right) + \frac{Cm}{18} \frac{18}{C} \ln\left(\frac{18}{C}\right) = \frac{C}{2} s \ln\left(\frac{eN}{9s}\right) - m \ln\left(\frac{C}{18}\right),
\end{aligned}
$$

where the last inequality was due to the decrease of $t \mapsto t \ln(t)$ on $(0, 1/e)$. Rearranging the latter gives

$$
m \geq \frac{C/18}{1 + \ln(C/18)} 9s \ln\left(\frac{eN}{9s}\right).
$$

By choosing C large enough, the hypothesis of Theorem B.11 can be met, thus guaranteeing the existence of a matrix $A \in \mathbb{R}^{m \times N}$ with the ℓ_1-restricted isometry property of order $9s$ with constant $\delta = 1/5$. Therefore, with $\Delta(y)$ denoting a minimizer of $\|z\|_1$ subject to $Az = y$, it follows from (14.4) with $p = 2$ that

$$
\|x - \Delta(Ax)\|_2 \leq \frac{C'}{\sqrt{s}} \mathrm{dist}_{\ell_1}(x, \Sigma_s^N) \leq \frac{C'}{\sqrt{s}} \|x\|_1 \qquad \text{for all } x \in \mathbb{R}^N.
$$

With $\Lambda \colon \mathbb{R}^N \to \mathbb{R}^m$ denoting the observation map associated with the matrix $A \in \mathbb{R}^{m \times N}$, taking the supremum over all $x \in B_1^N$ yields

$$
\mathrm{Err}_{B_1^N, \mathrm{Id}_{\ell_2^N}}(\Lambda, \Delta) \leq \frac{C'}{\sqrt{s}} \leq \frac{C'}{\sqrt{m/(C \ln(eN/m))}} = C'' \sqrt{\frac{\ln(eN/m)}{m}}.
$$

This bound provides the required upper estimate on the mth minimal intrinsic error $\mathrm{Err}^*_{B_1^N, \mathrm{Id}_{\ell_2^N}}(m)$.

For the lower estimate, one assumes that $\mathrm{E} := \mathrm{Err}^*_{B_1^N, \mathrm{Id}_{\ell_2^N}}(m) \leq 1/4$, otherwise there is nothing to do. One then selects an observation map $\Lambda \colon \mathbb{R}^N \to \mathbb{R}^m$ such that $\mathrm{Err}^*_{B_1^N, \mathrm{Id}_{\ell_2^N}}(\Lambda)$ is equal (or is arbitrarily close) to E. By Proposition 9.1, this implies that $\mathrm{Err}^0_{B_1^N, \mathrm{Id}_{\ell_2^N}}(\Lambda) \leq \mathrm{E}$. Thus, for any $v \in \ker(\Lambda)$, one has $\|v\|_2 \leq \mathrm{E} \|v\|_1$. Consequently, for any index set S of size $2s$, one obtains

$$
\|v_S\|_1 \leq \sqrt{2s} \|v_S\|_2 \leq \sqrt{2s} \|v\|_2 \leq \sqrt{2s} \, \mathrm{E} \|v\|_1.
$$

Defining $s := \lceil 1/(16\mathrm{E}^2) \rceil \geq 1$, one has $s < 1/(8\mathrm{E}^2)$, so that the matrix $A \in \mathbb{R}^{m \times N}$ associated with Λ satisfies the *null space property* of order $2s$ (in the form $\|v_S\|_1 < \|v\|_1/2$), meaning that $2s$-sparse recovery is possible via ℓ_1-minimization. This yields not only $m \geq 2(2s) \geq s$, but also $m \geq cs \ln(eN/s)$ thanks to Proposition 15.4. One derives that $m \geq c/(16\mathrm{E}^2) \ln(eN/m)$, which is rearranged to obtain the desired lower estimate $\mathrm{E} \geq c' \sqrt{\ln(eN/m)/m}$.   □

The relevant result from Banach space geometry concerns the so-called *Gelfand width*, defined inline below. The result is essentially a reformulation of the previous theorem, in view of the identification of Gelfand width and minimal intrinsic error, as uncovered in the following proof and highlighted earlier in Exercise 11.4.

Corollary 15.6 *For $m \leq N$, the mth Gelfand width of the unit ℓ_1^N-ball in the space ℓ_2^N satisfies*

$$d^m(B_1^N, \ell_2^N) := \inf_{\mathrm{codim}(\mathcal{U}) \leq m} \sup_{x \in B_1^N \cap \mathcal{U}} \|x\|_2 \asymp \min\left\{1, \sqrt{\frac{\ln(eN/m)}{m}}\right\}.$$

Proof Since the ball B_1^N is symmetric and convex, Theorem 9.4 guarantees that the intrinsic and null errors of an observation map $\Lambda : \mathbb{R}^N \mapsto \mathbb{R}^m$ coincide, i.e.,

$$\mathrm{Err}^*_{B_1^N, \mathrm{Id}_{\ell_2^N}}(\Lambda) = \mathrm{Err}^0_{B_1^N, \mathrm{Id}_{\ell_2^N}}(\Lambda) = \sup_{x \in \ker(\Lambda) \cap B_1^N} \|x\|_2.$$

Now taking the infimum over Λ while noticing that null spaces of linear maps from $\mathbb{R}^N$ to $\mathbb{R}^m$ are identifiable to subspaces of $\mathbb{R}^N$ of codimension at most m, one obtains $\mathrm{Err}^*_{B_1^N, \mathrm{Id}_{\ell_2^N}}(m) = d^m(B_1^N, \ell_2^N)$. The conclusion now simply follows from Theorem 15.5. □

Remark 15.7 Historically, the estimate for the Gelfand width of ℓ_1-balls, specifically the lower estimate, accounted for the optimality of Compressive Sensing results, i.e., for the fact that $m \asymp s \ln(eN/s)$ linear observations are necessary to achieve stability in sparse recovery. It is worth seeing how this original argument unravels when considering adaptive observations, leading to the realization that adaptivity does not help much here either. To do so, one assumes that (15.5) is achieved for $p = 2$, say, with some adaptive observation scheme. This assumption implies that $\mathrm{Err}^{*,\mathrm{ada}}_{B_1^N, \mathrm{Id}_{\ell_2^N}}(m) \leq C/\sqrt{s}$. Moreover, given that B_1^N is symmetric and convex, Theorem 11.3 allows one to write

$$\mathrm{Err}^{*,\mathrm{ada}}_{B_1^N, \mathrm{Id}_{\ell_2^N}}(m) \geq \frac{1}{2} \mathrm{Err}^*_{B_1^N, \mathrm{Id}_{\ell_2^N}}(m) = \frac{1}{2} d^m(B_1^N, \ell_2^N) \geq c' \min\left\{1, \sqrt{\frac{\ln(eN/m)}{m}}\right\}.$$

Leaving the case $c' \leq C/\sqrt{s}$ aside (which would mean that s is bounded), one obtains $c' \sqrt{\ln(eN/m)/m} \leq C/\sqrt{s}$, i.e., $m \geq c'' s \ln(eN/m)$. Some routine technical work allows one to transform this lower bound on the number of adaptive observations into the form $m \geq cs \ln(eN/s)$.

15.3 Irrelevance of ℓ_2-Stability

To close this chapter, one tackles a question which may have been on the reader's mind since the beginning: why ℓ_1-stability rather than ℓ_2-stability? In other words, why is the distance to sparse vectors measured with respect to the ℓ_1-norm rather than the ℓ_2-norm? The answer is that ℓ_2-stability can be achieved only when the number m of linear observations is proportional to the ambient dimension N, a situation which beats the very purpose of Compressive Sensing. Here is a precise statement.

Proposition 15.8 *If there exists a pair (A, Δ) of observation matrix $A \in \mathbb{R}^{m \times N}$ and recovery map $\Delta \colon \mathbb{R}^m \to \mathbb{R}^N$ such that*

$$\|x - \Delta(Ax)\|_2 \le C \operatorname{dist}_{\ell_2}(x, \Sigma_s^N) \quad \text{for all } x \in \mathbb{R}^N, \tag{15.11}$$

then the number of linear observations satisfies

$$m \ge c\,N$$

for some positive constant c depending only on C.

Proof For $v \in \ker(A)$, the stability property (15.11) yields bounds on both $\|v - \Delta(0)\|_2$ and on $\|(-v) - \Delta(0)\|_2$, which combine to give

$$\|v\|_2 \le C \operatorname{dist}_{\ell_2}(v, \Sigma_s^N) \le C \operatorname{dist}_{\ell_2}(v, \Sigma_1^N).$$

For any $j \in [1 : N]$, it follows that $\|v\|_2^2 \le C^2(\|v\|_2^2 - v_j^2)$, i.e., $|v_j| \le C' \|v\|_2$, where the constant $C' := \sqrt{(C^2 - 1)/C^2}$ is less than one. Now, with P denoting the orthogonal projector onto $\ker(A)$ and with $(e_1, \ldots, e_N)$ denoting the canonical basis of $\mathbb{R}^N$, one has

$$N - m \le \dim(\ker(A)) = \operatorname{tr}(P) = \sum_{j=1}^{N} (Pe_j)_j \le \sum_{j=1}^{N} C' \|Pe_j\|_2 \le C'N.$$

After a rearrangement, one obtains the required result with $c = 1 - C'$. □

Exercises

15.1 Explore numerically the lack of robustness of the *Prony method* for the exact recovery of s-sparse vectors $x \in \mathbb{R}^N$—treated as functions on $[0 : N - 1]$—from the $2s$ discrete Fourier coefficients $\hat{x}(0), \ldots, \hat{x}(2s - 1)$. This method consists in:

- observing that $\hat{p} * \hat{x} = 0$ for the auxiliary trigonometric polynomial defined by $p(t) := \prod_{k \in \operatorname{supp}(x)} (1 - e^{-i2\pi k/N} e^{i2\pi t/N})$;

- taking $\hat{p}(0) = 1$ and $\hat{p}(k) = 0$ for $k > s$ into account to write an $s \times s$ Toeplitz system with unknowns $\hat{p}(1), \ldots, \hat{p}(s)$;
- solving this system to determine $\hat{p}$, then p, next $\text{supp}(x)$, and finally x.

15.2 Given $p \in [1, 2]$, prove that the *m*th *Gelfand width* of the unit ℓ_1^N-ball in the space ℓ_p^N satisfies, for $m \leq N$,

$$d^m(B_1^N, \ell_p^N) \asymp \min\left\{1, \frac{\ln(eN/m)}{m}\right\}^{1-1/p}.$$

15.3 Consider the approximability set

$$\mathcal{K} = \{x \in \mathbb{R}^N : \text{dist}_{\ell_2}(x, \Sigma_s^N) \leq \varepsilon\},$$

as well as the quantity of interest Ave taking the average of the entries of a vector, i.e., $\text{Ave}(x) = (1/N) \sum_{j=1}^N x_j$ for $x \in \mathbb{R}^N$. Observe that the *m*th minimal intrinsic error for full approximation in ℓ_2^N over $\mathcal{K}$ cannot satisfy $\text{Err}^*_{\mathcal{K}, \text{Id}_{\ell_2^N}}(m) \leq C\varepsilon$ unless $m \geq cN$, while the *m*th minimal intrinsic error for Ave over $\mathcal{K}$ satisfies $\text{Err}^*_{\mathcal{K}, \text{Ave}}(m) \leq C\varepsilon$ with $m \asymp s\ln(eN/s)$.

15.4 Suppose that the matrix $A \in \mathbb{R}^{m \times N}$ satisfies the ℓ_1-restricted isometry property of order $2s$. By considering the (impractical) recovery map Δ defined for $y \in \mathbb{R}^m$ by

$$\Delta(y) \in \underset{z \in \mathbb{R}^N}{\text{argmin}} \|y - Az\|_1 \qquad \text{subject to } z \in \Sigma_s^N,$$

justify that the operator norm $\|A\|_{2 \to 1}$ cannot be bounded above by some absolute constant $C > 0$ unless $m \geq cN$ for some c depending on C.

16

Low-Rank Recovery from Linear Observations

In this chapter, the high-dimensional objects of interest change from sparse vectors $x \in \mathbb{R}^N$ to low-rank matrices $X \in \mathbb{R}^{n \times n}$. These matrices are acquired with $m \ll n^2$ linear observations, summarized as $y = \mathcal{A}(X)$ for some linear map $\mathcal{A} \colon \mathbb{R}^{n \times n} \to \mathbb{R}^m$. Intuitively, the number m of observations needed to recover rank-r matrices scales at least like the number of parameters used to describe them, i.e., roughly nr. It will be shown that $O(nr)$ linear observations are in fact sufficient for (stable and robust) rank-r recovery. By analogy with the vector case, a recovery method akin to ℓ_1-minimization will be introduced first. The success of this method will then be established for observation maps satisfying an adjusted version of the ℓ_1-restricted isometry property. At last, the practical implementation of the method as a semidefinite program will be highlighted.

16.1 Nuclear Norm Minimization

The analogy with the vector case is based on the fact that a matrix $X \in \mathbb{R}^{n \times n}$ has rank at most r if and only if the vector $x = [\sigma_1(X); \ldots; \sigma_n(X)]$ of its singular values is r-sparse. Thus, in lieu of the ℓ_1-norm, a central role is played by the *nuclear norm* of a matrix $Z \in \mathbb{R}^{n \times n}$, defined by

$$\|Z\|_* = \sum_{j=1}^{n} \sigma_j(Z), \qquad Z \in \mathbb{R}^{n \times n}.$$

Although positive definiteness ($\|Z\|_* = 0$ if and only if $Z = 0$) and absolute homogeneity ($\|cZ\|_* = |c|\,\|Z\|_*$) are readily seen, the triangle inequality is not immediate. It can be deduced from a weakened version of the *Mirsky inequality*

(Theorem D.6), namely from the inequality

$$\sum_{j=1}^{n} |\sigma_j(A) - \sigma_j(B)| \le \sum_{j=1}^{n} \sigma_j(A - B), \qquad A, B \in \mathbb{R}^{n \times n}. \tag{16.1}$$

To continue the analogy, one is compelled to attempt to recover a low-rank matrix $X \in \mathbb{R}^{n \times n}$ observed as $y = \mathcal{A}(X) \in \mathbb{R}^m$ by solving

$$\underset{Z \in \mathbb{R}^{n \times n}}{\text{minimize}} \ \|Z\|_* \quad \text{subject to } \mathcal{A}(Z) = y. \tag{16.2}$$

Not worrying for now about how this minimization program is performed in practice, a theoretical analysis is presented first, starting with a pendant of the *null space property*.

Theorem 16.1 *For $\mathcal{A}: \mathbb{R}^{n \times n} \to \mathbb{R}^m$, the following properties are equivalent:*

(i) *every $X \in \mathbb{R}^{n \times n}$ with $\text{rank}(X) \le r$ is the unique minimizer of $\|Z\|_*$ subject to $\mathcal{A}(Z) = \mathcal{A}(X)$;*

(ii) *for all $M \in \ker(\mathcal{A}) \setminus \{0\}$, one has $\sum_{j=1}^{r} \sigma_j(M) < \sum_{j=r+1}^{m} \sigma_j(M)$.*

Proof (i)$\Rightarrow$(ii). Let $M \in \ker(\mathcal{A}) \setminus \{0\}$ and let $\sigma_j = \sigma_j(M)$, $j \in [1:n]$, denote its singular values. The singular value decomposition of M reads $M = U\Sigma V^\top$, where $U, V \in \mathbb{R}^{n \times n}$ are orthogonal matrices and $\Sigma = \text{diag}[\sigma_1; \ldots; \sigma_n] \in \mathbb{R}^{n \times n}$ is a diagonal matrix. Writing $\Sigma = D - D'$ with $D := \text{diag}[\sigma_1; \ldots; \sigma_r; 0; \ldots; 0]$ and $D' := -\text{diag}[0; \ldots; 0; \sigma_{r+1}; \ldots; \sigma_n]$, the fact that $\mathcal{A}(M) = 0$ implies that $\mathcal{A}(UDV^\top) = \mathcal{A}(UD'V^\top)$. Now, since the matrix $UDV^\top$ has rank at most r, its nuclear norm must then be smaller than that of $UD'V^\top$. The desired inequality follows from $\|UDV^\top\|_* = \sum_{j=1}^{r} \sigma_j$ and $\|UD'V^\top\|_* = \sum_{\ell=r+1}^{n} \sigma_\ell$.

(ii)$\Rightarrow$(i). Consider $X \in \mathbb{R}^{n \times n}$ with $\text{rank}(X) \le r$ and $Z \in \mathbb{R}^{n \times n}$, $Z \ne X$, satisfying $\mathcal{A}(Z) = \mathcal{A}(X)$. With $M := X - Z \in \ker(\mathcal{A}) \setminus \{0\}$, inequality (16.1) ensures that

$$\|Z\|_* = \sum_{j=1}^{n} \sigma_j(X - M) \ge \sum_{j=1}^{n} |\sigma_j(X) - \sigma_j(M)|.$$

For $j \in [1:r]$, one has $|\sigma_j(X) - \sigma_j(M)| \ge \sigma_j(X) - \sigma_j(M)$, and for $j \in [r+1:n]$, in view of $\sigma_j(X) = 0$, one has $|\sigma_j(X) - \sigma_j(M)| = \sigma_j(M)$. It follows that

$$\|Z\|_* \ge \sum_{j=1}^{r} \sigma_j(X) - \sum_{j=1}^{r} \sigma_j(M) + \sum_{j=r+1}^{n} \sigma_j(M) > \sum_{j=1}^{r} \sigma_j(X) = \|X\|_*,$$

where the null space property (ii) was used in the last inequality. This proves that X is the unique nuclear norm minimizer. □

16.2 ℓ_1-Rank Restricted Isometry Property

At this time, some observation maps $\mathcal{A}\colon \mathbb{R}^{n\times n} \to \mathbb{R}^m$ satisfying the null space property of Theorem 16.1 need to be uncovered. As in the vector case, the main tool is a restricted isometry property featuring ℓ_1 as an inner norm, as opposed to ℓ_2 with a more standard approach.

Definition 16.2 A linear map $\mathcal{A}\colon \mathbb{R}^{n\times n} \to \mathbb{R}^m$ is said to satisfy the ℓ_1-*rank restricted isometry property* of order r with constants $\beta \ge \alpha > 0$ if

$$\alpha\|Z\|_F \le \|\mathcal{A}(Z)\|_1 \le \beta\|Z\|_F \qquad \text{whenever rank}(Z) \le r. \qquad (16.3)$$

This ℓ_1 version covers not only the typical observations processes where $\mathcal{A}(Z)_i = \langle A_i, Z \rangle_F$ for generic random matrices $A_1, \ldots, A_m \in \mathbb{R}^{n\times n}$ (as proved in Theorem 16.4 below), but also the more restricted observation processes where

$$\mathcal{A}(Z)_i = \langle b^{(i)}, Za^{(i)} \rangle = \langle A_i, Z \rangle_F, \qquad A_i := b^{(i)}a^{(i)\top},$$

for random vectors $a^{(1)}, \ldots, a^{(m)}, b^{(1)}, \ldots, b^{(m)} \in \mathbb{R}^n$ (see Theorem B.12). In the latter situation, however, the constants α and β cannot be arbitrarily close, i.e., they cannot be taken as $1 - \delta$ and $1 + \delta$. This is in fact of little importance, as demonstrated below.

Theorem 16.3 *Given* $\gamma \ge 1$, *if* $\mathcal{A}\colon \mathbb{R}^{n\times n} \to \mathbb{R}^m$ *satisfies the* ℓ_1-*rank restricted isometry property of order* $\lceil 4\gamma^2 r \rceil$ *with constants* $\beta \ge \alpha > 0$ *such that* $\beta/\alpha < \gamma$, *then it also satisfies the null space property of order* r.

Proof The argument relies on the noteworthy claim that any ℓ_1-restricted isometry condition guaranteeing sparse recovery automatically translates into an ℓ_1-rank restricted isometry condition guaranteeing low-rank recovery. Thus, the statement of the theorem is a consequence of Remark 14.5. Now, to justify the claim, suppose that $\mathcal{A}$ satisfies the ℓ_1-rank restricted isometry condition of order t with constants $\beta \ge \alpha$ and that the (vector) ℓ_1-restricted isometry condition with these parameters implies the (vector) null space property of order r. Consider a matrix $M \in \ker(\mathcal{A}) \setminus \{0\}$ and write its singular value decomposition as $M = U\Sigma V^\top$, where $U, V \in \mathbb{R}^{n\times n}$ are orthogonal matrices and $\Sigma = \text{diag}[\sigma_1; \ldots; \sigma_n] \in \mathbb{R}^{n\times n}$ is a diagonal matrix. The objective is to prove that

$$\sum_{j=1}^{r} \sigma_j < \sum_{j=r+1}^{n} \sigma_j. \qquad (16.4)$$

To attain this objective, introduce the matrix $A \in \mathbb{R}^{m\times n}$ of the linear map

$$z \in \mathbb{R}^n \mapsto \mathcal{A}(U \, \text{diag}[z]V^\top) \in \mathbb{R}^m.$$

This matrix is seen to satisfy the ℓ_1-restricted isometry property of order t with constants $\beta \geq \alpha$: indeed, when a vector z is t-sparse, the matrix $U \operatorname{diag}[z]V^\top$ has rank at most t, and so

$$\|A(z)\|_1 = \|\mathcal{A}(U \operatorname{diag}[z]V^\top)\|_1 = \begin{cases} \geq \alpha \|U \operatorname{diag}[z]V^\top\|_F = \alpha\|z\|_2, \\ \leq \beta \|U \operatorname{diag}[z]V^\top\|_F = \beta\|z\|_2. \end{cases}$$

Consequently, the matrix A satisfies the null space property of order r. Then, since the nonzero vector $v := [\sigma_1; \ldots; \sigma_n]$ belongs to $\ker(A)$, one derives that $\|v_{[1:r]}\|_1 < \|v_{[r+1:n]}\|_1$, which is the required inequality (16.4). □

It has been determined that low-rank recovery is achievable as soon as one can provide observation maps $\mathcal{A}: \mathbb{R}^{n \times n} \to \mathbb{R}^m$ satisfying the ℓ_1-rank restricted isometry property. This new quest is realized through probabilistic arguments, focusing on random observation maps $\mathcal{A}$ given by $\mathcal{A}(Z)_i = \langle A_i, Z \rangle_F$ for some independent gaussian matrices $A_1, \ldots, A_m \in \mathbb{R}^{n \times n}$. Observation maps $\mathcal{A}$ given by $\mathcal{A}(Z)_i = \langle b^{(i)}, Z a^{(i)} \rangle$ for some independent Rademacher vectors $a^{(1)}, \ldots, a^{(m)}$, $b^{(1)}, \ldots, b^{(m)}$ are covered in Appendix B as Theorem B.12. Regardless of the situation, the number m of observations needs only to be proportional to nr. This is a notable deviation from the vector case, where a logarithmic factor needed to appear.

Theorem 16.4 *Let $A_1, \ldots, A_m \in \mathbb{R}^{n \times n}$ be independent random matrices that are populated by independent gaussian variables with mean zero and standard deviation $\sqrt{\pi/2}/m$. Given $\delta \in (0, 1)$, if $m \geq C\delta^{-3}nr$, then the ℓ_1-rank restricted isometry property of order r with constants $1 - \delta$ and $1 + \delta$ holds with failure probability at most $2 \exp(-c\delta^2 m)$. The constants c and C can be chosen as $c = 1/(8\pi)$ and $C = 576\sqrt{2}\pi$.*

Proof For a fixed matrix $X \in \mathbb{R}^{n \times n}$ with $\operatorname{rank}(X) \leq r$, observe first that $\|\mathcal{A}(X)\|_1 = \sum_{i=1}^m |\langle A_i, X \rangle_F| = \sum_{i=1}^m |\langle a_i, x \rangle|$, where $a_i = \operatorname{vec}(A_i) \in \mathbb{R}^{n^2}$ stands for the vectorization of the matrix $A_i \in \mathbb{R}^{n \times n}$ and $x = \operatorname{vec}(X) \in \mathbb{R}^{n^2}$ for the vectorization of the matrix $X \in \mathbb{R}^{n \times n}$. Thus, according to the concentration inequality (B.18) proved in the appendix for the vector case, one has

$$\mathbb{P}\Big(\big|\|\mathcal{A}(X)\|_1 - \|X\|_F\big| > t\|X\|_F\Big) \leq 2 \exp\Big(-\frac{t^2 m}{\pi}\Big).$$

Then, the explanation for the disappearance of the logarithmic factor stems from the size of the covering number of Frobenius-normalized and low-rank matrices as estimated by Lemma A.8. This lemma establishes the existence of $K \leq (1 + 6/\rho)^{(2n+1)r} \leq \exp(18nr/\rho)$ matrices $X_1, \ldots, X_K$ that form a ρ-net for the set $\{X \in \mathbb{R}^{n \times n} : \|X\|_F = 1, \mathrm{rank}(X) \leq r\}$. By a union bound, one obtains

$$\mathbb{P}\left(\left|\||\mathcal{A}(X_k)\||_1 - \|X_k\|_F\right| > t\|X_k\|_F \text{ for some } k \in [1:K]\right) \leq K \times 2\exp\left(-\frac{t^2 m}{\pi}\right)$$

$$\leq 2\exp\left(-\frac{t^2 m}{\pi} + \frac{18nr}{\rho}\right). \tag{16.5}$$

Next, as in the second steps of the proofs of Theorems B.11 and B.12, choosing in particular $t = \delta/2$ and $\rho = \delta/(2\sqrt{2}(1+\delta))$, one derives that the ℓ_1-rank restricted isometry property of order r with constants $1 - \delta$ and $1 + \delta$ is highly likely to hold. Thanks to (16.5), the failure probability is actually bounded by

$$2\exp\left(-\frac{\delta^2 m}{4\pi} + \frac{72\sqrt{2}\,nr}{\delta}\right) \leq 2\exp\left(-\frac{\delta^2 m}{8\pi}\right)$$

so long as $72\sqrt{2}\,nr/\delta \leq \delta^2 m/(8\pi)$, i.e., $m \geq (576\sqrt{2}\,\pi/\delta^3)nr$. □

With all these ingredients in place, the following result can finally be stated.

Corollary 16.5 *If $m \geq Cnr$, then there exist linear maps $\mathcal{A}: \mathbb{R}^{n \times n} \to \mathbb{R}^m$ such that every matrix $X \in \mathbb{R}^{n \times n}$ with $\mathrm{rank}(X) \leq r$ can be exactly recovered by nuclear norm minimization from the mere knowledge of $y = \mathcal{A}(X) \in \mathbb{R}^m$.*

16.3 Semidefinite Programming Formulation

To complete this tour of low-rank recovery, it remains to justify that nuclear norm minimization is not just a theoretical scheme but can genuinely be solved in practice. Indeed, the program (16.2) is equivalent to the *semidefinite program*

$$\underset{Z,P,Q \in \mathbb{R}^{n \times n}}{\text{minimize}} \; \frac{1}{2}(\mathrm{tr}(P) + \mathrm{tr}(Q)) \qquad \text{s.to } \mathcal{A}(Z) = y$$

$$\text{and } \begin{bmatrix} P & | & Z \\ Z^\top & | & Q \end{bmatrix} \geq 0.$$

The equivalence is an instant consequence of the semidefinite characterization of the nuclear norm stated below.

Proposition 16.6 *The nuclear norm of a matrix $Z \in \mathbb{R}^{n \times n}$ can be expressed as*

$$\|Z\|_* = \underset{P,Q \in \mathbb{R}^{n \times n}}{\min} \left\{ \frac{1}{2}(\mathrm{tr}(P) + \mathrm{tr}(Q)) : \begin{bmatrix} P & | & Z \\ Z^\top & | & Q \end{bmatrix} \geq 0 \right\}. \tag{16.6}$$

Proof By duality between *Schatten norms* (see Section D.3), given that the nuclear norm is just the Schatten 1-norm, one obtains

$$\|Z\|_* = \max\{\operatorname{tr}(AZ) : A \in \mathbb{R}^{n \times n} \text{ satisfies } \|A\|_{2 \to 2} \leq 1\}.$$

Alternatively, this fact can be seen directly by considering the singular value decomposition $Z = U\Sigma V^\top$ and noticing that

$$\operatorname{tr}(AZ) = \operatorname{tr}(AU\Sigma V^\top) = \operatorname{tr}(V^\top AU\Sigma) = \sum_{j=1}^n \langle V^\top AU\Sigma e_j, e_j \rangle$$

$$= \sum_{j=1}^n \sigma_j \langle AUe_j, Ve_j \rangle \leq \sum_{j=1}^n \sigma_j \|A\|_{2 \to 2} \|Ue_j\|_2 \|Ve_j\|_2$$

$$= \|Z\|_* \|A\|_{2 \to 2},$$

so that $\operatorname{tr}(AZ) \leq \|Z\|_*$ when $\|A\|_{2 \to 2} \leq 1$, with equality occurring for $A = VU^\top$. Next, as a consequence of Theorem D.5 providing the eigendecomposition of the *self-adjoint dilation* of A, one has

$$\|A\|_{2 \to 2} \leq 1 \iff \left[\begin{array}{c|c} 0 & -A \\ \hline -A^\top & 0 \end{array}\right] \preceq I \iff \left[\begin{array}{c|c} I & A \\ \hline A^\top & I \end{array}\right] \succeq 0.$$

Thus, the nuclear norm of a matrix can be expressed as the maximum of a semidefinite program, namely as

$$\|Z\|_* = \max_{A \in \mathbb{R}^{n \times n}} \left\{ \operatorname{tr}(AZ) : \left[\begin{array}{c|c} I & A \\ \hline A^\top & I \end{array}\right] \succeq 0 \right\}. \tag{16.7}$$

Invoking duality in semidefinite programming, as stated in Theorem 21.7, this maximum can be transformed into the minimum of a semidefinite program. Exercise 16.4 invites the reader to verify carefully that the right-hand side of (16.7) indeed equals the right-hand side of (16.6). $\qquad\square$

Exercises

16.1 Let $x^{(1)}, \ldots, x^{(m)}$ be vectors in $\mathbb{R}^d$ with $m > d + 1$. Prove that the matrix $M \in \mathbb{R}^{m \times m}$ with entries $M_{i,j} = \|x^{(i)} - x^{(j)}\|_2^2$ has rank at most $d + 2$.

16.2 Generalize Corollary 16.5 for rank-r rectangular matrices $X \in \mathbb{R}^{n_1 \times n_2}$ under the condition that $m \geq Cnr$, $n := \max\{n_1, n_2\}$.

16.3 Explain why the ratio β/α in the ℓ_1-rank restricted isometry property (16.3) cannot be taken arbitrarily close to one for observations of the type $\mathcal{A}(Z)_i = \langle b^{(i)}, Za^{(i)} \rangle$, with $a^{(1)}, \ldots, a^{(m)}, b^{(1)}, \ldots, b^{(m)} \in \mathbb{R}^n$ being independent Rademacher vectors.

16.4 Justify in detail that the optimal values of the semidefinite programs (16.6) and (16.7) are identical.

17

Sparse Recovery from One-Bit Observations

Returning to sparse vectors $x \in \mathbb{R}^N$ as objects of interest, one contemplates in this chapter the practical obligation to quantize the linear observations made on x. As a matter of fact, the quantization scenario considered here is extreme: each observation is gathered using only one bit of information. Precisely, in the One-Bit Compressive Sensing setting, sparse vectors $x \in \mathbb{R}^N$ are acquired via

$$y_i = \text{sgn}\langle a^{(i)}, x \rangle, \qquad i \in [1:m]. \tag{17.1}$$

With $A \in \mathbb{R}^{m \times N}$ still denoting the matrix whose rows are (the transposes of) the vectors $a^{(1)}, \ldots, a^{(m)} \in \mathbb{R}^N$, this information is summarized as

$$y = \text{sgn}(Ax) \in \{-1, +1\}^m.$$

Of course, exact recovery is now impossible. Moreover, the information (17.1) makes it impossible to distinguish between x and any multiple γx with $\gamma > 0$. Thus, the question is phrased as: How many binary observations are needed to estimate the direction $x/\|x\|_2$ with accuracy ε? As is about to be revealed, the answer is $C_\varepsilon s \ln(eN/s)$. The simple arguments put forward in this chapter rely solely on the previously exploited ℓ_1-*restricted isometry property* but fail to uncover the optimal dependence of the constant C_ε on ε (some improvements are sketched in Exercise 17.2). Two recovery methods shall be highlighted: the first method is based on hard thresholding and the second method on linear programming. Both methods can be used to estimate the magnitude $\|x\|_2$, too, so long as the binary observations are somewhat enhanced.

17.1 Estimating the Direction via Hard Thresholding

The *hard thresholding operator* $H_s \colon \mathbb{R}^N \to \mathbb{R}^N$ appearing in this section outputs, for an input $z \in \mathbb{R}^N$, a (maybe nonunique) s-sparse vector $H_s(z) \in \mathbb{R}^N$

whose entries are equal to those of z on an index set of s largest absolute entries of z and to zero outside of this set. The recovery map $\Delta_{ht} : \{-1, +1\}^m \to \mathbb{R}^N$ under scrutiny is simply given as follows:

- for a sign vector $y \in \{-1, +1\}^m$, return the s-sparse vector

$$\Delta_{ht}(y) := H_s(A^\top y). \tag{17.2}$$

The key ingredient for the analysis of this procedure is given below.

Lemma 17.1 *If $A \in \mathbb{R}^{m \times N}$ satisfies the ℓ_1-restricted isometry property of order s with constant δ, then any ℓ_2-normalized vector $x \in \mathbb{R}^N$ supported on an index set $S \subseteq [1 : N]$ of size s is approximated by $(A^\top \, \mathrm{sgn}(Ax))_S$ with error*

$$\left\| x - (A^\top \, \mathrm{sgn}(Ax))_S \right\|_2 \leq \sqrt{5\delta}. \tag{17.3}$$

Proof By expanding the square, one sees that $\| x - (A^\top \, \mathrm{sgn}(Ax))_S \|_2^2$ equals

$$\| x \|_2^2 - 2\langle x, (A^\top \, \mathrm{sgn}(Ax))_S \rangle + \| (A^\top \, \mathrm{sgn}(Ax))_S \|_2^2. \tag{17.4}$$

The third term in (17.4) satisfies

$$
\begin{aligned}
\| (A^\top \, \mathrm{sgn}(Ax))_S \|_2^2 &= \langle A^\top \, \mathrm{sgn}(Ax), (A^\top \, \mathrm{sgn}(Ax))_S \rangle \\
&= \langle \mathrm{sgn}(Ax), A((A^\top \, \mathrm{sgn}(Ax))_S) \rangle \\
&\leq \| A((A^\top \, \mathrm{sgn}(Ax))_S) \|_1 \\
&\leq (1 + \delta) \| (A^\top \, \mathrm{sgn}(Ax))_S \|_2,
\end{aligned}
$$

where the last inequality was the upper bound in the ℓ_1-restricted isometry property. Therefore, after simplification, one has

$$\| (A^\top \, \mathrm{sgn}(Ax))_S \|_2 \leq (1 + \delta).$$

For the second term in (17.4), one notices that it satisfies

$$\langle x, (A^\top \, \mathrm{sgn}(Ax))_S \rangle = \langle x, A^\top \, \mathrm{sgn}(Ax) \rangle = \langle Ax, \mathrm{sgn}(Ax) \rangle = \| Ax \|_1 \geq (1 - \delta),$$

where the last inequality was the lower bound in the ℓ_1-restricted isometry property. The first term in (17.4) is simply $\| x \|_2^2 = 1$. Altogether, one arrives at

$$\| (A^\top \, \mathrm{sgn}(Ax))_S - x \|_2^2 \leq 1 - 2(1 - \delta) + (1 + \delta)^2 = 4\delta + \delta^2 \leq 5\delta,$$

which leads to the announced result after taking the square root. $\square$

The inequality (17.3) does not in itself provide the intended estimation for the direction of an s-sparse vector $x \in \mathbb{R}^N$ because the support of x is not directly available from $\mathrm{sgn}(Ax) \in \{-1, +1\}^m$. However, the bound plays the crucial role when proving the main result concerning the hard thresholding scheme, which is stated next. Notice that, setting $\varepsilon = C\sqrt{\delta}$ there and invoking Theorem B.11, one can deduce that direction estimation with accuracy ε is possible via hard thresholding with $m \asymp \varepsilon^{-6} s \ln(eN/s)$ binary observations of type (17.1). This is not optimal: different arguments (sketched in Exercise 17.2) would reveal that $m \asymp \varepsilon^{-2} s \ln(eN/s)$ suffice.

Theorem 17.2 *If $A \in \mathbb{R}^{m \times N}$ satisfies the ℓ_1-restricted isometry property of order $2s$ with constant δ, then the direction of any s-sparse vector $x \in \mathbb{R}^N$ observed via $y = \mathrm{sgn}(Ax) \in \{-1, +1\}^m$ is approximated by the output of the hard thresholding procedure (17.2) with error*

$$\left\| \frac{x}{\|x\|_2} - \Delta_{\mathrm{ht}}(y) \right\|_2 \le C\sqrt{\delta}.$$

Proof Let $\widehat{x} \in \mathbb{R}^N$ denote $\Delta_{\mathrm{ht}}(y) = H_s(A^\top \mathrm{sgn}(Ax))$ throughout the proof. With $S := \mathrm{supp}(x)$ and $T := \mathrm{supp}(\widehat{x})$, since $\widehat{x}$ is a best s-sparse approximant to $A^\top \mathrm{sgn}(Ax)$, and thus also to $(A^\top \mathrm{sgn}(Ax))_{S \cup T}$, one has

$$\left\| (A^\top \mathrm{sgn}(Ax))_{S \cup T} - \widehat{x} \right\|_2 \le \left\| (A^\top \mathrm{sgn}(Ax))_{S \cup T} - \frac{x}{\|x\|_2} \right\|_2 .$$

Then, a triangle inequality yields

$$\left\| \frac{x}{\|x\|_2} - \widehat{x} \right\|_2 \le \left\| (A^\top \mathrm{sgn}(Ax))_{S \cup T} - \widehat{x} \right\|_2 + \left\| (A^\top \mathrm{sgn}(Ax))_{S \cup T} - \frac{x}{\|x\|_2} \right\|_2$$

$$\le 2 \left\| (A^\top \mathrm{sgn}(Ax))_{S \cup T} - \frac{x}{\|x\|_2} \right\|_2 .$$

Since $x/\|x\|_2$ is supported on $S \cup T$, it now suffices to call upon Lemma 17.1 to obtain the desired result with $C = 2\sqrt{5}$. $\qquad\qquad\square$

17.2 Estimating the Direction via Linear Programming

This section examines another recovery procedure, inspired by the rationale that sparsity is created when minimizing an ℓ_1-norm. Compared to the previous procedure, this one has the advantage of not requiring any prior knowledge of the sparsity level s. Precisely, one considers here the optimization problem

$$\underset{z \in \mathbb{R}^N}{\text{minimize}} \ \|z\|_1 \quad \text{subject to } \mathrm{sgn}(Az) = y \quad \text{and} \quad \|Az\|_1 = 1. \qquad (17.5)$$

The constraint $\|Az\|_1 = 1$ serves as a normalization condition, given that z and any γz, $\gamma > 0$, share the same sign observations. The condition $\|z\|_2 = 1$ seems perhaps more natural, but it does not lead to a practical optimization program.

In contrast, the condition involving $\|Az\|_1$, which almost equals $\|z\|_2$ under the ℓ_1-restricted isometry property, leads to constraints turning out to be linear. Indeed, the constraint $\text{sgn}(Az) = y$ reads $y_i\langle a^{(i)}, z\rangle \geq 0$ for all $i \in [1:m]$ and then the constraint $\|Az\|_1 = 1$ reads $\sum_{i=1}^{m} y_i\langle a^{(i)}, z\rangle = 1$. Finally, introducing a vector of slack variables—say, $c \in \mathbb{R}^N$ such that $c \geq |z|$—makes it possible to transform (17.5) into a linear program. It is spelled out in the following description of the recovery map $\Delta_{\text{lp}} \colon \{-1, +1\}^m \to \mathbb{R}^N$ under consideration:

- for a sign vector $y \in \{-1, +1\}^m$, return a vector $\Delta_{\text{lp}}(y) = x^\#$, where $(x^\#, c^\#)$ solves the linear program

$$\underset{z, c \in \mathbb{R}^N}{\text{minimize}} \sum_{j=1}^{N} c_j \quad \text{s.to} \sum_{i=1}^{m} y_i\langle a^{(i)}, z\rangle = 1, \ \ y_i\langle a^{(i)}, z\rangle \geq 0, \ i \in [1:m],$$

$$\text{and} \ -c \leq z \leq c. \tag{17.6}$$

The argument developed below involves the notion of *effective sparsity*: a vector $z \in \mathbb{R}^N$ is said to be effectively s-sparse if

$$\|z\|_1 \leq \sqrt{s}\,\|z\|_2.$$

With this notion introduced, the key ingredient for the analysis of the above recovery procedure reads as follows.

Lemma 17.3 *If $A \in \mathbb{R}^{m \times N}$ satisfies the ℓ_1-restricted isometry property of order $9s$ with constant $\delta \leq 1/5$ and if $x \in \mathbb{R}^N$ is s-sparse and ℓ_2-normalized, then any convex combination of x and $\Delta_{\text{lp}}(\text{sgn}(Ax))$ is effectively $9s$-sparse.*

Proof Let $x^\#$ denote $\Delta_{\text{lp}}(\text{sgn}(Ax))$ throughout the proof. The defining property of $x^\#$, together with the sparsity of x and the ℓ_1-restricted isometry property, implies that

$$\|x^\#\|_1 \leq \left\|\frac{x}{\|Ax\|_1}\right\|_1 \leq \frac{\sqrt{s}\|x\|_2}{\|Ax\|_1} \leq \frac{\sqrt{s}}{1-\delta} \leq \frac{5\sqrt{s}}{4}.$$

With $\bar{x} = (1-\tau)x + \tau x^\#$, $\tau \in [0, 1]$, denoting a convex combination of x and $x^\#$, it follows that

$$\|\bar{x}\|_1 \leq (1-\tau)\|x\|_1 + \tau\|x^\#\|_1 \leq (1-\tau)\sqrt{s} + \tau\frac{5\sqrt{s}}{4} = \left(1 + \frac{\tau}{4}\right)\sqrt{s}.$$

Next, noticing that $\text{sgn}(A\bar{x}) = \text{sgn}(Ax^\#) = \text{sgn}(Ax)$ and using the ℓ_1-restricted isometry property, one has on the one hand

$$\|A\bar{x}\|_1 = (1 - \tau)\|Ax\|_1 + \tau\|Ax^\sharp\|_1 \geq (1 - \tau)(1 - \delta) + \tau \geq \frac{4}{5}\left(1 + \frac{\tau}{4}\right). \quad (17.7)$$

On the other hand, by the *sort-and-split technique*, considering an index set T_0 of $t := 9s$ largest absolute entries of $\bar{x}$, an index set T_1 of next t largest absolute entries of $\bar{x}$, an index set T_2 of next t largest absolute entries of $\bar{x}$, etc., one has, with the help of the ℓ_1-restricted isometry property once again,

$$\|A\bar{x}\|_1 \leq \sum_{k\geq 0}\|A\bar{x}_{T_k}\|_1 \leq (1 + \delta)\left(\|\bar{x}_{T_0}\|_2 + \sum_{k\geq 1}\|\bar{x}_{T_k}\|_2\right)$$

$$\leq (1 + \delta)\left(\|\bar{x}\|_2 + \sum_{k\geq 1}\frac{1}{\sqrt{t}}\|\bar{x}_{T_{k-1}}\|_1\right) \leq (1 + \delta)\left(\|\bar{x}\|_2 + \frac{1}{\sqrt{t}}\|\bar{x}\|_1\right)$$

$$\leq (1 + \delta)\left(\|\bar{x}\|_2 + \sqrt{\frac{s}{t}}\left(1 + \frac{\tau}{4}\right)\right) \leq \frac{6}{5}\left(\|\bar{x}\|_2 + \frac{1}{3}\left(1 + \frac{\tau}{4}\right)\right). \quad (17.8)$$

By combining (17.7) and (17.8), one derives that

$$\|\bar{x}\|_2 \geq \frac{1 + \tau/4}{3}.$$

Finally, the upper bound on $\|\bar{x}\|_1$ and the lower bound on $\|\bar{x}\|_2$ put together give

$$\frac{\|\bar{x}\|_1}{\|\bar{x}\|_2} \leq \frac{(1 + \tau/4)\sqrt{s}}{(1 + \tau/4)/3} = \sqrt{9s},$$

which means that $\bar{x}$ is effectively $9s$-sparse, as announced.   □

Before establishing the main result about the linear programming scheme, the additional fact that the ℓ_1-restricted isometry property for genuinely sparse vectors extends to effectively sparse vectors is singled out.

Lemma 17.4 *If $A \in \mathbb{R}^{m\times N}$ satisfies the ℓ_1-restricted isometry property of order $\lceil 9\delta^{-2}s\rceil$ with constant $\delta < 1/3$, then, for all effectively $9s$-sparse $z \in \mathbb{R}^N$,*

$$(1 - 3\delta)\|z\|_2 \leq \|Az\|_1 \leq (1 + 3\delta)\|z\|_2. \quad (17.9)$$

Proof Given an effectively $9s$-sparse vector $z \in \mathbb{R}^N$, let T_0, T_1, T_2, etc. be index sets of size $t := \lceil 9\delta^{-2}s\rceil$ supplied by the *sort-and-split technique* applied to z. From $z_{T_0^c} = \sum_{k\geq 1}z_{T_k}$ and $Az_{T_0^c} = \sum_{k\geq 1}Az_{T_k}$, one obtains

$$\|z_{T_0^c}\|_2 \leq \sum_{k\geq 1}\|z_{T_k}\|_2 \leq \sum_{k\geq 1}\frac{\|z_{T_k}\|_1}{\sqrt{t}} \leq \frac{\|z\|_1}{\sqrt{t}} \leq \sqrt{\frac{9s}{t}}\|z\|_2,$$

$$\|Az_{T_0^c}\|_1 \leq \sum_{k\geq 1}\|Az_{T_k}\|_2 \leq \sum_{k\geq 1}(1 + \delta)\|z_{T_k}\|_2 \leq (1 + \delta)\sqrt{\frac{9s}{t}}\|z\|_2,$$

where the last inequality was simply a repeat of the previous line. Then, writing $Az = Az_{T_0} + Az_{T_0^c}$, it follows on the one hand that

$$\|Az\|_1 \leq \|Az_{T_0}\|_2 + \|Az_{T_0^c}\|_2 \leq (1+\delta)\|z_{T_0}\|_2 + (1+\delta)\sqrt{\frac{9s}{t}}\|z\|_2$$

$$\leq (1+\delta)\left(1 + \sqrt{\frac{9s}{t}}\right)\|z\|_2, \tag{17.10}$$

and on the other hand that

$$\|Az\|_1 \geq \|Az_{T_0}\|_2 - \|Az_{T_0^c}\|_2 \geq (1-\delta)\|z_{T_0}\|_2 - \|Az_{T_0^c}\|_2$$

$$\geq (1-\delta)(\|z\|_2 - \|z_{T_0^c}\|_2) - \|Az_{T_0^c}\|_2 \geq \left(1 - \delta - 2\sqrt{\frac{9s}{t}}\right)\|z\|_2. \tag{17.11}$$

Taking the value of t into account in (17.10) and (17.11) leads to the two-sided estimate announced in (17.9). □

At last, it is time for the main recovery result of this section. Notice that, setting $\varepsilon = C\sqrt{\delta}$ below and invoking Theorem B.11, one can deduce that direction estimation with accuracy ε is possible via linear programming with $m \asymp \varepsilon^{-10} s \ln(eN/s)$ binary observations of type (17.1). Again, as with hard thresholding, this is not optimal in terms of power of ε^{-1}.

Theorem 17.5 *If $A \in \mathbb{R}^{m \times N}$ satisfies the ℓ_1-restricted isometry property of order $\lceil 9\delta^{-2}s \rceil$ with constant $\delta \leq 1/5$, then the direction of any s-sparse vector $x \in \mathbb{R}^N$ observed via $y = \text{sgn}(Ax) \in \{-1, +1\}^m$ is approximated by the output of the linear programming procedure (17.6) with error*

$$\left\| \frac{x}{\|x\|_2} - \Delta_{\text{lp}}(y) \right\|_2 \leq C\sqrt{\delta}.$$

Proof Let $x^{\#}$ denote $\Delta_{\text{lp}}(y)$ throughout the proof and let $x' = x/\|x\|_2$ denote the direction of x. The parallelogram law reads

$$\left\| \frac{x' + x^{\#}}{2} \right\|_2^2 + \left\| \frac{x' - x^{\#}}{2} \right\|_2^2 = \frac{\|x'\|_2^2 + \|x^{\#}\|_2^2}{2} = \frac{1 + \|x^{\#}\|_2^2}{2}. \tag{17.12}$$

Now, Lemma 17.3 implies that the vector $(x' + x^{\#})/2$ is effectively $9s$-sparse. From Lemma 17.4 and the fact that $\text{sgn}(Ax^{\#}) = \text{sgn}(Ax')$, one obtains

$$\left\| \frac{x' + x^{\#}}{2} \right\|_2 \geq \frac{1}{1+3\delta}\left\| A\left(\frac{x' + x^{\#}}{2}\right)\right\|_1 = \frac{1}{1+3\delta}\frac{\|Ax'\|_1 + \|Ax^{\#}\|_1}{2}$$

$$\geq \frac{1}{1+3\delta}\frac{(1-\delta) + 1}{2} = \frac{1 - \delta/2}{1+3\delta}. \tag{17.13}$$

Next, Lemma 17.3 also implies that $x^\#$ is effectively $9s$-sparse. It follows from Lemma 17.4 that

$$\|x^\#\|_2 \le \frac{1}{1-3\delta}\|Ax^\#\|_1 = \frac{1}{1-3\delta}. \tag{17.14}$$

Taking (17.13) and (17.14) into account in (17.12) yields

$$\left\|\frac{x'-x^\#}{2}\right\|_2^2 \le \frac{1+1/(1-3\delta)^2}{2} - \frac{(1-\delta/2)^2}{(1+3\delta)^2} \le C'\delta$$

for some absolute constant $C' > 0$. The announced result is deduced by taking the square root. □

17.3 Estimating Both the Direction and the Magnitude

As already remarked, the magnitude of an s-sparse vector $x \in \mathbb{R}^N$ cannot be estimated from standard binary observations of type (17.1). However, as one shall prove, it can be estimated from binary observations that incorporates some thresholds $\theta_1, \ldots, \theta_m \in \mathbb{R}$. Precisely, the binary observations considered in this section take the form

$$y_i = \text{sgn}(\langle a^{(i)}, x \rangle - \theta_i), \qquad i \in [1:m]. \tag{17.15}$$

The key insight consists in viewing them as standard binary observations made on the augmented vector $\widetilde{x} = [x; 1] \in \mathbb{R}^{N+1}$. Indeed, the vector $y \in \{-1, +1\}^m$ can be written as

$$y = \text{sgn}(\widetilde{A}\widetilde{x}), \qquad \text{where} \quad \widetilde{A} = \begin{bmatrix} a^{(1)\top} & | & -\theta_1 \\ \vdots & | & \vdots \\ a^{(m)\top} & | & -\theta_m \end{bmatrix} \in \mathbb{R}^{m\times(N+1)}.$$

In this case, the direction of the $(s+1)$-sparse vector $\widetilde{x}$ can be well estimated by the output of the hard thresholding or linear programming procedure carried out in the augmented space $\mathbb{R}^{N+1}$. Such a direction estimation in augmented space conceivably yields a full estimation in the original space—the following result demonstrates how.

Proposition 17.6 *The euclidean distance between two vectors $u, v \in \mathbb{R}^N$ is controlled by the euclidean distance between the directions of the augmented vectors $\widetilde{u} = [u; 1] \in \mathbb{R}^{N+1}$ and $\widetilde{v} = [v; 1] \in \mathbb{R}^{N+1}$ according to*

$$\|u - v\|_2 \le \|\widetilde{u}\|_2 \|\widetilde{v}\|_2 \left\| \frac{\widetilde{u}}{\|\widetilde{u}\|_2} - \frac{\widetilde{v}}{\|\widetilde{v}\|_2} \right\|_2.$$

Proof In order to derive the result, one simply writes

$$\|u - v\|_2 = \|\bar{u}\|_2 \left\| \frac{u}{\|\bar{u}\|_2} - \frac{v}{\|\bar{v}\|_2} + \frac{v}{\|\bar{v}\|_2} - \frac{v}{\|\bar{u}\|_2} \right\|_2$$

$$\leq \|\bar{u}\|_2 \left(\left\| \frac{u}{\|\bar{u}\|_2} - \frac{v}{\|\bar{v}\|_2} \right\|_2 + \|v\|_2 \left| \frac{1}{\|\bar{u}\|_2} - \frac{1}{\|\bar{v}\|_2} \right| \right)$$

$$\leq \|\bar{u}\|_2 \left(1 + \|v\|_2^2 \right)^{1/2} \left(\left\| \frac{u}{\|\bar{u}\|_2} - \frac{v}{\|\bar{v}\|_2} \right\|_2^2 + \left| \frac{1}{\|\bar{u}\|_2} - \frac{1}{\|\bar{v}\|_2} \right|^2 \right)^{1/2}$$

$$= \|\bar{u}\|_2 \|\bar{v}\|_2 \left\| \frac{\bar{u}}{\|\bar{u}\|_2} - \frac{\bar{v}}{\|\bar{v}\|_2} \right\|_2. \qquad \square$$

Without isolating a formal statement, one now explains more precisely how to utilize the nonstandard binary observations (17.15) in order to fully estimate an s-sparse vector $x \in \mathbb{R}^N$ with bounded magnitude, say $\|x\|_2 \leq 1$. First, by choosing the thresholds $\theta_1, \ldots, \theta_m$ as independent properly normalized mean-zero gaussian variables, a realization of the random matrix $\widetilde{A}$ satisfies the ℓ_1-restricted isometry property. Therefore, with $\widetilde{z} = [z; \zeta] \in \mathbb{R}^{N+1}$ denoting the output of one of the earlier recovery procedures carried out in the augmented space, the direction of the $(s + 1)$-sparse vector $\widetilde{x} \in \mathbb{R}^{N+1}$ is approximated by $\widetilde{z}$ with error

$$\left\| \frac{\widetilde{x}}{\|\widetilde{x}\|_2} - \widetilde{z} \right\|_2 \leq C \sqrt{\delta}. \qquad (17.16)$$

By looking at the first N entries and at the last entry, with δ chosen small enough for $C \sqrt{\delta} < 1/\sqrt{8}$ to hold, one derives in particular that

$$\left\| \frac{x}{\sqrt{1 + \|x\|_2^2}} - z \right\|_2 \leq C \sqrt{\delta}, \quad \text{so that} \quad \|z\|_2 \leq \frac{\|x\|_2}{\sqrt{1 + \|x\|_2^2}} + C \sqrt{\delta} \leq 1 + \frac{1}{\sqrt{8}},$$

$$\left| \frac{1}{\sqrt{1 + \|x\|_2^2}} - \zeta \right| \leq C \sqrt{\delta}, \quad \text{so that} \quad \zeta \geq \frac{1}{\sqrt{1 + \|x\|_2^2}} - C \sqrt{\delta} \geq \frac{1}{\sqrt{2}} - \frac{1}{\sqrt{8}}.$$

This implies that $\widetilde{x}^b := \widetilde{z}/\zeta = [x^b; 1] \in \mathbb{R}^{N+1}$, where $x^b := z/\zeta$, satisfies

$$\|\widetilde{x}^b\|_2^2 = \frac{\|z\|^2}{\zeta^2} + 1 \leq \frac{((\sqrt{8} + 1)/\sqrt{8})^2}{(1/\sqrt{8})^2} + 1 = 10 + 2\sqrt{8} \leq 16.$$

By also taking $\|\widetilde{x}\|_2^2 = \|x\|_2^2 + 1 \leq 2$ into account, Proposition 17.6 leads to

$$\|x - x^b\|_2 \leq \sqrt{32} \left\| \frac{\widetilde{x}}{\|\widetilde{x}\|_2} - \frac{\widetilde{x}^b}{\|\widetilde{x}^b\|_2} \right\|_2 = \sqrt{32} \left\| \frac{\widetilde{x}}{\|\widetilde{x}\|_2} - \frac{\widetilde{z}}{\|\widetilde{z}\|_2} \right\|_2. \qquad (17.17)$$

One now remarks that

$$\left\| \frac{\overline{x}}{\|\overline{x}\|_2} - \frac{\overline{z}}{\|\overline{z}\|_2} \right\|_2 \le \left\| \frac{\overline{x}}{\|\overline{x}\|_2} - \overline{z} \right\|_2 + \left\| \frac{\overline{z}}{\|\overline{z}\|_2} - \overline{z} \right\|_2 \le 2 \left\| \frac{\overline{x}}{\|\overline{x}\|_2} - \overline{z} \right\|_2, \quad (17.18)$$

where the last inequality used the fact that $\overline{z}/\|\overline{z}\|_2$ is the best ℓ_2-normalized approximant to $\overline{z}$. Together, the inequalities (17.17), (17.18), and (17.16) yield

$$\|x - x^b\|_2 \le D\sqrt{\delta}, \qquad D = 2\sqrt{32}\,C,$$

which is the intended full estimation of the vector x by a vector x^b efficiently constructed from the nonstandard binary observations $y = \mathrm{sgn}(Ax - \theta)$.

Exercises

17.1 The *sign product embedding property* of order s with constant $\delta \in (0,1)$ is a generalization of the ℓ_1-restricted isometry property which reads: for all s-sparse vectors $u, v \in \mathbb{R}^N$, u being ℓ_2-normalized,

$$|\langle \mathrm{sgn}(Au), Av \rangle - \langle u, v \rangle| \le \delta \|v\|_2.$$

Prove that it can be derived from the ℓ_1-restricted isometry property of order $2s$ with constant $\delta^2/5$.

17.2 The above sign product embedding property is known[1] to be satisfied by random matrices $A \in \mathbb{R}^{m \times N}$ populated with independent $\mathcal{N}(0, (\pi/2)/m^2)$ entries when $m \asymp \delta^{-2} s \ln(eN/s)$. Exploit it to establish that the direction of an s-sparse vector $x \in \mathbb{R}^N$ can be estimated with accuracy ε from $m \asymp \varepsilon^{-2} s \ln(eN/s)$ binary observations $y_i = \mathrm{sgn}\langle a^{(i)}, x \rangle$, $i \in [1:m]$.

17.3 Consider a linear map $\mathcal{A} : \mathbb{R}^{n \times m} \to \mathbb{R}^m$ satisfying the ℓ_1-rank restricted isometry property of order r with constants $1 - \delta$ and $1 + \delta$. Prove that any Frobenius-normalized matrix $X \in \mathbb{R}^{n \times n}$ belonging to a linear space $\mathcal{S} = \mathrm{span}\{u_1 v_1^\top, \ldots, u_r v_r^\top\}$ satisfies

$$\left\| X - P_{\mathcal{S}}(\mathcal{A}^*(\mathrm{sgn}(\mathcal{A}(X)))) \right\|_F \le \sqrt{5\delta},$$

where $P_{\mathcal{S}}$ denotes the orthogonal projector onto $\mathcal{S}$. Proceed to establish a generalization of Theorem 17.2 for low-rank recovery from one-bit observations.

17.4 For m_0 proportional to $s \ln(eN/s)$, let a matrix $A \in \mathbb{R}^{m_0 \times N}$ and a vector $\theta \in \mathbb{R}^{m_0}$ be chosen so that $\overline{A} = [A, -\theta]$ satisfies a suitable ℓ_1-restricted isometry property. Thus, there are recovery maps $\Delta : \{-1, +1\}^m \to \mathbb{R}^N$ for which $\|x - \Delta(\mathrm{sgn}(Ax - \theta))\|_2 \le \rho/4$ whenever $x \in \Sigma_s^N$ obeys $\|x\|_2 \le \rho$.

---

[1] See Bilyk and Lacey (2015) for details.

Consider now the following adaptive scheme for the one-bit observation and recovery of vectors $x \in \Sigma_s^N$ with $\|x\|_2 \leq 1$, starting with $x^0 = 0$:

$$x^{t+1} = H_s(x^t + \Delta(\text{sgn}(Ax - \theta^t))), \qquad \theta^t = Ax^t + \theta.$$

After T iterations, prove that $\|x - x^T\|_2 \leq 2^{-T}$ and remark that this means an exponential decay of the recovery error with the ratio $m/(s \ln(eN/s))$, where $m = Tm_0$ is the total number of binary observations.

18

Group Testing

This chapter describes another scenario where sparse vectors, or rather their supports, need to be recovered from few binary observations, the latter being outcomes of a testing procedure. As a prime example, consider the problem of identifying, out of a group of N individuals, the ones that are infected by a certain disease. Testing each individual separately requires performing N tests, which is wasteful if not many individuals are infected and if their samples can be probed simultaneously. Indeed, in case of just one infected individual, say, one can perform only about $\log_2(N)$ tests. To see this, suppose that $N = 2^n$: one starts by testing half of the group simultaneously, so that the patient is located in this half if the test outcome was positive and in the other half otherwise; next, one tests half of the resulting subgroup of size $N/2$, allowing one to locate the patient in a new subgroup of size $N/4$; etc. The patient is identified after n of these steps (since the size of the subgroup is then $N/2^n = 1$). The above testing procedure is *adaptive*, in the sense that a test is determined by the outcome of the previous tests. Such an adaptive procedure is not always practical, e.g. when samples must be sent to a laboratory for a time-consuming analysis. This chapter will focus on *nonadaptive* procedures. First, the so-called test matrix will be introduced to facilitate the study of conditions ensuring success of the recovery task at hand. Then, the minimal number of tests needed to realize these conditions will be determined. Finally, a simple recovery method will be presented.

18.1 Properties of the Test Matrix

In the formalization of nonadaptive group testing, the objects of interest are high-dimensional binary vectors $x \in \{0, 1\}^N$, where an index $j \in [1:N]$ is called active if $x_j = 1$ (corresponding e.g. to the jth individual being infected)

149

and inactive if $x_j = 0$. The task is to identify the set of active indices, i.e., the support S of x, from observations $y_1, \ldots, y_m \in \{0, 1\}$. Each observation represents the outcome of a test, with $y_i = 1$ meaning that the ith test is positive and $y_i = 0$ meaning that it is negative. Given that a test is positive when it includes an active index, one has $y_i = 1$ if and only if $R_i \cap S \neq \emptyset$, where $R_i \subseteq [1 : N]$ denotes the set of indices included in the ith test. The *test matrix* is the $m \times N$ matrix with entries $A_{i,j} = \mathbb{1}_{\{j \in R_i\}}$, which is either 0 or 1 according to

$$A_{i,j} = 1 \iff j \in R_i.$$

Observing that $|R_i \cap S| = \sum_{j=1}^{N} \mathbb{1}_{\{j \in R_i \cap S\}} = \sum_{j=1}^{N} A_{i,j} x_j = (Ax)_i$, the fact that the ith test queries whether $|R_i \cap S| \geq 1$ translates into

$$y_i = \begin{cases} 1 & \text{if } (Ax)_i \geq 1, \\ 0 & \text{if } (Ax)_i = 0. \end{cases}$$

These test outcomes are summarized through the vector

$$y = \chi(Ax) \in \{0, 1\}^m. \tag{18.1}$$

When seeking conditions on A ensuring that $y = \chi(Ax)$ uniquely determines a binary vector $x \in \{0, 1\}^N$ of a prescribed sparsity level, it is useful to identify the columns of $A \in \{0, 1\}^{m \times N}$ with subsets $C_1, \ldots, C_N$ of $[1 : m]$ according to

$$A_{i,j} = 1 \iff i \in C_j,$$

in the same way as rows of A were identified with subsets $R_1, \ldots, R_m$ of $[1 : N]$. The vector $y = \chi(Ax)$ can similarly be identified with the set $\cup_{j \in S} C_j$, where $S = \text{supp}(x)$. Thus, asking whether exactly s-sparse vectors $x \in \{0, 1\}^N$ are determined by $y = \chi(Ax)$ is equivalent to asking whether the sets $\cup_{j \in S} C_j$ are all distinct when S runs over all subsets of $[1 : N]$ with size $|S| = s$. This is the notion of s-separability. The related notion of $\bar{s}$-separability, which is the focus here, corresponds to vectors with sparsity level at most s rather than exactly s. It is formally defined below, along with two other notions that turn out to be closely related.

Definition 18.1 A test matrix with rows identified with $R_1, \ldots, R_m \subseteq [1 : N]$ and columns identified with $C_1, \ldots, C_N \subseteq [1 : m]$ is called:

- $\bar{s}$-*separable* if the sets $\cup_{j \in S} C_j$ are all distinct when S runs over all subsets of $[1 : N]$ with $|S| \leq s$;
- s-*disjunct* if there are no subsets $S \subseteq [1 : N]$ with $|S| = s$ and $\ell \notin S$ such that $C_\ell \subseteq \cup_{j \in S} C_j$;
- s-*strongly selective* if, for any subset $S \subseteq [1 : N]$ with $|S| \leq s$ and any $\ell \in S$, there exists $i \in [1 : m]$ such that $S \cap R_i = \{\ell\}$.

These properties are almost equivalent, as revealed by the following result.

Proposition 18.2 *For a test matrix $A \in \{0,1\}^{m \times N}$, disjunctiveness, strong selectivity, and separability are linked via the chain of implications*

$$s\text{-disjunct} \underset{(a)}{\Longrightarrow} (s+1)\text{-strongly selective} \underset{(b)}{\Longrightarrow} \bar{s}\text{-separable} \underset{(c)}{\Longrightarrow} (s-1)\text{-disjunct.}$$

Proof Throughout, let the sets $R_1, \ldots, R_m \subseteq [1:N]$ and $C_1, \ldots, C_N \subseteq [1:m]$ represent the rows and columns of A, respectively.

(a) Consider $S \subseteq [1:N]$ with $|S| \leq s+1$ and $\ell \in S$. By s-disjunctiveness, one has $C_\ell \not\subseteq \cup_{j \in S \setminus \{\ell\}} C_j$, so there is some $i \in C_\ell$ with $i \notin \cup_{j \in S \setminus \{\ell\}} C_j$. The first condition is similar to $A_{i,\ell} = 1$, or $\ell \in R_i$, while the second condition is similar to $A_{i,j} = 0$, or $j \notin R_i$, for all $j \in S \setminus \{\ell\}$, i.e., to $(S \setminus \{\ell\}) \cap R_i = \emptyset$. Now $\ell \in R_i$ and $(S \setminus \{\ell\}) \cap R_i = \emptyset$ also read $S \cap R_i = \{\ell\}$, which proves $(s+1)$-strong selectivity.

(b) Consider distinct $S, S' \subseteq [1:N]$ with $|S|, |S'| \leq s$ and suppose that $\cup_{j \in S} C_j = \cup_{j \in S'} C_j =: C$. Assume without loss of generality that $S' \setminus S \neq \emptyset$ and pick $\ell \in S' \setminus S$. By $(s+1)$-strong selectivity, there is some $i \in [1:m]$ such that $(S \cup \{\ell\}) \cap R_i = \{\ell\}$. On the one hand, one has $\ell \in R_i$, i.e., $A_{i,\ell} = 1$, so $i \in C_\ell \subseteq \cup_{j \in S'} C_j = C$. On the other hand, for any $j \in S$, one has $j \notin R_i$, i.e., $A_{i,j} = 0$, or $i \notin C_j$, so that $i \notin \cup_{j \in S} C_j = C$. This is a contradiction.

(c) Suppose that there exist $S \subseteq [1:N]$ with $|S| = s-1$ and $\ell \notin S$ such that $C_\ell \subseteq \cup_{j \in S} C_j$. This would imply that $\cup_{j \in S} C_j = \cup_{j \in S \cup \{\ell\}} C_j$, contradicting $\bar{s}$-separability. $\qquad \square$

18.2 Satisfying the Separabity Condition

The goal of this section is to determine how many nonadaptive tests must be performed for s-sparse vectors $x \in \{0,1\}^N$ to be recoverable from the binary information (18.1). As a preamble, consider the case $s = 1$: just like in the adaptive scenario, recovering a one-sparse vector $x \in \{0,1\}^N$ can be carried out using roughly $\log_2(N)$ tests. To see this, one considers the *bit-test matrix* $A \in \{0,1\}^{m \times N}$, $m = \lceil \log_2(N) \rceil$, whose entry $A_{i,j}$ represents the ith binary digit of $j - 1 \in [0:N-1]$, so that

$$j - 1 = A_{m,j} 2^{m-1} + A_{m-1,j} 2^{m-2} + \cdots + A_{2,j} 2 + A_{1,j}. \tag{18.2}$$

To locate the single active index $k \in [1:N]$ of x, note that $(Ax)_i = A_{i,k} \in \{0,1\}$, so that the ith test provides the value $y_i = A_{i,k}$. Forming $y_m 2^{m-1} + \cdots + y_1$ provides, according to (18.2), the value $k - 1$, and hence k is determined.

This special case is misleading, though. For $s > 1$, a noteworthy difference emerges between the adaptive and nonadaptive scenarios. Indeed, while it can be seen that $Cs\ln(N)$ adaptive tests are enough to distinguish all the s-sparse vectors $x \in \{0, 1\}^N$ using the information $y = \chi(Ax)$, this is not the case with nonadaptive tests, as a consequence of the result below.

Theorem 18.3 *Given $\varepsilon > 0$, if $N \geq (2s^2)^{1+\varepsilon}$ and if a test matrix $A \in \{0, 1\}^{m \times N}$ is s-disjunct, then*

$$m \geq c_\varepsilon \frac{s^2}{\ln(s)} \ln(N), \qquad (18.3)$$

where the constant c_ε can be taken as $c_\varepsilon = \varepsilon/(2e(1 + \varepsilon))$.

Proof As usual, one thinks of the columns of A as subsets $C_1, \ldots, C_N$ of $[1:m]$. Let $d := \lceil em/s^2 \rceil \geq 1$, so that $em/s^2 \leq d < em/s^2 + 1$. One partitions the whole index set as $[1:N] = J \cup J'$, where

$$J := \{\ell \in [1:N] : \text{there exists } D \subseteq C_\ell \text{ with } |D| = d \text{ such that}$$
$$D \not\subseteq C_j \text{ for any } j \in [1:N] \text{ distinct from } \ell\},$$
$$J' := \{\ell \in [1:N] : \text{for all } D \subseteq C_\ell \text{ with } |D| = d,$$
$$\text{there exists } j \in [1:N] \text{ distinct from } \ell \text{ such that } D \subseteq C_j\}.$$

For $\ell \in J$, if $D^{(\ell)}$ denotes the subset of C_ℓ with size d appearing in the definition of J, then $D^{(\ell)} \neq D^{(\ell')}$ whenever $\ell' \in J \setminus \{\ell\}$. This implies that the cardinality of J is at most the number of subsets of $[1:m]$ of size d; therefore,

$$|J| \leq \binom{m}{d} \leq \left(\frac{em}{d}\right)^d.$$

At this point, the objective reduces to establishing that $|J'| \leq s$, since then $|J| = N - |J'| \geq N - s \geq N/2$, so taking logarithms yields

$$\ln(N/2) \leq d \ln\left(\frac{em}{d}\right) \leq \left(\frac{em}{s^2} + 1\right)\ln(s^2).$$

By rearranging the latter before taking $N = N^{\frac{\varepsilon}{1+\varepsilon}} N^{\frac{1}{1+\varepsilon}} \geq N^{\frac{\varepsilon}{1+\varepsilon}} 2s^2$ into account, one obtains

$$\frac{em}{s^2} \geq \frac{\ln(N/2)}{\ln(s^2)} - 1 = \frac{\ln(N/(2s^2))}{\ln(s^2)} \geq \frac{\ln(N^{\frac{\varepsilon}{1+\varepsilon}})}{\ln(s^2)} = \frac{\varepsilon}{2(1 + \varepsilon)} \frac{\ln(N)}{\ln(s)},$$

which is the required estimate (18.3). It remains to bound the cardinality of J'. To this end, one first claims that, for $\ell \in J'$, $r \in [0:s]$, and any $j_1, \ldots, j_r$ distinct from ℓ, one has

$$|C_\ell \setminus (C_{j_1} \cup \cdots \cup C_{j_r})| > d(s - r).$$

If not, one could write $C_\ell \setminus (C_{j_1} \cup \cdots \cup C_{j_r}) = D_{r+1} \cup \cdots \cup D_s$ for some subsets $D_{r+1}, \ldots, D_s$ of C_ℓ of size d. But since $\ell \in J'$, there exist $j_{r+1}, \ldots, j_s \in [1:N]$

distinct from ℓ such that $D_{r+1} \subseteq C_{j_{r+1}}, \ldots, D_s \subseteq C_{j_s}$. This would imply that $C_\ell \subseteq C_{j_1} \cup \cdots \cup C_{j_r} \cup C_{j_{r+1}} \cup \cdots \cup C_{j_s}$ and would contradict the fact that A is s-disjunct. Thus, the claim is justified. Now suppose that J' had $s+1$ elements, say $j_0, j_1, \ldots, j_s$. One would then have

$$|C_{j_0} \cup C_{j_1} \cup \cdots \cup C_{j_s}| = |C_{j_0}| + |C_{j_1} \setminus C_{j_0}| + \cdots + |C_{j_s} \setminus (C_{j_0} \cup \cdots \cup C_{j_{s-1}})|$$

$$> ds + d(s-1) + \cdots + d(s-s) = d\frac{s(s+1)}{2} > \frac{em}{2},$$

but this is clearly impossible because $C_{j_0} \cup C_{j_1} \cup \cdots \cup C_{j_s}$ is a subset of $[1:m]$. It follows that $|J'| \leq s$, which concludes the proof. $\qquad\square$

The lower estimate (18.3) is accompanied by a matching upper estimate.[1] Giving up on the $\ln(s)$ term, a simple probabilistic argument (see Exercise 18.3) can be used to establish the existence of s-disjunct test matrices involving $m \leq Cs^2 \ln(N)$ tests. Uncharacteristically, the probabilistic construction can (almost) be matched by a deterministic construction, as highlighted below. The justification will make use of the following observation.

Lemma 18.4 *If a test matrix $A \in \{0,1\}^{m \times N}$ has the same number of 1 in every column, then it is s-disjunct whenever $s\mu < 1$, where μ denotes the coherence of (the column-renormalization of) A.*

Proof Suppose that A is not s-disjunct, i.e., that there exist $S \subseteq [1:N]$ with $|S| = s$ and $\ell \notin S$ such that $C_\ell \subseteq \cup_{j \in S} C_j$. With $A_1, \ldots, A_N \in \{0,1\}^m$ denoting the columns of A, the latter implies that $A_\ell \leq \sum_{j \in S} A_j$, where the inequality is understood entrywise. Writing κ for the number of 1 per column of A and taking the inner product with A_ℓ yields

$$\kappa = \|A_\ell\|_2^2 \leq \sum_{j \in S} \langle A_j, A_\ell \rangle \leq \sum_{j \in S} \mu \|A_j\|_2 \|A_\ell\|_2 = |S| \mu \kappa = (s\mu)\kappa.$$

When $s\mu < 1$, this is evidently impossible, so A is indeed s-disjunct. $\qquad\square$

It is now time to put forward a deterministically constructed test matrix achieving near-optimality in terms of number of tests.

Theorem 18.5 *Given a prime number $p \geq 3$ and an integer $d \leq p$, let $m := p^2$ and $N := p^d$. The $m \times N$ test matrix $A \in \{0,1\}^{m \times N}$ with rows indexed by couples $(i, j) \in \mathbb{Z}_p \times \mathbb{Z}_p$, columns indexed by polynomials f of degree less than d over $\mathbb{Z}_p$, and explicitly defined by*

$$A_{(i,j),f} = \begin{cases} 1, & \text{if } f(i) = j \pmod{p}, \\ 0, & \text{if } f(i) \neq j \pmod{p}, \end{cases} \tag{18.4}$$

is s-disjunct provided that $m \geq s^2 \ln(N)^2$.

---

[1] This upper estimate has been established in D'yachkov et al. (2014).

Proof   Notice first that the number of 1 in each column A_f of A is exactly equal to p, since

$$\sum_{(i,j)\in\mathbb{Z}_p\times\mathbb{Z}_p} A_{(i,j),f} = \sum_{(i,j)\in\mathbb{Z}_p\times\mathbb{Z}_p} \mathbb{1}_{\{f(i)=j\,(\mathrm{mod}\,p)\}} = \sum_{i=1}^{p} 1 = p.$$

This implies that $\|A_f\|_2 = \sqrt{p}$ for any polynomial f of degree $< d$ over $\mathbb{Z}_p$. Moreover, if g is another such polynomial, then

$$|\langle A_f, A_g\rangle| = \sum_{(i,j)\in\mathbb{Z}_p\times\mathbb{Z}_p} A_{(i,j),f}A_{(i,j),g} = \sum_{(i,j)\in\mathbb{Z}_p\times\mathbb{Z}_p} \mathbb{1}_{\{f(i)=j\,(\mathrm{mod}\,p)\}}\mathbb{1}_{\{g(i)=j\,(\mathrm{mod}\,p)\}}$$

$$= \sum_{i\in\mathbb{Z}_p} \mathbb{1}_{\{(f-g)(i)=0\,(\mathrm{mod}\,p)\}} \le d-1,$$

where the last inequality translates the fact that the number of roots in $\mathbb{Z}_p$ of a nonzero polynomial is at most equal to its degree. These considerations imply that the matrix A has coherence $\mu \le (d-1)/p < d/p$. Finally, in view of Lemma 18.4, one deduces that A is s-disjunct when $sd/p \le 1$, i.e., when $m \ge s^2d^2 = s^2(\ln(N)/\ln(p))^2$, which does occur for $m \ge s^2 \ln(N)^2$. $\square$

18.3 Recovery via a Linear Feasibility Program

Having found a test matrix $A \in \{0,1\}^{m\times N}$ such that s-sparse binary vectors $x \in \{0,1\}^N$ are uniquely determined by their test outcomes, it remains to devise a practical algorithm to actually recover x from the vector of test outcomes expressed in the form (18.1). As it turns out, a simple linear program does the trick.

Theorem 18.6   *Let $A \in \{0,1\}^{m\times N}$ be an s-disjunct test matrix. For an s-sparse vector $x \in \{0,1\}^N$ acquired through $y = \chi(Ax) \in \{0,1\}^m$, define*

$$I_0 := \{i \in [1:m] : y_i = 0\} \quad and \quad I_1 := \{i \in [1:m] : y_i = 1\}.$$

The support S of x is recovered as the support of a solution to the feasibility program

$$\text{find } z \in \mathbb{R}^N \quad \text{subject to} \quad z \ge 0, \quad (Az)_{I_0} = 0, \quad (Az)_{I_1} \ge 1. \tag{18.5}$$

Proof   The program (18.5) is feasible since the vector $x \in \{0,1\}^N$ satisfies the constraints. Let now $x' \in [0,\infty)^N$ denote any solution to (18.5) and let $S' := \{j \in [1:N] : x'_j > 0\}$ denote its support. Observe that $\mathbb{1}_{S'} \in \{0,1\}^N$ also admits $y \in \{0,1\}^m$ as a vector of test outcomes, in view of

$$(A\mathbb{1}_{S'})_i = 0 \iff S' \cap R_i = \emptyset \iff (Ax')_i = 0 \iff i \in I_0 \iff y_i = 0.$$

Therefore, as soon as one knows that S' has size at most s, one can conclude that $\mathbb{1}_{S'} = x$ using $\bar{s}$-separability—which, by Proposition 18.2, follows from s-disjunctiveness. To justify that $|S'| \leq s$, one shall prove that $S' \subseteq S$. Suppose on the contrary that there exists $\ell \in S'$, $\ell \notin S$. Invoking Proposition 18.2 again, the test matrix A is $(s+1)$-strongly selective, so there exists $i \in [1:m]$ such that $(S \cup \{\ell\}) \cap R_i = \{\ell\}$. This means that $\ell \in R_i$ and that $S \cap R_i = \emptyset$. The condition $\ell \in R_i$ implies that $(Ax')_i \geq x'_\ell > 0$, i.e., $i \notin I_0$, while the condition $S \cap R_i = \emptyset$ implies that $(Ax)_i = 0$, i.e., $i \in I_0$. This contradiction shows that $S' \subseteq S$ and hence concludes the proof. $\qquad\square$

Exercises

18.1 Extend the adaptive strategy outlined for one-sparse vectors to show that s-sparse vectors $x \in \{0, 1\}^N$ can be recovered from the outcomes of $O(s \ln(N))$ tests, without needing an upper estimate on s beforehand.

18.2 Prove that a test matrix is $\bar{s}$-separable if and only if it is s-separable and $(s-1)$-disjunct.

18.3 Let $C_1, \ldots, C_N$ be random subsets of $[1:m]$ with size $\kappa = 3s\lceil \ln(N) \rceil$, where $m = 2\kappa s = 6s^2\lceil \ln(N) \rceil$. Show that the random test matrix with columns (identified with) $C_1, \ldots, C_N$ is s-disjunct with probability at least $1 - N^{-s}$.

18.4 Suppose that a function $f : [0, 1]^N \to \mathbb{R}$ depends only on at most $s \ll N$ variables and that it increases strictly with each of these active variables. Find a deterministic observation scheme using $m \asymp s^2 \ln(N)^2$ points $x^{(1)}, \ldots, x^{(m)} \in [0, 1]^N$ that allows one to determine the unknown active variables via a practical algorithm with inputs $f(x^{(1)}), \ldots, f(x^{(m)})$.

PART FOUR

OPTIMIZATION

Executive Summary

Thinking back at the Data Science tour conducted up to this point, it is apparent that optimization programs have popped up repeatedly: one encountered, for instance, empirical risk minimization and support vector machines in Machine Learning, Chebyshev centers and the spline algorithm in Optimal Recovery, and ℓ_1-minimization and nuclear norm minimization in Compressive Sensing. It is therefore time to stop for a closer look at the theory of Optimization in order to grasp how the above problems are solved in practice.

Chapter 19 elucidates the important role played by convexity and introduces gradient descent algorithms for unconstrained convex optimization, finishing with stochastic gradient descent. Chapter 20 further concentrates on linear optimization by analyzing the simplex algorithm before going through a series of problems converted to linear programs. Next, Chapter 21 is concerned with duality theory: representative results are fully justified for linear programs and merely discussed for conic programs, including semidefinite programs, and their usefulness is illustrated with unusual examples of robust optimization. Semidefinite programs are the focus of Chapter 22, which highlights the sum-of-squares technique and the method of moments to deal with some variations of the spline algorithm. Finally, Chapter 23 turns to nonconvex optimization, with the objective of showcasing several situations where provable guarantees can be attached to nonconvex programs—these situations involve quadratically constrained quadratic programs, dynamic programs, and projected gradient descent.

Readers wishing to dig deeper in the theory of Optimization have several books available to them, e.g. Boyd and Vandenberghe (2004); Nesterov and Nemirovskii (1994); Nesterov (2013). A Data Science-oriented exposition is to be found in Wright and Recht (2022). If semidefinite programming and applications are more specifically targeted, then Lasserre (2010, 2015) can be consulted. Some personal contributions are reproduced in this part: the owl-norm minimization example of Chapter 21 is taken from Foucart (2021), the semidefinite examples of Chapter 22 are close to Foucart and Powers (2017) and Foucart and Lasserre (2019), and the dynamic programming example of Chapter 23 appeared in Foucart et al. (2015).

19

Basic Convex Optimization

A generic optimization program has the form

$$\underset{x \in \mathbb{R}^d}{\text{minimize}} f(x) \qquad \text{subject to } f_i(x) \le 0, \ i \in [1:n]. \qquad (19.1)$$

In this generic formalism, the functions $f, f_1, \ldots, f_n$ take values in $\mathbb{R} \cup \{+\infty\}$ and the domains of these functions are the sets of points where they take finite values. The function f is called the *objective function*, while the conditions $f_i(x) \le 0$ are called *inequality constraints*. Some *equality constraints* $g_i(x) = 0$ could be added, but this addition can be incorporated in the generic formalism, since each equality constraint $g_i(x) = 0$ can be interpreted as the two inequality constraints $g_i(x) \le 0$ and $-g_i(x) \le 0$. There could also be no constraints at all, in which case one talks about *unconstrained optimization*. A point $x \in \mathbb{R}^d$ satisfying all the constraints is called a *feasible point*. A *global minimizer* of (19.1) is a feasible point $x^* \in \mathbb{R}^d$ such that $f(x^*) \le f(x)$ for all feasible points $x \in \mathbb{R}^d$. A *local minimizer* of (19.1) is a feasible point $x^* \in \mathbb{R}^d$ such that $f(x^*) \le f(x)$ for all feasible points x belonging to some ball $B(x^*, \varepsilon)$ of radius $\varepsilon > 0$ centered at x^*. A *convex optimization program* is a program of the form (19.1) where $f, f_1, \ldots, f_n$ are all convex functions.

19.1 Gradient Descent for Unconstrained Convex Programs

The advantage of convex programs—constrained or unconstrained—is that local minimizers are automatically global minimizers, as demonstrated below.

Proposition 19.1 *If x^* is a local minimizer of a convex program, then it is also a global minimizer.*

Proof Given a local minimizer $x^* \in \mathbb{R}^d$, the goal is to show that $f(x^*) \le f(x)$ whenever the point $x \in \mathbb{R}^d$ is feasible, i.e., whenever $f_1(x) \le 0, \ldots, f_n(x) \le 0$.

Let $\tau \in (0, 1)$ be chosen small enough for the point $(1 - \tau)x^* + \tau x$ to belong to the ball $B(x^*, \varepsilon)$ of local optimality around x^*. This point obeys the inequality constraints, since the convexity of each f_i guarantees that

$$f_i((1 - \tau)x^* + \tau x) \le (1 - \tau)f_i(x^*) + \tau f_i(x) \le (1 - \tau) \times 0 + \tau \times 0 = 0.$$

Thus, the local optimality of x^* yields $f(x^*) \le f((1 - \tau)x^* + \tau x)$. Using the convexity of the function f, one deduces that $f(x^*) \le (1 - \tau)f(x^*) + \tau f(x)$. A rearrangement yields $f(x^*) \le f(x)$. □

Based on the above observation, solving convex optimization programs can be done by producing local minimizers. In turn, a possible strategy to produce local minimizers consists in generating a sequence $(x^t)_{t \ge 0}$ in such a way that the objective function decreases along the iterations, meaning that $f(x^{t+1}) \le f(x^t)$ for all $t \ge 0$. In unconstrained optimization, a family of such strategies consists of the *line search algorithms*, where the sequence $(x^t)_{t \ge 0}$ is constructed from x^0 via the iteration

$$x^{t+1} = x^t + \alpha^t v^t, \qquad t \ge 0.$$

Here, the vector $v^t \in \mathbb{R}^d$ represents a direction, i.e., it satisfies $\|v^t\|_2 = 1$, and the scalar $\alpha^t \in \mathbb{R}$ is a stepsize. A direction v is called a *descent direction* at a point $x \in \mathbb{R}^d$ if $f(x + \alpha v) < f(x)$ whenever $\alpha > 0$ is small enough. One can loosely write $f(x + \alpha v) \approx f(x) + \alpha \langle \nabla f(x), v \rangle$, so v is a descent direction when $\langle \nabla f(x), v \rangle < 0$ and the direction of steepest descent is $-\nabla f(x)/\|\nabla f(x)\|_2$. Choosing this descent direction without specifying the stepsize constitutes the family of *gradient descent algorithms*.

To make a reasoned choice of the stepsize, one relies on the Taylor theorem to express $f(x + \alpha v)$ for $\alpha > 0$ more precisely as

$$f(x + \alpha v) = f(x) + \alpha \langle \nabla f(x), v \rangle + \alpha \int_0^1 \langle \nabla f(x + t\alpha v) - \nabla f(x), v \rangle dt$$

$$\le f(x) + \alpha \langle \nabla f(x), v \rangle + \alpha \int_0^1 \|\nabla f(x + t\alpha v) - \nabla f(x)\|_2 dt. \quad (19.2)$$

Assuming that the function f is λ-smooth, i.e., that

$$\|\nabla f(z) - \nabla f(z')\|_2 \le \lambda \|z - z'\|_2 \qquad \text{for all } z, z' \in \mathbb{R}^d, \quad (19.3)$$

it follows that

$$f(x + \alpha v) \le f(x) + \alpha \langle \nabla f(x), v \rangle + \frac{\alpha^2 \lambda}{2}.$$

Now, for a given direction v, notice that the right-hand side is minimized when $\alpha = \alpha_v := -\langle \nabla f(x), v \rangle / \lambda$, yielding $f(x + \alpha_v v) \le f(x) - \langle \nabla f(x), v \rangle^2 / (2\lambda)$. Thus, this choice of stepsize, combined with the choice $v = -\nabla f(x)/\|\nabla f(x)\|_2$ as the direction of steepest descent, leads to the so-called *steepest descent algorithm*:

- start with some $x^0 \in \mathbb{R}^d$;
- for each $t \geq 0$, compute

$$x^{t+1} = x^t - \frac{1}{\lambda}\nabla f(x^t);$$

- stop at a predefined halting criterion.

Leaving aside the issue that implementing the steepest descent algorithm requires access to the gradient and knowledge of λ, one summarizes the above considerations as the guarantee that, for each $t \geq 0$,

$$f(x^{t+1}) \leq f(x^t) - \frac{\|\nabla f(x^t)\|_2^2}{2\lambda} = f(x^t) - \frac{\lambda}{2}\|x^{t+1} - x^t\|_2^2. \qquad (19.4)$$

19.2 Rates of Convergence for Steepest Descent

Even if the steepest descent algorithm produces a local minimizer, in general it will be one among many, so establishing the convergence of the values $f(x^t)$ towards the minimum of f based solely on (19.4) is inconceivable. Favorable properties of the objective function f must necessarily be invoked. The natural convexity assumption allows one not only to guarantee that a global minimizer is automatically produced, but also to quantify the rate of convergence.

Theorem 19.2 *If the function f is λ-smooth and convex, then the values $f(x^t)$ at the iterates of the steepest descent algorithm converge towards the value $f(x^*)$ at a mininizer x^* (assuming its existence) according to*

$$f(x^T) - f(x^*) \leq \frac{\lambda}{2T}\|x^0 - x^*\|_2^2, \qquad T \geq 1. \qquad (19.5)$$

Proof For any $t \geq 0$, one has $f(x^*) \geq f(x^t) + \langle \nabla f(x^t), x^* - x^t \rangle$ because a convex function is above all its tangent hyperplanes (see e.g. Exercise 19.2). In view of the definition of x^{t+1} written as $\nabla f(x^t) = -\lambda(x^{t+1} - x^t)$, and then in view of (19.4), one obtains

$$f(x^{t+1}) - f(x^*) \leq f(x^{t+1}) - f(x^t) + \lambda\langle x^{t+1} - x^t, x^* - x^t \rangle$$

$$\leq -\frac{\lambda}{2}(\|x^{t+1} - x^t\|_2^2 - 2\langle x^{t+1} - x^t, x^* - x^t \rangle)$$

$$= \frac{\lambda}{2}(\|x^t - x^*\|_2^2 - \|x^{t+1} - x^*\|_2^2).$$

Taking into account the fact that the sequence $(f(x^t))_{t\geq 0}$ is nonincreasing, it follows that

$$f(x^T) - f(x^*) \leq \frac{1}{T} \sum_{t=0}^{T-1} (f(x^{t+1}) - f(x^*)) \leq \frac{1}{T} \frac{\lambda}{2} (\|x^0 - x^*\|_2^2 - \|x^T - x^*\|_2^2)$$

$$\leq \frac{\lambda}{2T} \|x^0 - x^*\|_2^2,$$

which is the required result. □

A much better convergence rate can be obtained by assuming more than mere convexity. Namely, one considers functions f that are μ-*strongly convex* for some $\mu > 0$, meaning that, for all $x, x' \in \mathbb{R}^d$,

$$f(x') \geq f(x) + \langle \nabla f(x), x' - x \rangle + \frac{\mu}{2} \|x' - x\|_2^2. \tag{19.6}$$

It is not hard to see that a μ-strongly convex function has a unique global minimizer $x^* \in \mathbb{R}^d$. Fixing some $x \in \mathbb{R}^d$ for a while, the inequality (19.6) then yields

$$f(x^*) = \min_{x' \in \mathbb{R}^d} f(x')$$

$$\geq f(x) + \frac{\mu}{2} \min_{x' \in \mathbb{R}^d} \left(\|x' - x\|_2^2 + 2 \left\langle \frac{\nabla f(x)}{\mu}, x' - x \right\rangle \right)$$

$$= f(x) + \frac{\mu}{2} \min_{x' \in \mathbb{R}^d} \left(\left\| x' - x + \frac{\nabla f(x)}{\mu} \right\|_2^2 - \left\| \frac{\nabla f(x)}{\mu} \right\|_2^2 \right)$$

$$= f(x) - \frac{1}{2\mu} \|\nabla f(x)\|_2^2.$$

Therefore, a μ-strongly convex function f with global minimizer x^* satisfies, for any $x \in \mathbb{R}^d$,

$$\|\nabla f(x)\|_2^2 \geq 2\mu (f(x) - f(x^*)). \tag{19.7}$$

This inequality is crucial for improving the convergence rate of the steepest descent algorithm.

Theorem 19.3 *If the function f is λ-smooth and μ-strongly convex, then the values $f(x^t)$ at the iterates of the steepest descent algorithm converge towards the value $f(x^*)$ at the mininizer x^* according to*

$$f(x^T) - f(x^*) \leq \left(1 - \frac{\mu}{\lambda}\right)^T (f(x^0) - f(x^*)), \qquad T \geq 0. \tag{19.8}$$

Proof The estimate (19.8) is a straightforward consequence of

$$f(x^{t+1}) \leq f(x^t) - \frac{\mu}{\lambda} (f(x^t) - f(x^*)), \qquad t \geq 0,$$

which itself is easily derived from the general estimate (19.4) for $f(x^{t+1})$ when combined with (19.7).   □

For λ-smooth and μ-strongly convex functions, the above result implicitly shows that $\mu \le \lambda$. This can, of course, be derived more directly, for instance, by putting together the observation that

$$f(x) - f(x^*) \ge \frac{\mu}{2}\|x - x^*\|_2^2, \tag{19.9}$$

coming from (19.6) with $x = x^*$, and the observation that

$$2\mu(f(x) - f(x^*)) \le \|\nabla f(x) - \nabla f(x^*)\|_2^2 \le \lambda^2\|x - x^*\|_2^2, \tag{19.10}$$

coming from (19.7) and (19.3). Incidentally, these two observations reveal that Theorem 19.3 could alternatively be stated for the decay rate of $\|x^t - x^*\|_2$. Precisely, using (19.9), (19.8), and (19.10) in succession, one has

$$\|x^T - x^*\|_2^2 \le \frac{2}{\mu}(f(x^T) - f(x^*)) \le \frac{2}{\mu}\left(1 - \frac{\mu}{\lambda}\right)^T (f(x^0) - f(x^*))$$

$$\le \frac{\lambda^2}{\mu^2}\left(1 - \frac{\mu}{\lambda}\right)^T \|x^0 - x^*\|_2^2.$$

It is worth mentioning, albeit without proof,[1] that the rates (19.5) and (19.8) are improvable for algorithms constructing the new iterate x^{t+1} using more than the current iterate x^t. For instance, *Nesterov accelerated gradient methods* take the form

$$x^{t+1} = \widetilde{x}^t + \alpha^t\nabla f(\widetilde{x}^t), \qquad \widetilde{x}^t := x^t + \beta^t(x^t - x^{t-1}),$$

with constant stepsize $\alpha^t = -1/\lambda$ for λ-smooth functions, as before. It can be shown that:

- if f is convex, then the choice $\beta^t = \gamma^t(\gamma^{t-1})^2$, where $\gamma^t \in [0, 1]$ is defined inductively from $\gamma^0 = 0$ as the positive solution to the quadratic equation $\gamma^2 + (1 - (\gamma^{t-1})^2)\gamma - 1 = 0$, leads to

$$f(x^T) - f(x^*) \le \frac{2\lambda}{(T + 1)^2}\|x^0 - x^*\|_2^2, \quad T \ge 0;$$

- if f is μ-strongly convex, then the choice $\beta^t = (\sqrt{\lambda} - \sqrt{\mu})/(\sqrt{\lambda} + \sqrt{\mu})$ leads to

$$f(x^T) - f(x^*) \le 2\left(1 - \sqrt{\frac{\mu}{\lambda}}\right)^T (f(x^0) - f(x^*)), \quad T \ge 0.$$

---

[1] See e.g. Chapter 4 of Wright and Recht (2022) for more details.

19.3 Stochastic Gradient Descent

To close this chapter, a brief description of stochastic gradient descent is in order. This algorithm is used in situations where one does not have access to the exact gradient $\nabla f(x)$, but rather to a quantity $g_\xi(x)$ depending on a random variable ξ (vector, index, or other) in such a way that

$$\mathbb{E}[g_\xi(x)] = \nabla f(x) \qquad \text{for all } x \in \mathbb{R}^d.$$

A glaring example is provided by a *noisy gradient* $g_\xi(x) = \nabla f(x) + \xi$, in which $\xi \in \mathbb{R}^d$ is a mean-zero random vector. Another common example is provided by an *incremental gradient*, which occurs e.g. in empirical risk minimization where the objective function has the form $f = m^{-1} \sum_{i=1}^m f_i$. It is impractical to produce the exact gradient $\nabla f = m^{-1} \sum_{i=1}^m \nabla f_i$ because of the multitude of individual gradients ∇f_i to compute. Instead, one can simply pick an index ξ uniformly at random in $[1:m]$, so that $g_\xi(x) = \nabla f_\xi(x)$ has expectation $\nabla f(x)$. In any case, given a sequence $(\xi^0, \xi^1, \ldots)$ of independent random variables, the *stochastic gradient descent* algorithm reads:

- start with some $x^0 \in \mathbb{R}^d$;
- for each $t \geq 0$, compute the random vector

$$x^{t+1} = x^t - \alpha^t g_{\xi^t}(x^t)$$

with a stepsize $\alpha^t > 0$ to be chosen appropriately;
- stop at a predefined halting criterion.

In the representative result presented next, the *learning rate*—another term for the stepsize—is chosen constant on an *epoch*. When transitioning from one epoch to the next, the stepsize is divided by a constant while the size of the epoch is multiplied by that constant. For aesthetic's sake, the constant is chosen equal to two in the analysis below.

Theorem 19.4 *If the function f is μ-strongly convex and if there are some $\lambda \geq \mu$ and $\eta \geq 0$ such that*

$$\mathbb{E}\left[\|g_\xi(x)\|_2^2\right] \leq \lambda^2 \|x - x^*\|_2^2 + \eta^2 \qquad \text{for all } x \in \mathbb{R}^d, \tag{19.11}$$

then the iterates x^t of the stochastic gradient descent algorithm with stepsize $\alpha^t = (\mu/(4\lambda^2))2^{-k}$, $t \in [2^k - 1 : 2^{k+1} - 2]$, converge in expectation towards the global minimizer x^* according to

$$\mathbb{E}\left[\|x^{2^k-1} - x^*\|_2^2\right] \leq \exp\left(-\frac{\mu^2}{4\lambda^2}k\right)\left(\|x^0 - x^*\|_2^2 + \frac{\eta^2}{\lambda^2}\right), \qquad k \geq 0. \tag{19.12}$$

Before turning to the proof, one points out that assumption (19.11) holds:

- for noisy gradients when f is λ-smooth, since

$$\mathbb{E}\big[\|\nabla f(x) + \xi\|_2^2\big] = \|\nabla f(x)\|_2^2 + 2\langle \nabla f(x), \mathbb{E}(\xi)\rangle + \mathbb{E}(\|\xi\|_2^2)$$

$$\leq \lambda^2 \|x - x^*\|_2^2 + \sum_{j-1}^{d} \sigma_j^2,$$

with σ_j denoting the standard deviation of the jth entry of the vector ξ;
- for incremental gradients when each f_i is λ_i-smooth, since

$$\mathbb{E}\big[\|\nabla f_\xi(x)\|_2^2\big] = \frac{1}{m}\sum_{i=1}^{m}\|\nabla f_i(x)\|_2^2$$

$$\leq \frac{1}{m}\sum_{i=1}^{m}\big(2\|\nabla f_i(x) - \nabla f_i(x^*)\|_2^2 + 2\|\nabla f_i(x^*)\|_2^2\big)$$

$$\leq \frac{2}{m}\Big(\sum_{i=1}^{m}\lambda_i^2\Big)\|x - x^*\|_2^2 + \frac{2}{m}\sum_{i=1}^{m}\|\nabla f_i(x^*)\|_2^2.$$

Proof of Theorem 19.4 For $t \geq 0$, observe first that

$$\|x^{t+1} - x^*\|_2^2 = \|x^t - x^* - \alpha^t g_{\xi^t}(x^t)\|_2^2$$
$$= \|x^t - x^*\|_2^2 - 2\alpha^t\langle x^t - x^*, g_{\xi^t}(x^t)\rangle + (\alpha^t)^2\|g_{\xi^t}(x^t)\|_2^2. \qquad (19.13)$$

Next, notice that $\langle x^t - x^*, \nabla f(x^t)\rangle \geq \mu\|x^t - x^*\|_2^2$ as a consequence of (19.6) with $x = x^t$ and $x' = x^*$ and of (19.9). Thus, taking expectations in (19.13) and invoking (19.11), one obtains

$$\mathbb{E}\big[\|x^{t+1} - x^*\|_2^2\big] \leq (1 - 2\alpha^t\mu + (\alpha^t)^2\lambda^2)\mathbb{E}\big[\|x^t - x^*\|_2^2\big] + (\alpha^t)^2\eta^2.$$

Supposing for now that $\alpha^t \leq \mu/\lambda^2$ and making use of the shorthand notation $a_t := \mathbb{E}[\|x^t - x^*\|_2^2]$, one arrives at

$$a_{t+1} \leq (1 - \alpha^t\mu)a_t + (\alpha^t)^2\eta^2, \qquad t \geq 0. \qquad (19.14)$$

With $t_k := 2^k - 1$ for $k \geq 0$, one considers a piecewise constant stepsize α^t defined as follows:

$$\text{if } t \in [t_k : t_{k+1} - 1], \quad \text{then } \alpha^t = \frac{\alpha}{2^k}, \quad \text{where } \alpha := \frac{\mu}{4\lambda^2}.$$

Fixing $k \geq 0$, the inequality (19.14) reads

$$a_{t+1} \leq \Big(1 - \frac{\alpha\mu}{2^k}\Big)a_t + \frac{\alpha^2\eta^2}{2^{2k}}, \qquad t \in [t_k : t_{k+1} - 1].$$

By immediate induction on t, this implies that

$$a_{t_{k+1}} \leq \left(1 - \frac{\alpha\mu}{2^k}\right)^{2^k} a_{t_k} + \frac{\alpha^2\eta^2}{2^{2k}}\left(1 + \left(1 - \frac{\alpha\mu}{2^k}\right) + \left(1 - \frac{\alpha\mu}{2^k}\right)^2 + \cdots\right)$$

$$\leq \exp(-\alpha\mu)a_{t_k} + \frac{\alpha\eta^2}{\mu 2^k}.$$

Now, by immediate induction on k, the latter yields

$$a_{t_k} \leq \exp(-\alpha\mu)^k a_{t_0} + \frac{\alpha\eta^2}{\mu}\left(\frac{1}{2^{k-1}} + \frac{\exp(-\alpha\mu)}{2^{k-2}} + \cdots + \frac{\exp(-\alpha\mu)^{k-1}}{1}\right)$$

$$= \exp(-\alpha\mu)^k a_{t_0} + \frac{\alpha\eta^2}{\mu}\frac{\exp(-\alpha\mu)^k - 1/2^k}{\exp(-\alpha\mu) - 1/2}$$

$$\leq \exp(-\alpha\mu k)a_{t_0} + \frac{\alpha\eta^2}{\mu}\frac{\exp(-\alpha\mu k)}{\exp(-\alpha\mu) - 1/2}, \qquad (19.15)$$

where one made implicit use of $\exp(\alpha\mu) = \exp(\mu^2/(4\lambda^2)) \leq \exp(1/4) < 2$. Taking the value $\alpha = \mu/(4\lambda^2)$ into account, (19.15) reads

$$a_{t_k} \leq \exp\left(-\frac{\mu^2}{4\lambda^2}k\right)\left(a_{t_0} + \frac{\eta^2}{4\lambda^2}\frac{1}{\exp(-1/4) - 1/2}\right).$$

Finally, the estimate announced in (19.12) simply uses $\exp(-1/4) \geq 3/4$. $\quad\square$

The fact that (19.12) holds in expectation can look unsatisfying at first sight, as one would naturally prefer a result valid with high probability. Actually, a result in probability can be derived from (19.12). Indeed, the *Markov inequality* (see Lemma B.1) guarantees that

$$\mathbb{P}\left[\|x^{2^k-1} - x^*\|_2^2 > \exp\left(-\frac{\mu^2}{8\lambda^2}k\right)\left(\|x^0 - x^*\|_2^2 + \frac{\eta^2}{\lambda^2}\right)\right]$$

$$\leq \frac{\mathbb{E}\left[\|x^{2^k-1} - x^*\|_2^2\right]}{\exp\left(-\frac{\mu^2}{8\lambda^2}k\right)\left(\|x^0 - x^*\|_2^2 + \frac{\eta^2}{\lambda^2}\right)}$$

$$\leq \exp\left(-\frac{\mu^2}{8\lambda^2}k\right).$$

In other words, for a fixed $k \geq 0$, it occurs with probability exponentially close to one that $\|x^{2^k-1} - x^*\|_2^2$ is exponentially small. Results that are valid for whole ranges of k can be obtained via union bounds.

Exercises

19.1 Given a convex optimization program, prove that the set of feasible points
and the set of minimizers are both convex sets.

19.2 The objective of this exercise is to justify that a differentiable function
$f: \mathbb{R}^d \to \mathbb{R}$ is convex if and only if

$$f(x') \geq f(x) + \langle \nabla f(x), x' - x \rangle \qquad \text{for all } x, x' \in \mathbb{R}^d.$$

(a) In one direction, if f is convex, with $x_\tau = (1 - \tau)x + \tau x'$ for $\tau \in (0, 1)$,
prove that $f(x') \geq f(x) + (f(x_\tau) - f(x))/\tau$ before letting τ tend to zero.

(b) In the other direction, bound $\tau f(x') + (1 - \tau)f(x)$ from below using
two of the above inequalities featuring $\nabla f(x_\tau)$.

19.3 Observe that a function $f: \mathbb{R}^d \to \mathbb{R}$ is *μ-strongly convex* if and only if
the function $x \in \mathbb{R}^d \mapsto f(x) - (\mu/2)\|x\|_2^2$ is convex. Observe also that f
is μ-strongly convex if and only if

$$\langle \nabla f(x) - \nabla f(x'), x - x' \rangle \geq \mu\|x - x'\|_2^2 \qquad \text{for all } x, x' \in \mathbb{R}^d.$$

19.4 For a μ-strongly convex function f and under the assumption (19.11),
prove that the iterates of the stochastic gradient descent algorithm with
stepsize $\alpha^t = 2\mu/(2\lambda^2 + \mu^2 t)$ converge in expectation towards the global
minimizer x^* according to

$$\mathbb{E}\left[\|x^T - x^*\|_2^2\right] \leq \frac{\max\{2\lambda^2\|x^0 - x^*\|_2^2, 4\eta^2\}}{2\lambda^2 + \mu^2 T}, \qquad T \geq 0.$$

20
Snippets of Linear Programming

A *linear program* is a particular convex optimization program of the form

$$\underset{x\in\mathbb{R}^d}{\text{minimize}}\, f(x) \qquad \text{subject to } f_i(x) \le 0,\; i \in [1:n],$$

in which the objective function f as well as the constraint functions $f_1,\ldots,f_n$ are all *affine functions*, i.e., of the form $z \in \mathbb{R}^d \mapsto \langle a, z \rangle - b \in \mathbb{R}$. Thus, a linear program can be written in *inequality form* as

$$\underset{x\in\mathbb{R}^d}{\text{minimize}}\,\langle c, x \rangle \qquad \text{subject to } Ax \le b \qquad\qquad (20.1)$$

for some vectors $c \in \mathbb{R}^d$, $b \in \mathbb{R}^n$, and matrix $A \in \mathbb{R}^{n\times d}$. The *standard form* of a linear program is

$$\underset{x\in\mathbb{R}^d}{\text{minimize}}\,\langle c, x \rangle \qquad \text{subject to } Ax = b,\; x \ge 0. \qquad\qquad (20.2)$$

Any linear program in inequality form can be reformulated in standard form by introducing nonnegative vectors $v \in \mathbb{R}^n$ and $x^+, x^- \in \mathbb{R}^d$ of *slack variables* such that $Ax + v = b$ and $x = x^+ - x^-$. Once a linear program is in standard form, it can be solved exactly via the simplex algorithm. The main point of this chapter is to analyze this must-see algorithm. As shall be discussed first, the fact that the minimum occurs at an extreme point of a polytope is crucial. The chapter ends with examples of geometric problems that can be solved as linear programs.

20.1 Maximizers of a Convex Function

A linear program consists in minimizing over a convex set C (in actual fact, a convex polytope) a function which is linear, i.e., both convex and concave. The advantage of minimizing a convex function over C has already been pointed out: the local minimizers are automatically global minimizers. Minimizing a concave function—equivalently, maximizing a convex function—over C also has its advantage: (one of) the minimizer(s) is located at an *extreme point* of C.

Lemma 20.1 *If C is a compact convex set of $\mathbb{R}^d$ and if $f: C \to \mathbb{R}$ is a convex function, then f is maximized at an extreme point of C.*

Proof Let $x \in C$ be a maximizer of f. Since $C \subseteq \mathbb{R}^d$ is a compact convex set, the *Krein–Milman theorem* (Theorem C.14) implies that C is the convex hull of its extreme points. In view of the *Carathéodory theorem* (Theorem C.6), one can even write $x = \sum_{j=1}^{d+1} \tau_j x_j$ for some nonnegative numbers $\tau_1, \ldots, \tau_{d+1}$ summing up to one and some extreme points $x_1, \ldots, x_{d+1}$ of C. By convexity of f, one has $f(x) \le \sum_{j=1}^{d+1} \tau_j f(x_j)$. Thus, if $f(x_j) < \max\{f(z), z \in C\}$ for all $j \in [1 : d + 1]$, then one would obtain $f(x) < \max\{f(z), z \in C\}$, a contradiction. This proves that one of the x_j is a maximizer of f.   □

In some situations, this result is useless: for instance, if C is an ℓ_p-ball with $p \in (1, \infty)$, then every point of its boundary is an extreme point. It is useful, however, for linear programs where the convex set C is a polytope made of all feasible points—the *feasible polytope*—so the result ensures that the minimum of the linear objective function is achieved at one of its vertices. This suggests a simple strategy to solve a linear program: compute the values of f at each vertex of the feasible polytope and select the smallest of these values. This naive strategy does not translate into a practical algorithm, because deducing the vertex representation of a polytope from its half-space representation is not an easy task and because the number of vertices may be exponential in the problem size (e.g. the *Birkhoff theorem* says that the polytope of doubly stochastic matrices in $\mathbb{R}^{k \times k}$ has $k!$ vertices, namely the permutation matrices). Still, it is important to characterize the extreme points of the feasible polytope for a linear program in standard form.

Lemma 20.2 *For $A \in \mathbb{R}^{n \times d}$ and $b \in \mathbb{R}^n$, the extreme points of the polytope $\mathcal{F} = \{x \in \mathbb{R}^d : Ax = b, x \ge 0\}$ are given by*

$$\mathrm{Ex}(\mathcal{F}) = \left\{ x \in \mathbb{R}^d : \exists\, S \subseteq [1 : d] \text{ such that } \begin{array}{l} A_S \text{ is injective,} \\ x \text{ is supported on } S, \\ x_S \ge 0 \text{ satisfies } A_S x_S = b. \end{array} \right\}.$$

Proof To establish the $\subseteq$-part, let $x \in \mathbb{R}^d$ be an extreme point of $\mathcal{F}$. With $S := \mathrm{supp}(x)$, suppose that one can find $u \in \ker(A_S) \setminus \{0\}$. One could then write $x = (x - \tau u)/2 + (x + \tau u)/2$ with $x - \tau u$ and $x + \tau u$ both belonging to $\mathcal{F}$ when $\tau > 0$ is small enough, which would contradict the fact that x is an extreme point. One derives that $\ker(A_S) = \{0\}$, i.e., that A_S is injective. The facts that x is supported on S, that $x_S \geq 0$, and that $A_S x_S = b$ are obvious.

For the $\supseteq$-part, let $x \in \mathbb{R}^d$ be such that there exists $S \subseteq [1:d]$ for which A_S is injective, $x_{S^c} = 0$, $x_S \geq 0$, and $A_S x_S = b$. Suppose by contradiction that x is not an extreme point of $\mathcal{F}$, i.e., that there exist $\tau \in (0,1)$ and $u \neq u'$ such that $Au = Au' = b$, $u, u' \geq 0$, and $x = (1-\tau)u + \tau u'$. The latter yields $0 = (1-\tau)u_{S^c} + \tau u'_{S^c}$, leading to $u_{S^c} = u'_{S^c} = 0$, and in turn to $A_S u_S = A_S u'_S = b$. The injectivity of A_S now implies that $u_S = u'_S$, and hence $u = u'$, which is a contradiction. $\qquad \square$

Remark 20.3   Lemmas 20.1 and 20.2 offer an alternative explanation of a fact highlighted in Section 14.2, namely that (some) ℓ_1-minimizers are sparse. Indeed, given an observation matrix $A \in \mathbb{R}^{m \times N}$, minimizers of $\|z\|_1$ subject to $Az = y$ can be obtained by solving

$$\underset{[z^+; z^-] \in \mathbb{R}^{2N}}{\text{minimize}} \ \langle \mathbb{1}, [z^+; z^-] \rangle \qquad \text{subject to } [A, -A][z^+; z^-] = y, \ [z^+; z^-] \geq 0.$$

This linear program admits a solution $[\widehat{z^+}; \widehat{z^-}]$ which is an extreme point of the feasible polytope (it can e.g. be provided by the simplex algorithm; see below). As an extreme point, it is supported on a set S whose size is at most m, by the injectivity of $[A, -A]_S \in \mathbb{R}^{m \times |S|}$. Thus, the ℓ_1-minimizer $\widehat{z} = \widehat{z^+} - \widehat{z^-}$ is at most m-sparse.

20.2 The Simplex Algorithm

Instead of evaluating the linear objective function at all the (just characterized) vertices of the feasible polytope, a refined strategy consists in traveling through these vertices while decreasing the value of the objective function. This is the essence of the *simplex algorithm*, to be described below for a linear program in standard form. In order to simplify the presentation, it is assumed from now on that:

The $d > n$ columns of $A \in \mathbb{R}^{n \times d}$ are in general position.

This means that any n columns of A are linearly independent vectors in $\mathbb{R}^n$, so that A_S is invertible whenever $|S| = n$. In this case, it is readily seen that the set of extreme points of the feasible polytope $\mathcal{F} = \{x \in \mathbb{R}^d : Ax = b, x \geq 0\}$ reduces to

$$\text{Ex}(\mathcal{F}) = \{v \in \mathbb{R}^d : \exists S \subseteq [1:d], |S| = n, \text{ such that } v_{S^c} = 0 \text{ and } v_S = A_S^{-1} b \geq 0\}.$$

The following proposition provides a certificate for an extreme point of the feasible polytope to be a minimizer of a standard-form linear program with objective function $x \mapsto \langle c, x \rangle$.

Proposition 20.4 *Let $S \subseteq [1:d]$ with $|S| = n$ and let $v \in \mathbb{R}^d$ be the extreme point associated with S, i.e., $v_{S^c} = 0$ and $v_S = A_S^{-1}b \geq 0$. If*

$$c_{S^c} - A_{S^c}^\top A_S^{-\top} c_S \geq 0, \tag{20.3}$$

then v minimizes $\langle c, x \rangle$ subject to $Ax = b$ and $x \geq 0$.
Conversely, if v minimizes $\langle c, x \rangle$ subject to $Ax = b$ and $x \geq 0$ and if $v_S > 0$, then (20.3) holds.

Proof Let $x \in \mathbb{R}^d$ be such that $x \geq 0$ and $Ax = b$, i.e., $A_S x_S + A_{S^c} x_{S^c} = b$ or $x_S = A_S^{-1}(b - A_{S^c} x_{S^c})$. One observes that

$$
\begin{aligned}
\langle c, x \rangle - \langle c, v \rangle &= \langle c_S, x_S \rangle + \langle c_{S^c}, x_{S^c} \rangle - \langle c_S, v_S \rangle \\
&= \langle c_S, A_S^{-1}(b - A_{S^c} x_{S^c}) \rangle + \langle c_{S^c}, x_{S^c} \rangle - \langle c_S, A_S^{-1}b \rangle \\
&= \langle c_{S^c}, x_{S^c} \rangle - \langle c_S, A_S^{-1} A_{S^c} x_{S^c} \rangle \\
&= \langle c_{S^c} - A_{S^c}^\top A_S^{-\top} c_S, x_{S^c} \rangle. \tag{20.4}
\end{aligned}
$$

Consequently, if (20.3) holds, then $\langle c, x \rangle - \langle c, v \rangle \geq 0$, i.e., $\langle c, x \rangle \geq \langle c, v \rangle$ for all feasible points $x \in \mathbb{R}^d$. This establishes that the extreme point v is a minimizer of $\langle c, x \rangle$ subject to $Ax = b$ and $x \geq 0$.

Now assume that v is a minimizer of $\langle c, x \rangle$ subject to $Ax = b$ and $x \geq 0$ and that $v_S > 0$. With $i \in S^c$ and $t > 0$ small enough, define $x \in \mathbb{R}^d$ by $x_{S^c} = te_i$ and $x_S = v_S - tA_S^{-1}A_{S^c}e_i$. One notices that $Ax = b$ and $x \geq 0$, the latter being valid thanks to the assumption $v_S > 0$. Since x is a feasible point, one has $\langle c, x \rangle \geq \langle c, v \rangle$, which means by (20.4) that $(c_{S^c} - A_{S^c}^\top A_S^{-\top} c_S)_i \geq 0$. This being true for any $i \in S^c$, one concludes that (20.3) holds. $\square$

Under the assumptions that the columns of A are in general position and that none of the vectors $A_S^{-1}b$, $|S| = n$, have zero entries, Proposition 20.4 translates into the following description of the *simplex algorithm*:

- start at a vertex $v^0 \in \mathbb{R}^d$ associated with some $S_0 \subseteq [1:d]$ of size n;
- for each $k \geq 0$, so long as $(c_{S_k^c} - A_{S_k^c}^\top A_{S_k}^{-\top} c_{S_k})_i < 0$ for some $i \in S_k^c$,
  - consider the largest $t > 0$ keeping the vector $v_{S_k}^k - tA_{S_k}^{-1}A_{S_k^c}e_i$ nonnegative, hence making the entry at an index $j \in S_k$ vanish,
  - form the vertex $v^{k+1} \in \mathbb{R}^d$ associated with $S^{k+1} = S^k \cup \{i\} \setminus \{j\}$, as given by $v_{S_k^c}^{k+1} = te_i$ and $v_{S_k}^{k+1} = v_{S_k}^k - tA_{S_k}^{-1}A_{S_k^c}e_i$, yielding the inequality $\langle c, v^{k+1} \rangle < \langle c, v^k \rangle$ according to (20.4);
- stop when $c_{S_k^c} - A_{S_k^c}^\top A_{S_k}^{-\top} c_{S_k} \geq 0$ and return the vertex $v^k \in \mathbb{R}^d$.

The simplex algorithm is guaranteed to stop in a finite number of iterations, for otherwise the sequence $(\langle c, v^k \rangle)_{k \geq 0}$ would be strictly decreasing, which is impossible since there are only finitely many vertices to choose the v^k from. However, the number of vertices can be superpolynomial in d, and so can the number of iterations for some pathological examples rarely encountered in practice. Be that as it may, linear programs are solvable in polynomial time—this fact is established by relying on alternatives to the simplex algorithm, e.g. on interior-point methods.

The initialization of the algorithm requires greater scrutiny, as producing a vertex v^0 of the feasible polytope is not obvious at all. In fact, this task is performed by running the simplex algorithm on an auxiliary linear program that is easily initialized. With $B := \mathrm{diag}[\mathrm{sgn}(b)]$, this auxiliary program is

$$\underset{x \in \mathbb{R}^d, y \in \mathbb{R}^n}{\text{minimize }} \langle \mathbb{1}, y \rangle \qquad \text{subject to } Ax + By = b, \; x \geq 0, \; y \geq 0.$$

The vector $[0; |b|] \in \mathbb{R}^{d+n}$ is readily seen to be a vertex of the auxiliary feasible polytope. It serves as the initialization to a simplex algorithm that outputs a vertex $[v; w] \in \mathbb{R}^{d+n}$ minimizing $\langle \mathbb{1}, y \rangle$ subject to $Ax + By = b$, $x \geq 0$, and $y \geq 0$. As such, one must have $w = 0$, and hence v is a vertex of the original feasible polytope, used to initialize the original simplex algorithm.

20.3 Illustrative Linear Programs

This closing section presents a few examples of geometric problems that can be formulated, and hence solved, as linear programs. Several of these examples illustrate the usefulness of an opportune introduction of slack variables.

Example 20.5 Inscribed circle to a polytope.

One looks for a largest ball contained in a polytope $C = \{x \in \mathbb{R}^d : Ax \leq b\}$. In other words, one wants to find a center $c \in \mathbb{R}^d$ and the maximal radius r such that $B(c, r) \subseteq C$, i.e., such that $A(c + ru) \leq b$ whenever $\|u\| \leq 1$. Here, the underlying norm $\| \cdot \|$ is arbitrary and its dual norm is denoted by $\| \cdot \|^*$. With $a^{(1)}, \ldots, a^{(n)} \in \mathbb{R}^d$ representing the rows of A, it is required that, for any $i \in [1:n]$, $\langle a^{(i)}, c \rangle + \max_{\|u\| \leq 1} r \langle a^{(i)}, u \rangle \leq b_i$, i.e., $\langle a^{(i)}, c \rangle + r\|a^{(i)}\|^* \leq b_i$. One ends up having to solve

$$\underset{c \in \mathbb{R}^d, r \in \mathbb{R}}{\text{maximize }} r \qquad \text{subject to } \langle a^{(i)}, c \rangle + r\|a^{(i)}\|^* \leq b_i, \quad i \in [1:n],$$

which appears as a linear program in the variable $[c; r] \in \mathbb{R}^{d+1}$. □

Example 20.6 Best approximant from a polytope.

Given a polytope $C = \{x \in \mathbb{R}^d : Ax \le b\}$ and a point $v \in \mathbb{R}^d$, one wants to find the closest point to v from C. The norm of interest here is either the ℓ_1-norm or the ℓ_∞-norm—say, the ℓ_1-norm. Thus, one wants to solve

$$\underset{x \in \mathbb{R}^d}{\text{minimize}} \ \|v - x\|_1 \quad \text{subject to } Ax \le b.$$

Since $\|v - x\|_1 = \min\{\sum_{j=1}^d c_j : c \in \mathbb{R}^d$ satisfies $|v_j - x_j| \le c_j$ for all $j \in [1:d]\}$, by introducing a vector $c \in \mathbb{R}^d$ of slack variables such that $|v_j - x_j| \le c_j$, i.e., $-c_j \le v_j - x_j \le c_j$, for all $j \in [1:d]$, the above program becomes

$$\underset{x \in \mathbb{R}^d, c \in \mathbb{R}^d}{\text{minimize}} \ \sum_{j=1}^d c_j \quad \text{subject to } Ax \le b, \ -c \le v - x \le c,$$

which appears as a linear program in the variable $[x;c] \in \mathbb{R}^{2d}$. $\qquad \square$

Example 20.7 Proximity between two polytopes.

Given two polytopes $C = \{x \in \mathbb{R}^d : Ax \le b\}$ and $C' = \{x \in \mathbb{R}^d : A'x \le b'\}$, the quantity $\text{dist}(C, C') := \min\{\|x - x'\|, \ x \in C, x' \in C'\}$ was encountered in Chapter 7 (where C and C' were finite sets). It is called proximity, since it is not a distance, as $\text{dist}(C, C') = 0$ can occur with $C \ne C'$ so long as $C \cap C' \ne \emptyset$. The norm of interest here is again either the ℓ_1-norm or the ℓ_∞-norm—say, the ℓ_∞-norm. Thus, the proximity $\text{dist}(C, C')$ can be obtained as a solution to the convex program

$$\underset{x, x' \in \mathbb{R}^d}{\text{minimize}} \|x - x'\|_\infty \quad \text{subject to } Ax \le b, \ A'x' \le b'.$$

Introducing a slack variable $c \in \mathbb{R}$ such that $\|x - x'\|_\infty \le c$ results in the equivalent program

$$\underset{x, x' \in \mathbb{R}^d, c \in \mathbb{R}}{\text{minimize}} \ c \quad \text{subject to } Ax \le b, \ A'x' \le b', \ -c\mathbb{1} \le x - x' \le c\mathbb{1},$$

which appears as a linear program in the variable $[x; x'; c] \in \mathbb{R}^{2d+1}$. $\qquad \square$

Example 20.8 Hausdorff distance between two bounded polytopes.

Given two polytopes $C = \{x \in \mathbb{R}^d : Ax \le b\}$ and $C' = \{x \in \mathbb{R}^d : A'x \le b'\}$, the *Hausdorff distance* (genuinely a distance this time) between C and C' is defined by

$$\text{dist}_H(C, C') = \max\left\{ \sup_{x \in C} \inf_{x' \in C'} \|x - x'\|, \ \sup_{x' \in C'} \inf_{x \in C} \|x - x'\| \right\}.$$

The norm of interest here is again either the ℓ_1-norm or the ℓ_∞-norm—say, the ℓ_1-norm. Not always realistically, one assumes that the vertices $v_1, \ldots, v_K$ of C and $v'_1, \ldots, v'_{K'}$ of C' can be determined efficiently. One looks at each term inside the maximum separately, starting with the leftmost one. According to Lemma 20.1, and taking the convexity of $x \in C \mapsto \inf_{x' \in C'} \|x - x'\|_1$ for granted, this leftmost term can be written as

$$\sup_{x \in C} \inf_{x' \in C'} \|x - x'\|_1 = \max_{k \in [1:K]} \min_{x' \in C'} \|v_k - x'\|_1.$$

Therefore, in order to compute it, one can solve the K convex programs

$$\underset{x' \in \mathbb{R}^d}{\text{minimize}} \, \|v_k - x'\|_1 \qquad \text{subject to } A'x' \le b'.$$

As already done in Example 20.6, the latter is equivalent to the linear program

$$\underset{x' \in \mathbb{R}^d, c \in \mathbb{R}^d}{\text{minimize}} \sum_{j=1}^{d} c_j \qquad \text{subject to } A'x' \le b', \ -c \le v_k - x' \le c.$$

By employing the same strategy for the rightmost term inside the maximum, one concludes that the Hausdorff distance $\text{dist}_H(C, C')$ can be computed by solving $K + K'$ linear programs. $\qquad\qquad\square$

Exercises

20.1 Given an inequality-form feasible polytope $\mathcal{F} = \{x \in \mathbb{R}^d : Ax \le b\}$ where the matrix A has rows $a^{(1)}, \ldots, a^{(n)} \in \mathbb{R}^d$, prove that $v \in \mathcal{F}$ is an extreme point of $\mathcal{F}$ if and only if the system $(a^{(i)} : \langle a^{(i)}, v \rangle = b_i)$ spans $\mathbb{R}^d$.

20.2 For $x \in \mathbb{R}^d$, with $x_1^* \ge x_2^* \ge \cdots \ge x_d^* \ge 0$ denoting the nonincreasing rearrangement of $|x_1|, |x_2|, \ldots, |x_d|$, show that, for any $k \in [1:n]$,

$$\|x\|_2 \le \max\left\{1, \frac{\sqrt{d}}{k}\right\} \sum_{j=1}^{k} x_j^*$$

by relying on Lemma 20.1 for the maximization of the convex function $\alpha \in \mathbb{R}_+^d \mapsto \alpha_1^2 + \cdots + \alpha_d^2 \in \mathbb{R}$.

20.3 Consider a function f defined as the ratio of a convex piecewise affine function and an affine function, so that

$$f(x) = \frac{\max\{\langle a^{(i)}, x \rangle - b_i, i \in [1:n]\}}{\langle c, x \rangle - d}, \qquad x \in \mathbb{R}^d.$$

Prove that the minimal value of f over a feasible polytope included in the half-space $\mathcal{H} = \{x \in \mathbb{R}^d : \langle c, x \rangle - d > 0\}$ can be found by solving a linear program.

20.4 Experiment with Example 20.5 to guess the value of the inscribed radius
for the polytope $\{x \in \mathbb{R}^d : x_1,\ldots,x_d \geq 0, x_1 + \cdots + x_d \leq 1\}$ relatively to
the ℓ_p-norm.

21

Duality Theory and Practice

Consider a minimization program—the *primal program*—written in the form

$$\underset{x \in \mathbb{R}^d}{\text{minimize}} \ f(x) \quad \text{s.to } f_i(x) \le 0, \ i \in [1:m], \ g_j(x) = 0, \ j \in [1:n]. \quad (21.1)$$

The *Lagrangian* associated with this (not necessarily convex) program is the function L defined for $x \in \mathbb{R}^d$, $\lambda \in \mathbb{R}^m$, and $v \in \mathbb{R}^n$ by

$$L(x, \lambda, v) := f(x) + \sum_{i=1}^{m} \lambda_i f_i(x) + \sum_{j=1}^{n} v_j g_j(x).$$

The vectors λ and v are called *dual variables* (aka Lagrange multiplier vectors). The expression

$$F(\lambda, v) := \inf_{x \in \mathbb{R}^d} L(x, \lambda, v)$$

defines the so-called *Lagrange dual function*, which, as an infimum of affine functions, is always concave. Now, for any vector $x \in \mathbb{R}^d$ in the feasible set C of (21.1), one has $L(x, \lambda, v) \le f(x)$ whenever $\lambda \ge 0$. Consequently, for all $\lambda \in \mathbb{R}^m_+$ and $v \in \mathbb{R}^n$, one obtains

$$F(\lambda, v) \le \inf_{x \in C} L(x, \lambda, v) \le \inf_{x \in C} f(x).$$

Taking the supremum over the dual variables, it follows that

$$\sup_{\lambda \in \mathbb{R}^m, v \in \mathbb{R}^n} \{F(\lambda, v) : \lambda \ge 0\} \le \inf_{x \in \mathbb{R}^d} \{f(x) : f_i(x) \le 0, g_j(x) = 0\}.$$

The concave maximization program on the left-hand side is the *dual program*. As it turns out, the primal and dual programs often yield the same optimal value. This fact will be fully justified in the case of linear programs. The usefulness of the resulting duality theory will then be demonstrated by some examples of robust optimization. Finally, duality results for cone programs, including semidefinite programs, will be stated without detailed justification.

177

21.1 Duality in Linear Programming

Before establishing the main theoretical result, it is instructive to spell out the dual forms of some linear programs as generated by the Lagrangian formalism.

Proposition 21.1 *A primal linear program in inequality form and its dual program read:*

$$\underset{x\in\mathbb{R}^d}{\text{minimize}}\,\langle c, x\rangle \qquad \text{subject to}\quad Ax \le b, \tag{21.2}$$

$$\underset{\lambda\in\mathbb{R}^n}{\text{maximize}}\,\langle -b, \lambda\rangle \qquad \text{subject to}\quad A^{\top}\lambda + c = 0,\ \lambda \ge 0. \tag{21.3}$$

A primal linear program in standard form and its dual program read:

$$\underset{x\in\mathbb{R}^d}{\text{minimize}}\,\langle c, x\rangle \qquad \text{subject to}\quad Ax = b,\ x \ge 0, \tag{21.4}$$

$$\underset{v\in\mathbb{R}^n}{\text{maximize}}\,\langle -b, v\rangle \qquad \text{subject to}\quad A^{\top}v + c \ge 0. \tag{21.5}$$

Proof One verifies only the first statement, the verification of the second one being left as Exercise 21.1. Since there are no equality constraints in (21.2), one simply drops the dual variable v. With $a^{(1)}, \ldots, a^{(n)}$ representing the rows of A, the Lagrange dual function becomes

$$F(\lambda) = \inf_{x\in\mathbb{R}^d}\left\{\langle c, x\rangle + \sum_{i=1}^{n}\lambda_i(\langle a^{(i)}, x\rangle - b_i)\right\} = \inf_{x\in\mathbb{R}^d}\left\{\left\langle \sum_{i=1}^{n}\lambda_i a^{(i)} + c, x\right\rangle - \sum_{i=1}^{n}\lambda_i b_i\right\}$$

$$= \begin{cases} -\infty & \text{if } \sum_{i=1}^{n}\lambda_i a^{(i)} + c \ne 0, \\ \langle -b, \lambda\rangle & \text{if } \sum_{i=1}^{n}\lambda_i a^{(i)} + c = 0. \end{cases}$$

Thus, the maximum of $F(\lambda)$ over $\lambda \ge 0$ can occur only when the constraint $\sum_{i=1}^{n}\lambda_i a^{(i)} + c = 0$ is enforced. Since this constraint is just $A^{\top}\lambda + c = 0$, the dual program indeed takes the form announced in (21.3). □

After this preamble, one proceeds to the justification of the equality between the primal and dual optimal values for linear programs in yet another form, which offers greater symmetry between the primal and dual formulations.

Theorem 21.2 *Given $A \in \mathbb{R}^{n\times d}$, $b \in \mathbb{R}^n$, and $c \in \mathbb{R}^d$, the linear programs*

$$\underset{x\in\mathbb{R}^d}{\text{minimize}}\,\langle c, x\rangle \qquad \text{subject to}\quad Ax \ge b,\ x \ge 0$$

$$\underset{y\in\mathbb{R}^n}{\text{maximize}}\,\langle b, y\rangle \qquad \text{subject to}\quad A^{\top}y \le c,\ y \ge 0$$

have equal optimal values, provided feasible vectors $x \in \mathbb{R}^d$ and $y \in \mathbb{R}^n$ exist for each program.

The proof relies crucially on the nonhomogeneous *Farkas lemma* presented below. The homogeneous version is just the case $\alpha_0 = \alpha_1 = \cdots = \alpha_K = 0$.

Lemma 21.3 *Let $a_0, a_1, \ldots, a_K \in \mathbb{R}^n$ and $\alpha_0, \alpha_1, \ldots, \alpha_K \in \mathbb{R}$ be given. The following properties are equivalent:*

(i) *for any $x \in \mathbb{R}^n$, if $\langle a_1, x \rangle \geq \alpha_1, \ldots, \langle a_K, x \rangle \geq \alpha_K$, then $\langle a_0, x \rangle \geq \alpha_0$;*
(ii) *there exist some $t_1, \ldots, t_K \geq 0$ such that $a_0 = t_1 a_1 + \cdots + t_K a_K$ and $t_1 \alpha_1 + \cdots + t_K \alpha_K \geq \alpha_0$.*

Proof   The implication (ii)$\Rightarrow$(i) being obvious, one concentrates on proving the implication (i)$\Rightarrow$(ii). To do so, supposing that (i) holds, the goal is to show that $\widetilde{a}_0 := [a_0; -\alpha_0] \in \mathbb{R}^{n+1}$ belongs to the convex subset of $\mathbb{R}^{n+1}$ defined by

$$C = \{t_1 \widetilde{a}_1 + \cdots + t_K \widetilde{a}_K + u\widetilde{b}, \ t_1, \ldots, t_K, u \geq 0\},$$

where $\widetilde{a}_1 := [a_1; -\alpha_1], \ldots, \widetilde{a}_K := [a_K; -\alpha_K] \in \mathbb{R}^{n+1}$ and $\widetilde{b} := [0; 1] \in \mathbb{R}^{n+1}$. By way of contradiction, assume that $\widetilde{a}_0 \notin C$. Taking momentarily for granted that C is a closed subset of $\mathbb{R}^{n+1}$, a version of the *Hahn–Banach separation theorem* (Corollary C.12) guarantees the existence of a scalar $c \in \mathbb{R}$ and a vector $\widetilde{z} = [z; \zeta] \in \mathbb{R}^{n+1}$ such that

$$\langle \widetilde{a}_0, \widetilde{z} \rangle < c \leq \langle \widetilde{v}, \widetilde{z} \rangle \qquad \text{for all } \widetilde{v} \in C.$$

The latter reads, for any $t_1, \ldots, t_K, u \geq 0$,

$$\langle a_0, z \rangle - \alpha_0 \zeta < c \leq \sum_{k=1}^{K} t_k (\langle a_k, z \rangle - \alpha_k \zeta) + u\zeta. \tag{21.6}$$

Taking $t_1 = \cdots = t_K = 0$ and $u = 0$ leads to $c \leq 0$. Taking $t_1 = \cdots = t_K = 0$ and $u > 0$ arbitrarily large leads to $\zeta \geq 0$. For any $k \in [1:K]$, taking $t_k > 0$ arbitrarily large and $t_\ell = 0$ for $\ell \in [1:K] \setminus \{k\}$, as well as $u = 0$, leads to $\langle a_k, z \rangle - \alpha_k \zeta \geq 0$. Note that $\zeta = 0$ would give $\langle a_k, z \rangle \geq 0$ for all $k \in [1:K]$, which, in combination with $\langle a_0, z \rangle < c \leq 0$, would violate (i): indeed, given $x \in \mathbb{R}^n$ with $\langle a_1, x \rangle \geq \alpha_1, \ldots, \langle a_K, x \rangle \geq \alpha_K$, one would have, for $t > 0$ large enough, $\langle a_1, x + tz \rangle \geq \alpha_1, \ldots, \langle a_K, x + tz \rangle \geq \alpha_K$ but $\langle a_0, x + tz \rangle < \alpha_0$. With $\zeta > 0$ now acquired, one obtains $\langle a_k, z/\zeta \rangle \geq \alpha_k$ for all $k \in [1:K]$, therefore $\langle a_0, z/\zeta \rangle \geq \alpha_0$ by (i). This reads $\langle a_0, z \rangle - \alpha_0 \zeta \geq 0$, contradicting $\langle a_0, z \rangle - \alpha_0 \zeta < c$. This contradiction shows that $\widetilde{a}_0 \in C$.

It remains to justify that the *conic hull* of vectors $v_1, \ldots, v_K \in \mathbb{R}^d$, i.e.,

$$C = \{t_1 v_1 + \cdots + t_K v_K, \ t_1, \ldots, t_K \geq 0\},$$

is a closed subset of $\mathbb{R}^d$. This is done by induction on $K \geq 1$. The base case $K = 1$ being clear, one assumes that the induction hypothesis holds up to

$K - 1$ and aims at proving it for $K \geq 2$. There are two cases to consider. First, in case the system $(v_1, \ldots, v_K)$ is linearly independent, one completes it to a basis $(v_1, \ldots, v_K, v_{K+1}, \ldots, v_d)$ of $\mathbb{R}^d$. With A denoting the matrix whose columns are $v_1, \ldots, v_d$ and with B denoting its inverse, one has $C = A(\mathbb{R}_+^K \times \{0\})$, i.e., $C = B^{-1}(\mathbb{R}_+^K \times \{0\})$. Thus, the set C appears as the preimage of a closed set by a continuous function, and so it is closed as well. Second, in case the system $(v_1, \ldots, v_K)$ is linearly dependent, there exist scalars $\lambda_1, \ldots, \lambda_K$, not all zero, such that $\sum_{k=1}^K \lambda_k v_k = 0$. Then, any $v \in C$ written as $v = \sum_{k=1}^K t_k v_k$ with $t_1, \ldots, t_K \geq 0$ can also be written, for an arbitrary $t \in \mathbb{R}$, as $v = \sum_{k=1}^K (t_k - t\lambda_k)v_k$. Since one can always find $t \in \mathbb{R}$ such that $t_k - t\lambda_k \geq 0$ for all $k \in [1 : K]$ and $t_\ell - t\lambda_\ell = 0$ for some $\ell \in [1 : K]$, one deduces that

$$C = \bigcup_{\ell=1}^K \left\{ \sum_{k=1,k\neq\ell}^K t_k v_k, \ t_1, \ldots, t_{\ell-1}, t_{\ell+1}, \ldots, t_K \geq 0 \right\}.$$

Thus, the set C is as a finite union of closed sets (by the induction hypothesis), and so it is closed as well. The inductive proof is complete.   □

With the Farkas lemma now established, one can turn to the proof of the duality theorem for linear programming. Note that the Farkas lemma shall be used below in a condensed form, namely: given $A \in \mathbb{R}^{K \times n}$, $\alpha \in \mathbb{R}^K$, $a_0 \in \mathbb{R}^n$, and $\alpha_0 \in \mathbb{R}$,

$$\left[Ax \geq \alpha \Rightarrow a_0^\top x \geq \alpha_0 \right] \Leftrightarrow \left[A^\top t = a_0 \text{ and } \alpha^\top t \geq \alpha_0 \text{ for some } t \in \mathbb{R}_+^K \right]. \quad (21.7)$$

Proof of Theorem 21.2 Given vectors $x \in \mathbb{R}^d$ and $y \in \mathbb{R}^n$, their feasibility for the programs under consideration is equivalent to

$$\left[\begin{array}{c|c} A & 0 \\ \hline I_d & 0 \\ \hline 0 & -A^\top \\ \hline 0 & I_n \end{array} \right] \left[\begin{array}{c} x \\ y \end{array} \right] = \left[\begin{array}{c} Ax \\ x \\ -A^\top y \\ y \end{array} \right] \geq \left[\begin{array}{c} b \\ 0 \\ -c \\ 0 \end{array} \right],$$

and this feasibility implies that

$$\left[\begin{array}{c} c \\ -b \end{array} \right]^\top \left[\begin{array}{c} x \\ y \end{array} \right] = c^\top x - b^\top y \geq (A^\top y)^\top x - (Ax)^\top y = y^\top Ax - x^\top A^\top y = 0.$$

Therefore, by Lemma 21.3 in the form (21.7), there are nonnegative vectors $x', x'' \in \mathbb{R}^d$ and $y', y'' \in \mathbb{R}^n$ such that

$$\left[\begin{array}{c} c \\ -b \end{array} \right] = \left[\begin{array}{c|c|c|c} A^\top & I_d & 0 & 0 \\ \hline 0 & 0 & -A & I_n \end{array} \right] \left[\begin{array}{c} y' \\ x'' \\ x' \\ y'' \end{array} \right] \quad \text{and} \quad \left[\begin{array}{c} b \\ 0 \\ -c \\ 0 \end{array} \right]^\top \left[\begin{array}{c} y' \\ x'' \\ x' \\ y'' \end{array} \right] \geq 0.$$

These relations simply read

$$A^\top y' \le c, \qquad Ax' \ge b, \qquad b^\top y' - c^\top x' \ge 0.$$

In particular, the vectors x' and y' appear feasible for the appropriate programs. It is claimed that they are in fact optimal and that $c^\top x' = b^\top y'$. For the latter claim, since $c^\top x' \le b^\top y'$ is already acquired, one just needs to verify that $c^\top x' \ge b^\top y'$, which follows from

$$c^\top x' \ge (A^\top y')^\top x' = (y')^\top (Ax') \ge (y')^\top b = b^\top y'.$$

For the former claim, one verifies e.g. that x' is optimal, i.e., that $c^\top x' \le c^\top x$ whenever $Ax \ge b$ and $x \ge 0$. This is simply seen from

$$c^\top x' = b^\top y' \le (Ax)^\top y' = x^\top A^\top y' \le x^\top c = c^\top x.$$

A similar argument would prove the optimality of y'. $\qquad\qquad\square$

21.2 Examples of Robust Optimization

To continue the rundown on duality theory, one highlights that it is at the center of the field of *robust optimization*. This field is concerned with solving convex optimization problems under uncertainty. For instance, when minimizing over a vector variable x, inequality constraints of the type $Ax \le b$ are not enforced as such because the matrix A and the vector b may not be accurately known. Instead, it may be known only that (A, b) belongs to some uncertainty set $\mathcal{U}$—a ball centered at some $(\bar{A}, \bar{b})$, say. The constraint should then be replaced by $Ax \le b$ for all $(A, b) \in \mathcal{U}$, i.e., $\max\{Ax - b : (A, b) \in \mathcal{U}\} \le 0$. The basic idea is to express, for a fixed x, the latter in dual form as $\min\{f_x(y) : y \in \mathcal{V}\} \le 0$, i.e., as the existence of some $y \in \mathcal{V}$ such that $f_x(y) \le 0$. Then one performs a minimization over both x and a new variable y under the added constraints that $y \in \mathcal{V}$ and $f_x(y) \le 0$. Two examples are provided below to illustrate how such a strategy can sometimes be fruitful.

Example 21.4 Circumscribed circle to a polytope.

One looks for a smallest ball containing a polytope $C = \{x \in \mathbb{R}^d : Ax \le b\}$, which was called a *Chebyshev ball* in Chapter 9. In other words, one wants to find a center $c \in \mathbb{R}^d$ and a minimal radius r such that $C \subseteq B(c, r)$. Taking the underlying norm to be the ℓ_∞-norm, one has to solve

$$\underset{c \in \mathbb{R}^d, r \in \mathbb{R}}{\text{minimize}} \ r \qquad \text{subject to } \|x - c\|_\infty \le r \quad \text{for all } x \in C. \qquad (21.8)$$

The constraint in (21.8) is reformulated as $\max\{\|x - c\|_\infty : Ax \le b\} \le r$, or in fact as $2d$ constraints indexed by $j \in [1:d]$ and $\varepsilon_j \in \{-1, +1\}$, namely

$$\max_{x \in \mathbb{R}^d}\{\varepsilon_j(x - c)_j : Ax \le b\} = \max_{v \in \mathbb{R}^d}\{\langle-\varepsilon_j e_j, v\rangle : Av - Ac + b \ge 0\} \le r. \quad (21.9)$$

The above maximization has the form of the dual program (21.5), so its optimal value equals the optimal value of the primal program (21.4). Thus, each of the constraints (21.9) also reads

$$\min_{y \in \mathbb{R}^n}\{\langle-Ac + b, y\rangle : A^\top y = \varepsilon_j e_j, \ y \ge 0\} \le r,$$

i.e., it is seen to be equivalent to the existence of $y = y^{j,\varepsilon_j} \in \mathbb{R}^n$ such that $y \ge 0$, $A^\top y = \varepsilon_j e_j$, and $\langle-Ac + b, y\rangle = -\langle c, \varepsilon_j e_j\rangle + \langle b, y\rangle \le r$. All in all, the original problem (21.8) can be equivalently recast as

$$\begin{array}{ll} \underset{\substack{c \in \mathbb{R}^d, r \in \mathbb{R} \\ y^{1,\pm},\dots,y^{d,\pm} \in \mathbb{R}^n}}{\text{minimize}} \ r & \text{subject to} \quad y^{j,\pm} \ge 0, \ A^\top y^{j,\pm} = \pm e_j, \end{array}$$

$$\text{and} \quad \mp \langle c, e_j\rangle + \langle b, y^{j,\pm}\rangle \le r,$$

which appears as a linear program in $(2n + 1)d + 1$ variables. $\qquad\square$

Example 21.5 Owl-norm minimization.

Chapter 14 revealed the importance for sparse recovery of minimizing the ℓ_1-norm $\|z\|_1$ subject to observation constraints taking the form $Az = y$. In some situations, it is more relevant to solve

$$\underset{z \in \mathbb{R}^d}{\text{minimize}} \ \|z\|_{\text{owl}} \quad \text{subject to} \quad Az = y. \quad (21.10)$$

The *ordered weighted ℓ_1-norm* (*owl-norm* for short) featured above is defined relatively to some weights $w_1 \ge \cdots \ge w_n \ge 0$ by

$$\|z\|_{\text{owl}} = \sum_{j=1}^{d} w_j z_j^*, \quad (21.11)$$

where $z_1^* \ge \cdots \ge z_d^* \ge 0$ is the nonincreasing rearrangement of $|z_1|, \dots, |z_d|$. This expression is unfriendly for the program (21.10). But, by exploiting some rearrangement inequality (see Exercise 21.2), the owl-norm can be written as

$$\|z\|_{\text{owl}} = \max\left\{ \sum_{j=1}^{d} w_j |z_{\pi(j)}| : \pi \text{ is a permutation of } [1:d] \right\}.$$

Since permutation matrices constitute the extreme points of the set of doubly stochastic matrices—this is the *Birkhoff theorem* (Theorem C.13)—and in view of Lemma 20.1, one now has

$$\|z\|_{\text{owl}} = \max_{S \in \mathbb{R}^{d \times d}} \left\{ \sum_{j=1}^{d} w_j (S|z|)_j : \right.$$

$$\left. \sum_{i=1}^{d} S_{i,j} = \sum_{i=1}^{d} S_{j,i} = 1, j \in [1:d], \ S \geq 0 \right\}. \quad (21.12)$$

One recognizes a linear program of the form (21.3). By duality, its maximal value equals the minimal value of another linear program. Precisely, leaving the verification as Exercise 21.3, the owl-norm can be expressed as

$$\|z\|_{\text{owl}} = \min_{a,b \in \mathbb{R}^d} \left\{ \sum_{j=1}^{d} (a_j + b_j) : w_i|z_j| \leq a_i + b_j \text{ for all } i, j \in [1:d] \right\}. \quad (21.13)$$

This expression is now friendly for the program (21.10). Indeed, writing the constraints $w_i|z_j| \leq a_i + b_j$ as $-(a_i + b_j) \leq w_i z_j \leq (a_i + b_j)$, the owl-norm minimization can be reformulated as

$$\underset{z,a,b \in \mathbb{R}^d}{\text{minimize}} \sum_{j=1}^{d} (a_j + b_j) \quad \text{s.to} \ Az = y, \ -(a_i + b_j) \leq w_i z_j \leq (a_i + b_j), \ i, j \in [1:d],$$

which appears as a linear program in the variable $[z; a; b] \in \mathbb{R}^{3d}$. □

21.3 Duality in Conic Programming

Duality theory extends beyond linear programs. For instance, if one replaces the constraint $x \geq 0$ in a standard-form linear program by $x \in C$, where $C \subseteq \mathbb{R}^d$ is a closed convex cone, then one arrives at a standard-form cone program. It is possible to establish[1] the duality result stated below.

Theorem 21.6 *A primal cone program, written in standard form as*

$$\underset{x \in \mathbb{R}^d}{\text{minimize}} \langle c, x \rangle \quad \text{subject to } Ax = b, \ x \in C,$$

and its dual cone program, written as

$$\underset{v \in \mathbb{R}^n}{\text{maximize}} \langle -b, v \rangle \quad \text{subject to } A^\top v + c \in C^*,$$

have equal optimal values, provided that either the primal program or the dual program is strongly feasible.

---

[1] See e.g. Chapter 3 of Renegar (2001) or Appendix A of Ben-Tal et al. (2009) for details.

The terminology needs clarification. First, *strong feasibility* of the primal, respectively dual, program means that the program is feasible and remains so under small perturbation of b, respectively c; second, the notation C^* stands for the *dual cone* of $C \subseteq \mathbb{R}^d$, i.e., for

$$C^* = \{y \in \mathbb{R}^d : \langle x, y \rangle \geq 0 \text{ for all } x \in C\}.$$

Of particular interest is the *second-order cone* (aka the *Lorentz cone*) defined by

$$C_{\text{so}} = \left\{ x \in \mathbb{R}^d : x_d \geq 0, \sum_{j=1}^{d-1} x_j^2 \leq x_d^2 \right\}. \tag{21.14}$$

This cone is *self-dual*, in the sense that $C_{\text{so}}^* = C_{\text{so}}$, as verified in Exercise 21.4. In this exercise, identifying matrices $X, Y \in \mathbb{R}^{d \times d}$ with their vectorizations $x = \text{vec}(X), y = \text{vec}(Y) \in \mathbb{R}^{d^2}$ so that $\langle x, y \rangle$ agrees with the Frobenius inner product $\langle X, Y \rangle_F = \text{tr}(X^\top Y)$, readers are also invited to verify the self-duality of the *semidefinite cone*

$$C_{\text{sd}} = \{X \in \mathbb{R}^{d \times d} : X \text{ is positive semidefinite}\}. \tag{21.15}$$

As a reminder (see Appendix D for details), a symmetric matrix $M \in \mathbb{R}^{d \times d}$ is called *positive semidefinite*, which is abbreviated as $M \succeq 0$, if $\langle Mv, v \rangle \geq 0$ for all $v \in \mathbb{R}^d$, or equivalently if all its eigenvalues are nonnegative. A cone program for which $C = C_{\text{sd}}$ is a *semidefinite program* in *standard form*, which is thus written as

$$\underset{X \in \mathbb{R}^{d \times d}}{\text{minimize}} \ \text{tr}(C^\top X) \qquad \text{s.to } \text{tr}(A_i^\top X) = b_i, \ i \in [1 : n],$$

$$\text{and } X \succeq 0,$$

for some matrices $C, A_1, \ldots, A_n \in \mathbb{R}^{d \times d}$, assumed without loss of generality to be symmetric, and some numbers $b_1, \ldots, b_n \in \mathbb{R}$. Semidefinite programs encapsulate linear programs, since a standard-form linear program (20.2) can be reformulated as

$$\underset{X \in \mathbb{R}^{d \times d}}{\text{minimize}} \ \text{tr}(\text{diag}[c]^\top X) \qquad \text{s.to } \text{tr}(\text{diag}[a^{(i)}]^\top X) = b_i, \ i \in [1 : n],$$

$$\text{tr}(E_{k,\ell}^\top X) = 0, \ k \neq \ell \in [1 : d],$$

$$X \succeq 0,$$

where $a^{(1)}, \ldots, a^{(n)} \in \mathbb{R}^d$ denote the rows of $A \in \mathbb{R}^{n \times d}$ and where $E_{k,\ell} \in \mathbb{R}^{d \times d}$ denotes a matrix with all but its (k, ℓ)th entry equal to zero. In general, one can recast as a standard-form semidefinite program any optimization program that mixes vector or matrix variables, that features a linear objective function, and that involves linear inequality constraints in the regular or semidefinite sense, so the generic term semidefinite program is used to designate such programs. For illustration, as a direct consequence of Theorem D.5, the operator norm $\|M\|_{2\to 2}$ of a matrix $M \in \mathbb{R}^{d\times d}$ is the solution to the semidefinite program

$$\underset{c\in\mathbb{R}}{\text{minimize }} c \quad\text{s.to}\quad \left[\begin{array}{c|c} 0 & M \\ \hline M^\top & 0 \end{array}\right] \preceq c\, I_{2d}. \tag{21.16}$$

The following representative duality result instantiates Theorem 21.6 to the semidefinite case.

Theorem 21.7 *The primal and dual semidefinite programs*

$$\underset{X\in\mathbb{R}^{d\times d}}{\text{minimize }} \text{tr}(C^\top X) \qquad \text{s.to } \text{tr}(A_i^\top X) = b_i,\ i \in [1:n],$$

$$\text{and } X \succeq 0,$$

$$\underset{v\in\mathbb{R}^n}{\text{maximize }} \langle -b, v\rangle \qquad \text{s.to } v_1 A_1 + \cdots + v_n A_n + C \succeq 0$$

have equal optimal values, provided that either the primal program or the dual program is strongly feasible.

Exercises

21.1 Use the Lagrangian formalism to derive the dual form (21.5) of the standard-form linear program (21.4).

21.2 Given $a_1 \geq \cdots \geq a_n$, $b_1 \geq \cdots \geq b_n$, and a permutation π of $[1:n]$, use *summation by parts* to prove the *rearrangement inequalities*

$$\sum_{j=1}^n a_j b_{n+1-j} \leq \sum_{j=1}^n a_j b_{\pi(j)} \leq \sum_{j=1}^n a_j b_j. \tag{21.17}$$

21.3 Fill in the details allowing one to derive the expression (21.13) for the owl-norm from its expression (21.12).

21.4 Verify that the second-order cone and the semidefinite cone introduced respectively in (21.14) and (21.15) are both self-dual.

22

Semidefinite Programming in Action

In contrast with Chapter 20, this chapter is not concerned with any algorithmic solution. Instead, taking for granted that semidefinite programs can be solved efficiently, it merely illustrates the usefulness of semidefinite programming when optimizing in certain function spaces. The sum-of-squares technique and the method of moments are particularly emphasized. They appear in a series of three examples, all related to one problem stemming from the *spline algorithm* of Chapter 9. This problem is the formal optimization program

$$\underset{f \in \mathcal{T}_n^{\text{even}}}{\text{minimize}} \left\| f^{(k)} \right\|_{L_p(\mathbb{T})} \quad \text{subject to } f(x^{(i)}) = y_i, \ i \in [1:m]. \tag{22.1}$$

The highlight is put on the special cases $p = 2$, $p = \infty$, and $p = 1$. Compared to Theorem 9.6, the optimization space has been restricted from a whole Sobolev space W_2^k to a much smaller space $\mathcal{T}_n^{\text{even}} = \text{span}\{1, \cos, \ldots, \cos(n\cdot)\}$ of even trigonometric polynomials, implicitly assuming the appropriate symmetry in the data $(x^{(1)}, y_1), \ldots, (x^{(m)}, y_m)$. The overparametrized regime $n \geq m$ prevails here, otherwise at most one $f \in \mathcal{T}_n^{\text{even}}$ would obey the interpolatory constraints. The functions $f \in \mathcal{T}_n^{\text{even}}$ are represented by their coefficients $a \in \mathbb{R}^{n+1}$ on the basis $(1, \cos, \ldots, \cos(n\cdot))$, so that

$$f(x) = \sum_{j=0}^{n} a_j \cos(jx) \quad \text{and} \quad f^{(k)}(x) = \sum_{j=0}^{n} a_j j^k \cos^{(k)}(jx).$$

Thus, the interpolatory constraints on f translate into linear constraints on a of the form $Ma = y$, where the matrix $M \in \mathbb{R}^{m \times (n+1)}$ has entries $M_{i,j} = \cos(jx^{(i)})$ for $i \in [1:m]$ and $j \in [0:n]$.

186

22.1 Schur Complement

This section aims at solving the program (22.1) in the special case $p = 2$. Thanks to the orthogonality of the system $(j^k \cos(j\cdot), j \in [1:n])$, this instance of the program reduces to

$$\underset{a\in\mathbb{R}^{n+1}}{\text{minimize}} \ \|Da\|_2 \quad \text{subject to } Ma = y, \tag{22.2}$$

where the matrix $D = \sqrt{\pi} \, \text{diag}[0; 1^k; 2^k; \ldots; n^k] \in \mathbb{R}^{(n+1)\times(n+1)}$ is singular. The latter has a closed-form solution (see Exercise 22.1), so computing it as the output of an optimization program is an overkill. For sport, however, one notices that it can be recast as the semidefinite program

$$\underset{a\in\mathbb{R}^{n+1}, c\in\mathbb{R}}{\text{minimize}} \ c \quad \text{subject to } Ma = y \quad \text{and} \quad \left[\begin{array}{c|c} c\,I_{n+1} & Da \\ \hline (Da)^\top & c \end{array}\right] \geq 0.$$

This can be seen by introducing a slack variable $c \in \mathbb{R}$ such that $\|Da\|_2 \leq c$ and making use of the observation that, for a vector $v \in \mathbb{R}^d$ and a constant $c \in \mathbb{R}$,

$$\|v\|_2 \leq c \iff \left[\begin{array}{c|c} c\,I_d & v \\ \hline v^\top & c \end{array}\right] \geq 0.$$

This observation is a particular instance of equivalence (iii)⇔(ii) in the more general result below. In passing, one mentions that the matrix appearing in (i) is called the *Schur complement* of the upper left block of the matrix from (ii).

Proposition 22.1 *Given matrices A, B, and M, with A and B positive definite but not necessarily of the same size, the following properties are equivalent:*

(i) $B - M^\top A^{-1} M \geq 0$;

(ii) $\left[\begin{array}{c|c} A & M \\ \hline M^\top & B \end{array}\right] \geq 0$;

(iii) $\|A^{-1/2} M B^{-1/2}\|_{2\to2} \leq 1$.

Proof For all properly sized vectors u, v and all $t \in \mathbb{R}$, observe first that

$$\left\langle \left[\begin{array}{c|c} A & M \\ \hline M^\top & B \end{array}\right] \begin{bmatrix} u \\ tv \end{bmatrix}, \begin{bmatrix} u \\ tv \end{bmatrix} \right\rangle = \langle Au, u\rangle + 2t\langle u, Mv\rangle + t^2\langle Bv, v\rangle. \tag{22.3}$$

(i)⇒(ii). Writing (i) as $M^\top A^{-1} M \leq B$ allows one to obtain, for all properly sized vectors u, v,

$$|\langle u, Mv\rangle|^2 = |\langle A^{1/2}u, A^{-1/2}Mv\rangle|^2 \leq \|A^{1/2}u\|_2^2 \|A^{-1/2}Mv\|_2^2$$
$$= \langle Au, u\rangle \langle M^\top A^{-1} Mv, v\rangle \leq \langle Au, u\rangle \langle Bv, v\rangle.$$

According to the identity (22.3) with $t = 1$, it follows that

$$\left\langle \left[\begin{array}{c|c} A & M \\ \hline M^{\mathsf{T}} & B \end{array}\right] \left[\begin{array}{c} u \\ v \end{array}\right], \left[\begin{array}{c} u \\ v \end{array}\right] \right\rangle \geq \langle Au, u \rangle - 2\langle Au, u \rangle^{1/2} \langle Bv, v \rangle^{1/2} + \langle Bv, v \rangle$$

$$= (\langle Au, u \rangle^{1/2} - \langle Bv, v \rangle^{1/2})^2 \geq 0.$$

This proves the positive semidefiniteness of the matrix appearing in (ii).

(ii)$\Rightarrow$(iii). Under (ii), the quadratic expression of t in the right-hand side of (22.3) keeps a constant sign, so its discriminant must be nonpositive, i.e., $\langle u, Mv \rangle^2 - \langle Au, u \rangle \langle Bv, v \rangle \leq 0$. Replacing u by $A^{-1/2}u$ and v by $B^{-1/2}v$, this inequality reads $\langle u, A^{-1/2}MB^{-1/2}v \rangle^2 \leq \|u\|_2^2 \|v\|_2^2$ for all properly sized vectors u and v, meaning that $\|A^{-1/2}MB^{-1/2}\|_{2 \to 2} \leq 1$.

(iii)$\Rightarrow$(i). Under (iii), for any properly sized vector x written as $x = B^{-1/2}v$, one has

$$\langle (B - M^{\mathsf{T}}A^{-1}M)x, x \rangle = \|v\|_2^2 - \|A^{-1/2}MB^{-1/2}v\|_2^2 \geq 0.$$

This proves the positive semidefiniteness of the matrix appearing in (i).   □

22.2 Sum-of-Squares Technique

This section aims at solving the program (22.1) in the special case $p = \infty$. To begin with, introducing a slack variable $c \in \mathbb{R}$ allows one to reformulate the program as

$$\underset{a \in \mathbb{R}^{n+1}, c \in \mathbb{R}}{\text{minimize }} c \quad \text{s.to } Ma = y \quad \text{and} \quad \left\| \sum_{j=0}^{n} a_j j^k \cos^{(k)}(j \cdot) \right\|_{L_\infty(\mathbb{T})} \leq c. \quad (22.4)$$

At first sight, the latter L_∞-constraint looks like an infinite set of constraints. Indeed, assuming that $k \equiv 3 \pmod 4$ to fix the ideas, it reads

$$-c \leq \sum_{j=1}^{n} a_j j^k \sin(j\theta) \leq c \qquad \text{for all } \theta \in \mathbb{T}. \quad (22.5)$$

However, it can alternatively be interpreted as two nonnegativity conditions for trigonometric polynomials, and such conditions can actually be expressed as semidefinite constraints, as revealed by the result below. This result belongs to a set of *sum-of-squares* techniques, although only one square is involved in the sum here.

Theorem 22.2 *For a trigonometric polynomial written as $p(\theta) = \sum_{j=-n}^{n} c_j e^{-\mathrm{i}j\theta}$ with $c_{-j} = \overline{c_j}$ for all $j \in [0:n]$, the following properties are equivalent:*

(i) $p(\theta) \geq 0$ *for all $\theta \in \mathbb{T}$;*

(ii) $p(\theta) = |q(e^{-i\theta})|^2$ *for some algebraic polynomial q of degree at most n;*

(iii) *there exists a positive semidefinite matrix $Q \in \mathbb{C}^{(n+1)\times(n+1)}$ such that*

$$\sum_{i-j=\ell} Q_{i,j} = c_\ell \qquad \text{for all } \ell \in [0:n]. \tag{22.6}$$

Proof The equivalence (i)$\Leftrightarrow$(ii) is the *Riesz–Fejér theorem* (Theorem E.7), so only (ii)$\Rightarrow$(iii) and (iii)$\Rightarrow$(i) need to be justified.

(ii)$\Rightarrow$(iii). Writing $q(z) = \sum_{j=0}^{n} q_j z^j$, the relation $p(\theta) = |q(e^{-i\theta})|^2$ reads

$$p(\theta) = \left[\sum_{h=0}^{n} q_h e^{-ih\theta}\right]\left[\sum_{j=0}^{n} \overline{q_j} e^{ij\theta}\right] = \sum_{h,j=0}^{n} q_h \overline{q_j} e^{-i(h-j)\theta} = \sum_{\ell=-n}^{n}\left(\sum_{h-j=\ell} q_h \overline{q_j}\right) e^{-i\ell\theta}.$$

Defining the positive semidefinite matrix $Q \in \mathbb{C}^{(n+1)\times(n+1)}$ as $Q := qq^*$ and identifying the coefficient of $e^{-i\ell\theta}$ leads to (22.6) in the form

$$c_\ell = \sum_{h-j=\ell} q_h \overline{q_j} = \sum_{h-j=\ell} Q_{h,j} \qquad \text{for all } \ell \in [0:n].$$

(iii)$\Rightarrow$(i). With $v(\theta) := [1; e^{i\theta}; \ldots; e^{in\theta}] \in \mathbb{C}^{n+1}$, the expression (22.6) for the coefficients c_ℓ easily implies that $p(\theta) = \langle Qv(\theta), v(\theta)\rangle$. The fact that Q is positive semidefinite now ensures that $p(\theta) \geq 0$ for all $\theta \in \mathbb{T}$, as expected. $\square$

Returning to the conditions (22.5), one observes that they can be viewed as two polynomial nonnegativity conditions, namely

$$c \pm \sum_{j=1}^{n} a_j j^k \frac{e^{ij\theta} - e^{-ij\theta}}{2i} = \sum_{j=-n}^{n} c_j^\pm e^{-ij\theta} \geq 0 \qquad \text{for all } \theta \in \mathbb{T},$$

where $c_0^\pm := c$ and $c_j^\pm := \pm i a_{|j|} j^k / 2$ for $j \in [-n:n] \setminus \{0\}$, so that $c_j^\pm$ and $c_{-j}^\pm$ are indeed complex conjugate. According to Theorem 22.2, the optimization program (22.4) can then be recast as the semidefinite program

$$\underset{\substack{a\in\mathbb{R}^{n+1}, c\in\mathbb{R} \\ Q^+, Q^- \in \mathbb{C}^{(n+1)\times(n+1)}}}{\text{minimize}} \quad c \qquad \text{s.to } Ma = y,\ Q^\pm \geq 0,\ \sum_i Q_{i,i}^\pm = c,$$

$$\text{and } \sum_{i-j=\ell} Q_{i,j}^\pm = \pm \frac{i a_\ell \ell^k}{2} \quad \text{for all } \ell \in [1:n].$$

Although this semidefinite program differs slightly from the ones introduced in Chapter 21, which took place only in a real setting, this complex variant is also efficiently computable.

22.3 Method of Moments

This section aims at solving the program (22.1) in the special case $p = 1$. To fix the ideas, one assumes this time that k is even, so the program now reads

$$\underset{a \in \mathbb{R}^{n+1}}{\text{minimize}} \int_{\mathbb{T}} \left| \sum_{j=1}^{n} a_j j^k \cos(j\theta) \right| d\theta \qquad \text{subject to } Ma = y. \qquad (22.7)$$

With $\mathcal{M}(\mathbb{T})$, respectively $\mathcal{M}_+(\mathbb{T})$, denoting the set of signed, respectively nonnegative, Borel measures on $\mathbb{T}$, one introduces a slack variable $\mu \in \mathcal{M}(\mathbb{T})$ and considers its Jordan decomposition $\mu = \mu^+ - \mu^-$ with $\mu^+, \mu^- \in \mathcal{M}_+(\mathbb{T})$. Since the total variation of μ is $|\mu| = \mu^+ + \mu^-$, (22.7) becomes

$$\underset{\substack{a \in \mathbb{R}^{n+1} \\ \mu^+, \mu^- \in \mathcal{M}_+(\mathbb{T})}}{\text{minimize}} \int_{\mathbb{T}} d(\mu^+ + \mu^-) \quad \text{s.to } Ma = y$$

$$\text{and } d(\mu^+ - \mu^-)(\theta) = \sum_{j=1}^{n} a_j j^k \cos(j\theta) d\theta. \qquad (22.8)$$

As a first step, this minimization program over measures is to be rephrased as an infinite semidefinite program by replacing Borel measures with their sequences of trigonometric moments. Such a strategy is the essence of the *method of moments*, based on equivalences between measures and moments. The result stated below, whose proof is found in the appendix, relies on the so-called *discrete trigonometric moment problem* (Theorem E.8).[1]

Theorem 22.3 *Given an infinite sequence $u \in \mathbb{R}^{\mathbb{N}}$, there exists a nonnegative Borel measure $\mu \in \mathcal{M}_+(\mathbb{T})$ such that*

$$\int_{\mathbb{T}} \cos(\ell\theta) d\mu(\theta) = u_\ell \qquad \text{for all } \ell \geq 0$$

if and only if the infinite symmetric Toeplitz matrix built from u is positive semidefinite, i.e.,

$$\mathrm{Toep}_\infty(u) := \begin{bmatrix} u_0 & u_1 & u_2 & u_3 & \cdots \\ u_1 & u_0 & u_1 & u_2 & \\ u_2 & u_1 & u_0 & u_1 & \ddots \\ u_3 & u_2 & u_1 & \ddots & \ddots \\ \vdots & & \ddots & \ddots & \ddots \end{bmatrix} \succeq 0.$$

---

[1] A comprehensive treatment of various moment problems appears in Schmüdgen (2017).

Thinking in terms of moments rather than measures themselves, Theorem 22.3 guarantees that the program (22.8) is equivalent to

$$\underset{\substack{a \in \mathbb{R}^{n+1} \\ u^+, u^- \in \mathbb{R}^{\mathbb{N}}}}{\text{minimize}} (u_0^+ + u_0^-) \text{ s.to } Ma = y, \text{ Toep}_\infty(u^\pm) \succeq 0,$$

$$\text{and } u^+ - u^- = \pi [0; a_1; a_2 2^k; \ldots; a_n n^k; 0; 0; \ldots]. \quad (22.9)$$

Since this infinite semidefinite program cannot be solved exactly, a second step now consists in solving a truncated version while certifying that the resulting error is quantifiably small. Precisely, for some large enough integer $N \geq n$, one solves

$$\underset{\substack{a \in \mathbb{R}^{n+1} \\ u^+, u^- \in \mathbb{R}^{N+1}}}{\text{minimize}} (u_0^+ + u_0^-) \text{ s.to } Ma = y, \text{ Toep}_{N+1}(u^\pm) \succeq 0,$$

$$\text{and } u^+ - u^- = \pi [0; a_1; a_2 2^k; \ldots; a_n n^k; 0; \ldots; 0]. \quad (22.10)$$

It is to be shown that the trigonometric polynomial $f^{[N]} = \sum_{j=0}^{n} a_j^{[N]} \cos(j \cdot)$, with $a^{[N]} \in \mathbb{R}^{n+1}$ solving (22.10), approaches the minimizer $f^\#$ of the original program (22.1) with $p = 1$, written as $f^\# = \sum_{j=0}^{n} a_j^\# \cos(j \cdot)$ with $a^\# \in \mathbb{R}^{n+1}$ solving the equivalent programs (22.7), (22.8), and (22.9).

Proposition 22.4 *If (22.1) admits a unique solution $f^\#$ for $p = 1$, then*

$$f^{[N]} \longrightarrow f^\# \qquad \text{as} \quad N \longrightarrow +\infty.$$

Proof Let $\alpha^\# = \|f^\#\|_{L_1(\mathbb{T})} \in \mathbb{R}$ and $(a^\#, u^{+,\#}, u^{-,\#}) \in \mathbb{R}^{n+1} \times \mathbb{R}^{\mathbb{N}} \times \mathbb{R}^{\mathbb{N}}$ denote the minimal value and some minimizer of (22.9), respectively. For each $N \geq n$, let also $\alpha^{[N]} \in \mathbb{R}$ and $(a^{[N]}, u^{+,[N]}, u^{-,[N]}) \in \mathbb{R}^{n+1} \times \mathbb{R}^{N+1} \times \mathbb{R}^{N+1}$ denote the minimal value and some minimizer of (22.10), respectively. One starts by pointing out that $(\alpha^{[N]})_{N \geq n}$ is a nondecreasing sequence converging to some $\widetilde{\alpha} \leq \alpha^\#$. Indeed, the feasibility of $(a^{[N+1]}, u_{[0:N]}^{+,[N+1]}, u_{[0:N]}^{-,[N+1]})$ for (22.10) yields $\alpha^{[N]} \leq \alpha^{[N+1]}$ and the feasibility of $(a^\#, u_{[0:N]}^{+,\#}, u_{[0:N]}^{-,\#})$ for (22.10) yields $\alpha^{[N]} \leq \alpha^\#$.

Next, the convergence of $f^{[N]}$ to $f^\#$ being equivalent to the convergence of $a^{[N]}$ to $a^\#$, one proceeds by contradiction and assumes that there is an $\varepsilon > 0$ and an increasing sequence $(N_\ell)_{\ell \geq 1}$ of integers such that $\|a^{[N_\ell]} - a^\#\| \geq \varepsilon$ for all $\ell \geq 1$. Given $\ell \geq 1$, the positive semidefiniteness of $\text{Toep}_{N_\ell+1}(u^{\pm,[N_\ell]})$ implies that, for any $j \in [0 : N_\ell]$,

$$|u_j^{\pm,[N_\ell]}| \leq u_0^{\pm,[N_\ell]} \leq u_0^{+,[N_\ell]} + u_0^{-,[N_\ell]} = \alpha^{[N_\ell]} \leq \alpha^\#.$$

From the last constraint in (22.10), one deduces that the sequence $(a^{[N_\ell]})_{\ell \geq 1}$ is bounded. With the infinite vectors $(u^{\pm,[[N]]}) \in \mathbb{R}^{\mathbb{N}}$ representing the finite vectors $(u^{\pm,[N]}) \in \mathbb{R}^{N+1}$ padded with zeros, one remarks that the $\ell_\infty^{\mathbb{N}}$-valued sequences $(u^{\pm,[[N_\ell]]})_{\ell \geq 1}$ are bounded, too. Therefore, invoking the *sequential Banach–Alaoglu theorem*, there are convergent subsequences—still designated by $(a^{[N_\ell]})_{\ell \geq 1}$ and $(u^{\pm,[[N_\ell]]})_{\ell \geq 1}$ for ease of notation—converging to $\widetilde{a} \in \mathbb{R}^{n+1}$ and $\widetilde{u}^{\pm} \in \mathbb{R}^{\mathbb{N}}$, say, the last convergence being understood in the weak-star topology of $\ell_\infty^{\mathbb{N}}$. For any $j \in \mathbb{N}$, this weak-star convergence ensures that $u_j^{\pm,[[N_\ell]]} \to \widetilde{u}_j^{\pm}$. From here, the feasibility conditions $Ma^{[N_\ell]} = y$, $\mathrm{Toep}_\infty(u^{\pm,[[N_\ell]]}) \geq 0$, and $u^{+,[[N_\ell]]} - u^{-,[[N_\ell]]} = \pi[0; a_1^{[N_\ell]}; a_2^{[N_\ell]} 2^k; \ldots; a_n^{[N_\ell]} n^k; 0; 0; \ldots]$ pass to the limit and lead to $M\widetilde{a} = y$, $\mathrm{Toep}_\infty(\widetilde{u}^{\pm}) \geq 0$, and $\widetilde{u}^{+} - \widetilde{u}^{-} = \pi[0; \widetilde{a}_1; \widetilde{a}_2 2^k; \ldots; \widetilde{a}_n n^k; 0; 0; \ldots]$. This means that the triple $(\widetilde{a}, \widetilde{u}^{+}, \widetilde{u}^{-}) \in \mathbb{R}^{n+1} \times \mathbb{R}^{\mathbb{N}} \times \mathbb{R}^{\mathbb{N}}$ is feasible for the program (22.9). It is also a minimizer for this program, in view of

$$\widetilde{u}_0^{+} + \widetilde{u}_0^{-} = \lim_{\ell \to +\infty} (u_0^{+,[[N_\ell]]} + u_0^{-,[[N_\ell]]}) = \lim_{\ell \to +\infty} \alpha^{[N_\ell]} = \widetilde{\alpha} \leq \alpha^{\#}.$$

Consequently, the vector $\widetilde{a} \in \mathbb{R}^{n+1}$ turns out to be a minimizer for (22.7), and hence uniqueness implies that $\widetilde{a} = a^{\#}$. This conflicts with $\|\widetilde{a} - a^{\#}\| \geq \varepsilon$, obtained from $\|a^{[N_\ell]} - a^{\#}\| \geq \varepsilon$ by passing to the limit. This contradiction guarantees that $f^{[N]}$ converges to $f^{\#}$, as announced. $\qquad\square$

Remark 22.5 For a given $N \geq n$, after having solved (22.10) to produce $\alpha^{[N]}$ and $a^{[N]}$, one can then compute $\|f^{[N]}\|_{L_1(\mathbb{T})}$. Note that $\|f^{\#}\|_{L_1(\mathbb{T})} \leq \|f^{[N]}\|_{L_1(\mathbb{T})}$ because $a^{[N]}$ is feasible for (22.7). Note also that $\|f^{\#}\|_{L_1(\mathbb{T})} = \alpha^{\#} \geq \alpha^{[N]}$, as outlined in the above proof. In short, the minimal value of (22.7) is quantified through the two-sided estimate

$$\alpha^{[N]} \leq \|f^{\#}\|_{L_1(\mathbb{T})} \leq \|f^{[N]}\|_{L_1(\mathbb{T})}$$

with an error $\|f^{[N]}\|_{L_1(\mathbb{T})} - \alpha^{[N]}$ that can be numerically estimated for any given $N \geq n$. This error approaches zero as N increases, since Proposition 22.4 guarantees that $\|f^{[N]}\|_{L_1(\mathbb{T})} \to \|f^{\#}\|_{L_1(\mathbb{T})}$ and since it can be established that $\alpha^{[N]} \to \|f^{\#}\|_{L_1(\mathbb{T})}$; see Exercise 22.4.

Exercises

22.1 Writing $\Delta = \mathrm{diag}[1^k; 2^k; \ldots; n^k] \in \mathbb{R}^{n \times n}$ and $M = [\mathbb{1}; A\Delta]$ for some $A \in \mathbb{R}^{m \times n}$, prove that the constrained least-squares program (22.2) has solution $a^{\#} = [a_0^{\#}; \Delta^{-1} x^{\#}] \in \mathbb{R}^{n+1}$, where

$$a_0^{\#} = \frac{\sum_{i,j=1}^{n} y_i (AA^{\top})_{i,j}^{-1}}{\sum_{i,j=1}^{n} (AA^{\top})_{i,j}^{-1}} \in \mathbb{R} \quad \text{and} \quad x^{\#} = A^{\top}(AA^{\top})^{-1}(y - a_0^{\#}\mathbb{1}) \in \mathbb{R}^{n}.$$

22.2 With $T_0, T_1, \ldots, T_n$ denoting the Chebyshev polynomials of the first kind, show that the supremum norm of an algebraic polynomial $p = \sum_{j=0}^{n} a_j T_j$ can be expressed as

$$\|p\|_{C([-1,1])} = \min_{\substack{c \in \mathbb{R} \\ Q^{\pm} \in \mathbb{R}^{(n+1)\times(n+1)}}} \left\{ c : \sum_{i-j=\ell} Q_{i,j}^{\pm} = \left\{ \begin{array}{ll} c \pm a_0, & \ell = 0 \\ \pm \dfrac{a_\ell}{2}, & \ell \geq 1, \end{array} \right., Q^{\pm} \geq 0 \right\}$$

$$= \max_{u,v \in \mathbb{R}^{n+1}} \left\{ \langle a, u - v \rangle : u_0 + v_0 \leq 1, \operatorname{Toep}_{n+1}(u) \geq 0, \operatorname{Toep}_{n+1}(v) \geq 0 \right\}.$$

22.3 Prove the weakened version of the *sequential Banach–Alaoglu theorem* needed in the proof of Proposition 22.4, namely: if $(u^{(n)})_{n \geq 1}$ is a bounded sequence taking values in $\ell_\infty^{\mathbb{N}}$, then one can find an increasing sequence of integers $(n_k)_{k \geq 1}$ together with some $\widetilde{u} \in \ell_\infty^{\mathbb{N}}$ such that $\lim_{k \to +\infty} u_j^{(n_k)} = \widetilde{u}_j$ for all $j \geq 0$.

22.4 By revisiting the proof of Proposition 22.4 or otherwise, show that the minimal value $\alpha^{[N]}$ of (22.10) tends to the minimal value $\alpha^{\#}$ of (22.9) as N grows to infinity.

23

Instances of Nonconvex Optimization

This chapter is dedicated to minimization programs of the form

$$\underset{x}{\text{minimize}}\, f(x) \quad \text{subject to } x \in C, \tag{23.1}$$

where the function f or the set C (or both) are not convex. The various gradient descent methods from Chapter 19 could, of course, still be applied, but they would not come with any guarantee of success. Instead, the focus here is put on situations for which one can certify that the problem is solved (almost) exactly. Three illustrative examples are showcased: quadratically constrained quadratic programs, dynamic programming, and projected gradient descent.

23.1 Quadratically Constrained Quadratic Programs

By *quadratically constrained quadratic program*, one refers to a minimization program of the form (23.1) where f is a quadratic function and C is described as $C = \{x \in \mathbb{R}^d : g(x) \le 0\}$ for another quadratic function g. As an example, determining the operator norm $\|M\|_{2\to 2}$ of a symmetric matrix $M \in \mathbb{R}^{d\times d}$ could be viewed as a quadratically constrained quadratic program, since

$$-\|M\|_{2\to 2} = \min_{x\in\mathbb{R}^d} \{\langle -Mx, x\rangle : \langle x, x\rangle \le 1\}.$$

The method presented next should obviously not be invoked for this specific case, as it is more efficient to compute eigenvalues of M via the power method. As a more to-the-point example, the determination of the local worst-case error of a recovery map, which was introduced in Chapter 9, can be expressed as a quadratically constrained quadratic program and then transformed into a semidefinite program; see Exercise 23.2. The generic transformation of a quadratically constrained quadratic program into a semidefinite program, which constitutes the main result of this section, is elucidated below.

Theorem 23.1   *Given two quadratic functions f and g, written as*

$$f(x) = \langle Ax, x \rangle + 2\langle a, x \rangle + \alpha,$$
$$g(x) = \langle Bx, x \rangle + 2\langle b, x \rangle + \beta,$$

for symmetric matrices $A, B \in \mathbb{R}^{n \times n}$, vectors $a, b \in \mathbb{R}^n$, and scalars $\alpha, \beta \in \mathbb{R}$, consider the quadratically constrained quadratic program

$$\underset{x \in \mathbb{R}^n}{\text{minimize } f(x)} \quad \text{subject to} \quad g(x) \leq 0. \tag{23.2}$$

If there exists $x_* \in \mathbb{R}^n$ such that $g(x_*) < 0$, then its optimal value coincides with the optimal value of the semidefinite program

$$\underset{\gamma, \delta \in \mathbb{R}}{\text{maximize } \gamma} \quad \text{subject to} \quad \delta \geq 0, \quad \begin{bmatrix} A + \delta B & | & a + \delta b \\ a^\top + \delta b^\top & | & \alpha + \delta \beta - \gamma \end{bmatrix} \succeq 0. \tag{23.3}$$

The crucial ingredient for proving this theorem is the so-called *S-lemma*, stated below and fully justified in a short while.

Lemma 23.2   *Let $A, B \in \mathbb{R}^{n \times n}$ be symmetric matrices, let $a, b \in \mathbb{R}^n$ be vectors, and let $\alpha, \beta \in \mathbb{R}$ be scalars such that $\langle Bx_*, x_* \rangle + 2\langle b, x_* \rangle + \beta < 0$ for some $x_* \in \mathbb{R}^n$. The following properties are equivalent:*

(i) *for any $x \in \mathbb{R}^n$, if $\langle Bx, x \rangle + 2\langle b, x \rangle + \beta \leq 0$, then $\langle Ax, x \rangle + 2\langle a, x \rangle + \alpha \leq 0$;*
(ii) *there exists $\delta \geq 0$ such that $\langle Ax, x \rangle + 2\langle a, x \rangle + \alpha \leq \delta(\langle Bx, x \rangle + 2\langle b, x \rangle + \beta)$ for all $x \in \mathbb{R}^n$.*

The main result of this section can be swiftly deduced if the S-lemma is momentarily taken for granted.

Proof of Theorem 23.1   One starts by interpreting the optimum μ of (23.2) as

$$\mu = \underset{\gamma \in \mathbb{R}}{\max} \ \gamma \quad \text{subject to } \gamma \leq \inf\{f(x) : g(x) \leq 0\}$$

$$= \underset{\gamma \in \mathbb{R}}{\max} \ \gamma \quad \text{subject to } \gamma \leq f(x) \text{ whenever } g(x) \leq 0.$$

By Lemma 23.2, the latter constraint is equivalent to the existence of $\delta \geq 0$ such that $\gamma - f(x) \leq \delta g(x)$ for all $x \in \mathbb{R}^n$, i.e.,

$$\langle (A + \delta B)x, x \rangle + 2\langle a + \delta b, x \rangle + \alpha + \delta \beta - \gamma \geq 0$$

for all $x \in \mathbb{R}^n$. This itself is equivalent to

$$\left\langle \begin{bmatrix} A + \delta B & | & a + \delta b \\ a^\top + \delta b^\top & | & \alpha + \delta \beta - \gamma \end{bmatrix} \begin{bmatrix} x \\ 1 \end{bmatrix}, \begin{bmatrix} x \\ 1 \end{bmatrix} \right\rangle \geq 0$$

for all $x \in \mathbb{R}^n$, i.e., to the positive semidefiniteness of the above matrix. All in all, it has been shown that μ indeed appears as the optimal value of (23.3).   □

It remains to show the validity of the S-lemma, for which the following observation is key.

Lemma 23.3 *For symmetric matrices $A, B \in \mathbb{R}^{n \times n}$, if $\operatorname{tr}(A) > 0$ and $\operatorname{tr}(B) < 0$, then there exists a vector $v \in \mathbb{R}^{n \times n}$ such that $\langle Av, v \rangle > 0$ and $\langle Bv, v \rangle < 0$.*

Proof Consider the eigenvalue decomposition of A written as $A = UDU^\top$, where $U \in \mathbb{R}^{n \times n}$ is orthogonal and $D \in \mathbb{R}^{n \times n}$ is diagonal. On the one hand, for any $x \in \{-1, +1\}^n$, one has

$$\langle AUx, Ux \rangle = \langle U^\top AUx, x \rangle = \langle Dx, x \rangle = \sum_{i=1}^n d_{i,i} x_i^2 = \operatorname{tr}(D) = \operatorname{tr}(A) > 0.$$

On the other hand, one has

$$\sum_{x \in \{-1, +1\}^n} \langle BUx, Ux \rangle = \sum_{x \in \{-1, +1\}^n} \langle U^\top BUx, Ux \rangle = \sum_{x \in \{-1, +1\}^n} \sum_{i,j=1}^n (U^\top BU)_{i,j} x_i x_j$$

$$= \sum_{i,j=1}^n (U^\top BU)_{i,j} \sum_{x \in \{-1, +1\}^n} x_i x_j = \sum_{i,j=1}^n (U^\top BU)_{i,j} 2^n \delta_{i,j}$$

$$= 2^n \sum_{i=1}^n (U^\top BU)_{i,i} = 2^n \operatorname{tr}(U^\top BU) = 2^n \operatorname{tr}(B) < 0,$$

so there exists a vector $x \in \{-1, +1\}^n$ such that $\langle BUx, Ux \rangle < 0$. The required result is proved with the choice $v = Ux$. $\qquad\square$

Proof of Lemma 23.2 The implication (ii)$\Rightarrow$(i) being clear, one concentrates on proving the implication (i)$\Rightarrow$(ii). To this end, one first reformulates (i) as the statement that, for any $x \in \mathbb{R}^n$, the inequality $\langle \widetilde{B}\widetilde{x}, \widetilde{x} \rangle \leq 0$ implies the inequality $\langle \widetilde{A}\widetilde{x}, \widetilde{x} \rangle \leq 0$, where

$$\widetilde{A} = \left[\begin{array}{c|c} A & a \\ \hline a^\top & \alpha \end{array} \right], \qquad \widetilde{B} = \left[\begin{array}{c|c} B & b \\ \hline b^\top & \beta \end{array} \right], \qquad \widetilde{x} = \left[\begin{array}{c} x \\ 1 \end{array} \right].$$

Now consider the convex subsets of $\mathbb{R}^2$ defined by

$$C = \{ [\langle \widetilde{A}, X \rangle_F; \langle \widetilde{B}, X \rangle_F], X \succeq 0 \},$$
$$\mathcal{D} = \{ [u; v], u > 0, v < 0 \}.$$

One claims that the sets C and $\mathcal{D}$ are disjoint. Indeed, the contrary would mean that there exists a positive semidefinite matrix $X \in \mathbb{R}^{(n+1) \times (n+1)}$ such that $\langle \widetilde{A}, X \rangle_F = \operatorname{tr}(X^{1/2} \widetilde{A} X^{1/2}) > 0$ and $\langle \widetilde{B}, X \rangle_F = \operatorname{tr}(X^{1/2} \widetilde{B} X^{1/2}) < 0$. By Lemma 23.3, this implies the existence of $v \in \mathbb{R}^{n+1}$ such that $\langle \widetilde{A}v, v \rangle > 0$ and $\langle \widetilde{B}v, v \rangle < 0$. Writing $v = [z; \zeta]$ with $z \in \mathbb{R}^n$ and $\zeta \in \mathbb{R}$, one separates two cases: if $\zeta \neq 0$, then setting $x = z/\zeta$ leads to $\langle \widetilde{A}\widetilde{x}, \widetilde{x} \rangle > 0$ and $\langle \widetilde{B}\widetilde{x}, \widetilde{x} \rangle < 0$, which would contradict the reformulation of (i); if $\zeta = 0$, then $\langle Az, z \rangle > 0$ and $\langle Bz, z \rangle < 0$, and, for $|t|$ large enough, $\langle A(tz), (tz) \rangle + 2\langle a, (tz) \rangle + \alpha > 0$ and $\langle B(tz), (tz) \rangle + 2\langle b, (tz) \rangle + \beta < 0$, which would contradict (i) in its original form. Thus, the claim that C and $\mathcal{D}$ are disjoint is established.

Now, by the *Hahn–Banach separation theorem* (see Theorem C.11), one can find $(r, s) \in \mathbb{R}^2 \setminus \{(0, 0)\}$ and $t \in \mathbb{R}$ such that, for all $X \geq 0$, $u > 0$, and $v < 0$,

$$r\langle \widetilde{A}, X \rangle_F + s\langle \widetilde{B}, X \rangle_F \geq t > ru + sv. \tag{23.4}$$

Taking $X = 0$ shows that $t \leq 0$, and taking $(u, v) = (\varepsilon, -\varepsilon)$ for an arbitrarily small $\varepsilon > 0$ shows that $t \geq 0$, and hence $t = 0$. Next, taking $(u, v) = (\varepsilon, -1)$ leads to $s \geq 0$ and taking $(u, v) = (1, -\varepsilon)$ leads to $r \leq 0$. Note that $r = 0$ is impossible, for it would imply $s > 0$ and $s\langle \widetilde{B}, X \rangle_F \geq 0$ for all $X \geq 0$, and in particular $\langle \widetilde{B}\widetilde{x}, \widetilde{x} \rangle \geq 0$ for all $x \in \mathbb{R}^n$, which cannot occur when $x = x_*$. Now, setting $\delta = -s/r \geq 0$, the leftmost inequality in (23.4) with $X = \widetilde{x}\widetilde{x}^\top$ reads

$$\langle \widetilde{A}\widetilde{x}, \widetilde{x} \rangle - \delta \langle \widetilde{B}\widetilde{x}, \widetilde{x} \rangle \leq 0 \quad \text{for all } x \in \mathbb{R}^n,$$

which is the desired result. □

23.2 Dynamic Programming

In this section, the generic problem (23.1) is particularized to the situation where the objective function f equals the euclidean distance to the specific nonconvex set of s-sparse vectors in $\mathbb{R}^N$ having nonzero entries separated by at least k zero entries. More precisely, one takes C to be the set

$$\Sigma_{s,k}^N := \{ z \in \mathbb{R}^N : \|z\|_0 \leq s \text{ and } |i - j| > k \text{ whenever } i \neq j \in \operatorname{supp}(z) \}.$$

For $x \in \mathbb{R}^N$, if S denotes the support of the projection $x^* := P_{\Sigma_{s,k}^N}(x)$ of x onto $\Sigma_{s,k}^N$, then x^* coincides with x_S—the vector defined by $(x_S)_j = x_j$ when $j \in S$ and $(x_S)_j = 0$ when $j \notin S$. Thus, the projection of x could be found by looking at the minimal value of $\|x - x_S\|_2$ over all sets of size s with k-separated indices. But there are far too many such sets to make such a simplistic approach practical.

Yet, the problem can be solved rather efficiently. This is especially true for $k = 0$: in this case, the set $\Sigma_{s,0}^N$ reduces to the set Σ_s^N of s-sparse vectors and the projector $P_{\Sigma_{s,0}^N}$ reduces to the *hard thresholding operator* H_s defined by $H_s(x) = x_S$ where S is an index set of s largest absolute entries of x. The case $k \geq 1$ relies on *dynamic programming*, a method to solve a priori difficult problems by uncovering manageable recursions. Here, fixing a vector $x \in \mathbb{R}^N$, one introduces, for each $n \in [1 : N]$ and $r \in [0 : s]$, the projection $x^*(n, r)$ of

$x_{[1:n]}$ onto $\Sigma_{r,k}^n$ and the squared distance $F(n,r) = \|x_{[1:n]} - x^*(n,r)\|_2^2$ from $x_{[1:n]}$ to the set $\Sigma_{r,k}^n$. One also introduces the auxiliary quantities

$$F_1(n,r) := F(n-1,r) + x_n^2, \qquad F_2(n,r) := F(n-k-1,r-1) + \sum_{j=n-k}^{n-1} x_j^2.$$

The desired quantities $x^*(N,s)$ and $F(N,s)$ are obtained from the recursion formulas

$$F(n,r) = \min\{F_1(n,r), F_2(n,r)\}, \tag{23.5}$$

$$x^*(n,r) = \begin{cases} [x^*(n-1,r);0] & \text{if } F_1(n,r) < F_2(n,r), \\ [x^*(n-k-1,r-1);0;\ldots;0;x_n] & \text{otherwise.} \end{cases} \tag{23.6}$$

While the careful verification of these formulas is left to meticulous readers, an intuitive explanation consists in wondering whether the index n belongs to the support of the best approximant on $[1:n]$ with parameter r:

- if no, then the best approximation error is made of the best approximation error on $[1:n-1]$ with parameter r and the contribution from x_n^2;
- if yes, then the indices $n-k,\ldots,n-1$ are forced out of the support and the best approximation error is made of the best approximation error on $[1:n-k-1]$ with parameter $r-1$ and the contribution from $x_{n-k}^2 + \cdots + x_{n-1}^2$.

x	$F(n,r)$	$r=0$	$r=1$	$r=2$	$r=3$
1	$n=1$	1	0	0	0
0	$n=2$	1	0	0	0
1	$n=3$	2	1	0	0
1.1892	$n=4$	3.4142	2	1	1
1	$n=5$	4.4142	3	2	1.4142
0	$n=6$	4.4142	3	2	1.4142
0.7071	$n=7$	4.9142	3.5	2.5	1.9142

Figure 23.1 A tabular representation of the dynamic program that computes the projection x^* of $x = [1;0;1;2^{1/4};1;0;2^{-1/2}]$ onto $\Sigma_{s,k}^N$ with $N=7$, $s=3$, $k=1$: it is $x^* = [1;0;1;0;1;0;0]$.

The recursion (23.5), together with the initial values

$$F(n,0) = \|x_{[1:n]}\|_2^2, \qquad\qquad n \in [1:N],$$
$$F(n,r) = \|x_{[1:n]}\|_2^2 - \|x_{[1:n]}\|_\infty^2, \qquad n \in [1:k+1], r \in [1:s],$$

allows one to fill an $N \times (s+1)$ table of values $F(n,r)$. For each entry of the table, one can draw an arrow to keep track of the case yielding the minimum in (23.5). In this way, as shown in Figure 23.1, backtracking from the (N,s)th entry provides the projection $x^*(N,s)$ according to (23.6).

23.3 Projected Gradient Descent

Returning to the generic form of the nonconvex minimization program (23.1), one studies in this section the so-called *projected gradient descent* algorithm. With the projection $P_C(z)$ denoting as usual the point in C closest to z, this algorithm consists in producing a sequence $(x^t)_{t \geq 0}$ according to

$$x^{t+1} = P_C(x^t - \alpha^t \nabla f(x^t)), \qquad t \geq 0, \tag{23.7}$$

for a possibly iteration-dependent stepsize α^t. This is a rather natural strategy: by applying the projector P_C to otherwise standard gradient descent iterates, one guarantees that all the iterates belong to C. The projector P_C should of course be computable, such as for the set $C = \Sigma_{s,k}^N$ discussed in the previous section. Of particular interest is the case where the objective function has the form $f(x) = \|y - \mathcal{A}(x)\|_2^2$ for some $y \in \mathbb{R}^m$ and some linear map $\mathcal{A}$ taking values in $\mathbb{R}^m$— it is not written as a matrix $A \in \mathbb{R}^{m \times n}$ to allow the optimization variables x to be matrices, say. In this case, the projected gradient descent algorithm with a fixed stepsize becomes

$$x^{t+1} = P_C(x^t + \alpha \mathcal{A}^*(y - \mathcal{A}x^t)), \qquad t \geq 0, \tag{23.8}$$

where the linear map $\mathcal{A}^*$ denotes the adjoint of the linear map $\mathcal{A}$, characterized by the relation $\langle \mathcal{A}(x), u \rangle = \langle x, \mathcal{A}^*(u) \rangle$. For instance, when $C = \Sigma_s^N$ is the set of s-sparse vectors in $\mathbb{R}^N$, if $\mathcal{A}$ is represented by a matrix $A \in \mathbb{R}^{m \times N}$, then (23.8) with $\alpha = 1$ reads

$$x^{t+1} = H_s(x^t + A^\top(y - Ax^t)), \qquad t \geq 0. \tag{23.9}$$

This strategy constitutes the *iterative hard thresholding* algorithm popular in Compressive Sensing.

It shall be established that, under a favorable condition on the linear map $\mathcal{A}$, the projected gradient descent algorithm produces near-optimal solutions to the problem of minimizing $\|y - \mathcal{A}(x)\|_2^2$ subject to $x \in C$. The favorable condition, termed *restricted isometry property* on $C - C$ with constant $\delta \in (0, 1)$, stipulates that, for all $x, x' \in C$,

$$(1 - \delta)\|x - x'\|_2^2 \leq \|\mathcal{A}(x - x')\|_2^2 \leq (1 + \delta)\|x - x'\|_2^2. \tag{23.10}$$

A couple of comments are appropriate before making a formal statement. First, although the result below shows the convergence of the scalar sequence $(\|y - \mathcal{A}(x^t)\|_2)_{t \geq 0}$, the convergence of the vector sequence $(x^t)_{t \geq 0}$ itself is not necessarily guaranteed. In some cases (see Exercise 23.4), this can be acquired by adjusting the projected gradient descent algorithm. Second, the stepsize α influences the value of the constant $D \geq 1$ of near-optimality: with the choice $\alpha = 3/4$, it can be taken as an absolute constant when $\delta \leq 1/4$, say, while with the (unrealistic) choice $\alpha = 1/(1 + \delta)$, it can be chosen close to one, namely as $D = (1 + \delta)/(1 - 3\delta)$.

Theorem 23.4 *Suppose that $\mathcal{A}$ satisfies the restricted isometry property on $C - C$ with $\delta < 1/3$. Then, with $(x^t)_{t \geq 0}$ denoting the sequence of elements of C produced by the projected gradient descent algorithm (23.8) for a stepsize α satisfying*

$$1 + \delta \leq \frac{1}{\alpha} < 2(1 - \delta), \tag{23.11}$$

there is a constant $D \geq 1$ depending on α and δ such that

$$\lim_{t \to +\infty} \|y - \mathcal{A}(x^t)\|_2 \leq D \min\{\|y - \mathcal{A}(x)\|_2 : x \in C\}. \tag{23.12}$$

Proof For any $t \geq 0$, one observes first that

$$
\begin{aligned}
\|y - \mathcal{A}(x^{t+1})\|_2^2 - \|y - \mathcal{A}(x^t)\|_2^2 &= \|\mathcal{A}(x^t - x^{t+1}) + y - \mathcal{A}(x^t)\|_2^2 - \|y - \mathcal{A}(x^t)\|_2^2 \\
&= \|\mathcal{A}(x^t - x^{t+1})\|_2^2 + 2\langle \mathcal{A}(x^t - x^{t+1}), y - \mathcal{A}(x^t)\rangle \\
&= \|\mathcal{A}(x^t - x^{t+1})\|_2^2 + 2\langle x^t - x^{t+1}, \mathcal{A}^*(y - \mathcal{A}(x^t))\rangle. \tag{23.13}
\end{aligned}
$$

Next, the fact that $x^{t+1} \in C$ is a better approximant to $x^t + \alpha \mathcal{A}^*(y - \mathcal{A}(x^t))$ than $x^t \in C$ gives

$$\|x^t + \alpha \mathcal{A}^*(y - \mathcal{A}(x^t)) - x^{t+1}\|_2^2 \leq \|\alpha \mathcal{A}^*(y - \mathcal{A}(x^t))\|_2^2.$$

Expanding the squares and rearranging leads to

$$2\alpha\langle x^t - x^{t+1}, \mathcal{A}^*(y - \mathcal{A}(x^t))\rangle \leq -\|x^t - x^{t+1}\|_2^2.$$

Substituting the latter into (23.13) yields

$$
\begin{aligned}
\|y - \mathcal{A}(x^{t+1})\|_2^2 - \|y - \mathcal{A}(x^t)\|_2^2 &\leq \|\mathcal{A}(x^t - x^{t+1})\|_2^2 - \frac{1}{\alpha}\|x^t - x^{t+1}\|_2^2 \\
&\leq \left(1 - \frac{1}{\alpha(1 + \delta)}\right)\|\mathcal{A}(x^t - x^{t+1})\|_2^2,
\end{aligned}
$$

where the restricted isometry property (23.10) was exploited in the last step. Since the condition (23.11) ensures that $1 - 1/(\alpha(1 + \delta)) \le 0$, one obtains $\|y - \mathcal{A}(x^{t+1})\|_2^2 - \|y - \mathcal{A}(x^t)\|_2^2 \le 0$ for any $t \ge 0$. In other words, the sequence $(\|y - \mathcal{A}(x^t)\|_2^2)_{t \ge 0}$ of nonnegative numbers is nonincreasing, which justifies that the limit appearing on the left-hand side of (23.12) exists.

Now let $\bar{x} \in C$ denote a minimizer of $\|y - \mathcal{A}(x)\|_2^2$ subject to $x \in C$. Since $x^{t+1} \in C$ is also a better approximant to $x^t + \alpha \mathcal{A}^*(y - \mathcal{A}(x^t))$ than $\bar{x} \in C$, one has

$$\|x^t + \alpha \mathcal{A}^*(y - \mathcal{A}(x^t)) - x^{t+1}\|_2^2 \le \|x^t + \alpha \mathcal{A}^*(y - \mathcal{A}x^t) - \bar{x}\|_2^2.$$

This time, expanding the squares and rearranging leads to

$$2\alpha\langle x^t - x^{t+1}, \mathcal{A}^*(y - \mathcal{A}(x^t))\rangle$$
$$\le -\|x^t - x^{t+1}\|_2^2 + \|x^t - \bar{x}\|_2^2 + 2\alpha\langle x^t - \bar{x}, \mathcal{A}^*(y - \mathcal{A}(x^t))\rangle.$$

Substituting the latter into (23.13) yields

$$\|y - \mathcal{A}(x^{t+1})\|_2^2 - \|y - \mathcal{A}(x^t)\|_2^2 \le \|\mathcal{A}(x^t - x^{t+1})\|_2^2 - \frac{1}{\alpha}\|x^t - x^{t+1}\|_2^2$$
$$+ \frac{1}{\alpha}\|x^t - \bar{x}\|_2^2 + 2\langle \mathcal{A}(x^t - \bar{x}), y - \mathcal{A}(x^t)\rangle.$$

Then, in view of $\|\mathcal{A}(x^t - x^{t+1})\|_2^2 \le (1 + \delta)\|x^t - x^{t+1}\|_2^2 \le (1/\alpha)\|x^t - x^{t+1}\|_2^2$, of $(1 - \delta)\|x^t - \bar{x}\|_2^2 \le \|\mathcal{A}(x^t - \bar{x})\|_2^2$, and of

$$2\langle \mathcal{A}(x^t - \bar{x}), y - \mathcal{A}(x^t)\rangle = \|y - \mathcal{A}(\bar{x})\|_2^2 - \|\mathcal{A}(x^t - \bar{x})\|_2^2 - \|y - \mathcal{A}(x^t)\|_2^2,$$

one arrives at

$$\|y - \mathcal{A}(x^{t+1})\|_2^2 \le \left(\frac{1}{\alpha(1 - \delta)} - 1\right)\|\mathcal{A}(x^t - \bar{x})\|_2^2 + \|y - \mathcal{A}(\bar{x})\|_2^2.$$

The condition (23.11) ensures that

$$\rho := \frac{1}{\alpha(1 - \delta)} - 1 \in (0, 1).$$

Moreover, setting $\varepsilon := \|y - \mathcal{A}(\bar{x})\|_2$, a triangle inequality gives

$$\|y - \mathcal{A}(x^{t+1})\|_2^2 \le \rho(\|y - \mathcal{A}(x^t)\|_2 + \varepsilon)^2 + \varepsilon^2.$$

Thus, the limit λ of $\|y - \mathcal{A}(x^t)\|_2$ as $t \to \infty$ must satisfy $\lambda^2 \le \rho(\lambda + \varepsilon)^2 + \varepsilon^2$. Since the quadratic equation $(1 - \rho)\xi^2 - 2\rho\varepsilon\xi - (1 + \rho)\varepsilon^2 = 0$ has solutions $\xi = -\varepsilon$ and $\xi = ((1 + \rho)/(1 - \rho))\varepsilon$, one deduces that $\lambda \le ((1 + \rho)/(1 - \rho))\varepsilon$. In other words, the estimate announced in (23.12) has been proved in the form

$$\lim_{t \to +\infty} \|y - \mathcal{A}(x^t)\|_2 \le \frac{1 + \rho}{1 - \rho}\|y - \mathcal{A}(\bar{x})\|_2.$$

Note that $D = (1 + \rho)/(1 - \rho) = 1/(2\alpha(1 - \delta) - 1)$, so chosing $\alpha = 3/4$ yields $D = 2/(1 - 3\delta)$, and chosing $\alpha = 1/(1 + \delta)$ yields $D = (1 + \delta)/(1 - 3\delta)$, which is arbitrarily close to one when δ is arbitrarily close to zero.   □

Returning to the guiding example where $C = \Sigma_s^N$ is the set of s-sparse vectors in $\mathbb{R}^N$, a near-optimal estimate $\|y - \mathcal{A}(\widehat{x})\|_2 \le D \min\{\|y - \mathcal{A}(x)\|_2 : x \in C\}$ can also be derived from (14.7), say, with $\widehat{x} = H_s(x^\sharp)$ and $x^\sharp$ being an ℓ_1-minimizer. When considering $C = \Sigma_{s,k}^N$ with $k \ge 1$, as in the previous section, it is unclear if a near-optimal estimate can also be obtained by solving a convex optimization program instead of running the projected gradient descent algorithm. In view of $\Sigma_{s,k}^N \subseteq \Sigma_s^N$, it would actually be enough to perform ℓ_1-minimization when the restricted isometry property holds on $\Sigma_s^N - \Sigma_s^N$. However, there are regimes of parameters[1] for which the restricted isometry property holds on $\Sigma_{s,k}^N - \Sigma_{s,k}^N$ but not on $\Sigma_s^N - \Sigma_s^N$.

Exercises

23.1 Show that the existence of $x_* \in \mathbb{R}^n$ such that $\langle Bx_*, x_* \rangle + 2\langle b, x_* \rangle + \beta < 0$ is an essential hypothesis to reach the conclusion of the S-lemma.

23.2 With H denoting a finite-dimensional Hilbert space, let $\Lambda : H \to \mathbb{R}^m$ be an observation map, let $\Delta : \mathbb{R}^m \to H$ be a recovery map, and let $\mathcal{K} = \{f \in H : \mathrm{dist}_H(f, \mathcal{V}) \le \varepsilon\}$ be an *approximability set* relative to a linear subspace $\mathcal{V}$ of H and a parameter $\varepsilon > 0$. Write down explicitly a semidefinite program that outputs the *local worst-case error* at a given $y \in \Lambda(\mathcal{K})$, i.e.,

$$\mathrm{Err}_{\mathcal{K},\mathrm{Id}}^{\mathrm{loc}}(\Lambda, \Delta, y) = \sup_{f \in \mathcal{K}, \Lambda(f) = y} \|f - \Delta(y)\|_H.$$

23.3 Let $(x^{(1)}, y_1), \ldots, (x^{(m)}, y_m) \in \mathbb{R} \times \{0, 1\}$ and let $\mathcal{H}$ be the hypothesis class made of finite intervals $[a, b]$ with $-\infty < a \le b < +\infty$. Find a dynamic programming implementation of the empirical risk minimization for the 0/1-loss, so as to solve

$$\underset{a \le b}{\text{minimize}} \frac{1}{m} \sum_{i=1}^m \mathrm{Loss}_{0/1}(\mathbb{1}_{[a,b]}(x^{(i)}), y_i).$$

23.4 Instead of the iterative hard thresholding algorithm (23.9), consider a *hard thresholding pursuit* algorithm creating a sequence $(x^t)_{t \ge 0}$ according

---

[1] See Foucart et al. (2015) for more details.

to

S^{t+1} is an index set of s largest absolute entries of $x^t + \alpha A^\top(y - Ax^t)$,

$$x^{t+1} = \operatorname*{argmin}_{x \in \mathbb{R}^N} \|y - Ax\|_2 \quad \text{subject to supp}(x) \subseteq S^{t+1}.$$

By observing that the sequence of $(S^t)_{t \geq 0}$ of index sets is eventually periodic, prove that the sequence $(x^t)_{t \geq 0}$ converges in a finite number of iterations when the restricted isometry property holds on $\Sigma_s^N - \Sigma_s^N$ with constant δ satisfying $1 + \delta < 1/\alpha$.

23.5 Consider a nonconvex optimization program of the form

$$\operatorname*{minimize}_{u,v} f(u, v) \qquad \text{subject to } (u, v) \in C,$$

where, for each fixed u and v, the functions $f(u, \cdot)$ and $f(\cdot, v)$ are convex on sets $C_u := \{v' : (u, v') \in C\}$ and $C_v := \{u' : (u', v) \in C\}$ that are also convex. The *alternating minimization* heuristic creates a sequence $(u^t, v^t)_{t \geq 0}$ defined recursively by

$$u^{t+1} := \operatorname*{argmin}_u f(u, v^t) \qquad\qquad \text{subject to } u \in C_{v^t},$$

$$v^{t+1} := \operatorname*{argmin}_v f(u^{t+1}, v) \qquad\qquad \text{subject to } v \in C_{u^{t+1}}.$$

Verify that the objective function decreases along the iterations, i.e., that $f(u^{t+1}, v^{t+1}) \leq f(u^t, v^t)$ for all $t \geq 0$.

PART FIVE

NEURAL NETWORKS

Executive Summary

The 2010–20 decade saw the explosion of the field of Deep Learning, perhaps epitomized by the 2019 Turin Award presented to Yoshua Bengio, Geoffrey Hinton, and Yann LeCun. The field, loosely defined as a subset of Machine Learning that employs hypothesis classes made of functions generated by deep neural networks, still frenetically stimulates research in Data Science. This fifth part takes a partial (in both senses of the term) look at the theory of neural networks, including pieces that preceded the Deep Learning revolution.

Chapter 24 introduces the main notions, e.g. depth, width, and activation function. It focuses in particular on the so-called ReLU activation function, revealing a first effect of depth on the representation of multivariate continuous piecewise linear functions. Next, Chapter 25 concentrates on shallow networks. It features the universal approximation theorem, as well as a fairly precise quantitative evaluation of the approximation power of shallow ReLU networks. Chapter 26 then turns to deeper networks with the intention of showcasing some tokens that illustrate their superiority over shallow networks, notably in terms of approximation power. Chapter 27 finally touches on the training of neural networks. It explains how backpropagation facilitates gradient descent algorithms, hints at a reason for their empirical success despite nonconvexity, and briefly describes convolutional neural networks.

Readers interested in Deep Learning should consult the book by Goodfellow et al. (2016), even though the adopted viewpoint is not mathematical. A more mathematical, yet accessible, presentation can be found in Higham and Higham (2019). The set of three surveys (Bartlett et al., 2021; Belkin, 2021; DeVore et al., 2021) will also be valuable. The earlier survey by Pinkus (1999) was useful in preparing some of the material, together with more targeted articles. These include Ovchinnikov (2002) for the max-min representation of continuous piecewise linear functions, Yarotsky (2018) for the enhanced approximation power of deep ReLU networks, and Venturi et al. (2019) for the empirical risk landscape of overparametrized shallow networks.

24

First Encounter with ReLU Networks

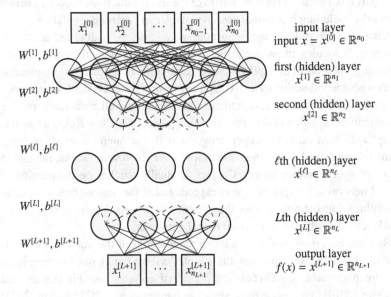

Figure 24.1 In this graphical representation of a neural network, the *depth* is the number L of (hidden) layers and the *width* of the ℓth layer is the number n_ℓ of circles in this layer. They are called *neurons*, while the edges between them are called *synapses*. At the ℓth layer, the ith neuron receives a linear combination $\sum_{j=1}^{n_{\ell-1}} W_{i,j}^{[\ell]} x_j^{[\ell-1]}$ of the states of the neurons at the $(\ell - 1)$st layer, adds a bias $b_i^{[\ell]}$ to it, and then the activation function is applied to determine the state $x_i^{[\ell]}$ of this neuron. In short, the *state vector* at a given layer is determined by the state vector at a previous layer according to $x^{[\ell]} = \phi(W^{[\ell]} x^{[\ell-1]} + b^{[\ell]})$, $\ell \in [1:L]$. At the output layer, the activation function is not applied, so that $x^{[L+1]} = W^{[L+1]} x^{[L]} + b^{[L+1]}$.

24.1 Some Terminology

A neural network is determined by an *activation function* $\phi\colon \mathbb{R} \to \mathbb{R}$ and by an architecture specified through a *depth* L and *widths* $n_0, n_1, \ldots, n_{L+1}$. The functions $f\colon \mathbb{R}^{n_0} \to \mathbb{R}^{n_{L+1}}$ generated by such a neural network are parametrized by *weight matrices* $W^{[1]} \in \mathbb{R}^{n_1 \times n_0}, \ldots, W^{[\ell]} \in \mathbb{R}^{n_\ell \times n_{\ell-1}}, \ldots, W^{[L+1]} \in \mathbb{R}^{n_{L+1} \times n_L}$ and by *bias vectors* $b^{[1]} \in \mathbb{R}^{n_1}, \ldots, b^{[\ell]} \in \mathbb{R}^{n_\ell}, \ldots, b^{[L+1]} \in \mathbb{R}^{n_{L+1}}$. Precisely, with affine functions $A^{[\ell]}\colon \mathbb{R}^{n_{\ell-1}} \to \mathbb{R}^{n_\ell}$ defined by $A^{[\ell]}(x) = W^{[\ell]}x + b^{[\ell]}$ for $x \in \mathbb{R}^{n_{\ell-1}}$, they take the form

$$f = A^{[L+1]} \circ \phi^{[L]} \circ A^{[L]} \circ \cdots \circ \phi^{[\ell]} \circ A^{[\ell]} \circ \cdots \circ \phi^{[1]} \circ A^{[1]}, \qquad (24.1)$$

where $\phi^{[\ell]}$, standing for the function ϕ that acts entrywise on n_ℓ-dimensional vectors, i.e., $\phi^{[\ell]}([x_1; \ldots; x_{n_\ell}]) = [\phi(x_1); \ldots; \phi(x_{n_\ell})]$, is often simply denoted by ϕ. Figure 24.1 gives a graphical representation of the architecture of neural network (with depth represented vertically and width horizontally, as they should!).

The number of weights is $\sum_{\ell=1}^{L+1} n_\ell n_{\ell-1}$ and the number of biases is $\sum_{\ell=1}^{L+1} n_\ell$. For neural networks of constant width n and generating univariate real-valued functions, i.e., for $n_0 = 1$, $n_1 = \cdots = n_L = n$, and $n_{L+1} = 1$, these numbers reduce to $(L-1)n^2 + 2n$ and to $Ln + 1$, respectively, meaning that the neural network is described by $(L-1)n^2 + (L+2)n + 1$ parameters. Note, however, that some of these parameters are superfluous, in the sense that different choices of parameters can generate the same function. Consider, for instance, univariate real-valued functions generated by a *shallow network*, i.e., one of depth $L = 1$. They take the form

$$f(x) = \sum_{i=1}^{n} w_i^{[2]} \phi(w_i^{[1]} x + b_i^{[1]}) + b^{[2]}, \qquad x \in \mathbb{R}.$$

One can always permute the neurons of the hidden layer and generate the same f. For activation functions ϕ that are positively homogeneous of degree one, one can also scale $w^{[1]}$ and $b^{[1]}$ by a factor $\gamma > 0$ and $w^{[2]}$ by a factor $1/\gamma$ and still generate the same f.

Among popular activation functions, one mentions in particular:

- the *logistic sigmoid function* defined by

$$\sigma(x) = \frac{1}{1 + e^{-x}}, \qquad x \in \mathbb{R},$$

which increases from $\sigma(-\infty) = 0$ to $\sigma(+\infty) = 1$ and whose derivative obeys $\sigma' = \sigma(1 - \sigma)$;

- the *rectified linear unit*, which is the function defined by

$$\text{ReLU}(x) = \max\{0, x\}, \quad x \in \mathbb{R},$$

and sometimes also written as $\text{ReLU}(x) = x_+$.

The rest of this chapter concentrates on the ReLU activation function, since it has become the standard choice in Deep Learning. Before anything else, one highlights that ReLU is positively homogeneous of degree one, i.e., that

$$\text{ReLU}(\gamma x) = \gamma \, \text{ReLU}(x) \quad \text{for all } x \in \mathbb{R} \text{ whenever } \gamma > 0. \tag{24.2}$$

It is also useful to put forward the simple relation

$$\text{ReLU}(x) - \text{ReLU}(-x) = x \quad \text{for all } x \in \mathbb{R}. \tag{24.3}$$

24.2 Shallow ReLU Networks and CPwL Functions

Since composing continuous piecewise linear (CPwL) functions yields CPwL functions and since affine functions and the ReLU function are themselves CPwL, the expression (24.1) shows that the functions generated by ReLU networks are CPwL functions. The converse is true, but there is a notable difference between the univariate and multivariate settings as far as depth is concerned. In this section, the depth is restricted to $L = 1$.

Theorem 24.1 *Every univariate continuous piecewise linear function can be generated by shallow ReLU networks. In contrast, there are multivariate continuous piecewise linear functions which cannot be generated by shallow ReLU networks.*

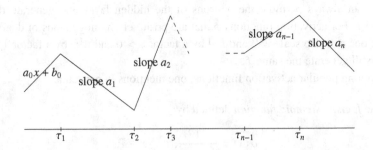

Figure 24.2 A univariate continuous piecewise linear function.

Proof of Theorem 24.1, Part 1   Let $f\colon \mathbb{R} \to \mathbb{R}$ be a univariate CPwL function. It is fully described (see Figure 24.2) by breakpoints $\tau_1 < \cdots < \tau_n$, by an affine function $x \mapsto a_0 x + b_0$ on $(-\infty, \tau_1)$, and by slopes $a_1, \ldots, a_{n-1}, a_n$ on $(\tau_1, \tau_2), \ldots, (\tau_{n-1}, \tau_n), (\tau_n, +\infty)$, respectively. Thus, one can write

$$f(x) = a_0 x + b_0 + \sum_{i=1}^{n} (a_i - a_{i-1}) \operatorname{ReLU}(x - \tau_i),$$

which, by virtue of $a_0 x + b_0 = \operatorname{ReLU}(a_0 x + b_0) - \operatorname{ReLU}(-a_0 x - b_0)$, establishes that f is generated by a shallow ReLU network of width $n + 2$.   □

As illustrated in Figure 24.3, the univariate *step function* and *tent function* can be generated by shallow ReLU networks using the process described above. They can also be generated by ReLU networks of depth two.

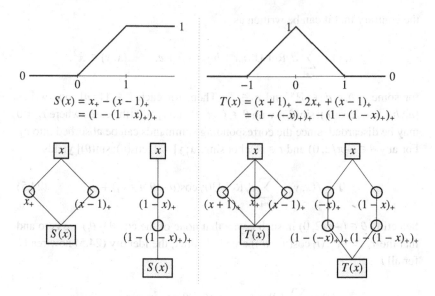

Figure 24.3 Univariate step function S and tent function T.

Proof of Theorem 24.1, Part 2   Let $f\colon \mathbb{R}^2 \to \mathbb{R}$ be the bivariate CPwL function depicted on Figure 24.4, i.e., the function defined by

$$f(x, y) = \min\{0, \max\{x, y\}\}, \qquad (x, y) \in \mathbb{R}^2. \tag{24.4}$$

To prove that it cannot be generated by a shallow ReLU network, assume on

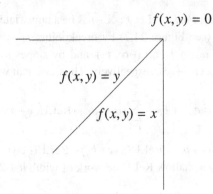

Figure 24.4 The counterexample for Theorem 24.1, Part 2.

the contrary that it can be written as

$$f(x, y) = \sum_{i=1}^{n} d_i \operatorname{ReLU}(a_i x + b_i y + c_i) + e, \qquad (x, y) \in \mathbb{R}^2,$$

for some $a, b, c, d \in \mathbb{R}^n$ and $e \in \mathbb{R}$. Then, for each $i \in [1:n]$, one writes $[a_i; b_i] = r_i [\cos(\theta_i); \sin(\theta_i)]$ with $\theta_i \in (-\pi, \pi]$ and $r_i > 0$ (the cases where $r_i = 0$ may be discarded, since the corresponding summands can be absorbed into e). For any $\theta \in (-\pi/2, 0)$ and $t \in \mathbb{R}$, choosing $[x; y] = t [\cos(\theta); \sin(\theta)]$ yields

$$0 = f(x, y) = \sum_{i=1}^{n} d_i \operatorname{ReLU}(r_i \cos(\theta - \theta_i)t + c_i) + e. \qquad (24.5)$$

Selecting $\theta \in (-\pi/2, 0)$ in such a way that none of the $\cos(\theta - \theta_i)$ are zero and that the $\tau_i := -c_i/(r_i \cos(\theta - \theta_i))$ are all distinct, the identity (24.5) now reads, for all $t \in \mathbb{R}$,

$$0 = \sum_{i=1}^{n} d_i \operatorname{ReLU}(r_i \cos(\theta - \theta_i)(t - \tau_i)) + e$$

$$= \sum_{i=1}^{n} d_i r_i |\cos(\theta - \theta_i)| \operatorname{ReLU}(t - \tau_i) + \ell(t), \qquad (24.6)$$

where ℓ is a univariate affine function. The last step relied on (24.2) and (24.3) to transform $\operatorname{ReLU}(\gamma_i(t - \tau_i))$, $\gamma_i := r_i \cos(\theta - \theta_i)$, into $\gamma_i \operatorname{ReLU}(t - \tau_i)$ when $\gamma_i > 0$ and into $-\gamma_i \operatorname{ReLU}(t - \tau_i) + \gamma_i(t - \tau_i)$ when $\gamma_i < 0$. The required contradiction follows from the fact that the CPwL function appearing in (24.6) have nonzero slopes and hence cannot be identically zero. □

24.3 Deep ReLU Networks and CPwL Functions

Having stressed the impossibility to generate all multivariate CPwL functions with ReLU networks of depth $L = 1$, one shall establish in this section the possibility to do so by allowing depths $L \geq 1$. As an example, the bivariate function (24.4) can be generated by a ReLU network of depth two, by virtue of $f(x, y) = - \max\{0, - \max\{x, y\}\} = - \text{ReLU}(- \max\{x, y\})$ and of

$$\max\{x, y\} = x + \max\{0, y - x\} = \text{ReLU}(x) - \text{ReLU}(-x) + \text{ReLU}(y - x).$$

The latter observation also guarantees that the trivariate maximum function can be generated by a ReLU network of depth two, by virtue of

$$\max\{x, y, z\} = \max\{\max\{x, y\}, z\}. \tag{24.7}$$

More generally, the d-variate maximum function can be generated by a ReLU network of depth $\lceil \log_2(d) \rceil$. Incidentally, the trivariate maximum function cannot be generated by a ReLU network of depth smaller than two: if it was, then writing the function (24.4) as

$$f(x, y) = \max\{x, y\} - \max\{x, y, 0\}$$

would imply that it could generated by a shallow ReLU network, which was proved impossible earlier.

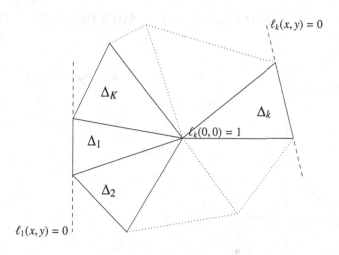

Figure 24.5 The continuous piecewise linear tent function T vanishing outside the convex cell $\Delta_1 \cup \cdots \cup \Delta_K$ and taking the value 1 at its center.

As a further example, consider the bivariate *tent function* T subordinated to the convex cell depicted in Figure 24.5. It cannot be generated by a shallow

ReLU network (see Theorem 26.2), but it can be explicitly generated by a deeper ReLU network. Indeed, it is readily verified that T can be expressed as

$$T(x,y) = \max\left\{0, \min_{k\in[1:K]} \ell_k(x,y)\right\}. \tag{24.8}$$

In fact, every CPwL has such a max-min representation, as established by the result below. The main statement of this section follows as a corollary.

Theorem 24.2 *Let $f: \mathbb{R}^d \to \mathbb{R}$ be a continuous piecewise linear function with affine pieces $f_1,\ldots,f_K$. There exists a family $\mathcal{S}$ of subsets S of $[1:K]$ such that, for any $x \in \mathbb{R}^d$,*

$$f(x) = \max_{S\in\mathcal{S}} \min_{k\in S} f_k(x). \tag{24.9}$$

Corollary 24.3 *Every mutlivariate continuous piecewise linear function can be generated by ReLU networks.*

Proof The result is an immediate consequence of (24.9), since it has been shown that maxima, hence minima, can be generated by ReLU networks, and then so can their compositions. □

Proof of Theorem 24.2 For all $x, y \in \mathbb{R}^d$, one first claims the existence of some $k \in [1:K]$ such that

$$f_k(x) \le f(x) \qquad \text{and} \qquad f_k(y) \ge f(y). \tag{24.10}$$

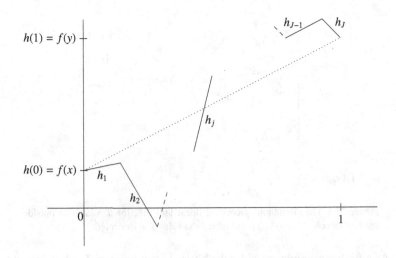

Figure 24.6 Illustration for the proof of Theorem 24.2.

To see this, consider the univariate CPwL function defined for $t \in [0, 1]$ by $h(t) = f((1-t)x+ty)$. Its linear pieces $h_1, \ldots, h_J$, enumerated from left to right, are given by $h_j(t) = f_{k_j}((1-t)x+ty)$, $t \in [0, 1]$, for some $k_1, \ldots, k_J \in [1:K]$. If the slope of h_1 or the slope of h_J equals at least the slope s of the line joining $(0, h(0))$ to $(1, h(1))$, then the result is acquired by taking $k = k_1$ or $k = k_J$. If both slopes are smaller than s, then there is some $j \in [2:J-1]$ such that h_j meets the line joining $(0, h(0))$ to $(1, h(1))$ with a slope larger than s, as shown in Figure 24.6. This implies that $h_j(0) < h(0)$, i.e., $f_{k_j}(x) < f(x)$, and that $h_j(1) > h(1)$, i.e., $f_{k_j}(y) > f(y)$, so that the claim is now fully justified.

Next, for every $x \in \mathbb{R}^d$, one considers the subset S_x of $[1:K]$ defined by $S_x := \{k \in [1:K] : f_k(x) \geq f(x)\}$. One subsequently introduces the family S of all S_x as x runs through $\mathbb{R}^d$. The objective is to prove that f coincides everywhere with the function $g := \max\{\min\{f_k, k \in S\}, S \in S\}$. Given $x \in \mathbb{R}^d$, one first notices that $g(x) \geq \min\{f_k(x), k \in S_x\} \geq f(x)$. Next, for $S \in S$, say $S = S_y$ with $y \in \mathbb{R}^d$, the claim (24.10) means that there exists $k \in S$ such that $f_k(x) \leq f(x)$. Thus, one has $\min\{f_k(x), k \in S\} \leq f(x)$, and taking the maximum over $S \in S$ yields $g(x) \leq f(x)$. In short, the desired equality $g(x) = f(x)$ has been obtained for all $x \in \mathbb{R}^d$. $\qquad\square$

Exercises

24.1 Propose yet another representation of the univariate tent function T by a ReLU network based on the identity $T(x) = (1 - |x|)_+$.

24.2 Build explicitly a ReLU network of depth n that outputs the maximum $\max\{x_1, \ldots, x_{2^n}\}$ of 2^n inputs $x_1, \ldots, x_{2^n}$.

24.3 Provide an explicit max-min representation of the form (24.9) for the d-variate function that outputs the jth largest element among d inputs.

24.4 Let f be a d-variate continuous piecewise linear function with linear pieces $f_1, \ldots, f_K$, where each region $\{x \in \mathbb{R}^d : f(x) = f_k(x)\}$ has a nonempty interior. If f is convex, prove that it can be written as

$$f = \max_{k \in [1:K]} f_k.$$

24.5 Invoke the inclusion-exclusion principle to verify the identity

$$\min\{a_1, \ldots, a_n\} = \sum_{k=1}^{n} (-1)^{k-1} \sum_{1 \leq i_1 < \cdots < i_k \leq n} \max\{a_{i_1}, \ldots, a_{i_k}\}.$$

Deduce that any multivariate continuous piecewise linear function is the difference of two convex continuous piecewise linear functions.

25

Expressiveness of Shallow Networks

This chapter is devoted to the approximation power of neural networks—their *expressive power*, in Deep Learning parlance. The first focal point is the famed *universal approximation theorem*, i.e., the fact that, for reasonable activation functions, every multivariate real-valued continuous function can be uniformly approximated on any compact set with arbitrary accuracy using functions that are generated by shallow networks. Next, concentrating on ReLU activation, the rate of approximation of Lipschitz functions by shallow networks is to be analyzed, leading to upper and lower estimates that almost match.

25.1 Activation Functions and Universal Approximation

In the univariate setting and with ReLU activation, the functions generated by shallow networks coincide with CPwL functions (see Theorem 24.1), so they are dense in any $C[a, b]$. This denseness result is to be extended to the multivariate setting and to other activation functions. In fact, the result below characterizes the activation functions for which denseness holds.

Theorem 25.1 *For a continuous activation function $\phi \colon \mathbb{R} \to \mathbb{R}$ and for a compact subset X of $\mathbb{R}^d$, let*

$$N_\phi(X) := \Big\{ g \in F(X, \mathbb{R}) : \text{there are } n \geq 1, \, a_1, \ldots, a_n \in \mathbb{R}^d, \text{ and } b, c \in \mathbb{R}^n$$

$$\text{such that } g(x) = \sum_{j=1}^{n} c_j \phi(\langle a_j, x \rangle + b_j) \text{ for all } x \in X \Big\} \quad (25.1)$$

denote the set of functions generated by shallow networks with the activation function ϕ. The following properties are equivalent:

(i) the set $N_\phi(X)$ is dense in $C(X)$;

(ii) the function ϕ is not a polynomial.

Proof of (i)⇒(ii) This implication is clear, because if ϕ was a polynomial, then the set $\mathcal{N}_\phi(X)$ would be contained in the space of polynomials of degree at most $\deg(\phi)$ and would therefore not be dense in $C(X)$. □

The core of the argument is the implication (ii)⇒(i). A first step consists in realizing that the problem can be reduced to the univariate case.

Proof of (ii)⇒(i), *Step 1* Suppose that the denseness result holds in the case $d = 1$. Now, for $d > 1$, it is easy to verify that the set

$$\mathcal{A} = \mathrm{span}\left\{ f \in F(X, \mathbb{R}) : f = \exp(\langle v, \cdot \rangle) \text{ for some } v \in \mathbb{R}^d \right\}$$

is a subalgebra of $C(X)$ that vanishes nowhere and separates points. Thus, by the *Stone–Weierstrass theorem* (Theorem E.3), it is dense in $C(X)$. Therefore, given a function $f \in C(X)$ and an accuracy $\varepsilon > 0$, one can find $k \geq 1$, $\gamma_1, \ldots, \gamma_k \in \mathbb{R}$, and $v_1, \ldots, v_k \in \mathbb{R}^d$ such that

$$\left| f(x) - \sum_{i=1}^{k} \gamma_i \exp(\langle v_i, x \rangle) \right| < \frac{\varepsilon}{2} \qquad \text{for all } x \in X. \tag{25.2}$$

For each $i \in [1:k]$, the set $\{\exp(\langle v_i, x \rangle), x \in X\}$ is a compact subset of $\mathbb{R}$, so by invoking the result for $d = 1$, one can find $n_i \geq 1$ and $a_i, b_i, c_i \in \mathbb{R}^{n_i}$ such that, for all $t \in \{\exp(\langle v_i, x \rangle), x \in X\}$,

$$\left| \exp(t) - \sum_{j=1}^{n_i} c_{i,j} \phi(a_{i,j} t + b_{i,j}) \right| < \frac{\varepsilon}{2 \sum_{\ell=1}^{k} |\gamma_\ell|}. \tag{25.3}$$

One deduces from (25.2) and (25.3) that, for all $x \in X$,

$$\left| f(x) - \sum_{i=1}^{k} \sum_{j=1}^{n_i} \gamma_i c_{i,j} \phi(a_{i,j} \langle v_i, x \rangle + b_{i,j}) \right|$$

$$\leq \left| f(x) - \sum_{i=1}^{k} \gamma_i \exp(\langle v_i, x \rangle) \right| + \sum_{i=1}^{k} |\gamma_i| \left| \exp(\langle v_i, x \rangle) - \sum_{j=1}^{n_i} c_{i,j} \phi(a_{i,j} \langle v_i, x \rangle + b_{i,j}) \right|$$

$$< \frac{\varepsilon}{2} + \sum_{i=1}^{k} |\gamma_i| \frac{\varepsilon}{2 \sum_{\ell=1}^{k} |\gamma_\ell|} = \varepsilon.$$

This means that f can be uniformly approximated by elements from $\mathcal{N}_\phi(X)$ with error at most ε. Since $f \in C(X)$ and $\varepsilon > 0$ were arbitrary, the denseness of $\mathcal{N}_\phi(X)$ in $C(X)$ is proved. □

The argument for the second step of the implication (ii)⇒(i) involves an identity known as the *Peano representation* of divided differences. Recall first that the *divided difference* of a function f at points $t_0 < t_1 < \cdots < t_{k-1} < t_k$ is defined inductively by $[t_0]f = f(t_0)$ and, for $k \geq 1$, by

$$[t_0, t_1, \ldots, t_{k-1}, t_k]f = \frac{[t_1, \ldots, t_{k-1}, t_k]f - [t_0, t_1, \ldots, t_{k-1}]f}{t_k - t_0}.$$

For a k-times differentiable function f, the divided difference $[t_0, t_1, \ldots, t_k]f$ provides a numerical approximation to $f^{(k)}(x)$ when $t_0, t_1, \ldots, t_{k-1}, t_k$ are all close to x. In fact, the divided difference can be represented as

$$[t_0, t_1, \ldots, t_{k-1}, t_k]f = \frac{1}{k!} \int_{t_0}^{t_k} M_{t_0, \ldots, t_k}(t) f^{(k)}(t) dt \qquad (25.4)$$

for some function $M_{t_0, \ldots, t_k}$ known as the L_1-normalized *B-spline* relative to $t_0, \ldots, t_k$. It is a piecewise polynomial of degree $< k$ with breakpoints $t_0, \ldots, t_k$, globally $(k - 2)$-times continuously differentiable, nonnegative on its support $[t_0, t_k]$, and integrating to one. The identity (25.4) can be verified (readers are invited to do so in Exercise 25.1) by relying on the inductive definition of B-splines, which is given by $M_{t_0, t_1}(t) = \mathbb{1}_{[t_0, t_1]}(t)/(t_1 - t_0)$ and, for $k \geq 2$,

$$M_{t_0, \ldots, t_k}(t) = \frac{k}{k-1}\left(\frac{t - t_0}{t_k - t_0} M_{t_0, \ldots, t_{k-1}}(t) + \frac{t_k - t}{t_k - t_0} M_{t_1, \ldots, t_k}(t)\right). \qquad (25.5)$$

Proof of (ii)$\Rightarrow$(i), *Step 2*   The objective is to establish the univariate result in the case $\phi \in C^{\infty}(\mathbb{R})$. Let a nonnegative integer k and a real number b be fixed for now. Given $x \in X$, the *Peano representation* (25.4) for the divided differences at the points $0, h, \ldots, kh$ of the function $f_x \colon t \in \mathbb{R} \mapsto \phi(tx + b) \in \mathbb{R}$ is written as

$$[0, h, \ldots, kh]f_x = \frac{1}{k!} \int_0^{kh} M_{0, h, \ldots, kh}(t) x^k \phi^{(k)}(tx + b) dt.$$

Setting $\gamma := \max\{|u|, u \in X\}$ and $\varepsilon_h := \max\{|\phi^{(k)}(v + b) - \phi^{(k)}(b)|, |v| \leq kh\gamma\}$, it follows that

$$\left|[0, h, \ldots, kh]f_x - \frac{\phi^{(k)}(b)}{k!}x^k\right| = \left|\frac{x^k}{k!} \int_0^{kh} M_{0, h, \ldots, kh}(t)(\phi^{(k)}(tx + b) - \phi^{(k)}(b))dt\right|$$

$$\leq \frac{\gamma^k}{k!} \int_0^{kh} M_{0, h, \ldots, kh}(t)\varepsilon_h dt = \frac{\gamma^k}{k!}\varepsilon_h.$$

Observing that the function $x \in X \mapsto [0, h, \ldots, kh]f_x$ belongs to $\mathcal{N}_\phi(X)$ and that the bound $(\gamma^k/k!)\varepsilon_h$ tends to zero as $h \to 0$ independently of $x \in X$, one deduces that the map $x \in X \mapsto (\phi^{(k)}(b)/k!)x^k$ belongs to the closure $\mathrm{cl}(\mathcal{N}_\phi(X))$ of $\mathcal{N}_\phi(X)$. Since there exists some $b \in \mathbb{R}$ such that $\phi^{(k)}(b) \neq 0$—otherwise ϕ would be a polynomial—one derives that the map $x \in X \mapsto x^k$ itself belongs to $\mathrm{cl}(\mathcal{N}_\phi(X))$. This being true for any integer $k \geq 0$, one concludes that

$cl(\mathcal{N}_\phi(X))$ contains all polynomials, and in turn, by the *Weierstrass theorem* (Theorem E.1), that $cl(\mathcal{N}_\phi(X))$ equals $C(X)$. $\square$

The argument for the implication (ii)$\Rightarrow$(i) now requires a final step to remove the assumption that $\phi \in C^\infty(\mathbb{R})$. It consists in selecting a compactly supported function $\psi \in C^\infty(\mathbb{R})$ and in considering its *convolution product* with a merely continuous function $\phi \colon \mathbb{R} \to \mathbb{R}$. This convolution product is defined for any $x \in \mathbb{R}$ by

$$(\phi * \psi)(x) = \int_{-\infty}^{\infty} \phi(x - y)\psi(y)dy. \tag{25.6}$$

It can be verified that the function $\phi * \psi$ belongs to $C^\infty(\mathbb{R})$. The same holds when convolving with $\psi_\varepsilon \colon x \in \mathbb{R} \mapsto \psi(x/\varepsilon)/\varepsilon$ for any $\varepsilon > 0$. By choosing e.g. ψ to be the *bump function* $x \in \mathbb{R} \mapsto \mathbb{1}_{[-1,1]}(x) \times \exp(-1/(1 - x^2))$ normalized so that $\int_{\mathbb{R}} \psi = 1$, there is the added bonus that $\phi * \psi_\varepsilon$ converges uniformly to ϕ on any compact subset of $\mathbb{R}$ when $\varepsilon \to 0$; see Exercise 25.2.

Proof of (ii)$\Rightarrow$(i), *Step 3*   For $\varepsilon > 0$, with the compactly supported function $\psi_\varepsilon \in C^\infty(\mathbb{R})$ chosen as above, one first observes that, for any $a, b \in \mathbb{R}$, the map

$$x \in X \mapsto (\phi * \psi_\varepsilon)(ax + b) = \int_{-\infty}^{\infty} \phi(ax + b - y)\psi_\varepsilon(y)dy$$

belongs to $cl(\mathcal{N}_\phi(X))$. It follows that $cl(\mathcal{N}_{\phi*\psi_\varepsilon}(X)) \subseteq cl(\mathcal{N}_\phi(X))$. Assume now that $cl(\mathcal{N}_\phi(X))$ is a proper subset of $C(X)$. Invoking the Weierstrass theorem again, there exists an integer $k \geq 0$ such that the map $x \in X \mapsto x^k$ does not belong to $cl(\mathcal{N}_\phi(X))$, and hence does not belong to $cl(\mathcal{N}_{\phi*\psi_\varepsilon}(X))$ either. However, according to Step 2, the map $x \in X \mapsto ((\phi * \psi_\varepsilon)^{(k)}(b)/k!)x^k$ belongs to $cl(\mathcal{N}_{\phi*\psi_\varepsilon}(X))$ for any $b \in \mathbb{R}$. This implies that $(\phi*\psi_\varepsilon)^{(k)}(b) = 0$ for any $b \in \mathbb{R}$, i.e., that $\phi * \psi_\varepsilon$ is a polynomial of degree $< k$. It follows that ϕ, as the limit of $\phi * \psi_\varepsilon$ when $\varepsilon \to 0$, is also a polynomial of degree $< k$, which is not the case. This contradiction finishes the proof that $\mathcal{N}_\phi(X)$ is dense in $C(X)$. $\square$

25.2 Approximation Rate with ReLU: Upper Bound

The universal approximation theorem (Theorem 25.1) is not quantitative: it says only that the error of best approximation to a given continuous function using shallow networks converges to zero as the width n goes to infinity, but it does not provide any information about the convergence speed. Concentrating on ReLU activation, one shall now target results about the approximation rate in terms of the number $(d + 2)n \asymp dn$ of parameters describing the set of

d-variate functions generated by shallow ReLU networks of width n. In the same spirit as in Theorem 25.1, this set is written as

$$\mathcal{N}^n_{\text{ReLU}} := \left\{ \sum_{j=1}^{n} c_j \, \text{ReLU}(\langle a_j, \cdot \rangle + b_j) : a_1, \dots, a_n \in \mathbb{R}^d \text{ and } b, c \in \mathbb{R}^n \right\}$$

without including a final bias, since it can be obtained by choosing one of the a_i to be zero. The worst-case considerations below involve *Lipschitz functions*. Precisely, one defines a model set (already encountered in Chapter 11) by

$$\mathcal{K}_{\text{Lip}} := \left\{ f \in C([0,1]^d) : |f|_{\text{Lip}} := \sup_{x \ne x' \in [0,1]^d} \frac{|f(x) - f(x')|}{\|x - x'\|_\infty} \le 1 \right\}.$$

The main result of this section consists of a nearly tight upper bound for the approximation rate of Lipschitz functions using shallow ReLU networks. The complete proof is omitted[1] and only the simple case of univariate functions is treated here.

Theorem 25.2 *There is a positive constant C_d such that, for any $n \ge 2$,*

$$\sup_{f \in \mathcal{K}_{\text{Lip}}} \inf_{g \in \mathcal{N}^n_{\text{ReLU}}} \|f - g\|_{C([0,1]^d)} \le C_d \ln(n) \frac{1}{n^{1/d}}. \tag{25.7}$$

Sketch of proof when $d = 1$ Let a function $f \in C([0,1])$ satisfy $|f|_{\text{Lip}} \le 1$. For $n \ge 2$, consider the continuous piecewise linear function g with breakpoints at $x_0 = 0, \dots, x_i = i/(n-1), \dots, x_{n-1} = 1$ that interpolates the values $f(x_0), \dots, f(x_i), \dots, f(x_{n-1})$ there. As outlined in the proof of Theorem 24.1, this function can be generated by a shallow ReLU network of width n, i.e., $g \in \mathcal{N}^n_{\text{ReLU}}$. Moreover, it also satisfies $|g|_{\text{Lip}} \le 1$, from where the inequality $\|f - g\|_{C([0,1])} \le 1/(n-1)$ can be easily obtained (an improved inequality is provided in Lemma 26.5). Indeed, for any $x \in [0,1]$, choosing $i \in [0:n-1]$ such that $|x - x_i| \le 1/(2(n-1))$ leads to

$$|f(x) - g(x)| \le |f(x) - f(x_i)| + |g(x_i) - g(x)| \le (|f|_{\text{Lip}} + |g|_{\text{Lip}})|x - x_i|$$

$$\le \frac{1}{n-1}.$$

In view of $n - 1 \ge n/2$, the bound $\inf \{\|f - g\|_{C([0,1])} : g \in \mathcal{N}^n_{\text{ReLU}}\} \le 2/n$ holds for any $f \in \mathcal{K}_{\text{Lip}}$, meaning that the estimate (25.7) is valid when $d = 1$ even without the logarithmic factor.   □

---

[1] The arguments are given in Bach (2017), with the result being stated in Subsection 4.7 there.

25.3 Approximation Rate with ReLU: Lower Bound

To justify the near-tightness of Theorem 25.2, this section provides a lower bound for the approximation rate of Lipschitz functions using shallow ReLU networks. Disregarding logarithmic factors, it matches the upper bound of the previous section.

Theorem 25.3 *There is a positive constant c_d such that, for any $n \geq 1$,*

$$\sup_{f \in \mathcal{K}_{\mathrm{Lip}}} \inf_{g \in \mathcal{N}_{\mathrm{ReLU}}^n} \|f - g\|_{C([0,1]^d)} \geq \frac{c_d}{\ln(2n)^{1/d}} \frac{1}{n^{1/d}}.$$

The result is a direct consequence of the following two observations, both of them being interesting in their own right.

Proposition 25.4 *Given any subset $\mathcal{G}$ of $C([0,1]^d)$, one has*

$$\sup_{f \in \mathcal{K}_{\mathrm{Lip}}} \inf_{g \in \mathcal{G}} \|f - g\|_{C([0,1]^d)} \geq \frac{1}{2 \, \mathrm{vc}(\mathbb{1}_{(0,+\infty)} \circ \mathcal{G})^{1/d}},$$

where $\mathbb{1}_{(0,+\infty)} \circ \mathcal{G}$ denotes the family of boolean functions of the form $\mathbb{1}_{(0,+\infty)} \circ g$ for some $g \in \mathcal{G}$.

Proposition 25.5 *The set of shallow ReLU networks of width $n \geq 1$ yields a VC-dimension satisfying*

$$\mathrm{vc}(\mathbb{1}_{(0,+\infty)} \circ \mathcal{N}_{\mathrm{ReLU}}^n) \leq Cdn \ln(2n)$$

for some absolute constant C that can be taken as $C = 40/\ln(2)$.

It now remains to justify these two propositions.

Proof of Proposition 25.4 The result is clear if $\delta \geq 1/2$, where

$$\delta := \sup_{f \in \mathcal{K}_{\mathrm{Lip}}} \inf_{g \in \mathcal{G}} \|f - g\|_{C([0,1]^d)}.$$

Thus, one assumes that $\delta < 1/2$ and considers the integer $n \geq 1$ such that $1/(2(n + 1)) \leq \delta < 1/(2n)$. Let $\mathfrak{X} = \{x^{(i)} = [i_1/n; \dots; i_d/n] : i \in [0:n]^d\}$ be the set of $(n + 1)^d$ nodes of the d-tensorized regular grid with spacing $1/n$. For each $i \in [0:n]^d$, let C_i denote the cell associated with $x^{(i)}$ in the Voronoi tessellation of $[0, 1]^d$ relative to the ℓ_∞-norm; see Figure 25.1. For any binary vector $\varepsilon \in \{0, 1\}^{[0:n]^d}$, the function f defined for $x \in [0, 1]^d$ by

$$f(x) = \sum_{i \in [0:n]^d} \widetilde{\varepsilon}_i \, \mathrm{dist}_{\ell_\infty}(x, [0, 1]^d \setminus C_i), \qquad \widetilde{\varepsilon}_i := 2\varepsilon_i - 1 \in \{-1, +1\}, \quad (25.8)$$

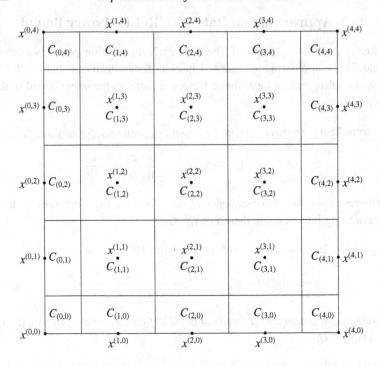

Figure 25.1 The cells $C_{\mathbf{i}}$ and their centers $x^{(\mathbf{i})}$ when $d = 2$ and $n = 4$.

can be verified to satisfy

$$|f|_{\text{Lip}} \leq 1 \quad \text{and} \quad f(x^{(\mathbf{i})}) = \frac{\widetilde{\varepsilon}_{\mathbf{i}}}{2n} \quad \text{for all } \mathbf{i} \in [0 : n^d].$$

Since there exists $g \in \mathcal{G}$ such that $|f(x) - g(x)| \leq \delta < 1/(2n)$ for all $x \in [0, 1]^d$, one deduces that $\text{sgn}(g(x^{(\mathbf{i})})) = \widetilde{\varepsilon}_{\mathbf{i}}$, i.e., that $(\mathbb{1}_{(0,+\infty)} \circ g)(x^{(\mathbf{i})}) = \varepsilon_{\mathbf{i}}$, for all $\mathbf{i} \in [0 : n]^d$. This fact means that the set $\mathfrak{X}$ is shattered by $\mathbb{1}_{(0,+\infty)} \circ \mathcal{G}$. Therefore,

$$\text{vc}(\mathbb{1}_{(0,+\infty)} \circ \mathcal{G}) \geq |\mathfrak{X}| = (n + 1)^d \geq (1/(2\delta))^d,$$

which is a rearrangement of the announced result.   □

Proof of Proposition 25.5   The main objective is to bound the *shatter function* (see Definition 2.1) of the family $\mathbb{1}_{(0,+\infty)} \circ \mathcal{N}^n_{\text{ReLU}}$ as follows: for $m \geq (d + 1)n$,

$$\tau(m) := \max_{x^{(1)}, \ldots, x^{(m)} \in \mathbb{R}^d} \left| \{[\mathbb{1}_{(0,+\infty)}(h(x^{(1)})); \ldots; \mathbb{1}_{(0,+\infty)}(h(x^{(m)}))], h \in \mathcal{N}^n_{\text{ReLU}}\} \right|$$

$$\leq \left(\frac{4m}{d\sqrt{n}}\right)^{4dn}. \tag{25.9}$$

From here, with $\overline{m}$ denoting the VC-dimension of $\mathbb{1}_{(0,+\infty)} \circ \mathcal{N}_{\text{ReLU}}^n$, one recalls that $\tau(\overline{m}) = 2^{\overline{m}}$. If $\overline{m} < (d+1)n$, then the result is immediately clear. If otherwise $\overline{m} \geq (d+1)n$, then the estimate (25.9) gives $2^{\overline{m}} \leq (4\overline{m}/(d\sqrt{n}))^{4dn}$. Taking the logarithm yields

$$\overline{m} \ln(2) \leq 4dn \ln\left(\frac{4\overline{m}}{d\sqrt{n}}\right), \quad \text{i.e.,} \quad \frac{4\overline{m}}{d\sqrt{n}} \leq \frac{16}{\ln(2)} \sqrt{n} \ln\left(\frac{4\overline{m}}{d\sqrt{n}}\right). \quad (25.10)$$

Since $\ln(t) < \sqrt{t}$ for any $t > 0$, this inequality implies

$$\frac{4\overline{m}}{d\sqrt{n}} \leq \frac{16}{\ln(2)} \sqrt{n} \sqrt{\frac{4\overline{m}}{d\sqrt{n}}}, \quad \text{and hence} \quad \frac{4\overline{m}}{d\sqrt{n}} \leq \frac{16^2}{\ln(2)^2} n \leq (2n)^{10}.$$

Substituting the latter into (25.10), one obtains the required estimate

$$\overline{m} \leq \frac{40}{\ln(2)} dn \ln(2n).$$

Turning to the justification of the bound (25.9), let $x^{(1)}, \ldots, x^{(m)} \in \mathbb{R}^d$ be fixed from now on. By the positive homogeneity of ReLU, any $h \in \mathcal{N}_{\text{ReLU}}^n$ can be written as $h = \sum_{j=1}^n \gamma_j \text{ReLU}(\langle a_j, \cdot \rangle + b_j)$ where $a_1, \ldots, a_n \in \mathbb{R}^d$, $b_1, \ldots, b_n \in \mathbb{R}$, and importantly, $\gamma_1, \ldots, \gamma_n \in \{-1, +1\}$. Thus, the goal is to bound the cardinality of the set $\mathcal{S} \in \{0, 1\}^m$ given by

$$\mathcal{S} := \bigcup_{\gamma_1, \ldots, \gamma_n \in \{-1, +1\}} \left\{ \left[\cdots ; \mathbb{1}_{(0,+\infty)}\left(\sum_{j=1}^n \gamma_j \text{ReLU}(\langle a_j, x^{(i)} \rangle + b_j) \right); \cdots \right] : \right.$$

$$\left. a_1, \ldots, a_n \in \mathbb{R}^d, b_1, \ldots, b_n \in \mathbb{R} \right\}. \quad (25.11)$$

For $a \in \mathbb{R}^d$ and $b \in \mathbb{R}$, notice that $\text{ReLU}(\langle a, x^{(i)} \rangle + b)$ reduces to $\varepsilon_i(\langle a, x^{(i)} \rangle + b)$ with $\varepsilon_i := \mathbb{1}_{(0,+\infty)}(\langle a, x^{(i)} \rangle + b)$ for $i \in [1:m]$. The binary vector $\varepsilon \in \{0, 1\}^m$ does not visit all 2^m possible configurations, though: it is restricted to a strict subset $\mathcal{E}$ of $\{0, 1\}^m$. Indeed, since each $\varepsilon \in \mathcal{E}$ corresponds to an intersection-of-half-spaces region $\{[a; b] \in \mathbb{R}^{d+1} : \text{sgn}(\langle a, x^{(i)} \rangle + b) = 2\varepsilon_i - 1, i \in [1:m]\}$ and since it is known (see Exercise 25.4 for the arguments) that the number of such intersection-of-half-spaces regions of $\mathbb{R}^k$ created by m hyperplanes is at most

$$R_{k,m} = 2\left[\binom{m-1}{0} + \binom{m-1}{1} + \cdots + \binom{m-1}{k-1} \right],$$

one obtains $|\mathcal{E}| \leq R_{d+1,m}$. Thus, for a particular choice of $\gamma_1, \ldots, \gamma_n \in \{-1, +1\}$, the set appearing in the union (25.11) is included in

$$\bigcup_{\varepsilon^{(1)},\dots,\varepsilon^{(n)}\in\mathcal{E}} \left\{ \left[\cdots ; \mathbb{1}_{(0,+\infty)}\left(\sum_{j=1}^{n}\gamma_j\varepsilon_i^{(j)}(\langle a_j, x^{(i)}\rangle + b_j)\right); \cdots\right] : \right.$$

$$\left. a_1,\dots,a_n \in \mathbb{R}^d, b_1,\dots,b_n \in \mathbb{R}\right\}. \quad (25.12)$$

For a particular choice of $\varepsilon^{(1)},\dots,\varepsilon^{(n)} \in \mathcal{E}$, the latter binary vectors correspond again to intersection-of-half-spaces regions created by m hyperplanes, but this time in the space $\mathbb{R}^{(d+1)n}$. Therefore, each set of binary vectors appearing in the union (25.12) has cardinality at most $R_{(d+1)n,m}$. All in all, the cardinality of the set (25.11) is bounded by $|S| \le 2^n \times (R_{d+1,m})^n \times R_{(d+1)n,m}$. Invoking the estimate established in Lemma 2.6, it follows that

$$|S| \le 2^n \times 2^n\left(\frac{e(m-1)}{d}\right)^{dn} \times 2\left(\frac{e(m-1)}{(d+1)n-1}\right)^{(d+1)n-1}$$

$$\le 2^n \times 2^n\left(\frac{em}{d}\right)^{dn} \times 2e^{-1}\left(\frac{em}{dn}\right)^{(d+1)n} \le 2^{2n}\left(\frac{em}{d}\right)^{2dn}\left(\frac{em}{dn}\right)^{2dn} \le \left(\frac{4m}{d\sqrt{n}}\right)^{4dn}.$$

Since this is true for any choice of $x^{(1)},\dots,x^{(m)} \in \mathbb{R}^d$, the bound announced in (25.9) is now justified. $\quad\square$

Exercises

25.1 Verify that the function $M_{t_0,\dots,t_k}$ given by the inductive definition (25.5) is a piecewise polynomial of degree $< k$ with breakpoints $t_0,\dots,t_k$, is globally $(k-2)$-times continuously differentiable, is nonnegative on its support $[t_0, t_k]$, and integrates to one. Verify also the validity of Peano representation (25.4) of divided differences.

25.2 Show that the convolution product (25.6) of a compactly supported and infinitely differentiable function $\psi \in C^\infty(\mathbb{R})$ with a merely continuous function $\phi \in C(\mathbb{R})$ is infinitely differentiable, i.e., that $\phi * \psi \in C^\infty(\mathbb{R})$. Furthermore, if ψ is nonnegative, is supported on $[-1, 1]$, and integrates to one, show that $|\phi(x) - (\phi * \psi_\varepsilon)(x)| \le \max\{|\phi(x) - \phi(x')|, |x - x'| \le \varepsilon\}$ for any $x \in \mathbb{R}$, where one defined $\psi_\varepsilon := \psi(\cdot/\varepsilon)/\varepsilon$ for $\varepsilon > 0$.

25.3 Fill in the details needed for a careful proof that the Lipschitz constant of the function f defined in (25.8) is at most one.

25.4 Let $R_{k,m}$, respectively $R_{k,m}^{\text{aff}}$, denote the number of regions in $\mathbb{R}^k$ created by m hyperplanes, respectively affine hyperplanes, in general position.

Prove by induction on $m \geq 1$ that

$$R_{k,m} = 2\left[\binom{m-1}{0} + \binom{m-1}{1} + \cdots + \binom{m-1}{k-1}\right],$$

$$R_{k,m}^{\text{aff}} = \binom{m}{0} + \binom{m}{1} + \cdots + \binom{m}{k}.$$

To do so, assume without loss of generality that the $(m + 1)$st (affine) hyperplane has equation $x_k = 0$ and count the number of regions added to the ones already created by the first m (affine) hyperplanes in order to obtain the recurrence relation

$$R_{k,m+1}^{(\text{aff})} = R_{k,m}^{(\text{aff})} + R_{k-1,m}^{(\text{aff})}.$$

26

Various Advantages of Depth

Deep neural networks have empirically proved to outperform their shallow counterparts in a variety of learning tasks. This chapter presents a selection of three theoretical observations to support the belief in the superiority of deep networks. The first observation is cautionary: with too much freedom for the activation function, depth-2 networks with a width that is fixed can strikingly approximate any continuous function arbitrarily well! Thus, one restricts the activation function to be ReLU in subsequent comparisons between deep and shallow networks. The second observation highlights that deep networks can generate compactly supported functions, which is not possible using shallow networks. The final observation concerns the approximation capabilities of ReLU networks and the fact that they are provably enhanced by depth.

26.1 Omnipotent Activation Functions

The purpose of this section is to point out that, for a depth $L > 1$, the activation function alone is powerful enough to enable the approximation of continuous multivariate functions with arbitrary precision while keeping the number of neurons bounded. Of course, this pathological situation is not encountered in practice, as one must work with manageable activation functions.

Theorem 26.1 *There is a continuous activation function $\phi \in C(\mathbb{R})$ such that the set of functions generated by networks of depth 2 and width $d(2d + 1)$ is dense in $C([0, 1]^d)$.*

Proof First, one points out that the set Q of univariate polynomials with rational coefficients is dense in $C([0, 1])$. Indeed, for any $f \in C([0, 1])$ and $\varepsilon > 0$, the existence of a polynomial p—written as $p(x) = \sum_{i=0}^{n} a_i x^i$—such that $\|f - p\|_{C([0,1])} \leq \varepsilon/2$ is guaranteed by the *Weierstrass theorem* (Theorem E.1),

226

so defining $q(x) = \sum_{i=0}^{n} b_i x^i$ with $b_i \in Q$ and $|a_i - b_i| \le \varepsilon/(2(n+1))$, $i \in [0:n]$, leads to $q \in Q$ and $\|f - q\|_{C([0,1])} \le \varepsilon$, given that, for any $x \in [0, 1]$,

$$|f(x) - q(x)| \le |f(x) - p(x)| + \sum_{i=0}^{n} |a_i - b_i| x^i \le \frac{\varepsilon}{2} + (n+1)\frac{\varepsilon}{2(n+1)} = \varepsilon.$$

Since the set Q is also countable, it can be enumerated as $Q = \{q_n, n \in \mathbb{Z}\}$. One then constructs a continuous function $\phi \in C(\mathbb{R})$ on $\cup_{n \in \mathbb{Z}}[2n, 2n+1]$ by

$$\phi(2n + x) = q_n(x), \qquad n \in \mathbb{Z}, \quad x \in [0, 1],$$

and somewhat arbitrarily on $\cup_{n \in \mathbb{Z}}(2n+1, 2n+2)$, so long as global continuity is achieved. This is the activation function being used. One remarks (with details left to the reader) that, in the univariate case $d = 1$, the announced result can be strengthened to the statement that even the set of functions generated by shallow ($L = 1$) and narrow ($W = 1$) networks is dense in $C([0, 1])$.

Turning to the result in the multivariate case $d \ge 2$, let $f \in C([0, 1]^d)$ and $\varepsilon > 0$. By the *Kolmogorov superposition theorem* (Theorem E.9), one can write

$$f(x) = \sum_{j=1}^{2d+1} \overline{f}\left(\sum_{i=1}^{d} \lambda_i \varphi_j(x_i)\right), \qquad x = (x_1, \ldots, x_d) \in [0, 1]^d,$$

for some univariate continuous function $\overline{f} \in C([0, 1])$ (depending on f), for some numbers $\lambda_1, \ldots, \lambda_d \ge 0$ (independent of f) satisfying $\sum_{i=1}^{d} \lambda_i = 1$, and some continuous functions $\varphi_1, \ldots, \varphi_{2d+1}$ (independent of f) mapping $[0, 1]$ into $[0, 1]$. In view of the denseness of Q and the definition of ϕ, one can find $\overline{n} \in \mathbb{Z}$ such that

$$\left|\overline{f}(y) - \phi(2\overline{n} + y)\right| < \frac{\varepsilon}{4d+2} \qquad \text{for all } y \in [0, 1]. \tag{26.1}$$

By the uniform continuity of $\phi(2\overline{n} + \cdot)$ on $[-1, 2]$, say, there exists $\delta > 0$ with $\delta < 1$, say, such that for all $y \in [0, 1]$,

$$|\phi(2\overline{n} + y) - \phi(2\overline{n} + y')| < \frac{\varepsilon}{4d+2} \qquad \text{whenever } |y - y'| < \delta.$$

Now, one selects integers $n_1, \ldots, n_{2d+1} \in \mathbb{Z}$ such that, for each $j \in [1:2d+1]$,

$$|\varphi_j(x) - \phi(2n_j + x)| < \delta \qquad \text{for all } x \in [0, 1].$$

It follows that, for each $j \in [1:2d+1]$,

$$\left|\sum_{i=1}^{d} \lambda_i \varphi_j(x_i) - \sum_{i=1}^{d} \lambda_i \phi(2n_j + x_i)\right| < \delta \qquad \text{for all } x \in [0, 1]^d.$$

In turn, one derives that, for all $x \in [0, 1]^d$,

$$\left|\phi\left(2\overline{n} + \sum_{i=1}^{d} \lambda_i \varphi_j(x_i)\right) - \phi\left(2\overline{n} + \sum_{i=1}^{d} \lambda_i \phi(2n_j + x_i)\right)\right| < \frac{\varepsilon}{4d+2}. \tag{26.2}$$

Finally, one defines the approximant h by

$$h(x) = \sum_{j=1}^{2d+1} \phi\left(2\bar{n} + \sum_{i=1}^{d} \lambda_i \phi(2n_j + x_i)\right), \qquad x \in [0, 1]^d,$$

which is claimed to yield $\|f - h\|_{C([0,1]^d)} < \varepsilon$. To verify this, one observes that, for any $x \in [0, 1]^d$,

$$|f(x) - h(x)| = \left| \sum_{j=1}^{2d+1} \left(\bar{f}\left(\sum_{i=1}^{d} \lambda_i \varphi_j(x_i)\right) - \phi\left(2\bar{n} + \sum_{i=1}^{d} \lambda_i \phi(2n_j + x_i)\right)\right) \right|$$

$$\leq \sum_{j=1}^{2d+1} \left| \bar{f}\left(\sum_{i=1}^{d} \lambda_i \varphi_j(x_i)\right) - \phi\left(2\bar{n} + \sum_{i=1}^{d} \lambda_i \varphi_j(x_i)\right) \right|$$

$$+ \sum_{j=1}^{2d+1} \left| \phi\left(2\bar{n} + \sum_{i=1}^{d} \lambda_i \varphi_j(x_i)\right) - \phi\left(2\bar{n} + \sum_{i=1}^{d} \lambda_i \phi(2n_j + x_i)\right) \right|$$

$$< \sum_{j=1}^{2d+1} \left(\frac{\varepsilon}{4d+2} + \frac{\varepsilon}{4d+2} \right) = \varepsilon,$$

where (26.1) and (26.2) were used for the last inequality. It remains to make sure that the function h is indeed generated by a network of depth 2 and width $d(2d+1)$ with activation function ϕ. This point is illustrated in Figure 26.1. $\quad\square$

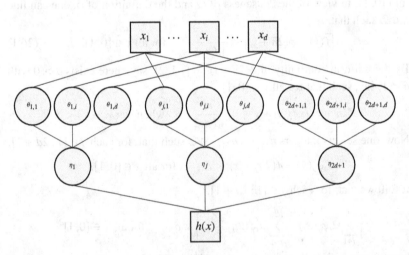

Figure 26.1 The network generating the approximant $h(x) = \sum_{j=1}^{2d+1} \eta_j$, where $\eta_j = \phi(2\bar{n} + \sum_{i=1}^{d} \lambda_i \theta_{j,i})$ and $\theta_{j,i} = \phi(2n_j + x_i)$.

26.2 Compact Supports

From now on, one imposes the activation function to be ReLU (although the result of this section extends to other activation functions; see Exercise 26.2). It was already revealed in Chapter 24 that the functions generated by ReLU networks are CPwL functions and, conversely, that every CPwL function can be generated by a deep network but not necessarily by a shallow one. Persisting in this direction, another merit of depth transpires from the inability of shallow ReLU networks to generate any function from the important class of compactly supported multivariate CPwL functions. Here is the formal statement.

Theorem 26.2 *For $d \geq 2$, there are no compactly supported functions, other than the zero function, in the linear space $N_{\mathrm{ReLU}}(\mathbb{R}^d)$ of d-variate functions generated by shallow ReLU networks.*

The full argument is postponed until the following identities are established.

Lemma 26.3 *For $\gamma \in \mathbb{R}$ and $t > |\gamma|$, setting*

$$I_\gamma(t) := \frac{1}{2} \int_{-\pi}^{\pi} \mathrm{ReLU}(t\cos(\theta) + \gamma)d\theta,$$

one has

$$I_\gamma(t) = t\sqrt{1 - \frac{\gamma^2}{t^2}} + \gamma \arccos\left(-\frac{\gamma}{t}\right) \quad and \quad I'_\gamma(t) = \sqrt{1 - \frac{\gamma^2}{t^2}}.$$

Proof The second identity is deduced by a routine differentiation from the first one. To verify this first identity in detail, notice that $\mathrm{ReLU}(t\cos(\theta) + \gamma)$ is activated only when $\cos(\theta) > -\gamma/t$—i.e., when $|\theta| < a := \arccos(-\gamma/t)$—so that

$$2I_\gamma(t) = \int_{-a}^{a} (t\cos(\theta) + \gamma)d\theta = \left[t\sin(\theta) + \gamma\theta\right]_{-a}^{a} = 2(t\sin(a) + \gamma a)$$

$$= 2\left(t\sqrt{1 - \frac{\gamma^2}{t^2}} + \gamma \arccos\left(-\frac{\gamma}{t}\right)\right),$$

which reduces to the announced identity. □

Proof of Theorem 26.2 By fixing some variables, it is enough to establish the result in the case $d = 2$. To this end, consider a compactly supported bivariate function of the form

$$f(x) = \sum_{j=1}^{n} c_j \mathrm{ReLU}(\langle a_j, x \rangle + b_j) + d,$$

where $a_1, \ldots, a_n \in \mathbb{R}^2$ and $b_1, \ldots, b_n, c_1, \ldots, c_n, d \in \mathbb{R}$. The objective is to prove that $f = 0$. It can be assumed without loss of generality that the a_j are ℓ_2-normalized. One then writes $a_j = [\cos(\theta_j); \sin(\theta_j)]$ for $\theta_j \in [-\pi, \pi]$, as well as $x = x_0 + t[\cos(\theta); \sin(\theta)]$ for $t > 0$, $\theta \in [-\pi, \pi]$, and $x_0 \in \mathbb{R}^2$ chosen so that the $\gamma_j = \langle a_j, x_0 \rangle + b_j$ and their opposites are all distinct (which is possible because the union of lines $\{v \in \mathbb{R}^2 : \langle a_j, v \rangle + b_j = \pm(\langle a_\ell, v \rangle + b_\ell)\}$ is of measure zero). Thus, one obtains

$$f(x_0 + t[\cos(\theta); \sin(\theta)]) = \sum_{j=1}^{n} c_j \operatorname{ReLU}(t \cos(\theta - \theta_j) + \gamma_j) + d. \qquad (26.3)$$

For $t \geq \max\{|\gamma_1|, \ldots, |\gamma_n|\}$ large enough so that $x_0 + t[\cos(\theta); \sin(\theta)] \notin \operatorname{supp}(f)$, integrating (26.3) over $\theta \in [-\pi, \pi]$ yields

$$\sum_{j=1}^{n} c_j I_{\gamma_j}(t) + \pi d = 0, \qquad \text{and hence} \qquad \sum_{j=1}^{n} c_j I'_{\gamma_j}(t) = 0,$$

where the notation of Lemma 26.3 has been used. This lemma now guarantees that, for $u > 0$ small enough (and playing the role of $1/t^2$), one has

$$\sum_{j=1}^{n} c_j \sqrt{1 - \gamma_j^2 u} = 0.$$

Differentiating the latter k times with respect to u before taking the limit as $u \to 0$ yields

$$\sum_{j=1}^{n} c_j \gamma_j^{2k} = 0, \qquad k \in [0 : n - 1].$$

This is an invertible Vandermonde linear system, only admitting the solution $c_1 = \cdots = c_n = 0$. It follows that $f(x) = d$ for all $x \in \mathbb{R}^2$. Since f is compactly supported, one concludes that $f = 0$, as desired. $\qquad \square$

26.3 Approximation Power

In this section, one is interested in the approximation rate for the nonlinear set of real-valued multivariate functions generated by ReLU networks of depth $L \geq 1$ and constant width $\bar{n} \geq 1$. Precisely, with $n_0 = d$, $n_1, \ldots, n_L = \bar{n}$, and $n_{L+1} = 1$, one considers the set

$$\mathcal{N}_{\operatorname{ReLU}}^{\bar{n},L} = \Big\{ A^{[L+1]} \circ \operatorname{ReLU} \circ A^{[L]} \circ \cdots \circ \operatorname{ReLU} \circ A^{[2]} \circ \operatorname{ReLU} \circ A^{[1]},$$

$$A^{[\ell]} : \mathbb{R}^{n_{\ell-1}} \to \mathbb{R}^{n_\ell} \text{ is an affine map for each } \ell \in [1 : L + 1] \Big\}.$$

The width $\bar{n}$ and the number d of variables are considered fixed quantities, so that the number $N = \bar{n}(\bar{n}+1)(L-1)+\bar{n}d+2\bar{n}+1$ of parameters describing $\mathcal{N}_{\text{ReLU}}^{\bar{n},L}$ is roughly proportional to the depth L. In terms of this number N, the result below provides $N^{-2/d}$ as an upper bound for the approximation rate over the set

$$\mathcal{K}_{\text{Lip}} := \left\{ f \in C([0,1]^d) : |f|_{\text{Lip}} := \sup_{x \neq x' \in [0,1]^d} \frac{|f(x) - f(x')|}{\|x - x'\|_\infty} \leq 1 \right\}.$$

Thus, the result establishes that deep ReLU networks are more powerful than shallow ones, since Theorem 25.3 showed that, up to a logarithmic factor, the approximation rate $N^{-1/d}$ over $\mathcal{K}_{\text{Lip}}$ could not be improved for shallow ReLU networks—there, the number N of parameters was roughly proportional to the width. One mentions without giving any details that this improvement comes at the price of the approximation scheme's stability.[1]

Theorem 26.4 *There is an integer $\bar{n} \geq 1$ and a positive constant C_d such that, for any $L \geq 1$,*

$$\sup_{f \in \mathcal{K}_{\text{Lip}}} \inf_{g \in \mathcal{N}_{\text{ReLU}}^{\bar{n},L}} \|f - g\|_{C([0,1]^d)} \leq C_d \frac{1}{L^{2/d}}.$$

One shall prove this result only in the univariate case,[2] starting with a few important observations.

Lemma 26.5 *Let f be a function defined on $[0,1]$. For $m \in [0 : M]$, consider $x_m := m/M$ and $y_m := \delta \lfloor f(x_m)/\delta + 1/2 \rfloor$ to be a closest element to $f(x_m)$ from a discretization grid with spacing δ. If $\widetilde{f}$ denotes the continuous piecewise linear function interpolating $y_0, y_1, \ldots, y_M$ at its breakpoints $x_0, x_1, \ldots, x_M$, then*

$$\|f - \widetilde{f}\|_{C([0,1])} \leq \frac{|f|_{\text{Lip}}}{2M} + \frac{\delta}{2} \quad \text{and} \quad |\widetilde{f}|_{\text{Lip}} \leq |f|_{\text{Lip}} + \delta M. \quad (26.4)$$

In particular, when there is no discretization ($\delta \to 0$), one has

$$\|f - \widetilde{f}\|_{C([0,1])} \leq \frac{|f|_{\text{Lip}}}{2M} \quad \text{and} \quad |\widetilde{f}|_{\text{Lip}} \leq |f|_{\text{Lip}}.$$

Proof Given $x \in [0,1]$, let $m \in [1 : M]$ be such that $x \in [x_{m-1}, x_m]$, and let subsequently $\tau \in [0,1]$ be such that $x = x_{m-1} + \tau(x_m - x_{m-1}) = (1-\tau)x_{m-1} + \tau x_m$. Since $\widetilde{f}$ is linear on $[x_{m-1}, x_m]$ with $\widetilde{f}(x_{m-1}) = y_{m-1}$ and $\widetilde{f}(x_m) = y_m$, one has $\widetilde{f}(x) = (1 - \tau)y_{m-1} + \tau y_m$. It follows that

$$f(x) - \widetilde{f}(x) = (1 - \tau)(f(x) - y_{m-1}) + \tau(f(x) - y_m)$$

$$= (1 - \tau)(f(x) - f(x_{m-1}) + f(x_{m-1}) - y_{m-1}) + \tau(f(x) - f(x_m) + f(x_m) - y_m).$$

---

[1] A thorough discussion can be found in DeVore et al. (2021).
[2] The general result for any number of variables is established in Yarotsky (2018).

Due to $|f(x) - f(x_{m-1})| \le |f|_{\text{Lip}}|x - x_{m-1}| = |f|_{\text{Lip}}\tau/M$, to $|f(x_{m-1}) - y_{m-1}| \le \delta/2$, to $|f(x) - f(x_m)| \le |f|_{\text{Lip}}|x - x_m| = |f|_{\text{Lip}}(1-\tau)/M$, and to $|f(x_m) - y_m| \le \delta/2$, one obtains

$$|f(x) - \widetilde{f}(x)| \le (1-\tau)(|f|_{\text{Lip}}\tau/M + \delta/2) + \tau(|f|_{\text{Lip}}(1-\tau)/M + \delta/2)$$
$$= 2(1-\tau)\tau|f|_{\text{Lip}}/M + \delta/2 \le |f|_{\text{Lip}}/(2M) + \delta/2.$$

This is the leftmost inequality of (26.4). The rightmost inequality is justified more easily, as the linear pieces of $\widetilde{f}$ on $[x_{m-1}, x_m]$, $m \in [1:M]$, have slopes $(y_m{-}y_{m-1})/(x_m{-}x_{m-1}) = (y_m{-}f(x_m){+}f(x_m){-}f(x_{m-1}){+}f(x_{m-1}){-}y_{m-1})/(x_m{-}x_{m-1})$, which are bounded by $(\delta/2)/(1/M) + |f|_{\text{Lip}} + (\delta/2)/(1/M) = |f|_{\text{Lip}} + \delta M$ in absolute value. □

Lemma 26.6 *The functions $\mathsf{M}^{(0)}$, $\mathsf{M}^{(1)}$, $\mathsf{M}^{(2)}$, $m^{(0)}$, $m^{(1)}$, and $m^{(2)}$ depicted in Figure 26.2 can be generated by ReLU networks of width 3 and depth M.*

Proof These functions take the form $x \in [0,1] \mapsto \sum_{i=1}^{M} c_i \operatorname{ReLU}(a_i x + b_i) \in \mathbb{R}$. As such, they could be generated by shallow ReLU networks of width M, but here one wants to generate them using a fixed width. To do so, one reserves a *source channel* that makes the input $x \in [0,1]$—which equals $\operatorname{ReLU}(x)$—available at each layer and a *collation channel* that aggregates the values of intermediate computations. Their purpose is illustrated in Figure 26.3, which shows the narrow ReLU network generating the desired function. □

Lemma 26.7 *For $z_1, z_2, \ldots, z_K \in \{0, 2, 4\}$, there is a width-5, depth-$(2K-1)$ ReLU network extracting from the input $\overline{z_1 z_2 \cdots z_K} := z_1/5 + z_2/5^2 + \cdots + z_K/5^K$ each quinary digit z_k at the $(2k)$th layer.*

Proof Consider the continuous piecewise linear function h with breakpoints at 1, 2, 3, 4 and values $h_{|(-\infty,1]} = 0$, $h_{|[2,3]} = 2$, $h_{|[4,+\infty)} = 4$. It can be generated by a shallow ReLU network of width 4. With $\zeta^{(1)} := \overline{z_1 z_2 \cdots z_K}$, notice that $5\zeta^{(1)} = z_1 + \xi$ with $\xi \in [0,1)$, so that z_1 can be extracted as $z_1 = h(5\zeta^{(1)})$ with one layer of a ReLU network. At the same time, one makes $\zeta^{(2)} := \overline{z_2 \cdots z_K}$ available as $\zeta^{(2)} = 5\zeta^{(1)} - z_1 = 5\zeta^{(1)} - h(5\zeta^{(1)})$. One repeats the process by applying h to $5\zeta^{(2)}$ to extract z_2 and making $\zeta^{(3)} := \overline{z_3 \cdots z_K}$ available, etc. The resulting ReLU network is shown in Figure 26.4. □

Proof of Theorem 26.4 Let a function $f \in C([0,1])$ satisfy $|f|_{\text{Lip}} \le 1$ and let an integer $M \ge 1$ be fixed throughout. One considers the continuous piecewise linear function $\widetilde{f}$ having breakpoints at the m/M, $m \in [0:M]$, and interpolating the values of f there. One derives $\|f - \widetilde{f}\|_{C([0,1])} \le 1/(2M)$ and $|\widetilde{f}|_{\text{Lip}} \le 1$ using Lemma 26.5, and hence $|f - \widetilde{f}|_{\text{Lip}} \le |f|_{\text{Lip}} + |\widetilde{f}|_{\text{Lip}} \le 2$. With the functions

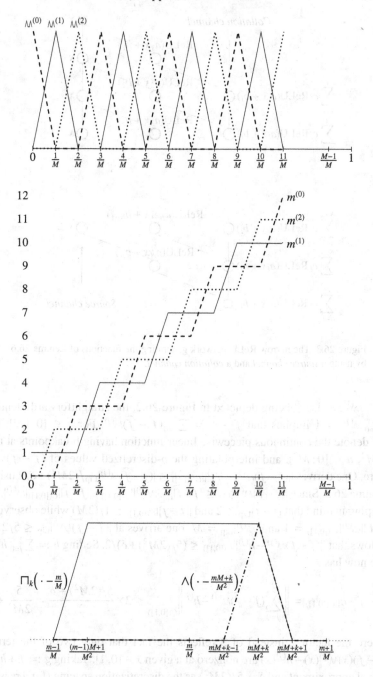

Figure 26.2 The functions involved in the proof of Theorem 26.4.

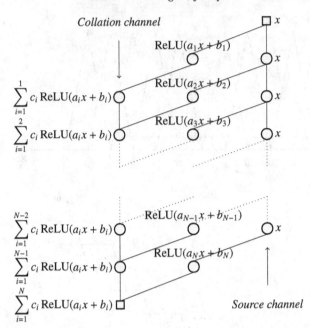

Figure 26.3 The narrow ReLU network generating the functions of Lemma 26.6 by using a *source channel* and a *collation channel*.

$\mathsf{M}^{(0)}$, $\mathsf{M}^{(1)}$, and $\mathsf{M}^{(2)}$ being depicted in Figure 26.2, the straightforward identity $\sum_{j=0}^{2} \mathsf{M}^{(j)} = 1$ implies that $f - \tilde{f} = \sum_{j=0}^{2}(f - \tilde{f})\mathsf{M}^{(j)}$. For $j \in \{0, 1, 2\}$, let $h^{(j)}$ denote the continuous piecewise linear function having breakpoints at the n/M^2, $n \in [0 : M^2]$, and interpolating the δ-discretized values of $(f - \tilde{f})\mathsf{M}^{(j)}$ there. One derives $\|(f-\tilde{f})\mathsf{M}^{(j)} - h^{(j)}\|_{C([0,1])} \leq |(f-\tilde{f})\mathsf{M}^{(j)}|_{\mathrm{Lip}}/(2M^2) + \delta/2$ using Lemma 26.5. Since $|(f-\tilde{f})\mathsf{M}^{(j)}|_{\mathrm{Lip}} \leq |f-\tilde{f}|_{\mathrm{Lip}}\|\mathsf{M}^{(j)}\|_{C([0,1])} + \|f-\tilde{f}\|_{C([0,1])}|\mathsf{M}^{(j)}|_{\mathrm{Lip}}$, keeping in mind that $|f-\tilde{f}|_{\mathrm{Lip}} \leq 2$ and $\|f-\tilde{f}\|_{C([0,1])} \leq 1/(2M)$ while observing that $\|\mathsf{M}^{(j)}\|_{C([0,1])} = 1$ and $|\mathsf{M}^{(j)}|_{\mathrm{Lip}} = M$, one arrives at $|(f - \tilde{f})\mathsf{M}^{(j)}|_{\mathrm{Lip}} \leq 5/2$. It follows that $\|(f-\tilde{f})\mathsf{M}^{(j)} - h^{(j)}\|_{C([0,1])} \leq (5/(2M^2)+\delta)/2$. Setting $h := \sum_{j=0}^{2} h^{(j)}$, one now has

$$\|f-\tilde{f}-h\|_{C([0,1])} = \left\| \sum_{j=0}^{2}(f-\tilde{f})\mathsf{M}^{(j)} - h^{(j)} \right\|_{C([0,1])} \leq 2 \times \frac{5/(2M^2)+\delta}{2} = \frac{5}{2M^2} + \delta,$$

where the factor 2 instead of 3 reflects the fact that only two of the terms $(f-\tilde{f})(x)\mathsf{M}^{(j)}(x) - h^{(j)}(x)$ are nonzero at a given $x \in [0, 1]$. Taking $g := \tilde{f} + h$ as a final approximant and $\delta = 5/(2M^2)$ as the discretization spacing (for a reason to become apparent soon), one obtains $\|f - g\|_{C([0,1])} \leq 5/M^2$, which is of the

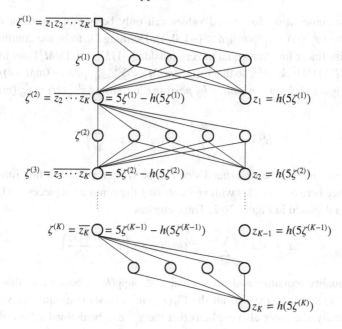

Figure 26.4 Bit extraction with the narrow ReLU network of Lemma 26.7.

order of the desired error if the parameter M and the depth L are comparable. Since the function $\widetilde{f}$ can be generated by a ReLU network of width 3 and depth M, similarly to what was done in Lemma 26.6, it remains to verify that the function h—in fact, each $h^{(j)}$—can be generated by a ReLU network of constant width and depth proportional to M.

To this end, fixing $j \in \{0, 1, 2\}$, one represents the δ-discretized values of $(f - \widetilde{f})_M{}^{(j)}$ on a grid with spacing $1/M^2$ through $y_k^{(j)}(m)$, where the parameter $m \in [1 : M - 1]$ accompanies a coarse grid with spacing $1/M$ and the parameter $k \in [-M : M]$ accompanies a refined grid with spacing $1/M^2$ around m/M. Precisely, one sets $y_k^{(j)}(m) = \delta\lfloor(f - \widetilde{f})_M{}^{(j)}((mM + k)/M^2) + 1/2\rfloor$. In this way, for $x \in \mathrm{supp}(h^{(j)})$, say, $x \in [(m - 1)/M, (m + 1)/M]$ for some $m \in j + 3\mathbb{Z}$, one has

$$h^{(j)}(x) = \sum_{k=-M}^{M} y_k^{(j)}(m) \wedge \left(x - \frac{mM + k}{M^2}\right), \tag{26.5}$$

where $\wedge$ is the tent function vanishing outside $[-1/M^2, 1/M^2]$, as depicted in Figure 26.2. Recalling that $|(f - \widetilde{f})_M{}^{(j)}|_{\mathrm{Lip}} \leq 5/2$, the nondiscretized values of $(f - \widetilde{f})_M{}^{(j)}$ at consecutive points of the refined grid differ by at most $5/(2M^2)$. Therefore, according to the choice $\delta = 5/(2M^2)$, the difference $y_k^{(j)}(m) - y_{k+1}^{(j)}(m)$

between consecutive discretized values can only be one of $-\delta$, 0, or δ, so $z_k^{(j)}(m) := (y_k^{(j)}(m) - y_{k+1}^{(j)}(m))/\delta \in \{-1, 0, 1\}$. Defining $\sqcap_k$ to be the continuous piecewise linear function equal to zero outside $[-1/M, (k+1)/M^2]$ and to one on $[-(M-1)/M^2, k/M^2]$, so that $\sqcap_k(x - m/M) = \sum_{\ell=-M+1}^{k} \wedge(x - (mM + \ell)/M^2)$ —see Figure 26.2—a *summation by parts* in (26.5) using $y_{-M}^{(j)}(m) = y_M^{(j)}(m) = 0$ gives

$$h^{(j)}(x) = \delta \sum_{k=-M+1}^{M-1} z_k^{(j)}(m) \sqcap_k \left(x - \frac{m}{M} \right).$$

The expression on the right-hand side can be written as a bona fide function of x, since here $m = m^{(j)}(x)$ with $m^{(j)}$ denoting the continuous piecewise linear function depicted in Figure 26.2. Thus, one has

$$h^{(j)}(x) = \delta \sum_{k=-M+1}^{M-1} z_k^{(j)}(m^{(j)}(x)) \sqcap_k \left(x - \frac{m^{(j)}(x)}{M} \right).$$

This equality remains valid even when $x \notin \mathrm{supp}(h^{(j)})$, because in this case $|x - m^{(j)}(x)/M| > 1/M$ and all the $\sqcap_k(x - m^{(j)}(x)/M)$ consequently vanish. Incidentally, the latter also explains that the $z_k^{(j)}$ can be defined arbitrarily on noninteger values. Now, to deal with the products appearing in the above sum, one remarks that, for $\eta \in \{-1, 0, 1\}$ and $\theta \in [0, 1]$,

$$\eta\theta = \mathrm{ReLU}(\theta + \eta) - \mathrm{ReLU}(\theta - \eta) - \mathrm{ReLU}(\eta) + \mathrm{ReLU}(-\eta). \qquad (26.6)$$

As such, the function $h^{(j)}$ can be written as the sum of four functions, the first of which is

$$h_1^{(j)}(x) = \delta \sum_{k=-M+1}^{M-1} \mathrm{ReLU}\left(z_k^{(j)}(m^{(j)}(x)) + \sqcap_k \left(x - \frac{m^{(j)}(x)}{M} \right) \right).$$

Finishing the proof requires a justification that all four of these functions can be represented by ReLU networks of constant width and depth proportional to M. This is done through Figure 26.5 for the particular case of $h_1^{(j)}$. In preparation for the application of the bit extraction technique of Lemma 26.7, one crucially observes that $z_k^{(j)}(m^{(j)}(x))$, or rather $2(z_k^{(j)}(m^{(j)}(x)) + 1) \in \{0, 2, 4\}$, is one of the quinary digits of $Z^{(j)}(x)$, where $Z^{(j)}$ is a continuous piecewise linear function defined when $m \in j + 3\mathbb{Z}$ by

$$Z^{(j)}(x) = \sum_{k=-M+1}^{M-1} \frac{2(z_k^{(j)}(m) + 1)}{5^{k+M}}, \qquad x \in \left[\frac{m-1}{M}, \frac{m+1}{M} \right].$$

Similarly to what was done in Lemma 26.6 for the function $m^{(j)}$, the function $Z^{(j)}$ can be generated by a ReLU network of constant width and depth M. $\square$

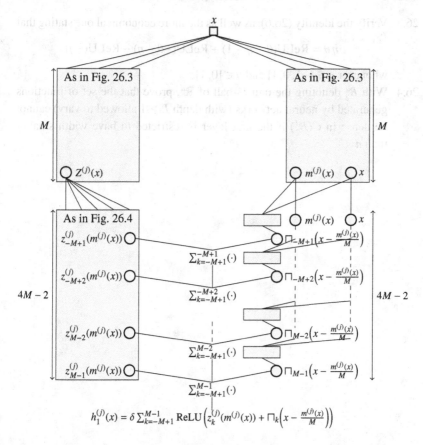

$$h_1^{(j)}(x) = \delta \sum_{k=-M+1}^{M-1} \text{ReLU}\left(z_k^{(j)}(m^{(j)}(x)) + \sqcap_k\left(x - \frac{m^{(j)}(x)}{M}\right)\right)$$

Figure 26.5 Illustration of the way the function $h_1^{(j)}$ can be generated by a ReLU network of constant width and depth proportional to M.

Exercises

26.1 Let the *nth sawtooth function* $S_n = T \circ \cdots \circ T : [0, 1] \to [0, 1]$ be the n-fold composition of the univariate tent function $T : [0, 1] \to [0, 1]$ shown in Figure 24.3. Prove that S_n can be generated by a ReLU network of width 3 and depth n but cannot be approximated with L_∞-accuracy $1/2$ using a shallow ReLU network of width smaller than 2^{n-1}.

26.2 For any univariate CPwL function ϕ, prove that the space $\mathcal{N}_\phi(\mathbb{R}^d)$ does not contain any nonzero compactly supported function when $d \geq 2$. For the logistic sigmoid function σ, prove that the space $\mathcal{N}_\sigma(\mathbb{R}^d)$ does not contain any nonzero compactly supported function even when $d \geq 1$.

26.3 Verify the identity (26.6), as well as the more economical one stating that

$$\eta\theta = \mathrm{ReLU}(\theta + \eta - 1) + \mathrm{ReLU}(-\theta - \eta) - \mathrm{ReLU}(-\eta)$$

whenever $\eta \in \{-1, 0, 1\}$ and $\theta \in [0, 1]$.

26.4 With B_2^d denoting the unit ℓ_2-ball of $\mathbb{R}^d$, prove that the set of functions generated by neural networks (with depth $L \geq 1$ allowed to vary) cannot be dense in $C(B_2^d)$ if the first layer is restricted to have width smaller than d.

27

Tidbits on Neural Network Training

The previous chapters focused on conceptual properties of neural networks, in particular in terms of approximation capability. But their success arguably owes more to the fact that they are skillfully trainable. Indeed, practice has suggested time and again that appropriate weights and biases can be learned when the empirical risk minimization strategy solicits various gradient descent algorithms despite the lack of convexity. This chapter examines some topics related to the learning stage. The first topic describes a way to compute the necessary gradients efficiently. The second topic elucidates the feasibility of producing global empirical risk minimizers in an overparametrized regime. The third and final topic concerns a specific network architecture utilized in image recognition.

27.1 Backpropagation

In this section, one returns to a learning strategy introduced in Chapter 1, namely *empirical risk minimization*. One recalls that, given a training sample $S = ((x^{(1)}, y_1), \ldots, (x^{(m)}, y_m)) \in (X \times Y)^m$, the objective is to minimize the empirical risk

$$\widehat{\text{Risk}}_S(h) = \frac{1}{m} \sum_{i=1}^{m} \text{Loss}(h(x^{(i)}), y_i) \qquad (27.1)$$

over functions h in a given hypothesis class. This class consists here of all functions generated by neural networks with prescribed activation function and architecture. Thus, when $X \subseteq \mathbb{R}^d$ and $Y \subseteq \mathbb{R}^k$, one first fixes a depth $L \geq 1$ and widths $n_0 = d, n_1, \ldots, n_L, n_{L+1} = k$, and then proceeds with the minimization of (27.1). The latter is understood as a function of the neural network weights $W^{[1]}, \ldots, W^{[L+1]}$ and biases $b^{[1]}, \ldots, b^{[L+1]}$, summarized as a vector $p \in \mathbb{R}^N$ of

239

parameters. Even though the function $p \in \mathbb{R}^N \mapsto \widehat{\mathrm{Risk}}_S(h)$ is not convex, and hence none of the guarantees of Chapter 19 apply, one attempts to perform the minimization via gradient descent. In fact, one executes the *stochastic gradient descent* algorithm, which involves an index $i(t)$ randomly chosen in $[1:m]$ at each iteration t. Precisely, for each $i \in [1:m]$, writing

$$C_i \colon p \in \mathbb{R}^N \mapsto \mathrm{Loss}(h(x^{(i)}), y_i) \in \mathbb{R}, \qquad \text{so that} \quad \widehat{\mathrm{Risk}}_S(h) = \frac{1}{m} \sum_{i=1}^{m} C_i(p),$$

and selecting possibly varying stepsizes $\alpha^{(t)} > 0$, one iterates the scheme

$$p^{(t+1)} = p^{(t)} - \alpha^{(t)} \nabla C_{i(t)}(p^{(t)}), \qquad t \geq 0, \tag{27.2}$$

after having initialized $p^{(0)}$, e.g. randomly. Therefore, one needs to be able, for fixed $(x, y) \in \mathbb{R}^d \times \mathbb{R}^k$, to efficiently compute the gradient of the generic map

$$C \colon p \in \mathbb{R}^N \mapsto \mathrm{Loss}(x^{[L+1]}, y) \in \mathbb{R}.$$

Here, one used the earlier notation $x^{[L+1]} \in \mathbb{R}^k$ for the neural network output obtained from the input $x^{[0]} = x \in \mathbb{R}^d$ by way of the state vectors $x^{[\ell]} \in \mathbb{R}^{n_\ell}$, $\ell \in [1:L]$. Recall that these state vectors are given recursively by

$$z^{[\ell]} = W^{[\ell]} x^{[\ell-1]} + b^{[\ell]}, \qquad x^{[\ell]} = \phi(z^{[\ell]}), \qquad \ell \in [1:L],$$

while one has $x^{[L+1]} = z^{[L+1]} = W^{[L+1]} x^{[L]} + b^{[L+1]}$ at the the output layer. The dependence of C on the parameter vector p is derived from the dependence of $x^{[L+1]}$ on the weights $W^{[1]}, \ldots, W^{[L+1]}$ and biases $b^{[1]}, \ldots, b^{[L+1]}$. Note that the dependence of $x^{[L+1]}$ on $W^{[L+1]}$ is immediate, its dependence on $W^{[L]}$ occurs by way of $x^{[L]}$, on $W^{[L-1]}$ by way of $x^{[L-1]}$, etc., so it makes intuitive sense that the gradient of C should be computed backwards. A precise formulation of this idea is the so-called *backpropagation*, established below as an elaborate consequence of the chain rule.

Proposition 27.1 *The gradient of C with respect to the parameters of the neural network has entries*

$$\frac{\partial C}{\partial W_{i,j}^{[\ell]}} = \gamma_i^{[\ell]} x_j^{[\ell-1]}, \qquad \frac{\partial C}{\partial b_i^{[\ell]}} = \gamma_i^{[\ell]}, \qquad \ell \in [1:L+1], \tag{27.3}$$

where the vectors $\gamma^{[1]}, \ldots, \gamma^{[L+1]}$ have entries $\gamma_i^{[\ell]} = \partial C / \partial z_i^{[\ell]}$. They can be computed backwards from $\gamma^{[L+1]} = \nabla \mathrm{Loss}(\cdot, y)$ according to the recursion

$$\gamma^{[\ell-1]} = \phi'(z^{[\ell-1]}) \odot (W^{[\ell]\top} \gamma^{[\ell]}), \qquad \ell \in [2:L+1], \tag{27.4}$$

where $\odot$ denotes the entrywise product.

Proof For $\ell \in [1 : L + 1]$, the identity $z^{[\ell]} = W^{[\ell]} x^{[\ell-1]} + b^{[\ell]}$ yields

$$\frac{\partial C}{\partial W_{i,j}^{[\ell]}} = \sum_k \frac{\partial C}{\partial z_k^{[\ell]}} \times \frac{\partial z_k^{[\ell]}}{\partial W_{i,j}^{[\ell]}} = \frac{\partial C}{\partial z_i^{[\ell]}} \times \frac{\partial z_i^{[\ell]}}{\partial W_{i,j}^{[\ell]}} = \gamma_i^{[\ell]} \times x_j^{[\ell-1]},$$

as well as

$$\frac{\partial C}{\partial b_i^{[\ell]}} = \sum_k \frac{\partial C}{\partial z_k^{[\ell]}} \times \frac{\partial z_k^{[\ell]}}{\partial b_i^{[\ell]}} = \frac{\partial C}{\partial z_i^{[\ell]}} \times \frac{\partial z_i^{[\ell]}}{\partial b_i^{[\ell]}} = \gamma_i^{[\ell]} \times 1 = \gamma_i^{[\ell]},$$

which completely justifies (27.3). To establish (27.4), one exploits the identity $z^{[\ell]} = W^{[\ell]} \phi(z^{[\ell-1]}) + b^{[\ell]}$ written for $\ell \in [2 : L + 1]$ to derive

$$\frac{\partial C}{\partial z_i^{[\ell-1]}} = \sum_k \frac{\partial C}{\partial z_k^{[\ell]}} \frac{\partial z_k^{[\ell]}}{\partial z_i^{[\ell-1]}} = \sum_k \frac{\partial C}{\partial z_k^{[\ell]}} \sum_j W_{k,j}^{[\ell]} \frac{\partial \phi(z_j^{[\ell-1]})}{\partial z_i^{[\ell-1]}} = \sum_k \gamma_k^{[\ell]} W_{k,i}^{[\ell]} \phi'(z_i^{[\ell-1]})$$

$$= \phi'(z_i^{[\ell-1]}) (W^{[\ell]\top} \gamma^{[\ell]})_i,$$

which is indeed (27.4). Finally, in view of the identity $x^{[L+1]} = z^{[L+1]}$, the ith entry of $\gamma^{[L+1]}$ becomes $\gamma_i^{[L+1]} = \partial \mathrm{Loss}(x^{[L+1]}, y)/\partial x_i^{[L+1]}$, i.e., $\gamma^{[L+1]}$ is the gradient of the loss function $\mathrm{Loss}(\cdot, y)$. $\qquad\square$

In order to genuinely compute the gradient of C, one needs two further items. The first item is the gradient of the loss function to initiate the process at $\gamma^{[L+1]}$, e.g. if $\mathrm{Loss}(x^{[L+1]}, y) = \|x^{[L+1]} - y\|_2^2/2$, then $\gamma^{[L+1]} = x^{[L+1]} - y$. The second item is the derivative of the activation function: if ϕ is the *rectified linear unit*, then $\phi'(z^{[\ell-1]})$ is conveniently equal to either zero or one (the nondifferentiability of ReLU at the origin being ignored) and if ϕ is the *logistic sigmoid function*, then $\phi'(z^{[\ell-1]}) = \phi(z^{[\ell-1]})(1 - \phi(z^{[\ell-1]})) = x^{[\ell-1]}(1 - x^{[\ell-1]})$. Note that $x^{[0]}, \ldots, x^{[L]}$ are available after the forward pass through the network that produced $x^{[L+1]}$.

In practice, the stochastic gradient descent strategy outlined above is tuned in several ways. As one example, instead of approximating the gradient of the empirical risk by the gradient of the loss function for a single datapair $(x^{(i)}, y_i)$, one can involve a *minibatch* of several such datapairs. As another example, instead of halfing the stepsize (aka *learning rate*) $\alpha^{(t)}$ at each duration-doubling *epoch*, as considered in Section 19.3, there are several methods[1] aiming for better choices of $\alpha^{(t)}$, which can even become a vector-valued quantity.

27.2 Overparametrized Empirical-Risk Landscapes

One continues to examine the minimization of the empirical risk (27.1), but this time one restricts the function h to be generated by a shallow network with

---

[1] See e.g. Section 8.5 in Goodfellow et al. (2016).

prescribed width n. In other words, with ϕ denoting the activation function, the hypothesis class is made of functions defined for $x \in \mathcal{X} \subseteq \mathbb{R}^d$ by

$$h_p(x) = \sum_{j=1}^{n} c_j \phi(\langle a_j, x \rangle + b_j), \qquad \text{or} \quad h_{c,W}(x) = \sum_{j=1}^{n} c_j \phi(\langle w_j, \widetilde{x} \rangle).$$

Here, the shorthand $\widetilde{x}$ stands for the augmented vector $[x; 1] \in \mathbb{R}^{d+1}$ and the vector $p \in \mathbb{R}^{(d+2)n}$ of parameters decomposes as $p = [c; W]$, where $W \in \mathbb{R}^{(d+1)n}$ contains the $w_j := [a_j; b_j] \in \mathbb{R}^{d+1}$, $j \in [1 : n]$. With such notation, one wishes to minimize over the parameter vector $p \in \mathbb{R}^{(d+2)n}$ the empirical risk now written as

$$\widehat{\text{Risk}}_S(h_p) = \frac{1}{m} \sum_{i=1}^{m} \text{Loss}(h_p(x^{(i)}), y_i). \qquad (27.5)$$

Producing a global minimizer presents some challenge because the objective function is generally nonconvex, even for shallow networks and for convex loss functions. Still, one typically applies a generic gradient descent algorithm in the hope that the output will be a global minimizer. Such a strategy finds a loose justification in the observation below. Without making a connection to the algorithm used, it establishes the existence of a path from any initial choice of parameters to a global minimizer along which the objective function decreases. This implies in particular that there are no strict local minimizers.

Proposition 27.2 *Let a sample $S = ((x^{(1)}, y_1), \ldots, (x^{(m)}, y_m)) \in (\mathbb{R}^d \times \mathbb{R})^m$ with distinct datapoints $x^{(1)}, \ldots, x^{(m)}$ be given. Consider a width $n \geq m$, a nonpolynomial activation function ϕ, and a loss function which is convex in its first variable. Assuming that minimizers of the empirical risk (27.5) exist, for any initial $p^{(0)} \in \mathbb{R}^{(d+2)n}$, there is a continuous map $t \in [0, 1] \rightarrow p(t) \in \mathbb{R}^{(d+2)n}$ starting at $p(0) = p^{(0)}$, ending at one of the minimizers $p(1) = p^{(1)}$, and such that, for $t, t' \in [0, 1]$,*

$$\widehat{\text{Risk}}_S(h_{p(t')}) \leq \widehat{\text{Risk}}_S(h_{p(t)}) \qquad \text{whenever } t \leq t'. \qquad (27.6)$$

Before turning to the proof, one draws attention to the fact that the empirical risk can always be made zero in this overparametrized regime $n \geq m$. The interpolation result below actually says a little more, as the first-layer weights can be chosen independently of the values $y_1, \ldots, y_m \in \mathbb{R}$ to interpolate.

Lemma 27.3 *Let ϕ be a nonpolynomial activation function. Given distinct datapoints $x^{(1)}, \ldots, x^{(m)} \in \mathbb{R}^d$, one can find $a_1, \ldots, a_m \in \mathbb{R}^d$ and $b_1, \ldots, b_m \in \mathbb{R}$ for which, whatever the values $y_1, \ldots, y_m \in \mathbb{R}$, there exist $c_1, \ldots, c_m \in \mathbb{R}$ such that $h = \sum_{j=1}^{m} c_j \phi(\langle a_j, \cdot \rangle + b_j)$ satisfies the interpolatory conditions $h(x^{(i)}) = y_i$, $i \in [1 : m]$.*

Proof The justification for any activation function is left as Exercise 27.2.[2] One concentrates here only on the case $\phi = \text{ReLU}$, for which the argument is constructive (and hence producing an empirical risk minimizer via gradient descent would be uncalled for). One first selects some vector $a \in \mathbb{R}^d$ in such a way that $t_1 := \langle a, x^{(1)} \rangle, \ldots, t_m := \langle a, x^{(m)} \rangle \in \mathbb{R}$ are all distinct, say in intervals $(\tau_1, \tau_2), \ldots, (\tau_m, +\infty)$. It is then possible to find $c_1, \ldots, c_m \in \mathbb{R}$ such that the function $g = \sum_{j=1}^m c_j \text{ReLU}(\cdot - \tau_j)$ satisfies $g(t_1) = y_1, \ldots, g(t_m) = y_m$. The function $h := g(\langle a, \cdot \rangle) = \sum_{j=1}^m c_j \text{ReLU}(\langle a, \cdot \rangle - \tau_j)$ now has the desired form and satisfies $h(x^{(1)}) = y_1, \ldots, h(x^{(m)}) = y_m$, as required. $\square$

Proof of Proposition 27.2 For $w \in \mathbb{R}^{d+1}$, it is convenient to use the notation

$$\varphi_w := [\phi(\langle w, \overline{x}^{(1)} \rangle); \ldots; \phi(\langle w, \overline{x}^{(m)} \rangle)] \in \mathbb{R}^m,$$

allowing one to rephrase Lemma 27.3 as the existence of $w_1, \ldots, w_m \in \mathbb{R}^{d+1}$ such that $(\varphi_{w_1}, \ldots, \varphi_{w_m})$ is a basis for $\mathbb{R}^m$. The required path is constructed in three pieces.

For the first piece, let $J \leq m$ be the maximal number of vectors $\varphi_{w_j^{(0)}}$ that form a linearly independent system. Up to reordering, it can be assumed that $(\varphi_{w_1^{(0)}}, \ldots, \varphi_{w_J^{(0)}})$ is such a maximal linearly independent system. Then, for each $k \in [J+1:N]$, since appending $\varphi_{w_k^{(0)}}$ results in a linearly dependent system, one must have $\varphi_{w_k^{(0)}} = \sum_{j=1}^J M_{j,k} \varphi_{w_j^{(0)}}$. It follows that, for every $i \in [1:m]$,

$$
\begin{aligned}
h_{p^{(0)}}(x^{(i)}) &= \sum_{j=1}^J c_j^{(0)} \phi(\langle w_j^{(0)}, \overline{x}^{(i)} \rangle) + \sum_{k=J+1}^n c_k^{(0)} \left(\sum_{j=1}^J M_{j,k} \phi(\langle w_j^{(0)}, \overline{x}^{(i)} \rangle) \right) \\
&= \sum_{j=1}^J \left(c_j^{(0)} + \sum_{k=J+1}^n M_{j,k} c_k^{(0)} \right) \phi(\langle w_j^{(0)}, \overline{x}^{(i)} \rangle) = \sum_{j=1}^n c_j^{(1/3)} \phi(\langle w_j^{(0)}, \overline{x}^{(i)} \rangle), \quad (27.7)
\end{aligned}
$$

where one has implicitly set $c_j^{(1/3)} = c_j^{(0)} + \sum_{k=J+1}^n M_{j,k} c_k^{(0)}$ for $j \in [1:J]$ and $c_j^{(1/3)} = 0$ for $j \in [J+1:n]$. One now creates the first piece of the path by defining $p(t)$ for $t \in [0, 1/3]$ via $c(t) = (1 - 3t)c^{(0)} + 3t c^{(1/3)}$ and $W(t) = W^{(0)}$. It is clear that $p(0) = p^{(0)}$ and that $p(1/3_-) = [c^{(1/3)}; W^{(0)}]$. One also sees that $\text{Risk}_S(h_{p(t)})$ is constant over $[0, 1/3]$—in fact, this holds for all $h_{p(t)}(x^{(i)})$, $i \in [1:m]$, by virtue of (27.7).

For the second piece, one starts by noticing that the linearly independent system $(\varphi_{w_1^{(0)}}, \ldots, \varphi_{w_J^{(0)}})$, when not already a basis for $\mathbb{R}^m$, can be completed into a still linearly independent system by appending an element from the

---

[2] Full details can be found in Theorem 5.1 of Pinkus (1999).

basis $(\varphi_{w_1}, \ldots, \varphi_{w_m})$. The process can be repeated until one obtains a basis $(\varphi_{w_1^{(2/3)}}, \ldots, \varphi_{w_m^{(2/3)}})$ for $\mathbb{R}^m$ which satisfies $w_j^{(2/3)} = w_j^{(0)}$ for $j \in [1:J]$. One further assigns $w_{m+1}^{(2/3)}, \ldots, w_n^{(2/3)} \in \mathbb{R}^{d+1}$ arbitrarily. One now creates the second piece of the path by defining $p(t)$ for $t \in [1/3, 2/3]$ via $c(t) = c^{(1/3)}$ and $W(t) = (2 - 3t)W^{(0)} + (3t - 1)W^{(2/3)}$. It is clear that $p(1/3_+) = [c^{(1/3)}; W^{(0)}]$, i.e., $p(1/3_+) = p(1/3_-)$, and that $p(2/3_-) = [c^{(1/3)}; W^{(2/3)}]$. One also sees that $\widehat{\mathrm{Risk}}_S(h_{p(t)})$ is constant over $[1/3, 2/3]$—again, this holds for all $h_{p(t)}(x^{(i)})$, $i \in [1:m]$, because the indices j causing a change in $w_j(t)$ come with $c_j(t) = 0$.

For the third piece, pick an empirical risk minimizer $p^* = [c^*; W^*] \in \mathbb{R}^{(d+2)n}$. Expanding each $\varphi_{w_j^*} \in \mathbb{R}^m$, $j \in [1:n]$, on the basis $(\varphi_{w_1^{(2/3)}}, \ldots, \varphi_{w_m^{(2/3)}})$ reads $\varphi_{w_j^*} = \sum_{\ell=1}^m N_{\ell,j} \varphi_{w_\ell^{(2/3)}}$. It follows that, for any $i \in [1:m]$,

$$
h_{p^*}(x^{(i)}) = \sum_{j=1}^n c_j^* \phi(\langle w_j^*, \overline{x}^{(i)} \rangle) = \sum_{j=1}^n c_j^* \left(\sum_{\ell=1}^m N_{\ell,j} \phi(\langle w_\ell^{(2/3)}, \overline{x}^{(i)} \rangle) \right)
$$

$$
= \sum_{\ell=1}^m \left(\sum_{j=1}^n N_{\ell,j} c_j^* \right) \phi(\langle w_\ell^{(2/3)}, \overline{x}^{(i)} \rangle) = \sum_{\ell=1}^n c_\ell^{(1)} \phi(\langle w_\ell^{(2/3)}, \overline{x}^{(i)} \rangle),
$$

where one has implicitly set $c_\ell^{(1)} = \sum_{j=1}^n N_{\ell,j} c_j^*$ for $\ell \in [1:m]$ and $c_\ell^{(1)} = 0$ for $\ell \in [m+1:n]$. Notice then that $p^{(1)} := [c^{(1)}; W^{(2/3)}]$ is also an empirical risk minimizer. One now creates the third piece of the path by defining $p(t)$ for $t \in [2/3, 1]$ via $c(t) = (3 - 3t)c^{(1/3)} + (3t - 2)c^{(1)}$ and $W(t) = W^{(2/3)}$. It is clear that $p(2/3_+) = [c^{(1/3)}; W^{(2/3)}] = p(2/3_-)$ and that $p(1) = p^{(1)}$. It remains to verify that $\widehat{\mathrm{Risk}}_S(h_{p(t)})$ decreases with $t \in [2/3, 1]$. To see this, let $t, t' \in [2/3, 1)$ with $t \leq t'$. Writing $t' = (1 - \tau)t + \tau$ for some $\tau \in [0, 1)$, one has $c(t') = (1 - \tau)c(t) + \tau c^{(1)}$ and, in turn, $h_{p(t')}(x^{(i)}) = (1 - \tau)h_{p(t)}(x^{(i)}) + \tau h_{p^{(1)}}(x^{(i)})$ for each $i \in [1:m]$. Thus, by the convexity of each $\mathrm{Loss}(\cdot, y_i)$, one obtains

$$
\widehat{\mathrm{Risk}}_S(h_{p(t')}) = \frac{1}{m} \sum_{i=1}^m \mathrm{Loss}(h_{p(t')}(x^{(i)}), y_i)
$$

$$
\leq \frac{1}{m} \sum_{i=1}^m \left((1 - \tau) \mathrm{Loss}(h_{p(t)}(x^{(i)}), y_i) + \tau \mathrm{Loss}(h_{p^{(1)}}(x^{(i)}), y_i) \right)
$$

$$
= (1 - \tau) \widehat{\mathrm{Risk}}_S(h_{p(t)}) + \tau \widehat{\mathrm{Risk}}_S(h_{p^{(1)}})
$$

$$
\leq (1 - \tau) \widehat{\mathrm{Risk}}_S(h_{p(t)}) + \tau \widehat{\mathrm{Risk}}_S(h_{p(t')}),
$$

where the fact that $p^{(1)}$ is an empirical risk minimizer was used in the last step. Rearranging this inequality leads to $\widehat{\mathrm{Risk}}_S(h_{p(t')}) \leq \widehat{\mathrm{Risk}}_S(h_{p(t)})$, as announced in (27.6). $\qquad \square$

27.3 Convolutional Neural Networks

This final section offers a brief glance at neural networks training specifically for image recognition, where the task consists in learning the function that takes as input a picture and outputs the object it contains, e.g. a bike or a car. As outlined in Subsection 6.3, this classification problem can be treated as a regression problem by outputting the likelihoods that certain objects are present in the picture. The task was revolutionized by Deep Learning, but the neural networks appearing in practice are not the ones that have been discussed so far. Indeed, the latter were fully connected neural networks, meaning that weights were attached to all possible synapses. However, when dealing with images, it is natural to believe that distant pixels do not cooperate. It is also natural to analyze all patches in a similar fashion. These two principles—*weight locality* and *weight sharing*—impose a specific structure on the first weight matrix $W^{[1]}$, also reproduced for the other weight matrices $W^{[\ell]}$. For simplicity, rather than considering that the inputs of a network are two-dimensional signals (Exercise 27.4 touches this situation), one considers inputs as one-dimensional periodic signals. This simplification leads to weight matrices that are k-banded (because of weight locality) and circulant (because of weight sharing), i.e., to matrices $W \in \mathbb{R}^{n \times n}$ of the form

$$
\begin{bmatrix}
w_0 & w_1 & \cdots & w_k & 0 & \ddots & & \ddots & 0 & w_{-k} & \cdots & w_{-1} \\
w_{-1} & w_0 & w_1 & \cdots & w_k & 0 & \ddots & & \ddots & 0 & \cdots & w_{-2} \\
\ddots & \ddots & \ddots & & \ddots & \ddots & & & & 0 & 0 & \ddots \\
\ddots & \ddots & \ddots & \ddots & & \ddots & & & 0 & 0 & & \ddots \\
0 & w_{-k} & \cdots & w_{-1} & w_0 & w_1 & \cdots & w_k & 0 & \cdots & \ddots & \cdots & 0 \\
0 & 0 & w_{-k} & \cdots & w_{-1} & w_0 & w_1 & \cdots & w_k & 0 & \cdots & \ddots & 0 \\
0 & \cdots & 0 & w_{-k} & \ddots & w_{-1} & w_0 & w_1 & \ddots & w_k & 0 & \cdots & 0 \\
0 & \ddots & \cdots & 0 & w_{-k} & \cdots & w_{-1} & w_0 & w_1 & \cdots & w_k & 0 & 0 \\
0 & \cdots & \ddots & \cdots & 0 & w_{-k} & \cdots & w_{-1} & w_0 & w_1 & \cdots & w_k & 0 \\
\ddots & & 0 & 0 & & \ddots & \ddots & & \ddots & & \ddots & & \ddots \\
\ddots & & 0 & 0 & & & \ddots & & & \ddots & \ddots & & \ddots \\
w_2 & \cdots & 0 & \ddots & & \ddots & 0 & w_{-k} & & w_{-1} & w_0 & w_1 \\
w_1 & \cdots & w_k & 0 & \ddots & & \ddots & 0 & w_{-k} & \cdots & w_{-1} & w_0
\end{bmatrix}.
$$

In terms of training cost, there is, of course, a huge saving owing to the number of parameters involved in the matrix W: there are now only $2k + 1 \leq n$ of them, as opposed to n^2 for full matrices. The term *convolutional neural network* is explained by the fact that the matrix-vector multiplication Wx reduces to the *convolution product* $\omega * x$ between the first row of W and the vector x (both indexed from 0 to $n-1$), as seen from

$$(Wx)_i = \sum_{j=0}^{n-1} W_{i,j} x_j = \sum_{j=0}^{n-1} \omega_{j-i \,(\mathrm{mod}\, n)} x_j = (\omega * x)_i, \qquad i \in [0:n-1].$$

Exercises

27.1 Given $\delta > 0$, the *Huber loss* function is defined for $y, y' \in \mathbb{R}^k$ by

$$\mathrm{Loss}_{\mathrm{Huber}}(y', y) = \begin{cases} \frac{1}{2}\|y' - y\|_2^2 & \text{if } \|y' - y\|_2 \le \delta, \\ \frac{1}{2}\left(2\delta\|y' - y\|_2 - \delta^2\right) & \text{if } \|y' - y\|_2 > \delta. \end{cases}$$

Determine the vector $\gamma^{[L+1]}$ that initiates backpropagation in this case.

27.2 Verify that Lemma 27.3 is indeed valid for any nonpolynomial activation function ϕ, for instance by:

- choosing $a \in \mathbb{R}^d$ such that the $\tau_i := \langle a, x^{(i)} \rangle$ are all distinct;
- remarking that the linear functional $\sum_{i=1}^m \gamma_i \delta_{\tau_i}$, $\gamma \ne (0, \ldots, 0)$, cannot annihilate all $\phi(t \cdot +b)$, $(t, b) \in \mathbb{R}^2$;
- deducing that the functions $f_i \colon (t, b) \in \mathbb{R}^2 \mapsto \phi(t\tau_i + b) \in \mathbb{R}$, $i \in [1:m]$, are linearly independent;
- showing that there are $(t_1, b_1), \ldots, (t_m, b_m) \in \mathbb{R}^2$ such that the vectors $[f_i(t_1, b_1); \ldots; f_i(t_m, b_m)] \in \mathbb{R}^m$, $i \in [1:m]$, are linearly independent;
- and deriving the final result from the observation that the linear map $c \in \mathbb{R}^m \mapsto \sum_{j=1}^m c_j [\phi(t_j\tau_1 + b_j); \ldots; \phi(t_j\tau_m + b_j)] \in \mathbb{R}^m$ is bijective.

27.3 Prove that $A \in \mathbb{C}^{n \times n}$ is a *circulant matrix* (i.e., the entries $A_{k,\ell}$ depend only on $k - \ell \,(\mathrm{mod}\, n)$) if and only if it diagonalizes in Fourier (i.e., there is a diagonal matrix $D \in \mathbb{C}^{n \times n}$ such that $A = FDF^*$, where the discrete Fourier matrix $F \in \mathbb{C}^{n \times n}$ has entries $F_{k,\ell} = \exp(\mathrm{i}2\pi k\ell/m)/\sqrt{m}$).

27.4 When the input x is an image, composed of $(n + 1)^2$ pixels indexed by $i, j \in [0:n]$, the output $y = Wx$ obtained by two-dimensional convolution may be composed of $(n - 1)^2$ pixels indexed by $i, j \in [1:n-1]$ and given by $y_{i,j} = \sum_{k,\ell \in \{-1,0,1\}} w_{i+k,j+\ell} x_{i+k,j+\ell}$. Observe that weight locality and weight sharing are in effect. Identify the matrices C, L, R, D, U in

$$W = w_{1,1} LU + w_{0,1} CU + w_{-1,1} RU + w_{1,0} L + w_{0,0} C + w_{-1,0} R$$
$$+ w_{1,-1} LD + w_{0,-1} CD + w_{-1,-1} RD$$

and verify for instance that $\partial y / \partial w_{1,-1} = LDx$.

APPENDICES

Appendix A

High-Dimensional Geometry

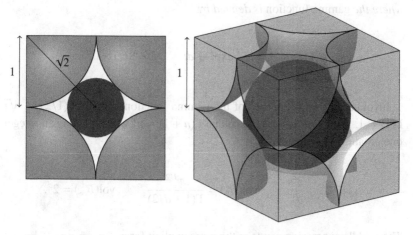

Figure A.1 The largest origin-centered ball avoiding all corner-centered balls.

Geometric intuition acquired in dimension two or three does not generally transpose to higher dimensions. As a first striking example, consider the unit cube $[-1, 1]^d$ in dimension d and consider the 2^d balls of unit radius centered at each of the corners of this cube. The origin is at a distance $\sqrt{d}$ of each of these corners, so it does not belong to the union of these balls. Now examine the largest ball centered at the origin that avoids these balls; see Figure A.1 for illustrations in the cases $d = 2$ and $d = 3$. The radius of this inner ball is $\sqrt{2}-1$ when $d = 2$, $\sqrt{3} - 1$ when $d = 3$, and $\sqrt{d} - 1$ when $d \geq 4$. This implies that the inner ball touches the boundary of the unit cube for $d = 4$ and even sticks out of the unit cube for $d \geq 5$.

A.1 Volumes

A second striking phenomenon is the fact that the gap between the unit ball
and the unit cube takes much of the volume of this cube. Precisely, the ratio
$\mathrm{vol}(B_2^d)/\mathrm{vol}(B_\infty^d)$ of the volume of the unit ball by the volume of the unit cube
decreases exponentially fast when the dimension d goes to infinity, as revealed
by the following volume formulas.

Theorem A.1   *For $p > 0$, the volume of the unit ℓ_p-ball in dimension d is*

$$\mathrm{vol}(B_p^d) = \frac{2^d \Gamma(1 + 1/p)^d}{\Gamma(1 + d/p)},$$

where the gamma function *is defined by*

$$\Gamma(z) = \int_0^\infty t^{z-1} \exp(-t)dt \qquad for \ \mathcal{R}(z) > 0.$$

Invoking known properties of the gamma function, namely $\Gamma(1/2) = \sqrt{\pi}$,
$\Gamma(1) = 1$, and $\Gamma(z + 1) = z\Gamma(z)$, so that $\Gamma(n + 1) = n!$ when $n \geq 0$ is an integer,
one obtains in particular

$$\mathrm{vol}(B_1^d) = \frac{2^d}{d!}, \qquad \mathrm{vol}(B_2^d) = \frac{\pi^{d/2}}{\Gamma(1 + d/2)}, \qquad \mathrm{vol}(B_\infty^d) = 2^d.$$

The middle expression can take the more explicit form

$$\mathrm{vol}(B_2^d) = \begin{cases} \dfrac{\pi^{d/2}}{(d/2)!}, & d \text{ even} \\[2ex] \dfrac{2^d \pi^{(d-1)/2}((d-1)/2)!}{d!}, & d \text{ odd} \end{cases} \sim \frac{1}{\sqrt{\pi d}} \sqrt{\frac{2e\pi}{d}}^{\,d},$$

where *Stirling formula* $n! \sim \sqrt{2\pi n}\,(n/e)^n$ was used in the last step.

Proof of Theorem A.1   Let ξ denote a mean-one exponential random variable.
Let also $B(\tau)$ denote, for each $\tau > 0$, the ℓ_p-ball of radius $\tau^{1/p}$. On the one

hand, expressing the volume as the integral of an indicator function, one has

$$\mathbb{E}[\text{vol}(B(\xi))] = \mathbb{E}\left[\int_{\mathbb{R}^d} \mathbb{1}_{\{(|x_1|^p+\cdots+|x_d|^p)^{1/p}\leq \xi^{1/p}\}} dx_1 \cdots dx_d\right]$$

$$= \int_{\mathbb{R}^d} \mathbb{P}[\xi \geq |x_1|^p + \cdots + |x_d|^p] dx_1 \cdots dx_d$$

$$= \int_{\mathbb{R}^d} \exp\left(-|x_1|^p - \cdots - |x_d|^p\right) dx_1 \cdots dx_d$$

$$= \prod_{k=1}^{d} \int_{-\infty}^{\infty} \exp\left(-|x_k|^p\right) dx_k$$

$$= \prod_{k=1}^{d} 2 \int_{0}^{\infty} \exp\left(-x_k^p\right) dx_k$$

$$= 2^d \Gamma\left(1 + \frac{1}{p}\right)^d, \tag{A.1}$$

where the last step relied on a change of variable to observe that

$$\int_{0}^{\infty} \exp(-x^p) dx = \frac{1}{p} \int_{0}^{\infty} t^{1/p-1} \exp(-t) dt = \frac{1}{p}\Gamma\left(\frac{1}{p}\right) = \Gamma\left(1 + \frac{1}{p}\right).$$

On the other hand, using the positive homogeneity of degree d for the volume in dimension d, one has

$$\mathbb{E}[\text{vol}(B(\xi))] = \mathbb{E}[\xi^{d/p} \text{vol}(B_p^d)] = \text{vol}(B_p^d) \int_{0}^{\infty} t^{d/p} \exp(-t) dt$$

$$= \text{vol}(B_p^d) \Gamma\left(1 + \frac{d}{p}\right). \tag{A.2}$$

Combining (A.1) and (A.2) yields the desired expression for $\text{vol}(B_p^d)$. □

The positive homogeneity for the volume also implies that, for any $\varepsilon > 0$ and any body $B \subseteq \mathbb{R}^d$,

$$\frac{\text{vol}((1-\varepsilon)B)}{\text{vol}(B)} = (1-\varepsilon)^d \leq \exp(-\varepsilon d),$$

which can be interpreted by saying that the volume of a high-dimensional body is concentrated near its surface. In a similar spirit, the surface of the high-dimensional sphere is concentrated near its equator. For instance, the region between latitudes $-\sqrt{3/d}$ and $\sqrt{3/d}$ makes for more than half of the surface of the sphere. This is obtained with $\varepsilon = \arcsin(\sqrt{3/d}) \geq \sqrt{3/d}$ in the formal statement below.

Theorem A.2 *Given $\varepsilon \in (0, 1/\sqrt{2})$, the d-dimensional spherical segment between the hyperplanes $x_d = -\varepsilon$ and $x_d = \varepsilon$ has a normalized surface area equal to at least $1 - 2\exp(-d\varepsilon^2/2)$.*

Proof Figure A.2 gives a geometric explanation of the equivalent statement that the spherical cap $S(\varepsilon) = \{x \in \mathbb{R}^d : x_1^2 + \cdots + x_d^2 = 1$ and $x_d \geq \varepsilon\}$ has a normalized surface area equal to at most $\exp(-d\varepsilon^2/2)$. □

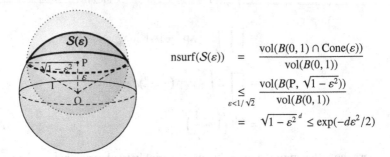

$$
\text{nsurf}(S(\varepsilon)) = \frac{\text{vol}(B(0,1) \cap \text{Cone}(\varepsilon))}{\text{vol}(B(0,1))}
$$

$$
\underset{\varepsilon < 1/\sqrt{2}}{\leq} \frac{\text{vol}(B(\text{P}, \sqrt{1-\varepsilon^2}))}{\text{vol}(B(0,1))}
$$

$$
= \sqrt{1-\varepsilon^2}^{\,d} \leq \exp(-d\varepsilon^2/2)
$$

Figure A.2 For large d, spherical caps $S(\varepsilon)$ have small normalized surface areas.

A.2 Covering and Packing Numbers

A third striking example of the peculiarities of high dimensions concerns the exponential number of directions with pairwise angle equal to at least $\pi/3$, say.

Theorem A.3 *Given $\varepsilon \in (0, 1/\sqrt{2})$, there exist $n = \lfloor \exp(d\varepsilon^2/4) \rfloor$ vectors $a_1, \ldots, a_n$ on the d-dimensional unit sphere that satisfy $|\langle a_i, a_j \rangle| \leq \varepsilon$ for all distinct $i, j \in [1:n]$.*

Proof Let $a_1, \ldots, a_n$ be drawn uniformly at random from the unit sphere. Selecting a pair of distinct indices $i, j \in [1:n]$ and defining the north pole as the position of a_i, one has $\mathbb{P}[|\langle a_i, a_j \rangle| > \varepsilon] \leq 2\exp(-d\varepsilon^2/2)$ as a consequence of Theorem A.2. By a union bound, it follows that

$$
\mathbb{P}[|\langle a_i, a_j \rangle| > \varepsilon \text{ for some } i \neq j \in [1:n]] \leq \binom{n}{2} 2\exp\left(-\frac{d\varepsilon^2}{2}\right)
$$

$$
< n^2 \exp\left(-\frac{d\varepsilon^2}{2}\right) \leq 1.
$$

This means that $|\langle a_i, a_j \rangle| \leq \varepsilon$ occurs for all distinct $i, j \in [1:n]$ with nonzero probability. □

In view of $\|a_i - a_j\|_2^2 = 2 - 2\langle a_i, a_j \rangle$, the previous observation equivalently indicates that there are exponentially many vectors on the d-dimensional unit sphere with pairwise euclidean distance at least equal to 1, say. The following considerations show that there cannot be more, even if noneuclidean distances were considered.

Definition A.4 Given a metric space $(\mathcal{X}, \text{dist})$, points $x_1, \ldots, x_n$ in a set $S \subseteq \mathcal{X}$ are said to form:

- a δ-*net* for S if, for any $x \in S$, $\text{dist}(x, x_i) \leq \delta$ for some $i \in [1:n]$;
- a δ-*separated* subset of S if $\text{dist}(x_i, x_j) > \delta$ for all $i \neq j \in [1:n]$.

The δ-*covering number* $N(S, \delta)$ of S is the smallest cardinality of a δ-net for S and the δ-*packing number* $\mathcal{P}(S, \delta)$ of S is the largest cardinality of a δ-separated subset of S.

The covering and packing numbers are closely tied to one another via

$$\mathcal{P}(S, 2\delta) \leq N(S, \delta) \leq \mathcal{P}(S, \delta).$$

To see the leftmost inequality, with $\{x_1, \ldots, x_n\}$ denoting a minimal δ-net, notice that no set $\{x_1', \ldots, x_p'\}$ with $p > n$ can be 2δ-separated, since there must exist a ball $B(x_k, \delta)$ containing two distinct points x_i' and x_j', implying that $\text{dist}(x_i', x_j') \leq 2\delta$. To see the rightmost inequality, notice that a maximal δ-separated set must be a δ-net, otherwise it would be possible to add a point to it while maintaining δ-separation.

There is a simple estimate for the covering number—in fact, for the packing number—that proves useful in many situations.

Theorem A.5 *If S is a subset of the unit ball in $\mathbb{R}^d$ relative to an arbitrary norm, then*

$$N(S, \delta) \leq \mathcal{P}(S, \delta) \leq \left(1 + \frac{2}{\delta}\right)^d. \tag{A.3}$$

Proof Let $\{x_1, \ldots, x_n\}$ be a δ-separated subset of S relative to the norm under consideration. Observing that the balls $B(x_1, \delta/2), \ldots, B(x_n, \delta/2)$ are disjoint and contained in $B(0, 1 + \delta/2)$, one has

$$\sum_{i=1}^{n} \text{vol}\,(B(x_i, \delta/2)) = \text{vol}\left(\bigcup_{i=1}^{n} B(x_i, \delta/2)\right) \leq \text{vol}\,(B(0, 1 + \delta/2)).$$

Using the translation invariance and the positive homogeneity of degree d for the volume, this reads

$$n\left(\frac{\delta}{2}\right)^d \text{vol}\,(B(0, 1)) \leq \left(1 + \frac{\delta}{2}\right)^d \text{vol}\,(B(0, 1)).$$

Eliminating $\mathrm{vol}\,(B(0,1)) > 0$ and rearranging yields $n \le (2/\delta + 1)^d$, which is the announced result. $\qquad\square$

Two consequences are of particular importance, notably in PART THREE on Compressive Sensing . The first consequence deals with sparse vectors.

Lemma A.6 *If S is the subset of $\mathbb{R}^N$ consisting of ℓ_2-normalized s-sparse vectors, then*

$$N(S,\delta) \le \binom{N}{s}\left(1 + \frac{2}{\delta}\right)^s \le \exp\left(s\ln\left(\frac{eN}{s}\right) + \frac{2s}{\delta}\right).$$

Proof For each index set $S \subseteq [1:N]$ of size s, let $\{x_1^S, \ldots, x_{n(S)}^S\}$ denote a δ-net for the unit sphere of the space $\{x \in \mathbb{R}^N : \mathrm{supp}(x) \subseteq S\}$ relative to the ℓ_2-norm. Since this space is identifiable with $\mathbb{R}^s$, Theorem A.5 guarantees that one can take $n(S) \le (1 + 2/\delta)^s$. Now, given an ℓ_2-normalized s-sparse vector $x \in \mathbb{R}^N$, if S denotes its support, then there is some $i \in [1:n(S)]$ such that $\|x - x_i^S\|_2 \le \delta$. This shows that a δ-net for S is provided by the set $\cup_{|S|=s}\{x_1^S, \ldots, x_{n(S)}^S\}$, which has cardinality at most $\binom{N}{s}(1 + 2/\delta)^s$, and hence proves the leftmost inequality in (A.3). The rightmost inequality simply reflects the facts that $\binom{N}{s} \le (eN/s)^s$ and that $1 + 2/\delta \le \exp(2/\delta)$. $\qquad\square$

Remark A.7 As apparent in the proof, for any ℓ_2-normalized s-sparse vector $x \in \mathbb{R}^N$, an element x_k from the δ-net satisfying $\|x - x_k\|_2 \le \delta$ can be chosen with $\mathrm{supp}(x_k)$ and $\mathrm{supp}(x)$ both included in a common index set S of size s, so that $x - x_k$ is s-sparse rather than simply $2s$-sparse.

The second consequence of Theorem A.5 deals with low-rank matrices.

Lemma A.8 *If S is the subset of $\mathbb{R}^{n \times n}$ consisting of Frobenius-normalized matrices of rank at most r, then*

$$N(S,\delta) \le \left(1 + \frac{6}{\delta}\right)^{(2n+1)r}.$$

Proof With $K \le (1 + 6/\delta)^r$, consider a $(\delta/3)$-net $\{x_1, \ldots, x_K\}$ for the unit sphere of $\mathbb{R}^r$ relative to the ℓ_2-norm. With $L \le (1 + 6/\delta)^{nr}$, consider also a $(\delta/3)$-net $\{W_1, \ldots, W_L\}$ for the subset $\{W \in \mathbb{R}^{n \times r} : W^\top W = I_r\}$ of the sphere of $\mathbb{R}^{n \times r}$ relative to the norm given for $W = \begin{bmatrix} W_1|\cdots|W_r \end{bmatrix} \in \mathbb{R}^{n \times r}$ by

$$\|W\|_{1 \to 2} = \max_{j \in [1:r]} \|W_j\|_2.$$

The coveted δ-net for S consists of all matrices $\widetilde{X} = \widetilde{U}\,\mathrm{diag}[\widetilde{x}]\widetilde{V}^\top \in S$, where $\widetilde{x}$ is chosen from $\{x_1, \ldots, x_K\}$ and $\widetilde{U}, \widetilde{V}$ are chosen from $\{W_1, \ldots, W_L\}$. Since this set has cardinality $KL^2 \le (1 + 6/\delta)^{(2n+1)r}$, it remains to verify that, for any

$X \in S$, i.e., $X \in \mathbb{R}^{n \times n}$ with $\|X\|_F = 1$ and $\text{rank}(X) \leq r$, one has $\|X - \widetilde{X}\|_F \leq \delta$ for some matrix $\widetilde{X}$ of the above form. To verify this, write the singular value decomposition of X as $X = U \text{diag}[x]V^\top$, with $x \in \mathbb{R}^r$ satisfying $\|x\|_2 = 1$ and $U, V \in \mathbb{R}^{n \times r}$ satisfying $U^\top U = I_r$ and $V^\top V = I_r$. Selecting $\widetilde{x} \in \mathbb{R}^r$ from $\{x_1, \ldots, x_K\}$ such that $\|x - \widetilde{x}\|_2 = \delta/3$, as well as $\widetilde{U}, \widetilde{V}$ from $\{W_1, \ldots, W_L\}$ such that $\|U - \widetilde{U}\|_{1 \to 2} \leq \delta/3$ and $\|V - \widetilde{V}\|_{1 \to 2} \leq \delta/3$, one defines $\widetilde{X} = \widetilde{U} \text{diag}[\widetilde{x}]\widetilde{V}^\top$ and writes $X - \widetilde{X}$ as

$$U\text{diag}[x](V^\top - \widetilde{V}^\top) + U(\text{diag}[x] - \text{diag}[\widetilde{x}])\widetilde{V}^\top + (U - \widetilde{U})\text{diag}[\widetilde{x}]\widetilde{V}^\top. \quad (A.4)$$

The middle term of (A.4) is bounded in the Frobenius norm via

$$\|U(\text{diag}[x] - \text{diag}[\widetilde{x}])\widetilde{V}^\top\|_F = \|(\text{diag}[x] - \text{diag}[\widetilde{x}])\|_F = \|x - \widetilde{x}\|_2 \leq \frac{\delta}{3}.$$

The rightmost term of (A.4) is bounded in the Frobenius norm via

$$\|(U - \widetilde{U})\text{diag}[\widetilde{x}]\widetilde{V}^\top\|_F^2 = \|(U - \widetilde{U})\text{diag}[\widetilde{x}]\|_F^2 = \sum_{j=1}^{r} \widetilde{x}_j^2 \|U_j - \widetilde{U}_j\|_2^2$$

$$\leq \sum_{j=1}^{r} \widetilde{x}_j^2 \|U - \widetilde{U}\|_{1 \to 2}^2 \leq \left(\frac{\delta}{3}\right)^2,$$

so that $\|(U - \widetilde{U})\text{diag}[\widetilde{x}]\widetilde{V}^\top\|_F \leq \delta/3$. As for the leftmost term of (A.4), one obtains in a similar fashion $\|U\text{diag}[x](V^\top - \widetilde{V}^\top)\|_F \leq \delta/3$. Finally, a triangular inequality in (A.4) yields $\|X - \widetilde{X}\|_F \leq (\delta/3) + (\delta/3) + (\delta/3) = \delta$, as expected. $\quad \square$

A.3 Projected Cross-Polytope

This final section highlights a fourth striking phenomenon occurring in high dimension, with connection to the theory of Compressive Sensing. As a starting point, consider the low-dimensional situation and imagine that a polyhedron is drawn on paper: effectively, one projects a three-dimensional polytope onto a two-dimensional space. There will be some hidden edges—these are not edges of the projected polytope. But in higher dimensions, all edges, and more generally all k-faces with small enough k, can survive projection, at least for the ℓ_1-ball (aka *cross polytope*). More surprisingly, the value of k is actually not that small: when projecting from $\mathbb{R}^N$ to $\mathbb{R}^m$, all k-faces can survive with $k \asymp m/\ln(eN/m)$. This phenomenon is related to the fact that all s-sparse vectors $x \in \mathbb{R}^N$ can be recovered from $Ax \in \mathbb{R}^m$ via ℓ_1-minimization when $s \asymp m/\ln(eN/m)$; see Chapter 14. The following result makes the relation precise.

Theorem A.9 *For $A \in \mathbb{R}^{m \times N}$, the following properties are equivalent:*

(i) *for all $k \in [0:s-1]$, every k-face of B_1^N is mapped to a k-face of $A(B_1^N)$;*
(ii) *every $x \in \Sigma_s^N$ is the unique minimizer of $\|z\|_1$ subject to $Az = Ax$.*

Proof (i)$\Rightarrow$(ii). Let $x \in \Sigma_s^N$ and let $z \in \mathbb{R}^N$, $z \neq x$, such that $Az = Ax$. The goal is to prove that $\|z\|_1 > \|x\|_1$. This being clear when $x = 0$, one assumes without loss of generality that $\|x\|_1 = 1$, so that $x \in B_1^N$. In fact, with $S := \operatorname{supp}(x)$ and $k := |S| - 1 \in [0:s-1]$, the vector x belongs to the k-face of B_1^N given by $\mathcal{F} = \operatorname{conv}\{\operatorname{sgn}(x_j)e_j, j \in S\}$. Since $A(\mathcal{F})$ is a face of $A(B_1^N)$, there exists $h \in \mathbb{R}^m$ such that, for all $y \in A(B_1^N)$, $\langle h, y \rangle \leq 1$ with equality if and only if $y \in A(\mathcal{F})$. In particular, for any $j \in [1:N]$, the fact that $A(\varepsilon e_j) \in A(B_1^N)$ for $\varepsilon = \pm 1$ yields $1 \geq \langle h, A(\varepsilon e_j) \rangle = \varepsilon(A^\top h)_j$, hence $|(A^\top h)_j| \leq 1$. It follows that

$$\|z\|_1 = \sum_{j=1}^N |z_j| \geq \sum_{j=1}^N (A^\top h)_j z_j = \langle A^\top h, z \rangle = \langle h, Az \rangle = \langle h, Ax \rangle = 1. \tag{A.5}$$

Suppose now that equality occurs in (A.5), i.e., that $|z_j| = (A^\top h)_j z_j$ for all $j \in [1:N]$. For $j \notin S$ and for $\varepsilon = \pm 1$, notice that $A(\varepsilon e_j)$, as a 0-face—in other words, as an extreme point—of $A(B_1^N)$, cannot belong to $A(\mathcal{F})$, which implies that $1 > \langle h, A(\varepsilon e_j) \rangle = \varepsilon(A^\top h)_j$, hence $|(A^\top h)_j| < 1$. Consequently, for $|z_j| = (A^\top h)_j z_j$ to hold, one must have $z_j = 0$ for all $j \notin S$, meaning that z is supported on S. For $j \in S$, notice that $A(\operatorname{sgn}(x_j)e_j) \in A(\mathcal{F})$, which implies that $1 = \langle h, A(\operatorname{sgn}(x_j)e_j) \rangle = \operatorname{sgn}(x_j)(A^\top h)_j$, hence $(A^\top h)_j = \operatorname{sgn}(x_j)$. One derives that the nonzero vector $u \in \mathbb{R}^S$ with entries $u_j := |z_j| - |x_j| = \operatorname{sgn}(x_j)(z_j - x_j)$ satisfies $\sum_{j \in S} u_j = \|z\|_1 - \|x\|_1 = 0$ and $\sum_{j \in S} u_j \operatorname{sgn}(x_j)Ae_j = Az - Ax = 0$. These observations indicate that the linear map f defined on the k-dimensional space $\{v \in \mathbb{R}^S : \sum_{j \in S} v_j = 0\}$ by $f(v) = \sum_{j \in S} v_j \operatorname{sgn}(x_j)Ae_j$ is not injective, so its range W has a dimension smaller than k. But this contradicts the fact that $A(\mathcal{F})$, whose affine hull is $Ax + W$, has an affine dimension equal to k. One concludes that equality does not occur in (A.5), i.e., the goal $\|z\|_1 > \|x\|_1$ is achieved.

(ii)$\Rightarrow$(i). Given $k \in [1:s-1]$, consider a k-face $\mathcal{F}$ of B_1^N. It can be written as $\mathcal{F} = \operatorname{conv}\{\varepsilon_j e_j, j \in S\}$ for some $S \subseteq [1:N]$ with $|S| = k+1$ and $\varepsilon \in \{-1, +1\}^S$. According to the *null space property* of order s (see Theorem 14.2), one has $\|v_S\|_1 < \|v_{S^c}\|_1$ for all $v \in \ker(A) \setminus \{0\}$. A compactness argument then ensures the existence of $\rho < 1$ such that $\|v_S\|_1 \leq \rho\|v_{S^c}\|_1$ for all $v \in \ker(A)$. One introduces the convex set

$$C := \{z \in \mathbb{R}^N : \|z_S\|_1 + \rho\|z_{S^c}\|_1 \leq 1\}$$

and notices that any $x \in \mathcal{F}$—e.g. $x = \sum_{j \in S} (\varepsilon_j/k)e_j$—belongs to C. One further notices that Ax is a boundary point of $A(C)$: indeed, the contrary would imply that there exists $t > 0$ such that $(1+t)Ax \in A(C)$, so that $v := (1+t)x-z \in \ker(A)$ for some $z \in C$, but then a contradiction would follow from

$$1 + t = \|(1 + t)x\|_1 = \|z_S + v_S\|_1 \le \|z_S\|_1 + \|v_S\|_1 \le \|z_S\|_1 + \rho\|v_{S^c}\|_1$$
$$= \|z_S\|_1 + \rho\|z_{S^c}\|_1 \le 1.$$

Therefore, by the *supporting hyperplane theorem* (Theorem C.8), one can find $h \in \mathbb{R}^m$ such that $\langle h, y \rangle \le \langle h, Ax \rangle = 1$ for all $y \in A(C)$. For $j \notin S$, taking $y = A((\varepsilon/\rho)e_j)$ with $\varepsilon = \pm 1$ yields $|(A^\top h)_j| \le \rho$. For $j \in S$, taking $y = A(\varepsilon e_j)$ with $\varepsilon = \pm 1$ yields $|(A^\top h)_j| \le 1$. In fact, in view of

$$1 = \langle h, Ax \rangle = \Big\langle A^\top h, \sum_{j \in S}(\varepsilon_j/k)e_j \Big\rangle = \sum_{j \in S}(\varepsilon_j/k)(A^\top h)_j \le \sum_{j \in S}(1/k) = 1,$$

one deduces that $(A^\top h)_j = \varepsilon_j$ for all $j \in S$. Now, given $y \in A(B_1^N)$ written as $y = Az$ for $z \in B_1^N$, one has

$$\langle h, y \rangle = \langle A^\top h, z \rangle = \sum_{j \in S}\varepsilon_j z_j + \sum_{j \notin S}(A^\top h)_j z_j \le \sum_{j \in S}|z_j| + \sum_{j \notin S}|z_j| = \|z\|_1 \le 1.$$

Equality occurs if and only if $\|z\|_1 = 1$, $z_j = 0$ for $j \notin S$, and $|z_j| = \varepsilon_j z_j$ for $j \in S$, i.e., if and only if $z \in \text{conv}\{\varepsilon_j e_j, j \in S\} = \mathcal{F}$. In short, for $y \in A(B_1^N)$, one has $\langle h, y \rangle \le 1$ with equality if and only if $y \in A(\mathcal{F})$. This means that $A(\mathcal{F})$ is a face of $A(B_1^N)$. It is a k-face because its affine hull takes the form $Ax + W$ for some linear space W of dimension k. Precisely, the space W is the range of the linear map f defined on the k-dimensional space $\{v \in \mathbb{R}^S : \sum_{j \in S} v_j = 0\}$ by $f(v) = \sum_{j \in S} v_j \, \text{sgn}(x_j)Ae_j$. Since this map is injective (as a consequence of the null space property), its range indeed has dimension k. $\qquad\square$

Exercises

A.1 Find the integer $d \ge 1$ that maximizes the volume of the d-dimensional unit euclidean ball.

A.2 For $p_1, \ldots, p_d > 0$ and $t > 0$, prove that the set

$$B^d_{p_1,\ldots,p_d}(t) = \{x \in \mathbb{R}^d : |x_1|^{p_1} + \cdots + |x_d|^{p_d} \le t\}$$

has a volume given by

$$\text{vol}\,(B^d_{p_1,\ldots,p_d}(t)) = \frac{2^d \Gamma(1 + 1/p_1) \cdots \Gamma(1 + 1/p_d)}{\Gamma(1 + 1/p_1 + \cdots + 1/p_d)} t^{1/p_1 + \cdots + 1/p_d}.$$

A.3 Establish that the surface areas of ℓ_1-, ℓ_2-, and ℓ_∞-balls are

$$\mathrm{surf}\,(B_1^d) = \frac{2^d \sqrt{d}}{(d-1)!}, \qquad \mathrm{surf}\,(B_2^d) = \frac{2\pi^{d/2}}{\Gamma(d/2)}, \qquad \mathrm{surf}\,(B_\infty^d) = d\,2^d.$$

A.4 The *Kashin decomposition theorem* is another striking result connected to Compressive Sensing. With $d = 2m$, it states that the space $\mathbb{R}^d$ can be decomposed as the orthogonal sum of two m-dimensional subspaces on each of which the ℓ_1-norm and ℓ_2-norm are comparable. Establish this result based on the following steps:

- given a matrix $G \in \mathbb{R}^{m \times m}$, defining $A, B \in \mathbb{R}^{m \times d}$ by $A = [I_m \,|\, G]$ and $B = [G^\top \,|\, -I_m]$, observe that $\ker(A)$ and $\ker(B)$ are two orthogonal m-dimensional spaces;
- now let $G \in \mathbb{R}^{m \times m}$ be a random matrix populated by independent $\mathcal{N}(0, 1/m)$ entries, take for granted (or prove along the same lines as Exercise B.3) that with nonzero probability the matrices $M = A$ and $M = B$ satisfy an ℓ_2-restricted isometry property of order $s = cm$ with fixed constant $\delta \in (0, 1)$, namely

$$(1 - \delta)\|z\|_2^2 \le \|Mz\|_2^2 \le (1 + \delta)\|z\|_2^2 \qquad \text{for all } z \in \Sigma_s^N;$$

- exploit the *sort-and-split technique* to show that $\|x\|_2 \le C\|x\|_1 / \sqrt{m}$ whenever $x \in \ker(A)$ or $x \in \ker(B)$;
- conclude.

Appendix B
Probability Theory

In this appendix, some probabilistic tools of absolute necessity for PART ONE and PART THREE—concentration inequalities in particular—are introduced. Readers can consult the books by Boucheron et al. (2013) and Buldygin and Kozachenko (2000) for supplementary material.

B.1 Tails and Moment Generating Functions

A crucial relation between the expectation of a nonnegative random variable Z and its *tails* $P[Z > z]$ is

$$\mathbb{E}[Z] = \int_0^\infty \mathbb{P}[Z > z]dz. \tag{B.1}$$

From there, one can easily derive the *Markov inequality*, an upper estimate for the tail of a nonnegative random variable in terms of its expectation.

Lemma B.1 *If Z is a nonnegative random variable, then*

$$\mathbb{P}[Z > t] \leq \frac{\mathbb{E}[Z]}{t} \qquad \text{for all } t \in (0, \infty). \tag{B.2}$$

Proof Given $t > 0$, invoke (B.1) to write

$$\mathbb{E}[Z] = \int_0^\infty \mathbb{P}[Z > z]dz \geq \int_0^t \mathbb{P}[Z > z]dz \geq \int_0^t \mathbb{P}[Z > t]dz$$
$$= t\,\mathbb{P}[Z > t],$$

which is just a rearrangement of (B.2). □

One can also derive a lower estimate for the tail of a bounded nonnegative random variable in terms of its expectation.

Lemma B.2 *If Z is a random variable with values in $[0, 1]$, then*

$$\mathbb{P}[Z > t] \geq \frac{\mathbb{E}[Z] - t}{1 - t} \qquad \text{for all } t \in (0, 1). \tag{B.3}$$

Proof The argument relies on (B.1) in the same spirit as above. Namely, given $t \in (0, 1)$, write

$$\mathbb{E}[Z] = \int_0^1 \mathbb{P}[Z > z]dz = \int_0^t \mathbb{P}[Z > z]dz + \int_t^1 \mathbb{P}[Z > z]dz$$

$$\leq \int_0^t 1dz + \int_t^1 \mathbb{P}[Z > t]dz = t + (1 - t)\mathbb{P}[Z > t].$$

This is just a rearrangement of (B.3).   □

Tails can be lower-bounded even if the nonnegative random variable is not bounded, as revealed by the *Paley–Zygmund inequality* below. The proof is left as Exercise B.1.

Lemma B.3 *If Z is a nonnegative random variable possessing a finite second moment $\mathbb{E}[Z^2]$, then*

$$\mathbb{P}[Z > t] \geq \frac{(\mathbb{E}[Z] - t)^2}{\mathbb{E}[Z^2]} \qquad \text{for all } t \in (0, \mathbb{E}[Z]). \tag{B.4}$$

For a random variable X, the function

$$t \mapsto \mathbb{E}[\exp(tX)] = \sum_{k=0}^{\infty} \frac{\mathbb{E}[X^k]}{k!} t^k$$

is called the *moment generating function*. The name originates from the fact that its knowledge is equivalent to the knowledge of all the moments $\mathbb{E}[X^k]$, $k \geq 0$. For instance, if $g \sim \mathcal{N}(0, 1)$ is a standard gaussian random variable, then

$$\mathbb{E}[\exp(tg)] = \exp\left(\frac{t^2}{2}\right), \qquad t \in \mathbb{R},$$

which yields the values of the even moments $\mathbb{E}[g^{2k}] = (2k)!/(2^k k!)$, $k \geq 0$. These values can be used to determine the moment generating function of the square of a standard gaussian random variable, which is

$$\mathbb{E}[\exp(tg^2)] = \frac{1}{\sqrt{1 - 2t}}, \qquad |t| < \frac{1}{2}. \tag{B.5}$$

An estimate for the moment generating function of the absolute value of a standard gaussian random variable will also turn out to be useful later.

Lemma B.4 *If $g \sim \mathcal{N}(0, 1)$ is a standard gaussian random variable, then*

$$\mathbb{E}[\exp(t|g|)] \leq \left(1 + \sqrt{\frac{2}{\pi}}t\right)\exp\left(\frac{t^2}{2}\right), \qquad t \in \mathbb{R}.$$

Proof The argument, technical but elementary, consists of the following steps:

$$\mathbb{E}[\exp(t|g|)] = \int_{-\infty}^{\infty} \exp(t|u|)\frac{\exp(-u^2/2)}{\sqrt{2\pi}}du$$

$$= \sqrt{\frac{2}{\pi}}\int_0^{\infty} \exp\left(tu - \frac{u^2}{2}\right)du$$

$$= \sqrt{\frac{2}{\pi}}\int_0^{\infty} \exp\left(-\frac{(u-t)^2}{2} + \frac{t^2}{2}\right)du$$

$$= \sqrt{\frac{2}{\pi}}\left(\int_{-t}^{\infty} \exp\left(-\frac{v^2}{2}\right)dv\right)\exp\left(\frac{t^2}{2}\right)$$

$$\leq \sqrt{\frac{2}{\pi}}\left(\int_{-t}^0 1\,dv + \int_0^{\infty} \exp\left(-\frac{v^2}{2}\right)dv\right)\exp\left(\frac{t^2}{2}\right)$$

$$= \sqrt{\frac{2}{\pi}}\left(t + \sqrt{\frac{\pi}{2}}\right)\exp\left(\frac{t^2}{2}\right),$$

which clearly simplifies to the announced upper bound. □

The moment generating function provides a convenient way to define *subgaussian random variables*. Namely, a random variable X is called subgaussian if there is some $c > 0$ such that

$$\mathbb{E}[\exp(tX)] \leq \exp\left(\frac{c^2t^2}{2}\right), \qquad t \in \mathbb{R}. \tag{B.6}$$

The smallest such $c > 0$ is sometimes called the *subgaussian standard* and is denoted as $\tau = \tau(X)$. Note that if X is subgaussian according to (B.6), then $\mathbb{E}[X] = 0$ and $\mathbb{E}[X^2] \leq \tau^2$. When $\mathbb{E}[X^2] = \tau^2$—i.e., when standard deviation and subgaussian standard coincide—one talks about *strictly subgaussian random variables*.

The expectation of the maximum of subgaussian random variables can be estimated using moment generating functions as follows.

Proposition B.5 *Let $X_1, \ldots, X_n$ be subgaussian random variables with subgaussian standard of at most τ. Then*

$$\mathbb{E}\left[\max_{i\in[1:n]} X_i\right] \leq \tau\sqrt{2\ln(n)}, \tag{B.7}$$

$$\mathbb{E}\left[\max_{i\in[1:n]} |X_i|\right] \leq \tau\sqrt{2\ln(2n)}. \tag{B.8}$$

Proof With $t > 0$ to be chosen later, one bounds the maximum by the *soft maximum* as follows:

$$t \max_{i \in [1:n]} X_i = \max_{i \in [1:n]} (tX_i) \le \ln \left(\exp(tX_1) + \cdots + \exp(tX_n) \right).$$

Taking the expectation and making use of the Jensen inequality yields

$$t\mathbb{E}\left[\max_{i \in [1:n]} X_i \right] \le \ln \left(\mathbb{E}[\exp(tX_1)] + \cdots + \mathbb{E}[\exp(tX_n)] \right) \le \ln \left(n \exp \left(\frac{\tau^2 t^2}{2} \right) \right).$$

Therefore, one arrives at

$$\mathbb{E}\left[\max_{i \in [1:n]} X_i \right] \le \frac{\ln(n)}{t} + \frac{\tau^2 t}{2} \le \tau \sqrt{2 \ln(n)},$$

where the optimal choice $t = \sqrt{2 \ln(n)}/\tau$ was made in the last step. This is the inequality (B.7). The inequality (B.8) is obtained by applying (B.7) to $X_1, \ldots, X_n, -X_1, \ldots, -X_n$.   □

B.2 Concentration Inequalities

The objective here is to establish the concentration inequalities of Hoeffding and of McDiarmid. The *Hoeffding inequality*, which is actually a consequence of the McDiarmid inequality, reads as follows.

Theorem B.6 *If $X_1, \ldots, X_n$ are independent random variables taking values in $[a_1, b_1], \ldots, [a_n, b_n]$, then*

$$\mathbb{P}\left[\frac{X_1 + \cdots + X_n}{n} - \mathrm{E} > \varepsilon \right] \le \exp \left(\frac{-2\varepsilon^2 n}{c^2} \right),$$

$$\mathbb{P}\left[\left| \frac{X_1 + \cdots + X_n}{n} - \mathrm{E} \right| > \varepsilon \right] \le 2 \exp \left(\frac{-2\varepsilon^2 n}{c^2} \right),$$

where $\mathrm{E} := \mathbb{E}[X_1 + \cdots + X_n]/n$ and $c^2 := ((b_1 - a_1)^2 + \cdots + (b_n - a_n)^2)/n$.

The argument starts by estimating the moment generating function of a bounded mean-zero random variable. This is the so-called *Hoeffding lemma*.

Lemma B.7 *A mean-zero random variable X taking values in $[a, b]$ has a moment generating function satisfying*

$$\mathbb{E}[\exp(tX)] \le \exp \left(\frac{(b-a)^2}{8} t^2 \right), \qquad t \in \mathbb{R}.$$

Proof Observe first that any $x \in [a, b]$ is a convex combination of the endpoints a and b, precisely

$$x = \frac{b - x}{b - a} a + \frac{x - a}{b - a} b.$$

Writing this for the random variable X, multiplying throughout by $t \in \mathbb{R}$, and applying the exponential function, which is convex, one derives that

$$\exp(tX) \le \frac{b - X}{b - a} \exp(at) + \frac{X - a}{b - a} \exp(bt).$$

Setting $u := (b - a)t$ and $c := -a/(b - a)$—which belongs to $[0, 1]$ since $\mathbb{E}[X] = 0$ imposes $a \le 0 \le b$—and taking the expectation gives

$$\mathbb{E}[\exp(tX)] \le \frac{b}{b - a} \exp(at) + \frac{-a}{b - a} \exp(bt) = \exp(at)[1 - c + c\exp((b - a)t)]$$

$$= \exp(-cu)[1 - c + c\exp(u)] =: \exp(f_c(u)). \tag{B.9}$$

The function f_c defined by $f_c(x) := -cx + \ln(1 - c + c\exp(x))$ satisfies $f_c(0) = 0$, as well as

$$f_c'(x) = -c + \frac{c\exp(x)}{1 - c + c\exp(x)}, \qquad \text{so that } f_c'(0) = 0,$$

$$f_c''(x) = \frac{(1 - c)c\exp(x)}{(1 - c + c\exp(x))^2}, \qquad \text{so that } f_c''(x) \le \frac{1}{4}.$$

Since $f_c(u) = f_c(0) + f_c'(0)u + f_c''(\xi)u^2/2 = f_c''(\xi)u^2/2$ for some $\xi \in \mathbb{R}$, one has $f_c(u) \le u^2/8$. Substituting the latter into (B.9) yields the desired result. $\square$

As an extension of the Hoeffding lemma, the moment generating function of a quantity depending on several random variables can be bounded as follows.

Lemma B.8 *Let F be an n-variate function and $c_1, \ldots, c_n > 0$ be such that, for all $i \in [1 : n]$ and for all $x_1, \ldots, x_{i-1}, x_i, x_i', x_{i+1}, \ldots, x_n$,*

$$|F(\ldots, x_{i-1}, x_i, x_{i+1}, \ldots) - F(\ldots, x_{i-1}, x_i', x_{i+1}, \ldots)| \le c_i. \tag{B.10}$$

If $X_1, \ldots, X_n$ are independent random variables and $\mathrm{E} := \mathbb{E}[F(X_1, \ldots, X_n)]$, then

$$\mathbb{E}[\exp(t\{F(X_1, \ldots, X_n) - \mathrm{E}\})] \le \exp\left(\frac{\sum_{i=1}^n c_i^2}{8} t^2\right).$$

Proof One proceeds by induction on $n \ge 1$. For $n = 1$, Condition (B.10) reads $|F(x) - F(x')| \le c$ for all x, x', implying that $F(X_1) - \mathrm{E}$ is contained in an interval $[a, b]$ of length $b - a = c$. The base case is then just an application of the *Hoeffding lemma* (Lemma B.7) to the mean-zero random variable $F(X_1) - \mathrm{E}$. Supposing now that the induction hypothesis holds up to an integer $n - 1 \ge 1$, one needs to prove that it holds for n as well. Given an n-variate function F satisfying Condition (B.10), one first remarks that the univariate function $F_{x_1,\ldots,x_{n-1}}$ and the $(n-1)$-variate function $\widetilde{F}$ defined by

$$F_{x_1,\ldots,x_{n-1}}(x) := F(x_1,\ldots,x_{n-1},x),$$

$$\widetilde{F}(x_1,\ldots,x_{n-1}) := \mathbb{E}_{X_n} F(x_1,\ldots,x_{n-1},X_n)$$

also satisfy conditions analog to (B.10). So, by the induction hypothesis,

$$\mathbb{E}[\exp(t\{F_{x_1,\ldots,x_{n-1}}(X_n) - \mathbb{E}_{x_1,\ldots,x_n}\})] \le \exp\left(\frac{c_n^2 t^2}{8}\right), \tag{B.11}$$

with $\mathbb{E}_{x_1,\ldots,x_{n-1}} := \mathbb{E}_{X_n}[F_{x_1,\ldots,x_{n-1}}(X_n)]$, as well as

$$\mathbb{E}[\exp(t\{\widetilde{F}(X_1,\ldots,X_{n-1}) - E\})] \le \exp\left(\frac{\sum_{i=1}^{n-1} c_i^2 t^2}{8}\right), \tag{B.12}$$

since $\mathbb{E}[\widetilde{F}(X_1,\ldots,X_{n-1})] = \mathbb{E}[F(X_1,\ldots,X_n)] = E$. Now, noticing that

$$\mathbb{E}_{X_1,\ldots,X_{n-1}} = \mathbb{E}_{X_n}[F(X_1,\ldots,X_{n-1},X_n)] = \widetilde{F}(X_1,\ldots,X_{n-1}),$$

one can write

$$\exp(t\{F(X_1,\ldots,X_n) - E\}) = \exp(t\{F_{x_1,\ldots,x_{n-1}}(X_n) - \mathbb{E}_{X_1,\ldots,X_{n-1}}\})$$
$$\times \exp(t\{\widetilde{F}(X_1,\ldots,X_{n-1}) - E\}).$$

Taking the expectation over X_n while keeping $X_1,\ldots,X_{n-1}$ fixed and using (B.11) yields

$$\mathbb{E}_{X_n}[\exp(t\{F(X_1,\ldots,X_n) - E\})] \le \exp\left(\frac{c_n^2 t^2}{8}\right)$$
$$\times \exp(t\{\widetilde{F}(X_1,\ldots,X_{n-1}) - E\}).$$

Next, taking the expectation over $X_1,\ldots,X_{n-1}$ and using (B.12) yields

$$\mathbb{E}[\exp(t\{F(X_1,\ldots,X_n) - E\})] \le \exp\left(\frac{c_n^2}{8}t^2\right) \times \exp\left(\frac{\sum_{i=1}^{n-1} c_i^2}{8}t^2\right)$$
$$= \exp\left(\frac{\sum_{i=1}^{n} c_i^2}{8}t^2\right).$$

This establishes that the induction hypothesis holds for n, and hence concludes the proof.   □

With the above lemma at hand, the coveted *McDiarmid inequality* follows without much difficulty. Note that the case $F(x_1,\ldots,x_n) = (x_1 + \cdots + x_n)/n$ yields the Hoeffding inequality (Theorem B.6).

Theorem B.9 *Let F be an n-variate function and $c_1, \ldots, c_n > 0$ be such that, for all $i \in [1:n]$ and all $x_1, \ldots, x_{i-1}, x_i, x_i', x_{i+1}, \ldots, x_n$,*

$$|F(\ldots, x_{i-1}, x_i, x_{i+1}, \ldots) - F(\ldots, x_{i-1}, x_i', x_{i+1}, \ldots)| \le c_i.$$

If $X_1, \ldots, X_n$ are independent random variables and $\mathbb{E} := \mathbb{E}[F(X_1, \ldots, X_n)]$, then

$$\mathbb{P}[\, F(X_1, \ldots, X_n) - \mathbb{E} > \varepsilon] \le \exp\left(-\frac{2\varepsilon^2}{\sum_{i=1}^n c_i^2}\right), \tag{B.13}$$

$$\mathbb{P}[\,|F(X_1, \ldots, X_n) - \mathbb{E}| > \varepsilon] \le 2\exp\left(-\frac{2\varepsilon^2}{\sum_{i=1}^n c_i^2}\right). \tag{B.14}$$

Proof For some $t > 0$ to be chosen soon, one can equivalently write the tail probability of (B.13) as

$$\mathbb{P} := \mathbb{P}[\exp(t\{F(X_1, \ldots, X_n) - \mathbb{E}\}) > \exp(t\varepsilon)]$$
$$\le \frac{\mathbb{E}[\exp(t\{F(X_1, \ldots, X_n) - \mathbb{E}\})]}{\exp(t\varepsilon)},$$

where the *Markov inequality* (Lemma B.1) was used in the last step. Then, using Lemma B.8, one derives that

$$\mathbb{P} \le \exp\left(\frac{\sum_{i=1}^n c_i^2}{8} t^2 - \varepsilon t\right) = \exp\left(-\frac{2\varepsilon^2}{\sum_{i=1}^n c_i^2}\right),$$

where the optimal choice $t = 4\varepsilon / \sum_{i=1}^n c_i^2$ was made in the last equality. Thus, the inequality (B.13) is established. Next, replacing F by $-F$, one can obtain a similar estimate for $\mathbb{P}[F(X_1, \ldots, X_n) - \mathbb{E} < -\varepsilon]$. Since $|F(X_1, \ldots, X_n) - \mathbb{E}| > \varepsilon$ occurs when $F(X_1, \ldots, X_n) - \mathbb{E} > \varepsilon$ or $F(X_1, \ldots, X_n) - \mathbb{E} < -\varepsilon$ occurs, the inequality (B.14) simply follows from a union bound. $\qquad\square$

As an illustration of the use of the McDiarmid inequality, the result below shows how the operator norm of a random symmetric matrix with bounded entries can be estimated from above.

Proposition B.10 *Let $A \in \mathbb{R}^{n \times n}$ be a symmetric random matrix whose upper entries $A_{i,j}$, $j \ge i$, are independent mean-zero random variables with values in $[-1, 1]$. If $\delta \in (0, 1/2)$, then, for any $t > 0$,*

$$\mathbb{P}\left[\|A\|_{2\to 2} > \frac{\sqrt{2} + t\sqrt{n}}{1 - 2\delta}\right] \le \exp\left(-\left(\frac{t^2}{4} - \ln\left(1 + \frac{2}{\delta}\right)\right)n\right).$$

Proof Thanks to the symmetry of A, its operator norm can be expressed as

$\|A\|_{2\to2} = \sup\{|\langle Ax, x\rangle|, \|x\|_2 = 1\}$. For a fixed $x \in \mathbb{R}^n$ satisfying $\|x\|_2 = 1$, one starts by studying the random variable

$$|\langle Ax, x\rangle| = \left|\sum_{i,j=1}^{n} A_{i,j}x_ix_j\right| = \left|\sum_{1\le i\le n} A_{i,i}x_i^2 + 2\sum_{1\le i<j\le n} A_{i,j}x_ix_j\right|$$

$$=: F\big((A_{i,j})_{1\le i\le j\le n}\big).$$

Notice that, for $a, a' \in [-1,1]^{n(n+1)/2}$ differing in only one position, say at (k, ℓ), one has

$$|F(a) - F(a')| \le \left|\sum_{1\le i\le n}(a_{i,i} - a'_{i,i})x_i^2 + 2\sum_{1\le i<j\le n}(a_{i,j} - a'_{i,j})x_ix_j\right|$$

$$= \begin{cases} |(a_{k,k} - a'_{k,k})x_k^2| \le 2x_k^2, & \text{if } \ell = k, \\ 2|(a_{k,\ell} - a'_{k,\ell})x_kx_\ell| \le 4|x_k||x_\ell|, & \text{if } \ell > k. \end{cases}$$

The sum of the squares of these upper bounds satisfies

$$4\sum_{1\le k\le n}x_k^4 + 16\sum_{1\le k<\ell\le n}x_k^2x_\ell^2 \le 8\sum_{1\le k,\ell\le n}x_k^2x_\ell^2 = 8\|x\|_2^4 = 8.$$

An application of the *McDiarmid inequality* (Theorem B.9) yields

$$\mathbb{P}\Big[|\langle Ax, x\rangle| > \mathrm{E} + t\sqrt{n}\Big] \le \exp\left(-\frac{t^2n}{4}\right), \tag{B.15}$$

where $\mathrm{E} := \mathbb{E}[|\langle Ax, x\rangle|]$. Decomposing $\langle Ax, x\rangle$ as the sum of two independent random variables, namely $\xi := \sum_{1\le i\le n} A_{i,i}x_i^2$ and $\zeta := 2\sum_{1\le i<j\le n} A_{i,j}x_ix_j$, one has $\mathbb{E}[\langle Ax, x\rangle^2] = \mathbb{E}[\xi^2] + \mathbb{E}[\zeta^2]$. Noticing that

$$\mathbb{E}[\xi^2] = \mathbb{E}\left[\sum_i A_{i,i}^2x_i^4 + \sum_{i\ne j}A_{i,i}A_{j,j}x_i^2x_j^2\right] = \mathbb{E}\left[\sum_i A_{i,i}^2x_i^4\right] \le \sum_i x_i^4,$$

$$\mathbb{E}[\zeta^2] = 4\mathbb{E}\left[\sum_{i<j}A_{i,j}^2x_i^2x_j^2 + \sum_{(i<j)\ne(k,\ell)}A_{i,j}A_{k,\ell}x_ix_jx_kx_\ell\right] = 4\mathbb{E}\left[\sum_{i<j}A_{i,j}^2x_i^2x_j^2\right]$$

$$\le 2\sum_{i\ne j}x_i^2x_j^2,$$

one obtains $\mathbb{E}[\langle Ax, x\rangle^2] \le 2\sum_{1\le i,j\le n}x_i^2x_j^2 = 2\|x\|_2^4 = 2$. Consequently, in view of $\mathrm{E} \le \mathbb{E}[\langle Ax, x\rangle^2]^{1/2} \le \sqrt{2}$, it follows from (B.15) that

$$\mathbb{P}\Big[|\langle Ax, x\rangle| > \sqrt{2} + t\sqrt{n}\Big] \le \exp\left(-\frac{t^2n}{4}\right).$$

Now let $\{x_1, \ldots, x_K\}$ be a δ-net for the unit sphere of $\mathbb{R}^n$. By Theorem A.5, it can be chosen to have $K \leq (1 + 2/\delta)^n$ elements. A union bound gives

$$\mathbb{P}\left[|\langle Ax_k, x_k\rangle| > \sqrt{2} + t\sqrt{n} \text{ for some } k \in [1:K]\right] \tag{B.16}$$

$$\leq \exp\left(-\frac{t^2 n}{4} + \ln\left(1 + \frac{2}{\delta}\right)n\right).$$

Let the favorable situation where $|\langle Ax_k, x_k\rangle| \leq \sqrt{2} + t\sqrt{n}$ for all $k \in [1:K]$ prevail. For $x \in \mathbb{R}^n$ with $\|x\|_2 = 1$, select $k \in [1:K]$ such that $\|x - x_k\|_2 \leq \delta$. Since A is a symmetric matrix, one has

$$\begin{aligned}
|\langle Ax, x\rangle| &= |\langle Ax_k, x_k\rangle + \langle A(x + x_k), (x - x_k)\rangle| \\
&\leq |\langle Ax_k, x_k\rangle| + |\langle A(x + x_k), (x - x_k)\rangle| \\
&\leq \sqrt{2} + t\sqrt{n} + \|A\|_{2\to 2}\|x + x_k\|_2\|x - x_k\|_2 \\
&\leq \sqrt{2} + t\sqrt{n} + 2\delta\|A\|_{2\to 2}.
\end{aligned}$$

By taking the maximum over x, one obtains

$$\|A\|_{2\to 2} \leq \sqrt{2} + t\sqrt{n} + 2\delta\|A\|_{2\to 2}, \quad \text{i.e.,} \quad \|A\|_{2\to 2} \leq \frac{\sqrt{2} + t\sqrt{n}}{1 - 2\delta}.$$

In view of (B.16), this event occurs with the announced failure probability. $\quad\square$

B.3 Restricted Isometry Properties

To close this appendix, the nonstandard restricted isometry properties at the center of the Compressive Sensing theory exposed in PART THREE shall be fully justified, starting with the situation involving sparse vectors.

Theorem B.11 *Consider a random matrix $A \in \mathbb{R}^{m\times N}$ whose entries are independent mean-zero gaussian variables with standard deviation $\sqrt{\pi/2}/m$. If $m \geq C\delta^{-3}s\ln(eN/s)$, then the ℓ_1-restricted isometry property of order s with constant δ, namely*

$$(1 - \delta)\|x\|_2 \leq \|Ax\|_1 \leq (1 + \delta)\|x\|_2 \quad \text{whenever } x \in \Sigma_s^N,$$

holds with probability at least $1 - 2\exp(-c\delta^2 m)$. The constants can be taken to be $C = 80\pi$ and $c = 1/(8\pi)$.

Proof As a first step, one looks at the concentration of $\|Ax\|_1$ around $\|x\|_2$ for a fixed $x \in \mathbb{R}^N$. Given that a linear combination of gaussian variables is still a gaussian variable, one can write, for each $i \in [1:m]$,

$$(Ax)_i = \sum_{j=1}^{N} A_{i,j} x_j = \frac{\sqrt{\pi/2}}{m}\|x\|_2 \, g_i,$$

where $g_i \sim \mathcal{N}(0, 1)$ is a standard gaussian variable. Since $\|Ax\|_1 = \sum_{i=1}^{m} |(Ax)_i|$, it follows that, for $t \in (0, 1)$,

$$\mathbb{P}[\|Ax\|_1 > (1 + t)\|x\|_2] = \mathbb{P}\left[\sum_{i=1}^{m} |g_i| > m\sqrt{2/\pi}(1 + t)\right]$$

$$= \mathbb{P}\left[\exp\left(u\sum_{i=1}^{m} |g_i|\right) > \exp\left(um\sqrt{2/\pi}(1 + t)\right)\right],$$

where the value of $u > 0$ is to be chosen soon. Using the *Markov inequality* (Lemma B.1) and the independence of the random variables $g_1, \ldots, g_m$, one derives

$$\mathbb{P}[\|Ax\|_1 > (1 + t)\|x\|_2] \le \frac{\mathbb{E}[\exp(u\sum_{i=1}^{m} |g_i|)]}{\exp(um\sqrt{2/\pi}(1 + t))} \qquad (\text{B.17})$$

$$= \prod_{i=1}^{m} \frac{\mathbb{E}[\exp(u|g_i|)]}{\exp(u\sqrt{2/\pi}(1 + t))}.$$

At this point, invoking Lemma B.4 to bound the moment generating function of the absolute value of g_i, one obtains

$$\frac{\mathbb{E}[\exp(u|g_i|)]}{\exp(u\sqrt{2/\pi}(1 + t))} \le \frac{(1 + \sqrt{2/\pi}u)\exp(u^2/2)}{\exp(u\sqrt{2/\pi}(1 + t))}$$

$$\le \exp\left(\frac{u^2}{2} - u\sqrt{2/\pi}t\right).$$

Substituting the latter into (B.17) while making the optimal choice $u = \sqrt{2/\pi}t$, one arrives at

$$\mathbb{P}[\|Ax\|_1 > (1 + t)\|x\|_2] \le \exp\left(-\frac{t^2 m}{\pi}\right).$$

A similar argument provides the exact same bound for $\mathbb{P}[\|Ax\|_1 < (1 - t)\|x\|_2]$. Altogether, for a fixed $x \in \mathbb{R}^N$, one can announce the following concentration inequality, valid for any $t \in (0, 1)$:

$$\mathbb{P}\left[\big|\|Ax\|_1 - \|x\|_2\big| > t\|x\|_2\right] \le 2\exp\left(-\frac{t^2 m}{\pi}\right). \qquad (\text{B.18})$$

As a second step, a covering argument is used to deduce a statement valid for all the vectors $x \in \mathbb{R}^N$ simultaneously. Precisely, with $\rho \le 1/2$, let $\{x_1, \ldots, x_K\}$ denote a ρ-net for the set $\overline{\Sigma}_s^N$ of ℓ_2-normalized s-sparse vectors in $\mathbb{R}^N$. According to Lemma A.6, it can be chosen with a number of elements satisfying

$$\ln(K) \le s \ln\left(\frac{eN}{s}\right) + \frac{2s}{\rho} \le \frac{s}{2\rho} \ln\left(\frac{eN}{s}\right) + \frac{2s}{\rho} \ln\left(\frac{eN}{s}\right) = \frac{5s}{2\rho} \ln\left(\frac{eN}{s}\right).$$

In view of (B.18) applied to each x_k, $k \in [1:K]$, a union bound yields

$$\mathbb{P}\Big[\big|\|Ax_k\|_1 - \|x_k\|_2\big| > t\|x_k\|_2 \text{ for some } k \in [1:K]\Big]$$

$$\le 2K \exp\left(-\frac{t^2 m}{\pi}\right) \le 2 \exp\left(-\frac{t^2 m}{\pi} + \frac{5s}{2\rho} \ln\left(\frac{eN}{s}\right)\right).$$

Consider the favorable situation where $1 - t \le \|Ax_k\|_1 \le 1 + t$ for all $k \in [1:K]$, which occurs with failure probability bounded by

$$2 \exp\left(-\frac{t^2 m}{\pi} + \frac{5s}{2\rho} \ln\left(\frac{eN}{s}\right)\right) \le 2 \exp\left(-\frac{t^2 m}{2\pi}\right),$$

provided m is chosen large enough so that $(5s/2\rho) \ln(eN/s) \le (t^2 m)/(2\pi)$, i.e., $m \ge (5\pi)/\rho t^2) s \ln(eN/s)$. One now needs to estimate

$$\alpha := \min_{x \in \Sigma_s^N} \|Ax\|_1 \qquad \text{and} \qquad \beta := \max_{x \in \Sigma_s^N} \|Ax\|_1.$$

For $x \in \widetilde{\Sigma}_s^N$, selecting $k \in [1:K]$ such that $\|x - x_k\|_2 \le \rho$ and $x - x_k \in \Sigma_s^N$ (see Remark A.7), one has

$$\|Ax\|_1 \le \|Ax_k\|_1 + \|A(x - x_k)\|_1 \le 1 + t + \beta\rho.$$

Taking the maximum over x and rearranging leads to

$$\beta \le \frac{1+t}{1-\rho}.$$

In a similar fashion, one has

$$\|Ax\|_1 \ge \|Ax_k\|_1 - \|A(x - x_k)\|_1 \ge 1 - t - \beta\rho,$$

which yields, after taking the minimum over x,

$$\alpha \ge 1 - t - \beta\rho.$$

With the choices $t = \delta/2$ and $\rho = \delta/(2(1 + \delta))$, one obtains $\beta \le 1 + \delta$ and in turn $\alpha \ge 1 - \delta$. This means that $(1 - \delta) \le \|Ax\|_1 \le (1 + \delta)$ for all $x \in \widetilde{\Sigma}_s^N$, i.e., the ℓ_1-restricted isometry property of order s with constant δ holds. The stated forms of the condition on m and of the success probability follow by taking the choices of t and ρ into account. $\qquad \square$

The restricted isometry property established next involves low-rank matrices instead of sparse vectors.

Theorem B.12 *Consider random vectors* $a^{(1)}, \ldots, a^{(m)}, b^{(1)}, \ldots, b^{(m)} \in \mathbb{R}^n$ *whose entries are independent Rademacher variables. If* $m \geq Cnr$, *then the linear map*

$$\mathcal{A}: X \in \mathbb{R}^{n \times n} \mapsto \frac{\sqrt{2}}{m} \big[\langle b^{(1)}, X a^{(1)} \rangle; \ldots; \langle b^{(m)}, X a^{(m)} \rangle \big] \in \mathbb{R}^m$$

satisfies the ℓ_1-*rank restricted isometry property of order r with constants* $1/2$ *and* 2, *namely*

$$\frac{1}{2} \|X\|_F \leq \|\mathcal{A}(X)\|_1 \leq 2 \|X\|_F \qquad \text{whenever} \ \operatorname{rank}(X) \leq r,$$

with probability at least $1 - 2 \exp(-cm)$. *The constants can be taken to be* $C = 2304(7 + 5\sqrt{2})$ *and* $c = (3 - 2\sqrt{2})/32$.

Proof As a first step, one considers a fixed matrix $X \in \mathbb{R}^{n \times n}$ and denotes its vectorization by $x = \operatorname{vec}(X) \in \mathbb{R}^N$, $N = n^2$. One can write

$$\|\mathcal{A}(X)\|_1 = \frac{\sqrt{2}}{m} \sum_{i=1}^{m} |\langle b^{(i)}, X a^{(i)} \rangle| = \frac{\sqrt{2}}{m} \sum_{i=1}^{m} \Big| \sum_{k,\ell=1}^{n} b_k^{(i)} a_\ell^{(i)} X_{k,\ell} \Big|$$

$$= \frac{\sqrt{2}}{m} \sum_{i=1}^{m} \Big| \sum_{j=1}^{N} \varepsilon_{i,j} x_j \Big| =: F(\varepsilon),$$

where the $\varepsilon_{i,j}$ are independent Rademacher variables. For $\eta, \eta' \in \{-1, +1\}^{mN}$ differing at only one place, say at (i, j), one has

$$|F(\eta) - F(\eta')| \leq \frac{\sqrt{2}}{m} |x_j| \, |\eta_{i,j} - \eta'_{i,j}| = \frac{2\sqrt{2}}{m} |x_j|.$$

An application of the *McDiarmid inequality* (Theorem B.9) gives

$$\mathbb{P}\big[\big| \|\mathcal{A}(X)\|_1 - \|\|X\|\| \big| > t \|\|X\|\| \big] \leq 2 \exp \Big(- \frac{t^2 \|\|X\|\|^2 m}{4 \|x\|_2^2} \Big),$$

where the notation $\|\|X\|\|$ stands for the expectation of $\sqrt{2} \sum_{i=1}^{m} |\langle b^{(i)}, X a^{(i)} \rangle| / m$, i.e.,

$$\|\|X\|\| = \sqrt{2} \, \mathbb{E}[|\langle b, Xa \rangle|],$$

with $a, b \in \mathbb{R}^n$ being random vectors with independent Rademacher entries. This expression defines a norm—the homogeneity and the triangle inequality are clear, while the positive definiteness follows from the yet-to-be-proved two-sided estimate

$$\frac{1}{\sqrt{2}} \|X\|_F \leq \mathbb{E}[|\langle b, Xa \rangle|] \leq \|X\|_F. \tag{B.19}$$

Accepting (B.19) for now, the fact that $\||X\|| \geq \|X\|_F = \|x\|_2$ yields

$$\mathbb{P}\big[\big|\|\mathcal{A}(X)\|_1 - \||X\||\big| > t\||X\||\big] \leq 2\exp\left(-\frac{t^2 m}{4}\right). \tag{B.20}$$

The second step is a covering argument. Precisely, let $\{X_1, \ldots, X_K\}$ denote a ρ-net for the set $\widetilde{\Sigma}_r^{n\times n}$ of Frobenius-normalized rank-r matrices. According to Lemma A.8, one can take

$$\ln(K) \leq (2n+1)r\ln\left(1 + \frac{6}{\rho}\right) \leq \frac{18nr}{\rho}.$$

In view of (B.20) applied to each X_k, $k \in [1:K]$, a union bound yields

$$\mathbb{P}\big[\big|\|\mathcal{A}(X_k)\|_1 - \||X_k\||\big| > t\||X_k\|| \text{ for some } k \in [1:K]\big]$$

$$\leq 2K\exp\left(-\frac{t^2 m}{4}\right) \leq 2\exp\left(-\frac{t^2 m}{4} + \frac{18nr}{\rho}\right).$$

Consider the favorable situation where $(1-t)\||X_k\|| \leq \|\mathcal{A}(X_k)\|_1 \leq (1+t)\||X_k\||$, and hence $(1-t) \leq \|\mathcal{A}(X_k)\|_1 \leq (1+t)\sqrt{2}$ for all $k \in [1:K]$. This occurs with failure probability

$$2\exp\left(-\frac{t^2 m}{4} + \frac{18nr}{\rho}\right) \leq 2\exp\left(-\frac{t^2 m}{8}\right),$$

when m is chosen large enough to have $18nr/\rho \leq t^2 m/8$, i.e., $m \geq (144/\rho t^2)nr$. One now needs to estimate

$$\alpha := \min_{X \in \widetilde{\Sigma}_r^{n\times n}} \|\mathcal{A}(X)\|_1 \qquad \text{and} \qquad \beta := \max_{X \in \widetilde{\Sigma}_r^{n\times n}} \|\mathcal{A}(X)\|_1.$$

Given $X \in \widetilde{\Sigma}_r^{n\times n}$, one selects $k \in [1:K]$ such that $\|X - X_k\|_F \leq \rho$. Since $X - X_K$ is a priori of rank $2r$ or less, one writes $X - X_k = U + V$ with $U, V \in \mathbb{R}^{n\times n}$ of rank r or less and satisfying $\|X - X_k\|_F^2 = \|U\|_F^2 + \|V\|_F^2$, so that $\|U\|_F + \|V\|_F \leq \sqrt{2}\rho$. It follows that $\|\mathcal{A}(X - X_k)\|_1 \leq \|\mathcal{A}(U)\|_1 + \|\mathcal{A}(V)\|_1 \leq \beta(\|U\|_F + \|V\|_F) \leq \sqrt{2}\beta\rho$. Then, in view of

$$\|\mathcal{A}(X)\|_1 \leq \|\mathcal{A}(X_k)\|_1 + \|\mathcal{A}(X - X_k)\|_1 \leq (1+t)\sqrt{2} + \sqrt{2}\beta\rho,$$

taking the maximum over X and rearranging leads to

$$\beta \leq \sqrt{2}\frac{1+t}{1 - \sqrt{2}\rho}.$$

In a similar fashion, one has

$$\|\mathcal{A}(X)\|_1 \geq \|\mathcal{A}(X_k)\|_1 - \|\mathcal{A}(X - X_k)\|_1 \geq 1 - t - \sqrt{2}\beta\rho,$$

which yields, after taking the minimum over X,

$$\alpha \geq 1 - t - \sqrt{2}\beta\rho.$$

With the choices $t = (\sqrt{2} - 1)/2$ and $\rho = (\sqrt{2} - 1)/4$, one obtains $\beta \leq 2$ and $\alpha \geq 1/2$. This means that $(1/2) \leq \|\mathcal{A}(X)\|_1 \leq 2$ for all $X \in \widetilde{\Sigma}_r^{n \times n}$, i.e., the ℓ_1-rank restricted isometry property of order r with constants $1/2$ and 2 holds. The stated forms of the condition on m and of the success probability follow by taking the choices of t and ρ into account.

It finally remains to prove the missing two-sided estimate (B.19). Writing $\langle b, Xa \rangle = \sum_{j=1}^{N} \varepsilon_j x_j$ where $\varepsilon_1, \dots, \varepsilon_N$ are independent Rademacher random variables and using the notation $\Delta := \{(j, j') \in [1 : N]^2 : j \neq j'\}$, one has

$$\langle b, Xa \rangle^2 = \sum_{j \in [1:N]} x_j^2 + \sum_{(j,j') \in \Delta} \varepsilon_j \varepsilon_{j'} x_j x_{j'} =: \|x\|_2^2 + G(\varepsilon). \tag{B.21}$$

The implicitly defined random quantity $G(\varepsilon)$ satisfies $\mathbb{E}[G(\varepsilon)] = 0$ and

$$G(\varepsilon)^2 = \sum_{(j,j') \in \Delta} x_j^2 x_{j'}^2 + \sum_{\substack{(j,j'),(\ell,\ell') \in \Delta \\ (j,j') \neq (\ell,\ell')}} \varepsilon_j \varepsilon_{j'} \varepsilon_\ell \varepsilon_{\ell'} x_j x_{j'} x_\ell x_{\ell'}, \tag{B.22}$$

so that $\mathbb{E}[G(\varepsilon)^2] = \sum_{(j,j') \in \Delta} x_j^2 x_{j'}^2 \leq \|x\|_2^4$. Thus, it follows from (B.21) and (B.22) that

$$\mathbb{E}[\langle b, Xa \rangle^2] = \|x\|_2^2 \quad \text{and} \quad \mathbb{E}[\langle b, Xa \rangle^4] \leq 2\|x\|_2^4.$$

The facts that $\mathbb{E}[|\langle b, Xa \rangle|] \leq (\mathbb{E}[\langle b, Xa \rangle^2])^{1/2}$ and that $\|x\|_2 = \|X\|_F$ now yield the rightmost estimate of (B.19), while the leftmost estimate relies on the Hölder inequality

$$\mathbb{E}[\langle b, Xa \rangle^2] = \mathbb{E}[|\langle b, Xa \rangle|^{2/3} |\langle b, Xa \rangle|^{4/3}] \leq \mathbb{E}[|\langle b, Xa \rangle|]^{2/3} \mathbb{E}[\langle b, Xa \rangle^4]^{1/3}$$

to arrive at

$$\mathbb{E}[|\langle b, Xa \rangle|] \geq \frac{\mathbb{E}[\langle b, Xa \rangle^2]^{3/2}}{\mathbb{E}[\langle b, Xa \rangle^4]^{1/2}} \geq \frac{\|x\|_2^3}{\sqrt{2}\|x\|_2^2} = \frac{1}{\sqrt{2}}\|x\|_2. = \frac{1}{\sqrt{2}}\|X\|_F.$$

With the two-sided estimate (B.19) now justified, the proof is complete. $\quad\square$

Exercises

B.1 Give a proof of the Paley–Zygmund inequality (Lemma B.3).

B.2 Verify that the moment generating function of a squared subgaussian random variable X with subgaussian standard τ satisfies

$$\mathbb{E}[\exp(tX^2)] \leq \frac{1}{\sqrt{1 - 2\tau^2 t}}, \qquad |t| < \frac{1}{2\tau^2}.$$

B.3 Establish the standard ℓ_2-restricted isometry property for a random matrix $A \in \mathbb{R}^{m \times N}$ whose entries are independent mean-zero gaussian variables with variance $1/m$. Precisely, prove that if $m \geq C\delta^{-2}s \ln(eN/s)$, then

$$(1 - \delta)\|x\|_2^2 \leq \|Ax\|_2^2 \leq (1 + \delta)\|x\|_2^2 \qquad \text{for all } x \in \Sigma_s^N \qquad \text{(B.23)}$$

holds with probability at least $1 - 2\exp(-c\delta^2 m)$. One can start with the concentration inequality from Lemma 8.3 and continue with a covering argument similar to the one used in the proof of Proposition B.10.

B.4 Consider random matrices $A \in \mathbb{R}^{m \times N}$ whose rows are independent copies of a random vector $a \in \mathbb{R}^N$. Suppose that, with failure probability at most $2\exp(-c_\delta m)$, these matrices satisfy the standard ℓ_2-restricted isometry property (B.23) of order s with constant δ provided $m \geq C_\delta s \ln(eN/s)$. Show that, with failure probability at most $2\exp(-c'_\delta m)$, the renormalized matrices $A/\sqrt{m} \in \mathbb{R}^{m \times N}$ satisfy the ℓ_1-*restricted isometry property* of order s with constants α_δ and β_δ provided $m \geq C'_\delta s \ln(eN/s)$. To this end, observe that, for any $y \in \mathbb{R}^m$ and any $m' < m$, there exists $I \subseteq [1 : m]$ with $|I| = m'$ such that $\|y_I\|_2 \leq \|y\|_1 / \sqrt{m - m'}$.

Appendix C
Functional Analysis

This appendix presents some functional analytic ingredients used throughout the book, especially in PART TWO and PART FOUR. Additional material can be found in classical texts, such as Rudin (1991) for functional analysis in general or Barvinok (2002) for the more targeted topic of convexity.

C.1 Completeness

A metric space X is called *complete* if every Cauchy sequence of points in X has a limit belonging to X. For instance, the set $\mathbb{R}$ of real numbers is complete, but the set $\mathbb{Q}$ of rational numbers is not. A fundamental result about complete metric spaces is the *Baire category theorem*, stated here without proof.

Theorem C.1 *If X is a complete metric space X, then any intersection of countably many open dense subsets of X is also a dense subset of X.*

A *Banach space X* is a normed space which is complete relative to the metric induced by its norm. In case of a norm derived from an inner product, one talks about a *Hilbert space*. The *dual space X^**—i.e., the set of continuous linear functionals on X—is always a Banach space, even if X is merely a normed space (see Exercise C.1). When X is actually a Hilbert space, its dual X^* is (isometric to) X itself. This is the content of the *Riesz representation theorem* for Hilbert spaces below.

Theorem C.2 *Let H be a Hilbert space with inner product $\langle \cdot, \cdot \rangle$. For every continuous linear functional $\lambda \in H^*$, there is a unique $v \in H$ such that*

$$\lambda(x) = \langle v, x \rangle \qquad \text{for all } x \in H. \tag{C.1}$$

Moreover, one has $\|\lambda\|^* := \sup\{|\lambda(x)| : \|x\| = 1\} = \|v\|$.

Proof The second part of the statement is rather straightforward. Indeed, on the one hand, one has $\|\lambda\|^* \geq \lambda(v/\|v\|) = \langle v, v/\|v\| \rangle = \|v\|$, and on the other hand, one also has $|\lambda(x)| = |\langle v, x \rangle| \leq \|v\| \|x\| = \|v\|$ whenever $\|x\| = 1$, so that $\|\lambda\|^* \leq \|v\|$. As for the first part of the statement, the uniqueness of $v \in H$ is straightforward, too: indeed, if $v, v' \in H$ both satisfy (C.1), then $\langle v - v', x \rangle = 0$ for all $x \in H$, and taking $x = v - v'$ yields $\|v - v'\|^2 = 0$, i.e., $v = v'$. It remains to establish the existence of a vector $v \in H$ satisfying (C.1). To this end, one considers a sequence $(u_n)_{n \geq 0}$ of unit vectors such that $(\lambda(u_n))_{n \geq 0}$ is a nondecreasing sequence that converges to $\|\lambda\|^*$. For integers $n, k \geq 0$, observe that $\|u_{n+k} + u_n\| \geq \lambda(u_{n+k} + u_n)/\|\lambda\|^* = (\lambda(u_{n+k}) + \lambda(u_n))/\|\lambda\|^* \geq 2\lambda(u_n)/\|\lambda\|^*$, so the parallelogram law $\|u_{n+k} + u_n\|^2 + \|u_{n+k} - u_n\|^2 = 2\|u_{n+k}\|^2 + 2\|u_n\|^2 = 4$ gives $\|u_{n+k} - u_n\|^2 \leq 4 - 4\lambda(u_n)^2/\|\lambda\|^{*2} \to 0$ as $n \to \infty$, independently of k. This proves that $(u_n)_{n \geq 0}$ is a Cauchy sequence, and hence it converges to some $u \in H$. Note that $\|u\| = \lim_{n \to \infty} \|u_n\| = 1$ and that $\lambda(u) = \lim_{n \to \infty} \lambda(u_n) = \|\lambda\|^*$. Now, for $x \in H$, the inequality $|\lambda(u + tx)| \leq \|\lambda\|^* \|u + tx\|$ squared and expanded around $t = 0$ gives $(\|\lambda\|^*)^2 + 2\|\lambda\|^* \lambda(x) t \leq (\|\lambda\|^*)^2 + 2(\|\lambda\|^*)^2 \langle u, x \rangle t + O(t^2)$, which implies that $\lambda(x) = \|\lambda\|^* \langle u, x \rangle$. Therefore, the required identity (C.1) is satisfied with $v = \|\lambda\|^* u$. □

Another classical Banach space is the set $C(X)$ of continuous functions on a compact (and implicitly Hausdorff) set X, equipped with the uniform norm defined for $f \in C(X)$ by $\|f\|_{C(X)} = \max\{|f(x)|, x \in X\}$. Its dual space can be identified with the set of signed Borel measures on X. This is the content of the *Riesz representation theorem* for $C(X)$, stated below without proof[1] for positive linear functionals only.

Theorem C.3 *Let X be a compact set. For every continuous linear functional $\lambda \in C(X)^*$ which is positive (in the sense that $f(x) \geq 0$ for all $x \in X$ implies that $\lambda(f) \geq 0$), there is a unique nonnegative Borel measure μ on X such that*

$$\lambda(f) = \int_X f(x) d\mu(x) \quad \text{for all } f \in C(X).$$

The *Tietze extension theorem* says that a function which is continuous on a closed subset of X can be extended to a continuous function on X while preserving the uniform norm. Here is a formal statement.

Theorem C.4 *Let X be a compact set and let $\mathcal{Y}$ be a closed subset of X. For $f \in C(\mathcal{Y})$, there exists $\widetilde{f} \in C(X)$ such that $\widetilde{f}_{|\mathcal{Y}} = f$ and $\|\widetilde{f}\|_{C(X)} = \|f\|_{C(\mathcal{Y})}$.*

The sketch of the argument will require the following ubiquitous result.

---

[1] A proof can be found in Rudin (1987), Theorem 6.19.

Theorem C.5   *A continuous linear map $L : X \to Y$ from a Banach space X to a normed space Y is surjective if one can find a dense subset S of Y and constants $C > 0$ and $\rho \in (0, 1)$ such that, for any $y \in S$,*

$$\text{there exists } x \in X \text{ such that } \|y - L(x)\| \le \rho\|y\| \text{ and } \|x\| \le C\|y\|. \qquad \text{(C.2)}$$

Moreover, if this condition holds with $S = Y$, then any $y \in Y$ has a preimage $x \in X$ satisfying $\|x\| \le (C/(1 - \rho))\|y\|$.

Proof   Consider first the case $S = Y$. Given $y \in Y$, construct a sequence $(x_n)_{n\ge 0}$ inductively by setting $x_0 = 0$ and, for $n \ge 1$, by defining x_n through an application of (C.2) to $y - L(x_0 + \cdots + x_{n-1})$, so that

$$\|y - L(x_0 + \cdots + x_{n-1}) - L(x_n)\| \le \rho\|y - L(x_0 + \cdots + x_{n-1})\|,$$

$$\|x_n\| \le C\|y - L(x_0 + \cdots + x_{n-1})\|.$$

By immediate induction, one derives that, for any $n \ge 1$,

$$\|y - L(x_0 + \cdots + x_n)\| \le \rho^n\|y\| \qquad \text{and} \qquad \|x_n\| \le C\rho^{n-1}\|y\|.$$

The latter inequality implies that the series $\sum x_n$ converges absolutely, so one can safely define $x := \sum_{n\ge 0} x_n$, and then the former inequality implies that $\|y - L(x)\| = 0$. Thus, for any $y \in Y$, one has found some $x \in X$ such that $L(x) = y$, which establishes the surjectivity of F. Note that this preimage of y has norm $\|x\| \le \sum_{n\ge 0} \|x_n\| \le \sum_{n\ge 1} C\rho^{n-1}\|y\| = (C/(1 - \rho))\|y\|$.

Consider now the case of a proper subset S dense in Y and choose $\varepsilon > 0$ such that $\varepsilon < (1 - \rho)/(1 + \rho)$. For $y \in Y$, there is some $z \in S$ such that $\|y - z\| \le \varepsilon\|y\|$. Then, according to (C.2), there exists $x \in X$ such that $\|z - L(x)\| \le \rho\|z\|$ and $\|x\| \le C\|z\|$. In view of $\|y - L(x)\| \le \|z - L(x)\| + \|y - z\| \le \rho\|z\| + \varepsilon\|y\|$ and of $\|z\| \le \|y\| + \|z - y\| \le \|y\| + \varepsilon\|y\|$, one obtains

$$\|y - L(x)\| \le (\rho + \rho\varepsilon + \varepsilon)\|y\| \qquad \text{and} \qquad \|x\| \le C(1 + \varepsilon)\|y\|.$$

In other words, for any $y \in Y$, condition (C.2) still holds with ρ replaced by $\rho + \rho\varepsilon + \varepsilon < 1$ and C replaced by $C(1 + \varepsilon)$. One has returned to the case $S = Y$, which has been treated earlier. Thus, the surjectivity of L is acquired. $\square$

To establish the Tietze extension theorem, one can use the above theorem together with the *Urysohn lemma*, which states that if $\mathcal{A}$, $\mathcal{B}$ are disjoint closed subsets of a compact set X, then there is a continuous function $f: X \to [0, 1]$ such that $f_{|\mathcal{A}} = 0$ and $f_{|\mathcal{B}} = 1$. This lemma is immediate when X is a compact metric space, as one can take $f(x) = \text{dist}(x, \mathcal{A})/(\text{dist}(x, \mathcal{A}) + \text{dist}(x, \mathcal{B}))$.

Proof of Theorem C.4   Part of the objective is to establish the surjectivity of the continuous linear map $L: \widetilde{f} \in C(X) \mapsto \widetilde{f}_{|\mathcal{Y}} \in C(\mathcal{Y})$. To do so, consider

$f \in C(\mathcal{Y})$ such that, without losing generality, $\|f\|_{C(\mathcal{Y})} = 1$. The Urysohn lemma applied to the disjoint closed sets $\mathcal{A} = \{x \in \mathcal{Y} : -1 \leq f(x) \leq -1/3\}$ and $\mathcal{B} = \{x \in \mathcal{Y} : 1/3 \leq f(x) \leq 1\}$ gives a continuous function $h : \mathcal{X} \to [0, 1]$ with $h_{|\mathcal{A}} = 0$ and $h_{|\mathcal{B}} = 1$. Defining a continuous function $\widetilde{f} : \mathcal{X} \to [-1/3, 1/3]$ by $\widetilde{f} := (2/3)h - (1/3)$, one easily verifies that

$$\left\| f - L(\widetilde{f}) \right\|_{C(\mathcal{Y})} \leq \frac{2}{3} \quad \text{and} \quad \left\| \widetilde{f} \right\|_{C(\mathcal{X})} \leq \frac{1}{3}.$$

This is condition (C.2) with $\rho = 2/3$ and $C = 1/3$. Thus, Theorem C.5 implies not only that any $f \in C(\mathcal{Y})$ comes with some $\widetilde{f} \in C(\mathcal{X})$ such that $L(\widetilde{f}) = f$, i.e., $\widetilde{f}_{|\mathcal{Y}} = f$, but also that this $\widetilde{f}$ obeys $\left\| \widetilde{f} \right\|_{C(\mathcal{X})} \leq (C/(1-\rho))\|f\|_{C(\mathcal{Y})} = \|f\|_{C(\mathcal{Y})}$. □

C.2 Convexity

Given two points x_0, x_1 in a vector space X, a convex combination of x_0 and x_1 is a point of the form $x_\tau = (1 - \tau)x_0 + \tau x_1$ for some $\tau \in [0, 1]$. More generally, a convex combination of points $x_1, \ldots, x_K$ is a point of the form $x = \sum_{k=1}^{K} \tau_k x_k$ with $\tau_1, \ldots, \tau_K \geq 0$ and $\sum_{k=1}^{K} \tau_k = 1$. A subset C of X is said to be a *convex set* if every convex combination of two points of C remains in C, i.e., if

$$x_0, x_1 \in C, \ \tau \in [0, 1] \implies x_\tau = (1 - \tau)x_0 + \tau x_1 \in C.$$

The *convex hull* conv(S) of a subset S of X is defined as the smallest convex set containing S. It can also be viewed as the intersection of all convex sets containing S or as the set of all convex combinations of points in S, i.e., as

$$\text{conv}(S) = \left\{ \sum_{k=1}^{K} \tau_k x_k : K \in \mathbb{N}^*, x_1, \ldots, x_K \in S, \tau_1, \ldots, \tau_K \geq 0, \sum_{k=1}^{K} \tau_k = 1 \right\}.$$

Several celebrated results involving convex sets are presented below, starting with the *Carathéodory theorem*. Note that this theorem implies that the convex hull of a compact subset of $\mathbb{R}^d$ is itself compact.

Theorem C.6 *If S is a subset of $\mathbb{R}^d$, then any point $x \in$ conv(S) is a convex combination of at most $d + 1$ points of S.*

Proof For $x \in$ conv(S), suppose by contradiction that $n > d + 1$, where n denotes the minimal number of points in a convex combination of points of S representing x. Write $x = \sum_{k=1}^{n} \tau_k x_k$ with $\tau_1, \ldots, \tau_n \geq 0$ and $\sum_{k=1}^{n} \tau_k = 1$, where none of the τ_k's are zero, otherwise x could be represented as a convex combination of less than n points of S. A dimension argument reveals that the linear map $u \in \mathbb{R}^n \mapsto \sum_{k=1}^{n} u_k[x_k; 1] \in \mathbb{R}^{d+1}$ cannot be injective. Thus, there is a nonzero $u \in \mathbb{R}^n$ such that $\sum_{k=1}^n u_k[x_k; 1] = 0$, and one can assume that $\max\{|u_k|/\tau_k\} =: |u_\ell|/\tau_\ell = 1$. Defining $\theta_k = \tau_k - \text{sgn}(u_\ell)u_k$, one observes that $\sum_{k=1}^n \theta_k x_k = x$, $\sum_{k=1}^n \theta_k = 1$, and $\theta_1, \ldots, \theta_n \geq 0$. But, since $\theta_\ell = 0$, it appears that x is a convex combination of less than n points of S, which is a contradiction. $\qquad\square$

Another celebrated result involving convex sets is the *Helly theorem*.

Theorem C.7 *Given a finite collection of convex sets in $\mathbb{R}^d$, if any $d + 1$ of these sets have a nonempty intersection, then the whole collection has a nonempty intersection.*

Proof One proves by induction on $n \geq d+1$ that any convex subsets $C_1, \ldots, C_n$ of $\mathbb{R}^d$ have a nonempty intersection as soon as any $d + 1$ of them have a nonempty intersection. The base case $n = d + 1$ is obvious. Assume now that the induction hypothesis holds for $n - 1$, $n \geq d + 2$. To prove that it holds for n, too, one considers n convex subsets $C_1, \ldots, C_n$ of $\mathbb{R}^d$, any $d + 1$ of which have a nonempty intersection. For any $i \in [1:n]$, applying the induction hypothesis to the C_j for $j \in [1:n] \setminus \{i\}$ produces a point $x_i \in \cap_{j \neq i} C_j$. By a dimension argument, the linear map $u \in \mathbb{R}^n \mapsto \sum_{k=1}^n u_k[x_k; 1] \in \mathbb{R}^{d+1}$ is not injective, so there is a nonzero $u \in \mathbb{R}^n$ such that $\sum_{k=1}^n u_k[x_k; 1] = 0$. Defining the nonempty index sets $K_+ := \{k \in [1:n] : u_k > 0\}$ and $K_- := \{k \in [1:n] : u_k < 0\}$, one has $\sum_{k \in K_+} u_k = \sum_{k \in K_-} (-u_k)$, which is assumed without loss of generality to equal one. Consequently, the point $x := \sum_{k \in K_+} u_k x_k = \sum_{k \in K_-} (-u_k)x_k$ belongs to $\text{conv}(\{x_k, k \in K_+\}) \cap \text{conv}(\{x_k, k \in K_-\})$. One claims that $x \in \cap_{i=1}^n C_i$. Indeed, consider an index $i \in [1:n]$, say, $i \in K_+$: for any $k \in K_-$, one has $x_k \in \cap_{j \neq k} C_j \subseteq C_i$, and in turn $x \in \text{conv}(\{x_k, k \in K_-\}) \subseteq C_i$. This justifies the claim that $\cap_{i=1}^n C_i$ contains x, and hence is nonempty. The induction hypothesis has been established for n and the inductive proof is complete. $\qquad\square$

The next celebrated result to be emphasized is the *supporting hyperplane theorem*.

Theorem C.8 *Let C be a convex subset of $\mathbb{R}^d$ and let $\overline{x}$ be a boundary point of C. There exists an affine hyperplane H containing $\overline{x}$ such that C lies entirely on one side of H, i.e., there exists $a \in \mathbb{R}^d \setminus \{0\}$ and $c \in \mathbb{R}$ such that $\sum_{i=1}^d a_i \overline{x}_i = c$ and $\sum_{i=1}^d a_i x_i \leq c$ for all $x \in C$.*

The proof of the supporting hyperplane theorem relies on the important *dominated extension theorem* below, which will also imply the Hahn–Banach theorems. To make sense of it, recall that a linear functional on a vector space X is a linear map from X into the scalar field (taken to be $\mathbb{R}$ throughout this appendix), while a *sublinear functional* on X is a map $f: X \to \mathbb{R}$ satisfying

$f(x + y) \leq f(x) + f(y)$ for all $x, y \in X$ and $f(tx) = tf(x)$ for all $t \geq 0$ and all $x \in X$.

Theorem C.9 *Let V be a linear subspace of a vector space X. If $\lambda: V \to \mathbb{R}$ is a linear functional such that $\lambda \leq f_{|V}$ for some sublinear functional $f: X \to \mathbb{R}$, then there exists a linear functional $\widetilde{\lambda}: X \to \mathbb{R}$ such that $\widetilde{\lambda}_{|V} = \lambda$ and $\widetilde{\lambda} \leq f$.*

Proof The first part of the argument consists in proving that λ can be extended from V to $V \oplus \text{span}\{w\}$, $w \notin V$, while preserving domination by f. To this end, for some suitable $\gamma \in \mathbb{R}$ uncovered below, one defines a linear functional $\widetilde{\lambda}$ on $V \oplus \text{span}\{w\}$ by $\widetilde{\lambda}(v + tw) = \lambda(v) + t\gamma$ for all $v \in V$ and $t \in \mathbb{R}$. This linear functional clearly extends λ, i.e., $\widetilde{\lambda}_{|V} = \lambda$. As for the domination by f, it holds if and only if $\lambda(v) + t\gamma \leq f(v + tw)$, or $t\gamma \leq f(v + tw) - \lambda(v)$, for all $v \in V$ and $t \in \mathbb{R}$. When $t > 0$, setting $v' := v/t$, this is equivalent to $\gamma \leq f(v' + w) - \lambda(v')$ for all $v' \in V$, and when $t < 0$, setting $v'' := -v/t$, this is equivalent to $\gamma \geq -f(v'' - w) + \lambda(v'')$ for all $v'' \in V$. Therefore, a suitable $\gamma \in \mathbb{R}$ exists if and only if $-f(v'' - w) + \lambda(v'') \leq f(v' + w) - \lambda(v')$, or $\lambda(v' + v'') \leq f(v' + w) + f(v'' - w)$, for all $v', v'' \in V$. This condition is indeed fulfilled since $\lambda(v' + v'') \leq f(v' + v'') = f(v' + w + v'' - w) \leq f(v' + w) + f(v'' - w)$.

The second part of the argument consists in transfinite induction (standard induction would be enough for a finite-dimensional space X). One introduces a set $\mathfrak{P} := \{(U, \mu) : U \text{ linear subspace of } X, \mu \text{ linear functional on } U, \mu \leq f_{|U}\}$ containing (V, λ). This is a partially ordered set for the binary relation defined by $(U', \mu') \geq (U, \mu)$ if and only if $U \subseteq U'$ and $\mu'_{|U} = \mu$. Notice that if $\mathfrak{Q}$ is a totally ordered subset of $\mathfrak{P}$ (aka a chain in $\mathfrak{P}$), then $\mathfrak{Q}$ has an upper bound (U', μ') in $\mathfrak{P}$: indeed, $U' := \bigcup_{(U,\mu)\in\mathfrak{Q}} U$ is a linear subspace of X on which μ' defined by $\mu'_{|U} = \mu$ for $(U, \mu) \in \mathfrak{Q}$ is a linear functional satisfying $\mu' \leq f_{|U'}$, so that $(U', \mu') \in \mathfrak{P}$, and one also clearly has $(U', \mu') \geq (U, \mu)$, i.e., $U \subseteq U'$ and $\mu'_{|U} = \mu$, for all $(U, \mu) \in \mathfrak{Q}$. Then, by the *Zorn lemma*, $\mathfrak{P}$ possesses a maximal element $(\overline{V}, \overline{\lambda}) \in \mathfrak{P}$. Suppose that $\overline{V}$ is a proper subspace of X, i.e., that there exists some $w \in X \setminus \overline{V}$. According to the first part, one can extend $\overline{\lambda}$ to a linear functional $\widehat{\lambda}$ defined on $\widehat{V} := \overline{V} \oplus \text{span}\{w\}$ such that $\widehat{\lambda}_{|\overline{V}} = \overline{\lambda}$ and $\widehat{\lambda} \leq f_{|\widehat{V}}$. The latter guarantees that $(\widehat{V}, \widehat{\lambda}) \in \mathfrak{P}$, implying that $(\widehat{V}, \widehat{\lambda}) \geq (\overline{V}, \overline{\lambda})$, and in turn that $\widehat{V} \subseteq \overline{V}$, which is impossible. This contradiction shows that $\overline{V} = X$. Now, the fact that $(\overline{V}, \overline{\lambda}) \in \mathfrak{P}$ yields $\overline{\lambda} \leq f_{|\overline{V}} = f$, while the fact that $(\overline{V}, \overline{\lambda}) \geq (V, \lambda)$ yields $\overline{\lambda}_{|V} = \lambda$. In other words, the linear functional $\overline{\lambda}$ fulfills the domination and extension requirements. □

The supporting hyperplane theorem can be deduced from the dominated extension theorem as follows.

Proof of Theorem C.8 (Sketch) If the interior of C was empty, then C would entirely lie in some hyperplane, which could then be taken as the supporting hyperplane. One now considers the case $\text{int}(C) \neq \emptyset$. Translating C if needed, one assumes that $0 \in \text{int}(C)$. It is easily verified that the *Minkowski functional* of C (aka its *gauge*) defined for $x \in \mathbb{R}^d$ by $f(x) = \inf\{t > 0 : x \in tC\}$ is a sublinear functional. For the linear functional λ defined on $V := \text{span}(\overline{x})$ by $\lambda(\overline{x}) = 1$, it is easily verified that $\lambda \leq f_{|V}$. Therefore, there is a linear functional $\widetilde{\lambda}$ defined on $\mathbb{R}^d$ such that $\widetilde{\lambda}_{|V} = \lambda$ and $\widetilde{\lambda} \leq f$. The former implies that $\widetilde{\lambda}(\overline{x}) = 1$, while the latter implies that $\widetilde{\lambda}(x) \leq 1$ for all $x \in C$ (since $f(x) \leq 1$ for all $x \in C$). It remains to write the linear functional $\widetilde{\lambda}$ as $\widetilde{\lambda} = \langle a, \cdot \rangle$ for some $a \in \mathbb{R}^d \setminus \{0\}$ while choosing $c = 1$. $\qquad\square$

As mentioned above, the dominated extension theorem is also the seed for two results routinely known as the Hahn–Banach theorems. The *Hahn–Banach extension theorem* is the following statement, obtained as a direct consequence of Theorem C.9 by taking the sublinear functional f to be $f(x) = \|\lambda\|_V^* \|x\|$.

Theorem C.10 *A continous linear functional λ on a linear subspace V of a normed space X can be extended to a continuous linear functional $\widetilde{\lambda}$ on the whole space X while preserving its norm, so that $\widetilde{\lambda}(v) = \lambda(v)$ for all $v \in V$ and $\|\widetilde{\lambda}\|_X^* := \max\{\widetilde{\lambda}(x)/\|x\| : x \in X \setminus \{0\}\} = \|\lambda\|_V^* := \max\{\lambda(v)/\|v\| : v \in V \setminus \{0\}\}$.*

In a vein of ideas more similar to the separating hyperplane theorem, the *Hahn–Banach separation theorem* reads as follows.

Theorem C.11 *Let C and $\mathcal{D}$ be disjoint convex subsets of a normed space X. If $\mathcal{D}$ is open, then there exist a continuous linear functional $\lambda \colon X \to \mathbb{R}$ and a number $c \in \mathbb{R}$ such that*

$$\lambda(x) \geq c > \lambda(y) \qquad \text{for all } x \in C \text{ and all } y \in \mathcal{D}.$$

Proof (Sketch) Fixing $x_0 \in C$ and $y_0 \in \mathcal{D}$, consider $\mathcal{E} := (\mathcal{D} - y_0) - (C - x_0)$, which is a convex open neighborhood of the origin. Let a sublinear functional f be given as the *Minkowski functional* of $\mathcal{E}$ and let a linear functional λ be defined on $V := \text{span}\{x_0 - y_0\}$ by $\lambda(x_0 - y_0) = 1$. From the convexity of C and $\mathcal{D}$, as well as their disjointness, one easily verifies that $\lambda \leq f_{|V}$. By Theorem C.9, there exists a linear functional $\widetilde{\lambda}$ defined on X such that $\widetilde{\lambda}_{|V} \leq \lambda$ and $\widetilde{\lambda} \leq f$. This linear functional is continuous, since it is bounded on an open neighborhood of the origin—indeed, $\widetilde{\lambda}(z) \leq f(z) \leq 1$ for all $z \in \mathcal{E}$. Now, for any $x \in C$ and $y \in \mathcal{D}$, one has $\widetilde{\lambda}(y) - \widetilde{\lambda}(x) + 1 = \widetilde{\lambda}(y - x + x_0 - y_0) \leq f(y - x + x_0 - y_0) < 1$, the last inequality being strict because $\mathcal{E}$ is open. Setting $c := \inf\{\widetilde{\lambda}(x) : x \in C\}$, one obtains that $\widetilde{\lambda}(x) \geq c$ for all $x \in C$ and that $c \geq \widetilde{\lambda}(y)$ for all $y \in \mathcal{D}$. But when $y \in \mathcal{D}$, because $y + \varepsilon(x_0 - y_0) \in \mathcal{D}$ for some small enough $\varepsilon > 0$, one actually has $c \geq \widetilde{\lambda}(y) + \varepsilon \widetilde{\lambda}(x_0 - y_0) = \widetilde{\lambda}(y) + \varepsilon$, so that $c > \widetilde{\lambda}(y)$. The result is now acquired for the continuous linear functional $\widetilde{\lambda} \colon X \to \mathbb{R}$. □

By taking $\mathcal{D}$ as an open ball centered at some point a and not intersecting C, Theorem C.11 readily implies the following result.

Corollary C.12 *Let C be a closed convex subset of a normed space X and let $a \notin C$. There exists a continuous linear functional $\lambda \colon X \to \mathbb{R}$ and a number $c \in \mathbb{R}$ such that*

$$\lambda(x) \geq c > \lambda(a) \qquad \text{for all } x \in C.$$

C.3 Extreme Points

Let $\mathcal{A}$ be a subset of a vector space X. A point $a \in \mathcal{A}$ is called an *extreme point* of $\mathcal{A}$ if it is not a strict convex combination of other points in $\mathcal{A}$, i.e., if

$$[(1 - \tau)x + \tau y = a \text{ for some } x, y \in \mathcal{A} \text{ and } \tau \in (0, 1)] \implies [x = y = a].$$

More generally, a subset $\mathcal{B}$ of $\mathcal{A}$ is called an *extreme set* of $\mathcal{A}$ if

$$[(1 - \tau)x + \tau y \in \mathcal{B} \text{ for some } x, y \in \mathcal{A} \text{ and } \tau \in (0, 1)] \implies [x, y \in \mathcal{B}].$$

The set of extreme points of $\mathcal{A}$ is denoted by $\mathrm{Ex}(\mathcal{A})$. When X is a normed space, one is often interested in the set $\mathrm{Ex}(B_X)$ of extreme points of the unit ball of X. An extreme point of B_X always has norm one, i.e., $\mathrm{Ex}(B_X) \subseteq S_X$. The case of equality $\mathrm{Ex}(B_X) = S_X$ defines a strictly convex space. For instance, the spaces ℓ_p^n are strictly convex for $p \in (1, \infty)$, but not for $p = 1$ or $p = \infty$, since $\mathrm{Ex}(B_1^n) = \{x \in \mathbb{R}^n : \exists i \in [1:n] \text{ such that } |x_j| = \delta_{i,j} \text{ for all } j \in [1:n]\}$ and $\mathrm{Ex}(B_\infty^n) = \{x \in \mathbb{R}^n : |x_j| = 1 \text{ for all } j \in [1:n]\}$. For the space $C(X)$ of continuous functions on a compact set X, one has $\mathrm{Ex}(B_{C(X)}) = \{-1, +1\}$ and $\mathrm{Ex}(B_{C(X)^*}) = \{f \in C(X) \mapsto f(x) \in \mathbb{R}, x \in X\}$. As a more delicate determination of extreme points, one now presents the *Birkhoff theorem*.

Theorem C.13 *Given $n \geq 1$, the set S of doubly stochastic $n \times n$ matrices, i.e.,*

$$S = \left\{ M \in \mathbb{R}^{n \times n} : M \geq 0, \sum_{j=1}^{n} M_{i,j} = 1 \text{ for all } i \in [1:n], \right.$$

$$\left. \text{and} \sum_{i=1}^{n} M_{i,j} = 1 \text{ for all } j \in [1:n] \right\}$$

has extreme points given by permutation matrices. In other words,

$$\mathrm{Ex}(S) = \Big\{P \in \mathbb{R}^{n \times n} : \text{there is a permutation } \pi \text{ of } [1:n]$$

$$\text{such that } P_{i,j} = \delta_{i,\pi(j)} \text{ for all } i, j \in [1:n]\Big\}.$$

Proof Let $\mathcal{P}$ be the set of permutation matrices. The inclusion $\mathcal{P} \subseteq \mathrm{Ex}(S)$ being easy to see, one concentrates on proving the inclusion $\mathrm{Ex}(S) \subseteq \mathcal{P}$, which is done by induction on $n \geq 1$. The base case $n = 1$ is clear. One now assumes that the induction hypothesis holds up to $n - 1$, $n \geq 2$. To show that it holds for n, too, one observes first that one of the $2n$ equality conditions defining doubly stochastic $n \times n$ matrices is redundant. For instance, the fact that the entries of the last column sum up to one follows from

$$\sum_{i=1}^{n} M_{i,n} = \sum_{i=1}^{n} \Big(1 - \sum_{j=1}^{n-1} M_{i,j}\Big) = n - \sum_{j=1}^{n-1} \sum_{i=1}^{n} M_{i,j} = n - (n-1) = 1.$$

Thus, with $x := \mathrm{vec}(M)$, the conditions for a matrix $M \in \mathbb{R}^{n \times n}$ to be doubly stochastic read $x \geq 0$ and $Ax = b$ for some $A \in \mathbb{R}^{(2n-1) \times n^2}$ and $b \in \mathbb{R}^{2n-1}$ that need not be specified. According to Lemma 20.2, an extreme point $P \in \mathrm{Ex}(S)$ has at most $2n - 1$ nonzero entries. Consequently, there is a row of P, say the kth row, containing less than two nonzero entries. Given that the entries along a row sum up to one, this means that the kth row has exactly one nonzero entry, say $P_{k,\ell}$, and that $P_{k,\ell} = 1$. This implies that the $(n-1) \times (n-1)$ matrix $\widetilde{P}$ obtained from P by removing the kth row and ℓth column is doubly stochastic, and in fact it is easily seen to be an extreme point of the set of $(n-1) \times (n-1)$ of doubly stochastic matrices. By the induction hypothesis, the matrix $\widetilde{P}$ is a permutation matrix, which implies that the matrix P itself is a permutation matrix. This establishes the induction hypothesis for n and concludes the proof.   □

Going further, it can also be said that any doubly stochastic matrix is a convex combination of permutation matrices. This fact follows not only from the Birkhoff theorem, but also from the *Krein–Milman theorem* stated below.

Theorem C.14 *If $\mathcal{A}$ is a nonempty compact subset of a normed space X, then the closed convex hulls of $\mathcal{A}$ and of $\mathrm{Ex}(\mathcal{A})$ are identical.*

Proof The first part consists in proving that the set of extreme points of a nonempty compact subset $\mathcal{A} \subseteq X$ is nonempty. To this end, one introduces the set $\mathfrak{P} := \{\mathcal{B} \subseteq \mathcal{A}, \mathcal{B} \text{ is a nonempty compact extreme set of } \mathcal{A}\}$, which appears as a partially ordered set with the inclusion $\subseteq$ playing the role of the binary relation $\geq$. Notice that if $\mathfrak{Q}$ is a totally ordered subset of $\mathfrak{P}$ (aka a chain in $\mathfrak{P}$), then $C := \bigcap_{\mathcal{B} \in \mathfrak{Q}} \mathcal{B}$ is an upper bound for $\mathfrak{Q}$ in $\mathfrak{P}$: indeed, one obviously has

$C \subseteq \mathcal{B}$ for all $\mathcal{B} \in \mathfrak{Q}$, and $C \in \mathfrak{P}$ holds because C is nonempty (otherwise, by compactness, a finite intersection of $\mathcal{B} \in \mathfrak{Q}$ would be empty, but such a finite intersection is one of the $\mathcal{B}$ since $\mathfrak{Q}$ is totally ordered), because C is compact (as an intersection of compact sets), and because C is an extreme set of $\mathcal{A}$ (as an intersection of extreme sets of $\mathcal{A}$). Then, by the *Zorn lemma*, $\mathfrak{P}$ possesses a maximal element $\mathcal{D} \in \mathfrak{P}$. One shall prove that $\mathcal{D}$ reduces to a singleton $\{d\}$, so the fact that $\mathcal{D}$ is an extreme set of $\mathcal{A}$ means that $d \in \mathrm{Ex}(\mathcal{A})$, and hence the part stating that $\mathrm{Ex}(\mathcal{A})$ is nonempty will be established. Thus, by way of contradiction, one assumes that $\mathcal{D}$, which is nonempty, contains two distinct elements d and d'. An application of the *Hahn–Banach extension theorem* to $\mathrm{span}\{d - d'\}$ shows that there exists some $\lambda \in X^*$ such that $\lambda(d) \neq \lambda(d')$. With $\gamma := \max\{\lambda(x), x \in \mathcal{D}\}$, it is not hard to see that $\mathcal{E} := \{x \in \mathcal{D} : \lambda(x) = \gamma\}$ is an extreme set of $\mathcal{D}$, which is itself an extreme set of $\mathcal{A}$, and therefore $\mathcal{E}$ is an extreme set of $\mathcal{A}$. Given that the set $\mathcal{E}$ is nonempty and compact, one obtains $\mathcal{E} \in \mathfrak{P}$. Now, $\mathcal{D}$ being a maximal element of $\mathfrak{P}$, it follows that $\mathcal{D} \subseteq \mathcal{E}$. In particular, one has $d, d' \in \mathcal{E}$, i.e., $\lambda(d) = \lambda(d') = \gamma$. This contradicts the fact that $\lambda(d) \neq \lambda(d')$ and finishes the justification of the first part.

For the second part, given the nonempty compact subset $\mathcal{A} \subseteq X$, one denotes by $\mathcal{B}$ and C the closed convex hulls of $\mathcal{A}$ and of $\mathrm{Ex}(\mathcal{A})$, respectively. Since $C \subseteq \mathcal{B}$ is immediate, one needs to prove that $\mathcal{B} \subseteq C$. To this end, it is enough to show that $\mathcal{A} \subseteq C$. Assume on the contrary that there exists $a \in \mathcal{A}$ with $a \notin C$. By Corollary C.12, one has $\alpha := \inf\{\lambda(x) : x \in C\} > \lambda(a)$ for some $\lambda \in X^*$. Setting $\beta := \inf\{\lambda(x) : x \in \mathcal{A}\}$, one considers the nonempty compact set $\mathcal{D} := \{x \in \mathcal{A} : \lambda(x) = \beta\}$. From the first part, it is known that $\mathrm{Ex}(\mathcal{D}) \neq \emptyset$, so one can select $z \in \mathrm{Ex}(\mathcal{D})$. In view of $z \in \mathcal{D}$, one observes that $\lambda(z) = \beta$. Furthermore, one claims that $z \in \mathrm{Ex}(\mathcal{A})$. Indeed, the contrary would mean that $z = (1 - \tau)a_0 + \tau a_1$ for some $\tau \in (0, 1)$ and $a_0 \neq a_1 \in \mathcal{A}$, but applying λ would give $\beta = (1 - \tau)\lambda(a_0) + \tau\lambda(a_1) \geq (1 - \tau)\beta + \tau\beta = \beta$, forcing $\lambda(a_0) = \lambda(a_1) = \beta$, i.e., $a_0, a_1 \in \mathcal{D}$, which is impossible because $z \in \mathrm{Ex}(\mathcal{D})$. Since $z \in \mathrm{Ex}(\mathcal{A}) \subseteq C$ is now established, it follows that $\lambda(z) \geq \alpha$, and in turn $\beta > \lambda(a)$. This violates the definition of β. The required contradiction having been obtained, the proof is complete. □

Exercises

C.1 Show that the dual of a normed space is always a Banach space.

C.2 In a Banach space, absolute convergence implies convergence. Prove conversely that if X is a normed space in which the convergence of $\sum \|x_n\|$ implies the convergence of $\sum x_n$, then X is a Banach space.

C.3   Given a subspace V of a vector space X, verify that $\{[x] := x + V, x \in V\}$ is a linear space. It is called the *quotient space* of X modulo V and is denoted by X/V. If X is a normed space and V is a closed subspace of X, prove that $\|[x]\|_{X/V} := \inf\{\|z\| : [z] = [x]\}$ defines a norm on X/V called the *quotient norm*. Furthermore, if X is a Banach space, prove that X/V is also a Banach space.

C.4   Let $x \in X$ be an element of a normed space X. Taking for granted that the *Krein–Milman theorem* also holds when $\mathcal{A}$ is a subset of X^* which is compact relatively to the weak-star topology, prove that there exists some $\lambda \in \mathrm{Ex}(B_{X^*})$ such that $\lambda(x) = \|x\|$.

Appendix D
Matrix Analysis

In this targeted summary of matrix analysis, of importance for PART THREE and PART FOUR, all the matrices have complex entries. The results remain valid for matrices having real entries provided some natural modifications are made, e.g. the transpose $A^\top$ should replace the adjoint A^*, orthogonal matrices should replace unitary matrices, etc. The books by Horn and Johnson (2013) and Bhatia (1997) provide more detailed treatments of the subject.

D.1 Eigenvalues of Self-Adjoint Matrices

The *adjoint* of a square matrix $A \in \mathbb{C}^{n \times n}$ is the matrix A^* with entries $A^*_{i,j} = \overline{A_{j,i}}$, $i, j \in [1:n]$. The matrix A is called *self-adjoint* if $A^* = A$. The eigenvalues of a self-adjoint matrix $A \in \mathbb{C}^{n \times n}$ are necessarily real: indeed, if $Ax = \lambda x$ for some $x \in \mathbb{C}^n \setminus \{0\}$, then taking the adjoint on both sides gives $x^* A^* = \overline{\lambda} x^*$, so that $\overline{\lambda} \|x\|_2^2 = x^* A^* x = x^* A x = \lambda \|x\|_2^2$, and hence $\overline{\lambda} = \lambda$. This observation ensures that the diagonal matrix D appearing in the *spectral theorem* below[1] turns out to be real when A is a self-adjoint matrix. The theorem more generally concerns normal matrices—in fact, it characterizes them. Recall that a square matrix $A \in \mathbb{C}^{n \times n}$ is called *normal* if $A^* A = A A^*$. Furthermore, if $A^* A = A A^* = I_n$, then $A \in \mathbb{C}^{n \times n}$ is called a *unitary* matrix.

Theorem D.1 *Given $A \in \mathbb{C}^{n \times n}$, the following statements are equivalent:*

  (i) *A is normal;*

  (ii) *A is unitarily diagonalizable, meaning that there exist a diagonal matrix $D \in \mathbb{C}^{n \times n}$ and a unitary matrix $V \in \mathbb{C}^{n \times n}$ such that $A = VDV^*$;*

  (iii) $\displaystyle\sum_{i,j=1}^{n} |A_{i,j}|^2 = \sum_{k=1}^{n} |\lambda_k(A)|^2$, $\lambda_1(A), \ldots, \lambda_n(A)$ *denoting the eigenvalues of A.*

---

[1] A proof of which can be found in Section 2.5 of Horn and Johnson (2013).

The (real) eigenvalues $\lambda_1(A), \ldots, \lambda_n(A)$ of a self-adjoint matrix $A \in \mathbb{C}^{n \times n}$ are traditionally ordered in a nonincreasing fashion, so that

$$\lambda_1(A) \geq \lambda_2(A) \geq \cdots \geq \lambda_n(A).$$

Each of these eigenvalues admits the minimax characterizations

$$\lambda_i(A) = \max_{\substack{\mathcal{V} \subseteq \mathbb{C}^n \\ \dim(\mathcal{V})=i}} \min_{\substack{x \in \mathcal{V} \\ \|x\|_2=1}} \langle Ax, x \rangle = \min_{\substack{\mathcal{V} \subseteq \mathbb{C}^n \\ \dim(\mathcal{V})=n-i+1}} \max_{\substack{x \in \mathcal{V} \\ \|x\|_2=1}} \langle Ax, x \rangle. \qquad \text{(D.1)}$$

In these characterizations, often referred to as the *Courant–Fischer theorem*, the term $\langle Ax, x \rangle$—or rather $\langle Ax, x \rangle / \|x\|_2^2$ when x is not ℓ_2-normalized—is called the *Rayleigh quotient*. The justification of (D.1) is postponed, as it is a special case of the Wielandt minimax principle (Theorem D.2 below). For now, note that the minimax characterizations provide a read-through proof of the fact that, for any $i \in [1:n]$, two self-adjoint matrices $B, C \in \mathbb{C}^{n \times n}$ satisfy

$$\lambda_i(B) \geq \lambda_i(C) \qquad \text{whenever } B \succeq C. \qquad \text{(D.2)}$$

The notation $B \succeq C$ means that $B - C \succeq 0$—in other words that $B - C$ is a positive semidefinite matrix. Recall that a square matrix $A \in \mathbb{C}^{n \times n}$ is called *positive semidefinite* if it is self-adjoint and if $\langle Ax, x \rangle \geq 0$ for all $x \in \mathbb{C}^n$. This is easily seen to be equivalent, using the spectral theorem, to the fact that A is self-adjoint and has all its eigenvalues nonnegative. To put an end to the positive semidefiniteness digression, notice in turn that a matrix $A \in \mathbb{C}^{n \times n}$ is positive semidefinite if and only if it can be written as $A = BB^*$ for some positive semidefinite matrix $B \in \mathbb{C}^{n \times n}$. It is now time for the awaited *Wielandt minimax principle*.

Theorem D.2 *Let $A \in \mathbb{C}^{n \times n}$ be a self-adjoint matrix. Given $k \in [1:n]$ and indices $i_1 < \cdots < i_k$ in $[1:n]$, one has*

$$\sum_{j=1}^{k} \lambda_{i_j}(A) = \max_{\substack{\mathcal{V}_1 \subseteq \cdots \subseteq \mathcal{V}_k \subseteq \mathbb{C}^n \\ \dim(\mathcal{V}_j)=i_j}} \min_{\substack{(x_1,\ldots,x_k) \text{ orthonormal} \\ x_1 \in \mathcal{V}_1, \ldots, x_k \in \mathcal{V}_k}} \sum_{j=1}^{k} \langle Ax_j, x_j \rangle.$$

Proof To establish the $\leq$-part, one needs to find subspaces $\mathcal{V}_1 \subseteq \cdots \subseteq \mathcal{V}_k$ of dimensions $i_1, \ldots, i_k$, respectively, such that $\sum_{j=1}^{k} \lambda_{i_j}(A) \leq \sum_{j=1}^{k} \langle Ax_j, x_j \rangle$ whenever $(x_1, \ldots, x_k)$ is an orthonormal system with $x_1 \in \mathcal{V}_1, \ldots, x_k \in \mathcal{V}_k$. Picking an orthonormal basis $(v_1, \ldots, v_n)$ of eigenvectors for the eigenvalues $\lambda_1(A) \geq \cdots \geq \lambda_n(A)$, it suffices to take $\mathcal{V}_j = \text{span}\{v_1, \ldots, v_{i_j}\}$, $j \in [1:k]$. Indeed, writing $x_j \in \mathcal{V}_j$ as $x_j = \sum_{\ell=1}^{i_j} c_{j,\ell} v_\ell$, one has $Ax_j = \sum_{\ell=1}^{i_j} c_{j,\ell} \lambda_\ell(A) v_\ell$ and $\sum_{\ell=1}^{i_j} c_{j,\ell}^2 = \|x_j\|_2^2 = 1$, so that $\langle Ax_j, x_j \rangle = \sum_{\ell=1}^{i_j} c_{j,\ell}^2 \lambda_\ell(A) \geq \lambda_{i_j}(A)$. Summing over $j \in [1:k]$ gives the required inequality.

For the $\geq$-part, one needs to show that, for all subspaces $\mathcal{V}_1 \subseteq \cdots \subseteq \mathcal{V}_k$ of dimensions $i_1, \ldots, i_k$, respectively, there is an orthonormal system $(x_1, \ldots, x_k)$ with $x_1 \in \mathcal{V}_1, \ldots, x_k \in \mathcal{V}_k$ such that $\sum_{j=1}^k \lambda_{i_j}(A) \geq \sum_{j=1}^k \langle Ax_j, x_j \rangle$. With $(v_1, \ldots, v_n)$ still denoting an orthonormal basis of eigenvectors for the eigenvalues $\lambda_1(A) \geq \cdots \geq \lambda_n(A)$, one considers the subspaces $\mathcal{W}_1, \ldots, \mathcal{W}_k$ defined by $\mathcal{W}_j = \mathrm{span}\{v_{i_j}, \ldots, v_n\}$, $j \in [1:k]$. In view of Exercise D.2, one can find orthonormal systems $(x_1, \ldots, x_k)$ and $(y_1, \ldots, y_k)$ spanning the same space S in such a way that $x_j \in \mathcal{V}_j$ and $y_j \in \mathcal{W}_j$ for all $j \in [1:k]$. Writing $y_j = \sum_{\ell=i_j}^n d_{j,\ell} v_\ell$, one has $Ay_j = \sum_{\ell=i_j}^n d_{j,\ell} \lambda_\ell(A) v_\ell$ and $\sum_{\ell=i_j}^n d_{j,\ell}^2 = \|y_j\|_2^2 = 1$, so that $\langle Ay_j, y_j \rangle = \sum_{\ell=i_j}^n d_{j,\ell}^2 \lambda_\ell(A) \leq \lambda_{i_j}(A)$. Summing over $j \in [1:k]$ leads to $\sum_{j=1}^k \langle Ay_j, y_j \rangle \leq \sum_{j=1}^k \lambda_{i_j}(A)$, which in turn implies the required inequality $\sum_{j=1}^k \langle Ax_j, x_j \rangle \leq \sum_{j=1}^k \lambda_{i_j}(A)$ because $\sum_{j=1}^k \langle Ax_j, x_j \rangle$ and $\sum_{j=1}^k \langle Ay_j, y_j \rangle$ are both equal to the trace of the compression of A to S.   □

The Wielandt minimax principle can be used to prove the next result, known as the *Lidskii inequality*. An alternative justification is nonetheless presented.

Theorem D.3   *Let* $A, B \in \mathbb{C}^{n \times n}$ *be two self-adjoint matrices. Given* $k \in [1:n]$ *and indices* $i_1 < \cdots < i_k$ *in* $[1:n]$, *one has*

$$\sum_{j=1}^k \lambda_{i_j}(A + B) \leq \sum_{j=1}^k \lambda_{i_j}(A) + \sum_{i=1}^k \lambda_i(B). \tag{D.3}$$

Proof   Since both sides of (D.3) are changed by the same quantity when B is replaced by $B - \lambda I_n$ for any $\lambda \in \mathbb{R}$, one can assume that $\lambda_{k+1}(B) = 0$. With $B = V \mathrm{diag}[\lambda_1(B); \ldots; \lambda_n(B)]V^*$ representing the eigendecomposition of B, one defines the matrix $B^+ = V \mathrm{diag}[\lambda_1(B); \ldots; \lambda_k(B); 0; \ldots; 0]V^*$. In view of $A + B \leq A + B^+$ and $A \leq A + B^+$, applying (D.2) yields $\lambda_i(A + B) \leq \lambda_i(A + B^+)$ and $\lambda_i(A) \leq \lambda_i(A + B^+)$ for all $i \in [1:n]$. It follows that

$$\sum_{j=1}^k (\lambda_{i_j}(A + B) - \lambda_{i_j}(A)) \leq \sum_{j=1}^k (\lambda_{i_j}(A + B^+) - \lambda_{i_j}(A))$$

$$\leq \sum_{i=1}^n (\lambda_i(A + B^+) - \lambda_i(A))$$

$$= \mathrm{tr}(A + B^+) - \mathrm{tr}(A) = \mathrm{tr}(B^+)$$

$$= \sum_{i=1}^k \lambda_i(B),$$

which is a rearrangement of the required inequality (D.3).   □

The *Weyl inequality*, stating that the eigenvalues of two self-adjoint matrices

$A, B \in \mathbb{C}^{n \times n}$ satisfy, for all $i \in [1:n]$,

$$\lambda_i(A) + \lambda_n(B) \leq \lambda_i(A + B) \leq \lambda_i(A) + \lambda_1(B),$$

is a particular case of the Lidskii inequality: the rightmost inequality is (D.3) directly applied with $k = 1$, while the leftmost inequality reduces to the rightmost one by changing A into $-A$, B into $-B$, and i into $n + 1 - i$. Finally, in view of $\|B\|_{2 \to 2} = \max\{|\lambda_1(B)|, |\lambda_n(B)|\}$, the Weyl inequality gives, for all $i \in [1:n]$,

$$|\lambda_i(A + B) - \lambda_i(A)| \leq \|B\|_{2 \to 2}. \tag{D.4}$$

D.2 Singular Values

While the concept of eigenvalues applies to square matrices only (with focus put even further on self-adjoint matrices in the previous section), the concept of singular values applies to rectangular matrices as well. It is based on the following fundamental result.[2]

Theorem D.4 *Given $A \in \mathbb{C}^{m \times n}$, there exist a nonnegative diagonal matrix $\Sigma \in \mathbb{R}^{m \times n}$ and unitary matrices $U \in \mathbb{C}^{m \times m}$ and $V \in \mathbb{C}^{n \times n}$ such that $A = U\Sigma V^*$.*

The nonnegative numbers on the diagonal of Σ are called *singular values* of A and are denoted by $\sigma_1(A) \geq \sigma_2(A) \geq \cdots \geq \sigma_\ell(A) \geq 0$, where the shorthand

$$\ell = \min\{m, n\}$$

is to be used for the rest of this appendix. Note that, similarly to eigenvalues, the singular values are traditionally arranged in a nonincreasing fashion. The singular value decomposition $A = U\Sigma V^*$ can also be written with $\Sigma \in \mathbb{R}^{\ell \times \ell}$ being a square matrix, in which case $U \in \mathbb{C}^{m \times \ell}$ and $V \in \mathbb{C}^{n \times \ell}$ are rectangular matrices having orthonormal columns. These columns, which are denoted by $u_1, \ldots, u_\ell$ and $v_1, \ldots, v_\ell$, are called left and right *singular vectors*, respectively. The decomposition $A = U\Sigma V^*$ equivalently reads $A = \sum_{k=1}^{\ell} \sigma_k(A) u_k v_k^*$, effortlessly showing that $Av_k = \sigma_k(A) u_k$ and that $u_k^* A = \sigma_k(A) v_k^*$ for all $k \in [1:\ell]$. In view of $AA^* = U\Sigma^2 U^* \in \mathbb{R}^{m \times m}$ and of $A^*A = V\Sigma^2 V^* \in \mathbb{R}^{n \times n}$, one sees that $\sigma_k(A) = \lambda_k(AA^*)^{1/2} = \lambda_k(A^*A)^{1/2}$ for all $k \in [1:\ell]$. The singular values of A are also related to the eigenvalues of another matrix associated with A, as revealed by the observation below.

---

[2] A proof of which can be found in Section 2.6 of Horn and Johnson (2013).

Theorem D.5 *The* self-adjoint dilation *of a matrix $A \in \mathbb{C}^{m \times n}$, defined by*

$$S(A) = \left[\begin{array}{c|c} 0 & A \\ \hline A^* & 0 \end{array}\right] \in \mathbb{C}^{(m+n)\times(m+n)},$$

has eigenvalues

$$\sigma_1(A) \geq \cdots \geq \sigma_\ell(A) \geq 0 = \cdots = 0 \geq -\sigma_\ell(A) \geq \cdots \geq -\sigma_1(A).$$

Proof Suppose for instance that $m \leq n$. If $A = \sum_{k=1}^{m} \sigma_k u_k v_k^*$ is the singular value decomposition of A and if $(v_{m+1}, \ldots, v_n)$ completes $(v_1, \ldots, v_m)$ to form an orthonormal basis of $\mathbb{C}^n$, then it is readily verified that, for all $k \in [1:m]$,

$$S(A)w_k^\pm = \pm\sigma_k w_k^\pm, \quad \text{where} \quad w_k^\pm := \frac{1}{\sqrt{2}}\left[\begin{array}{c} u_k \\ \pm v_k \end{array}\right],$$

and that, for all $k \in [m+1:n]$,

$$S(A)w_k^0 = 0, \quad \text{where} \quad w_k^0 := \left[\begin{array}{c} 0 \\ v_k \end{array}\right].$$

It is also readily verified that $(w_1^+, \ldots, w_m^+, w_{m+1}^0, \ldots, w_n^0, w_m^-, \ldots, w_1^-)$ forms an orthonormal basis for $\mathbb{C}^{m+n}$. This completes the argument in the case $m \leq n$. The case $m > n$ is treated in a similar way. □

The above observation, in combination with the Lidskii inequality, appears as a crucial ingredient in the proof of the *Mirsky inequality*, which is stated next.

Theorem D.6 *Let $A, B \in \mathbb{C}^{m \times n}$ be two matrices. Given $k \in [1:\ell]$ and indices $1 \leq i_1 < \cdots < i_k \leq \ell$, one has*

$$\sum_{j=1}^{k} |\sigma_{i_j}(A) - \sigma_{i_j}(B)| \leq \sum_{i=1}^{k} \sigma_i(A - B).$$

Proof In view of Theorem D.5, there is an index set $I \subseteq [1:m+n]$ of size k such that

$$\sum_{j=1}^{k} |\sigma_{i_j}(A) - \sigma_{i_j}(B)| = \sum_{i \in I} (\lambda_i(S(A)) - \lambda_i(S(B))).$$

It then follows from the *Lidskii inequality* (Theorem D.3) that

$$\sum_{j=1}^{k} |\sigma_{i_j}(A) - \sigma_{i_j}(B)| \leq \sum_{i=1}^{k} \lambda_i(S(A-B)) = \sum_{i=1}^{k} \sigma_i(A-B),$$

where Theorem D.5 was again called upon for the last equality. □

The following consequence of Theorem D.6 is worth pointing out.

Corollary D.7 *Let $A, B \in \mathbb{C}^{m \times n}$ be two matrices. Given nonincreasing weights $w_1 \geq \cdots \geq w_\ell \geq 0$, one has*

$$\sum_{i=1}^{\ell} w_i |\sigma_i(A) - \sigma_i(B)| \leq \sum_{i=1}^{\ell} w_i \sigma_i(A - B). \tag{D.5}$$

Proof By *summation by parts*, for any $s \in \mathbb{R}^\ell$, it holds that

$$\sum_{i=1}^{\ell} w_i s_i = w_\ell S_\ell + \sum_{i=1}^{\ell-1} (w_i - w_{i+1}) S_i, \tag{D.6}$$

where the S_i denote the partial sums $S_i := s_1 + \cdots + s_i$. Considering now $s_i := |\sigma_i(A) - \sigma_i(B)|$ and $s_i' := \sigma_i(A - B)$, Theorem D.6 guarantees that $S_i \leq S_i'$ for all $i \in [1 : \ell]$. In view of $w_\ell \geq 0$ and $w_i - w_{i+1} \geq 0$ for $i \in [1 : \ell - 1]$, the identity (D.6) implies that $\sum_{i=1}^{\ell} w_i s_i \leq \sum_{i=1}^{\ell} w_i s_i'$, which is the required result. □

Given $w_1 \geq \cdots \geq w_\ell \geq 0$, the weighted Mirsky inequality (D.5)—with A replaced by $A + B$—immediately implies that, for any $A, B \in \mathbb{C}^{m \times n}$,

$$\sum_{i=1}^{\ell} w_i \sigma_i(A + B) \leq \sum_{i=1}^{\ell} w_i \sigma_i(A) + \sum_{i=1}^{\ell} w_i \sigma_i(B). \tag{D.7}$$

The latter offers a neat (and not well-known) proof of the *von Neumann trace inequality*, which is stated below.

Theorem D.8 *Given two matrices $A, B \in \mathbb{C}^{m \times n}$, one has*

$$|\mathrm{tr}(A^* B)| \leq \sum_{i=1}^{\ell} \sigma_i(A) \sigma_i(B).$$

Proof Replacing A by $e^{i\theta} A$ for some appropriate $\theta \in \mathbb{T}$, one can assume that $|\mathrm{tr}(A^* B)| = \mathfrak{R}(\mathrm{tr}(A^* B))$, and hence

$$|\mathrm{tr}(A^* B)| = \mathfrak{R}(\langle A, B \rangle_F) = \frac{1}{2} \left(\|A + B\|_F^2 - \|A\|_F^2 - \|B\|_F^2 \right)$$

$$= \frac{1}{2} \left(\sum_{i=1}^{\ell} \sigma_i(A + B)^2 - \sum_{i=1}^{\ell} \sigma_i(A)^2 - \sum_{i=1}^{\ell} \sigma_i(B)^2 \right). \tag{D.8}$$

Now, using (D.7) first with $w_i = \sigma_i(A + B)$ and then with $w_i = \sigma_i(A) + \sigma_i(B)$, one obtains

$$\sum_{i=1}^{\ell} \sigma_i(A+B)^2 \leq \sum_{i=1}^{\ell} \sigma_i(A+B)(\sigma_i(A) + \sigma_i(B)) \leq \sum_{i=1}^{\ell} (\sigma_i(A) + \sigma_i(B))^2$$

$$= \sum_{i=1}^{\ell} \sigma_i(A)^2 + \sum_{i=1}^{\ell} \sigma_i(B)^2 + 2 \sum_{i=1}^{\ell} \sigma_i(A)\sigma_i(B). \tag{D.9}$$

Substituting (D.9) into (D.8) yields the desired result. □

D.3 Matrix Norms

The above argument for the von Neumann trace inequality implicitly required some knowledge about the *Frobenius norm* $\|A\|_F$ of a matrix $A \in \mathbb{C}^{m \times n}$. This is simply the euclidean norm of the vectorization of the matrix A. Thus, the *Frobenius inner product* between two matrices $A, B \in \mathbb{C}^{m \times n}$ is defined as $\langle A, B \rangle_F = \sum_{i=1}^{m} \sum_{j=1}^{n} \overline{A}_{i,j} B_{i,j}$. Importantly, it is also written as $\langle A, B \rangle_F = \mathrm{tr}(A^*B)$. Using the singular value decomposition of A and properties of the trace, this implies that the Frobenius norm of $A \in \mathbb{C}^{m \times n}$ coincides with the ℓ_2-norm of the vector $\sigma(A)$ of singular values of A. The ℓ_∞-norm of $\sigma(A)$ is the operator the *operator norm* $\|A\|_{2 \to 2}$ (from ℓ_2 to ℓ_2) and the ℓ_1-norm of $\sigma(A)$ is the so-called *nuclear norm* $\|A\|_*$. In brief, still using the shorthand $\ell = \min\{m, n\}$,

$$\|A\|_{2 \to 2} = \max\{\|Ax\|_2 : \|x\|_2 = 1\} \quad \text{is also} \quad \|A\|_{2 \to 2} = \sigma_1(A),$$

$$\|A\|_F = \left[\sum_{i=1}^{m} \sum_{j=1}^{n} |A_{i,j}|^2\right]^{1/2} \quad \text{is also} \quad \|A\|_F = \left[\sum_{k=1}^{\ell} \sigma_k(A)^2\right]^{1/2},$$

$$\text{and } \|A\|_*, \text{ by definition,} \quad \text{is just} \quad \|A\|_* = \sum_{k=1}^{\ell} \sigma_k(A).$$

For the operator and nuclear norms, the nontrivial part of the justification that they are indeed norms—proving the triangle inequality—follows from (D.7) with $w = [1; 0; \dots; 0]$ and $w = [1; 1; \dots; 1]$, respectively. Since the singular values of a matrix do not change when it is multiplied on the left or on the right by unitary matrices, the above norms do not change either. Thus, they each provide an example of a *unitarily invariant norm*, i.e., a norm $\| \cdot \|$ on $\mathbb{C}^{m \times n}$ such that $\|U^*AV\| = \|A\|$ for all $A \in \mathbb{C}^{m \times n}$ whenever U and V are unitary matrices. As it turns out, unitarily invariant norms are essentially determined by singular values.

Theorem D.9 *Unitarily invariant norms on $\mathbb{C}^{m \times n}$ are characterized by the identity*

$$\|A\| = \Phi(\sigma(A)), \qquad A \in \mathbb{C}^{m \times n},$$

where Φ is a symmetric gauge function, i.e., Φ is a norm on $\mathbb{R}^\ell$ that satisfies $\Phi([|x_{\pi(1)}|; \dots; |x_{\pi(\ell)}|]) = \Phi(x)$ for any $x \in \mathbb{R}^\ell$ and any permutation π of $[1 : \ell]$.

Proof Suppose first that $\| \cdot \|$ is a unitarily invariant norm on $\mathbb{C}^{m \times n}$. Defining Φ on $\mathbb{R}^{\ell}$ by $\Phi(x) = \| \operatorname{diag}[x] \|$ for any $x \in \mathbb{R}^{\ell}$, it is readily verified that Φ is a symmetric gauge function and that $\|A\| = \Phi(\sigma(A))$ holds for any $A \in \mathbb{C}^{m \times n}$.

Suppose conversely that Φ is a symmetric gauge function and then define $\|A\| = \Phi(\sigma(A))$ for all $A \in \mathbb{C}^{m \times n}$. The objective is to prove that $\| \cdot \|$ induces a unitarily invariant norm on $\mathbb{C}^{m \times n}$. The unitary invariance being immediate, as well as the positive definiteness and the absolute homogeneity, the remaining task is to show that $\| \cdot \|$ obeys the triangle inequality. A key ingredient is the remark that the dual norm Φ^* of Φ is also a symmetric gauge function. Indeed, for a vector $x \in \mathbb{R}^{\ell}$ and a permutation π of $[1 : \ell]$, one has

$$\Phi^*([|x_{\pi(1)}|; \ldots; |x_{\pi(\ell)}|]) = \max_{\Phi(u)=1} \sum_{k=1}^{\ell} u_k |x_{\pi(k)}| = \max_{\Phi(u)=1} \sum_{k=1}^{\ell} \operatorname{sgn}(x_k) u_{\pi^{-1}(k)} x_k$$

$$= \max_{\Phi(v)=1} \sum_{k=1}^{\ell} v_k x_k = \Phi^*(x),$$

where the fact that $\Phi(v) = \Phi(u)$ if $v = [\operatorname{sgn}(x_1) u_{\pi^{-1}(1)}; \ldots; \operatorname{sgn}(x_\ell) u_{\pi^{-1}(\ell)}]$ was used. Now, for $A, B \in \mathbb{C}^{m \times n}$, one writes $\Phi(\sigma(A + B)) = \langle w, \sigma(A + B) \rangle$ for some $w \in \mathbb{R}^{\ell}$ satisfying $\Phi^*(w) = 1$, hence $\Phi^*(\widetilde{w}) = 1$ with $\widetilde{w} \in \mathbb{R}_+^{\ell}$ denoting the non-increasing rearrangement of $|w| \in \mathbb{R}_+^{\ell}$. Keeping the rearrangement inequality (21.17) and the inequality (D.7) in mind, one derives that

$$\|A + B\| = \sum_{k=1}^{\ell} w_k \sigma_k(A + B) \leq \sum_{k=1}^{\ell} |w_k| \sigma_k(A + B) \leq \sum_{k=1}^{\ell} \widetilde{w}_k \sigma_k(A + B)$$

$$\leq \sum_{k=1}^{\ell} \widetilde{w}_k \sigma_k(A) + \sum_{k=1}^{\ell} \widetilde{w}_k \sigma_k(B) \leq \Phi^*(\widetilde{w}) \Phi(\sigma(A)) + \Phi^*(\widetilde{w}) \Phi(\sigma(B))$$

$$= \|A\| + \|B\|.$$

This justifies the triangle inequality and completes the proof. $\qquad\square$

From the characterization of a unitarily invariant norm as $\|A\| = \Phi(\sigma(A))$ for some symmetric gauge function, it is not hard to see that its dual norm is given by

$$\|A\|^* = \Phi^*(\sigma(A)), \qquad A \in \mathbb{C}^{m \times n},$$

where Φ^* is the dual gauge function of Φ. Thus, for $p \in [1, \infty]$, the *Schatten p-norm* (of which the operator, Frobenius, and nuclear norms are the special cases $p = \infty$, $p = 2$, and $p = 1$), which is defined by

$$\|A\|_{S_p} = \left[\sum_{k=1}^{\ell} \sigma_k(A)^p \right]^{1/p}, \qquad A \in \mathbb{C}^{m \times n},$$

admits as dual norm the Schatten p'-norm with conjugate exponent $p' \in [1, \infty]$ satisfying $1/p + 1/p' = 1$.

Another classical example of a unitarily invariant norm is provided by the *Ky Fan norm*, defined for $r \in [1 : \ell]$ by

$$\|A\|_{(r)} = \sum_{k=1}^{r} \sigma_k(A), \qquad A \in \mathbb{C}^{m \times n}.$$

Here is an alternative expression for the Ky Fan norm, as well as a simple expression for its dual norm.

Proposition D.10 *For any $A \in \mathbb{C}^{m \times n}$ and any $r \in [1 : \ell]$, one has*

$$\|A\|_{(r)} = \min \{\|B\|_* + r\|C\|_{2 \to 2} : A = B + C\}, \qquad (\text{D.10})$$

$$\|A\|_{(r)}^* = \max \{\|A\|_{2 \to 2}, \|A\|_*/r\}. \qquad (\text{D.11})$$

Proof For any decomposition $A = B + C$, it is clear that

$$\|A\|_{(r)} \le \|B\|_{(r)} + \|C\|_{(r)} \le \|B\|_* + r\|C\|_{2 \to 2}.$$

This justifies that $\|A\|_{(r)}$ is smaller than or equal to the minimum in question. To prove that it equals this minimum, one needs to find matrices B and C such that $A = B + C$ and $\|A\|_{(r)} = \|B\|_* + r\|C\|_{2 \to 2}$. From the singular value decomposition $A = \sum_{k=1}^{\ell} \sigma_k u_k v_k^*$, define $B = \sum_{k=1}^{\ell} \beta_k u_k v_k^*$ and $C = \sum_{k=1}^{\ell} \gamma_k u_k v_k^*$, where $\beta_k = \sigma_k - \sigma_r$ and $\gamma_k = \sigma_r$ for $k \le r$ and $\beta_k = 0$ and $\gamma_k = \sigma_k$ for $k > r$. One easily observes that $B + C = A$, while $\|B\|_* = (\sigma_1 - \sigma_r) + \cdots + (\sigma_r - \sigma_r)$ and $\|C\|_{2 \to 2} = \sigma_r$ yield $\|B\|_* + r\|C\|_{2 \to 2} = \sigma_1 + \cdots + \sigma_r = \|A\|_{(r)}$. Therefore, the identity (D.10) is established.

Turning to the identity (D.11), one introduces the norm defined for $Z \in \mathbb{C}^{m \times n}$ by $/\!\!/Z/\!\!/ = \max \{\|Z\|_{2 \to 2}, \|Z\|_*/r\}$. Then, considering a matrix $M \in \mathbb{C}^{m \times n}$ with $\|M\|_{(r)} = 1$ such that $\|A\|_{(r)}^* = \langle M, A \rangle_F$, one writes $M = B + C$ for some $B, C \in \mathbb{C}^{m \times n}$ satisfying $\|B\|_* + r\|C\|_{2 \to 2} = 1$. One has

$$\|A\|_{(r)}^* = \langle B, A \rangle_F + \langle C, A \rangle_F \le \|B\|_* \|A\|_{2 \to 2} + \|C\|_{2 \to 2} \|A\|_*$$

$$\le \|B\|_* /\!\!/ A /\!\!/ + r\|C\|_{2 \to 2} /\!\!/ A /\!\!/ = /\!\!/ A /\!\!/.$$

This proves the $\le$-part of (D.11). For the $\ge$-part, one writes $/\!\!/A/\!\!/ = \langle N, A \rangle_F$ for some $N \in \mathbb{C}^{m \times n}$ with $/\!\!/N/\!\!/^* = 1$. Endowing the space $\mathbb{C}^{m \times n} \times \mathbb{C}^{m \times n}$ with the norm $\|\|(X, Y)\|\| := \max \{\|X\|_{2 \to 2}, \|Y\|_*/r\}$, one defines a linear functional on the subspace $\{(X, X), X \in \mathbb{C}^{m \times n}\}$ by $\lambda((X, X)) = \langle N, X \rangle_F$. Using the *Hahn–Banach extension theorem* (Theorem C.10), one considers a norm-preserving extension $\widetilde{\lambda}$ of λ to the whole $\mathbb{C}^{m \times n} \times \mathbb{C}^{m \times n}$. One can then find $B, C \in \mathbb{C}^{m \times n}$ such that $\widetilde{\lambda}((X, Y)) = \langle B, X \rangle_F + \langle C, Y \rangle_F$ for all $X, Y \in \mathbb{C}^{m \times n}$. The fact that $\widetilde{\lambda}((X, X)) = \lambda((X, X))$ for all $X \in \mathbb{C}^{m \times n}$ translates into $B + C = N$. Next, the fact $\widetilde{\lambda}$ and λ have the same norm, i.e., that $\max\{\widetilde{\lambda}((X, Y)), \|\|(X, Y)\|\| = 1\}$ equals $\max\{\widetilde{\lambda}((X, X)), \|\|(X, X)\|\| = 1\}$ translates into $\|B\|_* + r\|C\|_{2\to 2} = /\!\!/ N /\!\!/^* = 1$, implying by (D.10) that $\|N\|_{(r)} \le 1$. It follows that $\|A\|^*_{(r)} \ge \langle A, N \rangle_F = /\!\!/ A /\!\!/$. The $\ge$-part of (D.11) is now established, which completes the proof. □

To end the discussion on unitarily invariant norms, one highlights the central theorem of low-rank approximation, namely the *Eckart–Young theorem*.

Theorem D.11 *Let* $\|\cdot\|$ *be a unitarily invariant norm on* $\mathbb{C}^{m\times n}$. *If* $A \in \mathbb{C}^{m\times n}$ *has singular value decomposition* $A = U \operatorname{diag}[\sigma_1; \ldots; \sigma_\ell] V^*$, $\ell = \min\{m, n\}$, *then the rank-r matrix* $A_r = U \operatorname{diag}[\sigma_1; \ldots; \sigma_r; 0; \ldots; 0] V^*$ *satisfies*

$$\|A - A_r\| \le \|A - B\| \quad \text{whenever } \operatorname{rank}(B) \le r,$$

i.e., it is a best approximant to A from the set of rank-r matrices with respect to the norm $\|\cdot\|$.

Proof Suppose for a moment that the result is acquired for all Ky Fan norms. Let Φ be a symmetric gauge function associated with the norm $\|\cdot\|$ and let Φ^* denote the dual symmetric gauge function. Consider $w \in \mathbb{R}^\ell$ with $\Phi^*(w) = 1$ such that $\|A - A_r\| = \Phi(\sigma(A - A_r)) = \langle w, \sigma(A - A_r) \rangle$ and notice that one can assume $w_1 \ge \cdots \ge w_\ell \ge 0$. For any $B \in \mathbb{C}^{m\times n}$ with $\operatorname{rank}(B) \le r$, in view of $\|A - B\| = \Phi(\sigma(A - B)) \ge \langle w, \sigma(A - B) \rangle$, *summation by parts* yields

$$\|A - B\| \ge \sum_{k=1}^{\ell} w_k \sigma_k(A - B) = w_\ell \|A - B\|_{(\ell)} + \sum_{k=1}^{\ell-1} (w_k - w_{k+1}) \|A - B\|_{(k)}$$

$$\ge w_\ell \|A - A_r\|_{(\ell)} + \sum_{k=1}^{\ell-1} (w_k - w_{k+1}) \|A - A_r\|_{(k)} = \sum_{k=1}^{\ell} w_k \sigma_k(A - A_r)$$

$$= \|A - A_r\|,$$

as desired. It now remains to establish the result for every Ky Fan k-norm, $k \in [1 : \ell]$. To this end, for any $B \in \mathbb{C}^{m\times n}$ with $\operatorname{rank}(B) \le r$, one shall invoke the *Mirsky inequality* (Theorem D.6) applied with indices $r + 1 < \cdots < r + k$ in case $k \le \ell - r$ and $r + 1 < \cdots < \ell$ in case $k > \ell - r$. In the former case, one has

$$\|A - B\|_{(k)} = \sum_{i=1}^{k} \sigma_i(A - B) \ge \sum_{i=1}^{k} |\sigma_{r+i}(A) - \sigma_{r+i}(B)| = \sum_{i=1}^{k} \sigma_{r+i}(A)$$

$$= \|A - A_r\|_{(k)},$$

where the facts that $\sigma_j(B) = 0$ for $j > r$ and $\sigma_i(A - A_r) = \sigma_{r+i}(A)$ for $i \le \ell - r$

have been used. In the latter case, one has

$$\|A - B\|_{(k)} = \sum_{i=1}^{k} \sigma_i(A - B) \geq \sum_{i=1}^{\ell-r} \sigma_i(A - B) \geq \sum_{i=1}^{\ell-r} |\sigma_{r+i}(A) - \sigma_{r+i}(B)|$$

$$= \sum_{i=1}^{\ell-r} \sigma_{r+i}(A) = \sum_{i=1}^{k} \sigma_{r+i}(A) = \|A - A_r\|_{(k)}.$$

All in all, the result for every Ky Fan k-norm has been shown and the proof is complete. □

Remark D.12 Despite the validity of the Eckart–Young theorem for arbitrary unitarily invariant norms, it is often applied specifically to the Frobenius norm. A simpler argument exists in this case. Namely, given a matrix $B \in \mathbb{C}^{m \times n}$ with rank$(B) \leq r$, the *von Neumann trace inequality* (Theorem D.8) guarantees that

$$\Re(\langle A, B \rangle_F) \leq \sum_{i=1}^{\ell} \sigma_i(A)\sigma_i(B) = \sum_{i=1}^{r} \sigma_i(A)\sigma_i(B).$$

The conclusion then follows from

$$\|A - B\|_F^2 - \|A - A_r\|_F^2 = \|A\|_F^2 - \|A - A_r\|_F^2 - 2\Re(\langle A, B \rangle_F) + \|B\|_F^2$$

$$\geq \sum_{i=1}^{r} \sigma_i(A)^2 - \sum_{i=1}^{r} \sigma_i(A)\sigma_i(B) + \sum_{i=1}^{r} \sigma_i(B)^2$$

$$= \sum_{i=1}^{r} (\sigma_i(A) - \sigma_i(B))^2 \geq 0.$$

Exercises

D.1 Prove that the self-adjointness condition in the definition of positive semidefiniteness is redundant in the complex setting. More precisely, given $A \in \mathbb{C}^{n \times n}$, prove that, if $\langle Ax, x \rangle \in \mathbb{R}$ for all $x \in \mathbb{C}^n$, then A is automatically self-adjoint.

D.2 Let $\mathcal{V}_1 \subset \cdots \subset \mathcal{V}_k$ and $\mathcal{W}_1 \supset \cdots \supset \mathcal{W}_k$ be subspaces of $\mathbb{C}^n$ satisfying $\dim(\mathcal{V}_j) + \dim(\mathcal{W}_j) = n + 1$ for all $j \in [1:k]$. Prove that there exist orthonormal systems $(x_1, \ldots, x_k)$ and $(y_1, \ldots, y_k)$ such that $x_j \in \mathcal{V}_j$ and $y_j \in \mathcal{W}_j$ for all $j \in [1:k]$, as well as span$\{x_1, \ldots, x_k\}$ = span$\{y_1, \ldots, y_k\}$.

D.3 Verify that the nuclear norm of a matrix $M \in \mathbb{C}^{n \times n}$ can be written as

$$\|M\|_* = \min_{UV^* = M} \|U\|_F \|V\|_F = \min_{UV^* = M} \frac{1}{2}(\|U\|_F^2 + \|V\|_F^2).$$

D.4 Prove that the *Ky Fan norm* of a matrix $A \in \mathbb{R}^{n \times n}$ has the semidefinite characterization

$$\|A\|_{(r)} = \min_{\substack{B,C,P,Q \in \mathbb{R}^{n \times n} \\ d \in \mathbb{R}}} \left\{ \frac{1}{2}(\text{tr}(P) + \text{tr}(Q)) + rd : B + C = A, \right.$$

$$\left. \left[\begin{array}{c|c} P & B \\ \hline B^{\mathsf{T}} & Q \end{array} \right] \geq 0, \left[\begin{array}{c|c} dI_n & C \\ \hline C^{\mathsf{T}} & dI_n \end{array} \right] \geq 0 \right\}.$$

Appendix E
Approximation Theory

This appendix establishes some required results from approximation theory. These results are invoked in PART TWO, PART FOUR, and PART FIVE. For a broader view of approximation theory, one can consult e.g. the books by Achieser (1992), Cheney (1966), and DeVore and Lorentz (1993).

E.1 Classic Uniform Approximation Theorems

Throughout this section, the set $C(X)$ represents the linear space of real-valued continuous functions defined on a compact set X. This space is equipped with the uniform norm

$$\|f\|_{C(X)} = \max_{x \in X} |f(x)|, \qquad f \in C(X).$$

The first result, known as the *Weierstrass theorem*, concerns the approximation of univariate functions by polynomials when $X = [a, b]$ is a compact interval.

Theorem E.1 *The set of algebraic polynomials is dense in $C([a, b])$, i.e., for every $f \in C([a, b])$ and every $\varepsilon > 0$, there exists an algebraic polynomial p such that $\|f - p\|_{C([a,b])} \le \varepsilon$.*

The Weierstrass theorem will in fact be established in two strengthened versions, the first of these versions being the *Stone–Weierstrass theorem*. To justify it, one begins by establishing an instantiation of the Weierstrass theorem with $f(x) = |x|$.

Lemma E.2 *The absolute value function can be uniformly approximated by algebraic polynomials on $[a, b]$.*

Proof A first step consists in justifying that the square-root function can be uniformly approximated by polynomials on $[0, 1]$. To this end, consider the sequence of functions $(p_n)_{n \geq 0}$ defined recursively for $t \in [0, 1]$ by

$$p_0(t) = 0 \quad \text{and} \quad p_{n+1}(t) = p_n(t) + \frac{t - p_n(t)^2}{2}, \quad n \geq 0.$$

It is easily verified by induction on $n \geq 0$ that p_n is a polynomial (of degree 2^{n-1} for $n \geq 1$) and that $0 \leq p_n(t) \leq \sqrt{t}$ for all $t \in [0, 1]$. As a consequence, fixing $t \in [0, 1]$, the sequence $(p_n(t))_{n \geq 0}$ is nondecreasing, bounded above by $\sqrt{t}$, and hence converges to a limit that can only be $\sqrt{t}$. Since the square-root function is continuous, the Dini lemma (see Exercise E.1) implies that the convergence of $(p_n(t))_{n \geq 0}$ towards $\sqrt{t}$ is uniform, thus concluding the first step.

For the second step, one turns to the absolute value function and assumes that $a < 0 < b$, otherwise there is nothing to do. In view of $x/(b - a) \in [-1, 1]$ whenever $x \in [a, b]$, one can define polynomials q_n for any $n \geq 0$ by

$$q_n(x) = (b - a) \, p_n\!\left(\left(\frac{x}{b - a}\right)^2\right), \quad x \in [a, b].$$

The uniform convergence of the sequence $(q_n)_{n \geq 0}$ towards the absolute value function follows from

$$\max_{x \in [a,b]} \bigl||x| - q_n(x)\bigr| = (b - a) \max_{x \in [a,b]} \left| \sqrt{\left(\frac{x}{b-a}\right)^2} - p_n\!\left(\left(\frac{x}{b-a}\right)^2\right) \right|$$

$$\leq (b - a) \bigl\| \sqrt{\cdot} - p_n \bigr\|_{C([0,1])} \xrightarrow[n \to \infty]{} 0. \qquad \square$$

It is time to state and prove the *Stone–Weierstrass theorem*. In its statement, a set $\mathcal{F}$ of functions defined on X is said to vanish nowhere if, for any $x \in X$, one can find $f \in \mathcal{F}$ such that $f(x) \neq 0$, and to separate points if, for any $x \neq y \in X$, one can find $f \in \mathcal{F}$ such that $f(x) \neq f(y)$.

Theorem E.3　*A subalgebra $\mathcal{A}$ of $C(X)$, X compact, that vanishes nowhere and separates points is dense in $C(X)$.*

Proof　Let $\overline{\mathcal{A}}$ denote the closure of $\mathcal{A}$, so that $\overline{\mathcal{A}}$ is a closed subalgebra of $C(X)$ that vanishes nowhere and separates points. First, one claims that $\overline{\mathcal{A}}$ is stable under composition with the absolute value function, i.e., that $|f| \in \overline{\mathcal{A}}$ whenever $f \in \overline{\mathcal{A}}$. Indeed, given $f \in \overline{\mathcal{A}}$, Lemma E.2 guarantees the existence of a sequence $(q_n)_{n \geq 0}$ of polynomials that approximate the absolute value function uniformly on an interval $[a, b]$ containing the compact set $f(X)$. Then, since $q_n(f) \in \overline{\mathcal{A}}$ for any $n \geq 0$, the observation that

$$\bigl\| |f| - q_n(f) \bigr\|_{C(X)} = \max_{x \in X} \bigl| |f(x)| - q_n(f(x)) \bigr| \leq \bigl\| |\cdot| - q_n \bigr\|_{C([a,b])} \xrightarrow[n \to \infty]{} 0$$

shows that $|f|$ belongs to the closure of $\overline{\mathcal{A}}$, which is $\overline{\mathcal{A}}$ itself. Next, one remarks that $\overline{\mathcal{A}}$ is also stable when taking maxima and minima. This simply follows from the previous claim and the facts that, for $f, g \in \overline{\mathcal{A}}$,

$$\max\{f, g\} = \frac{f + g + |f - g|}{2}, \qquad \min\{f, g\} = \frac{f + g - |f - g|}{2}.$$

Now, given $f \in C(X)$, the objective is to prove that, for any $\varepsilon > 0$, there exists some $g \in \overline{\mathcal{A}}$ such that $\|f - g\|_{C(X)} < \varepsilon$. One starts by observing that

for all $y \neq z \in X$, there exists $g_{y,z} \in \overline{\mathcal{A}}$ with $g_{y,z}(y) = f(y)$ and $g_{y,z}(z) = f(z)$.

To see this, one considers $u \in \overline{\mathcal{A}}$ such that $u(y) \neq u(z)$, which is possible because $\overline{\mathcal{A}}$ separates points. Assuming e.g. that $u(z) \neq 0$, one also considers $v \in \overline{\mathcal{A}}$ such that $v(z) \neq 0$, which is possible because $\overline{\mathcal{A}}$ vanishes nowhere. Then, for $t \in \mathbb{R}$ suitably chosen close to zero, the function $w := u + tv \in \overline{\mathcal{A}}$ satisfies $w(y) \neq 0$, $w(z) \neq 0$, and $w(y) \neq w(z)$. It follows that

$$\det \begin{bmatrix} w(y) & w(y)^2 \\ w(z) & w(z)^2 \end{bmatrix} = w(y)w(z)(w(z) - w(y)) \neq 0.$$

This means that the linear map $L : h \in \overline{\mathcal{A}} \mapsto [h(y); h(z)] \in \mathbb{R}^2$ is bijective on $\operatorname{span}\{w, w^2\} \subseteq \overline{\mathcal{A}}$, so it suffices to take $g_{y,z} = L^{-1}([f(y); f(z)])$.

Let $y \in X$ be fixed for a while. Let also $z \in X$ be distinct from y. Since the continuous functions f and $g_{y,z}$ agree at z, one can find an open neighborhood $O_{y,z}$ of z such that

$$\text{for all } x \in O_{y,z}, \quad f(x) < g_{y,z}(x) + \varepsilon. \tag{E.1}$$

By compactness of X, one extracts from the open covering $X = \cup_{z \in X} O_{y,z}$ a finite covering $X = \cup_{z \in Z} O_{y,z}$ where Z is a finite subset of X. One then considers the function $g_y := \max_{z \in Z} g_{y,z}$, which belongs to $\overline{\mathcal{A}}$ by an earlier remark. From (E.1), one derives that

$$\text{for all } x \in X, \quad f(x) < g_y(x) + \varepsilon. \tag{E.2}$$

Next, since the continuous functions f and g_y agree at y, one can find an open neighborhood O'_y of y such that

$$\text{for all } x \in O'_y, \quad f(x) > g_y(x) - \varepsilon. \tag{E.3}$$

Again by compactness of X, one extracts from the open covering $X = \cup_{y \in X} O'_y$ a finite covering $X = \cup_{y \in \mathcal{Y}} O'_y$ where $\mathcal{Y}$ is a finite subset of X. One then considers the function $g := \min_{y \in \mathcal{Y}} g_y$, which belongs to $\overline{\mathcal{A}}$ by an earlier remark. From (E.3), one derives that

$$\text{for all } x \in X, \quad f(x) > g(x) - \varepsilon.$$

One also deduces as a direct consequence of (E.2) that

$$\text{for all } x \in X, \qquad f(x) < g(x) + \varepsilon.$$

Altogether, the objective $\|f - g\|_{C(X)} < \varepsilon$ has been attained for some $g \in \overline{\mathcal{A}}$. This establishes that any $f \in C(X)$ belongs to the closure of $\overline{\mathcal{A}}$, i.e., to $\overline{\mathcal{A}}$ itself. In other words, the subalgebra $\mathcal{A}$ is dense in $C(X)$.   □

Although the Stone–Weierstrass theorem implies the Weierstrass theorem, and even its d-variate version (given that multivariate polynomials form a subalgebra of $C(X)$ for any compact set $X \subseteq \mathbb{R}^d$), it does not offer a way to construct a sequence of polynomials approximating a given function. The *Korovkin theorem*, stated below, does.

Theorem E.4 *Let $(U_n)_{n \geq 0}$ be a sequence of positive linear operators defined on $C(X)$, X compact. Suppose that one can find functions $a_1, \ldots, a_L \in C(X)$ and $f_1, \ldots, f_L \in C(X)$ such that*

(i) for all $(t, x) \in X \times X$, the inequality $p(t, x) := \sum_{\ell=1}^{L} a_\ell(t) f_\ell(x) \geq 0$ holds, with equality occurring if and only if $t = x$;

(ii) for all $f \in \{f_1, \ldots, f_L\}$, one has $U_n(f) \longrightarrow f$ as $n \to \infty$.

Then it is guaranteed that $U_n(f) \longrightarrow f$ as $n \to \infty$ for all $f \in C(X)$.

Proof Consider a function $q \in \operatorname{span}\{f_1, \ldots, f_L\}$ such that $q(x) > 0$ for all $x \in X$ (e.g. $q = p(t, \cdot) + p(t', \cdot)$ with $t \neq t'$) and let $q_{\min} := \min\{q(x), x \in X\} > 0$. Let $C > 0$ be a constant such that $\|U_n(q)\|_{C(X)} \leq C$ for all $n \geq 0$ (it exists because the sequence $(U_n(q))_{n \geq 0}$ converges to q in the uniform norm) and let $\alpha_1, \ldots, \alpha_L > 0$ be constants such that $|a_1(t)| \leq \alpha_1, \ldots, |a_L(t)| \leq \alpha_L$ for all $t \in X$ (they exist by the continuity of the a_ℓ and the compactness of X).

Now, given $f \in C(X)$ and $\varepsilon > 0$, the objective is to find an integer N such that $|U_n(f)(x) - f(x)| \leq \varepsilon$ for all $x \in X$ whenever $n \geq N$. One considers the function F defined by

$$F(t, x) = f(x) - \frac{f(t)}{q(t)} q(x), \qquad (t, x) \in X \times X.$$

The idea is to write $f = F(t, \cdot) + (f(t)/q(t))q$ specified for $t = x \in X$ to deduce

$$U_n(f)(x) = U_n(F(x, \cdot))(x) + \frac{f(x)}{q(x)} U_n(q)(x),$$

then to show, for all $x \in X$ simultaneously, that $|U_n(F(x, \cdot))(x)| \leq \varepsilon_1, \varepsilon_1 := \varepsilon/2$, and that $|U_n(q)(x) - q(x)| \leq \varepsilon_2, \varepsilon_2 := \varepsilon/(2\|f/q\|_{C(X)})$, whenever n exceeds some integer N. This implies that $|U_n(f)(x) - f(x)| \leq \varepsilon_1 + \|f/q\|_{C(X)} \varepsilon_2 = \varepsilon$ for all $x \in X$ whenever n exceeds this integer N. The existence of N such that $\max\{|U_n(q)(x) - q(x)|, x \in X\} \le \varepsilon_2$ whenever $n > N$ is an immediate consequence of the uniform convergence of $U_n(q)$ to q.

Thus, it remains to find some N such that $\max\{|U_n(F(\cdot, x))(x)|, x \in X\} \le \varepsilon_1$ whenever $n > N$. To this end, consider the compact subset of $X \times X$ defined by $\Delta := \{(t, x) \in X \times X : |F(t, x)| \ge \varepsilon'\}$ for some $\varepsilon' > 0$ to be chosen later, and let $\delta := \min\{p(t, x) : (t, x) \in \Delta\} > 0$. Notice that $|F(t, x)| < \varepsilon'$ when $(t, x) \notin \Delta$ and that $|F(t, x)| \le \|F\|_{C(X \times X)} \le (\|F\|_{C(X \times X)}/\delta)p(t, x)$ when $(t, x) \in \Delta$. It follows that

$$|F(t, x)| \le \varepsilon' + \frac{\|F\|_{C(X \times X)}}{\delta} p(t, x) \qquad \text{for all } (t, x) \in X \times X.$$

The positivity of the operators U_n then ensures that, for any $t \in X$,

$$|U_n(F(t, \cdot))| \le U_n(|F(t, \cdot)|) \le \varepsilon' U_n(\mathbb{1}) + \frac{\|F\|_{C(X \times X)}}{\delta} U_n(p(t, \cdot)). \tag{E.4}$$

Besides, in view of $q_{\min}\mathbb{1} \le q$, one has $q_{\min} U_n(\mathbb{1}) \le U_n(q) \le C$. Substituting the latter into (E.4) while specifying $t = x$ for an arbitrary $x \in X$, one obtains

$$|U_n(F(x, \cdot))(x)| \le \varepsilon' \frac{C}{q_{\min}} + \frac{\|F\|_{C(X \times X)}}{\delta} U_n(p(x, \cdot))(x)$$

$$= \frac{\varepsilon_1}{2} + \frac{\|F\|_{X \times X}}{\delta} (U_n(p(x, \cdot)) - p(x, \cdot))(x), \tag{E.5}$$

where the choice $\varepsilon' := (\varepsilon_1 q_{\min})/(2C)$ was made. Moreover, one observes that, for any $x \in X$,

$$(U_n(p(x, \cdot)) - p(x, \cdot))(x) \le \left\| U_n(p(x, \cdot)) - p(x, \cdot) \right\|_{C(X)}$$

$$= \left\| \sum_{\ell=1}^{L} a_\ell(x)(U_n(f_\ell) - f_\ell) \right\|_{C(X)}$$

$$\le \sum_{\ell=1}^{L} \alpha_\ell \|U_n(f_\ell) - f_\ell\|_{C(X)}.$$

Since the latter sum is independent of $x \in X$ and approaches zero as $n \to \infty$, there is an integer N such that $(U_n(p(x, \cdot)) - p(x, \cdot))(x) \le (\varepsilon_1 \delta)/(2\|F\|_{C(X \times X)})$ for all $x \in X$ whenever $n > N$. Thus, when $n > N$, one concludes from (E.5) that $|U_n(F(x, \cdot))(x)| \le \varepsilon_1$ for all $x \in X$, which was the remaining objective. $\square$

The Korovkin theorem provides a relatively simple proof of the fact that any continuous function on $[0, 1]$ is the uniform limit of its sequence of *Bernstein polynomials* (see Exercise E.2). But nothing has yet been said about the rate of approximation. As mentioned at the beginning of Chapter 10, this rate is intimately related to the smoothness of f. The relation exists both in $C([0, 1])$ and in $C(\mathbb{T})$, but it is much nicer looking in $C(\mathbb{T})$ when using trigonometric polynomials. The *Jackson theorem* (aka the *direct theorem*) expresses one part of this relation approximability–smoothness.

Theorem E.5 *Given an integer $k \geq 1$, if $f \in C(\mathbb{T})$ has a continuous kth derivative, then* $\text{dist}_{C(\mathbb{T})}(f, \mathcal{T}_n) = O(n^{-k})$.

Proof The crucial point of the argument is to prove that there is a constant $C > 0$ such that, for any $f \in C^1(\mathbb{T})$,

$$\text{dist}_{C(\mathbb{T})}(f, \mathcal{T}_n) \leq \frac{C}{n} \|f'\|_{C(\mathbb{T})}, \qquad n \geq 1. \tag{E.6}$$

From here, one can deduce that, for any $f \in C^1(\mathbb{T})$,

$$\text{dist}_{C(\mathbb{T})}(f, \mathcal{T}_n) \leq \frac{2C}{n} \, \text{dist}_{C(\mathbb{T})}(f', \mathcal{T}_n), \qquad n \geq 1. \tag{E.7}$$

To see this, let $p \in \mathcal{T}_n$ be such that $\text{dist}_{C(\mathbb{T})}(f', \mathcal{T}_n) = \|f' - p\|_{C(\mathbb{T})}$. Let also P be an antiderivative of $p - c$, where c represents the constant term in p, so that $P \in \mathcal{T}_n$. One has

$$\text{dist}_{C(\mathbb{T})}(f, \mathcal{T}_n) \leq \|f - P\|_{C(\mathbb{T})} \leq \frac{C}{n} \|f' - (p - c)\|_{C(\mathbb{T})} \leq \frac{C}{n} (\|f' - p\|_{C(\mathbb{T})} + |c|).$$

In view of $\int_{\mathbb{T}} f' = 0$, the announced inequality (E.7) follows from

$$|c| = \left| \frac{1}{2\pi} \int_{\mathbb{T}} p(t) dt \right| = \left| \frac{1}{2\pi} \int_{\mathbb{T}} (p(t) - f'(t)) dt \right| \leq \frac{1}{2\pi} \int_{\mathbb{T}} |p(t) - f'(t)| dt$$
$$\leq \|f' - p\|_{C(\mathbb{T})}.$$

Now, for $f \in C^k(\mathbb{T})$, applying (E.7) to $f, f', \ldots, f^{(k-1)}$ yields the required result in the form

$$\text{dist}_{C(\mathbb{T})}(f, \mathcal{T}_n) \leq \frac{(2C)^k}{n^k} \|f^{(k)}\|_{C(\mathbb{T})}, \qquad n \geq 1.$$

It remains to justify (E.6). This is done with the help of the *Jackson kernel* defined for $t \in \mathbb{T}$ by

$$J_n(t) = \gamma_n \left(\frac{\sin(mt/2)}{\sin(t/2)} \right)^4, \qquad m = \left\lceil \frac{n}{2} \right\rceil,$$

where the normalizing constant γ_n is chosen such that $\int_{\mathbb{T}} J_n = 1$. Notice that J_n belongs to $\mathcal{T}_n$ since it is a multiple of the square of the *Fejér kernel* F_m, which belongs to $\mathcal{T}_{m-1}$ (see Exercise E.3). Therefore, the *convolution product* $J_n * f$ defined for $x \in \mathbb{T}$ by

$$(J_n * f)(x) = \int_{\mathbb{T}} J_n(x - y) f(y) dy$$

belongs to $\mathcal{T}_n$, which implies that $\text{dist}_{C(\mathbb{T})}(f, \mathcal{T}_n) \leq \|f - J_n * f\|_{C(\mathbb{T})}$. Taking into account that, for any $x \in \mathbb{T}$,

$$\left| f(x) - (J_n * f)(x) \right| = \left| \int_{\mathbb{T}} J_n(x-y)(f(x)-f(y))dy \right| \leq \int_{\mathbb{T}} J_n(x-y)|f(x)-f(y)|dy$$

$$\leq \int_{\mathbb{T}} J_n(x-y)\|f'\|_{C(\mathbb{T})}|x-y|dy = 2\|f'\|_{C(\mathbb{T})} \int_0^{\pi} J_n(t)t\,dt,$$

the desired inequality (E.6) will be validated as soon as one shows that the latter integral is $O(n^{-1})$. To see this, remembering that $2\theta/\pi \leq \sin(\theta) \leq \theta$ for $\theta \in [0, \pi/2]$, one writes

$$\int_0^{\pi} J_n(t)t\,dt = \gamma_n \int_0^{\pi} \frac{\sin^4(mt/2)}{\sin^4(t/2)} t\,dt \leq \gamma_n \int_0^{\pi} \frac{\sin^4(mt/2)}{(t/\pi)^4} t\,dt$$

$$= \pi^4 \frac{m^2}{4} \gamma_n \int_0^{m\pi/2} \frac{\sin^4(\tau)}{\tau^3} d\tau \leq C'n^2\gamma_n, \qquad (E.8)$$

where the latter inequality holds because $\sin^4(\tau)/\tau^3$ is integrable on $(0, \infty)$. Since the normalization condition $\int_{\mathbb{T}} J_n = 1$ ensures that

$$\frac{1}{2\gamma_n} = \int_0^{\pi} \frac{\sin^4(mt/2)}{\sin^4(t/2)} dt \geq \int_0^{\pi/m} \frac{(mt/\pi)^4}{(t/2)^4} dt = \frac{16}{\pi^3} m^3 \geq c'n^3,$$

the integral (E.8) is indeed bounded above by $C''n^{-1}$ with $C'' = C'/(2c')$. $\qquad \square$

The second part of the relation approximability–smoothness is expressed by the *Bernstein theorem* (aka the *inverse theorem*).

Theorem E.6 *Given an integer $k \geq 0$ and $\alpha \in (0,1)$, if $f \in C(\mathbb{T})$ satisfies $\text{dist}_{C(\mathbb{T})}(f, \mathcal{T}_n) = O(n^{-(k+\alpha)})$, then $f^{(k)}$ exists and is α-Hölder continuous.*

Proof For each integer $n \geq 1$, let $p_n \in \mathcal{T}_n$ be such that $\|f - p_n\|_{C(\mathbb{T})} \leq Cn^{-k-\alpha}$. With $P_0 := p_1$ and $P_m := p_{2^m} - p_{2^{m-1}}$ for $m \geq 1$, one notices the identity $f = \sum_{m \geq 0} P_m$, with absolute and uniform convergence justified by the fact that

$$\|P_m\|_{C(\mathbb{T})} \leq \|p_{2^m} - f\|_{C(\mathbb{T})} + \|f - p_{2^{m-1}}\|_{C(\mathbb{T})} \leq C(2^m)^{-k-\alpha} + C(2^{m-1})^{-k-\alpha}$$

$$\leq C'2^{-m(k+\alpha)}. \qquad (E.9)$$

One considers first the case $k = 0$. For $x, x' \in \mathbb{T}$, set $\delta := |x - x'|$ and choose an integer $M \geq 0$ such that $2^{-(M+1)} < \delta/\pi \leq 2^{-M}$. One has

$$|f(x) - f(x')| \leq \sum_{m \geq 0} |P_m(x) - P_m(x')| \leq \sum_{m=0}^{M-1} \|P'_m\|_{C(\mathbb{T})}|x-x'| + \sum_{m=M}^{\infty} 2\|P_m\|_{C(\mathbb{T})}$$

$$\leq \sum_{m=0}^{M-1} 2^m \|P_m\|_{C(\mathbb{T})}\delta + 2\sum_{m=M}^{\infty} \|P_m\|_{C(\mathbb{T})},$$

where the *Bernstein inequality* (see Exercise E.4) was used in the last step. In view of (E.9), it follows that

$$|f(x) - f(x')| \leq \sum_{m=0}^{M-1} C' 2^{m(1-\alpha)} \delta + 2 \sum_{m=M}^{\infty} C' 2^{-m\alpha} \leq C'' \left(2^{M(1-\alpha)} \delta + 2^{-M\alpha} \right)$$
$$\leq C''' \delta^\alpha,$$

where the last inequality relied on the choice of M. This justifies that f is α-Hölder continuous.

Next, one considers the case $k \geq 1$. By applying the *Bernstein inequality* k times and keeping (E.9) in mind, one obtains

$$\|P_m^{(k)}\|_{C(\mathbb{T})} \leq (2^m)^k \|P_m\|_{C(\mathbb{T})} \leq C' 2^{-m\alpha}.$$

Therefore, the series $\sum_{m \geq 0} P_m^{(k)}$ converges absolutely and uniformly, so that $f^{(k)}$ exists, is continuous, and satisfies $f^{(k)} = \sum_{m \geq 0} P_m^{(k)}$. Moreover, for each $n \geq 1$, choosing $M \geq 0$ such that $2^M \leq n < 2^{M+1}$, one has

$$\text{dist}_{C(\mathbb{T})}(f^{(k)}, \mathcal{T}_n) \leq \left\| f^{(k)} - \sum_{m=0}^{M} P_m^{(k)} \right\|_{C(\mathbb{T})} = \left\| \sum_{m=M+1}^{\infty} P_m^{(k)} \right\|_{C(\mathbb{T})} \leq \sum_{m=M+1}^{\infty} \|P_m^{(k)}\|_{C(\mathbb{T})}$$
$$\leq \sum_{m=M+1}^{\infty} C' 2^{-m\alpha} \leq C'' 2^{-M\alpha} \leq C''' n^{-\alpha}.$$

The argument already presented for the case $k = 0$ now guarantees that $f^{(k)}$ is α-Hölder continuous.   □

E.2 Riesz–Fejér and Carathéodory–Toeplitz Theorems

This section establishes the results underlying the sum-of-squares technique and the method of moments, which were both used in Chapter 22. It starts with the *Riesz–Fejér theorem*.

Theorem E.7 *For a trigonometric polynomial written as* $p(\theta) = \sum_{j=-n}^{n} c_j e^{-ij\theta}$ *with* $c_{-j} = \overline{c_j}$, $j \in [0:n]$, *if* $p(\theta) \geq 0$ *for all* $\theta \in \mathbb{T}$, *then there exists an algebraic polynomial* q *of degree at most* n *such that* $p(\theta) = |q(e^{-i\theta})|^2$ *for all* $\theta \in \mathbb{T}$.

Proof Setting $P(z) = \sum_{j=-n}^{n} c_j z^j$, one has $P(e^{-i\theta}) \geq 0$ for all $\theta \in [-\pi, \pi]$. Assuming without loss of generality that $c_n \neq 0$, the degree-$2n$ polynomial $T(z) := z^n P(z)$ does not vanish at 0, and hence has the same (nonzero) roots as P. In view of $P(1/\overline{z}) = \overline{P(z)}$, each root ζ_k of T outside the unit circle comes with the root $\overline{\zeta_k}^{-1}$ of T inside the unit circle (with the same multiplicity). Thus, one can write

$$T(z) = \prod_{k=1}^{m} (z - \zeta_k)(z - \overline{\zeta_k}^{-1}) S(z)$$

for some $m \in [0:n]$ and some polynomial S of degree $2n - 2m$ with roots on the unit circle. It follows that

$$P(z) = \prod_{k=1}^{m} (z - \zeta_k)(z^{-1} - \overline{\zeta_k}) \frac{R(z)}{z^{n-m}},$$

where R, being a multiple of S, is a polynomial of degree $2n - 2m$ with roots on the unit circle, say at $e^{-i\theta_\ell}$ for $\ell \in [1:2n-2m]$. Since both $P(e^{-i\theta})$ and $\prod_{k=1}^{m}(e^{-i\theta} - \zeta_k)(e^{i\theta} - \overline{\zeta_k})$ are nonnegative for all $\theta \in [-\pi, \pi]$, one derives that

$$\frac{R(e^{-i\theta})}{e^{-i(n-m)\theta}} = a \prod_{\ell=1}^{2n-2m} \frac{e^{-i\theta} - e^{-i\theta_\ell}}{e^{-i\theta/2}} = a \prod_{\ell=1}^{2n-2m} (-2ie^{-i\theta_\ell/2}) \sin((\theta - \theta_\ell)/2) \geq 0$$

for all $\theta \in [-\pi, \pi]$. This would not be possible if the multiplicity of one of the θ_ℓ was odd. So $R(z)$ in fact takes the form $R(z) = a \prod_{\ell=1}^{n-m}(z - e^{-i\theta_\ell})^2$, and hence $R(z)/z^{n-m} = a' \prod_{\ell=1}^{n-m}(z - e^{-i\theta_\ell})(z^{-1} - e^{i\theta_\ell})$. All in all, one arrives at

$$P(z) = a' \left(\prod_{k=1}^{m}(z - \zeta_k) \prod_{\ell=1}^{n-m}(z - e^{-i\theta_\ell}) \right) \left(\prod_{k=1}^{m}(z^{-1} - \overline{\zeta_k}) \prod_{\ell=1}^{n-m}(z^{-1} - e^{i\theta_\ell}) \right) =: a' Q(z)\overline{Q(\overline{z}^{-1})}.$$

Taking $z = e^{-i\theta}$ shows that $a' \geq 0$. The result follows by setting $q = \sqrt{a'} Q$. $\square$

The Riesz–Fejér theorem turns out to be one of the main ingredients in the proof of the *Carathéodory–Toeplitz theorem*, which states that the terms of an infinite sequence $u \in \mathbb{C}^{\mathbb{N}}$ are realized as trigonometric moments $\int_{\mathbb{T}} e^{-i\ell\theta} d\mu(\theta)$, $\ell \in \mathbb{N}$, of a nonnegative Borel measure $\mu \in \mathcal{M}_+(\mathbb{T})$ if and only if the infinite symmetric Toeplitz matrix built from u is positive semidefinite. This complex version of the *discrete trigonometric moment problem* implies a real version— the one needed below—which can also be proved directly.

Theorem E.8 *For an infinite sequence $u \in \mathbb{R}^{\mathbb{N}}$, the following are equivalent:*
 (i) there exists a nonnegative Borel measure $\mu \in \mathcal{M}_+(\mathbb{T})$ such that

$$\int_{\mathbb{T}} \cos(\ell\theta) d\mu(\theta) = u_\ell \qquad \text{for all } \ell \geq 0;$$

 (ii) the infinite symmetric Toeplitz matrix built from u is positive semidefinite, meaning that, for every finite sequence $c \in \mathbb{R}^{\mathbb{N}}$,

$$\sum_{k,\ell=0}^{\infty} c_k c_\ell u_{|k-\ell|} \geq 0.$$

Proof (i)$\Rightarrow$(ii). For a sequence $c \in \mathbb{R}^{\mathbb{N}}$ such that $c_j = 0$ if $j > N$, say, observe that

$$\sum_{k,\ell=0}^{\infty} c_k c_\ell u_{|k-\ell|} = \sum_{k,\ell=0}^{N} c_k c_\ell \int_{\mathbb{T}} \cos((k-\ell)\theta) d\mu(\theta)$$

$$= \int_{\mathbb{T}} \sum_{k,\ell=0}^{N} c_k c_\ell (\cos(k\theta)\cos(\ell\theta) + \sin(k\theta)\sin(\ell\theta)) d\mu(\theta)$$

$$= \int_{\mathbb{T}} \left(\left(\sum_{k=0}^{N} c_k \cos(k\theta) \right)^2 + \left(\sum_{k=0}^{N} c_k \sin(k\theta) \right)^2 \right) d\mu(\theta) \geq 0.$$

(ii)$\Rightarrow$(i). Consider the linear functional λ defined on the space $\mathcal{T} = \cup_{n \geq 0} \mathcal{T}_n$ of trigonometric polynomials by

$$\lambda(\cos(\ell \cdot)) = u_\ell \quad \text{and} \quad \lambda(\sin(\ell \cdot)) = 0, \qquad \ell \geq 0.$$

Given $p \in \mathcal{T}$ with $p \geq 0$, the *Riesz–Fejér theorem* (Theorem E.7) guarantees that there exist $c_0, c_1, \ldots, c_n \in \mathbb{C}$ such that, for all $\theta \in \mathbb{T}$,

$$p(\theta) = \left(\sum_{k=0}^{n} c_k e^{-ik\theta} \right) \overline{\left(\sum_{\ell=0}^{n} c_\ell e^{-i\ell\theta} \right)} = \sum_{k,\ell=0}^{n} c_k \overline{c_\ell} e^{-i(k-\ell)\theta}$$

$$= \sum_{k,\ell=0}^{n} (\Re(c_k \overline{c_\ell}) \cos((k-\ell)\theta) + \Im(c_k \overline{c_\ell}) \sin((k-\ell)\theta)).$$

Applying the linear functional λ to p and introducing the real and imaginary parts $a_j, b_j \in \mathbb{R}$ of each c_j, one obtains

$$\lambda(p) = \sum_{k,\ell=0}^{n} \Re(c_k \overline{c_\ell}) u_{|k-\ell|} = \sum_{k,\ell=0}^{n} (a_k a_\ell + b_k b_\ell) u_{|k-\ell|} \geq 0.$$

This shows that the linear functional λ is positive on $\mathcal{T}$. It can be extended to a positive linear functional $\widetilde{\lambda}$ on the whole $C(\mathbb{T})$ as follows: first, the expression $v(f) = \inf\{\lambda(p) : p \in \mathcal{T}, p \geq f\}$ defines a sublinear functional on $C(\mathbb{T})$ satisfying $v(p) = \lambda(p)$ for $p \in \mathcal{T}$; second, the *dominated extension theorem* (Theorem C.9) yields a linear functional $\widetilde{\lambda}$ on $C(\mathbb{T})$ such that $\widetilde{\lambda}_{|\mathcal{T}} = \lambda$ and $\widetilde{\lambda} \leq v$; third, the linear functional $\widetilde{\lambda}$ is seen to be positive because $f \geq 0$ implies that $\widetilde{\lambda}(-f) \leq v(-f) \leq \lambda(0) = 0$. Then, by the *Riesz representation theorem* (Theorem C.3), there is a nonnegative Borel measure $\mu \in \mathcal{M}_+(\mathbb{T})$ such that $\widetilde{\lambda}(f) = \int_{\mathbb{T}} f(\theta) d\mu(\theta)$ for all $f \in C(\mathbb{T})$. For each $\ell \geq 0$, specifying this to $f = \cos(\ell \cdot)$ gives $u_\ell = \int_{\mathbb{T}} \cos(\ell\theta) d\mu(\theta)$, as desired. $\square$

E.3 Kolmogorov Superposition Theorem

The *Kolmogorov superposition theorem* gave a negative answer to Hilbert's 13th problem. In its original form, it states that any multivariate continuous function f defined on $[0, 1]^n$ can be represented as

$$f(x_1, \ldots, x_n) = \sum_{j=1}^{2n+1} \overline{f}_j \left(\sum_{i=1}^{n'} \varphi_{i,j}(x_i) \right)$$

where the $\overline{f}_j$ and $\varphi_{i,j}$ are univariate continuous functions, each $\varphi_{i,j}$ being nondecreasing on $[0, 1]$ and independent of f. A slightly stronger form of the result is presented below.

Theorem E.9 *For $n \geq 2$, let $\lambda_1, \ldots, \lambda_n$ be rationally independent positive numbers summing up to one. For quasi-all univariate functions $\varphi_1, \ldots, \varphi_{2n+1}$ that are continuous and nondecreasing from $[0, 1]$ into $[0, 1]$, any multivariate continuous function $f \in C([0, 1]^n)$ can be represented as*

$$f(x_1, \ldots, x_n) = \sum_{j=1}^{2n+1} \overline{f} \left(\sum_{i=1}^{n} \lambda_i \varphi_j(x_i) \right) \tag{E.10}$$

for some univariate continuous function $\overline{f} \in C([0, 1])$.

Proof Let Φ be the complete subset of $C([0, 1])$ defined as

$$\Phi = \{\varphi \in C([0, 1]) : \varphi \text{ is nondecreasing from } [0, 1] \text{ into } [0, 1]\}.$$

With π_i denoting the projection $x \in [0, 1]^n \mapsto x_i \in [0, 1]$, the objective is to show that, for all $\phi = (\varphi_1, \ldots, \varphi_{2n+1})$ in a dense subset of Φ^{2n+1} (this is the meaning of "quasi-all"), the linear map

$$L_\phi : \overline{f} \in C([0, 1]) \mapsto \sum_{j=1}^{2n+1} \overline{f} \left(\sum_{i=1}^{n} \lambda_i \varphi_j \circ \pi_i \right) \in C([0, 1]^n)$$

is surjective. According to Theorem C.5, with $\mathcal{F}$ denoting a countable dense subset of $C([0, 1]^n)$, e.g. the set of polynomials with rational coefficients, it is enough to find constants $C > 0$ and $\rho \in (0, 1)$ such that, for all $f \in \mathcal{F}$,

there exists $\overline{f} \in C([0, 1])$: $\begin{cases} \|f - L_\phi(\overline{f})\|_{C([0,1]^n)} < \rho \|f\|_{C([0,1]^n)}, \\ \|\overline{f}\|_{C([0,1])} \leq C \|f\|_{C([0,1]^n)}. \end{cases}$ (E.11)

For $f \in \mathcal{F}$, consider the set $\Omega(f)$ of $\phi \in \Phi^{2n+1}$ for which (E.11) holds: it is an open and dense subset of Φ^{2n+1}, as shall be established soon. Therefore, by the *Baire category theorem* (Theorem C.1), the set $\Omega = \cap_{f \in \mathcal{F}} \Omega(f)$ is a dense subset of Φ^{2n+1}. According to the previous considerations, choosing any of

$\phi = (\varphi_1, \ldots, \varphi_{2n+1})$ from this set Ω allows one to reach the conclusion of the theorem.

It remains to prove that, taking $C = 1/(2n + 1)$ and $\rho \in (1 - 1/(2n + 1), 1)$, the set

$$\Omega(f) = \left\{ \phi = (\varphi_1, \ldots, \varphi_{2n+1}) \in \Phi^{2n+1} : \text{ there exists } \overline{f} \in C([0, 1]) \text{ such that} \right.$$

$$\left. \|f - L_\phi(\overline{f})\|_{C([0,1]^n)} < \rho \|f\|_{C([0,1]^n)} \text{ and } \|\overline{f}\|_{C([0,1])} \leq C \|f\|_{C([0,1]^n)} \right\}$$

is an open and dense subset of Φ^{2n+1} for every $f \in \mathcal{F}$—in fact, for every $f \in C([0, 1]^n)$. Since openness is easy to verify, one concentrates on proving denseness from now on. For this purpose, let O denote an open neighborhood of some $\phi^0 = (\varphi_1^0, \ldots, \varphi_{2n+1}^0) \in \Phi^{2n+1}$. For a small $\delta > 0$ to be chosen later, one defines $\mathcal{I}_1, \ldots, \mathcal{I}_{2n+1}$ as unions of intervals given, for each $j \in [1 : 2n + 1]$, by

$$\mathcal{I}_j := \bigcup_{k \in \mathbb{Z}} I_{j,k}, \qquad I_{j,k} := (j - 1)\delta + (2n + 1)k\delta + [0, 2n\delta);$$

see Figure E.1. Furthermore, one defines $C_1, \ldots, C_{2n+1}$ as unions of hypercubes given, for each $j \in [1 : 2n + 1]$, by

$$C_j := \bigcup_{k_1, \ldots, k_n \in \mathbb{Z}} C_{j,k_1,\ldots,k_n}, \qquad C_{j,k_1,\ldots,k_n} = I_{j,k_1} \times \cdots \times I_{j,k_n}.$$

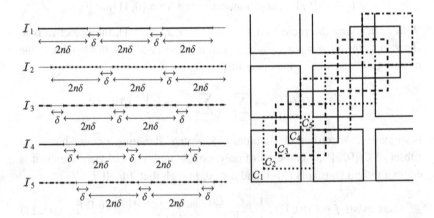

Figure E.1 The sets $\mathcal{I}_1, \ldots, \mathcal{I}_{2n+1}$ (left), as well as the set C_1 and parts of the sets $C_2, \ldots, C_{2n+1}$ (right) when $n = 2$.

Notice that each $\xi \in [0, 1]$ is missed by exactly one of the sets $\mathcal{I}_1, \ldots, \mathcal{I}_{2n+1}$, i.e., that $|\{j \in [1 : 2n + 1] : \xi \notin \mathcal{I}_j\}| = 1$. Consequently, each $x \in [0, 1]^n$ is missed by exactly n of the sets $C_1, \ldots, C_{2n+1}$, i.e.,

$$|J_x| = n, \qquad \text{where } J_x := \{j \in [1 : 2n+1] : x \notin C_j\}.$$

For $j \in [1 : 2n+1]$, one defines a continuous function φ_j which is equal to a rational number $y_{j,k} \in [0,1]$ on each interval $I_{j,k}$ and is linear between these intervals. A proper choice of the $y_{j,k}$ guarantees that each φ_j is nondecreasing, so that $\phi = (\varphi_1, \ldots, \varphi_{2n+1}) \in \Phi^{2n+1}$. Combined with a proper choice of $\delta > 0$, one can make ϕ close enough to ϕ^0 to ensure that $\phi \in O$. One now observes that the functions $\psi_j := \sum_{i=1}^n \lambda_i \varphi_j \circ \pi_i$ are constant on the hypercubes $C_{j,k_1,\ldots,k_n}$, since $x \in C_{j,k_1,\ldots,k_n}$ yields

$$\psi_j(x) = \sum_{i=1}^n \lambda_i \varphi_j(x_i) = \sum_{i=1}^n \lambda_i y_{j,k_i} =: t_{j,k_1,\ldots,k_n}.$$

These numbers $t_{j,k_1,\ldots,k_n} \in [0,1]$ are all distinct by the rational independence of $\lambda_1, \ldots, \lambda_n$. With $c_{j,k_1,\ldots,k_n}$ denoting the centers of the hypercubes $C_{j,k_1,\ldots,k_n}$, one can then find, by the *Tietze extension theorem* (Theorem C.4), a function $\overline{f} \in C([0,1])$ such that

$$\overline{f}(t_{j,k_1,\ldots,k_n}) = \frac{1}{2n+1} f(c_{j,k_1,\ldots,k_n}) \qquad \text{and} \qquad \|\overline{f}\|_{C([0,1])} \leq \frac{1}{2n+1} \|f\|_{C([0,1]^n)}.$$

For $x \in [0,1]^n$ and $j \in [1 : 2n+1]$, the simple triangle inequality

$$\left| \frac{1}{2n+1} f(x) - \overline{f}(\psi_j(x)) \right| \leq \frac{1}{2n+1} \|f\|_{C([0,1]^n)} + \|\overline{f}\|_{C([0,1])} \leq \frac{2}{2n+1} \|f\|_{C([0,1]^n)}$$

can be much improved when $j \notin J_x$. Indeed, in this case, one has $x \in C_j$, say $x \in C_{j,k_1,\ldots,k_n}$, so that

$$\left| \frac{1}{2n+1} f(x) - \overline{f}(\psi_j(x)) \right| = \frac{1}{2n+1} |f(x) - f(c_{j,k_1,\ldots,k_n})| \leq \frac{1}{2n+1} \omega(f, n\delta),$$

where $\omega(f, \cdot)$ denotes the modulus of continuity of the function f. It follows that, for any $x \in [0,1]^n$,

$$\left| (f - L_\phi(\overline{f}))(x) \right| = \left| f(x) - \sum_{j=1}^{2n+1} \overline{f}(\psi_j(x)) \right| = \left| \sum_{j=1}^{2n+1} \left(\frac{1}{2n+1} f(x) - \overline{f}(\psi_j(x)) \right) \right|$$

$$\leq \sum_{j \in J_x} \left| \frac{1}{2n+1} f(x) - \overline{f}(\psi_j(x)) \right| + \sum_{j \notin J_x} \left| \frac{1}{2n+1} f(x) - \overline{f}(\psi_j(x)) \right|$$

$$\leq n \frac{2}{2n+1} \|f\|_{C([0,1]^n)} + (n+1) \frac{1}{2n+1} \omega(f, n\delta).$$

Since $\omega(f, n\delta)$ can be made arbitrarily small, an appropriate choice of $\delta > 0$ yields $\|f - L_\phi(\overline{f})\|_{C([0,1]^n)} \leq \rho \|f\|_{C([0,1]^n)}$. At this point, it has been established that $\phi \in O \cap \Omega(f)$, which finally justifies that $\Omega(f)$ is dense in Φ^{2n+1}. $\qquad \square$

Exercises

E.1   Give a proof of the *Dini lemma*, which reads:

If a monotone sequence of continuous functions defined on a compact set converges pointwise to a continuous function, then the convergence is uniform.

E.2   For a function $f \in C([0,1])$, its *Bernstein polynomials* of degree (at most) n are defined by

$$B_n(f)(x) := \sum_{k=0}^{n} f\left(\frac{k}{n}\right)\binom{n}{k}x^k(1-x)^{n-k}, \qquad x \in [0,1].$$

Prove that the sequence $(B_n(f))_{n\geq 0}$ converges uniformly to f.

E.3   For $n \geq 1$, prove that every $p \in \mathcal{T}_n$ obeys the relation

$$p(x) = \int_{\mathbb{T}} D_n(x-t)p(t)dt, \qquad x \in \mathbb{T},$$

where the *Dirichlet kernel* $D_n \in \mathcal{T}_n$ is given for $x \in \mathbb{T}$ by

$$D_n(x) := 1 + 2\cos(x) + \cdots + 2\cos(nx) = \frac{\sin((2n+1)x/2)}{\sin(x/2)}.$$

Prove also that the *Fejér kernel* $F_n \in \mathcal{T}_{n-1}$ satisfies, for any $x \in \mathbb{T}$,

$$F_n(x) := \frac{1}{n}(D_0(x) + D_1(x) + \cdots + D_{n-1}(x)) = \frac{1}{n}\left(\frac{\sin(nx/2)}{\sin(x/2)}\right)^2.$$

E.4   Observe that the *Bernstein inequality*, which states that, for any $n \geq 0$,

$$\|p'\|_{C(\mathbb{T})} \leq n\|p\|_{C(\mathbb{T})}, \qquad p \in \mathcal{T}_n,$$

is a consequence of the inequality

$$p'(0)^2 + n^2p(0)^2 \leq n^2\|p\|_{C(\mathbb{T})}^2, \qquad p \in \mathcal{T}_n.$$

To prove the latter inequality, consider $\gamma > \|p\|_{C(\mathbb{T})}$ and $\theta \in (0, \pi/n)$ such that $\cos(n\theta) = -\text{sgn}(p'(0))p(0)/\gamma$, verify that $q \in \mathcal{T}_n$ defined by $q(x) = \gamma\cos(nx) + \text{sgn}(p'(0))p(x-\theta)$ has exactly one root in each interval $((k-1)\pi/n, k\pi/n)$, $k \in [1:2n]$, deduce that $q'(\theta) \leq 0$ for the root θ belonging to $(0, \pi/n)$, and conclude.

References

Achieser, N. I. 1992. *Theory of Approximation*. Dover Publications, Inc.

Bach, F. 2017. Breaking the curse of dimensionality with convex neural networks. *Journal of Machine Learning Research*, **18**(1), 629–681.

Bartlett, P. L, Montanari, A., and Rakhlin, A. 2021. Deep learning: a statistical viewpoint. *Acta Numerica*, **30**, 87–201.

Barvinok, A. 2002. *A Course in Convexity*. American Mathematical Society.

Belkin, M. 2021. Fit without fear: remarkable mathematical phenomena of deep learning through the prism of interpolation. *Acta Numerica*, **30**, 203–248.

Ben-Tal, A., El Ghaoui, L., and Nemirovski, A. 2009. *Robust Optimization*. Princeton University Press.

Bhatia, R. 1997. *Matrix Analysis*. Springer Science & Business Media.

Bilyk, D., and Lacey, M. T. 2015. Random tessellations, restricted isometric embeddings, and one bit sensing. *arXiv preprint arXiv:1512.06697*.

Binev, P., Cohen, A., Dahmen, W., DeVore, R. A., Petrova, G., and Wojtaszczyk, P. 2017. Data assimilation in reduced modeling. *SIAM/ASA Journal on Uncertainty Quantification*, **5**(1), 1–29.

Boucheron, S., Lugosi, G., and Massart, P. 2013. *Concentration Inequalities: A Nonasymptotic Theory of Independence*. Oxford University Press.

Boyd, S., and Vandenberghe, L. 2004. *Convex Optimization*. Cambridge University Press.

Buldygin, V. V., and Kozachenko, Yu. V. 2000. *Metric Characterization of Random Variables and Random Processes*. American Mathematical Society.

Chazelle, B. 2001. *The Discrepancy Method: Randomness and Complexity*. Cambridge University Press.

Cheney, E. W. 1966. *Introduction to Approximation Theory*. McGraw-Hill.

Cheney, E. W., and Light, W. A. 2009. *A Course in Approximation Theory*. American Mathematical Society.

DeVore, R., and Lorentz, G. G. 1993. *Constructive Approximation*. Springer Science & Business Media.

DeVore, R., Foucart, S., Petrova, G., and Wojtaszczyk, P. 2019. Computing a quantity of interest from observational data. *Constructive Approximation*, **49**(3), 461–508.

DeVore, R., Hanin, B., and Petrova, G. 2021. Neural network approximation. *Acta Numerica*, **30**, 327–444.

Dey, T. K., and Wang, Y. 2022. *Computational Topology for Data Analysis*. Cambridge University Press.

Dick, J., and Pillichshammer, F. 2010. *Digital Nets and Sequences: Discrepancy Theory and Quasi-Monte Carlo Integration*. Cambridge University Press.

Dick, J., Kuo, F. Y., and Sloan, I. H. 2013. High-dimensional integration: the quasi-Monte Carlo way. *Acta Numerica*, **22**, 133–288.

Du, D., and Hwang, F. K. 2000. *Combinatorial Group Testing and Its Applications*. World Scientific.

D'yachkov, A. G., Vorob'ev, I. V., Polyansky, N. A., and Shchukin, V. Yu. 2014. Bounds on the rate of disjunctive codes. *Problems of Information Transmission*, **50**(1), 27–56.

Eldar, Y. C., and Kutyniok, G. 2012. *Compressed Sensing: Theory and Applications*. Cambridge University Press.

Foucart, S. 2017. Flavors of compressive sensing. Pages 61–104 of: *Approximation Theory XV: San Antonio 2016*. Springer Proceedings in Mathematics & Statistics. Springer.

Foucart, S. 2019. Sampling schemes and recovery algorithms for functions of few coordinate variables. *Journal of Complexity*, 101457.

Foucart, S. 2021. Facilitating OWL norm minimizations. *Optimization Letters*, **15**(1), 263–269.

Foucart, S., and Lasserre, J. B. 2019. Computation of Chebyshev polynomials for union of intervals. *Computational Methods and Function Theory*, **19**(4), 625–641.

Foucart, S., and Powers, V. 2017. Basc: constrained approximation by semidefinite programming. *IMA Journal of Numerical Analysis*, **37**(2), 1066–1085.

Foucart, S., and Rauhut, H. 2013. *A Mathematical Introduction to Compressive Sensing*. Applied and Numerical Harmonic Analysis. Birkhäuser/Springer.

Foucart, S., Minner, M. F., and Needham, T. 2015. Sparse disjointed recovery from non-inflating measurements. *Applied and Computational Harmonic Analysis*, **39**(3), 558–567.

Goodfellow, I., Bengio, Y., and Courville, A. 2016. *Deep Learning*. MIT Press.

Hastie, T., Tibshirani, R., and Friedman, J. 2009. *The Elements of Statistical Learning*. Second edn. Springer.

Higham, C. F., and Higham, D. J. 2019. Deep learning: an introduction for applied mathematicians. *SIAM Review*, **61**(4), 860–891.

Horn, R. A., and Johnson, C. R. 2013. *Matrix Analysis*. Second edn. Cambridge University Press.

König, H. 1986. *Eigenvalue Distribution of Compact Operators*. Birkhäuser Verlag.

Lasserre, J. B. 2010. *Moments, Positive Polynomials and Their Applications*. World Scientific.

Lasserre, J. B. 2015. *An Introduction to Polynomial and Semi-Algebraic Optimization*. Cambridge University Press.

Law, K., Stuart, A., and Zygalakis, K. 2015. *Data Assimilation: A Mathematical Introduction*. Springer International Publishing.

Matousek, J. 2009. *Geometric Discrepancy: An Illustrated Guide*. Springer Science & Business Media.

Micchelli, C. A., and Rivlin, T. J. (eds). 1977. *Optimal Estimation in Approximation Theory*. Plenum Press.

Mohri, M., Rostamizadeh, A., and Talwalkar, A. 2018. *Foundations of Machine Learning*. MIT Press.

Muthukrishnan, S. 2005. Data streams: algorithms and applications. *Foundations and Trends® in Theoretical Computer Science*, **1**(2), 117–236.

Nesterov, Yu. 2013. *Introductory Lectures on Convex Optimization: A Basic Course*. Springer Science & Business Media.

Nesterov, Yu., and Nemirovskii, A. 1994. *Interior-Point Polynomial Algorithms in Convex Programming*. SIAM.

Novak, E., and Woźniakowski, H. 2008. *Tractability of Multivariate Problems: Linear Information*. European Mathematical Society.

Ovchinnikov, S. 2002. Max-min representation of piecewise linear functions. *Contributions to Algebra and Geometry*, **43**(1), 297–302.

Pinkus, A. 1999. Approximation theory of the MLP model in neural networks. *Acta Numerica*, **8**, 143–195.

Renegar, J. 2001. *A Mathematical View of Interior-Point Methods in Convex Optimization*. SIAM.

Rudin, W. 1987. *Real and Complex Analysis*. Third edn. McGraw-Hill.

Rudin, W. 1991. *Functional Analysis*. Second edn. McGraw-Hill.

Schmüdgen, K. 2017. *The Moment Problem*. Springer.

Scholkopf, B., and Smola, A. J. 2001. *Learning with Kernels: Support Vector Machines, Regularization, Optimization, and Beyond*. MIT Press.

Shalev-Shwartz, S., and Ben-David, S. 2014. *Understanding Machine Learning: From Theory to Algorithms*. Cambridge University Press.

Sloan, I. H., and Woźniakowski, H. 1998. When are quasi-Monte Carlo algorithms efficient for high dimensional integrals? *Journal of Complexity*, **14**(1), 1–33.

Smith, R. C. 2013. *Uncertainty Quantification: Theory, Implementation, and Applications*. SIAM.

Sukharev, A. G. 1979. Optimal numerical integration formulas for some classes of functions of several variables. Pages 282–285 of: *Doklady Akademii Nauk*, vol. 246. Russian Academy of Sciences.

Sutton, R. S., and Barto, A. G. 2018. *Reinforcement Learning: An Introduction*. MIT Press.

Venturi, L., Bandeira, A. S., and Bruna, J. 2019. Spurious valleys in one-hidden-layer neural network optimization landscapes. *Journal of Machine Learning Research*, **20**(133), 1–34.

Vershynin, R. 2018. *High-Dimensional Probability: An Introduction with Applications in Data Science*. Cambridge University Press.

Vybíral, J. 2020. A variant of Schur's product theorem and its applications. *Advances in Mathematics*, **368**, 107140.

Wendland, H. 2004. *Scattered Data Approximation*. Cambridge University Press.

Wright, S. J., and Recht, B. 2022. *Optimization for Data Analysis*. Cambridge University Press.

Yarotsky, D. 2018. Optimal approximation of continuous functions by very deep ReLU networks. Pages 639–649 of: *Conference on Learning Theory*. Proceedings of Machine Learning Research.

Index

315

Printed in the United States
by Baker & Taylor Publisher Services

Printed in the United States
by Baker & Taylor Publisher Services